ANTIAIRCRAFT ARTILLERY BATTALIONS OF THE US ARMY
VOLUME II

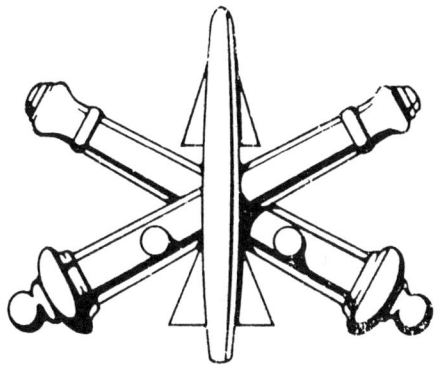

By James A. Sawicki

WYVERN PUBLICATIONS

Copyright © 1991 by James A. Sawicki

All rights reserved. No part of this book may be reproduced or utilized in any form or by any means, electronic or mechanical, including photocopying, recording or by an information storage and retrieval system, without permission in writing from the author, except by a reviewer who may quote brief passages in a review. Inquiries should be addressed to Wyvern Publications, Post Office Box 188, Dumfries, Virginia 22026.

Library of Congress Catalog Card Number 91-065688

ISBN 0-9602404-8-9

Published by Wyvern Publications, Post Office Box 188, Dumfries, Virginia 22026

Manufactured in the United States of America

300th ANTIAIRCRAFT ARTILLERY SEARCHLIGHT BATTALION

Constituted 27 May 1942 in the Army of the United States as 3d Battalion, 210th Coast Artillery (Antiaircraft) and activated 15 June 1942 at Everett, Washington. (Departed Seattle Port of Embarkation 29 June 1942 for overseas service and arrived in Alaska on 5 July 1942). Reorganized on Adak Island and redesignated 14 February 1944 as 300th Antiaircraft Artillery Searchlight Battalion. (Returned from overseas service and arrived at the Seattle Port of Embarkation on 1 May 1944). Inactivated 30 November 1944 at Fort Bliss, Texas.

Consolidated 3 November 1955 with Headquarters and Headquarters Battery, 210th Antiaircraft Artillery Group.

CAMPAIGN STREAMERS
World War II
Aleutian Islands

DECORATIONS
None

COAT OF ARMS
None

DISTINCTIVE INSIGNIA
None

300th ANTIAIRCRAFT ARTILLERY BATTALION

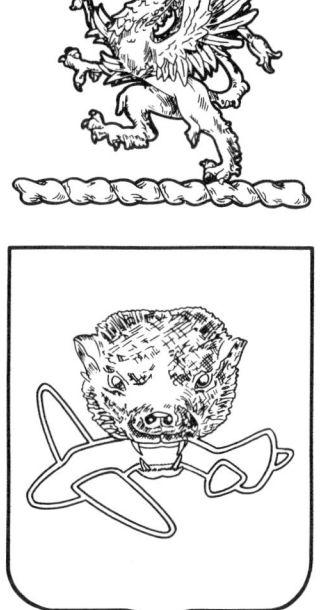

Constituted 22 May 1946 as the 593d Antiaircraft Artillery Automatic Weapons Battalion and allotted to the Michigan National Guard. Organized and Federally recognized 1 November 1949 with Headquarters at Kingsford. Reorganized and redesignated 1 October 1950 as 300th

Antiaircraft Artillery Gun Battalion with Headquarters and Medical Detachment at Kingsford; Battery A at Manistee; Battery B at Iron River; Battery C at Baraga and Battery D at Ironwood. Redesignated 5 October 1953 as 300th Antiaircraft Artillery Battalion.

Consolidated 15 March 1959 with the 182d Artillery, a parent regiment under the Combat Arms Regimental System.

CAMPAIGN STREAMERS
None

DECORATIONS
None

COAT OF ARMS
SHIELD: Gules, a wolverine's head caboshed or bearing in its jaws a crushed airplane sable, fimbriated of the second.

CREST: That for the regiments and separate battalions of the Michigan Army National Guard: On a wreath of the colors (or and gules) a griffin segreant or.

MOTTO: *Defendamus* (We Defend)

The colors scarlet and yellow are used for Artillery. The wolverine refers to the nickname of Michigan where the unit was organized and its home area. The crushed black airplane symbolizes the antiaircraft mission of the organization.

DISTINCTIVE INSIGNIA
The insignia is the shield and motto of the coat of arms. The sample of the insignia depicted was approved for wear on 6 September 1956.

301st COAST ARTILLERY BARRAGE BALLOON BATTALION

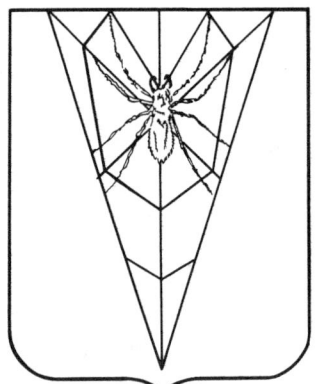 

Constituted 28 April 1941 in the Regular Army as the 301st Coast Artillery Battalion, Separate (Barrage Balloon) and activated 1 May 1941 at Camp Davis, North Carolina. Redesignated 1 July 1941 as the 301st Coast Artillery Barrage Balloon Battalion. (Departed Norfolk, Virginia 20 December 1941 for overseas service and arrived in Panama, Canal Zone on 30 December 1941. Returned to the United States and arrived at the San Francisco Port or Embarkation on 16 December 1943).

Redesignated 10 April 1944 as the 47th Signal Light Construction Battalion.

CAMPAIGN STREAMERS
World War II
American Theater without inscription

DECORATIONS
None

COAT OF ARMS
SHIELD: Gules, on a pile or a field spider spinning a web of the first.

CREST: None

MOTTO: *Cave Plexum* (Beware The Web)

The shield is red for Artillery and the gold pile represents a searchlight beam. The field spider spinning his web in the sky makes reference to the activities and the locality of the organization.

DISTINCTIVE INSIGNIA
The insignia is the shield and motto of the coat of arms. The insignia depicted was never made for nor worn by this organization.

302d ANTIAIRCRAFT BALLOON BATTALION

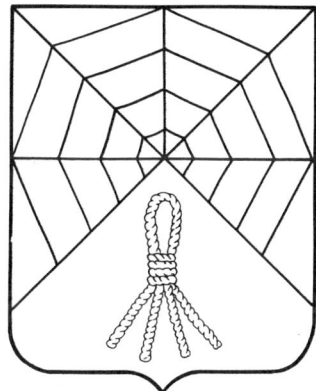 

Constituted in the Regular Army as the 302d Coast Artillery Barrage Balloon Battalion and activated 1 November 1941 at Camp Davis, North Carolina. Redesignated 15 July 1943 as the 302d Antiaircraft Balloon Battalion, Very Low Altitude. Inactivated 1 August 1944 at Camp Breckenridge, Kentucky. Disbanded 26 October 1944.

CAMPAIGN STREAMERS
None

DECORATIONS
None

COAT OF ARMS
SHIELD: Per chevron or and gules, on the first a spider web of the last, on the second a rope maneuvering spider of the first.

CREST: None

MOTTO: *Amat Victoria Curam* (Victory Favors The Watchful)

The division of the shield represents the derivation of the Barrage Balloon units from the Artillery, the web a symbolism of the web of protection woven over the cities. A maneuvering spider is a snatch block or a loop of rope with four (4) or more handling lines attached to it. It may be attached to the balloon cable and enables a balloon to be hauled down when the winch is out of order or the cable has fouled by having a crew walk along the ground.

DISTINCTIVE INSIGNIA

The insignia is the shield and motto of the coat of arms. The insignia depicted was never made for nor worn by this organization.

303d COAST ARTILLERY BARRAGE BALLOON BATTALION

Constituted in the Regular Army as the 303d Coast Artillery Barrage Balloon Battalion and activated 1 November 1941 at Camp Davis, North Carolina. Disbanded 9 September 1943 at Fort Custer, Michigan.

CAMPAIGN STREAMERS
None

DECORATIONS
None

COAT OF ARMS
SHIELD: Gules, a mullet azure, fimbriated or.

CREST: None

MOTTO: *In Coelibus Regnamus* (We Rule The Skies)

The shield is blue and refers to the area of operation while red signifies the Coast Artillery. Gold, or yellow represents the influence of the Air Corps on balloon development and also signifies cooperation between the two arms. The star indicates that the unit was the third Barrage Balloon Battalion organized at the Barrage Balloon Training Center.

DISTINCTIVE INSIGNIA
The insignia is the shield and motto of the coat of arms. The insignia depicted was never made for nor worn by this organization.

304th COAST ARTILLERY BARRAGE BALLOON BATTALION

Constituted in the Regular Army as the 304th Coast Artillery Barrage Balloon Battalion and activated 1 November 1941 at Camp Davis, North Carolina. Disbanded 9 September 1943 at Fort Custer, Michigan.

CAMPAIGN STREAMERS
None

DECORATIONS
None

COAT OF ARMS
None

DISTINCTIVE INSIGNIA
None

305th COAST ARTILLERY BARRAGE BALLOON BATTALION

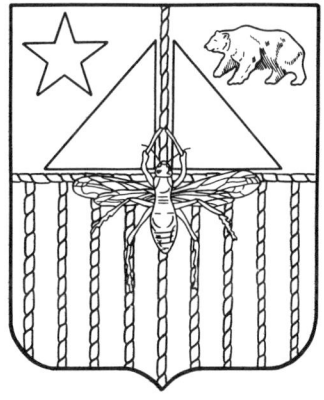 

Constituted in the Regular Army as the 305th Coast Artillery Barrage Balloon Battalion and activated 1 November 1941 at Camp Davis, North Carolina. (Departed San Francisco Port of Embarkation 8 July 1942 for overseas service and arrived in Hawaii on 16 July 1942). Inactivated 5 November 1943 at Fort Kamehameha, Territory of Hawaii. Disbanded 14 June 1944.

CAMPAIGN STREAMERS
World War II
Pacific Theater with out inscription

DECORATIONS
None

COAT OF ARMS
SHIELD: Per fess azure and gules, on the first a triangle point to chief between a mullet and a bear passant or, issuant from chief a cable or fimbriated of the first, supporting a horizontal cable with nine of the like therefrom to base throughout of the third, at fess point a hornet of the second.

CREST: None

MOTTO: Forever On Guard

The shield is red for Artillery while the chief is blue and refers to the area of operations. The triangle represents a balloon barrage impeding attack from the sky while the cables are those of the barrage balloon. The star and hornet refer to North Carolina, the state of activation while the bear is for California and commemorates its defense of Mare Island, California during World War II.

DISTINCTIVE INSIGNIA
The insignia is the shield and motto of the coat of arms. The insignia depicted was unofficially worn by this battalion in Hawaii during 1943.

306th COAST ARTILLERY BARRAGE BALLOON BATTALION

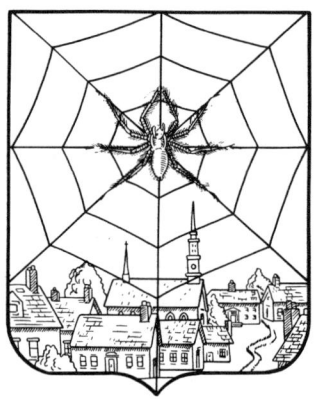 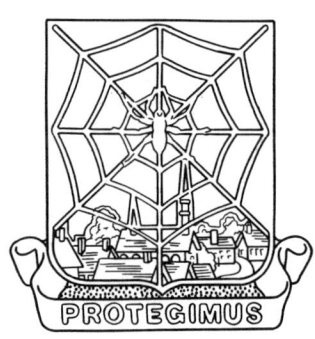

Constituted 19 January 1942 in the Army of the United States as the 306th Coast Artillery Barrage Balloon Battalion and activated 1 February 1942 at Camp Tyson, Tennessee. Disbanded 9 September 1943 at Fort Custer, Michigan.

CAMPAIGN STREAMERS
None

DECORATIONS
None

COAT OF ARMS
SHIELD: Or, in base a city gules, overall an American garden spider in its web in pale, head to chief of the second.

CREST: None

MOTTO: *Protegimus* (We Cover Before)

• Red and gold are the colors for the Coast Artillery. The shield graphically illustrates the protective function of the organization, the spider weaving a net of protection over its charge. The spider is symbolical of tenacity, wisdom and prudence.

DISTINCTIVE INSIGNIA
The insignia is the shield and motto of the coat of arms. The insignia depicted was never made for nor worn by this organization.

307th COAST ARTILLERY BARRAGE BALLOON BATTALION

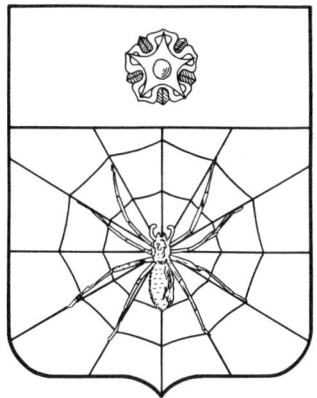 

Constituted 31 January 1942 in the Army of the United States as the 307th Coast Artillery Barrage Balloon Battalion and activated 1 February 1942 at Camp Tyson, Tennessee. Disbanded 9 September 1943 at Fort Custer, Michigan.

CAMPAIGN STREAMERS
None

DECORATIONS
None

COAT OF ARMS
SHIELD: Gules, a field spider in its web or, on a chief argent a rose of the field, barbed and seeded proper.

CREST: None

MOTTO: *Aude Retam* (Dare And Share)

The shield is scarlet, the color of the Coast Artillery. The functions of the battalion are aptly shown in the protecting net woven by the spider. The rose is the heraldic mark of cadency for the seventh son.

DISTINCTIVE INSIGNIA
The insignia is the shield and motto of the coat of arms. The insignia depicted was never made for nor worn by this organization.

308th COAST ARTILLERY BARRAGE BALLOON BATTALION

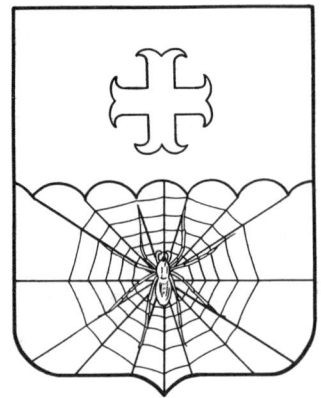 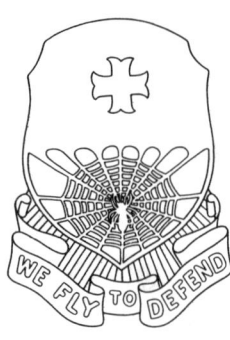

Constituted 31 January 1942 in the Army of the United States as the 308th Coast Artillery Barrage Balloon Battalion and activated 1 March 1942 at Camp Tyson, Tennessee. Disbanded 9 September 1943 at Fort Custer, Michigan.

CAMPAIGN STREAMERS
None

DECORATIONS
None

COAT OF ARMS
SHIELD: Per cross engrailed or and gules, in chief a cross moline azure, in base an American field spider spinning its web of the first.

CREST: None

MOTTO: We Fly To Defend

The shield is red and yellow, the colors of the Coast Artillery. The nature of the activities of the organization is symbolized by the spider in its web. The moline cross is the heraldic mark of cadency for the eighth son.

DISTINCTIVE INSIGNIA
The insignia is the shield and motto of the coat of arms. The insignia depicted was unofficially worn by this organization during 1942 and 1943 at Keyport, Washington.

308th ANTIAIRCRAFT ARTILLERY BATTALION

Constituted 9 July 1946 as the 308th Antiaircraft Artillery Searchlight Battalion and allotted to the New Jersey National Guard. Redesignated 1 December 1947 as the 308th Antiaircraft Artillery Gun Battalion (90mm). Organized and Federally recognized 9 January 1950 with Headquarters at Rio Grande and elements at Rio Grande, Ocean City and Wildwood. Redesignated 13 April 1953 as the 308th Antiaircraft Artillery Battalion (90mm Gun).

Redesignated 1 February 1955 as the 286th Armored Field Artillery Battalion.

CAMPAIGN STREAMERS
None

DECORATIONS
None

COAT OF ARMS

SHIELD: Gules, seme of bird-bolts palewise or, in honor point a horse's head couped at the withers of the second.

CREST: That for the regiments and separate battalions of the New Jersey Army National Guard: On a wreath of the colors (or and gules) a lion's head erased or, collared four fusils gules.

MOTTO: *Nos Acies est in Caelo* (Our Battle Line In The Sky)

The colors red and yellow are for Artillery. The bird-bolts, ancient arrows for killing birds, symbolize antiaircraft. The horse's head, adapted from the New Jersey State Seal, represents the origin of the organization.

DISTINCTIVE INSIGNIA

The insignia is the shield and motto of the coat of arms. The sample of the insignia depicted was approved for wear on 19 November 1953.

309th COAST ARTILLERY BARRAGE BALLOON BATTALION

Constituted 31 January 1942 in the Army of the United States as the 309th Coast Artillery Barrage Balloon Battalion and activated 1 April 1942 at Camp Tyson, Tennessee. Disbanded 9 September 1943 at Fort Custer, Michigan.

CAMPAIGN STREAMERS
None

DECORATIONS
None

COAT OF ARMS
SHIELD: Per bend engrailed gules and or, on the first an octofoil of the second, in base a field spider in its web azure.

CREST: None

MOTTO: Aloft And Alert

The tinctures gules and or are the colors of the Coast Artillery. Red is also symbolic of war and being to chief is significant of war in the air. The engrailed division of the shield is symbolic of the barrage balloon representing the catenary curtain of the dilatable balloon. The spider hanging in the web represents the lethal devices which may be attached to the cables to render them more effective. The tincture of the spider, azure, when taken with that of the surrounding field or, commemorates the part played by the Air Corps in the development of the barrage balloon. The octofoil is the sign of the ninth son and symbolizes the fact that this was the ninth Barrage Balloon Battalion to be organized.

DISTINCTIVE INSIGNIA
The insignia is the shield and motto of the coat of arms. The insignia depicted was never made for nor worn by this organization.

309th ANTIAIRCRAFT ARTILLERY AUTOMATIC WEAPONS BATTALION

Constituted 20 July 1940 as 2d Battalion, 261st Coast Artillery (Harbor Defense) and allotted to the New Jersey National Guard. Organized and Federally recognized 25 November 1940 at Jersey City. Redesignated 15 January 1941 as the 122d Separate Battalion Coast Artillery (Antiaircraft) (Gun). Inducted into Federal service 27 January 1941 at Jersey City. Redesignated 10 September 1943 as 122d Antiaircraft Artillery Gun Battalion (Semimobile). (Departed Seattle Port of Embarkation 23 July 1944 for overseas service; arrived at Amchitka, Alaska 3 August 1944 and moved to Shemya, Alaska on 5 November 1944). Inactivated 3 February 1945 at Shemya. Redesignated 28 June 1946 as the 309th Antiaircraft Artillery Automatic Weapons Battalion. Reorganized and Federally recognized 15 April 1947 at Jersey City.

Redesignated 1 March 1949 as the 650th Antiaircraft Artillery Automatic Weapons Battalion.

CAMPAIGN STREAMERS
World War II
Pacific Theater without inscription

DECORATIONS
None

COAT OF ARMS
None

DISTINCTIVE INSIGNIA
None

310th COAST ARTILLERY BARRAGE BALLOON BATTALION

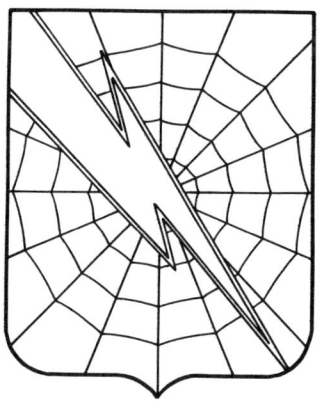 

Constituted 5 May 1942 in the Army of the United States as the 310th Coast Artillery Barrage Balloon Battalion and activated 5 June 1942 at Camp Tyson, Tennessee. Disbanded 9 September 1943 at Fort Custer, Michigan.

CAMPAIGN STREAMERS
None

DECORATIONS
None

COAT OF ARMS
SHIELD: Gules, a spider web or, overall issuing from dexter chief a ray bevilled bendwise of the last, fimbriated azure.

CREST: None

MOTTO: *Caveat Volator* (Flyer Beware)

The shield is in the colors of the Coast Artillery, red and yellow. The spider web is symbolic of the mission of the barrage balloon, to keep away the hostile flyer and to bring him down if he fails to do so. The ray bevilled is symbolic of the lightning flash and the lethal devices which serve to make the barrage balloon a potent defensive weapon.

DISTINCTIVE INSIGNIA
The insignia is the shield and motto of the coat of arms. The insignia depicted was never made for nor worn by this organization.

310th ANTIAIRCRAFT ARTILLERY AUTOMATIC WEAPONS BATTALION

Constituted 9 July 1946 as the 310th Antiaircraft Artillery Automatic Weapons Battalion and allotted to the New Jersey National Guard. Organized and Federally recognized 18 June 1948 at Jersey City. Disbanded 31 July 1952 at Jersey City when Federal recognition was withdrawn.

CAMPAIGN STREAMERS
None

DECORATIONS
None

COAT OF ARMS
None

DISTINCTIVE INSIGNIA
None

311th COAST ARTILLERY BARRAGE BALLOON BATTALION

Constituted 5 May 1942 in the Army of the United States as the 311th Coast Artillery Barrage

Balloon Battalion and activated 5 June 1942 at Camp Tyson, Tennessee. Disbanded 9 September 1943 at Fort Custer, Michigan.

CAMPAIGN STREAMERS
None

DECORATIONS
None

COAT OF ARMS
SHIELD: Gules, an American field spider hanging in web throughout or, on a chief azure a fillet invected, in honor point three mullets two and one of the second.

CREST: None

MOTTO: *Dominus Caelorum* (Lord Of The Heavens)

The shield is scarlet for the Coast Artillery. The spider in the web is symbolic of the mission of a Barrage Balloon Battalion. The spider being the symbol of wisdom and sagacity in defense and the web symbolizes the net of cables of the barrage.

DISTINCTIVE INSIGNIA
The insignia is the shield and motto of the coat of arms. The insignia depicted was never made for nor worn by this organization.

311th ANTIAIRCRAFT ARTILLERY AUTOMATIC WEAPONS BATTALION

Constituted 9 July 1946 as the 311th Antiaircraft Artillery Automatic Weapons Battalion and allotted to the New Jersey National Guard. Organized and Federally recognized 21 November 1947 at Newark. Disbanded 6 July 1954 at Newark when Federal recognition was withdrawn.

CAMPAIGN STREAMERS
None

DECORATIONS
None

COAT OF ARMS
None

DISTINCTIVE INSIGNIA
None

312th COAST ARTILLERY BARRAGE BALLOON BATTALION

Constituted 9 May 1942 in the Army of the United States as the 312th Coast Artillery Barrage Balloon Battalion and activated 5 June 1942 at Camp Tyson, Tennessee. Disbanded 9 September 1943 at Fort Custer, Michigan.

CAMPAIGN STREAMERS
None

DECORATIONS
None

COAT OF ARMS
SHIELD: Gules, a spider web of nine radiating and fifty-four cross strands or, overall six mullets, three, one and two azure, fimbriated of the second.

CREST: None

MOTTO: Silent Defenders

Scarlet is the color of the Coast Artillery. The spider web is symbolic of the functions of a barrage balloon organization while the stars represent the numerical designation of the organization.

DISTINCTIVE INSIGNIA
The insignia is the shield and motto of the coat of arms. The insignia depicted was never made for nor worn by this organization.

313th ANTIAIRCRAFT BALLOON BATTALION

Constituted 27 May 1942 in the Army of the United States as the 313th Coast Artillery Barrage Balloon Battalion and activated 15 June 1942 at Fort Randolph, Canal Zone. (Moved to the United States and landed at the Hampton Roads Port of Embarkation on 27 December 1943). Redesignated 27 January 1944 as the 313th Antiaircraft Balloon Battalion, Low Altitude.

Redesignated 10 April 1944 as the 48th Signal Light Construction Battalion.

CAMPAIGN STREAMERS
World War II
American Theater without inscription

DECORATIONS
None

COAT OF ARMS
None

DISTINCTIVE INSIGNIA
None

313th ANTIAIRCRAFT ARTILLERY BATTALION

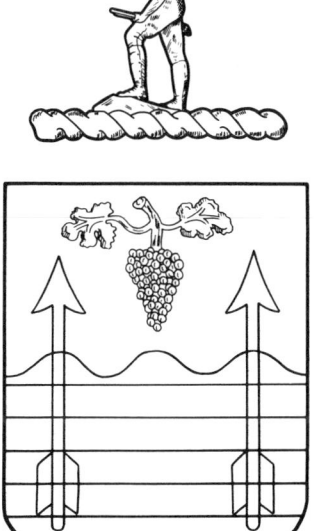

Constituted 25 February 1943 in the Army of the United States as Headquarters and Headquarters Battery, 103d Antiaircraft Artillery Group and activated 5 July 1943 at Orlando, Florida. (Departed for overseas service 6 October 1944; arrived in England 18 October 1944 and landed in France on 2 December 1944). Inactivated 15 March 1946 at Heidelberg, Germany. Redesignated Headquarters and Headquarters Battery, 313th Harbor Defense and allotted to the Organized Reserves on 6 December 1946. Activated 17 December 1946 at New York, New York. (Organized Reserves redesignated 25 March 1948 as Organized Reserve Corps). Reorganized and redesignated 30 December 1949 as Headquarters and Headquarters Battery, 313th Antiaircraft Artillery Automatic Weapons Battalion; concurrently, remainder of battalion organized from existing Coast Artillery Batteries in the Organized Reserve Corps as follows: 336th Coast Artillery Gun Battery as Battery A; 355th Coast Artillery Searchlight Battery as Battery B; 359th Coast Artillery Searchlight Battery as Battery C; and 373d Coast Artillery Searchlight Battery as Battery D. Reorganized and redesignated 1 January 1951 as the 313th Antiaircraft Artillery Gun Battalion. (Organized Reserve Corps redesignated 9 July 1952 as Army Reserve). Redesignated 1 September 1953 as the 313th Antiaircraft Artillery Battalion. Inactivated 30 June 1959 at Watertown, New York.

CAMPAIGN STREAMERS
World War II
Tunisia
Sicily
Naples-Foggia
Rome-Arno
Rhineland
Ardennes-Alsace
Central Europe

DECORATIONS
None

COAT OF ARMS
SHIELD: Per fess wavy or and barry of six gules and the first, overall two arrows counterchanged and in chief a bunch of grapes proper.

CREST: That for the regiments and separate battalions of the Army Reserve: On a wreath of the colors (or and gules) the Lexington Minute Man proper. The statue of the Minute Man, Captain John Parker (H. H. Kitson, sculptor), stands on the common in Lexington, Massachusetts.

MOTTO: *Semper ad Caelum* (Always Toward Heaven)

The colors red and yellow are used for Artillery. The wavy partition line alludes to the historic harbor defense role of the organization and symbolically divides the shield into sky and ground. The upward-pointing arrows represent the swift effectiveness of the battalion's antiaircraft artillery. The grapes, indicative of the Rhineland, and six bars symbolize the battalion's campaigns in Europe and North Africa during World War II.

DISTINCTIVE INSIGNIA
The insignia is the shield and motto of the coat of arms. The sample of the insignia depicted was approved for wear 21 April 1955.

314th ANTIAIRCRAFT ARTILLERY BATTALION

Organized in the Maine National Guard as 2d Battalion, 152d Field Artillery and Federally recognized 3 April 1929 with Headquarters at Bangor and batteries at Bangor and Brewer. (Headquarters relocated to Waterville on 21 July 1934 and back to Bangor on 8 January 1938). Inducted into Federal service 24 February 1941 at home stations. Redesignated 19 February 1942 as the 152d Field Artillery Battalion and assigned to the 43d Infantry Division. Inactivated 14 October 1945 at Camp Stoneman, California. Redesignated 21 May 1946 as the 203d Field

Artillery Battalion. Relieved from the 43d Infantry Division and redesignated 1 July 1946 as the 314th Antiaircraft Artillery Automatic Weapons Battalion (Mobile). Reorganized and Federally recognized 19 December 1946 with Headquarters at Bangor and batteries at Belfast, Brewer, Calais and Millinocket. Reorganized and redesignated 1 December 1950 as 314th Antiaircraft Artillery Gun Battalion (90mm). Reorganized and redesignated 1 July 1951 as 314th Antiaircraft Artillery Automatic Weapons Battalion (Mobile). Redesignated 1 October 1953 as 314th Antiaircraft Artillery Battalion (Automatic Weapons) (Mobile). Reorganized and redesignated 1 January 1956 as 314th Antiaircraft Artillery Battalion (75mm Gun).

Reorganized and redesignated 15 May 1959 as the 240th Artillery, a parent regiment under the Combat Arms Regimental System.

CAMPAIGN STREAMERS
World War II
Guadalcanal
New Guinea
Northern Solomons
Luzon (with arrowhead)

DECORATIONS
Philippine Presidential Unit Citation, Streamer embroidered *17 OCTOBER 1944 TO 4 JULY 1945* (152d FA Bn cited; DAGO 47, 1950)

COAT OF ARMS
SHIELD: Gules, a phoenix rising out of flames or, on a canton of the first fimbriated of the second a projectile bendwise, scintillant of the last.

CREST: That for the regiments and separate battalions of the Maine Army National Guard: On a wreath of the colors (argent and gules) a pine tree proper.

MOTTO: *Tantum dic Verbum* (Only Say The Word)

The red shield with the gold scintillating projectile on a canton was the coat of arms of the 152d Field Artillery Battalion during World War II. The phoenix a symbol of rejuvenation, refers to the rejuvenation of the battalion following World War II service.

DISTINCTIVE INSIGNIA
The insignia is the shield and motto of the coat of arms. The sample of the insignia depicted was approved for wear 5 April 1956.

315th COAST ARTILLERY BARRAGE BALLOON BATTALION

Constituted 12 July 1942 in the Army of the United States as the 315th Coast Artillery Barrage Balloon Battalion and activated 20 July 1942 at Camp Tyson, Tennessee. Disbanded 9 September 1943 at Fort Custer, Michigan.

CAMPAIGN STREAMERS
None

DECORATIONS
None

COAT OF ARMS
SHIELD: Per fess dancette or and gules, on the first a spider web throughout azure.

CREST: None

MOTTO: Our Ramparts We Guard

Red and yellow are the colors of the Coast Artillery while blue and yellow commemorate the Air Corps and the part it played in development of the barrage balloon. The dancette division of the shield is symbolic of the ramparts to be guarded and the spider web to chief refers to the web of cables extending into the heavens which are the weapons that make the barrage effective.

DISTINCTIVE INSIGNIA
The insignia is the shield and motto of the coat of arms. The insignia depicted was never made for nor worn by this organization.

316th ANTIAIRCRAFT BALLOON BATTALION

Constituted 26 August 1942 in the Army of the United States as the 316th Coast Artillery Barrage Balloon Battalion and activated 5 December 1942 at Camp Tyson, Tennessee. Redesignated 15 July 1943 as the 316th Antiaircraft Balloon Battalion, Very Low Altitude.

Redesignated 7 April 1944 as the 49th Signal Light Construction Battalion.

CAMPAIGN STREAMERS
None

DECORATIONS
None

COAT OF ARMS
SHIELD: Gules, a dragon fly volant in chief bendwise sable, fimbriated or; overall a spider web throughout of the last.

CREST: None

MOTTO: *Dominus Retae* (Master Of The Snare)

The spider web is distinctive of a Barrage Balloon Battalion The scarlet of the shield is for the Coast Artillery Corps. The dragon fly represents the enemy aircraft while the spider web indicates the web of cable which not only blocks out, but enmeshes and destroys enemy aircraft.

DISTINCTIVE INSIGNIA
The insignia is the shield and motto of the coat of arms. The insignia depicted was never made for nor worn by this organization.

317th ANTIAIRCRAFT BALLOON BATTALION

Constituted 26 August 1942 in the Army of the United States as the 317th Coast Artillery Barrage Balloon Battalion and activated 5 December 1942 at Camp Tyson, Tennessee. Redesignated 15 July 1943 as the 317th Antiaircraft Balloon Battalion, Very Low Altitude. Inactivated 1 August 1944 at Camp Breckenridge, Kentucky. Disbanded 26 October 1944.

CAMPAIGN STREAMERS
None

DECORATIONS
None

COAT OF ARMS
None

DISTINCTIVE INSIGNIA
None

317th ANTIAIRCRAFT ARTILLERY BATTALION

Constituted 2 June 1942 in the Army of the United States as Headquarters and Headquarters Battery, 86th Coast Artillery (Antiaircraft) (Semimobile) and activated 4 June 1942 at Camp Haan, California. Reorganized at Camp Haan and redesignated 20 January 1943 as Headquarters and Headquarters Battery, 109th Coast Artillery Group (Antiaircraft). Redesignated 26 May 1943 as Headquarters and Headquarters Battery, 109th Antiaircraft Artillery Group. (Departed New York Port of Embarkation 3 December 1943 for overseas service; arrived in England on 9 December 1943 and landed on the Beaches of Normandy on 6 June 1944. Returned from overseas service and arrived at the Hampton Roads Port of Embarkation on 2 November 1945). Inactivated 2 November 1945 at Camp Patrick Henry, Virginia. Redesignated Headquarters and Headquarters Battery, 317th Harbor Defense and allotted to the Organized Reserve Corps on 6 December 1946. Activated 17 December 1946 at Boston, Massachusetts. (Organized Reserve Corps redesignated Organized Reserves on 25 March 1948). Reorganized and redesignated 6 October 1949 as Headquarters and Headquarters Battery, 317th Antiaircraft Artillery Gun Battalion; concurrently, remainder of battalion organized by redesignation of existing units as follows: 302d Coast Artillery Searchlight Battery as Battery A; 365th Coast Artillery Gun Battery as Battery B; 366th Coast Artillery Gun Battery as Battery C and 367th Coast Artillery Gun Battery as Battery D. (Organized Reserves redesignated 9 July 1952 as Army Reserve). Redesignated 30 November 1953 as the 317th Antiaircraft Artillery Battalion. Inactivated 11 May 1959 at Boston.

CAMPAIGN STREAMERS
World War II
Normandy (with arrowhead)
Northern France
Rhineland
Ardennes-Alsace
Central Europe
New Guinea

DECORATIONS
None

COAT OF ARMS
SHIELD: Per bend gules and or, on a bend two arrows parallel, all counterchanged.

CREST: That for the regiments and separate battalions of the Army Reserve: On a wreath of the colors (or and gules) the Lexington Minute Man proper. The status of the Minute Man, Captain John Parker (H.H. Kitson, sculptor), stands on the common in Lexington, Massachusetts.

MOTTO: *Ex Coelo Descendant* (Let Them Fall From The Heavens)

Red and yellow are used for Artillery. The bend represents a baldric or sword scarf and is a mark of military honor. The arrows allude to the antiaircraft functions of the battalion and also represent combat service in both the European and Pacific Theaters during World War II.

DISTINCTIVE INSIGNIA
The insignia is the shield and motto of the coat of arms. The sample of the insignia depicted was approved for wear on 12 January 1953.

318th ANTIAIRCRAFT BALLOON BATTALION

Constituted 26 August 1942 in the Army of the United States as the 318th Coast Artillery Barrage Balloon Battalion and activated 10 December 1942 at Camp Tyson, Tennessee. Redesignated 1 August 1943 as the 318th Antiaircraft Balloon Battalion, Low Altitude. Reorganized and redesignated 25 September 1943 as the 318th Antiaircraft Balloon Battalion, Very Low Altitude.

Redesignated 17 April 1944 as the 78th Signal Light Construction Battalion.

CAMPAIGN STREAMERS
None

DECORATIONS
None

COAT OF ARMS
None

DISTINCTIVE INSIGNIA
None

318th ANTIAIRCRAFT ARTILLERY GUN BATTALION

Constituted 29 July 1921 in the Organized Reserves as 1st Battalion, 510th Artillery (Antiaircraft), Coast Artillery Corps, allotted to the Third Corps Area and assigned to III Corps. Organized during February 1922 with Headquarters at Chester, Pennsylvania. Redesignated 30 June 1924 as 1st Battalion, 510th Coast Artillery (Antiaircraft). Ordered into active military service, less personnel and equipment, at Fort Sheridan, Illinois on 15 November 1942. Reorganized at Fort Sheridan on 20 January 1943 and redesignated 164th Coast Artillery Battalion (Antiaircraft) (Gun). Redesignated 7 June 1943 as 164th Antiaircraft Artillery Gun Battalion. (Departed San Francisco Port of Embarkation 8 October 1943 for overseas service and arrived at Guadalcanal on 11 November 1943. Moved to Russell Island on 29 November 1943; to New Guinea on 2 January 1945 and to San Narciso on 14 August 1945). Inactivated 15 April 1946 at San Narciso. (Organized Reserves redesignated Organized Reserve Corps on 25 March 1948). Redesignated 318th Antiaircraft Artillery Gun Battalion. Assigned to First Army and activated 2 October 1948 at Georgetown, Delaware. Inactivated 1 December 1950 at Georgetown. (Organized Reserve Corps redesignated Army Reserve on 9 July 1952).

Redesignated 16 October 1952 as the 164th Antiaircraft Artillery Gun Battalion.

CAMPAIGN STREAMERS
World War II
Pacific Theater without inscription

DECORATIONS
None

COAT OF ARMS
None

DISTINCTIVE INSIGNIA
None

319th ANTIAIRCRAFT BALLOON BATTALION

Constituted 26 August 1942 in the Army of the United States as the 319th Coast Artillery Barrage Balloon Battalion (Colored) and activated 10 December 1942 at Camp Tyson, Tennessee. Redesignated 1 August 1943 as the 319th Antiaircraft Balloon Battalion, Very Low Altitude (Colored). Inactivated 29 February 1944 at Camp Tyson. Disbanded 14 June 1944.

CAMPAIGN STREAMERS
None

DECORATIONS
None

COAT OF ARMS
None

DISTINCTIVE INSIGNIA
None

319th ANTIAIRCRAFT ARTILLERY BATTALION

Constituted 19 May 1944 in the Army of the United States as Headquarters and Headquarters Battery, 144th Coast Artillery Group (155mm Gun) and activated 31 May 1944 at Fort Ruger, Hawaii. (Moved to New Caledonia on 22 February 1945 and to Okinawa on 23 June 1945). Inactivated 10 October 1945 on Okinawa. Redesignated Headquarters and Headquarters Battery, 319th Harbor Defense, allotted to the Organized Reserves and assigned to Sixth Army on 4 December 1946. Activated 31 December 1946 at San Francisco, California. (Organized Reserves redesignated 25 March 1948 as Organized Reserve Corps). Reorganized and redesignated 1 September 1949 as Headquarters and Headquarters Battery, 319th Antiaircraft Artillery Gun Battalion; concurrently, remainder of battalion organized by redesignation of 331st, 858th, 857th, and 859th Coast Artillery Gun Batteries as Batteries A-D, respectively. (Organized Reserve Corps redesignated 9 June 1952 as Army Reserve). Redesignated 15 April 1953 as the 319th Antiaircraft Artillery Battalion. Inactivated 1 December 1957 at San Francisco.

CAMPAIGN STREAMERS
World War II
Ryukyus

DECORATIONS
None

COAT OF ARMS
SHIELD: Gules, on a pale or issuant from base a dexter cubit arm erect grasping a broken aircraft overall counterchanged, in chief a pomme.

CREST: That for the regiments and separate battalions of the Army Reserve: On a wreath of the colors (or and gules) the Lexington Minute Man proper. The statue of the Minute Man, Captain John Parker (H. H. Kitson, sculptor), stands on the common in Lexington, Massachusetts.

MOTTO: *Aetherem Possidemus* (We Possess The Skies)

Scarlet and yellow are used for Artillery. The roundel indicates an island and symbolizes service on Okinawa during World War Ii. The hand grasping and bending an aircraft denotes the organization's mission, that of defense against enemy air attack.

DISTINCTIVE INSIGNIA

The insignia is the shield and motto of the coat of arms. The insignia depicted was never made for nor worn by this organization.

320th ANTIAIRCRAFT BALLOON BATTALION

Constituted 26 August 1942 in the Army of the United States as the 320th Coast Artillery Barrage Balloon Battalion (Colored) and activated 10 December 1942 at Camp Tyson, Tennessee. Redesignated 15 July 1943 as the 320th Antiaircraft Balloon Battalion, Very Low Altitude (Colored). (Departed New York Port of Embarkation 17 November 1943 for overseas service; arrived in England on 24 November 1943 and landed in France on 6 June 1944. Returned from overseas service and arrived at the New York Port of Embarkation on 26 November 1944. Departed Seattle Port of Embarkation 29 April 1945 and arrived in Hawaii on 6 May 1945). Inactivated 14 December 1945 at Camp Aiea, Honolulu, Territory of Hawaii.

CAMPAIGN STREAMERS
World War II
Normandy (with arrowhead)
Northern France
Pacific Theater without inscription

DECORATIONS
None

COAT OF ARMS
SHIELD: Gules, a griffin's head erased or, on a chief invected argent a spider web azure.

CREST: None

MOTTO: *Ex Terra Volamus* (Out Of The Earth We Fly)

The scarlet is the color of the Coast Artillery Corps. The functions of the organization are allegorically implied by the griffin's head, that animal which heraldically sets forth the property of a valorous soldier whose magnanimity is such that he will dare all danger, and even death itself, and has also been regarded as a symbol of vigilancy. The invected partition line of the shield denotes clouds, and the spider web is a guard against enemy encroachment.

DISTINCTIVE INSIGNIA
The insignia is the shield and motto of the coat of arms. The insignia depicted was never made for nor worn by this organization.

321st ANTIAIRCRAFT BALLOON BATTALION

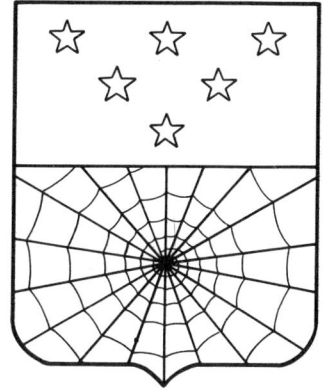 

Constituted 26 August 1942 in the Army of the United States as the 321st Coast Artillery Barrage Balloon Battalion (Colored) and activated 10 December 1942 at Camp Tyson, Tennessee. Redesignated 15 July 1943 as the 321st Antiaircraft Balloon Battalion, Very Low Altitude (Colored). Inactivated 29 February 1944 at Camp Tyson. Disbanded 14 June 1944.

CAMPAIGN STREAMERS
None

DECORATIONS
None

COAT OF ARMS
SHIELD: Per fess enhanced gules and or, on the first six mullets three, two and one of the last, on the second a spider web throughout of the first.

CREST: None

MOTTO: *Caveant aves* (Let The Birds Beware)

The tinctures of the shield, gules and or, are the colors of the Coast Artillery Corps to which the battalion belongs. The red to chief and the stars are symbolic of the war above and the spider web to base is symbolic of the mission of the battalion to spread a web of cables from the earth to the heavens.

DISTINCTIVE INSIGNIA
The insignia is the shield and motto of the coat of arms. The insignia depicted was never made for nor worn by this organization.

321st ANTIAIRCRAFT ARTILLERY AUTOMATIC WEAPONS BATTALION

Constituted 17 October 1946 in the Organized Reserves as the 321st Antiaircraft Artillery Automatic Weapons Battalion and assigned to the Seventh United States Army. Activated 28 October 1946 at Tuscaloosa, Alabama. Relieved from the Seventh United States Army and assigned to the Third United States Army 15 March 1947. (Organized Reserves redesignated 25 March 1948 as Organized Reserve Corps). Inactivated 31 December 1950 at Tuscaloosa.

CAMPAIGN STREAMERS
None

DECORATIONS
None

COAT OF ARMS
None

DISTINCTIVE INSIGNIA
None

322d ANTIAIRCRAFT ARTILLERY AUTOMATIC WEAPONS BATTALION

Constituted 7 May 1946 in the Army of the United States as the 322d Antiaircraft Artillery Automatic Weapons Battalion. Activated 25 May 1946 at Fort Bliss, Texas; inactivated 31 October 1946 at Fort Bliss. Allotted to the Organized Reserves and assigned to Sixth United States Army 23 December 1946. Activated 20 January 1947 with Headquarters at Seattle, Washington. (Organized Reserves redesignated 25 March 1948 as Organized Reserve Corps). Assigned to the 104th Infantry Division 28 March 1949. Relieved from the 104th Infantry Division and disbanded 1 May 1952 at Seattle.

CAMPAIGN STREAMERS
None

DECORATIONS
None

COAT OF ARMS
None

DISTINCTIVE INSIGNIA
None

323d ANTIAIRCRAFT ARTILLERY AUTOMATIC WEAPONS BATTALION

Constituted 1 July 1946 in the Organized Reserves as the 323d Antiaircraft Artillery Automatic Weapons Battalion. Activated 1 August 1946 at Billings, Montana. (Organized Reserves redesignated 25 March 1948 as Organized Reserve Corps). Assigned to the 96th Infantry Division on 31 March 1949. Relieved from the 96th Infantry Division and disbanded 1 March 1952 at Billings.

CAMPAIGN STREAMERS
None

DECORATIONS
None

COAT OF ARMS
None

DISTINCTIVE INSIGNIA
None

324th ANTIAIRCRAFT ARTILLERY GUN BATTALION

Constituted 1 April 1942 in the Army of the United States as the 3d Battalion, 211th Coast Artillery (Antiaircraft) and activated 15 June 1952 at Vallejo, California. Reorganized and redesignated 10 September 1943 as the 324th Antiaircraft Artillery Searchlight Battalion. Inactivated, less Battery B, 30 August 1944 at Vallejo; Battery B inactivated 10 January 1946 at Fort Lawton, Washington. (3d Battalion, 241st Coast Artillery reconstituted and consolidated with the 324th Antiaircraft Artillery Searchlight Battalion on 25 August 1945). Allotted to the Massachusetts National Guard, 8 July 1946. Redesignated 1 December 1947 as the 324th Antiaircraft Artillery Gun Battalion. Reorganized and Federally recognized 16 February 1948 with Headquarters and Headquarters Battery, Battery A and Medical Detachment at New Bedford, Battery B at Taunton, Battery C at Braintree, and Battery D at South Weymouth. Redesignated 1 February 1949 as the 126th Antiaircraft Artillery Automatic Weapons Battalion.

CAMPAIGN STREAMERS
Civil War
Virginia 1861
North Carolina 1862
North Carolina 1863

World War I
Aisne-Marne
Champagne
Oise-Aisne
Meuse-Argonne

World War II
Pacific Theater without inscription

DECORATIONS
None

COAT OF ARMS
None

DISTINCTIVE INSIGNIA
None

325th ANTIAIRCRAFT ARTILLERY BATTALION

Constituted 25 February 1943 in the Army of the United States as the 325th Antiaircraft Artillery Searchlight Battalion and activated 30 April 1943 at Camp Haan, California. (Departed San Francisco Port of Embarkation 14 March 1944 for overseas service; arrived in Hawaii on 20 March 1944 and relocated to Okinawa on 4 June 1945). Inactivated 30 December 1946 at Gofuji, Okinawa. Redesignated 325th Antiaircraft Artillery Automatic Weapons Battalion, allotted to the Organized Reserve Corps and assigned to the 81st Infantry Division on 1 March 1952. Activated 1 June 1952 with Headquarters at La Grange, Georgia. (Organized Reserve Corps redesignated 9 July 1952 as Army Reserve). (Headquarters relocated to Atlanta, Georgia 22 April 1955). Redesignated 31 January 1953 as the 325th Antiaircraft Artillery Battalion. Inactivated 1 May 1959 at Atlanta.

CAMPAIGN STREAMERS
World War II
Ryukyus

DECORATIONS
None

COAT OF ARMS
None

DISTINCTIVE INSIGNIA
None

326th ANTIAIRCRAFT ARTILLERY SEARCHLIGHT BATTALION

Constituted 25 February 1943 in the Army of the United States as the 326th Antiaircraft Artillery Searchlight Battalion and activated 10 June 1943 at Fort Bliss, Texas. Inactivated 25 February 1945 at Fort Bliss. Disbanded 10 October 1952.

CAMPAIGN STREAMERS
None

DECORATIONS
None

COAT OF ARMS
None

DISTINCTIVE INSIGNIA
None

326th ANTIAIRCRAFT ARTILLERY BATTALION

Constituted 1 May 1955 as the 326th Antiaircraft Artillery Battalion and allotted to the Arkansas Army National Guard. Organized and Federally recognized 22 June 1955 with

Headquarters at West Memphis, and Batteries at Harrisburg, Marked Tree, West Helena and West Memphis.

Consolidated 1 June 1959 with the 206th Artillery, a parent regiment under the Combat Arms Regimental System.

CAMPAIGN STREAMERS
None

DECORATIONS
None

COAT OF ARMS
SHIELD: Per pale nebuly or and gules, issuant from sinister base a 40mm gun muzzle bendwise and in sinister chief a lozenge, all counterchanged.

CREST: That for the regiments and separate battalions of the Arkansas Army National Guard: On a wreath of the colors (or and gules) above two sprays of apple blossoms proper a diamond argent charged with four mullets azure, one in upper point and three in lower, within a bordure of the last bearing twenty-five mullets of the second.

MOTTO: Born To Battle

The colors scarlet and yellow are for Artillery. The nebuly partition line, a heraldic representation of air, is crossed by the gun muzzle to indicate the battalion's antiaircraft mission. The diamond shape symbolizes the allotment of the organization to Arkansas, the only state in the country where diamonds are found.

DISTINCTIVE INSIGNIA
The insignia is the shield and motto of the coat of arms. The sample of the insignia depicted was approved for wear on 15 November 1956.

327th ANTIAIRCRAFT ARTILLERY SEARCHLIGHT BATTALION

Constituted 25 February 1943 in the Army of the United States as the 327th Antiaircraft Artillery Searchlight Battalion and activated 10 June 1943 at Camp Edwards, Massachusetts. Inactivated 30 November 1944 at Camp Livingston, Louisiana. Disbanded 10 October 1952.

CAMPAIGN STREAMERS
None

DECORATIONS
None

COAT OF ARMS
None

DISTINCTIVE INSIGNIA
None

327th ANTIAIRCRAFT ARTILLERY BATTALION

Constituted in the Arkansas Army National Guard as the 327th Antiaircraft Artillery Battalion and Federally recognized 22 September 1955 at Jonesboro.

Converted and redesignated 1 June 1959 as the 875th Engineer Battalion.

CAMPAIGN STREAMERS
None

DECORATIONS
None

COAT OF ARMS
None

DISTINCTIVE INSIGNIA
None

328th ANTIAIRCRAFT ARTILLERY SEARCHLIGHT BATTALION

Constituted 27 May 1942 in the Army of the United States as the 3d Battalion, 85th Coast Artillery (Antiaircraft) and activated 28 May 1942 at Newport News, Virginia. Reorganized and redesignated 1 September 1943 as the 328th Antiaircraft Artillery Searchlight Battalion. Inactivated 8 August 1944 at Camp Rucker, Alabama. Disbanded 26 October 1944.

CAMPAIGN STREAMERS
None

DECORATIONS
None

COAT OF ARMS
None

DISTINCTIVE INSIGNIA
None

329th ANTIAIRCRAFT ARTILLERY SEARCHLIGHT BATTALION

Constituted 25 February 1943 in the Army of the United States as the 329th Antiaircraft Artillery Searchlight Battalion and activated 10 July 1943 at Camp Davis, North Carolina. Inactivated 15 November 1944 at Camp Gordon, Georgia. Disbanded 10 October 1952.

CAMPAIGN STREAMERS
None

DECORATIONS
None

COAT OF ARMS
None

DISTINCTIVE INSIGNIA
None

330th ANTIAIRCRAFT ARTILLERY SEARCHLIGHT BATTALION

Constituted 25 February 1943 in the Army of the United States as the 330th Antiaircraft Artillery Searchlight Battalion and activated 10 July 1943 at Camp Haan, California. Inactivated 11 December 1944 at Camp Hood, Texas. Disbanded 10 October 1952.

CAMPAIGN STREAMERS
None

DECORATIONS
None

COAT OF ARMS
None

DISTINCTIVE INSIGNIA
None

330th ANTIAIRCRAFT ARTILLERY BATTALION

Constituted 15 October 1954 in the Tennessee Army National Guard as the 330th Antiaircraft Artillery Battalion (Automatic Weapons) (Self Propelled), assigned to the 30th Armored Division and organized 27 October 1954 from existing units as follows:

Headquarters and Headquarters Company, 2d Battalion, 278th Infantry (organized and Federally recognized 11 April 1938 at Kingsport as Battery F, 115th Field Artillery; redesignated 1 February 1940 as Battery F, 191st Field Artillery; inducted into Federal service 24 February 1941 at Kingsport; redesignated 8 February 1943 as Battery C, 959th Field Artillery Battalion; inactivated 5 March 1946 at Camp Kilmer, New Jersey; redesignated 31 July 1946 as Headquarters and Headquarters Company, 2d Battalion 278th Infantry; reorganized and Federally recognized 15 April 1947 at Kingsport; ordered into active Federal service 1 September 1950 at Kingsport; released from active Federal service 8 September 1954 and resumed State status), redesignated Headquarters and Headquarters Battery

Battery H, 278th Infantry (constituted 31 July 1946 in the Tennessee National Guard and organized and Federally recognized 15 April 1947 at Kingsport; ordered into active Federal service 1 September 1950 at Kingsport; released from active Federal service 8 September 1954 and resumed State status), redesignated Battery A

Company L, 278th Infantry (organized and Federally recognized 13 April 1953 at Bristol as Company L, 278th Infantry [NGUS] and redesignated 8 September 1954 as Company L, 278th Infantry), redesignated Battery B

Company G, 278th Infantry (organized and Federally recognized 13 June 1933 at Bristol as Company C, 117th Infantry; redesignated 1 May 1938 as Howitzer Company, 117th Infantry; redesignated 26 September 1939 as Company D, 117th Infantry; inducted into Federal service 16 September 1940 at Bristol; inactivated 24 November 1945 at Fort Jackson, South Carolina; redesignated 31 July 1946 as Company G, 278th Infantry; reorganized and Federally recognized 25 April 1947 at Bristol; ordered into active Federal service 1 September 1950 at Bristol; released from active Federal service 8 September 1954 and resumed State status), redesignated Battery C

Company E, 278th. Infantry (organized and Federally recognized 24 May 1922 at Elizabethton as Company A, 117th Infantry; inducted into Federal service 16 September 1940; inactivated 24 November 1945 at Fort Jackson, South Carolina; redesignated 31 July 1946 as Company E, 278th Infantry; reorganized and Federally recognized 10 April 1947 at Elizabethton; ordered into active Federal service 1 September 1950 at Elizabethton; released from active Federal service 8 September 1954 and resumed State status), redesignated Battery D

Relieved from the 30th Armored Division and consolidated 1 March 1959 with the 117th Infantry, a parent regiment under the Combat Arms Regimental System.

CAMPAIGN STREAMERS
World War II
Normandy
Northern France
Rhineland
Ardennes-Alsace
Central Europe

DECORATIONS
Presidential Unit Citation (Army), Streamer embroidered *MORTAIN* (1st Bn 117th Inf cited for action on 7 Aug 1944; WDGO 12, 1945)

Presidential Unit Citation (Army), Streamer embroidered *ST. BARTHELMY* (1st Bn 117th Inf cited for action on 2 Oct 1944; WDGO 70, 1946)

French Croix de Guerre with Palm, World War II, Streamer embroidered *MORTAIN* (1st Bn 117th Inf cited for action on 7 Aug 1944; DAGO 43, 1952)

French Croix de Guerre with Palm, World War II, Streamer embroidered *FRANCE* (30th Inf Div cited; DAGO 14, 1959)

French Croix de Guerre with Silver Star, Streamer embroidered *SCHERPENSEEL* (117th Inf cited for period 2-11 Oct 1944; DAGO 43, 1950)

Belgian Fourragere 1940 (117th Inf cited; DAGO 43, 1950)

Cited in the Order of the Day of the Belgian Army for action in *BELGIUM* (117th Inf cited for period 4-10 Sep 1944; DAGO 43, 1950)

Cited in the Order of the Day of the Belgian Army for action in the *ARDENNES* (117th Inf cited for period 17-27 Jan 1945; DAGO 43, 1950)

COAT OF ARMS
SHIELD: Per chevron gules and azure, on a chevron rompu or, the upper sides of the chevron coinciding with the partition line, three mullets of the second, in nombril point a fleur-de-lis of the third.

CREST: That for the regiments and separate battalions of the Tennessee Army National Guard: On a wreath of the colors (or and gules), upon a mount vert a hickory tree proper charged with three mullets, one and two argent.

MOTTO: *Spectamus et Servamus* (Watch And Serve)

The colors scarlet and yellow are used for Artillery. The color blue, the rompu chevron and the three stars are taken from the coat of arms of the 117th Infantry and refer to the origin of elements of the battalion. The fleur-de-lis on a blue background represents combat service as Infantry in Europe during World War II.

DISTINCTIVE INSIGNIA
The insignia is the shield and motto of the coat of arms. The sample of the insignia depicted was approved for wear on 9 August 1956.

331st ANTIAIRCRAFT ARTILLERY SEARCHLIGHT BATTALION

Constituted 27 May 1942 in the Army of the United States as the 3d Battalion, 62d Coast Artillery (Antiaircraft) and activated 15 June 1942 near Fort Totten, New York. (Departed New York Port of Embarkation 31 August 1942 for overseas service; arrived in England on 6 September 1942; landed in North Africa on 11 November 1942 and moved to Sicily in 1944). Reorganized at Palmero, Sicily and redesignated 24 March 1944 as the 331st Antiaircraft Artillery Searchlight Battalion. (Relocated to Italy on 9 June 1944). Disbanded 4 December 1944 at Pozzouli, Italy. Reconstituted 5 August 1958 in the Regular Army.

Consolidated 24 June 1961 with the 62d Artillery, a parent regiment under the Combat Arms Regimental System.

CAMPAIGN STREAMERS
World War II
Algeria-French Morocco
Rome-Arno

DECORATIONS
None

COAT OF ARMS
None

DISTINCTIVE INSIGNIA
None

332d ANTIAIRCRAFT ARTILLERY SEARCHLIGHT BATTALION

Constituted 27 May 1942 in the Army of the United States as the 3d Battalion, 89th Coast Artillery (Antiaircraft) and activated 15 June 1942 at Washington, District of Columbia. Reorganized at Washington and redesignated 1 September 1943 as 332d Antiaircraft Artillery Searchlight Battalion. Inactivated 12 June 1944 at Camp Davis, North Carolina. Disbanded 26 June 1944.

CAMPAIGN STREAMERS
None

DECORATIONS
None

COAT OF ARMS
None

DISTINCTIVE INSIGNIA
None

333d ANTIAIRCRAFT ARTILLERY SEARCHLIGHT BATTALION

Constituted 1 April 1942 in the Army of the United States as the 3d Battalion, 75th Coast Artillery (Antiaircraft) and activated 1 August 1942 at Fort Richardson, Alaska. (Departed Alaska and arrived at the Seattle Port of Embarkation on 3 February 1944). Reorganized and redesignated 20 February 1944 as the 333d Antiaircraft Artillery Searchlight Battalion. Inactivated 18 August 1944 at Camp Carson, Colorado. Disbanded 26 October 1944.

CAMPAIGN STREAMERS
World War II
Pacific Theater without inscription

DECORATIONS
None

COAT OF ARMS
None

DISTINCTIVE INSIGNIA
None

334th ANTIAIRCRAFT ARTILLERY SEARCHLIGHT BATTALION

Constituted 27 May 1942 in the Army of the United States as the 3d Battalion, 90th Coast Artillery (Antiaircraft) (Semimobile) (Colored) and activated 15 June 1942 at Camp Stewart, Georgia. (Departed New York Port of Embarkation 2 April 1943 for overseas service and arrived in North Africa on 12 April 1943). Reorganized at Oran, Algeria and redesignated 9 March 1944 as 334th Antiaircraft Artillery Searchlight Battalion (Colored). (Relocated to Corsica on 27 May 1944). Disbanded 9 December 1944 on Corsica.

CAMPAIGN STREAMERS
World War II
Rome-Arno

DECORATIONS
None

COAT OF ARMS
None

DISTINCTIVE INSIGNIA
None

335th ANTIAIRCRAFT ARTILLERY SEARCHLIGHT BATTALION

Constituted 27 May 1942 in the Army of the United States as the 3d Battalion, 209th Coast Artillery (Antiaircraft) and activated 7 July 1942 in North Ireland. (Moved to England on 12 December 1942. Landed in North Africa on 3 January 1943 and moved to Italy on 28 October 1943). Reorganized at Bari, Italy and redesignated 1 May 1944 as the 335th Antiaircraft Artillery Searchlight Battalion. Inactivated 9 December 1944 at Naples, Italy.

CAMPAIGN STREAMERS
World War II
Tunisia
Naples-Foggia
Rome-Arno

DECORATIONS
None

COAT OF ARMS
None

DISTINCTIVE INSIGNIA
None

336th ANTIAIRCRAFT ARTILLERY SEARCHLIGHT BATTALION

Constituted 27 May 1942 in the Army of the United States as the 3d Battalion, 212th Coast Artillery (Antiaircraft) and activated 15 June 1942 at Seattle, Washington. Reorganized at Seattle and redesignated 10 September 1943 as the 336th Antiaircraft Artillery Searchlight Battalion. Disbanded 26 June 1944 at Camp Gruber, Oklahoma. Reconstituted 27 May 1946 and allotted to the New York National Guard.

CAMPAIGN STREAMERS
None

DECORATIONS
None

COAT OF ARMS
None

DISTINCTIVE INSIGNIA
None

336th ANTIAIRCRAFT ARTILLERY GUN BATTALION

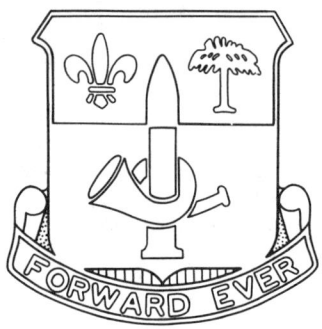

Constituted in the New York National Guard as the 16th Battalion of Infantry and organized 21 March 1898 from existing companies of the Third Brigade at Utica, including the 28th Separate Company (organized 9 June 1873) and the 44th Separate Company (organized 20 December 1837). Redesignated 19 April 1899 as 4th Battalion of Infantry, New York National Guard. Redesignated 1 May 1905 as 1st Battalion, 1st Infantry, New York National Guard. Mustered into Federal service 16 July-3 August 1917; drafted into Federal service 5 August 1917. Redesignated 4 January 1918 as 1st Battalion, 1st Pioneer Infantry. Demobilized 13 July 1919 at Camp Zachary Taylor, Kentucky. Reorganized in the New York National Guard as 3d Battalion, 10th Infantry and Federally recognized 15 February 1922 with Headquarters at Utica. Inducted into Federal service 15 October 1940 at home stations. Redesignated 11 December 1940 as 3d Battalion, 106th Infantry. Inactivated 31 December 1945 at Fort Lawton, Washington. Redesignated 27 September 1946 as 336th Antiaircraft Artillery Gun Battalion. Reorganized and Federally recognized 30 October 1947 with Headquarters at Utica. Ordered into active Federal service 15 May 1951 at home stations. Released from active Federal service 14 March 1953 and resumed State status.

Converted and redesignated 15 March 1953 as 3d Battalion, 101st Armored Cavalry.

CAMPAIGN STREAMERS
World War I
Aisne-Marne
Oise-Aisne

World War II
Eastern Mandates (with arrowhead)
Western Pacific
Ryukyus

DECORATIONS
None

COAT OF ARMS

SHIELD: Per fess enhanced gules and or, an antiaircraft projectile and case counterchanged, interlaced with a bugle horn azure between in chief a fleur-de-lis and a palm tree of the second.

CREST: That for the regiments and separate battalions of the New York Army National Guard: On a wreath of the colors (or and gules) the full rigged ship *Half Moon*, all proper.

MOTTO: Forward Ever

Red and yellow are used for Artillery. The antiaircraft projectile indicates the mission of the Battalion. The bugle horn, a symbol for Infantry, shows the long service as Infantry and is taken from the coat of arms of the 10th Infantry, New York National Guard. The fleur-de-lis is for service in France during World War I and the palm tree is for service in the Pacific Theater during World War II.

DISTINCTIVE INSIGNIA

The insignia is the shield and motto of the coat of arms. The insignia depicted was never made for nor worn by this organization.

336th ANTIAIRCRAFT ARTILLERY GUN BATTALION

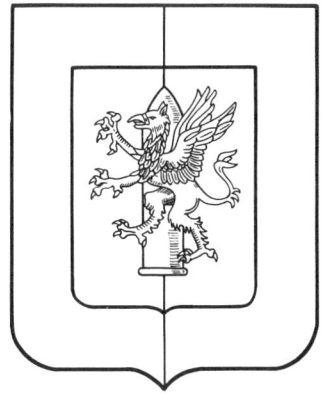

Constituted 23 July 1940 in the New York National Guard as the 2d Battalion, 209th Coast Artillery (Antiaircraft). Organized in northwestern New York State and Federally recognized 16 October 1940 with Headquarters at Rochester. Inducted into Federal service 10 February 1941 at home stations. (Departed New York Port of Embarkation 11 May 1942 for overseas service; arrived in Northern Ireland on 18 May 1942 and moved to England on 12 December 1942. Landed in North Africa on 3 January 1943 and moved to Italy on 28 October 1943). Reorganized at Montesarcchio, Italy and redesignated 18 March 1944 as the 898th Antiaircraft Artillery Automatic Weapons Battalion (Mobile). (Following service on Corsica and in France, returned

from overseas service and arrived at the Boston Port of Embarkation on 2 November 1945). Inactivated 3 November 1945 at Camp Myles Standish, Massachusetts. Redesignated 16 March 1953 as the 336th Antiaircraft Artillery Gun Battalion. Reorganized in northwestern New York State and Federally recognized 23 March 1953 with Headquarters at Niagara Falls. Redesignated 1 October 1953 as the 336th Antiaircraft Artillery Battalion (Gun).

Redesignated 1 October 1957 as the 106th Antiaircraft Artillery Battalion.

CAMPAIGN STREAMER
World War II
Tunisia
Naples-Foggia
Rome-Arno
Rhineland
Ardennes-Alsace
Central Europe

DECORATIONS
None

COAT OF ARMS

SHIELD: Per pale gules and or, an antiaircraft shell of the second, overall a griffin segreant argent, all within a bordure per pale of the second and the first.

CREST: That for the regiments and separate battalions of the New York Army National Guard: On a wreath of the colors (or and gules) the full rigged ship *Half Moon*, all proper.

MOTTO: *Defensores Caeli* (Defenders Of The Heaven)

The shield is that of the coat of arms of the old 209th Coast Artillery within a border to indicate the descent of the 336th Antiaircraft Artillery Battalion from the 2d Battalion of that regiment. The colors red and yellow and the shell symbolize the Artillery character of the battalion. The griffin, emblematic of the first ship to sail the Great Lakes above Niagara Falls, refers to the home area of the unit in the Great Lakes area.

DISTINCTIVE INSIGNIA
The insignia is the shield and motto of the coat of arms. The sample of the insignia depicted was approved for wear on 26 January 1955.

337th ANTIAIRCRAFT ARTILLERY BATTALION

Constituted 27 May 1942 in the Pennsylvania National Guard as the 3d Battalion, 213th Coast Artillery (Antiaircraft) and organized 15 June 1942 at Bayonne, New Jersey. (Departed New York Port of Embarkation 1 November 1942 for overseas service and arrived at Casablanca, North Africa on 18 November 1942. After service in Algeria and Tunisia moved to Italy on 9 September 1943). Reorganized 1 April 1944 at Arco Felice, Italy and redesignated 337th Antiaircraft Artillery Searchlight Battalion. Inactivated 24 September 1944 at Citiavecchia, Italy. Reorganized and Federally recognized 9 December 1946 with Headquarters at Reading and batteries at Reading and Hamburg. Reorganized and redesignated 1 December 1947 as the 337th Antiaircraft Artillery Gun Battalion. Ordered into active Federal service 1 May 1951 at Hamburg. Released from active Federal service 31 December 1952 and resumed State status. Redesignated 1 October 1953 as the 337th Antiaircraft Artillery Battalion (90mm Gun).

Consolidated 1 June 1959 with the 213th Artillery, a parent regiment under the Combat Arms Regimental System.

CAMPAIGN STREAMERS
World War II
Naples-Foggia
Rome-Arno

COAT OF ARMS
SHIELD: Or, a Maltese cross azure between a pairle six fleurs-de-lis gules.

CREST: That for the regiments and separate battalions of the Pennsylvania Army National Guard: On a wreath of the colors (or and azure) a lion rampant guardant proper, holding in dexter paw a naked scimitar agent, hilted or and in sinister an escutcheon argent, on a fess sable three plates.

MOTTO: Cannoneers Of The Blue

The descent from the 213th Coast Artillery is symbolized by the use of symbols from the coat of arms of that regiment. These symbols are arranged to form a similar design.

DISTINCTIVE INSIGNIA
The insignia is the shield and motto of the coat of arms. The sample of the insignia depicted was approved for wear on 2 December 1952.

338th ANTIAIRCRAFT ARTILLERY SEARCHLIGHT BATTALION

Constituted 27 May 1942 in the Army of the United States as the 3d Battalion, 99th Coast Artillery (Antiaircraft) (Semimobile) and organized 15 June 1942 at Fort Read, Trinidad with Negro enlisted personnel. (Returned from overseas service and arrived at the New York Port of Embarkation on 4 December 1943). Reorganized at Camp Stewart, Georgia and redesignated 29 February 1944 as 338th Antiaircraft Artillery Searchlight Battalion (Semimobile) (Colored). Disbanded 31 July 1944 at Camp Rucker, Alabama.

CAMPAIGN STREAMERS
World War II
American Theater without inscription

DECORATIONS
None

COAT OF ARMS
None

DISTINCTIVE INSIGNIA
None

339th ANTIAIRCRAFT ARTILLERY SEARCHLIGHT BATTALION

Constituted 27 May 1942 as the 3d Battalion, 206th Coast Artillery (Antiaircraft) and allotted to the Arkansas National Guard. Activated 1 August 1942 at Fort Mears, Alaska. (Returned from overseas service and arrived at the Seattle Port of Embarkation on 27 February 1944). Reorganized and redesignated 1 April 1944 as 339th Antiaircraft Artillery Searchlight Battalion. Inactivated 12 June 1944 at Fort Bliss, Texas. Disbanded 26 June 1944.

Reconstituted 27 May 1946 in the Arkansas National Guard as the 125th Medical Battalion.

CAMPAIGN STREAMERS
World War II
Aleutian Islands

DECORATIONS
None

COAT OF ARMS
None

DISTINCTIVE INSIGNIA
None

340th ANTIAIRCRAFT ARTILLERY MISSILE BATTALION

Constituted 27 May 1942 in the District of Columbia National Guard as the 3d Battalion, 260th Coast Artillery (Antiaircraft) and organized 15 June 1942 at Retsil, Washington. Reorganized and redesignated 10 September 1943 as 340th Antiaircraft Artillery Searchlight Battalion. Converted and redesignated 17 April 1944 as the 76th Signal Light Construction Battalion. Reorganized and redesignated 26 June 1944 as 76th Signal Heavy Construction Battalion. Inactivated 25 October 1945 at Manila, Philippine Islands. Redesignated 8 May 1946 as 340th Antiaircraft Artillery Searchlight Battalion. Reorganized at Washington and Federally recognized 4 October 1946. Reorganized and redesignated 1 December 1947 as 340th Antiaircraft Artillery Automatic Weapons Battalion. Reorganized and redesignated 1 September 1950 as 340th Antiaircraft Artillery Gun Battalion. Redesignated 15 November 1953 as 340th Antiaircraft Artillery Battalion (120mm Gun). Reorganized and redesignated 10 February 1958 as 340th Antiaircraft Artillery Missile Battalion (NIKE). Battalion, less Headquarters and Headquarters Battery disbanded 1 March 1959 when Federal recognition was withdrawn; concurrently, Headquarters and Headquarters Battery converted and redesignated as the 107th Engineer Company.

CAMPAIGN STREAMERS
World War II
Rhineland

DECORATIONS
None

COAT OF ARMS
SHIELD: Gules, on a pile bendwise or two projectiles sable between in chief a billet argent surmounted by a lozenge of the first charged with a fleur-de-lis of the second and in base a prickly pear cactus of the like within a diminished border engrailed per border of the third and gold.

CREST: That for the regiments and separate battalions of the District of Columbia Army National Guard: On a wreath of the colors (or and gules) the dome of the United States Capitol proper in front of a rising sun or.

MOTTO: *Gardez Bien* (Guard Well)

The 340th Antiaircraft Artillery Missile Battalion descended from the 3d Battalion of the 260th Coast Artillery, therefore the coat of arms of the parent organization has been placed within a gold engrailed border to indicate this descent. The border has been made engrailed and divided gold and black to distinguish it from the coat of arms of the 380th Antiaircraft Artillery Battalion which also descended from the 260th Coast Artillery.

DISTINCTIVE INSIGNIA
The insignia is the shield and motto of the coat of arms. The sample of the insignia depicted was approved for wear on 16 December 1952.

341st ANTIAIRCRAFT ARTILLERY SEARCHLIGHT BATTALION

Constituted 25 February 1943 in the Army of the United States as the 341st Antiaircraft Artillery Searchlight Battalion and activated 5 September 1943 at Fort Brooke, Puerto Rico. Disbanded 1 June 1944 at Camp O'Reilly, Puerto Rico.

CAMPAIGN STREAMERS
World War II
American Theater without inscription

DECORATIONS
None

COAT OF ARMS
None

DISTINCTIVE INSIGNIA
None

341st ANTIAIRCRAFT ARTILLERY BATTALION

Constituted 1 April 1955 as the 341st Antiaircraft Artillery Battalion and allotted to the Alabama Army National Guard. Organized and Federally recognized 10 May 1955 with Headquarters and Headquarters Battery and Medical Detachment at Jasper; Battery A at Vernon; Battery B at Double Springs; Battery C at Carbon Hill; and Battery D at Dora. Battalion broken up 2 May 1959 and elements converted, reorganized, consolidated and/or redesignated as follows: Headquarters and Headquarters Battery at Jasper redesignated Headquarters and Headquarters Detachment, 111th Ordnance Battalion; Battery A at Vernon consolidated with Company C, 877th Engineer Battalion; Battery B at Double Springs and Battery C at Carbon Hill consolidated and redesignated Company B, 1343d Engineer Battalion; and Battery D at Dora redesignated 402d Ordnance Company.

CAMPAIGN STREAMERS
None

DECORATIONS
None

COAT OF ARMS

SHIELD: Per fess wavy or and gules, in honor point a Chinese sun counterchanged.

CREST: That for the regiments and separate battalions of the Alabama Army National Guard: On a wreath of the colors (or and gules), a slip of cotton plant with full bursting boll proper.

MOTTO: Fuglemen

The colors scarlet and yellow are for Artillery. The Chinese sun and waves represent overseas service in World War II in the China-Burma-India area.

DISTINCTIVE INSIGNIA

The insignia is the shield and motto of the coat of arms. The sample of the insignia depicted was approved for wear on 27 December 1957.

342d ANTIAIRCRAFT ARTILLERY SEARCHLIGHT BATTALION

Constituted 25 February 1943 in the Army of the United States as the 342d Antiaircraft Artillery Searchlight Battalion and activated 15 February 1943 at Fort Randolph, Panama Canal Zone. Disbanded 1 February 1946 at Fort Randolph.

CAMPAIGN STREAMERS
World War II
American Theater without inscription

DECORATIONS
None

COAT OF ARMS
None

DISTINCTIVE INSIGNIA
None

343d ANTIAIRCRAFT ARTILLERY SEARCHLIGHT BATTALION

Constituted 25 February 1943 in the Army of the United States as the 343d Antiaircraft Artillery Searchlight Battalion and activated 15 September 1943 at Fort Sherman, Panama Canal Zone. Disbanded 1 February 1946 at Fort Sherman.

CAMPAIGN STREAMERS
World War II
American Theater without inscription

DECORATIONS
None

COAT OF ARMS
None

DISTINCTIVE INSIGNIA
None

343d ANTIAIRCRAFT ARTILLERY GUN BATTALION

Constituted 25 February 1943 as the 143d Antiaircraft Artillery Gun Battalion (Mobile) and activated 10 July 1943 at Camp Haan, California. (Departed New York Port of Embarkation 26 July 1944 for overseas service; arrived in England 6 August 1944 and landed in France on 31 August 1944. Returned from overseas service and arrived in the New York Port of Embarkation on 21 December 1945). Inactivated 22 December 1945 at Camp Kilmer, New Jersey. Redesignated 343d Antiaircraft Artillery Automatic Weapons Battalion, allotted to the Organized Reserve Corps and assigned to Fourth Army on 2 March 1949. Activated 18 March 1949 at New Orleans, Louisiana; inactivated 24 January 1950 at New Orleans. (Organized Reserve Corps redesignated Army Reserve on 15 July 1952).

Redesignated 16 October 1952 as the 143d Antiaircraft Artillery Gun Battalion.

CAMPAIGN STREAMERS
World War II
Northern France
Rhineland
Ardennes-Alsace
Central Europe

DECORATIONS
Presidential Unit Citation (Army), Streamer embroidered *ARDENNES* (143d AAA Gun Bn cited for period 18-24 Dec 1944; WDGO 113, 1946)

Cited in the Order of the Day of the Belgian Army for action in the *ARDENNES* (143d AAA Gun Bn cited for period 17-25 Jan 1945; DAGO 43, 1950)

COAT OF ARMS
None

DISTINCTIVE INSIGNIA
None

344th ANTIAIRCRAFT ARTILLERY SEARCHLIGHT BATTALION

Constituted 27 May 1942 in the Minnesota National Guard as the 3d Battalion, 217th Coast Artillery (Antiaircraft) (Semimobile) and activated 15 June 1942 near Oakland, California. Reorganized and redesignated 10 September 1943 as the 344th Antiaircraft Artillery Searchlight Battalion. Inactivated 12 June 1944 at Camp Haan, California.

Consolidated 21 June 1946 with the 136th Infantry.

CAMPAIGN STREAMERS
None

DECORATIONS
None

COAT OF ARMS
None

DISTINCTIVE INSIGNIA
None

345th ANTIAIRCRAFT ARTILLERY SEARCHLIGHT BATTALION

Constituted 25 February 1943 in the Army of the United States as the 345th Antiaircraft Artillery Searchlight Battalion and activated 15 September 1943 at Fort Clayton, Panama Canal Zone. Disbanded 1 February 1946 at Fort Clayton.

CAMPAIGN STREAMERS
World War II
American Theater without inscription

DECORATIONS
None

COAT OF ARMS
None

DISTINCTIVE INSIGNIA
None

346th ANTIAIRCRAFT ARTILLERY SEARCHLIGHT BATTALION

Constituted 25 February 1943 in the Army of the United States as the 346th Antiaircraft Artillery Searchlight Battalion and activated 15 September 1943 at Fort Clayton, Panama Canal Zone. Disbanded 1 February 1946 at Fort Clayton.

CAMPAIGN STREAMERS
World War II
American Theater without inscription

DECORATIONS
None

COAT OF ARMS
None

DISTINCTIVE INSIGNIA
None

347th ANTIAIRCRAFT ARTILLERY SEARCHLIGHT BATTALION

Constituted 27 May 1942 in the Minnesota National Guard as the 3d Battalion, 215th Coast Artillery (Antiaircraft) (Semimobile) and activated 1 August 1942 at Fort Greely, Kodiak, Alaska. (Returned from overseas service and arrived at the Seattle Port of Embarkation on 29 February 1944). Reorganized at Fort Bliss, Texas and redesignated 1 July 1944 as the 347th Antiaircraft Artillery Searchlight Battalion. Inactivated 18 August 1944 at Camp Carson, Colorado.

CAMPAIGN STREAMERS
World War II
American Theater without inscription

DECORATIONS
None

COAT OF ARMS
None

DISTINCTIVE INSIGNIA
None

348th ANTIAIRCRAFT ARTILLERY SEARCHLIGHT BATTALION

Constituted 27 May 1942 in the Army of the United States as the 3d Battalion, 605th Coast Artillery (Antiaircraft) and activated 15 June 1942 at Camp Stewart, Georgia. Reorganized at Boston, Massachusetts on 1 September 1943 and redesignated as the 348th Antiaircraft Artillery Searchlight Battalion. Inactivated 12 June 1944 at Camp Stewart. Disbanded 26 June 1944.

CAMPAIGN STREAMERS
None

DECORATIONS
None

COAT OF ARMS
None

DISTINCTIVE INSIGNIA
None

350th ANTIAIRCRAFT ARTILLERY SEARCHLIGHT BATTALION

Constituted 1 January 1942 in the Army of the United States as the 350th Coast Artillery Searchlight Battalion and activated 1 May 1942 at Camp Stewart, Georgia. Redesignated 10 April 1943 as the 350th Antiaircraft Artillery Searchlight Battalion. (Departed San Francisco Port of Embarkation 27 October 1943 for overseas service and arrived in Australia on 13 November 1943. Moved to New Guinea on 19 February 1944 and then to the Philippines on 7 April 1945). Inactivated 21 February 1946 on Luzon, Philippine Islands.

Redesignated 16 May 1946 as the 194th Antiaircraft Artillery Searchlight Battalion.

CAMPAIGN STREAMERS
World War II
New Guinea
Luzon

DECORATIONS
Philippine Presidential Unit Citation, Streamer embroidered *17 OCTOBER 1944 TO 4 JULY 1945* (350th AAA SL Bn cited; DAGO 47, 1950)

COAT OF ARMS
None

DISTINCTIVE INSIGNIA
None

351st ANTIAIRCRAFT ARTILLERY MISSILE BATTALION

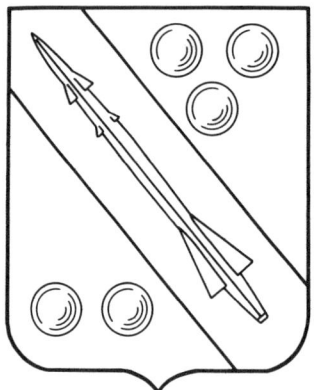 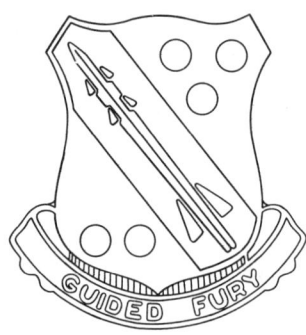

Constituted 1 January 1942 in the Army of the United States as the 351st Coast Artillery Searchlight Battalion and activated 12 January 1942 at Camp Haan, California. (Departed New York Port of Embarkation 13 January 1943 for overseas service; arrived in North Africa on 27 January 1943 and moved to Italy on 10 October 1943). Redesignated 24 May 1944 as the 351st Antiaircraft Artillery Searchlight Battalion. Disbanded 28 October 1944 in Italy. Reconstituted 5 June 1956 in the Regular Army as the 351st Antiaircraft Artillery Missile Battalion. Activated 15 July 1956 at Cleveland, Ohio; inactivated 1 September 1958 at Cleveland.

CAMPAIGN STREAMERS
World War II
Tunisia
Naples-Foggia
Rome-Arno
North Apennines
Po Valley

DECORATIONS
None

COAT OF ARMS
SHIELD: Or, on a bend gules a missile of the field between five gunstones, three and two.

CREST: None

MOTTO: Guided Fury

The colors scarlet and yellow are used for Artillery. The five gunstones commemorate the World War II campaigns of the unit while the missile represents the current mission.

DISTINCTIVE INSIGNIA
The insignia is the shield and motto of the coat of arms. The sample of the insignia depicted was approved for wear on 16 October 1957.

352d ANTIAIRCRAFT ARTILLERY SEARCHLIGHT BATTALION

Constituted 31 January 1942 in the Army of the United States as the 352d Coast Artillery Searchlight Battalion and activated 1 March 1942 at Camp Haan, California. Redesignated 8 May 1943 as the 352d Antiaircraft Artillery Searchlight Battalion. Inactivated 3 January 1945 at

Fort Jackson, South Carolina. Disbanded 10 October 1952.

CAMPAIGN STREAMERS
None

DECORATIONS
None

COAT OF ARMS
None

DISTINCTIVE INSIGNIA
None

353d ANTIAIRCRAFT ARTILLERY SEARCHLIGHT BATTALION

Constituted 31 January 1942 in the Army of the United States as the 353d Separate Coast Artillery Searchlight Battalion and activated 1 May 1942 at Camp Stewart, Georgia. Redesignated 17 February 1944 as the 353d Antiaircraft Artillery Searchlight Battalion. (Departed New York Port of Embarkation 7 February 1943 for overseas service; landed in North Africa on 21 February 1943 and moved to France on 17 September 1944. Returned from overseas service and arrived at the New York Port of Embarkation on 1 January 1946). Inactivated 2 January 1946 at Camp Kilmer, New Jersey.

Allotted to the Texas National Guard on 2 July 1946; concurrently, battalion broken up and elements redesignated as follows: Headquarters and Headquarters Battery as Headquarters and Headquarters Battery, 270th Coast Artillery Battalion; Battery A as 924th Coast Artillery Battery (12-inch); Battery B as 949th Coast Artillery Battery (90mm AMTB) and Battery C as 956th Coast Artillery Battery (6-inch).

CAMPAIGN STREAMERS
World War II
Tunisia
Rome-Arno
Rhineland
Ardennes-Alsace
Central Europe

DECORATIONS
None

COAT OF ARMS

SHIELD: Per fess enhanced azure and gules, two searchlights issuing from dexter and sinister base respectively, sable fimbriated or with beams throughout crossing at honor point of the last.

CREST: None

MOTTO: We Pierce The Blue

In the predominating scarlet and gold of the Coast Artillery arm the separate searchlight mobile functions of the organization are appropriately symbolized by the searchlights piercing the sky, represented by the blue upper portion of the shield. The motto *We Pierce The Blue* is expressive of the successful accomplishment of the tasks allotted to the organization.

DISTINCTIVE INSIGNIA

The insignia is the shield and motto of the coat of arms. The insignia depicted was never made for nor worn by this organization.

354th ANTIAIRCRAFT ARTILLERY SEARCHLIGHT BATTALION

Constituted 24 April 1942 in the Army of the United States as the 354th Coast Artillery Searchlight Battalion and activated 1 May 1942 at Los Angeles, California. (Departed New York Port of Embarkation 7 February 1943 for overseas service; arrived in North Africa 21 February 1943 and moved to Italy on 3 March 1944). Redesignated 1 May 1944 as the 354th Antiaircraft Artillery Searchlight Battalion. Disbanded 9 December 1944 at Botinuccio, Italy.

CAMPAIGN STREAMERS
World War II
Tunisia
Rome-Arno

DECORATIONS
None

COAT OF ARMS

SHIELD: Sable, two diminutive piles issuing from dexter and sinister chief in saltire and extending to dexter and sinister nombril points respectively argent, in the intersection the silhouette of an aircraft of the first, in base a baton palewise or surmounted by four laurel leaves fructed of four vert, fimbriated of the fourth.

CREST: None

MOTTO: *Cepimus* (We Have Caught It)

The upper half of the shield is symbolic of the tactics and the high altitude illuminations developed by the First Provisional Searchlight Battalion of which this Battalion was an offspring. The two white searchlight beams intersect on a field of midnight with the intersection well toward the top of the shield. In the center of the intersection is a bomber. The lower half of the shield is symbolic of the origin of the battalion. Beneath the intersection is a sprig of laurel with four green berries, held aloft by a golden baton; the four green berries represent the four untrained units which made up the First Provisional Searchlight Battalion; Battery A, 207th Coast Artillery, Battery A, 209th Coast Artillery, Battery A, 212th Coast Artillery, and Battery A, 214th Coast Artillery. The golden baton represents the leadership of LTC Arthur B. Nicholson, CAC which ripened the berries or developed the untrained units into one well integrated unit capable of handling a new tactical idea and of illuminating targets at an altitude thrice that of which, at the time, was considered the maximum working ceiling of searchlights.

DISTINCTIVE INSIGNIA
The insignia is the shield and motto of the coat of arms. The insignia depicted was never made for nor worn by this organization.

355th ANTIAIRCRAFT ARTILLERY SEARCHLIGHT BATTALION

Constituted 24 April 1942 in the Army of the United States as the 355th Coast Artillery Searchlight Battalion and activated 1 May 1942 at Los Angeles, California. (Departed New York Port of Embarkation 14 January 1943 for overseas service; arrived in North Africa 27 January 1943 and moved to Italy on 23 February 1944). Redesignated 1 May 1944 as the 355th Antiaircraft Artillery Searchlight Battalion. Disbanded 20 December 1944 at Oran, North Africa.

CAMPAIGN STREAMERS
World War II
Tunisia
Rome-Arno

DECORATIONS
None

COAT OF ARMS
None

DISTINCTIVE INSIGNIA
None

356th ANTIAIRCRAFT ARTILLERY SEARCHLIGHT BATTALION

Constituted 5 May 1942 in the Army of the United States as the 3d Battalion, 504th Coast Artillery (Antiaircraft) (Semimobile) and activated 1 July 1942 at Camp Hulen, Texas. Reorganized at Camp Hulen and redesignated 20 January 1943 as the 356th Coast Artillery Searchlight Battalion. Redesignated 3 March 1943 as the 356th Antiaircraft Artillery Searchlight Battalion. (Departed San Francisco Port of Embarkation for overseas service 11 December 1943 and arrived on Guadalcanal 30 December 1943. Moved to the Philippine Islands 4 April 1945. Returned to the United States and arrived at the San Francisco Port of Embarkation 27

December 1945). Inactivated 28 December 1945 at Camp Stoneman, California.

CAMPAIGN STREAMERS
World War II
Leyte

DECORATIONS
Philippine Presidential Unit Citation, Streamer embroidered *17 OCTOBER 1944 TO 4 JULY 1945* (356th AAA SL Bn cited; DAGO 47, 1950)

COAT OF ARMS
None

DISTINCTIVE INSIGNIA
None

357th ANTIAIRCRAFT ARTILLERY SEARCHLIGHT BATTALION

Constituted 19 December 1942 in the Army of the United States as the 357th Coast Artillery Searchlight Battalion and activated 20 January 1943 at Camp Stewart, Georgia. Redesignated 27 April 1943 as the 357th Antiaircraft Artillery Searchlight Battalion. (Departed New York Port of Embarkation 6 October 1944 for overseas service; arrived in England on 18 October 1944 and landed in France on 27 December 1944). Returned from overseas service and inactivated 27 December 1945 at Camp Patrick Henry, Virginia.

CAMPAIGN STREAMERS
World War II
Central Europe

DECORATIONS
None

COAT OF ARMS
None

DISTINCTIVE INSIGNIA
None

358th ANTIAIRCRAFT ARTILLERY SEARCHLIGHT BATTALION

Constituted 19 December 1942 in the Army of the United States as the 358th Coast Artillery Searchlight Battalion and activated 20 January 1943 at Camp Stewart, Georgia. Redesignated 1 May 1943 as the 358th Antiaircraft Artillery Searchlight Battalion. Inactivated 30 January 1945 at Fort Jackson, South Carolina. Disbanded 10 October 1952.

CAMPAIGN STREAMERS
None

DECORATIONS
None

COAT OF ARMS
None

DISTINCTIVE INSIGNIA
None

359th ANTIAIRCRAFT ARTILLERY SEARCHLIGHT BATTALION

Constituted 19 December 1942 in the Army of the United States as the 359th Coast Artillery Searchlight Battalion and activated 10 January 1943 at Camp Edwards, Massachusetts. Redesignated 24 April 1943 as the 359th Antiaircraft Artillery Searchlight Battalion. Inactivated 8 November 1944 at Camp Gordon, Georgia. Disbanded 10 October 1952.

CAMPAIGN STREAMERS
None

DECORATIONS
None

COAT OF ARMS
None

DISTINCTIVE INSIGNIA
None

360th ANTIAIRCRAFT ARTILLERY SEARCHLIGHT BATTALION

Constituted 27 May 1942 in the Organized Reserves as the 3d Battalion, 508th Coast Artillery (Antiaircraft) (Semimobile) and activated 1 September 1942 at Camp Stewart, Georgia. Reorganized at Camp Stewart and redesignated 20 January 1943 as the 360th Coast Artillery Searchlight Battalion (Antiaircraft). (Departed New York Port of Embarkation 5 March 1943 for overseas service; arrived at Casablanca, French Morocco, North Africa 18 March 1943 and landed near Naples, Italy on 3 March 1944). Redesignated 1 May 1944 as the 360th Antiaircraft Artillery Searchlight Battalion. Disbanded 15 December 1944 at Villanova, Italy.

CAMPAIGN STREAMERS
World War II
Naples-Foggia
Rome-Arno
North Apennines

DECORATIONS
None

COAT OF ARMS
None

DISTINCTIVE INSIGNIA
None

361st COAST ARTILLERY SEARCHLIGHT BATTALION

Constituted 17 December 1942 in the Army of the United States as the 361st Coast Artillery Searchlight Battalion (Colored). (1st Platoon, Battery A activated 1 January 1943 at Fort Jackson, South Carolina and inactivated 15 October 1943 in Liberia). Battalion disbanded 14 June 1944.

CAMPAIGN STREAMERS
None

DECORATIONS
None

COAT OF ARMS
None

DISTINCTIVE INSIGNIA
None

362d ANTIAIRCRAFT ARTILLERY SEARCHLIGHT BATTALION

Constituted 27 May 1942 in the Army of the United States as the 3d Battalion, 512th Coast Artillery (Antiaircraft) (Semimobile) and activated 15 June 1942 at Fort Bliss, Texas. Reorganized at Fort Bliss and redesignated 20 January 1943 as the 362d Coast Artillery Searchlight Battalion. Redesignated 3 March 1943 as the 362d Antiaircraft Artillery Searchlight Battalion. (Departed San Francisco Port of Embarkation 27 July 1943 for overseas service and arrived on Guadalcanal 6 September 1943. Moved to New Guinea on 11 January 1945 and to the Philippines on 20 April 1945). Disbanded 21 April 1945 at Alabang, Luzon, Philippine Islands.

CAMPAIGN STREAMERS
World War II
Luzon

DECORATIONS
Philippine Presidential Unit Citation, Streamer embroidered *17 OCTOBER 1944 TO 4 JULY 1945* (362d AAA SL Bn cited; DAGO 47, 1950)

COAT OF ARMS
None

DISTINCTIVE INSIGNIA
None

363d ANTIAIRCRAFT ARTILLERY SEARCHLIGHT BATTALION

Constituted 1 April 1942 in the Army of the United States as the 3d Battalion, 514th Coast Artillery (Antiaircraft) and activated at Camp Davis, North Carolina. Reorganized and redesignated 20 January 1943 as the 363d Coast Artillery Searchlight Battalion. Redesignated 3 March 1943 as the 363d Antiaircraft Artillery Searchlight Battalion. Inactivated 31 October 1944 at Camp Gordon, Georgia. Disbanded 10 October 1952.

CAMPAIGN STREAMERS
None

DECORATIONS
None

COAT OF ARMS
None

DISTINCTIVE INSIGNIA
None

364th ANTIAIRCRAFT ARTILLERY BATTALION

Constituted 2 October 1942 in the Army of the United States as the 685th Coast Artillery Battery (Antiaircraft) (Automatic Weapons) and activated 10 October 1942 at Camp Stewart, Georgia. Redesignated 10 June 1943 as the 685th Antiaircraft Artillery Machine Gun Battery. Disbanded 10 July 1945. Reconstituted as the 356th Coast Artillery Gun Battery, allotted to the Organized Reserves and assigned to First Army on 5 June 1947. Activated 17 June 1947 at Brooklyn, New York. (Organized Reserves redesignated 25 March 1948 as Organized Reserve Corps). Reorganized and redesignated 6 October 1949 as Headquarters and Headquarters Battery, 364th Antiaircraft Artillery Gun Battalion; concurrently, remainder of battalion organized from individual batteries as follows: 360th Coast Artillery Gun Battery redesignated Battery A; 364th Coast Artillery Gun Battery redesignated as Battery B; 368th Coast Artillery Gun Battery redesignated as Battery C and 369th Coast Artillery Battery redesignated Battery D. Relocated to Fort Tilden, New York 8 November 1949; to Long Island City on 15 January 1951 and back to Brooklyn on 2 July 1951. (Organized Reserve Corps redesignated 9 July 1952 as Army Reserve). Redesignated 1 September 1953 as the 364th Antiaircraft Artillery Battalion. Inactivated 31 May 1959 at Brooklyn.

CAMPAIGN STREAMERS
World War II
India-Burma
Central Burma

DECORATIONS
None

COAT OF ARMS
None

DISTINCTIVE INSIGNIA
None

365th ANTIAIRCRAFT ARTILLERY SEARCHLIGHT BATTALION

Constituted 31 January 1942 in the Army of the United States as the 3d Battalion, 501st Coast Artillery (Antiaircraft) (Semimobile) and activated 1 April 1942 at Camp Haan, California. Reorganized and redesignated 10 September 1943 at San Francisco, California as the 365th Antiaircraft Artillery Searchlight Battalion. Inactivated 18 August 1944 at Camp Carson, Colorado. Disbanded 26 October 1944.

CAMPAIGN STREAMERS
None

DECORATIONS
None

COAT OF ARMS
None

DISTINCTIVE INSIGNIA
None

365th ANTIAIRCRAFT ARTILLERY BATTALION

Constituted 30 September 1949 in the Organized Reserve Corps as the 365th Antiaircraft Artillery Gun Battalion and organized by redesignation of existing batteries as follows: 339th Coast Artillery Searchlight Battery (constituted 14 October 1944 as the 730th Coast Artillery Battery) redesignated Headquarters Battery; 335th Coast Artillery Gun Battery (constituted 11 March 1943 as Battery C 283d Coast Artillery Battalion) redesignated Battery A; 337th Coast Artillery Gun Battery (constituted 20 June 1942 as the 692d Coast Artillery Battery) redesignated Battery B; 352d Coast Artillery Gun Battery (constituted 26 December 1942 as the 677th Coast Artillery Battery) redesignated Battery C; and 361st Coast Artillery Gun Battery (constituted 2 October 1942 as the 690th Coast Artillery Battery) redesignated Battery D. Activated 8 November 1949 at Long Island City, New York. (Organized Reserve Corps redesignated 9 July 1952 as Army Reserve). Redesignated 1 September 1953 as the 365th Antiaircraft Artillery Battalion. Inactivated 1 May 1959 at Long Island City.

CAMPAIGN STREAMERS
World War II
Sicily (with arrowhead)
Naples-Foggia (with arrowhead)
Anzio (with arrowhead)
Rome-Arno

DECORATIONS
None

COAT OF ARMS
None

DISTINCTIVE INSIGNIA
None

366th ANTIAIRCRAFT ARTILLERY SEARCHLIGHT BATTALION

Constituted 31 January 1942 in the Army of the United States as 3d Battalion, 502d Coast Artillery (Antiaircraft) (Semimobile) and activated 1 May 1942 at Fort Sheridan, Illinois. Reorganized at Paterson, New Jersey and redesignated 1 September 1943 as the 366th Antiaircraft Artillery Searchlight Battalion (Mobile). Inactivated 28 July 1944 at Camp Chaffee, Arkansas. Disbanded 26 October 1944.

CAMPAIGN STREAMERS
None

DECORATIONS
None

COAT OF ARMS
None

DISTINCTIVE INSIGNIA
None

367th ANTIAIRCRAFT ARTILLERY SEARCHLIGHT BATTALION

Constituted 27 May 1942 in the Army of the United States as 3d Battalion, 507th Coast Artillery (Antiaircraft), and activated 1 August 1942 at Camp Haan, California. Reorganized at North Long Beach, California and redesignated 10 September 1943 as 367th Antiaircraft Artillery Searchlight Battalion. Inactivated 12 June 1944 at Camp Haan. Disbanded 26 June 1944.

CAMPAIGN STREAMERS
None

DECORATIONS
None

COAT OF ARMS
None

DISTINCTIVE INSIGNIA
None

367th ANTIAIRCRAFT ARTILLERY BATTALION

Constituted 10 October 1956 as the 367th Antiaircraft Artillery Battalion (90mm Gun) and allotted to the Army National Guard of the Territory of Hawaii. Withdrawn from allotment to the Army National Guard of the Territory of Hawaii on 15 January 1959 and returned to Department of Army control.

CAMPAIGN STREAMERS
None

DECORATIONS
None

COAT OF ARMS
None

DISTINCTIVE INSIGNIA
None

368th ANTIAIRCRAFT ARTILLERY SEARCHLIGHT BATTALION

Constituted 20 September 1942 as 3d Battalion, 701st Coast Artillery (Antiaircraft) and activated 1 October 1942 at Fort Totten, New York. Reorganized and redesignated 1 September 1943 as 368th Antiaircraft Artillery Searchlight Battalion. Inactivated 15 August 1944 at Fort Jackson, South Carolina. Disbanded 26 October 1944.

CAMPAIGN STREAMERS
None

DECORATIONS
None

COAT OF ARMS
None

DISTINCTIVE INSIGNIA
None

369th ANTIAIRCRAFT ARTILLERY BATTALION

Constituted 2 June 1913 in the New York National Guard as 1st Battalion, 15th Infantry (Colored). Organized and Federally recognized 29 June 1916 at New York City. Mustered into Federal service 25 July 1917 at Camp Whitman, New York and drafted into Federal service on 5 August 1917. Redesignated 1 March 1918 as 1st Battalion, 369th Infantry and assigned to the 93d Division. Relieved from the 93d Division and demobilized 28 February 1919 at Camp Upton, New York. Consolidated with the 1st Battalion, 15th Infantry, New York Guard (organized 31 July 1918 at New York City) and redesignated 11 October 1921 as 1st Battalion, 369th Infantry (Colored). Reorganized and Federally recognized 6 September 1924 at New York City. Converted, reorganized and redesignated 30 August 1940 as 1st Battalion, 369th Coast Artillery (Antiaircraft) (Colored). Inducted into Federal service 13 January 1941 at New York City. (Departed San Francisco Port of Embarkation 16 June 1942 for overseas service and arrived in Hawaii 21 June 1942). Reorganized and redesignated 12 December 1943 as 369th Antiaircraft Artillery Gun Battalion (Colored). (Moved to Okinawa on 12 August 1945. Returned from overseas service and arrived at the Los Angeles Port of Embarkation on 20 January 1946). Inactivated 21 January 1946 at Camp Anza, Arlington, California. Reorganized and Federally recognized 29 October 1947 at New York City. Ordered into active Federal service 11 September 1950 at New York City. Released from active Federal service 10 September 1952 and resumed State status. Redesignated 1 October 1953 as the 369th Antiaircraft Artillery Battalion (90mm Gun).

Redesignated 1 April 1955 as the 569th Field Artillery Battalion.

CAMPAIGN STREAMERS
World War I
Champagne-Marne
Meuse-Argonne
Champagne 1918
Alsace 1918

World War II
Pacific Theater without inscription

DECORATIONS
French Croix de Guerre with Silver Star, World War I, Streamer embroidered *MEUSE-ARGONNE* (369th Inf cited; WDGO 11, 1924)

COAT OF ARMS
SHIELD: Per chevron azure and gules, a chevron wavy argent between in chief five poplar trees or and in base a rattlesnake ready to strike of the third, and for unofficial use pendant from the escutcheon the French Croix de Guerre with Silver Star, all proper.

CREST: That for the regiments and separate battalions of the New York Army National Guard: On a wreath of the colors (argent and azure) the full rigged ship *Half Moon*, all proper.

MOTTO: Don't Tread On Me

The blue, white and red of the shield represent the Tricolor of France and commemorates the fact that the entire combat service of the organization during World War I was with the French Army. The wavy chevron represents the first front line sector held by the organization at the junction of the Aisne and Tourbe Rivers in the general outline of a wavy chevron. The five poplar trees represent the Argonne Forest and the five days of combat during the Meuse-Argonne offensive. The rattlesnake perpetuates the distinctive insignia adopted in April 1918 and worn by the organization throughout the remainder of its service in France. The Motto, "Don't Tread On Me", was adopted at the same time as the insignia.

DISTINCTIVE BADGE
On a blue shield a silver rattlesnake coiled to strike. The sample of the badge depicted was originally approved 23 February 1924 for wear by the 369th Infantry.

370th ANTIAIRCRAFT ARTILLERY SEARCHLIGHT BATTALION

Constituted 4 May 1943 in the Army of the United States as the 370th Coast Artillery Searchlight Battalion and activated 1 June 1943 at Fort Buchanan, Puerto Rico. Redesignated 15 October 1943 as the 370th Antiaircraft Artillery Searchlight Battalion. Disbanded 1 June 1944 at Camp O'Reilly, Puerto Rico.

CAMPAIGN STREAMERS
World War II
American Theater without inscription

DECORATIONS
None

COAT OF ARMS
None

DISTINCTIVE INSIGNIA
None

371st ANTIAIRCRAFT ARTILLERY SEARCHLIGHT BATTALION

Constituted 14 May 1943 in the Army of the United States as the 371st Antiaircraft Artillery Searchlight Battalion and activated 24 May 1943 at Portsmouth, Virginia. Inactivated 12 June 1944 at Camp Davis, North Carolina. Disbanded 26 June 1944.

CAMPAIGN STREAMERS
None

DECORATIONS
None

COAT OF ARMS
None

DISTINCTIVE INSIGNIA
None

372d ANTIAIRCRAFT ARTILLERY SEARCHLIGHT BATTALION

Constituted 14 May 1943 in the Army of the United States as the 372d Antiaircraft Artillery Searchlight Battalion and activated 24 May 1943 at Buffalo, New York. Inactivated 12 June 1944 at Camp Davis, North Carolina. Disbanded 26 June 1944.

CAMPAIGN STREAMERS
None

DECORATIONS
None

COAT OF ARMS
None

DISTINCTIVE INSIGNIA
None

372d ANTIAIRCRAFT ARTILLERY GUN BATTALION

Constituted 25 February 1943 in the Army of the United States as the 132d Coast Artillery Battalion (Separate) (Antiaircraft) (Gun) (Mobile) and activated 15 June 1943 at Camp Edwards, Massachusetts. Redesignated 28 June 1943 as the 132d Antiaircraft Artillery Gun Battalion (Mobile). (Departed New York Port of Embarkation 23 July 1944 for overseas service; arrived in England on 28 July 1944 and landed in France on 23 August 1944. Returned from overseas service and arrived at the New York Port of Embarkation on 19 February 1946). Inactivated 20 February 1946 at Camp Kilmer, New Jersey. Redesignated 372d Antiaircraft Artillery Gun Battalion and allotted to the Organized Reserves on 18 October 1948. Activated 26 October 1948 at Baltimore, Maryland; inactivated 29 August 1950 at Baltimore.

CAMPAIGN STREAMERS
World War II
Northern France
Rhineland
Central Europe

DECORATIONS
None

COAT OF ARMS
None

DISTINCTIVE INSIGNIA
None

373d ANTIAIRCRAFT ARTILLERY SEARCHLIGHT BATTALION

Constituted 27 May 1942 as 3d Battalion, 198th Coast Artillery (Antiaircraft) and allotted to the Delaware National Guard. Activated 1 January 1943 on Bora Bora, Society Islands. Reorganized and redesignated 1 March 1944 as 373d Antiaircraft Artillery Searchlight Battalion. Inactivated 29 December 1945 at Camp Stoneman, California.

Consolidated 16 May 1946 with Headquarters and Headquarters Battery 198th Antiaircraft Artillery Group.

CAMPAIGN STREAMERS
World War II
Northern Solomons (with arrowhead)
Luzon

DECORATIONS
Philippine Presidential Unit Citation, Streamer embroidered *17 OCTOBER 1944 TO 4 JULY 1945* (373d AAA SL Bn cited; DAGO 47, 1950)

COAT OF ARMS
None

DISTINCTIVE INSIGNIA
None

374th ANTIAIRCRAFT ARTILLERY SEARCHLIGHT BATTALION

Constituted 27 May 1942 in the Army of the United States as 3d Battalion, 77th Coast Artillery (Antiaircraft) (Semimobile) (Colored) and activated 20 January 1943 on Tongatabu Island, South Tonga Islands. Relocated to New Hebrides on 18 April 1943. Reorganized and redesignated 1 November 1943 as the 374th Antiaircraft Artillery Searchlight Battalion (Colored). (Moved to New Georgia in 1944 and later stationed in the Admiralty Islands and in New Guinea). Disbanded 25 June 1945 at Hollandia, New Guinea.

CAMPAIGN STREAMERS
World War II
Bismarck Archipelago
Northern Solomons

DECORATIONS
None

COAT OF ARMS
None

DISTINCTIVE INSIGNIA
None

374th ANTIAIRCRAFT ARTILLERY BATTALION

Constituted 29 July 1921 in the Organized Reserves as Headquarters and Headquarters Battery, 510th Artillery (Antiaircraft), Coast Artillery Corps and organized during February 1922 at Chester, Pennsylvania. Redesignated 30 June 1924 as Headquarters and Headquarters Battery, 510th Coast Artillery (Antiaircraft). Ordered into active military service, less personnel and equipment, 15 November 1942 at Fort Sheridan, Illinois. Reorganized and redesignated 20 January 1943 as Headquarters and Headquarters Battery, 112th Coast Artillery Group. Redesignated 26 May 1943 as Headquarters and Headquarters Battery, 112th Antiaircraft Artillery Group. (Departed New York Port of Embarkation 17 November 1943 for the European Theater of Operations and served in England, France, Germany, and Austria; returned to the United States and arrived at the Hampton Roads Port of Embarkation on 18 October 1945). Inactivated 18 October 1945 at Camp Patrick Henry, Virginia. Redesignated Headquarters and Headquarters Battery, 374th Harbor Defense and assigned to Sixth Army on 11 March 1947. Activated 10 April 1947 at Los Angeles, California. (Organized Reserves redesignated 25 March 1948 as Organized Reserve Corps). Reorganized and redesignated 1 September 1949 as Headquarters and Headquarters Battery, 374th Antiaircraft Artillery Gun Battalion; concurrently, remainder of battalion organized from new and existing units as follows: Battery A constituted new and 330th, 811th and 861st Coast Artillery Gun Batteries redesignated Batteries B, C, and D respectively. (Organized Reserve Corps redesignated 9 June 1952 as Army Reserve). Redesignated 15 April 1953 as the 374th Antiaircraft Artillery Battalion. Inactivated 1 May 1959 at Los Angeles.

CAMPAIGN STREAMERS
World War II
Normandy
Northern France
Rhineland
Ardennes-Alsace
Central Europe

DECORATIONS
None

COAT OF ARMS
None

DISTINCTIVE INSIGNIA
None

375th ANTIAIRCRAFT ARTILLERY AUTOMATIC WEAPONS BATTALION

Constituted 29 July 1921 in the Organized Reserves as 2d Battalion, 510th Artillery (Antiaircraft), Coast Artillery Corps, allotted to the Third Corps Area and assigned to III Corps. Organized during February 1922 with Headquarters at Chester, Pennsylvania. Ordered into active military service, less personnel and equipment, at Fort Sheridan, Illinois on 15 November

1942. Reorganized at Fort Sheridan on 20 January 1943 and redesignated 198th Coast Artillery Battalion (Antiaircraft) (Automatic Weapons). Redesignated 30 April 1943 as 198th Antiaircraft Artillery Automatic Weapons Battalion. (Departed San Francisco Port of Embarkation 8 May 1944 for overseas service; arrived in New Guinea on 30 July 1944 and moved to the Philippine Islands on 9 January 1945). Inactivated 31 August 1945 at Manila, Philippine Islands. Redesignated 375th Antiaircraft Artillery Automatic Weapons Battalion, assigned to Sixth Army and activated 15 June 1947 at Logan, Utah. (Organized Reserves redesignated Organized Reserve Corps on 25 March 1948). Inactivated 10 November 1950 at Logan.

CAMPAIGN STREAMERS
World War II
New Guinea
Luzon (with arrowhead)

DECORATIONS
Philippine Presidential Unit Citation, Streamer embroidered *7 OCTOBER 1944 TO 4 JULY 1945* (198th AAA AW Bn cited; DAGO 47, 1950)

COAT OF ARMS
None

DISTINCTIVE INSIGNIA
None

376th ANTIAIRCRAFT ARTILLERY BATTALION

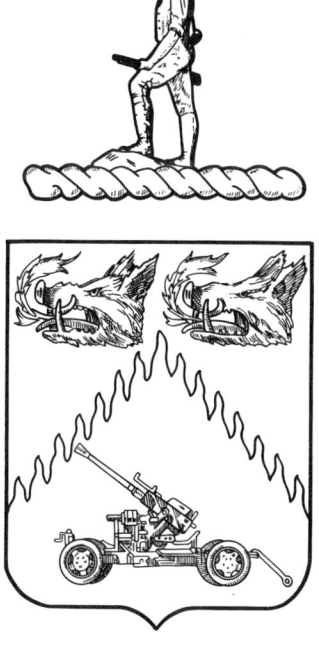
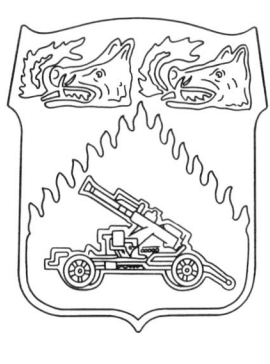

Constituted 6 July 1942 in the Army of the United States as the 376th Coast Artillery Battalion (Antiaircraft) (Automatic Weapons) and activated 15 July 1942 at Camp Stewart, Georgia. Redesignated 27 February 1943 as the 376th Antiaircraft Artillery Automatic Weapons Battalion (Mobile). (Departed New York Port of Embarkation 5 September 1943 for overseas service; arrived in England 15 September 1943 and landed in France on 15 June 1944. Returned from overseas service and arrived at the New York Port of Embarkation 1 December 1945).

Inactivated 2 December 1945 at Camp Kilmer, New Jersey. Allotted to the Organized Reserves, assigned to Seventh Army and activated 28 October 1946 at Charleston, South Carolina. Relieved from Seventh Army and assigned to Third Army 15 March 1947. (Organized Reserves redesignated 25 March 1948 as Organized Reserve Corps and 9 July 1952 as Army Reserve). Redesignated 19 January 1954 as the 376th Antiaircraft Artillery Battalion. (Headquarters relocated to Spartanburg, South Carolina on 1 May 1957). Inactivated 25 June 1959 at Spartanburg.

CAMPAIGN STREAMERS
World War II
Normandy
Northern France
Rhineland
Ardennes-Alsace
Central Europe

DECORATIONS
Belgian Fourragere 1940 (376th AAA AW Bn cited; DAGO 43, 1950)

Cited in the Order of the Day of the Belgian Army for action along the *MEUSE RIVER* (376th AAA AW Bn cited for period 3-13 Sept 1944; DAGO 43, 1950)

Cited in the Order of the Day of the Belgian Army for action in the *ARDENNES* (376th AAA AW Bn cited for period 20 Dec 1944-26 Jan 1945; DAGO 43, 1950)

COAT OF ARMS
SHIELD: Per chevron radiant or and gules, in chief two boars' heads couped, fire issuing from the mouth proper, in base a 40mm AA gun of the first.

CREST: That for the regiments and separate battalions of the Army Reserve: On a wreath of the colors (or and gules) the Lexington Minute Man proper. The statue of the Minute Man, Captain John Parker (H.H. Kitson, sculptor), stands on the common in Lexington, Massachusetts.

MOTTO: *Monitus Munitus* (Forewarned, Forearmed)

The scarlet of the shield is for the Coast Artillery Corps. The boars' heads symbolize the courage of the organization in the performance of its allotted duties and the chevron is symbolic of protection, used heraldically to represent the saddle of a war horse; the 40mm gun is representative of the antiaircraft functions of the Battalion.

DISTINCTIVE INSIGNIA
The insignia is the shield and motto of the coat of arms. The insignia depicted was unofficially worn by this battalion after World War II.

377th ANTIAIRCRAFT ARTILLERY BATTALION

Constituted 6 July 1942 in the Army of the United States as the 377th Coast Artillery Battalion (Antiaircraft) (Automatic Weapons) and activated 15 July 1942 at Camp Stewart, Georgia. Redesignated 15 May 1943 as the 377th Antiaircraft Artillery Automatic Weapons Battalion (Mobile). (Departed New York Port of Embarkation 5 September 1943 for overseas service; arrived in England 15 September 1943 and landed in France on 14 June 1944. Returned from overseas service and arrived at the New York Port of Embarkation 28 January 1946). Inactivated 29 January 1946 at Camp Kilmer, New Jersey. Allotted to the Organized Reserves and assigned to Second Army on 2 January 1947. Activated 8 January 1947 at Pittsburgh, Pennsylvania. (Organized Reserves redesignated 25 March 1948 as Organized Reserve Corps). Inactivated 19 October 1950 at Pittsburgh. (Organized Reserve Corps redesignated 9 July 1952 as Army Reserve). Redesignated 18 January 1956 as the 377th Antiaircraft Artillery Battalion. Activated 14 February 1956 with Headquarters at Erie, Pennsylvania; inactivated 1 June 1959 at Erie.

CAMPAIGN STREAMERS
World War II
Normandy
Northern France
Rhineland
Ardennes-Alsace
Central Europe

DECORATIONS
Belgian Fourragere 1940 (377th AAA AW Bn cited; DAGO 43, 1950)

Cited in the Order of the Day of the Belgian Army for action in *BELGIUM* (377th AAA AW Bn cited for period 7-13 Sept 1944; DAGO 43, 1950)

Cited in the Order of the Day of the Belgian Army for action in the *ARDENNES* (377th AAA AW Bn cited for period 16-21 Dec 1944; DAGO 43, 1950)

COAT OF ARMS

SHIELD: Gules, a pile throughout or surmounted by a fess azure charged with a winged projectile of the second.

CREST: That for the regiments and separate battalions of the Army Reserve: On a wreath of the colors (or and gules) the Lexington Minute Man proper. The statue of the Minute Man, Captain John Parker (H.H. Kitson, sculptor), stands on the common in Lexington, Massachusetts.

MOTTO: *Caela Purgamus* (We Clean The Skies)

The winged projectile and the searchlight like beam in ultramarine blue and gold, represent an antiaircraft shell shot into the blue sky. This also symbolizes the function of the organization.

DISTINCTIVE INSIGNIA

The insignia is the shield and motto of the coat of arms. The sample of the insignia depicted was approved for wear on 6 February 1943.

378th ANTIAIRCRAFT ARTILLERY BATTALION

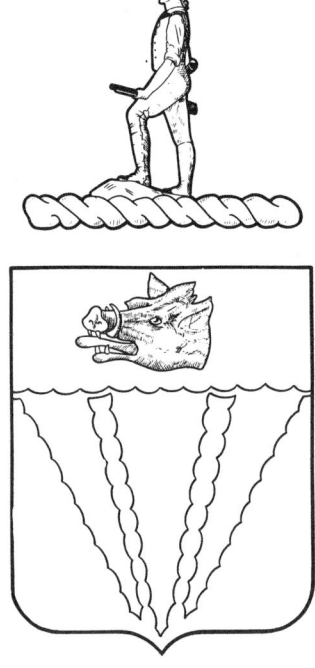
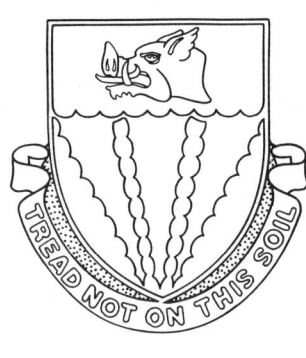

Constituted 6 July 1942 in the Army of the United States as the 378th Coast Artillery Battalion (Antiaircraft) (Automatic Weapons) and activated 15 July 1942 at Camp Stewart, Georgia. (Departed Boston Port of Embarkation 10 February 1943 and arrived in Iceland 25 February 1943). Redesignated 10 November 1943 as the 378th Antiaircraft Artillery Automatic Weapons Battalion (Mobile). (Returned from overseas service and arrived at the New York Port of Embarkation on 27 December 1944). Inactivated 12 February 1945 at Fort Bragg, North Carolina. Allotted to the Organized Reserves and assigned to Seventh Army 31 October 1946. Activated 8 November 1946 at Wilmington, North Carolina. Relieved from the Seventh Army and assigned to Third Army 15 March 1947. (Organized Reserves redesignated 25 March 1948 as Organized Reserve Corps). Inactivated 31 December 1950 at Wilmington.

CAMPAIGN STREAMERS
World War II
American Theater without inscription

DECORATIONS
None

COAT OF ARMS

SHIELD: Gules, three piles engrailed in point or, on a chief invected azure fimbriated of the second, a boar's head couped of the like.

CREST: That for the regiments and separate battalions of the Organized Reserve Corps: On a wreath of the colors (or and gules) the Lexington Minute Man proper. The statue of the Minute Man, Captain John Parker (H.H. Kitson, sculptor), stands on the common in Lexington, Massachusetts.

MOTTO: Tread Not On This Soil

The scarlet is the color of the Coast Artillery Corps. The three engrailed piles are representative of the wedge driven into enemy territory by the organization as well as the equivalent of searchlight beams and refer to the antiaircraft functions of the organization. The engrailed division of the chief represents clouds and the position itself signifies determination and authority as well as successful command in war. The State of activation, Georgia, is indicated by the boar's head taken from the crest of that State.

DISTINCTIVE INSIGNIA
The insignia is the shield and motto of the coat of arms. The insignia depicted was never made for nor worn by this organization.

379th ANTIAIRCRAFT ARTILLERY AUTOMATIC WEAPONS BATTALION

Constituted 6 July 1942 in the Army of the United States as the 379th Coast Artillery Battalion (Antiaircraft) (Automatic Weapons) and activated 15 July 1942 at Camp Stewart, Georgia. Redesignated 10 May 1943 as the 379th Antiaircraft Artillery Automatic Weapons Battalion (Mobile). (Departed New York Port of Embarkation 1 December 1944 for overseas service; arrived in England on 12 December 1944 and landed in France 19 February 1945). Inactivated 5 June 1946 in Germany. Allotted to the Organized Reserves and assigned to Fifth Army 1 November 1946. Activated 14 November 1946 at Minneapolis, Minnesota. (Organized Reserves redesignated 25 March 1948 as Organized Reserve Corps). Inactivated 4 December 1950 at Minneapolis.

CAMPAIGN STREAMERS
World War II
Rhineland
Central Europe

DECORATIONS
None

COAT OF ARMS
None

DISTINCTIVE INSIGNIA
None

380th ANTIAIRCRAFT ARTILLERY MISSILE BATTALION

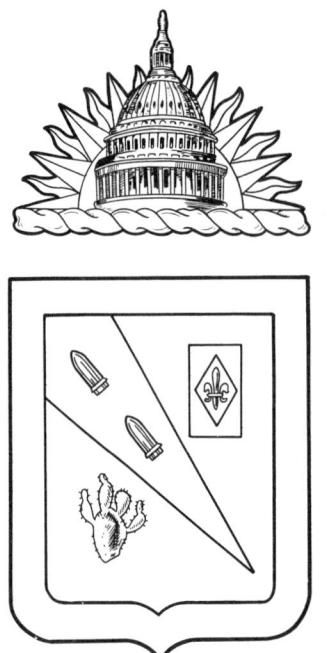

Constituted 17 June 1924 as the 2d Battalion, 260th Coast Artillery (Harbor Defense) and allotted to the District of Columbia National Guard. Redesignated 1 August 1929 as the 2d Battalion, 260th Coast Artillery (Antiaircraft). Organized new at Washington between 19 June 1930 and 1 April 1939. Inducted into Federal service at Washington on 6 January 1941. Reorganized and redesignated 10 September 1943 as the 380th Antiaircraft Artillery Automatic Weapons Battalion. Inactivated 6 December 1944 at Camp Livingston, Louisiana. Reorganized at Washington and Federally recognized 10 October 1946. Reorganized and redesignated 1 September 1950 as the 380th Antiaircraft Artillery Gun Battalion. Ordered into active Federal service at Washington, 15 May 1951. Released from active Federal service 14 April 1953 and resumed District status. Redesignated 15 November 1953 as the 380th Antiaircraft Artillery Battalion (120mm Gun). Reorganized and redesignated 10 February 1958 as the 380th Antiaircraft Artillery Missile Battalion (NIKE).

Broken up 1 March 1959 and elements converted or disbanded as follows: Headquarters and Headquarters Battery redesignated 105th Military Police Detachment; Battery A redesignated 114th Engineer Company; and Federal recognition withdrawn from Batteries B, C, and D.

CAMPAIGN STREAMERS
None

DECORATIONS
None

COAT OF ARMS
SHIELD: Gules, on a pile bendwise or two projectiles sable between in chief a billet argent surmounted by a lozenge of the first charged with a fleur-de-lis of the second and in base a prickly pear cactus of the like within a diminished bordure or.

CREST: That for the regiments and separate battalions of the District of Columbia Army National Guard: On a wreath of the colors (or and gules) the dome of the United States Capitol proper in front of a rising sun or.

MOTTO: *Dieu Defend le Droit* (God Defends The Right)

The 380th Antiaircraft Artillery Missile Battalion descended from the 2d Battalion of the 260th Coast Artillery, therefore the coat of arms of the parent organization has been placed within a diminished border to indicate this descent.

DISTINCTIVE INSIGNIA
The insignia is the shield and motto of the coat of arms. The sample of the insignia depicted was approved for wear on 22 December 1952.

381st ANTIAIRCRAFT ARTILLERY AUTOMATIC WEAPONS BATTALION

Constituted 19 December 1942 in the Army of the United States as the 381st Coast Artillery Battalion (Antiaircraft) (Automatic Weapons) and activated 20 January 1943 at Fort Sheridan, Illinois. Redesignated 30 April 1943 as the 381st Antiaircraft Artillery Automatic Weapons Battalion (Semimobile). (Departed San Francisco Port of Embarkation 20 January 1945 for overseas service and arrived in the Philippine Islands on 17 February 1945). Disbanded 15 March 1945 at Tacloban, Leyte, Philippine Islands.

CAMPAIGN STREAMERS
World War II
Leyte

DECORATIONS
Philippine Presidential Unit Citation, Streamer embroidered *17 OCTOBER 1944 TO 4 JULY 1945* (381st AAA AW Bn cited; DAGO 47, 1950)

COAT OF ARMS
None

DISTINCTIVE INSIGNIA
None

382d ANTIAIRCRAFT ARTILLERY AUTOMATIC WEAPONS BATTALION

Constituted 19 December 1942 in the Army of the United States as the 382d Coast Artillery Battalion (Antiaircraft) (Automatic Weapons) and activated 10 January 1943 at Camp Hulen, Texas. Redesignated 30 April 1943 as the 382d Antiaircraft Artillery Automatic Weapons Battalion (Semimobile). (Departed Portland Sub Port of Embarkation 23 March 1944 for overseas service; arrived in New Guinea on 21 April 1944 and moved to the Philippines on 13 March 1945). Inactivated 30 June 1946 at Yokohama, Japan. Allotted to the Organized Reserves and assigned to Sixth Army on 7 November 1946. Activated 1 December 1946 at Oakland, California. (Organized Reserves redesignated 25 March 1948 as Organized Reserve Corps). Inactivated 30 November 1950 at Oakland.

CAMPAIGN STREAMERS
World War II
New Guinea
Luzon

DECORATIONS
Philippine Presidential Unit Citation, Streamer embroidered *17 OCTOBER 1944 TO 4 JULY 1945* (382d AAA AW Bn cited; DAGO 47, 1950)

COAT OF ARMS
None

DISTINCTIVE INSIGNIA
None

383d ANTIAIRCRAFT ARTILLERY BATTALION

Constituted 19 December 1942 in the Army of the United States as the 383d Coast Artillery Battalion (Antiaircraft) (Automatic Weapons) and activated 10 January 1943 at Fort Bliss, Texas. Redesignated 30 April 1943 as the 383d Antiaircraft Artillery Automatic Weapons Battalion (Semimobile). (Departed San Francisco Port of Embarkation 23 November 1943 for overseas service and arrived in Australia on 19 December 1943; after service in New Guinea, on Morotai Island and in the Philippines, returned to San Francisco Port of Embarkation 16 December 1945). Inactivated 18 December 1945 at Camp Stoneman, California. Allotted to the Organized Reserves and assigned to Fifth Army on 18 November 1946. Activated 26 November 1946 with Headquarters at Chicago, Illinois. (Organized Reserves redesignated 25 March 1948 as Organized Reserve Corps). Inactivated 15 November 1950 at Chicago. (Organized Reserve Corps redesignated 9 July 1952 as Army Reserve). Redesignated 383d Antiaircraft Artillery Battalion and activated 19 July 1956 with Headquarters at Evanston, Illinois. Inactivated 30 September 1959 at Evanston.

CAMPAIGN STREAMERS
World War II
New Guinea (with arrowhead)
Leyte

DECORATIONS
Philippine Presidential Unit Citation, Streamer embroidered *17 OCTOBER 1944 TO 4 JULY 1945* (383d AAA AW Bn cited; DAGO 47, 1950)

COAT OF ARMS

SHIELD: Per chevron enhanced or and gules, a Philippine sun surmounted by a New Guinea drum charged with a stylized figure, all counterchanged.

CREST: That for the regiments and separate battalions of the Army Reserve: On a wreath of the colors (or and gules) the Lexington Minute Man proper. The statue of the Minute Man, Captain John Parker (H.H. Kitson, sculptor), stands on the common in Lexington, Massachusetts.

MOTTO: None Shall Get By

Scarlet is the color for Artillery. The dominant peak symbolizes the volcanic origin of New Guinea and the Philippines where the battalion served during World War II. The Philippines are represented by their decorative sun and New Guinea by the stylized native drum.

DISTINCTIVE INSIGNIA

The insignia is the shield and motto of the coat of arms. The sample of the insignia depicted was approved for wear on 22 August 1958.

384th ANTIAIRCRAFT ARTILLERY AUTOMATIC WEAPONS BATTALION

Constituted 2 May 1918 in the Regular Army as the 2d Battalion, 71st Artillery, Coast Artillery Corps and organized 12 May 1918 at various Forts in the Coast Defenses of Boston. Demobilized 6 March 1919 at Camp Devens, Massachusetts. Reconstituted 1 July 1940 in the Regular Army as the 2d Battalion, 71st Coast Artillery (Antiaircraft) (Semimobile). Activated 3 January 1941 at Fort Monroe, Virginia. Reorganized at Washington, District of Columbia and redesignated 1 September 1943 as the 384th Antiaircraft Artillery Automatic Weapons Battalion. Inactivated 18 August 1944 at Camp Pickett, Virginia and disbanded 26 October 1944. Reconstituted 23 April 1946 in the Regular Army as the 384th Antiaircraft Artillery Gun Battalion. Activated 8 May 1946 at Fort Bliss, Texas; disbanded 31 January 1949 at Fort Bliss.

Reconstituted 28 June 1950 in the Regular Army and consolidated with the 41st Antiaircraft Artillery Gun Battalion.

CAMPAIGN STREAMERS
World War I
Streamer without inscription

DECORATIONS
None

COAT OF ARMS
None

DISTINCTIVE INSIGNIA
None

385th ANTIAIRCRAFT ARTILLERY BATTALION

Constituted 19 December 1942 in the Army of the United States as the 385th Coast Artillery Battalion (Antiaircraft) (Automatic Weapons) and activated 10 January 1943 at Camp Edwards, Massachusetts. Redesignated 30 April 1943 as the 385th Antiaircraft Artillery Automatic Weapons Battalion (Semimobile). (Departed New York Port of Embarkation 29 January 1944 for overseas service; arrived in England on 5 February 1944 and landed in France on 12 July 1944). Inactivated 30 October 1945 in Germany. Allotted to the Organized Reserves 19 November 1946. Activated 29 November 1946 with Headquarters at Detroit, Michigan. (Organized Reserves redesignated 25 March 1948 as Organized Reserve Corps). Assigned to the 21st Armored Division 25 November 1949. Relieved from the 21st Armored Division and assigned to the 70th Infantry Division 1 March 1952. (Organized Reserve Corps redesignated 9 July 1952 as Army Reserve). Redesignated 15 December 1952 as the 385th Antiaircraft Artillery Battalion. Inactivated 12 July 1954 at Detroit. Activated 1 August 1955 at Royal Oak, Michigan. Disbanded 1 May 1959 at Royal Oak.

CAMPAIGN STREAMERS
World War II
Normandy
Northern France
Rhineland
Ardennes-Alsace
Central Europe

DECORATIONS
None

COAT OF ARMS
SHIELD: Gules, on a bend enhanced or four fleurs-de-lis azure palewise, in base a mailed fist of the second.

CREST: That for the regiments and separate battalions of the Army Reserve: On a wreath of the colors (or and gules) the Lexington Minute Man proper. The statue of the Minute Man, Captain John Parker (H.H. Kitson, sculptor), stands on the common in Lexington, Massachusetts.

MOTTO: Power, Prestige, Pride

Scarlet and yellow are the colors for Artillery. The four fleurs-de-lis symbolize the organization's campaigns in Europe during World War II. The mailed fist represents the power with which the battalion's functions are performed.

DISTINCTIVE INSIGNIA
The insignia is the shield and motto of the coat of arms. The insignia depicted was never made for nor worn by this organization.

386th ANTIAIRCRAFT ARTILLERY AUTOMATIC WEAPONS BATTALION

Constituted 19 December 1942 in the Army of the United States as the 386th Coast Artillery Battalion (Antiaircraft) (Automatic Weapons) and activated 10 January 1943 at Camp Edwards, Massachusetts. Redesignated 30 April 1943 as the 386th Antiaircraft Artillery Automatic Weapons Battalion (Semimobile). (Departed New York Port of Embarkation 11 February 1944 for overseas service; arrived in England 18 February 1944 and landed in France 11 July 1944). Inactivated 30 October 1945 in Germany. Allotted to the Organized Reserves and assigned to Fifth Army on 19 November 1946. Activated 29 November 1946 at Detroit, Michigan. (Organized Reserves redesignated 25 March 1948 as Organized Reserve Corps). Inactivated 15 November 1950 at Detroit.

CAMPAIGN STREAMERS
World War II
Normandy
Northern France
Rhineland
Ardennes-Alsace
Central Europe

DECORATIONS
None

COAT OF ARMS
None

DISTINCTIVE INSIGNIA
None

387th ANTIAIRCRAFT ARTILLERY BATTALION

Constituted 19 December 1942 in the Army of the United States as the 387th Coast Artillery Battalion (Antiaircraft) (Automatic Weapons) and activated 20 January 1943 at Camp Edwards, Massachusetts. Redesignated 10 April 1943 as the 387th Antiaircraft Artillery Automatic Weapons Battalion (Self Propelled). (Departed New York Port of Embarkation 10 April 1944 for overseas service; arrived in England 16 April 1944 and landed in France 29 June 1944). Inactivated 30 June 1946 in Germany. Allotted to the Organized Reserves and assigned to First Army 6 December 1946. Activated 17 December 1946 with Headquarters at Wilmington, Delaware. (Organized Reserves redesignated 25 March 1948 as Organized Reserve Corps and redesignated 9 July 1952 as Army Reserve). Redesignated 15 October 1953 as the 387th Antiaircraft Artillery Battalion. Inactivated 9 April 1954 at Wilmington.

CAMPAIGN STREAMERS
World War II
Normandy
Northern France
Rhineland
Ardennes-Alsace
Central Europe

DECORATIONS
Presidential Unit Citation (Army), Streamer embroidered *HURTGEN FOREST* (Btry C 387th AAA AW Bn cited for period 29 Nov-8 Dec 1944; WDGO 31, 1947)

COAT OF ARMS
SHIELD: Gules, five fleurs-de-lis, three and two or above a lozenge fesswise of the like bearing the head of a crowing cock erased azure, armed, eyed and jelloped of the first.

CREST: That for the regiments and separate battalions of the Army Reserve: On a wreath of the colors (or and gules) the Lexington Minute Man proper. The statue of the Minute Man, Captain John Parker (H.H. Kitson, sculptor), stands on the common

in Lexington, Massachusetts.

MOTTO: Look To The Sky

The colors red and yellow are used for Artillery. The five fleurs-de-lis represent the campaigns of the organization in Europe during World War II. The lozenge is from the Delaware State flag. The blue cock's head is a reference to the tradition of "the blue hen's chicken" which has been associated with Delaware's fighting men since the Revolution.

DISTINCTIVE INSIGNIA
The insignia is the shield and motto of the coat of arms. The sample of the insignia depicted was approved for wear on 21 August 1953.

388th ANTIAIRCRAFT ARTILLERY BATTALION

Constituted 19 January 1942 in the Army of the United States as the 2d Battalion, 85th Coast Artillery (Antiaircraft) (Semimobile) and activated 26 January 1942 at Camp Davis, North Carolina. Reorganized at Norfolk, Virginia and redesignated 1 September 1943 as the 388th Antiaircraft Artillery Automatic Weapons Battalion (Self Propelled). (Departed Seattle Port of Embarkation 29 March 1945 for overseas service; arrived in Hawaii on 6 April 1945 and landed on Ie Shima, Ryukyu Islands on 10 May 1945). Inactivated 15 February 1946 in Korea. Allotted to the Organized Reserves and assigned to Fifth Army on 19 December 1946. Activated 15 January 1947 at Milwaukee, Wisconsin. (Organized Reserves redesignated 25 March 1948 as Organized Reserve Corps and further redesignated 9 July 1952 as Army Reserve). Redesignated 12 March 1954 as the 388th Antiaircraft Artillery Battalion. Inactivated 18 May 1959 at Milwaukee.

CAMPAIGN STREAMERS
World War II
Ryukyus

DECORATIONS
None

COAT OF ARMS
None

DISTINCTIVE INSIGNIA
None

389th ANTIAIRCRAFT ARTILLERY AUTOMATIC WEAPONS BATTALION

Constituted 19 December 1942 in the Army of the United States as the 389th Coast Artillery Battalion (Antiaircraft) (Automatic Weapons) and activated 20 January 1943 at Camp Haan, California. Redesignated 30 April 1943 as the 389th Antiaircraft Artillery Automatic Weapons Battalion (Semimobile). (Departed Portland Sub Port of Embarkation 31 March 1944 for overseas service and arrived in New Guinea on 1 May 1944; moved to Morotai Island on 16 September 1944 and landed in the Philippines on 21 July 1945). Inactivated 30 January 1946 on Luzon, Philippine Islands. Allotted to the Organized Reserves and assigned to Fourth Army on 20 January 1947. Activated 30 January 1947 at Waco, Texas. (Organized Reserves redesignated 25 March 1948 as Organized Reserve Corps). Inactivated 1 March 1952 at Waco.

CAMPAIGN STREAMERS
World War II
New Guinea

DECORATIONS
None

COAT OF ARMS
None

DISTINCTIVE INSIGNIA
None

390th ANTIAIRCRAFT ARTILLERY AUTOMATIC WEAPONS BATTALION

Constituted 19 December 1942 in the Army of the United States as the 390th Coast Artillery Battalion (Antiaircraft) (Automatic Weapons) and activated 20 January 1943 at Camp Haan, California. Redesignated 10 April 1943 as the 390th Antiaircraft Artillery Automatic Weapons Battalion (Self Propelled). (Departed Boston Port of Embarkation 22 June 1944 for overseas service; arrived in England 29 June 1944 and landed in France on 27 July 1944). Inactivated 15 September 1946 at Munich, Germany. Allotted to the Organized Reserves and assigned to Sixth Army 6 February 1947. Activated 5 April 1947 at Portland, Oregon. (Organized Reserves redesignated 25 March 1948 as Organized Reserve Corps). Inactivated 31 August 1950 at Portland.

CAMPAIGN STREAMERS
World War II
Northern France
Rhineland
Ardennes-Alsace
Central Europe

DECORATIONS
French Croix de Guerre with Gold Star, World War II, Streamer embroidered *NORMANDY* (390th AAA AW Bn cited; DAGO 43, 1950)

Cited in the Order of the Day of the Belgian Army for action in the *ARDENNES* (390th AAA AW Bn cited for period 20 Dec 1944-26 Jan 1945; DAGO 43, 1950)

COAT OF ARMS
None

DISTINCTIVE INSIGNIA
None

391st ANTIAIRCRAFT ARTILLERY BATTALION

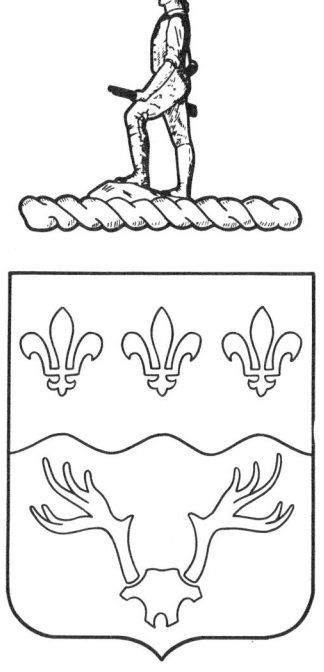

Constituted 19 December 1942 in the Army of the United States as the 391st Coast Artillery Battalion (Antiaircraft) (Automatic Weapons) and activated 10 January 1943 at Camp Davis, North Carolina. Redesignated 30 April 1943 as the 391st Antiaircraft Artillery Automatic Weapons Battalion (Semimobile). (Departed Boston Port of Embarkation 27 February 1944 for overseas service; arrived in England 8 March 1944 and landed in France on 14 July 1944. Returned from overseas service and arrived at the New York Port of Embarkation on 27 December 1945). Inactivated 27 December 1945 at Camp Kilmer, New Jersey. Allotted to the Organized Reserves 7 March 1947 and activated 24 March 1947 at Oklahoma City, Oklahoma. (Organized Reserves redesignated 25 March 1948 as Organized Reserve Corps). Redesignated 495th Antiaircraft Artillery Automatic Weapons Battalion and assigned to the 95th Infantry Division 30 June 1949. (Headquarters relocated to Antlers, Oklahoma on 1 October 1950). Redesignated 1 March 1952 as the 391st Antiaircraft Artillery Automatic Weapons Battalion. (Organized Reserve Corps redesignated 9 July 1952 as Army Reserve). Redesignated 9 January 1953 as the 391st Antiaircraft Artillery Battalion (Automatic Weapons). Disbanded 1 April 1959 at Antlers.

CAMPAIGN STREAMERS
World War II
Normandy
Northern France
Rhineland

DECORATIONS
None

COAT OF ARMS
SHIELD: Per fess enhanced wavy or and gules, in chief three fleurs-de-lis and in base a pair of deer antlers, all counterchanged.

CREST: That for the regiments and separate battalions of the Army Reserve: On a wreath of the colors (or and gules) the Lexington Minute Man proper. The statue of the Minute Man, Captain John Parker (H.H. Kitson, sculptor), stands on the common in Lexington, Massachusetts.

MOTTO: Little Dixie's Finest

The colors red and yellow are for Artillery. The entire field represents the State of Oklahoma, the horizontal wavy line referring to the Canadian River which roughly divides the State into north and south sections. The deer antlers allude to Antlers – the headquarters of the battalion – and are placed in the lower part of the field, the southern part of Oklahoma being the home area of the organization. The three fleurs-de-lis represent the three campaigns of the unit in Europe during World War II.

DISTINCTIVE INSIGNIA
The insignia is the shield and motto of the coat of arms. The sample of the insignia depicted was approved for wear on 1 March 1957.

392d ANTIAIRCRAFT ARTILLERY AUTOMATIC WEAPONS BATTALION

Constituted 5 August 1942 in the Army of the United States as the 2d Battalion, 89th Coast Artillery (Antiaircraft) (Semimobile) and activated 10 August 1942 at Washington, District of Columbia. Reorganized at Washington and redesignated 1 September 1943 as the 392d Antiaircraft Artillery Automatic Weapons Battalion (Semimobile). (Departed Seattle Port of Embarkation 12 November 1944 for overseas service and arrived in Hawaii on 17 November 1944). Inactivated 15 May 1946 at Fort Ruger, Oahu, Territory of Hawaii. Allotted to the Organized Reserve Corps on 8 February 1949 and assigned to Sixth Army on 17 February 1949. Activated 5 March 1949 at San Jose, California; inactivated 31 August 1950 at San Jose.

CAMPAIGN STREAMERS
World War II
Pacific Theater without inscription

DECORATIONS
None

COAT OF ARMS
None

DISTINCTIVE INSIGNIA
None

393d ANTIAIRCRAFT ARTILLERY AUTOMATIC WEAPONS BATTALION

Constituted 19 December 1942 in the Army of the United States as the 393d Coast Artillery Battalion (Antiaircraft) (Automatic Weapons) and activated 20 January 1943 at Camp Davis, North Carolina. Redesignated 30 April 1943 as the 393d Antiaircraft Artillery Automatic Weapons Battalion (Semimobile). Disbanded 1 September 1944 at Fort Dix, New Jersey.

CAMPAIGN STREAMERS
None

DECORATIONS
None

COAT OF ARMS
None

DISTINCTIVE INSIGNIA
None

393d ANTIAIRCRAFT ARTILLERY GUN BATTALION

Constituted in the Organized Reserves during July 1923 as the 1st Battalion, 513th Artillery, Coast Artillery Corps (Antiaircraft) and allotted to the Second Corps area. Organized in New York State during October 1923 with Headquarters at Syracuse. Redesignated 30 June 1924 as the 1st Battalion, 513th Coast Artillery (Antiaircraft). Ordered into active military service, less personnel and equipment and organized 1 September 1942 at Fort Bliss, Texas. Reorganized at Fort Bliss and redesignated 20 January 1943 as the 166th Coast Artillery Battalion (Antiaircraft) (Gun) (Semimobile) (Separate). Redesignated 19 June 1943 as the 166th Antiaircraft Artillery Gun Battalion (Semimobile). (Departed San Francisco Port of Embarkation 24 September 1943 for overseas service and arrived in Australia on 9 October 1943. Moved to New Guinea 5 February 1944 and landed in the Philippines on 20 November 1944). Inactivated 11 February 1946 on Leyte, Philippine Islands. Redesignated 393d Antiaircraft Artillery Automatic Weapons Battalion, assigned to First Army and activated at Boston, Massachusetts on 21 February 1947. (Organized Reserves redesignated 25 March 1948 as Organized Reserve Corps). Inactivated 31 August 1950 at Fort Rodman, Massachusetts. Redesignated 393d Antiaircraft Artillery Gun Battalion and activated at Boston on 15 October 1950. Inactivated 15 June 1951 at Boston. (Organized Reserve Corps redesignated 9 July 1952 as Army Reserve).

Redesignated 16 October 1952 as the 166th Antiaircraft Artillery Battalion.

CAMPAIGN STREAMERS
World War II
New Guinea
Leyte
Luzon
Southern Philippines (with arrowhead)

DECORATIONS
Presidential Unit Citation (Army), Streamer embroidered *MINDORO* (166th AAA Gun Bn cited for period 15 Dec 1944-6 Jan 1945; WDGO 110, 1946)

Philippine Presidential Unit Citation, Streamer embroidered *17 OCTOBER 1944 TO 4 JULY 1945* (166th AAA Gun Bn cited; DAGO 47, 1950)

COAT OF ARMS
None

DISTINCTIVE INSIGNIA
None

394th ANTIAIRCRAFT ARTILLERY AUTOMATIC WEAPONS BATTALION

Constituted 19 December 1942 in the Army of the United States as the 394th Coast Artillery Battalion (Antiaircraft) (Automatic Weapons) (Colored) and activated 20 January 1943 at Camp Davis, North Carolina. Redesignated 30 April 1943 as the 394th Antiaircraft Artillery Automatic Weapons Battalion (Semimobile) (Colored). (Departed San Francisco Port of Embarkation 20 January 1945 for overseas service and arrived in New Guinea on 4 February 1945). Disbanded 18 March 1945 at Hollandia, New Guinea.

CAMPAIGN STREAMERS
World War II
Pacific Theater without inscription

DECORATIONS
None

COAT OF ARMS
None

DISTINCTIVE INSIGNIA
None

394th ANTIAIRCRAFT ARTILLERY GUN BATTALION

Constituted 27 May 1942 in the Organized Reserves as the 3d Battalion, 513th Coast Artillery (Antiaircraft) and activated 1 September 1942 at Fort Bliss, Texas. Reorganized at Fort Bliss and redesignated 20 January 1943 as the 227th Coast Artillery Searchlight Battalion. Redesignated 3 March 1943 as the 227th Antiaircraft Artillery Searchlight Battalion. (Departed San Francisco Port of Embarkation 6 November 1943 for overseas service and arrived in Australia on 21 November 1943. Moved to New Guinea 5 April 1944 and landed in the Philippines on 23 March 1945. Returned from overseas service and arrived at the New York Port of Embarkation on 7 February 1946). Inactivated 9 February 1946 at Camp Kilmer, New Jersey. Redesignated 394th Antiaircraft Artillery Automatic Weapons Battalion and assigned to First Army on 6 February 1947. Activated 21 February 1947 at Hartford, Connecticut. (Organized Reserves redesignated 25 March 1948 as Organized Reserve Corps). Reorganized and redesignated 10 November 1948 as the 394th Antiaircraft Artillery Gun Battalion. Reorganized 22 April 1949 at Bangor, Maine. Inactivated 28 June 1950 at Bangor.

CAMPAIGN STREAMERS
World War II
New Guinea
Luzon

DECORATIONS
Philippine Presidential Unit Citation, Streamer embroidered *17 OCTOBER 1944 TO 4 JULY 1945* (227th AAA SL Bn cited; DAGO 47, 1950)

COAT OF ARMS
None

DISTINCTIVE INSIGNIA
None

395th ANTIAIRCRAFT ARTILLERY AUTOMATIC WEAPONS BATTALION

Constituted 19 December 1942 in the Army of the United States as the 395th Coast Artillery Battalion (Antiaircraft) (Automatic Weapons) (Colored) and activated 10 January 1943 at Camp Davis, North Carolina. Redesignated 30 April 1943 as the 395th Antiaircraft Artillery Automatic Weapons Battalion (Semimobile) (Colored). (Departed San Francisco Port of Embarkation 16 June 1944 for overseas service and arrived in New Guinea on 5 July 1944). Disbanded 15 March 1945 at Finschafen, New Guinea.

CAMPAIGN STREAMERS
World War II
Pacific Theater without inscription

DECORATIONS
None

COAT OF ARMS
None

DISTINCTIVE INSIGNIA
None

396th ANTIAIRCRAFT ARTILLERY AUTOMATIC WEAPONS BATTALION

Constituted 1 October 1920 as the 2d Battalion, 6th Infantry and allotted to the Illinois National Guard. Converted and redesignated 19 March 1921 as 2d Battalion, 1st Artillery (Antiaircraft), Coast Artillery Corps. Redesignated 13 December 1921 as 2d Battalion, 202d Artillery (Antiaircraft), Coast Artillery Corps. Organized and Federally recognized 15 May 1922 at Chicago. Redesignated 7 December 1923 as 2d Battalion, 202d Artillery (Antiaircraft), Coast Artillery Corps. Redesignated 26 August 1924 as 2d Battalion, 202d Coast Artillery (Antiaircraft). Inducted into Federal service 16 September 1940 at Chicago. Reorganized at Bremerton, Washington and redesignated 10 September 1943 as the 396th Antiaircraft Artillery Automatic Weapons Battalion. Inactivated 9 January 1945 at Camp Livingston, Louisiana.

Redesignated 5 July 1946 as the 693d Antiaircraft Artillery Automatic Weapons Battalion.

CAMPAIGN STREAMERS
None

DECORATIONS
None

COAT OF ARMS
None

DISTINCTIVE INSIGNIA
None

396th ANTIAIRCRAFT ARTILLERY AUTOMATIC WEAPONS BATTALION

Organized in the Illinois National Guard as the 2d Battalion, 108th Quartermaster Regiment and Federally recognized 7 June 1937 at Bloomington. Inducted into Federal service 5 March 1941 at Bloomington. Broken up 12 February 1942 at Camp Forrest, Tennessee; Headquarters, 2d Battalion disbanded and Companies C and D consolidated, reorganized and redesignated Company A, 108th Quartermaster Battalion. (Company A, 108th Quartermaster Battalion consolidated 28 October 1942 with 33d Quartermaster Company and inactivated 5 February 1946 at Kobe, Japan). Former 2d Battalion, 108th Quartermaster Regiment reconstituted 5 July 1946 as the 396th Antiaircraft Artillery Automatic Weapons Battalion. Reorganized and Federally recognized 3 June 1947 with Headquarters and Batteries A and B at Bloomington; Battery C at LeRoy and Battery D at Gibson City.

Redesignated 15 February 1949 as the 144th Antiaircraft Artillery Automatic Weapons Battalion.

CAMPAIGN STREAMERS
World War II
New Guinea
Luzon

DECORATIONS
Meritorious Unit Commendation, Streamer embroidered *PACIFIC THEATER* (33d QM Co cited for period 1 Aug 1944-1 Feb 1945; GO 128, Hq 33d Inf Div dated 14 Jun 1945)

Philippine Presidential Unit Citation, Streamer embroidered *17 OCTOBER 1944 TO 4 JULY 1945* (33d QM Co cited; DAGO 47, 1950)

COAT OF ARMS
None

DISTINCTIVE INSIGNIA
None

397th ANTIAIRCRAFT ARTILLERY BATTALION

Constituted 19 December 1942 in the Army of the United States as the 397th Coast Artillery Battalion (Antiaircraft) (Automatic Weapons) and activated 20 February 1943 at Fort Sheridan, Illinois. Redesignated 30 April 1943 as the 397th Antiaircraft Artillery Automatic Weapons Battalion (Semimobile). (Departed Boston Port of Embarkation 27 February 1944 for overseas service and arrived in England on 8 March 1944. Temporarily reorganized as the 397th Antiaircraft Artillery Machine Gun Battalion [Provisional] for the invasion of Continental Europe and landed in France on 6 June 1944. Returned from overseas service and arrived at the New York Port of Embarkation on 3 December 1945). Inactivated 4 December 1945 at Camp Kilmer, New Jersey. Allotted to the Organized Reserves and assigned to First Army 15 April 1947. Activated 1 May 1947 at Jamaica, New York. (Organized Reserves redesignated 25 March 1948 as Organized Reserve Corps). Relocated to New York, New York on 24 January 1951. (Organized Reserve Corps redesignated 9 July 1952 as Army Reserve). Redesignated 19 January 1954 as the 397th Antiaircraft Artillery Battalion. Inactivated 10 August 1959 at New York.

CAMPAIGN STREAMERS
World War II
Normandy (with arrowhead)
Northern France
Rhineland
Ardennes-Alsace
Central Europe

DECORATIONS
Presidential Unit Citation (Army), Streamer embroidered *BEACHES OF NORMANDY* (397th AA MG Bn [Prov] cited for action on 6 Jun 1944; WDGO 76, 1944)

COAT OF ARMS
None

DISTINCTIVE INSIGNIA
None

398th ANTIAIRCRAFT ARTILLERY BATTALION

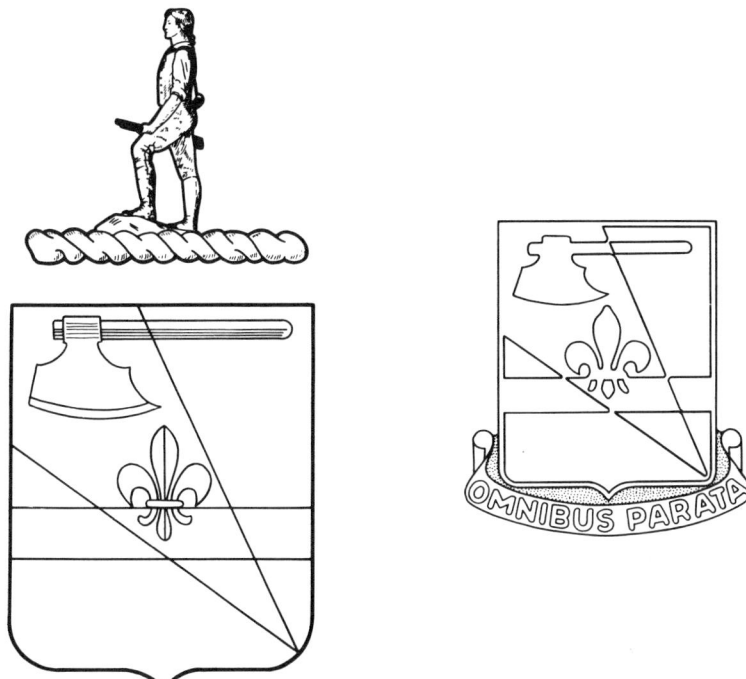

Constituted 19 December 1942 in the Army of the United States as the 398th Coast Artillery Battalion (Antiaircraft) (Automatic Weapons) and activated 20 February 1943 at Camp Edwards, Massachusetts. Redesignated 1 May 1943 as the 398th Antiaircraft Artillery Automatic Weapons Battalion (Self Propelled). (Departed Boston Port of Embarkation 22 June 1944 for overseas service; arrived in England on 29 June 1944 and landed in France on 26 July 1944. Returned from overseas service and arrived at the New York Port of Embarkation on 29 April 1946). Inactivated 30 April 1946 at Camp Kilmer, New Jersey. Allotted to the Organized Reserves and assigned to First Army 6 February 1947. Activated 21 February 1947 at Manchester, New Hampshire. (Organized Reserves redesignated 25 March 1948 as Organized Reserve Corps). Ordered into active military service at Manchester on 11 September 1950. (Organized Reserve Corps redesignated 9 July 1952 as Army Reserve). Redesignated 13 December 1954 as the 398th Antiaircraft Artillery Battalion (Automatic Weapons) (Self Propelled). Released from active military service on 20 December 1954 and resumed reserve status. Inactivated 30 June 1959 at Manchester.

CAMPAIGN STREAMERS

World War II
Northern France
Rhineland
Ardennes-Alsace
Central Europe

Korean War
Third Korean Winter
Korea Summer 1953

DECORATIONS

Republic of Korea Presidential Unit Citation, Streamer embroidered *KOREA* (398th AAA AW Bn cited for period 16 Jan 1953-1 May 1954; DAGO 51, 1957)

COAT OF ARMS

SHIELD: Gules, on a pile issuing from dexter chief or and a bar debased a fleur-de-lis and in chief a battle axe fesswise, all counterchanged.

CREST: That for the regiments and separate battalions of the Army Reserve: On a wreath of the colors (or and gules) the Lexington Minute Man proper. The statue of the Minute Man, Captain John Parker (H.H. Kitson, sculptor), stands on the common in Lexington, Massachusetts.

MOTTO: *Omnibus Parata* (Ready For Anything)

The shield is in the colors of Artillery. The pile symbolizes a "cone of fire". The bar represents interdiction of the aerial enemy through any visible handicaps. The fleur-de-lis symbolizes the organization's service in France while the battle axe, a favorite Teutonic weapon and heraldic charge through the medieval period, represents the battalion's World War II campaigns east of the Rhine.

DISTINCTIVE INSIGNIA

The insignia is the shield and motto of the coat of arms. The sample of the insignia depicted was approved for wear on 22 May 1953.

399th ANTIAIRCRAFT BALLOON BATTALION

Constituted 25 March 1942 in the Army of the United States as the 399th Coast Artillery Barrage Balloon Battalion and activated 15 October 1942 at Fort Brady, Michigan. Redesignated 1 September 1943 as the 399th Antiaircraft Balloon Battalion, Low Altitude. Disbanded 30 September 1943 at Fort Sheridan, Illinois.

CAMPAIGN STREAMERS
None

DECORATIONS
None

COAT OF ARMS

SHIELD: Gules, frette or, on a chief arched of the last an American field spider in its web of the first.

CREST: None

MOTTO: *In solo Regit qui Degit in Coelo* (He Who Lives In Heaven Rules On Earth)

The scarlet is for Artillery while the gold interlacing of the shield symbolizes protection. The arched form of the chief alludes to the clouds. The American field spider and the web is representative of the barrage balloon.

DISTINCTIVE INSIGNIA
The insignia is the shield and motto of the coat of arms. The insignia depicted was never made for nor worn by this organization.

399th ANTIAIRCRAFT ARTILLERY AUTOMATIC WEAPONS BATTALION

Constituted 29 July 1921 in the Organized Reserves as the 2d Battalion, 511th Artillery (Antiaircraft), Coast Artillery Corps, allotted to the Fifth Corps area and assigned to V Corps. Organized in Indiana during May 1922 with Headquarters at Laconia. Redesignated 30 June 1924 as 2d Battalion, 511th Coast Artillery (Antiaircraft). Ordered into active military service, less personnel and equipment, 15 November 1942 at Camp Haan, California. Reorganized at Camp Haan and redesignated 20 January 1943 as the 199th Coast Artillery Battalion (Antiaircraft) (Automatic Weapons) (Semimobile) (Separate). Redesignated 30 April 1943 as the 199th Antiaircraft Artillery Automatic Weapons Battalion (Semimobile). (Departed San Francisco Port of Embarkation 16 August 1943 for overseas service; arrived on Guadalcanal 21 September 1943 and moved to Bougainville on 15 January 1944. After service in the Philippines returned from overseas service and arrived at the Los Angeles Port of Embarkation on 3 January 1946). Inactivated 4 January 1946 at Camp Anza, Arlington, California. Redesignated 10 December 1946 as the 399th Antiaircraft Artillery Automatic Weapons Battalion. Activated 20 December 1946 with Headquarters at Cleveland, Ohio. (Organized Reserves redesignated Organized Reserve Corps on 25 March 1948).

Redesignated 10 April 1952 as the 199th Antiaircraft Artillery Automatic Weapons Battalion.

CAMPAIGN STREAMERS
World War II
Northern Solomons
Leyte

DECORATIONS
Philippine Presidential Unit Citation, Streamer embroidered *17 OCTOBER 1944 TO 4 JULY 1945* (199th AAA AW Bn cited; DAGO 47, 1950)

COAT OF ARMS
None

DISTINCTIVE INSIGNIA
None

400th ANTIAIRCRAFT ARTILLERY BATTALION

Constituted July 1923 in the Organized Reserves as the 2d Battalion, 513th Artillery (Antiaircraft), Coast Artillery Corps and allotted to the Second Corps area. Organized during October 1923 with Headquarters at Syracuse, New York. Redesignated 30 June 1924 as 2d Battalion, 513th Coast Artillery (Antiaircraft). Ordered into active military service, less personnel and equipment and organized 1 September 1942 at Fort Bliss, Texas. Reorganized and redesignated 20 January 1943 as the 200th Coast Artillery Battalion (Antiaircraft) (Automatic Weapons). Redesignated 19 March 1943 at Camp Pickett, Virginia as the 400th Coast Artillery Battalion (Antiaircraft) (Automatic Weapons). (Departed Hampton Roads Port of Embarkation 8 June 1943 for overseas service and arrived in North Africa on 22 June 1943. After service in Sicily, Italy, Corsica and France returned to Hampton Roads Port of Embarkation on 15 November 1945). Inactivated 15 November 1945 at Camp Patrick Henry, Virginia. Activated 21 February 1947 with Headquarters at Rochester, New York. (Organized Reserves redesignated 25 March 1948 as Organized Reserve Corps). Redesignated 8 July 1949 as the 498th Antiaircraft Artillery Automatic Weapons Battalion and assigned to the 98th Infantry Division. Redesignated 4 April 1952 as the 400th Antiaircraft Artillery Automatic Weapons Battalion. (Organized Reserve Corps redesignated 9 July 1952 as Army Reserve). Redesignated 1 January 1953 as the 400th Antiaircraft Artillery Battalion (Automatic Weapons) (Self Propelled). Relieved from the 98th Infantry Division and disbanded 1 May 1959 at Rochester.

CAMPAIGN STREAMERS
World War II
Sicily (with arrowhead)
Naples-Foggia
Rome-Arno
Rhineland

DECORATIONS
None

COAT OF ARMS

SHIELD: Gules, on a bend azure fimbriated or a hawk volant pierced by an arrow, bird and bolt both reversed, in sinister chief a winged cannon bendwise and in dexter base a clenched hand palewise erased at the wrist, habited in a gauntlet, all of the third, all within a bordure of the like.

CREST: That for the regiments and separate battalions of the Army Reserve: On a wreath of the colors (or and gules) the Lexington Minute Man proper. The statue of the Minute Man, Captain John Parker (H.H. Kitson, sculptor), stands on the common in Lexington, Massachusetts.

MOTTO: *Ab Armis Arcendum* (Defense With Arms)

The shield of the coat of arms of the old 513th Coast Artillery, within a border, is used to indicate descent from that regiment. The shield is scarlet for Artillery. The bend represents the sky, the hawk the target and the bolt a hit. The winged cannon indicates the type of artillery, antiaircraft. The clenched hand and gauntlet symbolize determination to defend.

DISTINCTIVE INSIGNIA

The insignia is the shield and motto of the coat of arms. The sample of the insignia depicted was approved for wear on 29 October 1956.

401st ANTIAIRCRAFT ARTILLERY MISSILE BATTALION

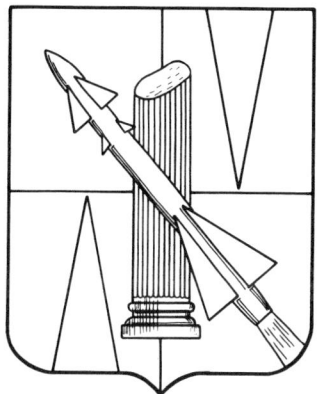 

Constituted 31 January 1942 in the Army of the United States as the 401st Separate Coast Artillery Battalion (Antiaircraft) (Gun) and activated 1 April 1942 at Camp Haan, California. Redesignated 22 May 1942 as the 401st Coast Artillery Battalion (Separate) (Antiaircraft) (Gun). Redesignated 27 May 1942 as the 401st Separate Coast Artillery Battalion (Antiaircraft) (Gun). (Departed Hampton Roads Port of Embarkation 24 April 1943 for overseas service and arrived in North Africa on 26 May 1943. Moved to Sicily on 11 July 1943 and landed in Italy on 9 November 1943). Redesignated 12 December 1943 as the 401st Antiaircraft Artillery Gun Battalion (Mobile). Inactivated 15 October 1945 at Cecchignola, Italy. Redesignated as the 401st Antiaircraft Artillery Missile Battalion and allotted to the Regular Army, 18 April 1956. Activated 1 May 1956 at Milwaukee, Wisconsin; inactivated 1 September 1958 at Hale Corners, Wisconsin.

CAMPAIGN STREAMERS
World War II
Sicily (with arrowhead)
Naples-Foggia
Rome-Arno
North Apennines
Po Valley

DECORATIONS
None

COAT OF ARMS
SHIELD: Per cross gules and or two piles, one reversed, issuant respectively from sinister chief and dexter base terminating in fess, a broken column in pale surmounted by a missile with trail bendwise, all counterchanged of the field.

CREST: None

MOTTO: *Defense pour la Liberte* (Defense For Freedom)

Scarlet and yellow are used for Artillery. The missile represents the antiaircraft missile function of the unit. The four main divisions together with the column symbolize the five campaigns in the Mediterranean Theater of Operations during World War II. The basic partition of the shield also refers to the cross on the Italian flag. One of the triangular segments indicates the assault landing in Sicily while the other depicts the organization's original service as a Coast Artillery Battalion.

DISTINCTIVE INSIGNIA
The insignia is the shield and motto of the coat of arms. The sample of the insignia depicted was approved for wear on 18 April 1958.

402d ANTIAIRCRAFT ARTILLERY GUN BATTALION

Constituted 31 January 1942 in the Army of the United States as the 402d Separate Coast Artillery Battalion (Antiaircraft) (Gun) and activated 1 May 1942 at Fort Bliss, Texas. Redesignated 1 September 1943 as the 402d Antiaircraft Artillery Gun Battalion (Semimobile).

Redesignated 1 May 1944 as the 940th Field Artillery Battalion.

CAMPAIGN STREAMERS
None

DECORATIONS
None

COAT OF ARMS
None

DISTINCTIVE INSIGNIA
None

402d ANTIAIRCRAFT ARTILLERY AUTOMATIC WEAPONS BATTALION

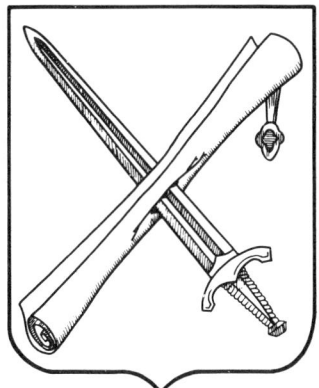

Constituted 6 August 1942 in the Army of the United States as the 454th Coast Artillery Battalion (Antiaircraft) (Automatic Weapons) and activated 1 September 1942 at Camp Stewart, Georgia. (Departed Hampton Roads Port of Embarkation 10 May 1943 for overseas service; arrived in North Africa on 2 June 1943 and moved to Italy in 1944). Reorganized and redesignated 1 May 1944 as the 454th Antiaircraft Artillery Automatic Weapons Battalion (Mobile). Disbanded 25 September 1944 in Italy. Reconstituted 30 November 1948 in the Organized Reserve Corps. Activated 18 January 1949 with Headquarters at Kansas City, Missouri. Redesignated 402d Antiaircraft Artillery Automatic Weapons Battalion and assigned to the 102d Infantry Division on 25 November 1949. Headquarters relocated to St. Louis, Missouri on 15 March 1951. (Organized Reserve Corps redesignated 9 July 1952 as Army Reserve).

Redesignated 15 December 1952 as the 454th Antiaircraft Artillery Automatic Weapons Battalion.

CAMPAIGN STREAMERS
World War II
Rome-Arno

DECORATIONS
None

COAT OF ARMS
SHIELD: Gules, a scroll bend sinisterwise pierced by a sword in bend, point to chief or.

CREST: None

MOTTO: *Audax et Vigilans* (Daring And Vigilant)

In the scarlet and gold of the Coast Artillery arm the functions of the organization, allegorically illustrated by the protecting sword piercing the scroll, alludes to the record which the organization made for itself during World War II.

DISTINCTIVE INSIGNIA
The insignia is the shield and motto of the coat of arms. The insignia depicted was never made for nor worn by this organization.

403d ANTIAIRCRAFT ARTILLERY GUN BATTALION

Constituted 13 April 1942 in the Army of the United States as the 403d Coast Artillery Battalion (Antiaircraft) (Gun) and activated 1 June 1942 at Camp Hulen, Texas. (Departed New York Port of Embarkation 28 April 1943 for overseas service and arrived in North Africa on 11 May 1943. Moved to Sicily on 15 August 1943 and landed in Italy on 23 October 1943). Redesignated 12 December 1943 as the 403d Antiaircraft Artillery Gun Battalion (Mobile). Disbanded 15 September 1945 at Palermo, Sicily.

CAMPAIGN STREAMERS
World War II
Sicily
Naples-Foggia
Rome-Arno
North Apennines
Po Valley

DECORATIONS
None

COAT OF ARMS
SHIELD: Gules, on a fess nebuly between three portcullis or, a mullet azure.

CREST: None

MOTTO: We Protect

In the scarlet and gold of the Coast Artillery arm the portcullis heraldically signifies an effective protection in an emergency. The nebuly formation of the horizontal band denotes clouds of air, both symbols being representative of the antiaircraft functions of the organization. The blue star is representative of the State of activation, Texas and also of the blue sky overhead.

DISTINCTIVE INSIGNIA
The insignia is the shield and motto of the coat of arms. The insignia depicted was never made for nor worn by this organization.

403d ANTIAIRCRAFT ARTILLERY AUTOMATIC WEAPONS BATTALION

Constituted 9 May 1942 in the Army of the United States as the 438th Coast Artillery Battalion

(Antiaircraft) (Automatic Weapons) and activated 6 June 1942 at Camp Edwards, Massachusetts. Redesignated 15 May 1943 as the 438th Antiaircraft Artillery Automatic Weapons Battalion (Mobile). (Departed New York Port of Embarkation 17 November 1943 for overseas service; arrived in England on 24 November 1943 and landed in France on 17 June 1944. Returned from overseas service and arrived at the New York Port of Embarkation on 20 March 1946). Inactivated 21 March 1946 at Camp Kilmer, New Jersey. Allotted to the Organized Reserves and assigned to Fifth Army, 27 August 1947. Activated 15 October 1947 with Headquarters at Cedar Rapids, Iowa. (Organized Reserves redesignated 25 March 1948 as Organized Reserve Corps. Relieved from Fifth Army, redesignated 403d Antiaircraft Artillery Automatic Weapons Battalion (Self Propelled) and assigned to the 103d Infantry Division, 25 November 1949.

Redesignated 1 April 1952 as the 438th Antiaircraft Artillery Automatic Weapons Battalion.

CAMPAIGN STREAMERS
World War II
Normandy
Northern France
Rhineland
Ardennes-Alsace
Central Europe

DECORATIONS
None

COAT OF ARMS
None

DISTINCTIVE INSIGNIA
None

HEADQUARTERS AND HEADQUARTERS DETACHMENT 404th COAST ARTILLERY BATTALION

Organized 11 May 1818 at Providence as an element of the 1st Light Infantry Company, 2d Regiment, Rhode Island Militia. Relieved from the 2d Regiment in April 1842. Mustered into Federal service 2 May 1861 at Washington, District of Columbia as Company D, 1st Rhode Island Volunteer Infantry; mustered out 2 August 1861 at Providence and resumed State status as an element of the 1st Light Infantry Company. Expanded and redesignated Company D, 1st Light Infantry, Rhode Island Militia in January 1872. Redesignated 1 May 1875 as Company D, 1st Battalion of Infantry, Rhode Island Militia. Redesignated 24 May 1887 as Company D, 1st Regiment of Infantry, Rhode Island Militia. Mustered into Federal service 14 May 1898 at North Kingston as Company D, 1st Rhode Island Volunteer Infantry; mustered out 30 March 1899 at Columbia, South Carolina and resumed State status. Converted and redesignated 4 November 1908 as 4th Company, 1st Artillery District, Coast Artillery Corps. Redesignated 3 September 1914 as 4th Company, 1st Coast Defense Command, Coast Artillery Corps. Redesignated 18 December 1916 as 4th Company, 1st Coast Artillery District, Coast Artillery Corps. Redesignated 2 January 1917 as 4th Company, Coast Artillery Corps, Rhode Island National Guard. Mustered into Federal service 2 April 1917 at Providence and drafted into Federal service on 5 August 1917. Redesignated 31 August 1917 as 13th Company, Coast Defense of Narragansett Bay. Demobilized at Fort Getty, Rhode Island in December 1918. Reorganized and Federally recognized 6 January 1920 at Providence as 4th Company, 1st Coast Defense Command, Coast Artillery Corps. Redesignated 31 January 1922 as 348th Company, 1st Coast Defense Command, Coast Artillery Corps. Redesignated 1 October 1923 as Battery D, 243d Artillery, Coast Artillery Corps. Redesignated 11 July 1924 as Battery D, 243d Coast Artillery (Harbor Defense). Inducted into Federal service 16 September 1940 at Providence. Redesignated 13 September 1943 as Battery I, 8th Coast Artillery. Inactivated 18 April 1944 at Camp Shelby, Mississippi. Disbanded 31 May 1944. Reconstituted 2 July 1946 as Headquarters and Headquarters Detachment, 404th Coast Artillery Battalion (Harbor Defense) and allotted to the Rhode Island National Guard. Withdrawn from allotment to the Rhode Island National Guard on 1 May 1949 and returned to Department of the Army control.

CAMPAIGN STREAMERS
Civil War
Bull Run

DECORATIONS
None

COAT OF ARMS
None

DISTINCTIVE INSIGNIA
None

405th ANTIAIRCRAFT ARTILLERY BATTALION

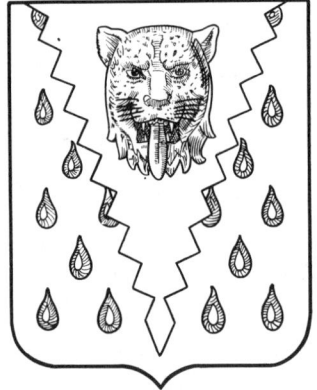

Constituted 5 May 1942 in the Army of the United States as the 405th Coast Artillery Battalion (Antiaircraft) (Gun) and activated 1 July 1942 at Fort Sheridan, Illinois. Redesignated 7 June 1943 as the 405th Antiaircraft Artillery Gun Battalion (Semimobile). (Departed New York Port of Embarkation 21 October 1943 for overseas service; arrived in England on 3 November 1943 and landed in France on 18 July 1944). Inactivated 30 April 1946 in France. Allotted to the Organized Reserve Corps and assigned to Sixth Army, 2 March 1950. Activated 15 July 1950 at Seattle, Washington. (Organized Reserve Corps redesignated 9 July 1952 as Army Reserve). Redesignated 15 April 1953 as the 405th Antiaircraft Artilery Battalion. Inactivated 1 August 1959 at Seattle.

CAMPAIGN STREAMERS
World War II
Normandy
Northern France
Rhineland
Ground Combat-European Theater

DECORATIONS
Belgian Fourragere 1940 (405th AAA Gun Bn cited; DAGO 43, 1950)

Cited in the Order of the Day of the Belgian Army for *DEFENSE OF ANTWERP* (405th AAA Gun Bn cited for period 25 Oct-28 Nov 1944; DAGO 43, 1950)

Cited in the Order of the Day of the Belgian Army for *DEFENSE OF ANTWERP HARBOR* (405th AAA Gun Bn cited for action on 16 Dec 1944; DAGO 43, 1950)

COAT OF ARMS
SHIELD: Or, gutte-de-larmes, on a pile indented gules a leopard's face of the first.

CREST: That for the regiments and separate battalions of the Army Reserve: On a wreath of the colors (or and gules) the Lexington Minute Man proper. The statue of the Minute Man, Captain John Parker (H. H. Kitson, sculptor), stands on the common in Lexington, Massachusetts.

MOTTO: *Moneo et Munio* (I Warn And I Protect)

The scarlet is for Artillery. The functions of the organization are illustrated by the wedge-shaped pile representative of the driving force into enemy opposition. The leopard's face heraldically represents a valiant and hardy warrior who accomplishes hazardous things by force and courage. The drops are added for design.

DISTINCTIVE INSIGNIA
The insignia is the shield and motto of the coat of arms. The insignia depicted was never made for nor worn by this organization.

406th ANTIAIRCRAFT ARTILLERY GUN BATTALION

Constituted 5 May 1942 in the Army of the United States as the 406th Separate Coast Artillery Battalion (Antiaircraft) (Gun) and redesignated 27 May 1942 as the 406th Coast Artillery Battalion (Antiaircraft) (Gun). Activated 1 July 1942 at Fort Sheridan, Illinois. (Departed New York Port of Embarkation 28 April 1943 for overseas service; arrived in North Africa on 11 May 1943 and moved to Sicily on 10 August 1943. Returned to North Africa on 15 November 1943 and moved to Corsica on 13 December 1943). Redesignated 31 December 1943 as the 406th Antiaircraft Artillery Gun Battalion. (Landed in France on 14 November 1944). Disbanded 31 December 1944 at St. Victoret, France.

CAMPAIGN STREAMERS
World War II
Sicily
Naples-Foggia
Rome-Arno

DECORATIONS
None

COAT OF ARMS
None

DISTINCTIVE INSIGNIA
None

407th ANTIAIRCRAFT ARTILLERY GUN BATTALION

Constituted 21 May 1942 in the Army of the United States as the 407th Coast Artillery Battalion (Antiaircraft) (Gun) and activated 10 January 1943 at Camp Haan, California. Redesignated 7 June 1943 as the 407th Antiaircraft Artillery Gun Battalion (Semimobile). (Departed Boston Port of Embarkation 27 February 1944 for overseas service; arrived in England 8 March 1944 and landed in France on 23 June 194). Inactivated 30 April 1946 in France. Allotted to the Organized Reserve Corps 8 March 1949 and assigned to Fifth Army 11 March 1949. Activated 5 April 1949 at Chicago, Illinois; inactivated 15 November 1950 at Chicago.

CAMPAIGN STREAMERS
World War II
Normandy
Northern France
Rhineland

DECORATIONS
Belgian Fourragere 1940 (407th AAA Gun Bn cited; DAGO 43, 1950)

Cited in the Order of the Day of the Belgian Army for *DEFENSE OF ANTWERP* (407th AAA Gun Bn cited for period 25 Oct-28 Nov 1944; DAGO 43, 1950)

Cited in the Order of the Day of the Belgian Army for *DEFENSE OF ANTWERP HARBOR* (407th AAA Gun Bn cited for action on 16 Dec 1944; DAGO 43, 1950)

COAT OF ARMS
None

DISTINCTIVE INSIGNIA
None

409th ANTIAIRCRAFT ARTILLERY GUN BATTALION

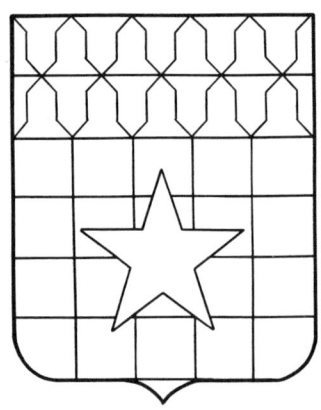 

Constituted 9 May 1942 in the Army of the United States as the 409th Separate Coast Artillery Battalion (Antiaircraft) (Gun) and redesignated 27 May 1942 as the 409th Coast Artillery Battalion (Antiaircraft) (Gun). Activated 1 August 1942 at Fort Bliss, Texas. (Departed Hampton Roads Port of Embarkation 10 May 1943; arrived in North Africa on 23 May 1943 and landed in Italy on 19 September 1943). Redesignated 12 December 1943 as the 409th Antiaircraft Artillery Gun Battalion (Semimobile). (Moved to Corsica on 8 April 1944 and landed in France on 1 November 1944). Disbanded at Marseille, France; Gun Batteries on 31 December 1944 and Headquarters and Headquarters Battery on 25 January 1945.

CAMPAIGN STREAMERS
World War II
Naples-Foggia
Rome-Arno

DECORATIONS
None

COAT OF ARMS
SHIELD: Checky gules and or, a mullet argent, a chief vair.

CREST: None

MOTTO: With Courage And Arms

Scarlet is the color of the Coast Artillery Corps. The vair is symbolic of dignity while the checky portion of the shield is representative of constancy while the star is indicative of the State of activation, Texas.

DISTINCTIVE INSIGNIA
The insignia is the shield and motto of the coat of arms. The sample of the insignia depicted was never made for nor worn by this organization.

410th ANTIAIRCRAFT ARTILLERY GUN BATTALION

Constituted 9 May 1942 in the Army of the United States as the 410th Coast Artillery Battalion (Antiaircraft) (Gun) and activated 15 June 1942 at Fort Bliss, Texas. (Departed New York Port of Embarkation 28 April 1943 and arrived in North Africa on 11 May 1943; moved to Sicily on 15 August 1943 and landed in Italy on 20 October 1943). Redesignated 12 December 1943 as the 410th Antiaircraft Artillery Gun Battalion (Semimobile). (Moved to Corsica on 21 March 1944 and landed in France on 14 November 1944). Disbanded 31 December 1944 at Miramas, France.

CAMPAIGN STREAMERS
World War II
Sicily
Naples-Foggia
Rome-Arno

DECORATIONS
None

COAT OF ARMS

SHIELD: Per pale gules and azure a bascle or, in chief a fountain.

CREST: None

MOTTO: I Wait My Time

The scarlet of the shield is for the Coast Artillery Corps while the blue portion of the shield is for the sky, the area of operations. The counter weighted drawbridge was used over moats in medieval times for protection and is representative of the protection afforded by the organization. The fountain is symbolic of water and represents overseas service.

DISTINCTIVE INSIGNIA

The insignia is the shield and motto of the coat of arms. The sample of the insignia depicted was never made for nor worn by this organization.

411th ANTIAIRCRAFT ARTILLERY BATTALION

Constituted 21 May 1942 in the Army of the United States as the 411th Coast Artillery Battalion (Antiaircraft) (Gun) and activated 1 September 1942 at Camp Davis, North Carolina. Redesignated 28 June 1943 as the 411th Antiaircraft Artillery Gun Battalion (Mobile). (Departed New York Port of Embarkation 1 January 1944 for overseas service; arrived in England on 27 January 1944 and landed in France on 9 June 1944. Returned from overseas service and arrived at the Hampton Roads Port of Embarkation on 23 October 1945). Inactivated 23 October 1945 at Camp Patrick Henry, Virginia. Allotted to the Organized Reserve Corps, assigned to Third Army and activated 7 December 1948 at Montgomery, Alabama. (Headquarters relocated to Tuscaloosa, Alabama on 12 December 1950). (Organized Reserve Corps redesignated 9 July 1952 as Army Reserve). Redesignated 31 May 1953 as the 411th Antiaircraft Artillery Battalion. Inactivated 25 June 1959 at Tuscaloosa.

CAMPAIGN STREAMERS
World War II
Normandy
Northern France
Rhineland
Ardennes-Alsace
Central Europe

DECORATIONS
French Croix de Guerre with Gold Star, World War II, Streamer embroidered *NORMANDY* (411th AAA Gun Bn cited for period 1-31 Aug 1944; DAGO 43, 1950)

COAT OF ARMS

SHIELD: Per fess raguly azure and gules, issuant from base the silhouette of a 90mm antiaircraft gun or.

CREST: That for the regiments and separate battalions of the Army Reserve: On a wreath of the colors (or and azure) the Lexington Minute Man proper. The statue of the Minute Man, Captain John Parker (H. H. Kitson, sculptor), stands on the common in Lexington, Massachusetts.

MOTTO: Until The Final Gun

The scarlet is the color of the Coast Artillery Corps. The blue refers to the sky while the 90mm gun in silhouette depicts the principal weapon with which the battalion was equipped.

DISTINCTIVE INSIGNIA
The insignia is the shield and motto of the coat of arms. The sample of the insignia depicted was unofficially worn in Germany by this organization during the fall of 1945.

412th ANTIAIRCRAFT ARTILLERY AUTOMATIC WEAPONS BATTALION

Constituted 27 September 1946 as the 412th Antiaircraft Artillery Automatic Weapons Battalion (Semimobile) and allotted to the New York National Guard. Withdrawn from allotment to the New York Army National Guard and returned to Department of Army control about 1949.

CAMPAIGN STREAMERS
None

DECORATIONS
None

COAT OF ARMS
None

DISTINCTIVE INSIGNIA
None

413th ANTIAIRCRAFT ARTILLERY GUN BATTALION

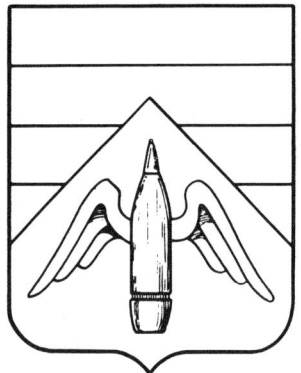 

Constituted 13 April 1942 in the Army of the United States as the 413th Coast Artillery Battalion (Antiaircraft) (Gun) and activated 1 June 1942 at Camp Haan, California. Redesignated 28 June 1943 as the 413th Antiaircraft Artillery Gun Battalion. (Departed New York Port of Embarkation 15 November 1943 for overseas service; arrived in England on 20 November 1943 and landed in France on 7 June 1944. Returned from overseas service and arrived at Hampton Roads Port of Embarkation on 27 October 1945). Inactivated 27 October 1945 at Camp Patrick Henry, Virginia.

Redesignated 28 June 1950 as the 91st Antiaircraft Artillery Battalion.

CAMPAIGN STREAMERS
World War II
Normandy (with arrowhead)
Northern France
Rhineland
Ardennes-Alsace
Central Europe

DECORATIONS
Cited in the Order of the Day of the Belgian Army for action in the *ARDENNES* (413th AAA Gun Bn cited for period 20 Dec 1944-26 Jan 1945; DAGO 43, 1950)

COAT OF ARMS
SHIELD: Per chevron barry of four azure and gules, and or, on the last a winged shell palewise sable.

CREST: None

MOTTO: *Non Nolis Tantum Nati* (We Were Not Born For Ourselves Alone)

Scarlet is the color of the Coast Artillery Corps. The winged shell represents antiaircraft artillery and the triangle formed by the per chevron division of the shield denotes three beams. The numerical designation is indicated by the four divisions of the shield, the winged shell and the three angles formed by the per chevron division. The motto is expressive of the obligation placed upon the personnel of the organization for the protection of their country and countrymen.

DISTINCTIVE INSIGNIA
The insignia is the shield and motto of the coat of arms. The sample of the insignia depicted was never made for nor worn by this organization.

414th ANTIAIRCRAFT ARTILLERY BATTALION

Constituted 9 May 1942 in the Army of the United States as the 414th Separate Coast Artillery Battalion (Antiaircraft) (Gun) and redesignated 27 May 1942 as the 414th Coast Artillery Battalion (Antiaircraft) (Gun). Activated 9 June 1942 at Camp Stewart, Georgia. (Departed New York Port of Embarkation 26 September 1942 for overseas service and arrived in Iceland on 22 October 1942). Redesignated 22 June 1943 as the 414th Antiaircraft Artillery Gun Battalion (Semimobile). (Moved to England on 10 March 1944 and landed in France on 8 July 1944. Returned from overseas service and arrived at the New York Port of Embarkation on 13 December 1945). Inactivated 15 December 1945 at Camp Kilmer, New Jersey. Allotted to the Organized Reserve Corps on 8 November 1948 and activated 1 February 1949 with Headquarters at Lafayette, Indiana. (Organized Reserve Corps redesignated 9 July 1952 as Army Reserve). Redesignated 16 March 1953 as the 414th Antiaircraft Artillery Battalion. Inactivated 1 May 1959 at Lafayette.

CAMPAIGN STREAMERS
World War II
Normandy
Northern France
Rhineland
Ardennes-Alsace
Ground Combat-European Theater

DECORATIONS
None

COAT OF ARMS
SHIELD: Gules, a pale between eight martlets palewise, four and four or.

CREST: That for the regiments and separate battalions of the Army Reserve: On a wreath of the colors (or and gules) the Lexington Minute Man proper. The statue of the Minute Man, Captain John Parker (H. H. Kitson, sculptor), stands on the common in Lexington, Massachusetts.

MOTTO: No Trespassing

In the scarlet and gold of the Coast Artillery arm the pale, a medieval symbol of protection, and the eight martlets, the martlet being the heraldic symbol of cadency for the fourth son and alluding to the aircraft functions of the organization, are representative of the protective task of the battalion. The mobility of the unit is contained in the flying martlets. The numerical designation is also indicated by the arrangement of the four martlets, the one pale, and the four martlets.

DISTINCTIVE INSIGNIA
The insignia is the shield and motto of the coat of arms. The sample of the insignia depicted was approved for wear on 9 March 1954.

415th ANTIAIRCRAFT ARTILLERY AUTOMATIC WEAPONS BATTALION

Constituted 18 July 1942 in the Army of the United States as the 415th Coast Artillery Battalion (Antiaircraft) (Automatic Weapons). (Battery A activated 22 July 1942 at Sault Ste. Marie, Michigan and Battery B activated 22 July 1942 at Fort Ord, California). Redesignated 13 July 1943 as the 415th Antiaircraft Artillery Automatic Weapons Battalion. (Batteries A and B inactivated 1 April 1944 on New Caledonia). Disbanded 1 April 1944.

CAMPAIGN STREAMERS
World War II
Pacific Theater without inscription

DECORATIONS
None

COAT OF ARMS
None

DISTINCTIVE INSIGNIA
None

416th ANTIAIRCRAFT ARTILLERY BATTALION

Constituted 24 May 1946 as the 416th Antiaircraft Artillery Automatic Weapons Battalion (Mobile) and allotted to the National Guard of the Commonwealth of Pennsylvania. Organized and Federally recognized 1 October 1946 with Headquarters at Philadelphia and batteries at Philadelphia and Sellersville. Reorganized and redesignated 1 June 1951 as 416th Antiaircraft Artillery Gun Battalion (90mm). Redesignated 1 October 1953 as the 416th Antiaircraft Artillery Battalion (90mm Gun). Disbanded 11 October 1953 at Philadelphia when Federal recognition was withdrawn.

CAMPAIGN STREAMERS
None

DECORATIONS
None

COAT OF ARMS
None

DISTINCTIVE INSIGNIA
None

417th ANTIAIRCRAFT ARTILLERY SEARCHLIGHT BATTALION

Constituted 18 July 1942 in the Army of the United States as the 417th Coast Artillery Searchlight Battalion. (1st Platoon, Battery A activated 22 July 1942 at Fort Ord, California and 1st Platoon, Battery B activated 22 July 1942 at Sault Ste. Marie, Michigan). Redesignated 13 July 1943 as the 417th Antiaircraft Artillery Searchlight Battalion. (Detachments of Batteries A and B inactivated 1 April 1944 on New Caledonia). Disbanded 1 April 1944.

CAMPAIGN STREAMERS
None

DECORATIONS
None

COAT OF ARMS
None

DISTINCTIVE INSIGNIA
None

418th ANTIAIRCRAFT ARTILLERY BATTALION

Constituted 2 July 1946 as the 418th Antiaircraft Artillery Automatic Weapons Battalion and allotted to the Virginia National Guard. Redesignated 5 September 1951 as the 418th Antiaircraft Artillery Gun Battalion. Organized and Federally recognized 17 October 1951 with Headquarters at Danville and batteries at Danville, Altavista, Rocky Mount and Chatham. Redesignated 1 October 1953 as the 418th Antiaircraft Artillery Battalion (90mm Gun). (Headquarters relocated to Chatham on 1 March 1956).

Consolidated 1 June 1959 with the 246th Artillery, a parent regiment under the Combat Arms Regimental System.

CAMPAIGN STREAMERS
None

DECORATIONS
None

COAT OF ARMS
None

DISTINCTIVE INSIGNIA
None

419th COAST ARTILLERY BATTALION

Constituted 28 August 1942 in the Army of the United States as the 419th Coast Artillery Battalion (Antiaircraft) (Composite) and activated 3 September 1942 on Adak Island, Alaska. (Returned from overseas service and arrived at the Seattle Port of Embarkation in April 1944). Inactivated 31 July 1944 at Camp Swift, Texas. Disbanded 26 October 1944.

CAMPAIGN STREAMERS
World War II
Aleutian Islands

DECORATIONS
None

COAT OF ARMS
None

DISTINCTIVE INSIGNIA
None

420th COAST ARTILLERY BATTALION

Constituted 8 March 1942 in the Army of the United States as the 420th Coast Artillery Battalion (Composite) (Semimobile) and activated 17 April 1942 in Alaska with Headquarters at Fort Raymond. (Returned from overseas service and arrived at the Seattle Port of Embarkation in April 1944). Inactivated 29 July 1944 at Camp Howze, Texas. Disbanded 16 October 1944.

CAMPAIGN STREAMERS
World War II
Aleutian Islands

DECORATIONS
None

COAT OF ARMS
None

DISTINCTIVE INSIGNIA
None

420th ANTIAIRCRAFT ARTILLERY BATTALION

Constituted 5 July 1946 as the 420th Antiaircraft Artillery Gun Battalion and allotted to the Washington National Guard. Organized and Federally recognized 14 November 1947 with Headquarters at Yakima and batteries at Prosser, Pasco and Yakima. Ordered into active Federal service 1 May 1951 at home stations. Released from active Federal service 31 December 1952 and resumed State status. (Headquarters relocated to Ephrata on 1 February 1953). Redesignated 1 October 1953 as 420th Antiaircraft Artillery Battalion (90mm Gun).

Consolidated 15 April 1959 with the 205th Artillery, a parent regiment under the Combat Arms Regimental System.

CAMPAIGN STREAMERS
None

DECORATIONS
None

COAT OF ARMS
None

DISTINCTIVE INSIGNIA
None

421st ANTIAIRCRAFT ARTILLERY BATTALION

 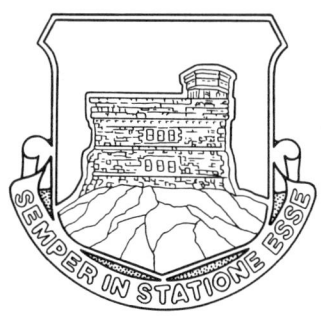

Constituted 9 July 1941 in the Regular Army as the 421st Separate Coast Artillery Battalion (Antiaircraft) and activated 1 August 1941 at St. Johns, Newfoundland. Redesignated 20 September 1941 as the 421st Coast Artillery Battalion (Antiaircraft) (Composite) and further redesignated 11 November 1943 as the 421st Antiaircraft Artillery Battalion (Composite) (Semimobile). (Returned from overseas service and arrived at the New York Port of Embarkation 2 January 1944). Inactivated 15 January 1944 at Camp McCoy, Wisconsin. Disbanded 6 December 1944.

CAMPAIGN STREAMERS
World War II
American Theater without inscription

DECORATIONS
None

COAT OF ARMS
SHIELD: Gules, on a mount issuing from base the Cabot Tower at St. Johns, Newfoundland or.

CREST: None

MOTTO: *Semper in Statione esse* (Always On The Alert)

The shield is red for Artillery and the Cabot Tower commemorates the activation and service of the Battalion in Newfoundland.

DISTINCTIVE INSIGNIA
The insignia is the shield and motto of the coat of arms. The insignia depicted was never made for nor worn by this organization.

421st ANTIAIRCRAFT ARTILLERY BATTALION

Constituted 3 November 1928 in the Nevada National Guard as 2d Battalion, 115th Engineers and assigned to the 40th Division. Organized and Federally recognized 1 May 1936 with Headquarters at Reno and companies at Reno, Winnemucca, Elko and Las Vegas. Relieved from the 40th Division, converted, reorganized and redesignated 1 January 1941 as the 121st Separate Coast Artillery Battalion (Antiaircraft) (Gun). Inducted into Federal service 23 June 1941 at home stations. Redesignated 10 September 1943 as the 121st Antiaircraft Artillery Gun Battalion (Mobile). Reorganized at Fort Sill, Oklahoma and redesignated 4 January 1945 as the 1st Rocket Battalion. Reorganized and redesignated 13 April 1945 as the 421st Rocket Field

Artillery Battalion (4.5" Rocket-Truck Drawn). (Departed Seattle Port of Embarkation 6 June 1945 for overseas service; arrived in Hawaii on 12 June 1945 and landed on Okinawa on 24 July 1945. Returned from overseas service and arrived at the Seattle Port of Embarkation on 14 January 1946). Inactivated 15 January 1946 at Fort Lawton, Washington. Reorganized as the 421st Antiaircraft Artillery Gun Battalion and Federally recognized 23 January 1948 with Headquarters at Las Vegas and batteries at Carson City, Winnemucca, Elko and Ely. (Headquarters relocated to Reno on 19 January 1949). Reorganized and redesignated 1 December 1952 as 421st Antiaircraft Artillery Automatic Weapons Battalion. Redesignated 1 October 1953 as 421st Antiaircraft Artillery Battalion (Automatic Weapons) (Mobile).

Consolidated 1 April 1959 with the 221st Artillery, a parent regiment under the Combat Arms Regimental System.

CAMPAIGN STREAMERS
World War II
Ryukyus

DECORATIONS
None

COAT OF ARMS
None

DISTINCTIVE INSIGNIA
None

422d ANTIAIRCRAFT ARTILLERY BATTALION

Constituted 13 January 1942 in the Army of the United States as the 422d Coast Artillery Battalion (Antiaircraft) (Composite) and activated 21 January 1942 at Camp Edwards, Massachusetts. (Departed New York Port of Embarkation 6 April 1942 for overseas service and arrived in Newfoundland on 14 April 1942). Redesignated 11 November 1943 as the 422d Antiaircraft Artillery Battalion (Composite) (Semimobile). (Returned from overseas service and arrived at the New York Port of Embarkation on 2 January 1944). Battalion, less Batteries B and C, inactivated 15 January 1944 at Camp McCoy, Wisconsin; concurrently, Batteries B and C redesignated as separate Antiaircraft Artillery batteries. Disbanded 6 December 1944.

CAMPAIGN STREAMERS
World War II
American Theater without inscription

DECORATIONS
None

COAT OF ARMS
None

DISTINCTIVE INSIGNIA
None

422d ANTIAIRCRAFT ARTILLERY BATTALION

Constituted 1 December 1952 in the Nevada Army National Guard as 422d Antiaircraft Artillery Automatic Weapons Battalion and organized from new and existing units as follows:

Battery A, 421st Antiaircraft Artillery Automatic Weapons Battalion (organized and Federally recognized 13 February 1941 at Las Vegas as Battery D, 121st Separate Battalion, Coast Artillery [Antiaircraft]; inducted into Federal service 23 June 1941 at Las Vegas; redesignated 10 September 1943 as Battery D, 121st Antiaircraft Artillery Gun Battalion; redesignated 4 January 1945 as Battery D, 1st Rocket Battalion; redesignated 13 April 1945 as Battery D, 421st Rocket Field Artillery Battalion; inactivated 15 January 1946 at Fort Lawton, Washington; reorganized and Federally recognized 23 January 1948 at Las Vegas as Headquarters Battery, 421st Antiaircraft Artillery Gun Battalion; and redesignated 1 December 1949 as Battery A, 421st Antiaircraft Artillery Automatic Weapons Battalion), redesignated Headquarters and Headquarters Battery

216th Transportation Truck Company (organized and Federally recognized 18 February 1952 at Boulder City), redesignated Battery A

122d Transportation Truck Company (organized and Federally recognized 10 January 1952 at Yerington), redesignated Battery B

Battery C organized new and Federally recognized 4 December 1952 at Hawthorne

Battery D, 421st Antiaircraft Artillery Gun Battalion (organized and Federally recognized 25 June 1948 at Ely), redesignated Battery D

Medical Detachment organized new and Federally recognized 7 January 1955 at Las Vegas

Redesignated 1 October 1953 as 422d Antiaircraft Artillery Battalion (Automatic Weapons) (Mobile). Reorganized and redesignated 1 January 1956 as 422d Antiaircraft Artillery Battalion (75mm Gun).

Consolidated 1 April 1959 with the 421st Artillery, a parent regiment under the Combat Arms Regimental System.

CAMPAIGN STREAMERS
World War II
Ryukyus

DECORATIONS
None

COAT OF ARMS
SHIELD: Per fess abased dancette gules and or, overall issuing from the fess point of an ogress in base the rising cloud of an atomic bomb explosion proper, fimbriated of the second.

CREST: That for the regiments and separate battalions of the Nevada Army National Guard: On a wreath of the colors (or and gules) within a garland of sagebrush a sledge and miner's drill crossed in saltire behind a pickax in pale proper.

MOTTO: *Sobre todo* (Above The Rest)

Red and yellow are used for Artillery. The jagged gold section is used to represent the Spring Mountains to the west of Las Vegas where the Headquarters of the battalion was located. The black circle indicates the Nevada Atomic Proving Grounds which is a short distance from the Las Vegas Armory. The atomic bomb burst signifies that the battalion was the first National Guard unit in history to witness and participate in one of the atomic exercises at the Proving Grounds.

DISTINCTIVE INSIGNIA
The insignia is the shield, crest and motto of the coat of arms. The sample of the insignia depicted was approved for wear on 27 July 1954.

423d ANTIAIRCRAFT ARTILLERY BATTALION

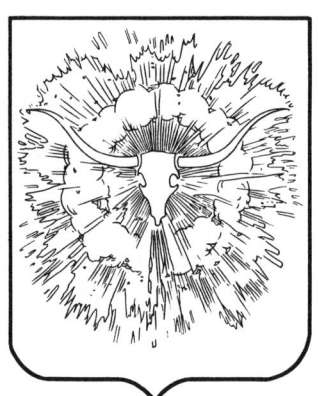

Constituted 27 August 1941 in the Regular Army as the 423d Separate Coast Artillery Battalion (Antiaircraft) and activated 10 September 1941 at Fort Bliss, Texas. Redesignated 20 September 1941 as the 423d Coast Artillery Battalion (Antiaircraft) (Composite). (Departed Charleston Sub Port of Embarkation 3 February 1942 for overseas service and arrived in Bermuda on 6 February 1942). Redesignated 1 June 1944 as the 423d Antiaircraft Artillery Battalion (Composite) (Semimobile); concurrently, organic batteries inactivated in Bermuda. (Remainder of battalion returned from overseas service and arrived at the Boston Port of Embarkation on 14 May 1945). Inactivated 30 June 1945 at Fort Bliss, Texas.

CAMPAIGN STREAMERS
World War II
American Theater without inscription

DECORATIONS
None

COAT OF ARMS
SHIELD: Gules, on a shellburst proper the skull and horns of a Texas Longhorn steer sable.

CREST: None

MOTTO: *Guarda el Cielo* (We Guard The Sky)

The shield is red for Coast Artillery. The design is symbolic of the fighting force of the Battalion in that every shell burst from the guns of the unit has the power of a charging Longhorn Bull. The Longhorn is representative of the State of Texas where the Battalion was activated.

DISTINCTIVE INSIGNIA
The insignia is the shield and motto of the coat of arms. The insignia depicted was never made for nor worn by this organization.

424th ANTIAIRCRAFT ARTILLERY AUTOMATIC WEAPONS BATTALION

Constituted 12 December 1942 in the Army of the United States as the 424th Coast Artillery Battalion (Antiaircraft) (Composite) and activated 2 January 1943 at Camp Edwards, Massachusetts. (Departed Boston Port of Embarkation 1 August 1943 and arrived in Greenland on 21 August 1943). Redesignated 28 September 1943 as the 424th Antiaircraft Artillery Automatic Weapons Battalion (Semimobile). (Returned from overseas service and arrived at the Boston Port of Embarkation on 26 July 1944). Disbanded 20 September 1944 at Camp Davis, North Carolina.

CAMPAIGN STREAMERS
World War II
European Theater without inscription

DECORATIONS
None

COAT OF ARMS
None

DISTINCTIVE INSIGNIA
None

425th ANTIAIRCRAFT ARTILLERY BATTALION

Constituted 25 February 1943 in the Army of the United States as the 125th Coast Artillery Battalion (Separate) (Antiaircraft) (Gun) (Mobile) and activated 24 May 1943 at Camp Haan, California. Redesignated 28 June 1943 as the 125th Antiaircraft Artillery Gun Battalion (Mobile). (Departed Boston Port of Embarkation 1 July 1944 for overseas service; arrived in England 8 July 1944 and landed in France on 23 September 1944. Returned from overseas service and arrived at the New York Port of Embarkation on 26 March 1946). Inactivated 27 March 1946 at Camp Kilmer, New Jersey. Redesignated 28 March 1946 as the 425th Antiaircraft Artillery Gun Battalion. Redesignated 425th Antiaircraft Artillery Battalion and allotted to the Regular Army on 9 February 1955. Activated 10 March 1955 at Camp Stewart, Georgia. Inactivated 1 September 1958 at the Savannah River Project, Georgia.

CAMPAIGN STREAMERS
World War II
Ardennes-Alsace
Rhineland
England 1944

DECORATIONS
Belgian Fourragere 1940 (125th AAA Gun Bn cited; DAGO 43, 1950)

Cited in the Order of the Day of the Belgian Army for *DEFENSE OF ANTWERP* (125th AAA Gun Bn cited for period 25 Oct-28 Nov 1944; DAGO 43, 1950)

Cited in the Order of the Day of the Belgian Army for *DEFENSE OF ANTWERP HARBOR* (125th AAA Gun Bn cited for action on 16 Dec 1944; DAGO 43, 1950)

COAT OF ARMS
SHIELD: Gules, in chief two projectiles bendwise and bend sinisterwise above a three-towered fortress issuant from base or.

CREST: None

MOTTO: Engage And Destroy

The colors scarlet and yellow are for Artillery. The fortress is taken from the arms of the city of Antwerp and alludes to the battalion's service in defense of that city and harbor during World War II. The projectiles represent antiaircraft fire.

DISTINCTIVE INSIGNIA
The insignia is the shield and motto of the coat of arms. The sample of the insignia depicted was approved for wear on 29 January 1957.

427th ANTIAIRCRAFT ARTILLERY BATTALION

Constituted 30 April 1942 in the Army of the United States as the 427th Coast Artillery Battalion (Antiaircraft) (Composite) and activated 2 May 1942 at Camp Davis, North Carolina. Disbanded 10 August 1942 at Washington, District of Columbia. Reconstituted 14 August 1943 in the Army of the United States as the 427th Antiaircraft Artillery Battalion (Composite) (Semimobile) and activated 1 September 1943 at Fort Brady, Michigan. Inactivated 10 May 1944 at Camp Pickett, Virginia. Disbanded 26 June 1944.

CAMPAIGN STREAMERS
None

DECORATIONS
None

COAT OF ARMS
None

DISTINCTIVE INSIGNIA
None

427th ANTIAIRCRAFT ARTILLERY AUTOMATIC WEAPONS BATTALION

Constituted 19 December 1942 in the Army of the United States as the 113th Coast Artillery Battalion (Separate) (Antiaircraft) (Gun) (Semimobile) and activated 10 February 1943 at Fort Bliss, Texas. Redesignated 28 June 1943 as the 113th Antiaircraft Artillery Gun Battalion (Semimobile). (Departed New York Port of Embarkation 21 August 1943 for overseas service; arrived in North Africa on 2 September 1943, moved to England on 10 August 1944 and landed in France on 30 August 1944. Returned from overseas service and arrived at the New York Port of Embarkation on 1 January 1946). Inactivated 2 January 1946 at Camp Kilmer, New Jersey. Redesignated 427th Antiaircraft Artillery Automatic Weapons Battalion and allotted to the Organized Reserves on 15 February 1949. Assigned to Second Army, 24 February 1949. Activated 10 March 1949 at Louisville, Kentucky. Relocated to Pittsburgh, Pennsylvania on 21 January 1950. Inactivated 30 June 1950 at Pittsburgh.

CAMPAIGN STREAMERS
World War II
Rhineland
Ardennes-Alsace
Central Europe

DECORATIONS
Belgian Fourragere 1940 (113th AAA Gun Bn cited; DAGO 43, 1950)

Cited in the Order of the Day of the Belgian Army for the *DEFENSE OF LIEGE* (113th AAA Gun Bn cited for period 27 Nov-14 Dec 1944; DAGO 43, 1950)

Cited in the Order of the Day of the Belgian Army for the *DEFENSE OF THE MEUSE RIVER* (113th AAA Gun Bn cited for period 16 Dec 1944-25 Jan 1945); DAGO 43, 1950)

COAT OF ARMS
None

DISTINCTIVE INSIGNIA
None

428th COAST ARTILLERY BATTALION

Constituted 2 August 1942 in the Army of the United States as the 428th Separate Coast Artillery Battalion (Antiaircraft) (Composite) and activated 10 August 1942 at Fort Shafter, Territory of Hawaii. (Relocated to Canton Island on 26 August 1942).

Reorganized, expanded and redesignated 13 May 1943 as the 428th Coast Artillery.

CAMPAIGN STREAMERS
World War II
Pacific Theater without inscription

DECORATIONS
None

COAT OF ARMS
None

DISTINCTIVE INSIGNIA
None

HEADQUARTERS AND HEADQUARTERS DETACHMENT 428th COAST ARTILLERY BATTALION

Constituted 15 March 1945 in the Army of the United States as Headquarters and Headquarters Detachment, 58th Coast Artillery Battalion (Harbor Defense) and activated 10 April 1945 at Fort Kamehameha, Territory of Hawaii. Inactivated 10 December 1946 at Fort Kamehameha. Redesignated Headquarters and Headquarters Detachment, 428th Coast Artillery Battalion (Harbor Defense), allotted to the Organized Reserves and assigned to Sixth Army on 19 January 1948. Activated 14 February 1948 at Long Beach, California. (Organized Reserves redesignated 25 March 1948 as Organized Reserve Corps). Inactivated 6 December 1948 at Long Beach.

CAMPAIGN STREAMERS
World War II
Pacific Theater without inscription

DECORATIONS
None

COAT OF ARMS
None

DISTINCTIVE INSIGNIA
None

429th ANTIAIRCRAFT ARTILLERY BATTALION

Constituted 19 January 1942 in the Army of the United States as the 429th Separate Coast Artillery Battalion (Antiaircraft) and redesignated 13 May 1943 as the 429th Coast Artillery Battalion (Antiaircraft) (Composite). Organized by elements at Christmas Island as follows: Headquarters and Headquarters Battery and Battery A activated 13 May 1943; Batteries B and C activated 30 June 1942. (Returned from overseas service and arrived in Hawaii on 28 September 1943). Redesignated 26 December 1943 as the 429th Antiaircraft Artillery Battalion (Composite) (Semimobile); concurrently, Battery A redesignated 716th Antiaircraft Searchlight Battery. Disbanded 26 May 1944 at Aiea, Oahu, Territory of Hawaii.

CAMPAIGN STREAMERS
World War II
Pacific Theater without inscription

DECORATIONS
None

COAT OF ARMS
None

DISTINCTIVE INSIGNIA
None

429th ANTIAIRCRAFT ARTILLERY AUTOMATIC WEAPONS BATTALION

Constituted 21 May 1942 in the Army of the United States as 2d Battalion, 612th Coast Artillery (Antiaircraft) (Colored) and activated 1 September 1942 at Camp Stewart, Georgia. Reorganized at Camp Stewart on 20 January 1943 and redesignated as 207th Coast Artillery Battalion (Antiaircraft) (Automatic Weapons) (Battalion) (Separate) (Colored). Redesignated 30 April 1943 as 207th Antiaircraft Artillery Automatic Weapons Battalion (Semimobile) (Colored). (Departed San Francisco Port of Embarkation 6 September 1943 for overseas service; arrived in Australia on 28 September 1943 and moved to New Guinea on 3 December 1943. Returned from overseas service and arrived at the Los Angeles Port of Embarkation on 25 January 1946). Inactivated 26 January 1946 at Camp Anza, Arlington, California. Redesignated 429th Antiaircraft Artillery Automatic Weapons Battalion, allotted to the Organized Reserves and assigned to Fourth Army on 23 June 1947. Activated 3 July 1947 at Dallas, Texas. (Organized Reserves redesignated Organized Reserve Corps on 25 March 1948). Inactivated 9 January 1950 at Dallas.

CAMPAIGN STREAMERS
World War II
New Guinea

DECORATIONS
None

COAT OF ARMS
None

DISTINCTIVE INSIGNIA
None

430th ANTIAIRCRAFT ARTILLERY BATTALION

Constituted 31 January 1942 in the Army of the United States as the 430th Separate Coast Artillery Battalion (Antiaircraft) (Automatic Weapons) and activated 1 March 1942 at Camp Davis, North Carolina. Redesignated 15 May 1943 as the 430th Antiaircraft Artillery Automatic Weapons Battalion (Mobile). (Departed Boston Port of Embarkation 20 October 1943 for overseas service; arrived in England on 2 November 1943 and landed in France on 13 June 1944. Returned from overseas service and arrived at Hampton Roads Port of Embarkation on 10 December 1945). Inactivated at Camp Patrick Henry, Virginia; Battalion, less Batteries B and D on 11 December 1945 and Batteries B and D on 16 December 1945. Allotted to the Organized Reserves on 28 March 1947 and activated 27 May 1947 at Brooklyn, New York. (Organized Reserves redesignated 25 March 1948 as Organized Reserve Corps). Relocated to Newark, New Jersey on 9 December 1948. Redesignated 478th Antiaircraft Artillery Automatic Weapons Battalion and assigned to the 78th Infantry Division, 8 July 1949. Relocated to East Orange, New Jersey on 20 September 1950. Redesignated 1 April 1952 as 430th Antiaircraft Artillery Automatic Weapons Battalion. (Organized Reserve Corps redesignated 25 July 1952 as Army Reserve). Redesignated 15 December 1952 as the 430th Antiaircraft Artillery Battalion (Automatic Weapons). Disbanded 1 May 1959 at East Orange.

CAMPAIGN STREAMERS
World War II
Normandy
Northern France
Rhineland
Central Europe

DECORATIONS
None

COAT OF ARMS
SHIELD: Gules, upon water issuant from base six duck decoys in front of a duck blind, rifle barrels protruding, all or.

CREST: That for the regiments and separate battalions of the Army Reserve: On a wreath of the colors (or and gules) the Lexington Minute Man proper. The statue of the Minute Man, Captain John Parker (H. H. Kitson, sculptor), stands on the common in Lexington, Massachusetts.

MOTTO: We Bag Them

In the scarlet and gold of the Coast Artillery the functions of the organization are aptly illustrated by the story of the duck hunters, a pastime engaged in, in the State of activation, North Carolina. The motto is expressive of the determination of the personnel to annihilate all opposition, a positive declaration of accomplishment.

DISTINCTIVE INSIGNIA
The insignia is the shield and motto of the coat of arms. The sample of the insignia depicted was approved for wear on 18 May 1956.

431st ANTIAIRCRAFT ARTILLERY AUTOMATIC WEAPONS BATTALION

Constituted 31 January 1942 in the Army of the United States as the 431st Separate Coast Artillery Battalion (Antiaircraft) (Automatic Weapons) and activated 1 March 1942 at Camp Stewart, Georgia. Redesignated 22 May 1942 as the 431st Coast Artillery Battalion (Antiaircraft) (Automatic Weapons). (Departed New York Port of Embarkation 5 August 1942 for overseas service; arrived in England on 20 August 1942 and landed in North Africa on 8 November 1942). Redesignated 13 November 1943 as the 431st Antiaircraft Artillery Automatic Weapons Battalion (Mobile). (After service in Sicily and Sardinia landed in Southern France on 8 November 1944. Returned from overseas service and arrived at the Boston Port of Embarkation on 16 October 1945). Inactivated 17 October 1945 at Camp Myles Standish, Massachusetts. Allotted to the Organized Reserves and assigned to Seventh Army on 14 March 1947. Relieved from the Seventh Army and assigned to Third Army on 15 March 1947. Activated 28 March 1947 at Atlanta, Georgia. (Organized Reserves redesignated 25 March 1948 as Organized Reserve Corps). Inactivated 1 December 1950 at Atlanta.

CAMPAIGN STREAMERS
World War II
Algeria-French Morocco (with arrowhead)
Tunisia
Sicily
Rhineland
Ardennes-Alsace
Central Europe

DECORATIONS
None

COAT OF ARMS
SHIELD: Gules, a porcupine passant or.

CREST: None

MOTTO: *Memo me Impune Lacessit* (No One Provokes Me With Impunity)

Red and yellow are the colors associated with Artillery. The stiff, sharp, erectile spines, often more than a foot long, mingled with the hair of the porcupine, readily become detached. The implication obviously is that a warm reception awaits anyone attempting to close quarters with the organization.

DISTINCTIVE INSIGNIA
The insignia is the shield and motto of the coat of arms. The sample of the insignia depicted was never made for nor worn by this organization.

432d ANTIAIRCRAFT ARTILLERY BATTALION

Constituted 31 January 1942 in the Army of the United States as the 432d Separate Coast Artillery Battalion (Antiaircraft) (Automatic Weapons) and activated 1 March 1942 at Camp Hulen, Texas. Redesignated 22 May 1942 as the 432d Coast Artillery Battalion (Antiaircraft) (Automatic Weapons). (Departed New York Port of Embarkation 5 August 1942 for overseas service; arrived in England on 20 August 1942, landed in North Africa on 23 November 1942 and moved to Italy on 20 October 1943). Redesignated 5 December 1943 as the 432d Antiaircraft Artillery Automatic Weapons Battalion (Self Propelled). Inactivated 20 September 1945 at Caserta, Italy. Allotted to the Organized Reserves and assigned to Sixth Army on 6 May 1947. Activated 12 June 1947 at Salt Lake City, Utah. (Organized Reserves redesignated 25 March 1948 as Organized Reserve Corps). Relocated to Vallejo, California on 10 January 1949. Inactivated 14 November 1949 at Vallejo. Redesignated 18 August 1950 as the 432d Antiaircraft Artillery Gun Battalion. Activated 1 September 1950 at Oakland, California. (Organized Reserve Corps redesignated 9 July 1952 as Army Reserve). Redesignated 15 April 1953 as the 432d Antiaircraft Artillery Battalion. Inactivated 17 May 1954 at Oakland.

CAMPAIGN STREAMERS
World War II
Tunisia
Naples-Foggia
Rome-Arno
North Apennines
Po Valley

DECORATIONS
None

COAT OF ARMS
None

DISTINCTIVE INSIGNIA
None

433d ANTIAIRCRAFT ARTILLERY MISSILE BATTALION

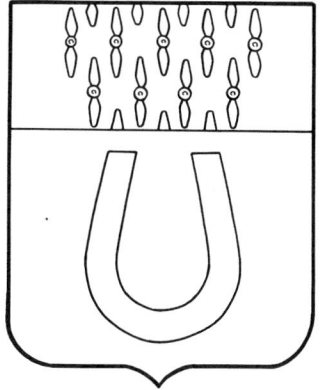 

Constituted 31 January 1942 in the Army of the United States as the 433d Separate Coast Artillery Battalion (Antiaircraft) (Automatic Weapons) and activated 1 March 1942 at Camp Stewart, Georgia. Redesignated 22 May 1942 as the 433d Coast Artillery Battalion (Antiaircraft) (Automatic Weapons). (Departed New York Port of Embarkation 7 February 1943 for overseas service; landed in North Africa on 19 February 1943 and moved to Sicily on 11 July 1943). Redesignated 13 November 1943 as the 433d Antiaircraft Artillery Automatic Weapons Battalion (Mobile). (Moved to Italy on 29 November 1943 and landed in Southern France on 15 September 1944). Inactivated 6 October 1945 in Germany. Allotted to the Organized Reserves and assigned to Sixth Army on 6 May 1947. Activated 2 June 1947 with Headquarters at Monrovia, California. (Organized Reserves redesignated 25 March 1948 as Organized Reserve Corps). Reorganized and redesignated 10 February 1949 as the 433d Antiaircraft Artillery Gun Battalion. Headquarters relocated to Pasadena, California on 26 April 1949. Inactivated 15 September 1950 at Pasadena. (Organized Reserve Corps redesignated 9 July 1952 as Army Reserve). Withdrawn from the Army Reserve, redesignated 433d Antiaircraft Artillery Missile Battalion (NIKE) (Continental) and allotted to the Regular Army on 22 August 1955. Activated 7 September 1955 at Fort Lawton, Washington; inactivated 1 September 1958 at Midway, Washington.

CAMPAIGN STREAMERS
World War II
Sicily (with arrowhead)
Naples-Foggia
Rome-Arno
Anzio
Southern France (with arrowhead)
Rhineland
Ardennes-Alsace
Central Europe

DECORATIONS
None

COAT OF ARMS
SHIELD: Gules, a horseshoe magnet, poles to chief or, on a chief of the last semee of propeller blades palewise in pile of the field.

CREST: None

MOTTO: We Bring Them Down

The functions of the organization are implied in the attraction of the propellers to the poles of the magnet, thus bringing down enemy ships within the scope of the battalion's range. The horseshoe-like magnet, an emblem of good luck, enhances the attractive arrangement. The motto is expressive of the determination of the personnel to fulfill their allotted tasks with thoroughness, an inspiring battle slogan.

DISTINCTIVE INSIGNIA
The insignia is the shield of the coat of arms. A sample of the insignia depicted, although not in conformity with official authority, was approved for wear on 14 August 1957.

434th ANTIAIRCRAFT ARTILLERY AUTOMATIC WEAPONS BATTALION

Constituted 31 January 1942 in the Army of the United States as 434th Coast Artillery Battalion (Antiaircraft) (Automatic Weapons) and activated 1 March 1942 at Camp Hulen, Texas. (Departed New York Port of Embarkation 4 August 1942 for overseas service; arrived in Scotland 17 August 1942 and landed in England on 19 August 1942. Relocated to North Africa on 19 January 1943 and then moved to Italy on 10 October 1943). Redesignated 5 December 1943 as the 434th Antiaircraft Artillery Automatic Weapons Battalion (Self Propelled). Disbanded 14 January 1945 at Montecatini, Italy and personnel transferred to the 473d Infantry. Reconstituted 20 March 1951 and consolidated with the 2d Antiaircraft Artillery Automatic Weapons Battalion.

CAMPAIGN STREAMERS
World War II
Tunisia
Rome-Arno
Anzio
North Apennines

DECORATIONS
None

COAT OF ARMS
SHIELD: Gules, a buzzard volant sable, armed and legged of the field, fimbriated or, collared with a rope extending to base throughout of the last.

CREST: None

MOTTO: Our Reception

The scarlet is the color of the Coast Artillery. The antiaircraft functions of this organization are illustrated in the lassoed buzzard implying that all enemy trespassing will be dealt with summarily.

DISTINCTIVE INSIGNIA
The insignia is the shield and motto of the coat of arms. The insignia depicted was never made for nor worn by this unit.

435th ANTIAIRCRAFT ARTILLERY AUTOMATIC WEAPONS BATTALION

Constituted 31 January 1942 in the Army of the United States as 435th Coast Artillery Battalion (Antiaircraft) (Automatic Weapons) and activated 1 March 1942 at Fort Bliss, Texas. (Departed Boston Port of Embarkation 28 April 1943 for overseas service; arrived in North Africa on 11 May 1943 and moved to Italy on 22 September 1943). Redesignated 12 December 1943 as the 435th Antiaircraft Artillery Automatic Weapons Battalion (Semimobile). Disbanded 19 December 1944 at Montecatini, Italy and personnel transferred to the 473d Infantry.

CAMPAIGN STREAMERS
World War II
Naples-Foggia
Anzio
Rome-Arno
North Apennines

DECORATIONS
None

COAT OF ARMS
None

DISTINCTIVE INSIGNIA
None

436th ANTIAIRCRAFT ARTILLERY MISSILE BATTALION

Constituted 10 April 1942 in the Army of the United States as 436th Coast Artillery Battalion (Antiaircraft) (Automatic Weapons) and activated 20 April 1942 at Camp Hulen, Texas. (Departed Hampton Roads Port of Embarkation 27 October 1942 for overseas service; arrived

in North Africa on 8 November 1942 and landed in Sicily on 9 July 1943). Redesignated 13 November 1943 as the 436th Antiaircraft Artillery Automatic Weapons Battalion (Mobile). (Relocated to Southern France on 18 September 1944. Returned from overseas service and arrived at the New York Port of Embarkation 8 October 1945). Inactivated 9 October 1945 at Camp Shanks, New York. Allotted to the Organized Reserves and assigned to Sixth Army on 6 May 1947. Activated 2 June 1947 at Long Beach, California. (Organized Reserves redesignated 25 March 1948 as Organized Reserve Corps). Inactivated 30 November 1950 at Long Beach. (Organized Reserve redesignated 9 July 1952 as Army Reserve). Withdrawn from the Army Reserve, redesignated 436th Antiaircraft Artillery Battalion and allotted to the Regular Army,, 9 November 1954. Activated 6 January 1955 at Travis Air Force Base, California. Reorganized and redesignated 5 January 1957 as the 436th Antiaircraft Artillery Missile Battalion. Inactivated 1 September 1958 at Travis Air Force Base.

CAMPAIGN STREAMERS
World War II
Algeria-French Morocco (with arrowhead)
Tunisia
Sicily (with arrowhead)
Rome-Arno
Southern France
Rhineland
Ardennes-Alsace
Central Europe

DECORATIONS
None

COAT OF ARMS
SHIELD: Gules, a representation of the mythological Hindu god Indra astride an elephant richly caprisoned, all or.

CREST: None

MOTTO: Defend And Spare Not

Indra was the chief of the Hindu gods, the strongest of them all and the god of the atmospheric regions, wielder of the thunderbolt, lord of the plains, bull of the heavens, conqueror of the malignant, gatherer of clouds, dispenser of rain, and generator of fire in the clouds (lightning), thus overcoming all enemies; all of which are symbolical of the protective functions of the unit. The motto is allusive to the protection afforded by the Battalion.

DISTINCTIVE INSIGNIA
The insignia is the shield of the coat of arms. The sample of the insignia depicted was approved for wear on 23 January 1956.

437th ANTIAIRCRAFT ARTILLERY AUTOMATIC WEAPONS BATTALION

Constituted 10 April 1942 in the Army of the United States as 437th Coast Artillery Battalion (Antiaircraft) (Automatic Weapons) and activated 20 April 1942 at Camp Hulen, Texas. (Departed New York Port of Embarkation 2 November 1942; arrived in North Africa on 11 November 1942 and landed in Italy on 30 November 1943). Reorganized and redesignated 12 December 1943 as the 437th Antiaircraft Artillery Automatic Weapons Battalion (Mobile). (Relocated to Southern France on 30 August 1944). Disbanded 26 October 1944 at Marseilles, France.

CAMPAIGN STREAMERS
World War II
Naples-Foggia
Rome-Arno
Southern France

DECORATIONS
None

COAT OF ARMS
None

DISTINCTIVE INSIGNIA
None

438th ANTIAIRCRAFT ARTILLERY BATTALION

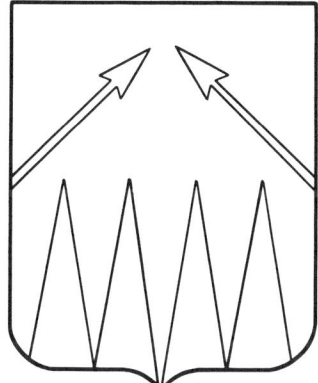

Constituted 9 May 1942 in the Army of the United States as the 438th Coast Artillery Battalion (Antiaircraft) (Automatic Weapons) and activated 6 June 1942 at Camp Edwards, Massachusetts. Redesignated 15 May 1943 as the 438th Antiaircraft Artillery Automatic Weapons Battalion (Mobile). (Departed New York Port of Embarkation 17 November 1943 for overseas service; arrived in England on 24 November 1943 and landed in France on 17 June 1944. Returned from overseas service and arrived at the New York Port of Embarkation on 20 March 1946). Inactivated 21 March 1946 at Camp Kilmer, New Jersey. Allotted to the Organized Reserves and assigned to Fifth Army, 27 August 1947. Activated 15 October 1947 with Headquarters at Cedar Rapids, Iowa. (Organized Reserves redesignated 25 March 1948 as Organized Reserve Corps). Relieved from Fifth Army, redesignated 403d Antiaircraft Artillery Automatic Weapons Battalion (Self Propelled) and assigned to the 103d Infantry Division, 25 November 1949. Redesignated 1 April 1952 as the 438th Antiaircraft Artillery Automatic Weapons Battalion (Self Propelled). (Organized Reserve Corps redesignated 9 July 1952 as Army Reserve). Redesignated 15 December 1952 as the 438th Antiaircraft Artillery Battalion (Automatic Weapons) (Self Propelled). Relieved from the 103d Infantry Division and inactivated 18 May 1959 at Cedar Rapids.

CAMPAIGN STREAMERS
World War II
Normandy
Northern France
Rhineland
Ardennes-Alsace
Central Europe

DECORATIONS
None

COAT OF ARMS
SHIELD: Gules, two javelins issuant from dexter and sinister fess chevronwise, issuant from base four piles or.

CREST: That for the regiments and separate battalions of the Army Reserve: On a wreath of the colors (or and gules) the Lexington Minute Man proper. The statue of the Minute Man, Captain John Parker (H. H. Kitson, sculptor), stands on the common in Lexington, Massachusetts.

MOTTO: *Audacia Vincit* (Courage Conquers)

In the scarlet and gold of the Coast Artillery arm the two javelins are in the form of a driving wedge.

DISTINCTIVE INSIGNIA
The insignia is the shield and motto of the coat of arms. The sample of the insignia depicted was approved for wear on 19 April 1958.

439th ANTIAIRCRAFT ARTILLERY GUN BATTALION

Constituted 9 May 1942 in the Army of the United States as 439th Coast Artillery Battalion (Antiaircraft) (Automatic Weapons) and activated 6 June 1942 at Camp Hulen, Texas. (Departed New York Port of Embarkation 28 April 1943; arrived in North Africa on 11 May 1943 and landed in Italy on 13 November 1943). Reorganized and redesignated 12 December 1943 as the 439th Antiaircraft Artillery Automatic Weapons Battalion (Semimobile). (Relocated to Southern France on 18 September 1944). Inactivated 30 October 1945 in Germany. Allotted to the Organized Reserves and assigned to Fourth Army on 9 June 1947. Activated 24 June 1947 at Houston, Texas. (Organized Reserves redesignated 25 March 1948 as Organized Reserve Corps). Reorganized and redesignated 17 December 1948 as the 439th Antiaircraft Artillery Gun Battalion. Inactivated 15 December 1950 at Houston.

CAMPAIGN STREAMERS
World War II
Naples-Foggia
Rome-Arno
Southern France
Rhineland
Ardennes-Alsace
Central Europe

DECORATIONS
French Croix de Guerre with Palm, World War II, Streamer embroidered *CENTRAL ITALY* (439th AAA AW Bn cited for period 1 Dec 1943-31 Jul 1944; DAGO 43, 1950)

COAT OF ARMS
None

DISTINCTIVE INSIGNIA
None

440th ANTIAIRCRAFT ARTILLERY BATTALION

Constituted 5 May 1942 in the Army of the United States as 440th Coast Artillery Battalion (Antiaircraft) (Automatic Weapons) and activated 1 July 1942 at Camp Haan, California. Reorganized and redesignated 15 May 1943 as the 440th Antiaircraft Artillery Automatic Weapons Battalion (Mobile). (Departed New York Port of Embarkation 29 December 1943; arrived in England on 9 January 1944 and landed in France on 7 July 1944. Returned from overseas and arrived at the New York Port of Embarkation on 21 November 1945). Inactivated 22 November 1945 at Camp Shanks, New York. Allotted to the Organized Reserves and assigned to Fifth Army on 27 August 1947. Activated 24 September 1947 at St. Louis, Missouri. (Organized Reserves redesignated 25 March 1948 as Organized Reserve Corps). Inactivated 15 November 1950 at St. Louis. Assigned to the 75th Infantry Division and activated 1 May 1952 with Headquarters at Waco, Texas. Redesignated 9 January 1953 as the 440th Antiaircraft Artillery Battalion. (Organized Reserve Corps redesignated 25 July 1952 as Army Reserve). Inactivated 31 January 1955 at Waco.

CAMPAIGN STREAMERS
World War II
Normandy
Northern France
Rhineland
Ardennes-Alsace
Central Europe

DECORATIONS
French Croix de Guerre with Silver Star, World War II, Streamer embroidered *GOUVY BELGIUM* (440th AAA AW Bn cited for period 17-22 Dec 1944; DAGO 43, 1950)

COAT OF ARMS
None

DISTINCTIVE INSIGNIA
None

441st ANTIAIRCRAFT ARTILLERY MISSILE BATTALION

 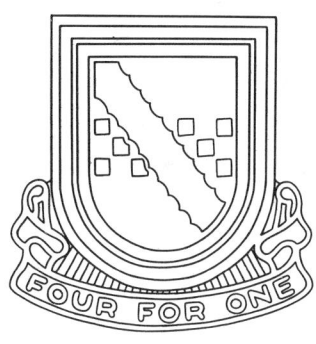

Constituted 21 May 1942 in the Army of the United States as 441st Coast Artillery Battalion (Antiaircraft) (Gun). Redesignated 27 May 1942 as the 441st Coast Artillery Battalion (Antiaircraft) (Automatic Weapons) and activated 1 June 1942 at Camp Stewart, Georgia. (Departed Hampton Roads Port of Embarkation 8 June 1943 for overseas service; landed in North Africa on 22 June 1943 and moved to Sicily on 9 July 1943. Participated in assault landings at Salerno, Italy on 10 September 1943 and in Southern France on 15 August 1944. Returned from overseas and arrived at Hampton Roads Port of Embarkation on 18 October 1945).

Inactivated 18 October 1945 at Camp Patrick Henry, Virginia. Allotted to the Organized Reserves and assigned to Fifth Army on 27 April 1947. Activated 24 September 1947 at Chicago, Illinois. (Organized Reserves redesignated 25 March 1948 as the Organized Reserve Corps). Inactivated 15 November 1950 at Chicago. (Organized Reserve Corps redesignated 9 July 1952 as Army Reserve). Withdrawn from the Army Reserve, redesignated 441st Antiaircraft Artillery Missile Battalion (NIKE) (Continental) and allotted to the Regular Army on 21 July 1955. Activated 1 August 1955 at Fort Cronkhite, California; inactivated 1 September 1958 at San Pablo, California.

CAMPAIGN STREAMERS
World War II
Sicily (with arrowhead)
Naples-Foggia (with arrowhead)
Rome-Arno
Anzio (with arrowhead)
Southern France (with arrowhead)
Rhineland
Ardennes-Alsace
Central Europe

DECORATIONS
Presidential Unit Citation (Army), Streamer embroidered *COLMAR* (441st AAA AW Bn cited for period 22 Jan-6 Feb 1945; WDGO 44, 1945)

COAT OF ARMS
SHIELD: Or a fess checky azure and of the first, a bend engrailed within a double tressure gules.

CREST: None

MOTTO: Four For One

Scarlet is the color of the Coast Artillery. The design is based upon the activation of the organization at Camp Stewart, Georgia, the shield being similar to that of the Stewart Clan of Scotland. The checkered horizontal fess is the heraldic representation of the military belt or girdle of honor; the diagonal bend denotes the scarf of a military commander. The engrailed line represents fire and speed, and the double tressure represents the protection afforded by the battalion as the tressure heraldically represents the moat dug around medieval castles.

DISTINCTIVE INSIGNIA
The insignia is the shield and motto of the coat of arms. The sample of the insignia depicted was approved for wear on 6 September 1956.

442d ANTIAIRCRAFT ARTILLERY AUTOMATIC WEAPONS BATTALION

Constituted 21 May 1942 in the Army of the United States as the 442d Coast Artillery Battalion (Antiaircraft) (Automatic Weapons) and activated 1 June 1942 at Fort Bliss, Texas. (Departed Hampton Roads Port of Embarkation 10 May 1943 for overseas service and arrived in North Africa on 2 June 1943). Reorganized and redesignated 28 May 1943 as the 442d Antiaircraft Artillery Automatic Weapons Battalion (Semimobile). Disbanded 22 July 1944 at Oran, North Africa.

CAMPAIGN STREAMERS
World War II
European Theater without inscription

DECORATIONS
None

COAT OF ARMS
None

DISTINCTIVE INSIGNIA
None

443d ANTIAIRCRAFT ARTILLERY BATTALION

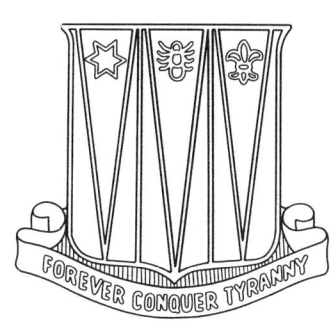

Constituted 10 April 1942 in the Army of the United States as the 443d Coast Artillery Battalion (Antiaircraft) (Automatic Weapons) and activated 20 April 1942 at Fort Sheridan, Illinois. (Departed New York Port of Embarkation 26 October 1942 for overseas service and arrived in North Africa on 10 November 1942. Participated in assault landing on Sicily on 9 July 1943 and moved to Italy on 20 October 1943). Reorganized and redesignated 14 April 1944 as the 443d Antiaircraft Artillery Automatic Weapons Battalion (Self Propelled). (Returned from overseas service and arrived at the New York Port of Embarkation on 16 February 1946). Inactivated 17 February 1946 at Camp Kilmer, New Jersey. Redesignated 443d Antiaircraft Artillery Automatic Weapons Battery and activated at Fort Bliss, Texas on 1 August 1946. Allotted to the Regular Army, 24 February 1949. Reorganized and redesignated 8 June 1949 as the 443d Antiaircraft Artillery Automatic Weapons Battalion. Redesignated 1 October 1953 as the 443d Antiaircraft Artillery Battalion (Automatic Weapons). Inactivated 1 September 1958 in Germany.

CAMPAIGN STREAMERS
World War II
Algeria-French Morocco (with arrowhead)
Tunisia
Sicily (with arrowhead)
Naples-Foggia
Rome-Arno
Southern France (with arrowhead)
Rhineland
Ardennes-Alsace
Central Europe

DECORATIONS
None

COAT OF ARMS
SHIELD: Gules a pale or, three searchlight beams issuant from base and charged in chief

with a mullet of six points bendwise, a tarantula and a fleur-de-lis all counterchanged.

CREST: None

MOTTO: Forever Conquer Tyranny

The colors red and yellow are used for Artillery. The shield is divided into nine sections which allude to the nine campaigns of the organization. The pale is symbolical of strength. The three searchlight beams refer to the functional nature of the organization and also represent its three assault landings: that beam charged with the six-pointed star for Algeria-French Morocco, that with the tarantula for Sicily and that with the fleur-de-lis for Southern France.

DISTINCTIVE INSIGNIA
The insignia is the shield and motto of the coat of arms. The sample of the insignia depicted was approved for wear on 14 March 1952.

444th AIRBORNE ANTIAIRCRAFT BATTALION

Constituted 5 May 1942 in the Army of the United States as the 444th Coast Artillery Battalion (Antiaircraft) (Automatic Weapons) and activated 1 July 1942 at Camp Haan, California. Reorganized and redesignated 24 May 1943 as the 444th Antiaircraft Artillery Automatic Weapons Battalion (Mobile). (Departed New York Port of Embarkation 20 February 1945 for overseas service and landed in France on 27 February 1945. Returned from overseas service and arrived at the Boston Port of Embarkation on 16 November 1945). Inactivated 17 November 1945 at Camp Myles Standish, Massachusetts. Redesignated 444th Airborne Antiaircraft Battalion and allotted to the Organized Reserve Corps on 25 March 1948. Activated 1 May 1948 at San Juan, Puerto Rico; inactivated 30 November 1949 at San Juan.

CAMPAIGN STREAMERS
World War II
Rhineland
Central Europe

DECORATIONS
None

COAT OF ARMS
None

DISTINCTIVE INSIGNIA
None

445th ANTIAIRCRAFT ARTILLERY BATTALION

Constituted 5 May 1942 in the Army of the United States as the 445th Separate Coast Artillery Battalion (Antiaircraft) (Automatic Weapons) and activated 1 July 1942 at Camp Davis, North Carolina. Redesignated 10 October 1942 as the 445th Coast Artillery Battalion (Antiaircraft) (Automatic Weapons). Reorganized and redesignated 15 May 1943 as the 445th Antiaircraft Artillery Automatic Weapons Battalion (Semimobile). (Departed New York Port of Embarkation 21 February 1944 for overseas service; arrived in England on 28 February 1944 and landed in France on 9 July 1944). Inactivated 29 June 1946 in Holland. Allotted to the Organized Reserve Corps on 25 March 1948 and activated 1 May 1948 at San Juan, Puerto Rico. (Organized Reserve Corps redesignated 9 July 1952 as Army Reserve). Redesignated 8 November 1953 as the 445th Antiaircraft Artillery Battalion. Inactivated 1 August 1959 at San Juan.

CAMPAIGN STREAMERS
World War II
Normandy
Northern France
Rhineland
Central Europe
England 1944

DECORATIONS
None

COAT OF ARMS
SHIELD: Gules a leopard statant, spotted, the dexter paw upraised or, the sinister resting upon a crushed tank argent, issuant from dexter honor point a silhouette of an aircraft of the last.

CREST: That for the regiments and separate battalions of the Army Reserve: On a wreath of the colors (or and gules) the Lexington Minute Man proper. The statue of the Minute Man, Captain John Parker (H. H. Kitson, sculptor), stands on the common in Lexington, Massachusetts.

MOTTO: *Dum Vigilo curo* (While I Watch, I Take Care)

The crouching alert position of the leopard symbolizes the dual purpose of offensive and defensive action; the outstretched paw reaching for the plane denotes the primary purpose of the antiaircraft; the crushed tank under the paw indicates the secondary purpose of tank destruction. The leopard, being one of the smaller animals, is symbolic of the smaller, streamlined organizations. As it is a sleek, fast moving, agile animal, the leopard represents the mobility, speed, and automatic weapons of the organization; its spots indicate the technique of camouflage.

DISTINCTIVE INSIGNIA
The insignia is the shield and motto of the coat of arms. The sample of the insignia depicted was approved for wear 14 October 1954.

446th ANTIAIRCRAFT ARTILLERY BATTALION

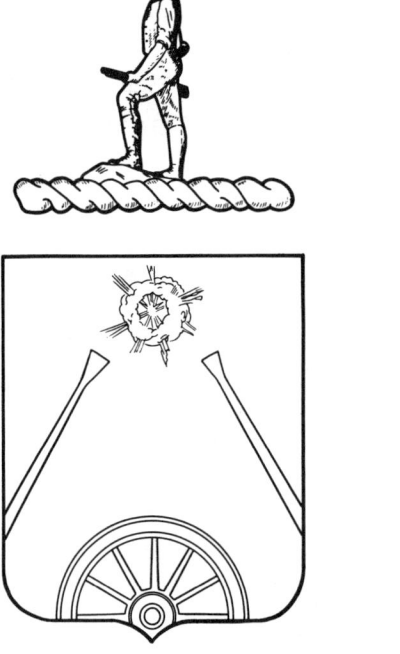

Constituted 5 May 1942 in the Army of the United States as the 446th Coast Artillery Battalion (Antiaircraft) (Automatic Weapons) and activated 1 July 1942 at Camp Davis, North Carolina. Reorganized and redesignated 15 May 1943 as the 446th Antiaircraft Artillery Automatic Weapons Battalion (Semimobile). (Departed New York Port of Embarkation 29 September 1944 for overseas service and landed in France on 10 October 1944. Returned from overseas service and arrived at Hampton Roads Port of Embarkation 23 October 1945). Inactivated 23 October 1945 at Camp Patrick Henry, Virginia. Redesignated 446th Antiaircraft Artillery Gun Battalion and allotted to the Organized Reserve Corps on 25 March 1948. Activated 1 May 1948 at San Juan, Puerto Rico. (Organized Reserve Corps redesignated 9 July 1952 as Army Reserve). Redesignated 1 June 1953 as the 446th Antiaircraft Artillery Battalion. Inactivated 28 February 1959 at San Juan.

CAMPAIGN STREAMERS
World War II
Rhineland
Ardennes-Alsace
Central Europe

DECORATIONS
None

COAT OF ARMS
SHIELD: Gules two gun tubes (Bofors 40mm AA guns) issuing chevronwise or between a shell burst in chief argent and a demi wheel issuant from base of the second.

CREST: That for the regiments and separate battalions of the Army Reserve: On a wreath of the colors (or and gules) the Lexington Minute Man proper. The statue of the Minute Man, Captain John Parker (H. H. Kitson, sculptor), stands on the common in Lexington, Massachusetts.

MOTTO: *Ad Accutissimum Corona* (To The Most Alert The Crown Of Victory)

In the scarlet and gold of the Coast Artillery arm the antiaircraft functions of the organization are indicated by the two Bofors 40mm AA guns typified by the shape of the muzzle or flash hider, and the half wheel signifying semimobility. The shell burst in the center is white for contrast and indicates speed of action.

DISTINCTIVE INSIGNIA
The insignia is the shield and motto of the coat of arms. The sample of the insignia depicted was approved for wear 23 December 1952.

447th ANTIAIRCRAFT ARTILLERY BATTALION

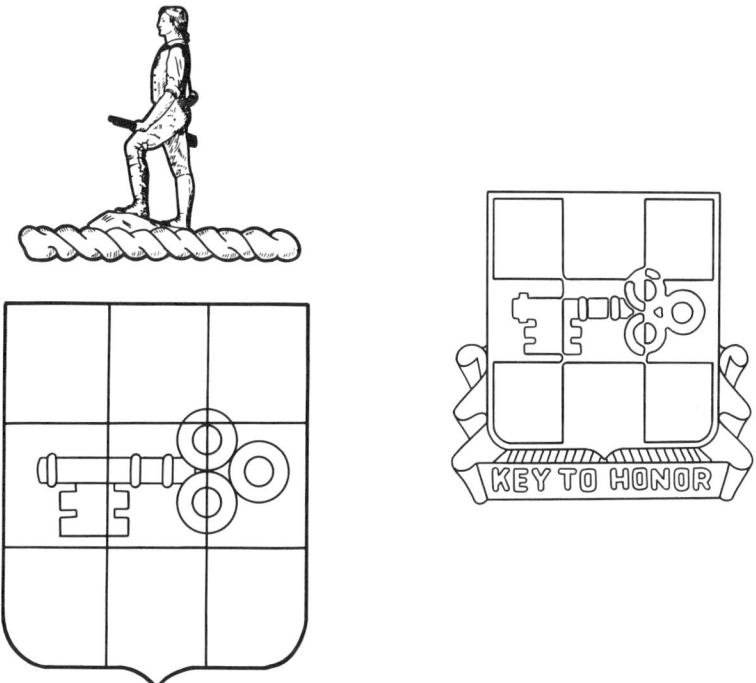

Constituted 5 May 1942 in the Army of the United States as the 447th Coast Artillery Battalion (Antiaircraft) (Automatic Weapons) and activated 1 July 1942 at Fort Bliss, Texas. Reorganized and redesignated 15 May 1943 as the 447th Antiaircraft Artillery Automatic Weapons Battalion (Semimobile). (Departed New York Port of Embarkation 11 February 1944 for overseas service; arrived in England on 23 February 1944 and participated in assault landing on beaches of Normandy, 6 June 1944. Returned from overseas service and arrived at Boston Port of Embarkation 24 October 1945). Inactivated 25 October 1945 at Camp Myles Standish,

Massachusetts. Allotted to the Organized Reserve Corps and assigned to United States Army, Caribbean on 25 March 1948. Activated 1 May 1948 at Mayaguez, Puerto Rico. Redesignated 19 May 1952 as the 447th Antiaircraft Artillery Automatic Weapons Battalion, Mobile. (Organized Reserve Corps redesignated 9 July 1952 as Army Reserve). Redesignated 8 November 1953 as the 447th Antiaircraft Artillery Battalion. Inactivated 1 October 1959 at Mayaguez.

CAMPAIGN STREAMERS
World War II
Normandy (with arrowhead)
Northern France
Rhineland
Ardennes-Alsace
Central Europe

DECORATIONS
Presidential Unit Citation (Army), Streamer embroidered *ARDENNES* (Btry C 447th AAA AW Bn cited for period 16-24 Dec 1944; DAGO 63, 1947)

COAT OF ARMS
SHIELD: Gules, a pale and a fess or counterchanged, overall a key of the last.

CREST: That for the regiments and separate battalions of the Army Reserve: On a wreath of the colors (or and gules) the Lexington Minute Man proper. The statue of the Minute Man, Captain John Parker (H. H. Kitson, sculptor), stands on the common in Lexington, Massachusetts.

MOTTO: Key To Honor

The colors scarlet and yellow are used for Artillery. The five red squares represent the five campaigns of the battalion in Europe during World War II. The nine divisions of the shield symbolize the nine enemy divisions against which Battery C fought to win its Presidential Unit Citation. The key is for the assault on Normandy Beach, symbolic of opening "Fortress Europa".

DISTINCTIVE INSIGNIA
The insignia is the shield and motto of the coat of arms. The sample of the insignia depicted was approved for wear 29 May 1958.

448th ANTIAIRCRAFT ARTILLERY BATTALION

Constituted 5 May 1942 in the Army of the United States as the 448th Coast Artillery Battalion (Antiaircraft) (Automatic Weapons) and activated 1 July 1942 at Fort Bliss, Texas. Reorganized and redesignated 15 May 1943 as the 448th Antiaircraft Artillery Automatic Weapons Battalion (Semimobile). (Departed New York Port of Embarkation 29 December 1943 for overseas service; arrived in Scotland on 11 January 1944, moved to England on 27 March 1944 and landed in France on 19 June 1944. Returned from overseas service and arrived at Boston Port of Embarkation 11 December 1945). Inactivated 12 December 1945 at Camp Myles Standish, Massachusetts. Redesignated 448th Antiaircraft Artillery Gun Battalion and allotted to the Organized Reserve Corps 22 June 1948. Activated 20 July 1948 at Ponce, Puerto Rico. (Organized Reserve Corps redesignated 9 July 1952 as Army Reserve). Redesignated 1 June 1953 as the 448th Antiaircraft Artillery Battalion. Inactivated 1 May 1955 at Ponce. Activated 29 November 1955 at Humacao, Puerto Rico; inactivated 30 April 1959 at Humacao.

CAMPAIGN STREAMERS
World War II
Normandy
Northern France
Rhineland
Ardennes-Alsace
Central Europe
England 1944

DECORATIONS
None

COAT OF ARMS
SHIELD: Gules a leopard's head erased affronte or, gorged with a collar azure, holding in the mouth a rat fesswise sable.

CREST: That for the regiments and separate battalions of the Army Reserve: On a wreath of the colors (or and gules) the Lexington Minute Man proper. The statue of the Minute Man, Captain John Parker (H. H. Kitson, sculptor), stands on the common in Lexington, Massachusetts.

MOTTO: Our Trap Springs

The scarlet is the color of the Coast Artillery Corps. The functions of the organization are illustrated by the ferocious leopard's head which heraldically signifies a valiant and hardy warrior who enterprises hazardous things by force and courage. The black rat in the leopard's mouth indicates the reception accorded enemy opposition. The motto is expressive of the symbolism of the shield.

DISTINCTIVE INSIGNIA
The insignia is the shield and motto of the coat of arms. The sample of the insignia depicted was approved for wear 15 April 1954.

449th ANTIAIRCRAFT ARTILLERY GUN BATTALION

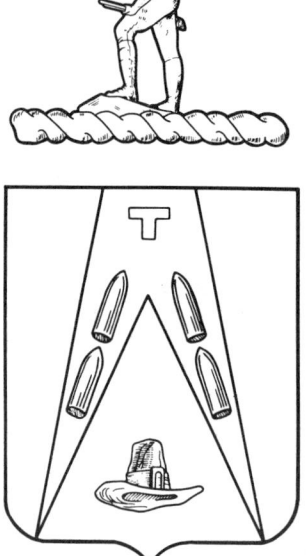

Constituted 5 May 1942 in the Army of the United States as the 449th Coast Artillery Battalion (Antiaircraft) (Automatic Weapons) and activated 1 July 1942 at Camp Edwards, Massachusetts. Reorganized and redesignated 25 May 1943 as the 449th Antiaircraft Artillery Automatic Weapons Battalion (Semimobile). (Departed New York Port of Embarkation 5 December 1943 for overseas service; arrived in England on 16 December 1943 and landed in France on 14 July 1944. Returned from overseas service and arrived at New York Port of Embarkation 25 November 1945). Inactivated 26 November 1945 at Camp Kilmer, New Jersey. Redesignated 449th Antiaircraft Artillery Gun Battalion, allotted to the Organized Reserve Corps and assigned to Fourth Army, 14 September 1948. Activated 27 September 1948 at Shreveport, Louisiana; inactivated 16 November 1950 at Shreveport.

CAMPAIGN STREAMERS
World War II
Normandy
Northern France
Rhineland
Ardennes-Alsace
Central Europe

DECORATIONS
None

COAT OF ARMS
SHIELD: Gules, on two piles issuing from middle chief to dexter and sinister base or four projectiles and a conventionalized target of the first, in base a Pilgrim's hat of the second.

CREST: That for the regiments and separate battalions of the Organized Reserve Corps: On a wreath of the colors (or and gules) the Lexington Minute Man proper. The statue of the Minute Man, Captain John Parker (H. H. Kitson, sculptor), stands on the common in Lexington, Massachusetts.

MOTTO: *Caveant hostes* (Let The Enemy Beware)

Scarlet is the color of the Coast Artillery. The two piles represent the searchlight beams and the antiaircraft automatic weapons of the organization are indicated by two streams of projectiles directed at a conventionalized target. New England, the place of activation, is indicated by the Pilgrim's hat.

DISTINCTIVE INSIGNIA
The insignia is the shield and motto of the coat of arms. The insignia depicted was never made for nor worn by this organization.

450th ANTIAIRCRAFT ARTILLERY BATTALION

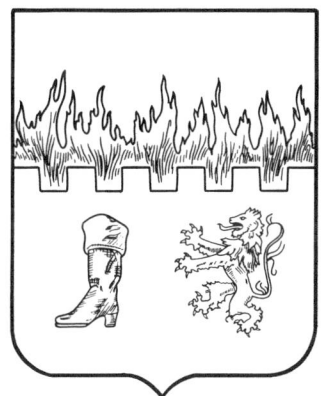 

Constituted 8 May 1942 in the Army of the United States as the 450th Coast Artillery Battalion (Antiaircraft) (Automatic Weapons) (Colored) and activated 11 May 1942 at Camp Davis, North Carolina. (Departed New York Port of Embarkation 6 January 1943 for overseas service and arrived in England on 11 January 1943. Moved to North Africa on 23 March 1943 and relocated to Italy on 28 October 1943). Reorganized and redesignated 12 December 1943 as the 450th Antiaircraft Artillery Automatic Weapons Battalion (Semimobile) (Colored). (Relocated to Southern France on 21 October 1944). Disbanded at Miramas, France; Batteries A, B and C on 31 December 1944 and remainder of Battalion on 25 January 1945. Reconstituted in the Regular Army on 17 June 1946 and activated 2 July 1946 at Fort Bliss, Texas. Redesignated 12 October 1950 as the 450th Antiaircraft Artillery Battalion (Automatic Weapons). Inactivated 1 November 1957 at Eielson Air Force Base, Alaska.

CAMPAIGN STREAMERS
World War II
Naples-Foggia
Rome-Arno
North Apennines
Po Valley
England 1943

DECORATIONS
None

COAT OF ARMS
SHIELD: Party per fess embattled gules and or, enflamed to chief, in base a boot and a lion rampant counterchanged.

CREST: None

MOTTO: A Wall Of Fire

Red and yellow are the Artillery colors and are used pictorially to depict the motto "a wall of fire". The boot, for Italy and a lion, symbolic of Great Britain, represent the battle honors earned during World War II.

DISTINCTIVE INSIGNIA
The insignia is the shield and motto of the coat of arms. The sample of the insignia depicted was approved for wear on 18 December 1951.

451st ANTIAIRCRAFT ARTILLERY BATTALION

Constituted 9 May 1942 in the Army of the United States as the 451st Coast Artillery Battalion (Antiaircraft) (Automatic Weapons) and activated 1 August 1942 at Camp Stewart, Georgia. (Departed New York Port of Embarkation 5 March 1943 for overseas service; arrived in North Africa on 18 March 1943 and moved to Italy on 16 September 1943). Reorganized and redesignated 12 December 1943 as the 451st Antiaircraft Artillery Automatic Weapons Battalion (Semimobile). (Participated in Southern France assault landing on 15 August 1944. Returned from overseas service and arrived at Hampton Roads Port of Embarkation on 6 November 1945). Inactivated 6 November 1945 at Camp Patrick Henry, Virginia. Allotted to the Organized Reserves on 27 February 1947 and activated 12 March 1947 at Newark, New Jersey. (Organized Reserves redesignated 25 March 1948 as Organized Reserve Corps). Headquarters relocated to Brooklyn, New York on 9 December 1948 and then to Hackensack, New Jersey on 8 November 1949. Inactivated 31 August 1950 at Hackensack. (Organized Reserve Corps redesignated 9 July 1952 as Army Reserve). Withdrawn from the Army Reserve, redesignated 451st Antiaircraft Artillery Battalion and allotted to the Regular Army, 9 November 1954. Activated 6 January 1955 at March Air Force Base, California; inactivated 15 June 1957 at March Air Force Base.

CAMPAIGN STREAMERS
World War II
Naples-Foggia
Anzio
Rome-Arno
Southern France (with arrowhead)
Rhineland
Ardennes-Alsace
Central Europe

DECORATIONS
Belgian Fourragere 1940 (451st AAA AW Bn cited; DAGO 43, 1950)

Cited in the Order of the Day of the Belgian Army for the *DEFENSE OF LIEGE* (451st AAA AW Bn cited for period 27 Nov-14 Dec 1944; DAGO 43, 1950)

Cited in the Order of the Day of the Belgian Army for *DEFENSE OF THE MEUSE RIVER* (451st AAA AW Bn cited for period 16 Dec 1944-25 Jan 1945; DAGO 43, 1950)

COAT OF ARMS
SHIELD: Gules, a cross argent between in chief a fleur-de-lis and a battle axe palewise or, in fess palewise overall a pheon of the last fimbriated of the first.

CREST: None

MOTTO: Vigilance And Power

The colors scarlet and yellow are used for Artillery. The white cross on the red field is from the arms of Savoy and represents service in Italy. The fleur-de-lis is for France and the Teutonic battle axe is for service in the Rhineland and Central Europe. The pheon, an early form of artillery, is used to indicate the assault landing in Southern France.

DISTINCTIVE INSIGNIA
The insignia is the shield and motto of the coat of arms. The sample of the insignia depicted was approved for wear on 19 April 1956.

452d ANTIAIRCRAFT ARTILLERY AUTOMATIC WEAPONS BATTALION

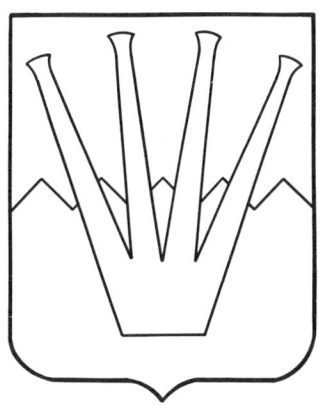 

Constituted 9 May 1942 in the Army of the United States as the 452d Coast Artillery Battalion (Antiaircraft) (Automatic Weapons) (Colored) and activated 1 August 1942 at Camp Stewart, Georgia. Redesignated 15 May 1943 as the 452d Antiaircraft Artillery Automatic Weapons Battalion (Colored). (Departed New York Port of Embarkation for overseas service 21 October 1943; arrived in England 2 November 1943 and landed in France on 9 July 1944. Returned from overseas service and arrived at the Boston Port of Embarkation on 15 November 1945).

Inactivated 16 November 1945 at Camp Myles Standish, Massachusetts. Activated 17 June 1946 in Korea; inactivated 15 December 1946 in Korea.

Redesignated 13 October 1948 as the 30th Antiaircraft Artillery Automatic Weapons Battalion.

CAMPAIGN STREAMERS
World War II
Normandy
Northern France
Rhineland
Ardennes-Alsace
Central Europe
England 1944

DECORATIONS
None

COAT OF ARMS
SHIELD: Per fess indented of five azure and gules, issuant from nombril point four 40mm gun barrels in arc to chief conjoined, couped or.

CREST: None

MOTTO: We Guard The Skyways

Red is the color of Artillery. The four gun barrels are symbolic of the firing functions of the organization and represent the crown of victory with which the efforts of the battalion were rewarded. The numerical designation is indicated by the four gun barrels, the five indentations, and the two divisions of the shield. The motto is expressive of the protection afforded by the battalion.

DISTINCTIVE INSIGNIA
The insignia is the shield and motto of the coat of arms. The insignia depicted was never made for nor worn by this organization.

452d ANTIAIRCRAFT ARTILLERY AUTOMATIC WEAPONS BATTALION

Constituted 25 February 1943 in the Army of the United States as the 134th Antiaircraft Artillery Gun Battalion (Mobile) and activated 10 June 1943 at Fort Sheridan, Illinois. (Departed Boston Port of Embarkation 3 July 1944 for overseas service; arrived in England on 12 July 1944 and landed in France on 26 September 1944. Returned from overseas service and arrived at the New York Port of Embarkation on 19 February 1946). Inactivated 20 February 1946 at Camp Kilmer, New Jersey. Redesignated as the 452d Antiaircraft Artillery Automatic Weapons Battalion and allotted to the Organized Reserve Corps on 25 February 1949. Activated 5 April 1949 at Chicago, Illinois.

Redesignated 25 November 1949 as the 485th Antiaircraft Artillery Automatic Weapons Battalion.

CAMPAIGN STREAMERS
World War II
Rhineland
Ardennes-Alsace
Central Europe
England 1944

DECORATIONS
None

COAT OF ARMS
None

DISTINCTIVE INSIGNIA
None

453d ANTIAIRCRAFT ARTILLERY BATTALION

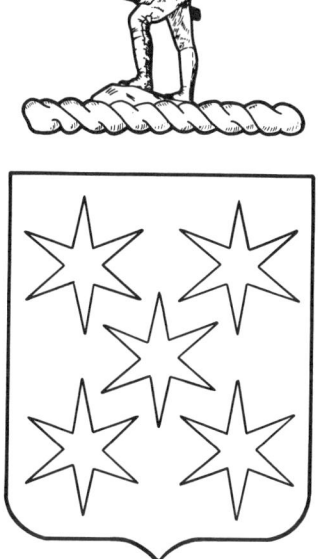 

Constituted 9 May 1942 in the Army of the United States as the 453d Coast Artillery Battalion (Antiaircraft) (Automatic Weapons) and activated 1 August 1942 at Fort Bliss, Texas. Reorganized and redesignated 5 June 1943 as the 453d Antiaircraft Artillery Automatic Weapons Battalion (Semimobile). (Departed New York Port of Embarkation 11 February 1944 for overseas service; arrived in England on 23 February 1944 and landed in France on 18 June 1944. Returned from overseas service and arrived at the New York Port of Embarkation on 25 January 1946). Inactivated 26 January 1946 at Camp Kilmer, New Jersey. Allotted to the Organized Reserve Corps and assigned to Second Army on 8 September 1948. Activated 22 September 1948 with Headquarters at Fort Myer, Virginia; inactivated 14 September 1950 at Fort Myer. Assigned to the 83d Infantry Division on 18 April 1952. (Organized Reserve Corps redesignated 9 July 1952 as Army Reserve). Activated 20 May 1952 in Ohio with Headquarters at Columbus, and Batteries at Loudonville, Logan, Ravenna and Mansfield. Redesignated 27 December 1952 as the 453d Antiaircraft Artillery Battalion (Automatic Weapons) (Self Propelled). Headquarters relocated to Mansfield, Ohio on 23 February 1955. Inactivated 20 March 1959 at Mansfield.

CAMPAIGN STREAMERS
World War II
Normandy
Northern France
Rhineland
Ardennes-Alsace
Central Europe

DECORATIONS
None

COAT OF ARMS
SHIELD: Gules, five mullets of six points, two, one and two, or.

CREST: That for the regiments and separate battalions of the Army Reserve: On a wreath of the colors (or and gules) the Lexington Minute Man proper. The statue of the Minute Man, Captain John Parker (H. H. Kitson, sculptor), stands on the common in Lexington, Massachusetts.

MOTTO: Victory Our Task

The colors red and yellow are used for Artillery. Antiaircraft is symbolized by the six-pointed star — representing an air burst of a shell — five in number for the campaigns of the organization in Europe during World War II.

DISTINCTIVE INSIGNIA
The insignia is the shield and motto of the coat of arms. The sample of the insignia depicted was approved for wear on 19 June 1956.

454th ANTIAIRCRAFT ARTILLERY BATTALION

Constituted 6 August 1942 in the Army of the United States as the 454th Coast Artillery Battalion (Antiaircraft) (Automatic Weapons) and activated 1 September 1942 at Camp Stewart, Georgia. (Departed Hampton Roads Port of Embarkation 10 May 1943 for overseas service; arrived in North Africa on 2 June 1943 and moved to Italy in 1944). Reorganized and redesignated 1 May 1944 as the 454th Antiaircraft Artillery Automatic Weapons Battalion (Mobile). Disbanded 25 September 1944 in Italy. Reconstituted 30 November 1948 in the Organized Reserve Corps. Activated 18 January 1949 with Headquarters at Kansas City, Missouri. Redesignated 402d Antiaircraft Artillery Automatic Weapons Battalion and assigned to the 102d Infantry Division on 25 November 1949. Headquarters relocated to St. Louis,

Missouri on 15 March 1951. (Organized Reserve Corps redesignated 9 July 1952 as Army Reserve). Redesignated 15 December 1952 as the 454th Antiaircraft Artillery Automatic Weapons Battalion. Redesignated 1 October 1953 as the 454th Antiaircraft Artillery Battalion. Inactivated 31 May 1959 at St. Louis.

CAMPAIGN STREAMERS
World War II
Rome-Arno

DECORATIONS
None

COAT OF ARMS
SHIELD: Gules, a scroll bend sinisterwise pierced by a sword in bend, point to chief or.

CREST: That for the regiments and separate battalions of the Army Reserve: On a wreath of the colors (or and gules) the Lexington Minute Man proper. The statue of the Minute Man, Captain John Parker (H. H. Kitson, sculptor), stands on the common in Lexington, Massachusetts.

MOTTO: *Audax et Vigilans* (Daring and Vigilant)

In the scarlet and gold of the Coast Artillery arm the functions of the organization, allegorically illustrated by the protecting sword piercing the scroll, alludes to the record which the organization made for itself during World War Ii.

DISTINCTIVE INSIGNIA
The insignia is the shield and motto of the coat of arms. The sample of the insignia depicted was approved for wear on 26 October 1953.

455th ANTIAIRCRAFT ARTILLERY AUTOMATIC WEAPONS BATTALION

Constituted 3 August 1942 in the Army of the United States as the 455th Coast Artillery Battalion (Antiaircraft) (Automatic Weapons) and activated 1 September 1942 at Camp Stewart, Georgia. Reorganized and redesignated 31 May 1943 as the 455th Antiaircraft Artillery Automatic Weapons Battalion (Mobile). (Departed New York Port of Embarkation 5 September 1943 for overseas service; arrived in England on 18 September 1943 and landed in France on 8 July 1944. Returned from overseas service and arrived at the Boston Port of Embarkation on 16 October 1945). Inactivated 17 October 1945 at Camp Myles Standish, Massachusetts. Allotted to the Organized Reserve Corps and assigned to Second Army on 12 October 1948. Activated 22 October 1948 with Headquarters at Huntington, West Virginia; inactivated 28 November 1950 at Huntington.

CAMPAIGN STREAMERS
World War II
Normandy
Northern France
Rhineland
Ardennes-Alsace
Central Europe

DECORATIONS
None

COAT OF ARMS
None

DISTINCTIVE INSIGNIA
None

456th ANTIAIRCRAFT ARTILLERY BATTALION

Constituted 3 August 1942 in the Army of the United States as the 456th Coast Artillery Battalion (Antiaircraft) (Automatic Weapons) and activated 1 September 1942 at Fort Sheridan, Illinois. Reorganized and redesignated 1 June 1943 as the 456th Antiaircraft Artillery Automatic Weapons Battalion (Mobile). (Departed New York Port of Embarkation 21 October 1943 for overseas service; arrived in England on 3 November 1943 and landed in France on 1 July 1944. Returned from overseas service and arrived at the Hampton Roads Port of Embarkation on 23 October 1945). Inactivated 23 October 1945 at Camp Patrick Henry, Virginia. Allotted to the Organized Reserve Corps 3 November 1948 and assigned to First Army on 8 November 1948. Activated 19 November 1948 at Providence, Rhode Island. Redesignated 19 January 1954 as the 456th Antiaircraft Artillery Battalion. Inactivated 18 April 1955 at Providence.

CAMPAIGN STREAMERS
World War II
Normandy
Northern France
Rhineland
Ardennes-Alsace
Central Europe
England 1944

DECORATIONS
None

COAT OF ARMS
None

DISTINCTIVE INSIGNIA
None

457th ANTIAIRCRAFT ARTILLERY BATTALION

Constituted 3 August 1942 in the Army of the United States as the 457th Coast Artillery Battalion (Antiaircraft) (Automatic Weapons) and activated 1 September 1942 at Camp Hulen, Texas. Reorganized and redesignated 15 May 1943 as the 457th Antiaircraft Artillery Automatic

Weapons Battalion (Mobile). (Departed New York Port of Embarkation 5 December 1943 for overseas service; arrived in England on 15 December 1943 and landed in France on 28 June 1944. Returned from overseas service and arrived at the Boston Port of Embarkation on 20 November 1945). Inactivated 21 November 1945 at Camp Myles Standish, Massachusetts. Allotted to the Organized Reserve Corps 18 October 1948. Activated 26 October 1948 with Headquarters at Baltimore, Maryland. (Organized Reserve Corps redesignated 9 July 1952 as Army Reserve). Redesignated 12 October 1953 as the 457th Antiaircraft Artillery Battalion. Headquarters relocated to Pittsburgh, Pennsylvania on 19 November 1955. Inactivated 6 April 1959 at Pittsburgh.

CAMPAIGN STREAMERS
World War II
Normandy (with arrowhead)
Northern France
Rhineland
Ardennes-Alsace
Central Europe
England 1944

DECORATIONS
None

COAT OF ARMS
SHIELD: Per bend embattled of five gules and or, in chief a mullet and in base a cross bottony counterchanged.

CREST: That for the regiments and separate battalions of the Army Reserve: On a wreath of the colors (or and gules) the Lexington Minute Man proper. The statue of the Minute Man, Captain John Parker (H. H. Kitson, sculptor), stands on the common in Lexington, Massachusetts

MOTTO: We Attack, We Defend

The colors red and yellow are used for Artillery. The activation of the unit in Texas during World War II is symbolized by the star from the State Flag and its reactivation in Maryland after the war is represented by the cross from the flag of that State. The embattlements represent the five campaigns in Europe during World War II.

DISTINCTIVE INSIGNIA
The insignia is the shield and motto of the coat of arms. The sample of the insignia depicted was approved for wear on 28 April 1953.

458th ANTIAIRCRAFT ARTILLERY AUTOMATIC WEAPONS BATTALION

Constituted 2 August 1942 in the Army of the United States as the 458th Coast Artillery Battalion (Antiaircraft) (Automatic Weapons) (Colored) and activated 1 September 1942 at Camp Stewart, Georgia. Reorganized and redesignated 30 April 1943 as the 458th Antiaircraft Artillery Automatic Weapons Battalion (Mobile) (Colored). Disbanded 24 April 1944 at Camp Patrick Henry, Virginia.

CAMPAIGN STREAMERS
None

DECORATIONS
None

603

COAT OF ARMS
None

DISTINCTIVE INSIGNIA
None

458th ANTIAIRCRAFT ARTILLERY BATTALION

Constituted 25 February 1943 in the Army of the United States as the 133d Coast Artillery Battalion (Antiaircraft) (Gun) and activated 15 June 1943 at Camp Edwards, Massachusetts. Reorganized and redesignated 28 June 1943 as the 133d Antiaircraft Artillery Gun Battalion (Mobile). (Departed New York Port of Embarkation 24 July 1944 for overseas service; arrived in England 31 July 1944 and landed in France on 23 August 1944). Inactivated 31 July 1946 in Austria. Redesignated 458th Antiaircraft Artillery Gun Battalion and allotted to the Organized Reserve Corps, 1 November 1948. Activated 19 November 1948 at Cincinnati, Ohio; inactivated 29 August 1950 at Cincinnati. Activated 3 November 1950 with Headquarters at Rochester, New York. (Headquarters relocated to Buffalo, New York on 15 May 1952). (Organized Reserve Corps redesignated 9 July 1952 as Army Reserve). Redesignated 1 September 1953 as the 458th Antiaircraft Artillery Battalion (Gun). Inactivated 1 May 1959 at Buffalo.

CAMPAIGN STREAMERS
World War II
Northern France
Rhineland
Central Europe

DECORATIONS
None

COAT OF ARMS
SHIELD: Gules, a bend wavy between a fleur-de-lis in chief and a battle axe bendwise in base, all or.

CREST: That for the regiments and separate battalions of the Army Reserve: On a wreath of the colors (or and gules) the Lexington Minute Man proper. The statue of the Minute Man, Captain John Parker (H. H. Kitson, sculptor), stands on the common in Lexington, Massachusetts.

MOTTO: The Lead Is Ours

The shield is in the colors of Artillery. The fleur-de-lis represents the Northern France campaign. The wavy bend is taken from the corporate arms of Rheinprovinz, the province in which the Rhineland campaign occurred. The battle axe, a favorite Teutonic weapon and heraldic charge throughout the medieval period, symbolizes the Central Europe campaign.

DISTINCTIVE INSIGNIA
The insignia is the shield and motto of the coat of arms. The sample of the insignia depicted was approved for wear on 27 May 1955.

459th ANTIAIRCRAFT ARTILLERY BATTALION

Constituted 6 August 1942 in the Army of the United States as the 459th Coast Artillery Battalion (Antiaircraft) (Automatic Weapons) and activated 1 September 1942 at Camp Hulen, Texas. Reorganized and redesignated 15 May 1943 as the 459th Antiaircraft Artillery Automatic Weapons Battalion (Mobile). (Departed New York Port of Embarkation 21 October 1943 for overseas service; arrived in England 3 November 1943 and landed in France on 12 June 1944. Returned from overseas service and arrived at the Boston Port of Embarkation on 24 October 1945). Inactivated 25 October 1945 at Camp Myles Standish, Massachusetts. Allotted to the Organized Reserve Corps, 8 November 1948. Activated 6 December 1948 at Pittsburgh, Pennsylvania. Ordered into active military service 11 September 1950 at Pittsburgh. Redesignated 13 December 1950 as the 459th Antiaircraft Artillery Battalion. (Organized Reserve Corps redesignated 9 July 1952 as Army Reserve). Released from active military service 6 January 1955 at Travis Air Force Base, California and resumed Reserve status. Inactivated 8 July 1955 at Pittsburgh.

CAMPAIGN STREAMERS
World War II
Normandy
Northern France
Rhineland
Central Europe

DECORATIONS
None

COAT OF ARMS
None

DISTINCTIVE INSIGNIA
None

460th ANTIAIRCRAFT ARTILLERY BATTALION

Constituted 3 August 1942 in the Army of the United States as the 460th Coast Artillery Battalion (Antiaircraft) (Automatic Weapons) and activated 1 September 1942 at Camp Hulen, Texas. Reorganized and redesignated 15 May 1943 as the 460th Antiaircraft Artillery Automatic Weapons Battalion (Mobile). (Departed New York Port of Embarkation 21 February 1944 for overseas service; arrived in England 28 February 1944 and landed in France on 12 June 1944). Inactivated 30 April 1946 in France. Allotted to the Organized Reserve Corps and assigned to Second Army on 17 November 1948. Activated 8 December 1948 at Kokomo, Indiana. Relocated to South Bend, Indiana on 31 December 1948. (Organized Reserve Corps redesignated 9 July 1952 as Army Reserve). Redesignated 1 February 1954 as the 460th Antiaircraft Artillery Battalion. Inactivated 1 September 1959 at South Bend.

CAMPAIGN STREAMERS
World War II
Normandy
Northern France
Rhineland
Ardennes-Alsace
Central Europe

DECORATIONS
None

COAT OF ARMS

SHIELD: Per chevron abased or and gules, in chief a vol sable pierced by three lightning flashes radiant from fess point argent, fimbriated of the second, in base a lion affronte passant of the first.

CREST: That for the regiments and separate battalions of the Army Reserve: On a wreath of the colors (or and gules) the Lexington Minute Man proper. The statue of the Minute Man, Captain John Parker (H. H. Kitson, sculptor), stands on the common in Lexington, Massachusetts.

MOTTO: *Caveat Aggressio* (Aggressor Beware)

Scarlet and yellow are used for Artillery. Wings pierced by lightning flashes symbolize the antiaircraft function of the battalion and the effective action of its automatic weapons. The lion is taken from the coat of arms of the French province of Normandy and symbolizes the unit's baptism of fire in Europe during World War II.

DISTINCTIVE INSIGNIA
The insignia is the shield and motto of the coat of arms. The sample of the insignia depicted was approved for wear on 21 May 1953.

461st ANTIAIRCRAFT ARTILLERY BATTALION

Constituted 6 August 1942 in the Army of the United States as the 461st Coast Artillery Battalion (Antiaircraft) (Automatic Weapons) and activated 1 September 1942 at Camp Haan, California. (Departed New York Port of Embarkation 7 July 1943 for overseas service; arrived in England 15 July 1943 and landed in France on 13 June 1944). Reorganized and redesignated 20 August 1943 as the 461st Antiaircraft Artillery Automatic Weapons Battalion (Mobile). (Returned from overseas service and arrived at the New York Port of Embarkation on 23 November 1945). Inactivated 24 November 1945 at Camp Kilmer, New Jersey. Allotted to the Organized Reserve Corps, 19 November 1948. Activated 2 December 1948 with Headquarters at Bangor, Maine. (Headquarters relocated to Hartford, Connecticut on 22 April 1949). Assigned to the 76th Infantry Division on 31 May 1949. Redesignated 8 July 1949 as the 476th Antiaircraft Artillery Automatic Weapons Battalion. Redesignated 15 April 1952 as the 461st Antiaircraft Artillery Automatic Weapons Battalion. Redesignated 1 January 1953 as the 461st Antiaircraft Artillery Battalion. Disbanded 1 May 1959 at Hartford.

CAMPAIGN STREAMERS
World War II
Normandy
Northern France
Rhineland
Ardennes-Alsace
Central Europe

DECORATIONS
None

COAT OF ARMS
SHIELD: Per fess abased gules and sable, in chief a lion passant guardant or holding in dexter forepaw a woodsman's axe and a key saltirewise of the like, and in base two pallets of the last.

CREST: That for the regiments and separate battalions of the Army Reserve: On a wreath of the colors (or and gules) the Lexington Minute Man proper. The statue of the Minute Man, Captain John Parker (H. H. Kitson, sculptor), stands on the common in Lexington, Massachusetts.

MOTTO: *Debellare Superbos* (To Conquer The Proud)

The colors red and yellow are for Artillery. The two vertical bars on the black background represent antiaircraft fire directed vertically. The gold lion is taken from the arms of Normandy and holds in his paw two charges — the key and axe — of frequent occurrence in the arms of the areas in which the battalion participated in combat during World War II.

DISTINCTIVE INSIGNIA
The insignia is the shield and motto of the coat of arms. The sample of the insignia depicted was approved for wear on 12 April 1956.

462d ANTIAIRCRAFT ARTILLERY AUTOMATIC WEAPONS BATTALION

Constituted 6 August 1942 in the Army of the United States as the 462d Coast Artillery Battalion (Antiaircraft) (Automatic Weapons) and activated 1 September 1942 at Camp Haan, California. Reorganized and redesignated 15 May 1943 as the 462d Antiaircraft Artillery Automatic Weapons Battalion (Mobile). (Departed Boston Port of Embarkation 6 November 1943 for overseas service; arrived in England 16 November 1943 and landed in France on 11 June 1944. Returned from overseas service and arrived at the New York Port of Embarkation on 5 October 1945). Inactivated 6 October 1945 at Camp Shanks, New York.

Redesignated 9 December 1948 as the 82d Antiaircraft Artillery Automatic Weapons Battalion

CAMPAIGN STREAMERS
World War II
Normandy
Northern France
Rhineland
Ardennes-Alsace
Central Europe

DECORATIONS
Belgian Fourragere 1940 (462d AAA AW Bn cited; DAGO 43, 1950)

Cited in the Order of the Day of the Belgian Army for action in the *ARDENNES* (462d AAA AW Bn cited for period 13-19 Dec 1944; DAGO 43, 1950)

Cited in the Order of the Day of the Belgian Army for action on *ELSENBORN CREST* (462d AAA AW Bn cited for period 19-30 Dec 1944; DAGO 43, 1950)

COAT OF ARMS
None

DISTINCTIVE INSIGNIA
None

462d ANTIAIRCRAFT ARTILLERY GUN BATTALION

Constituted 25 February 1943 in the Army of the United States as the 135th Antiaircraft Artillery Gun Battalion (Mobile) and activated 15 June 1943 at Camp Edwards, Massachusetts. (Departed New York Port of Embarkation 28 August 1944 for overseas service; arrived in England on 3 September 1944 and landed in France on 29 September 1944. Returned from overseas service and arrived at the New York Port of Embarkation on 20 February 1946). Inactivated 22 February 1946 at Camp Kilmer, New Jersey. Redesignated 462d Antiaircraft Artillery Gun Battalion and allotted to the Organized Reserve Corps on 25 February 1949. Assigned to Fifth Army on 3 March 1949. Activated 5 April 1949 with Headquarters at Linden, New Jersey. Headquarters relocated to Flint, Michigan on 2 June 1949. Inactivated 4 December 1950 at Flint.

CAMPAIGN STREAMERS
World War II
Rhineland
Central Europe

DECORATIONS
None

COAT OF ARMS
None

DISTINCTIVE INSIGNIA
None

463d ANTIAIRCRAFT ARTILLERY BATTALION

Constituted 6 August 1942 in the Army of the United States as the 463d Coast Artillery Battalion (Antiaircraft) (Automatic Weapons) and activated 1 September 1942 at Camp Haan, California. Reorganized and redesignated 15 May 1943 as the 463d Antiaircraft Artillery

Automatic Weapons Battalion (Mobile). (Departed New York Port of Embarkation 22 February 1944 for overseas service; arrived in England 4 March 1944 and landed in France on 28 June 1944. Returned from overseas service and arrived at the New York Port of Embarkation on 16 March 1946). Inactivated 17 March 1946 at Camp Kilmer, New Jersey. Allotted to the Organized Reserve Corps and assigned to First Army, 19 November 1948. Activated 14 December 1948 with Headquarters at East Orange, New Jersey; inactivated 31 August 1950 at East Orange. Assigned to the 79th Infantry Division, 21 May 1952. Activated 10 June 1952 at Philadelphia, Pennsylvania. (Organized Reserve Corps redesignated 9 July 1952 as Army Reserve). Redesignated 27 December 1952 as the 463d Antiaircraft Artillery Battalion. Relieved from the 79th Infantry Division and inactivated 11 May 1959 at Philadelphia.

CAMPAIGN STREAMERS

World War II
Normandy
Northern France
Rhineland
Ardennes-Alsace
Central Europe

DECORATIONS

French Croix de Guerre with Palm, World War II, Streamer embroidered *NORMANDY TO PARIS* (463d AAA AW Bn cited for period 19 Jun-27 Aug 1944; DAGO 43, 1950)

French Croix de Guerre with Palm, World War II, Streamer embroidered *PARROY FOREST* (463d AAA AW Bn cited for period 21-24 Nov 1944; DAGO 43, 1950)

Fourragere in the colors of the French Croix de Guerre, World War II (463d AAA AW Bn cited; DAGO 43, 1950)

COAT OF ARMS

SHIELD: Per chevron rayonne or and gules, on the second a unicorn salient argent.

CREST: That for the regiments and separate battalions of the Army Reserve: On a wreath of the colors (or and gules) the Lexington Minute Man proper. The statue of the Minute Man, Captain John Parker (H. H. Kitson, sculptor), stands on the common in Lexington, Massachusetts.

MOTTO: *Semper Saliens* (Always Forward)

Red and yellow are the colors for Artillery. The piercing fire power of the battalion's antiaircraft automatic weapons is represented by the peaked flame-like partition line. The unicorn, taken from the coat of arms of St. Lo in Normandy, symbolizes the organization's first campaign during World War II. This fabulous animal, which according to legend could not be taken alive, also indicates the organization's fighting valor.

DISTINCTIVE INSIGNIA

The insignia is the shield and motto of the coat of arms. The sample of the insignia depicted was approved for wear on 29 October 1953.

464th ANTIAIRCRAFT ARTILLERY BATTALION

Constituted 30 August 1942 in the Army of the United States as the 464th Coast Artillery Battalion (Separate) (Antiaircraft) and activated 15 October 1942 at Camp Davis, North Carolina. (Departed New York Port of Embarkation 9 May 1943 for overseas service and arrived in India 23 June 1943 via Brazil, Madagascar, and Ceylon). Redesignated 28 April 1944 as the 464th Antiaircraft Artillery Automatic Weapons Battalion. (Moved to Burma 12 January 1945 and returned to India on 18 April 1945). Disbanded 10 July 1945 at Kancharapara, India. Reconstituted 24 July 1946 and allotted to the Alabama National Guard. Reorganized and Federally recognized 9 January 1947 with Headquarters and Headquarters Battery and Medical Detachment at Talladega; Battery A at Sylacauga; Battery B at Anniston; Battery C at Arab and Battery D at Jasper. Ordered into active Federal service 23 January 1951 at home stations. Released from active Federal service 22 December 1952 and resumed State status. Redesignated 1 January 1953 as the 464th Antiaircraft Artillery Battalion.

Consolidated 2 May 1959 with the 203d Artillery, a parent regiment under the Combat Arms Regimental System.

CAMPAIGN STREAMERS
World War II
India Burma
Central Burma
China Defensive

DECORATIONS
None

COAT OF ARMS
SHIELD: Gules, in chief a mullet with a smaller mullet in each angle and in base a Chinese sword fesswise, all or.

CREST: That for the regiments and separate battalions of the Alabama Army National Guard: On a wreath of the colors (or and gules) a slip of cotton plant with full bursting boll proper.

MOTTO: Defenders Of Right

Red and yellow are the colors for Artillery. The group of stars taken from the flag of Burma is symbolic of the organization's service in Burma while the Chinese sword represents the China Defensive Campaign of World War II.

DISTINCTIVE INSIGNIA
The insignia is the shield and motto of the coat of arms. The sample of the insignia depicted was approved for wear on 19 March 1957.

465th ANTIAIRCRAFT ARTILLERY MISSILE BATTALION

Constituted 30 August 1942 in the Army of the United States as the 465th Coast Artillery Battalion (Antiaircraft) (Automatic Weapons) and activated 15 October 1942 at Camp Davis, North Carolina. Reorganized and redesignated 1 February 1943 as the 465th Antiaircraft Artillery Automatic Weapons Battalion (Semimobile). (Departed Boston Port of Embarkation 22 June 1944 for overseas service; arrived in England 29 June 1944 and landed in France on 30 July 1944). Converted and redesignated 1 May 1946 as Constabulary School Squadron. Inactivated 30 June 1948 in Germany. Converted and redesignated 11 December 1951 as the 465th Antiaircraft Artillery Battalion. Redesignated 465th Antiaircraft Artillery Missile Battalion and allotted to the Regular Army, 3 May 1956. Activated 1 June 1956 at Fort Niagara, Youngstown, New York. Inactivated 1 September 1958 at Lancaster, New York.

CAMPAIGN STREAMERS
World War II
Northern France
Rhineland
Ardennes-Alsace
Central Europe

DECORATIONS
French Croix de Guerre with Gold Star, World War II, Streamer embroidered *NORMANDY BEACHHEAD* (465th AAA AW Bn cited for period 1-31 Aug 1944; DAGO 43, 1950)

COAT OF ARMS
SHIELD: Per pale gules and or, two piles in point counterchanged, in base two battle axes in saltire proper.

CREST: None

MOTTO: *Credo et Videbo* (I Believe And I Shall See)

The scarlet is for the Coast Artillery Corps. The functions of the organization are allegorically illustrated by the wedge-shaped pile meeting in point, representing both searchlight beams and the fire of the battalion. The ability to protect their allotted territory is indicated by the crossed battle axes, an ancient weapon of defense. The motto is expressive of the performance of Coast Artillery functions, and the faith of the personnel in the successful outcome of allotted duties.

DISTINCTIVE INSIGNIA
The insignia is the shield and motto of the coat of arms. The sample of the insignia depicted was approved for wear on 12 December 1956.

466th ANTIAIRCRAFT ARTILLERY BATTALION

Constituted 30 August 1942 in the Army of the United States as the 466th Coast Artillery Battalion (Antiaircraft) (Automatic Weapons) (Colored) and activated 15 October 1942 at Camp Stewart, Georgia. Reorganized and redesignated 30 April 1943 as the 466th Antiaircraft Artillery Automatic Weapons Battalion (Semimobile) (Colored). (Departed San Francisco Port of Embarkation 29 September 1943 for overseas service and arrived on Espiritu Santo 16 October 1943; moved to New Britain on 20 May 1944 and then to New Guinea on 7 December 1944). Inactivated 30 November 1945 at Finschhafen, New Guinea. Allotted to the Organized Reserves on 8 November 1946 and activated 19 November 1946 with Headquarters at Richmond, Virginia. (Organized Reserves redesignated 25 March 1948 as Organized Reserve Corps). Ordered into active military service at Richmond on 11 September 1950. Redesignated 13 December 1950 as the 466th Antiaircraft Artillery Battalion. (Organized Reserve Corps redesignated 9 July 1952 as Army Reserve). Released from active military service 6 January 1955 and resumed Reserve status. Reorganized at Glassmere, Pennsylvania on 21 March 1955. Inactivated 1 June 1959 at Glassmere.

CAMPAIGN STREAMERS
World War II
Bismarck Archipelago
New Guinea

DECORATIONS
None

COAT OF ARMS
SHIELD: Or, within a double treasure a pale gules fretty of the field in front of six bars wavy azure.

CREST: That for the regiments and separate battalions of the Army Reserve: On a wreath of the colors (or and gules) the Lexington Minute Man proper. The statue of the Minute Man, Captain John Parker (H. H. Kitson, sculptor), stands on the common in Lexington, Massachusetts.

MOTTO: Firm And Determined

The scarlet is for the Coast Artillery Corps. The vertical pale denotes military strength and fortitude, and anciently was bestowed upon those who had defended cities or supported the government; the fretty interlacing also being symbolic or protection. The six wavy blue bars, representing the seas, refer to the coastal territory covered by the organization. The scarlet double treasure is representative of the moat anciently used in the protection of medieval castles. The motto is expressive of the characteristics of the personnel in the performance of their duties.

DISTINCTIVE INSIGNIA
The insignia is the shield and motto of the coat of arms. The sample of the insignia depicted was approved for wear on 15 July 1952.

467th ANTIAIRCRAFT ARTILLERY AUTOMATIC WEAPONS BATTALION

Constituted 29 August 1942 in the Army of the United States as the 467th Coast Artillery Battalion (Antiaircraft) (Automatic Weapons) and activated 15 October 1942 at Camp Stewart, Georgia. Reorganized and redesignated 13 February 1943 as the 467th Antiaircraft Artillery Automatic Weapons Battalion (Semimobile). (Departed New York Port of Embarkation 19 January 1944 for overseas service; arrived in England on 30 January 1944 and landed in France on 6 June 1944. Returned from overseas service and arrived at the New York Port of Embarkation on 15 April 1946). Inactivated 16 April 1946 at Camp Kilmer, New Jersey. Allotted to the Organized Reserve Corps on 24 November 1948 and assigned to Third Army on 13 December 1948. Activated 3 January 1949 at Tampa, Florida. Assigned to the 87th Infantry Division on 15 April 1949.

Redesignated 18 May 1949 as the 487th Antiaircraft Artillery Automatic Weapons Battalion.

CAMPAIGN STREAMERS
World War II
Normandy (with arrowhead)
Northern France
Rhineland
Ardennes-Alsace
Central Europe

DECORATIONS
None

COAT OF ARMS
None

DISTINCTIVE INSIGNIA
None

468th ANTIAIRCRAFT ARTILLERY AUTOMATIC WEAPONS BATTALION

Constituted 30 August 1942 in the Army of the United States as the 468th Coast Artillery Battalion (Antiaircraft) (Automatic Weapons) and activated 15 October 1942 at Camp Haan, California. Reorganized and redesignated 13 February 1943 as the 468th Antiaircraft Artillery Automatic Weapons Battalion (Semimobile). (Departed New York Port of Embarkation 2 July 1944 for overseas service; arrived in England on 12 July 1944 and landed in France on 28 August 1944). Inactivated 10 June 1946 at Berchesgaden, Germany. Allotted to the Organized Reserve Corps and assigned to Fourth Army on 1 November 1948. Activated 19 November 1948 at New Orleans, Louisiana; inactivated 17 October 1950 at New Orleans.

CAMPAIGN STREAMERS
World War II
Normandy
Northern France
Rhineland
Ardennes-Alsace
Central Europe

DECORATIONS
None

COAT OF ARMS
None

DISTINCTIVE INSIGNIA
None

469th ANTIAIRCRAFT ARTILLERY BATTALION

Constituted 30 August 1942 in the Army of the United States as the 469th Coast Artillery Battalion (Antiaircraft) (Automatic Weapons) and activated 15 October 1942 at Camp Davis, North Carolina. Reorganized and redesignated 30 April 1943 as the 469th Antiaircraft Artillery

Automatic Weapons Battalion (Semimobile). (Departed San Francisco Port of Embarkation 28 August 1943 for overseas service and arrived in Australia on 29 September 1943. After service in New Guinea and on New Britain landed in the Philippine Islands on 20 October 1944. Returned from overseas service and arrived at the San Francisco Port of Embarkation on 20 January 1946). Inactivated 22 January 1946 at Camp Stoneman, California. Allotted to the Organized Reserve Corps on 19 November 1948. Activated 14 December 1948 at New York, New York. Redesignated 477th Antiaircraft Artillery Automatic Weapons Battalion and assigned to the 77th Infantry Division on 8 July 1949. Redesignated 4 April 1952 as the 469th Antiaircraft Artillery Automatic Weapons Battalion. Redesignated 1 January 1953 as the 469th Antiaircraft Artillery Battalion. Inactivated 1 May 1959 at New York.

CAMPAIGN STREAMERS
World War II
New Guinea (with arrowhead)
Bismarck Archipelago
Leyte (with arrowhead)
Luzon

DECORATIONS
Philippine Presidential Unit Citation, Streamer embroidered *17 OCTOBER 1944 TO 4 JULY 1945* (469th AAA AW Bn cited; DAGO 47, 1950)

COAT OF ARMS
SHIELD: Gules, out of bulrushes in base proper a griffin salient, armed azure.

CREST: That for the regiments and separate battalions of the Army Reserve: On a wreath of the colors (or and gules) the Lexington Minute Man proper. The statue of the Minute Man, Captain John Parker (H. H. Kitson, sculptor), stands on the common 'in Lexington, Massachusetts.

MOTTO: No Encroachment

Scarlet is the color of the Coast Artillery. The griffin is symbolic of a valorous soldier whose magnanimity is such that he will dare all dangers and is representative of the zealous spirit of the personnel of the organization in the performance of their duties. The griffin is also a symbol of vigilance and is suggestive of the alertness of the organization in its antiaircraft functions.

DISTINCTIVE INSIGNIA
The insignia is the shield and motto of the coat of arms. The sample of the insignia depicted was approved for wear on 10 June 1954.

470th ANTIAIRCRAFT ARTILLERY BATTALION

Constituted 30 August 1942 in the Army of the United States as the 470th Coast Artillery Battalion (Antiaircraft) (Automatic Weapons) and activated 15 October 1942 at Camp Davis, North Carolina. Reorganized and redesignated 30 April 1943 as the 470th Antiaircraft Artillery Automatic Weapons Battalion (Semimobile). (Departed San Francisco Port of Embarkation 28 August 1943 for overseas service and arrived in Australia on 29 September 1943. After service in New Guinea and on Woodlark Island, landed in the Philippine Islands on 9 January 1945. Returned from overseas service and arrived at the Seattle Port of Embarkation on 23 January 1946). Inactivated 24 January 1946 at Fort Lewis, Washington. Redesignated 470th Antiaircraft Artillery Gun Battalion, allotted to the Organized Reserve Corps and assigned to First Army on 19 November 1948. Activated 14 December 1948 at New York, New York. (Organized Reserve Corps redesignated 9 July 1952 as Army Reserve). Redesignated 1 September 1953 as the 470th Antiaircraft Artillery Battalion. Inactivated 30 June 1959 at New York.

CAMPAIGN STREAMERS
World War II
New Guinea
Bismarck Archipelago
Luzon (with arrowhead)
Southern Philippines

DECORATIONS
Philippine Presidential Unit Citation, Streamer embroidered *17 OCTOBER 1944 TO 4 JULY 1945* (470th AAA AW Bn cited; DAGO 47, 1950)

COAT OF ARMS
SHIELD: Per chevron embowed in point or and gules, in chief four pomeis two and two and in base a sea lion holding in dexter paw a sword of the first.

CREST: That for the regiments and separate battalions of the Army Reserve: On a wreath of the colors (or and gules) the Lexington Minute Man proper. The statue of the Minute Man, Captain John Parker (H. H. Kitson, sculptor), stands on the common

in Lexington, Massachusetts.

MOTTO: *Columna Ignis* (Pillar Of Fire)

The colors scarlet and yellow are used for Artillery. The sea lion holding the sword is taken from the coat of arms of the Philippines and commemorates the Philippine Presidential Unit Citation awarded the battalion. The four roundels represent the four Pacific Island campaigns of World War II. The curved partition line with the upward thrust symbolizes the antiaircraft mission of the organization.

DISTINCTIVE INSIGNIA
The insignia is the shield and motto of the coat of arms. The insignia depicted was unofficially worn by this organization between 1955 and 1959.

471st ANTIAIRCRAFT ARTILLERY BATTALION

Constituted 29 August 1942 in the Army of the United States as the 471st Coast Artillery Battalion (Antiaircraft) (Automatic Weapons) and activated 15 October 1942 at Camp Stewart, Georgia. Reorganized and redesignated 30 April 1943 as the 471st Antiaircraft Artillery Automatic Weapons Battalion (Semimobile). (Departed San Francisco Port of Embarkation 5 July 1943 for overseas service and arrived on Guadalcanal on 23 August 1943. After service on Florida and Emirau Islands, landed in the Philippine Islands on 21 January 1945. Returned from overseas service and arrived at the Seattle Port of Embarkation on 23 January 1946). Inactivated 24 January 1946 at Fort Lewis, Washington. Allotted to the Organized Reserve Corps 3 December 1948 and assigned to Fourth Army on 15 December 1948. Activated 28 December 1948 with Headquarters at Tulsa, Oklahoma. (Assigned to the 22d Armored Division on 25 August 1949. Headquarters relocated to El Paso, Texas on 1 July 1950). Relieved from the 22d Armored Division and inactivated at El Paso on 1 March 1952. (Organized Reserve Corps redesignated 9 July 1952 as Army Reserve). Redesignated 20 August 1956 as the 471st Antiaircraft Artillery Battalion. Activated 1 September 1956 with Headquarters at El Paso, Texas; inactivated 1 April 1959 at El Paso.

CAMPAIGN STREAMERS
World War II
Bismarck Archipelago
Northern Solomons
Luzon

DECORATIONS
Philippine Presidential Unit Citation, Streamer embroidered *17 OCTOBER 1944 TO 4 JULY 1945* (471st AAA AW Bn cited; DAGO 47, 1950)

COAT OF ARMS
SHIELD: Or, on a pile invected inverted gules a boar's head erased of the field between two flaunches of the second, each charged with a portcullis of the first.

CREST: That for the regiments and separate battalions of the Army Reserve: On a wreath of the colors (or and gules) the Lexington Minute Man proper. The statue of the Minute Man, Captain John Parker (H. H. Kitson, sculptor), stands on the common in Lexington, Massachusetts.

MOTTO: *Maneo et Munio* (I Remain And Defend)

The scarlet is the color of the Coast Artillery Corps. The functions of the battalion are symbolized by the wedge shaped pile driving into enemy territory. The flaunche is the heraldic representation of learning and protection which function is enhanced by the medieval portcullis used to bar the entrance of ancient drawbridges and castles. The State of activation, Georgia, is indicated by the boar's head taken from the coat of arms of Sir James Olgethorpe, the founder of the Georgia colony.

DISTINCTIVE INSIGNIA
The insignia is the shield and motto of the coat of arms. The insignia depicted was never made for nor worn by this organization.

472d ANTIAIRCRAFT ARTILLERY AUTOMATIC WEAPONS BATTALION

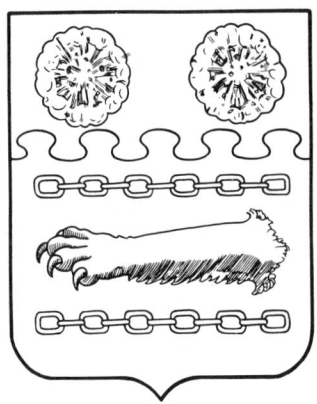

Constituted 30 August 1942 in the Army of the United States as the 472d Coast Artillery Battalion (Antiaircraft) (Automatic Weapons) and activated 15 October 1942 at Camp Stewart, Georgia. Reorganized and redesignated 30 April 1943 as the 472d Antiaircraft Artillery Automatic Weapons Battalion (Semimobile). (Departed San Francisco Port of Embarkation 27 August 1943 for overseas service and arrived in Australia on 14 September 1943. After service in New Guinea, moved to the Philippine Islands on 25 March 1945. Returned from overseas service and arrived at the San Francisco Port of Embarkation on 30 December 1945). Inactivated 1 January 1946 at Camp Stoneman, California. Allotted to the Organized Reserve Corps 25 January 1949 and activated 1 March 1949 with Headquarters at Columbus, Ohio. Assigned to the 83d Infantry Division on 18 July 1949. Relieved from the 83d Infantry Division and inactivated 20 May 1952 at Columbus.

CAMPAIGN STREAMERS
World War II
New Guinea
Luzon

DECORATIONS
Philippine Presidential Unit Citation, Streamer embroidered *17 OCTOBER 1944 TO 4 JULY 1945* (472d AAA AW Bn cited; DAGO 47, 1950)

COAT OF ARMS
SHIELD: Gules a lion's gamb erased fesswise between two chains in a similar position or, on a chief nebule of the last two bomb bursts proper.

CREST: That for the regiments and separate battalions of the Organized Reserve Corps: On a wreath of the colors (or and gules) the Lexington Minute Man proper. The statue of the Minute Man, Captain John Parker (H. H. Kitson, sculptor), stands on the common in Lexington, Massachusetts.

MOTTO: *In Vigilia sic Vinces* (In Watchfulness Thus You Will Conquer)

The scarlet of the shield is for the Coast Artillery Corps. The lion's paw is symbolic of the courage and fighting spirit of the organization while the chains are representative of the chain of obligation placed upon the organization in the fulfillment of its allotted duties. The nebule division of the shield, representative of clouds, together with the bomb bursts, are symbolic of the antiaircraft activities of the battalion.

DISTINCTIVE INSIGNIA
The insignia is the shield and motto of the coat of arms. The insignia depicted was never made for nor worn by this organization.

473d ANTIAIRCRAFT ARTILLERY AUTOMATIC WEAPONS BATTALION

Constituted 30 August 1942 in the Army of the United States as the 473d Coast Artillery Battalion (Antiaircraft) (Automatic Weapons) and activated 10 February 1943 at Camp Hulen, Texas. Reorganized and redesignated 10 April 1943 as the 473d Antiaircraft Artillery Automatic Weapons Battalion (Semimobile). (Departed New York Port of Embarkation 7 April 1944 for overseas service; arrived in England on 15 April 1944 and landed in France on 10 July 1944. Returned from overseas service and arrived at the New York Port of Embarkation on 30 April 1946). Inactivated 1 May 1946 at Camp Kilmer, New Jersey. Allotted to the Organized Reserve Corps 25 January 1949 and assigned to First Army on 15 February 1949. Activated 25 February 1949 at Boston, Massachusetts; inactivated 8 July 1949 at Boston.

CAMPAIGN STREAMERS
World War II
Normandy
Northern France
Rhineland
Central Europe
England 1944

DECORATIONS
None

COAT OF ARMS
None

DISTINCTIVE INSIGNIA
None

474th ANTIAIRCRAFT ARTILLERY BATTALION

Constituted 3 November 1942 in the Army of the United States as the 474th Coast Artillery Battalion (Antiaircraft) (Automatic Weapons) and activated 15 November 1942 at Camp Edwards, Massachusetts. Reorganized and redesignated 1 February 1943 as the 474th Antiaircraft Artillery Automatic Weapons Battalion (Semimobile). (Departed New York Port of Embarkation 29 January 1944 for overseas service; arrived in England on 5 February 1944 and landed in France on 6 June 1944). Converted and redesignated 1 May 1946 as the 74th Constabulary Squadron. Inactivated 20 September 1947 at Augsburg, Germany. Converted and redesignated 11 December 1951 as the 474th Antiaircraft Artillery Battalion. Allotted to the Regular Army and assigned to the 69th Infantry Division, 23 April 1954. Activated 1 May 1954 at Fort Dix, New Jersey. Relieved from the 69th Infantry Division and inactivated 16 March 1956 at Fort Dix.

CAMPAIGN STREAMERS
World War II
Normandy (with arrowhead)
Northern France
Rhineland
Ardennes-Alsace
Central Europe

DECORATIONS
None

COAT OF ARMS
SHIELD: Or, a chevronel in point embowed sable between three fleurs-de-lis gules, on a chief of the last a lion passant guardant grasping a pheon, all of the first.

CREST: None

MOTTO: My Claw Is Sharp

The colors red and yellow are used for Artillery. The gold lion on the red chief grasping the pheon symbolizes the organization's participation in the assault landing at Normandy on 6 June 1944. The black chevronel represents the Ardennes-Alsace campaign while the fleurs-de-lis represents the unit's other campaigns in Europe during World War II.

DISTINCTIVE INSIGNIA
The insignia is the shield and motto of the coat of arms. The insignia depicted was never made for nor worn by this organization.

475th ANTIAIRCRAFT ARTILLERY AUTOMATIC WEAPONS BATTALION

Constituted 3 November 1942 in the Army of the United States as the 475th Coast Artillery Battalion (Antiaircraft) (Automatic Weapons) and activated 15 November 1942 at Camp Edwards, Massachusetts. Reorganized and redesignated 30 April 1943 as the 475th Antiaircraft Artillery Automatic Weapons Battalion (Semimobile). (Departed San Francisco Port of Embarkation 1 October 1943 for overseas service and arrived on Guadalcanal on 21 October 1943. After service in New Guinea, moved to the Philippine Islands on 14 July 1945. Returned from overseas service and arrived at the San Francisco Port of Embarkation on 9 January 1946). Inactivated 11 January 1946 at Camp Stoneman, California.

CAMPAIGN STREAMERS
World War II
Pacific Theater without inscription

DECORATIONS
None

COAT OF ARMS
None

DISTINCTIVE INSIGNIA
None

476th ANTIAIRCRAFT ARTILLERY AUTOMATIC WEAPONS BATTALION

Constituted 3 November 1942 in the Army of the United States as the 476th Coast Artillery Battalion (Antiaircraft) (Automatic Weapons) and activated 15 November 1942 at Fort Sheridan, Illinois. Reorganized and redesignated 30 April 1943 as the 476th Antiaircraft Artillery Automatic Weapons Battalion (Semimobile). (Departed San Francisco Port of Embarkation 27 October 1943 for overseas service and arrived in Australia on 13 November 1943. After service in New Guinea and on Biak Island, moved to the Philippine Islands on 9 February 1945). Inactivated 15 December 1945 at Zamboanga, Mindanao, Philippine Islands. Redesignated 24 May 1949 as the 851st Antiaircraft Artillery Automatic Weapons Battalion. Redesignated 476th Antiaircraft Artillery Automatic Weapons Battalion and allotted to the Regular Army 16 October 1952.

CAMPAIGN STREAMERS
World War II
New Guinea (with arrowhead)
Luzon
Southern Philippines

DECORATIONS
Presidential Unit Citation (Army), Streamer embroidered *BIAK ISLAND* (476th AAA AW Bn cited for period 27 May-3 Jun 1944; DAGO 45, 1945)

Philippine Presidential Unit Citation, Streamer embroidered *17 OCTOBER 1944 TO 4 JULY 1945* (476th AAA AW Bn cited; DAGO 47, 1950)

COAT OF ARMS
None

DISTINCTIVE INSIGNIA
None

476th ANTIAIRCRAFT ARTILLERY AUTOMATIC WEAPONS BATTALION

Constituted 6 August 1942 in the Army of the United States as the 461st Coast Artillery Battalion (Antiaircraft) (Automatic Weapons) and activated 1 September 1942 at Camp Haan, California. (Departed New York Port of Embarkation 7 July 1943 for overseas service; arrived in England 15 July 1943 and landed in France on 13 June 1944). Reorganized and redesignated 20 August 1943 as the 461st Antiaircraft Artillery Automatic Weapons Battalion (Mobile). (Returned from overseas service and arrived at the New York Port of Embarkation on 23 November 1945). Inactivated 24 November 1945 at Camp Kilmer, New Jersey. Allotted to the Organized Reserve Corps, 19 November 1948. Activated 2 December 1948 with Headquarters at Bangor, Maine. (Headquarters relocated to Hartford, Connecticut on 22 April 1949). Assigned to the 76th Infantry Division on 31 May 1949. Redesignated 8 July 1949 as the 476th Antiaircraft Artillery Automatic Weapons Battalion.

Redesignated 15 April 1952 as the 461st Antiaircraft Artillery Automatic Weapons Battalion.

CAMPAIGN STREAMERS
World War II
Normandy
Northern France
Rhineland
Ardennes-Alsace
Central Europe

DECORATIONS
None

COAT OF ARMS
None

DISTINCTIVE INSIGNIA
None

477th ANTIAIRCRAFT ARTILLERY AUTOMATIC WEAPONS BATTALION

Constituted 3 November 1942 in the Army of the United States as the 477th Coast Artillery Battalion (Antiaircraft) (Automatic Weapons) (Colored) and activated 10 November 1942 at Camp Stewart, Georgia. Reorganized and redesignated 30 April 1943 as the 477th Antiaircraft Artillery Automatic Weapons Battalion (Semimobile) (Colored). (Departed San Francisco Port of Embarkation 23 August 1943 for overseas service and arrived in Australia on 7 September 1943. After service in New Guinea, moved to the Philippine Islands on 11 October 1945). Inactivated 20 January 1946 in the Philippine Islands.

Redesignated 13 October 1948 as the 32d Antiaircraft Artillery Automatic Weapons Battalion.

CAMPAIGN STREAMERS
World War II
New Guinea

DECORATIONS
None

COAT OF ARMS
None

DISTINCTIVE INSIGNIA
None

477th ANTIAIRCRAFT ARTILLERY AUTOMATIC WEAPONS BATTALION

Constituted 30 August 1942 in the Army of the United States as the 469th Coast Artillery Battalion (Antiaircraft) (Automatic Weapons) and activated 15 October 1942 at Camp Davis, North Carolina. Reorganized and redesignated 30 April 1943 as the 469th Antiaircraft Artillery Automatic Weapons Battalion (Semimobile). (Departed San Francisco Port of Embarkation 28 August 1943 for overseas service and arrived in Australia on 29 September 1943. After service in New Guinea and on New Britain landed in the Philippine Islands on 20 October 1944. Returned from overseas service and arrived at the San Francisco Port of Embarkation on 20 January 1946). Inactivated 22 January 1946 at Camp Stoneman, California. Allotted to the Organized Reserve Corps on 19 November 1948. Activated 14 December 1948 at New York, New York. Redesignated 477th Antiaircraft Artillery Automatic Weapons Battalion and assigned to the 77th Infantry Division on 8 July 1949.

Redesignated 4 April 1952 as the 469th Antiaircraft Artillery Automatic Weapons Battalion.

CAMPAIGN STREAMERS
World War II
New Guinea (with arrowhead)
Bismarck Archipelago
Leyte (with arrowhead)
Luzon

DECORATIONS
Philippine Presidential Unit Citation, Streamer embroidered *17 OCTOBER 1944 TO 4 JULY 1945* (469th AAA AW Bn cited; DAGO 47, 1950)

COAT OF ARMS
SHIELD: Gules, out of bulrushes in base proper a griffin salient, armed azure.

CREST: That for the regiments and separate battalions of the Organized Reserve Corps:

On a wreath of the colors (or and gules) the Lexington Minute Man proper. The statue of the Minute Man, Captain John Parker (H. H. Kitson, sculptor), stands on the common in Lexington, Massachusetts.

MOTTO: No Encroachment

Scarlet is the color of the Coast Artillery. The griffin is symbolic of a valorous soldier whose magnanimity is such that he will dare all dangers and is representative of the zealous spirit of the personnel of the organization in the performance of their duties. The griffin is also a symbol of vigilance and is suggestive of the alertness of the organization in its antiaircraft functions.

DISTINCTIVE INSIGNIA
The insignia is the shield and motto of the coat of arms. The insignia depicted was never made for nor worn by this organization.

478th ANTIAIRCRAFT ARTILLERY BATTALION

Constituted 3 November 1942 in the Army of the United States as the 478th Coast Artillery Battalion (Antiaircraft) (Automatic Weapons) and activated 20 November 1942 at Camp Davis, North Carolina. Reorganized and redesignated 30 April 1943 as the 478th Antiaircraft Artillery Automatic Weapons Battalion (Semimobile). (Departed San Francisco Port of Embarkation 27 September 1943 for overseas service and arrived in Australia on 15 October 1943. After service in New Guinea, moved to the Philippine Islands on 22 February 1945. Returned from overseas service and arrived at the San Francisco Port of Embarkation on 2 January 1946). Inactivated 4 January 1946 at Camp Stoneman, California. Redesignated 24 May 1949 as the 854th Antiaircraft Artillery Automatic Weapons Battalion. Redesignated 16 October 1952 as the 478th Antiaircraft Artillery Automatic Weapons Battalion and allotted to the Regular Army. Redesignated 9 February 1955 as the 478th Antiaircraft Artillery Battalion. Activated 25 March 1955 at Camp Stewart, Georgia; inactivated 15 February 1958 at the Savannah River Project, Georgia.

CAMPAIGN STREAMERS
World War II
New Guinea
Leyte
Southern Philippines (with arrowhead)

DECORATIONS
Philippine Presidential Unit Citation, Streamer embroidered *17 OCTOBER 1944 TO 4 JULY 1945* (478th AAA AW Bn cited; DAGO 47, 1950)

COAT OF ARMS
SHIELD: Barry wavy of six or and gules, three gunstones one and two fimbriated of the first,

that in chief bearing a pheon of the last.

CREST: None

MOTTO: *Gladiatores Libertate* (Defenders Of Freedom)

The colors yellow and scarlet are for Artillery. The wavy background symbolizes overseas service. The three gunstones represent the three island areas of New Guinea, Leyte, and the Southern Philippines. The pheon, representing an early type of artillery, symbolizes the assault landing in the Philippines.

DISTINCTIVE INSIGNIA
The insignia is the shield and motto of the coat of arms. The sample of the insignia depicted was approved for wear on 27 June 1956.

478th ANTIAIRCRAFT ARTILLERY AUTOMATIC WEAPONS BATTALION

Constituted 31 January 1942 in the Army of the United States as the 430th Separate Coast Artillery Battalion (Antiaircraft) (Automatic Weapons) and activated 1 March 1942 at Camp Davis, North Carolina. Redesignated 15 May 1943 as the 430th Antiaircraft Artillery Automatic Weapons Battalion (Mobile). (Departed Boston Port of Embarkation 20 October 1943 for overseas service; arrived in England on 2 November 1943 and landed in France on 13 June 1944. Returned from overseas service and arrived at Hampton Roads Port of Embarkation on 10 December 1945). Inactivated at Camp Patrick Henry, Virginia: Battalion, less Batteries B and D on 11 December 1945 and Batteries B and D on 16 December 1945. Allotted to the Organized Reserves on 28 March 1947 and activated 27 May 1947 at Brooklyn, New York. (Organized Reserves redesignated 25 March 1948 as Organized Reserve Corps). Relocated to Newark, New Jersey on 9 December 1948. Redesignated 478th Antiaircraft Artillery Automatic Weapons Battalion and assigned to the 78th Infantry Division, 8 July 1949. Relocated to East Orange, New Jersey on 20 September 1950.

Redesignated 1 April 1952 as the 430th Antiaircraft Artillery Automatic Weapons Battalion.

CAMPAIGN STREAMERS
World War II
Normandy
Northern France
Rhineland
Central Europe

DECORATIONS
None

COAT OF ARMS
None

DISTINCTIVE INSIGNIA
None

479th ANTIAIRCRAFT ARTILLERY AUTOMATIC WEAPONS BATTALION

Constituted 3 November 1942 in the Army of the United States as the 479th Coast Artillery Battalion (Antiaircraft) (Automatic Weapons) and activated 20 November 1942 at Camp Davis, North Carolina. Redesignated 30 April 1943 as the 479th Antiaircraft Artillery Automatic

Weapons Battalion.

Converted and redesignated 7 December 1944 at Camp Shelby, Mississippi as the 71st Chemical Mortar Battalion.

CAMPAIGN STREAMERS
None

DECORATIONS
None

COAT OF ARMS
None

DISTINCTIVE INSIGNIA
None

479th ANTIAIRCRAFT ARTILLERY AUTOMATIC WEAPONS BATTALION

Constituted 1 April 1942 in the Army of the United States as the 3d Battalion, 510th Coast Artillery (Antiaircraft) and activated 15 November 1942 at Fort Sheridan, Illinois. Reorganized at Fort Sheridan and redesignated 20 January 1943 as the 225th Coast Artillery Searchlight Battalion. Redesignated 3 March 1943 as the 225th Antiaircraft Artillery Searchlight Battalion. (Departed New York Port of Embarkation 23 December 1943 for the European Theater of Operations; arrived in England on 18 January 1944 and landed in France on 18 June 1944). Inactivated 31 December 1945 in Germany. Redesignated 5 November 1948 as the 633d Antiaircraft Artillery Automatic Weapons Battalion and allotted to the Organized Reserve Corps. Assigned to Second Army and activated at Philadelphia, Pennsylvania on 7 December 1948. Relieved from Second Army, redesignated as the 479th Antiaircraft Artillery Automatic Weapons Battalion, and assigned to the 79th Infantry Division on 15 July 1949.

Relieved from the 79th Infantry Division, inactivated at Philadelphia and redesignated 225th Antiaircraft Artillery Battalion on 10 June 1952.

CAMPAIGN STREAMERS
World War II
Normandy
Northern France
Rhineland
Central Europe

DECORATIONS
None

COAT OF ARMS
None

DISTINCTIVE INSIGNIA
None

480th ANTIAIRCRAFT ARTILLERY AUTOMATIC WEAPONS BATTALION

Constituted 3 November 1942 in the Army of the United States as the 480th Coast Artillery Battalion (Antiaircraft) (Automatic Weapons) and activated 15 November 1942 at Fort Bliss,

Texas. Reorganized and redesignated 30 April 1943 as the 480th Antiaircraft Artillery Automatic Weapons Battalion (Semimobile). (Departed New York Port of Embarkation 11 February 1944 for overseas service; arrived in England on 18 February 1944 and landed in France on 12 July 1944. Returned from overseas service and arrived at the New York Port of Embarkation on 27 November 1945). Inactivated 28 November 1945 at Camp Shanks, New York.

CAMPAIGN STREAMERS
World War II
Normandy
Northern France
England 1944

DECORATIONS
None

COAT OF ARMS
None

DISTINCTIVE INSIGNIA
None

481st ANTIAIRCRAFT ARTILLERY BATTALION

Constituted 3 November 1942 in the Army of the United States as the 481st Coast Artillery Battalion (Antiaircraft) (Automatic Weapons) and activated 20 November 1942 at Camp Davis, North Carolina. Reorganized and redesignated 30 April 1943 as the 481st Antiaircraft Artillery Automatic Weapons Battalion (Semimobile). (Departed New York Port of Embarkation 11 February 1944 for overseas service; arrived in England on 23 February 1944 and landed in France on 12 July 1944. Returned from overseas service and arrived at the Hampton Roads Port of Embarkation on 10 December 1945). Inactivated 10 December 1945 at Camp Patrick Henry, Virginia. Allotted to the Organized Reserve Corps and assigned to the 81st Infantry Division on 6 May 1949. Activated 1 September 1949 with Headquarters at Statesville, North Carolina.

Relieved from the 81st Infantry Division and assigned to the 108th Infantry Division on 1 March 1952. (Organized Reserve Corps redesignated 9 July 1952 as Army Reserve). Redesignated 31 January 1953 as the 481st Antiaircraft Artillery Battalion (Automatic Weapons). Disbanded 1 May 1959 at Statesville.

CAMPAIGN STREAMERS
World War II
Normandy
Northern France
Rhineland
Central Europe
England 1944

DECORATIONS
None

COAT OF ARMS
SHIELD: Gules, a semee-de-lis or, a dragon's sinister wing argent charged with a cross of the first.

CREST: That for the regiments and separate battalions of the Army Reserve: On a wreath of the colors (or and gules) the Lexington Minute Man proper. The statue of the Minute Man, Captain John Parker (H. H. Kitson, sculptor), stands on the common in Lexington, Massachusetts.

MOTTO: Courage, Strength, Honor

Red is the branch color for Artillery. The fleur-de-lis, used so frequently in European and especially French arms, represents the battalion's campaigns in Europe during World War II. The white dragon's wing charged with a red cross is the crest of the city of London, the "mighty heart" of England, which the battalion helped to defend in 1944.

DISTINCTIVE INSIGNIA
The insignia is the shield of the coat of arms. The insignia depicted was never made for nor worn by this organization.

482d ANTIAIRCRAFT ARTILLERY BATTALION

Constituted 19 December 1942 in the Army of the United States as the 482d Coast Artillery Battalion (Antiaircraft) (Automatic Weapons) and activated 20 February 1943 at Camp Hulen, Texas. Reorganized and redesignated 1 May 1943 as the 482d Antiaircraft Artillery Automatic Weapons Battalion (Self Propelled). (Departed New York Port of Embarkation 11 August 1944 for overseas service; arrived in England on 22 August 1944 and landed in France on 23 September 1944. Returned from overseas service and arrived at the New York Port of Embarkation on 29 April 1946). Inactivated 30 April 1946 at Camp Kilmer, New Jersey. Allotted to the Organized Reserve Corps and assigned to the 100th Infantry Division on 18 April 1952. Activated 12 May 1952 with Headquarters at Fort Thomas, Kentucky. (Organized Reserve Corps redesignated 9 July 1952 as Army Reserve). Disbanded 5 March 1959 at Fort Thomas.

CAMPAIGN STREAMERS
World War II
Rhineland
Ardennes-Alsace
Central Europe

DECORATIONS
Presidential Unit Citation (Army), Streamer embroidered *ARDENNES* (Btry A 482d AAA AW Bn cited for period 17-26 Dec 1944; WDGO 24, 1945)

Presidential Unit Citation (Army), Streamer embroidered *BASTOGNE* (Btry C 482d AAA AW Bn cited for period 18-27 Dec 1944; WDGO 17, 1945)

Presidential Unit Citation (Army), Streamer embroidered *REMAGEN BRIDGEHEAD* (482d AAA AW Bn cited for period 28 Feb-9 Mar 1945; WDGO 72, 1945)

Cited in the Order of the Day of the Belgian Army for action as *ST VITH* (Btry B 482d AAA AW Bn cited for period 16-31 Dec 1944; DAGO 43, 1950)

COAT OF ARMS
None

DISTINCTIVE INSIGNIA
None

483d ANTIAIRCRAFT ARTILLERY MISSILE BATTALION

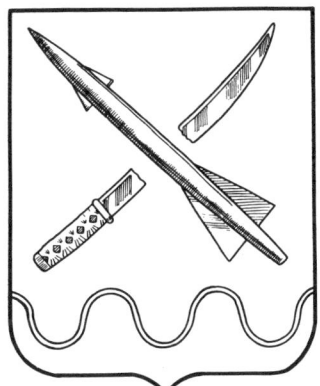

Constituted 19 December 1942 in the Army of the United States as the 483d Coast Artillery Battalion (Antiaircraft) (Automatic Weapons) and activated 10 February 1943 at Fort Bliss, Texas. Reorganized and redesignated 30 April 1943 as the 483d Antiaircraft Artillery Automatic Weapons Battalion (Semimobile). (Departed Seattle Port of Embarkation 17 June 1944 for overseas service and arrived in Hawaii on 24 June 1944. After service on Anguar Island and Ulithi Atoll, moved to Iwo Jima, Volcano Islands on 25 February 1945). Inactivated 15 January 1946 on Iwo Jima. Redesignated as the 483d Antiaircraft Artillery Missile Battalion and allotted to the Regular Army, 16 February 1955. Activated 11 March 1955 at Fort Hancock, New Jersey; inactivated 1 September 1958 at Camp Kilmer, New Jersey.

CAMPAIGN STREAMERS
World War II
Western Pacific
Air Offensive-Japan

DECORATIONS
None

COAT OF ARMS
SHIELD: Gules, saltirewise a broken Japanese sword and an antiaircraft artillery missile or, a foot wavy azure fimbriated of the second.

CREST: None

MOTTO: Vigilance And Valor

The shield is red for Artillery. The wavy blue section, representing the sea, refers to the organization's service in the Pacific during World War II. The missile indicates the function of artillery and the broken sword alludes to the battalion's participation in the air offensive against Japan.

DISTINCTIVE INSIGNIA
The insignia is the shield and motto of the coat of arms. The sample of the insignia depicted was approved for wear on 29 March 1956.

484th ANTIAIRCRAFT ARTILLERY AUTOMATIC WEAPONS BATTALION

Constituted 3 November 1942 in the Army of the United States as the 484th Coast Artillery Battalion (Antiaircraft) (Automatic Weapons) (Colored) and activated 10 December 1942 at Camp Stewart, Georgia. Redesignated 30 April 1943 as the 484th Antiaircraft Artillery Automatic Weapons Battalion (Colored). (Departed San Francisco Port of Embarkation 31 July 1943 for overseas service; arrived in India on 5 September 1943 and relocated to Burma on 22 November 1944. Returned from overseas service and arrived at the New York Port of Embarkation on 5 January 1946). Inactivated 6 January 1946 at Camp Kilmer, New Jersey.

Redesignated 13 October 1948 as the 34th Antiaircraft Artillery Automatic Weapons Battalion.

CAMPAIGN STREAMERS
World War II
Central Burma
India-Burma

DECORATIONS
None

COAT OF ARMS
None

DISTINCTIVE INSIGNIA
None

485th ANTIAIRCRAFT ARTILLERY MISSILE BATTALION

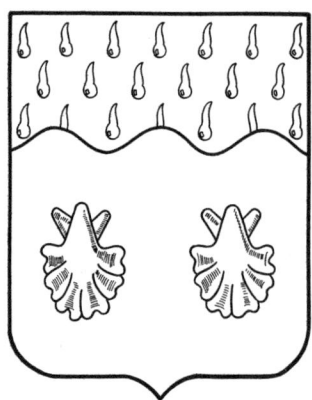

Constituted 2 November 1942 in the Army of the United States as the 485th Coast Artillery Battalion (Antiaircraft) (Automatic Weapons) and activated 10 February 1943 at Camp Hulen, Texas. Reorganized and redesignated 30 April 1943 as the 485th Antiaircraft Artillery Automatic

Weapons Battalion (Semimobile). (Departed San Francisco Port of Embarkation 16 February 1944 for overseas service and arrived in Hawaii on 21 February 1944. Moved to the Philippine Islands on 20 October 1944 and participated in the initial landings on Okinawa on 1 April 1945). Inactivated 20 February 1946 on Okinawa. Redesignated 10 November 1949 as the 646th Antiaircraft Artillery Automatic Weapons Battalion. Redesignated as the 485th Antiaircraft Artillery Automatic Weapons Battalion and allotted to the Regular Army on 16 October 1952. Redesignated 17 February 1955 as the 485th Antiaircraft Artillery Missile Battalion. Activated 1 March 1955 at Fort Sheridan, Illinois; inactivated 1 September 1958 at Chicago, Illinois.

CAMPAIGN STREAMERS
World War II
Leyte (with arrowhead)
Ryukyus (with arrowhead)

DECORATIONS
Philippine Presidential Unit Citation, Streamer embroidered *17 OCTOBER 1944 TO 4 JULY 1945* (485th AAA AW Bn cited; DAGO 47, 1950)

COAT OF ARMS
SHIELD: Gules two escallops or, on a chief wavy of the last guttee du sang.

CREST: None

MOTTO: *Pared de Fuego* (Wall Of Fire)

The shield is scarlet and yellow for Artillery. The escallops symbolize the unit's two campaigns in the Pacific Theater during World War II. The drops of blood on the wavy chief recall the unit's Philippine Presidential Unit Citation for the assault landing on Leyte.

DISTINCTIVE INSIGNIA
The insignia is the shield and motto of the coat of arms. The sample of the insignia depicted was approved for wear on 28 March 1956.

485th ANTIAIRCRAFT ARTILLERY AUTOMATIC WEAPONS BATTALION

Constituted 25 February 1943 in the Army of the United States as the 134th Antiaircraft Artillery Gun Battalion (Mobile) and activated 10 June 1943 at Fort Sheridan, Illinois. (Departed Boston Port of Embarkation 3 July 1944 for overseas service; arrived in England on 12 July 1944 and landed in France on 26 September 1944. Returned from overseas service and arrived at the New York Port of Embarkation on 19 February 1946). Inactivated 20 February 1946 at Camp Kilmer, New Jersey. Redesignated 452d Antiaircraft Artillery Automatic Weapons Battalion and allotted to the Organized Reserve Corps on 25 February 1949. Activated 5 April 1949 at Chicago, Illinois. Redesignated 485th Antiaircraft Artillery Automatic Weapons Battalion and assigned to the 85th Infantry Division on 25 November 1949.

Redesignated 1 March 1952 as the 134th Antiaircraft Artillery Automatic Weapons Battalion.

CAMPAIGN STREAMERS
World War II
Rhineland
Ardennes-Alsace
Central Europe
England 1944

DECORATIONS
None

COAT OF ARMS
None

DISTINCTIVE INSIGNIA
None

486th ANTIAIRCRAFT ARTILLERY BATTALION

Constituted 2 November 1942 in the Army of the United States as the 486th Coast Artillery Battalion (Antiaircraft) (Automatic Weapons) and activated 10 December 1942 at Camp Davis, North Carolina. Reorganized and redesignated 13 February 1943 as the 486th Antiaircraft Artillery Automatic Weapons Battalion (Self Propelled). (Departed New York Port of Embarkation 3 December 1943 for overseas service; arrived in England on 9 December 1943 and landed in France on 23 June 1944). Inactivated 1 June 1946 at Heilbronn, Germany. Allotted to the Organized Reserve Corps and assigned to the 80th Infantry Division on 18 April 1952. Activated 10 May 1952 with Headquarters at Richmond, Virginia. Redesignated 27 May 1952 as the 486th Antiaircraft Artillery Battalion. (Organized Reserve Corps redesignated 9 July 1952 as Army Reserve). Relieved from the 80th Infantry Division and disbanded 23 March 1959 at Richmond.

CAMPAIGN STREAMERS
World War II
Normandy
Northern France
Rhineland
Ardennes-Alsace
Central Europe

DECORATIONS
Belgian Fourragere 1940 (486th AAA AW Bn cited; DAGO 43, 1950)

Cited in the Order of the Day of the Belgian Army for action in *BELGIUM* (486th AAA AW

Bn cited for period 3-13 Sept 1944; DAGO 43, 1950)

Cited in the Order of the Day of the Belgian Army for action in the *ARDENNES* (486th AAA AW Bn cited for period 20 Dec 1944-31 Jan 1945; DAGO 43, 1950)

COAT OF ARMS
SHIELD: Per chevron flory counter flory gules and or, in base a lion rampant sable.

CREST: That for the regiments and separate battalions of the Army Reserve: On a wreath of the colors (or and gules) the Lexington Minute Man proper. The statue of the Minute Man, Captain John Parker (H. H. Kitson, sculptor), stands on the common in Lexington, Massachusetts.

MOTTO: *Hoeders van de Lucht* (Guardian Of The Skies)

The shield is red and yellow for Artillery. The five fleurs-de-lis represent the battalion's campaigns in Europe during World War II. The lion, from the Belgian coat of arms, commemorates the action for which the organization was decorated by the Belgian Government.

DISTINCTIVE INSIGNIA
The insignia is the shield and motto of the coat of arms. The sample of the insignia depicted was approved for wear on 27 July 1954.

487th ANTIAIRCRAFT ARTILLERY AUTOMATIC WEAPONS BATTALION

Constituted 2 November 1942 in the Army of the United States as the 487th Coast Artillery Battalion (Antiaircraft) (Automatic Weapons) and activated 10 December 1942 at Camp Haan, California. Reorganized and redesignated 30 April 1943 as the 487th Antiaircraft Artillery Automatic Weapons Battalion (Semimobile). (Departed Portland Sub Port of Embarkation 31 March 1944 for overseas service and arrived in New Guinea on 12 May 1944. After service on Noemfoor Island moved to the Philippine Islands on 17 April 1945). Inactivated 15 February 1946 in the Philippine Islands.

Redesignated 24 May 1949 as the 852d Antiaircraft Artillery Automatic Weapons Battalion.

CAMPAIGN STREAMERS
World War II
New Guinea (with arrowhead)
Luzon
Southern Philippines

DECORATIONS
Philippine Presidential Unit Citation, Streamer embroidered *17 OCTOBER 1944 TO 4 JULY 1945* (487th AAA AW Bn cited; DAGO 47, 1950)

COAT OF ARMS
None

DISTINCTIVE INSIGNIA
None

487th ANTIAIRCRAFT ARTILLERY BATTALION

Constituted 29 August 1942 in the Army of the United States as the 467th Coast Artillery Battalion (Antiaircraft) (Automatic Weapons) and activated 15 October 1942 at Camp Stewart, Georgia. Reorganized and redesignated 13 February 1943 as the 467th Antiaircraft Artillery Automatic Weapons Battalion (Semimobile). (Departed New York Port of Embarkation 19 January 1944 for overseas service; arrived in England on 30 January 1944 and landed in France on 6 June 1944. Returned from overseas service and arrived at the New York Port of Embarkation on 15 April 1946). Inactivated 16 April 1946 at Camp Kilmer, New Jersey. Allotted to the Organized Reserve Corps on 24 November 1948 and assigned to Third Army on 13 December 1948. Activated 3 January 1949 at Tampa, Florida. Assigned to the 87th Infantry Division on 15 April 1949. Redesignated 18 May 1949 as the 487th Antiaircraft Artillery Automatic Weapons Battalion. (Headquarters relocated to Bartow, Florida on 1 February 1950; to Jackson, Mississippi on 1 June 1951 and to Jacksonville, Florida on 1 March 1952). (Organized Reserve Corps redesignated 9 July 1952 as Army Reserve). Redesignated 31 January 1953 as the 487th Antiaircraft Artillery Battalion. Inactivated 28 February 1954 at Jacksonville.

CAMPAIGN STREAMERS
World War II
Normandy (with arrowhead)
Northern France
Rhineland
Ardennes-Alsace
Central Europe

DECORATIONS
None

COAT OF ARMS
None

DISTINCTIVE INSIGNIA
None

488th ANTIAIRCRAFT ARTILLERY AUTOMATIC WEAPONS BATTALION

Constituted 19 November 1942 in the Army of the United States as the 488th Coast Artillery Battalion (Antiaircraft) (Automatic Weapons) and activated 10 February 1943 at Fort Bliss, Texas. Reorganized and redesignated 30 April 1943 as the 488th Antiaircraft Artillery Automatic Weapons Battalion (Semimobile). Inactivated 5 August 1944 at Camp Maxey, Texas. Disbanded 26 October 1944.

CAMPAIGN STREAMERS
None

DECORATIONS
None

COAT OF ARMS
None

DISTINCTIVE INSIGNIA
None

489th ANTIAIRCRAFT ARTILLERY BATTALION

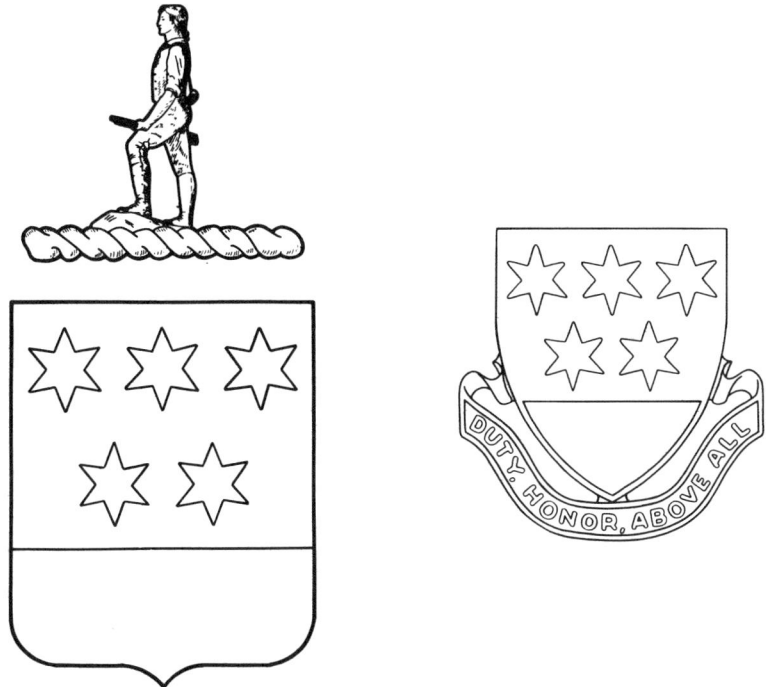

Constituted 19 December 1942 in the Army of the United States as the 489th Coast Artillery Battalion (Antiaircraft) (Automatic Weapons) and activated 10 February 1943 at Fort Bliss, Texas. Reorganized and redesignated 1 May 1943 as the 489th Antiaircraft Artillery Automatic Weapons Battalion (Self Propelled). (Departed New York Port of Embarkation 27 February 1944 for overseas service; arrived in England 9 March 1944 and landed in France on 13 July 1944). Inactivated 30 June 1946 in Germany. Allotted to the Organized Reserve Corps, 11 February 1949 and assigned to the 89th Infantry Division on 18 February 1949. Activated 20 September 1949 with Headquarters at Fort Dodge, Kansas. (Organized Reserve Corps redesignated 9 July 1952 as Army Reserve). Redesignated 15 December 1952 as the 489th Antiaircraft Artillery Battalion. (Headquarters relocated to Dodge City, Kansas on 14 December 1953). Disbanded 30 September 1959 at Dodge City.

CAMPAIGN STREAMERS
World War II
Normandy
Northern France
Rhineland
Ardennes-Alsace
Central Europe

DECORATIONS
Presidential Unit Citation (Army), Streamer embroidered *ARDENNES* (489th AAA AW Bn cited for period 22 Dec 1944-27 Mar 1945; WDGO 54, 1943)

French Croix de Guerre with Palm, World War II, Streamer embroidered *NORMANDY* (489th AAA AW Bn cited for period 27 Jul-11 Aug 1944; DAGO 43, 1950)

French Croix de Guerre with Palm, World War II, Streamer embroidered *MOSELLE RIVER* (489th AAA AW Bn cited for period 12-29 Sept 1944; DAGO 43, 1950)

Fourragere in the colors of the French Croix de Guerre, World War II (489th AAA AW Bn cited; DAGO 43, 1950)

COAT OF ARMS

SHIELD: Or, five mullets of six points, three and two, and a base gules.

CREST: That for the regiments and separate battalions of the Army Reserve: On a wreath of the colors (or and gules) the Lexington Minute Man proper. The statue of the Minute Man, Captain John Parker (H. H. Kitson, sculptor), stands on the common in Lexington, Massachusetts.

MOTTO: Duty, Honor, Above All

The shield is in the colors of Artillery. The partition line represents the horizon. The mullets, symbolizing flak bursts, form a "box" of flak: one burst for each of the organization's campaigns in Europe during World War II.

DISTINCTIVE INSIGNIA

The insignia is the shield and motto of the coat of arms. The sample of the insignia depicted was approved for wear on 22 December 1953.

490th ANTIAIRCRAFT ARTILLERY AUTOMATIC WEAPONS BATTALION

Constituted 19 December 1942 in the Army of the United States as the 490th Coast Artillery Battalion (Antiaircraft) (Automatic Weapons) and activated 10 February 1943 at Camp Stewart, Georgia. Reorganized and redesignated 10 April 1943 as the 490th Antiaircraft Artillery Automatic Weapons Battalion (Self Propelled). Inactivated 1 December 1944 at Camp Livingston, Louisiana. Disbanded 10 October 1952.

CAMPAIGN STREAMERS
None

DECORATIONS
None

COAT OF ARMS
None

DISTINCTIVE INSIGNIA
None

491st ANTIAIRCRAFT ARTILLERY BATTALION

Constituted 19 December 1942 in the Army of the United States as the 491st Coast Artillery Battalion (Antiaircraft) (Automatic Weapons) and activated 10 February 1943 at Camp Stewart, Georgia. Reorganized and redesignated 30 April 1943 as the 491st Antiaircraft Artillery Automatic Weapons Battalion (Semimobile). (Departed New York Port of Embarkation 10 April 1944 for overseas service; arrived in England 16 April 1944 and landed in France on 14 July 1944. Returned from overseas service and arrived at the New York Port of Embarkation 1 December 1945). Inactivated 3 December 1945 at Camp Kilmer, New Jersey. Allotted to the Organized Reserve Corps 10 January 1949 and assigned to Sixth Army 28 February 1949. Assigned to the 91st Infantry Division and activated at San Francisco, California on 25 March 1949. (Organized Reserve Corps redesignated 9 July 1952 as Army Reserve). Redesignated 15 November 1952 as the 491st Antiaircraft Artillery Battalion. (Relocated to San Jose, California on 1 September 1955). Disbanded 1 May 1959 at San Jose.

CAMPAIGN STREAMERS
World War II
Normandy
Northern France
Central Europe
England 1944

COAT OF ARMS

SHIELD: Or, in fess on a cross patee throughout gules a lion passant guardant of the field.

CREST: That for the regiments and separate battalions of the Army Reserve: On a wreath of the colors (or and gules) the Lexington Minute Man proper. The statue of the Minute Man, Captain John Parker (H. H. Kitson, sculptor), stands on the common in Lexington, Massachusetts

MOTTO: *Peto Sustineo Destruo* (Seek Support Destroy)

Scarlet is for Artillery. The yellow rays formed by the arms of the cross represent searchlights used in antiaircraft combat. The lion, taken from the coat of arms of Great Britain and Normandy, refers to service in those respective areas during World War II.

DISTINCTIVE INSIGNIA
The insignia is the shield and motto of the coat of arms. The sample of the insignia depicted was approved for wear on 18 June 1958.

492d ANTIAIRCRAFT ARTILLERY AUTOMATIC WEAPONS BATTALION

Constituted 19 December 1942 in the Army of the United States as the 492d Coast Artillery Battalion (Antiaircraft) (Automatic Weapons) (Colored) and activated 10 February 1943 at Camp Stewart, Georgia. Reorganized and redesignated 30 April 1943 as the 492d Antiaircraft Artillery Automatic Weapons Battalion (Semimobile) (Colored). (Departed New York Port of Embarkation 28 March 1944 for overseas service and landed in North Africa on 6 April 1944). Disbanded 15 May 1944 in North Africa.

CAMPAIGN STREAMERS
World War II
European Theater without inscription.

DECORATIONS
None

COAT OF ARMS
None

DISTINCTIVE INSIGNIA
None

492d AIRBORNE ANTIAIRCRAFT BATTALION

Constituted 15 February 1946 in the Organized Reserves as the 492d Airborne Antiaircraft Battalion and assigned to the 100th Airborne Division. Activated 3 February 1947 at Louisville, Kentucky. (Organized Reserves redesignated 25 March 1948 as Organized Reserve Corps). Relieved from the 100th Airborne Division and disbanded 12 May 1952 at Fort Thomas, Kentucky.

CAMPAIGN STREAMERS
None

DECORATIONS
None

COAT OF ARMS
None

DISTINCTIVE INSIGNIA
None

493d ANTIAIRCRAFT ARTILLERY AUTOMATIC WEAPONS BATTALION

Constituted 19 December 1942 in the Army of the United States as the 493d Coast Artillery Battalion (Antiaircraft) (Automatic Weapons) (Colored) and activated 10 February 1943 at Camp Stewart, Georgia. Reorganized and redesignated 30 April 1943 as the 493d Antiaircraft Artillery Automatic Weapons Battalion (Semimobile) (Colored). (Departed Hampton Roads Port of Embarkation 28 March 1944 for overseas service and landed in North Africa on 6 April 1944). Disbanded 15 May 1944 in North Africa.

CAMPAIGN STREAMERS
World War II
European Theater without inscription

DECORATIONS
None

COAT OF ARMS
None

DISTINCTIVE INSIGNIA
None

494th ANTIAIRCRAFT ARTILLERY BATTALION

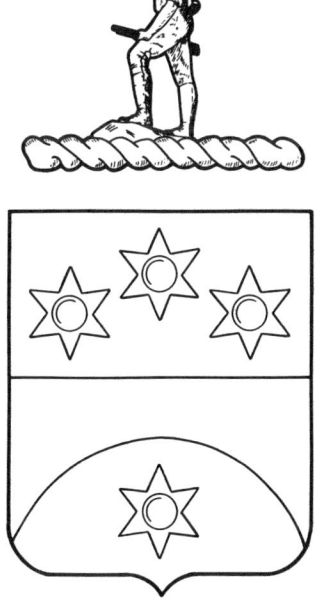 

Constituted 15 June 1942 in the Army of the United States as the 494th Coast Artillery Battalion (Antiaircraft) (Gun) and activated 10 July 1942 in Iceland with personnel from the 61st Coast Artillery. Reorganized and redesignated 5 September 1943 as the 494th Antiaircraft Artillery Gun Battalion (Semimobile). (Moved to England on 4 November 1943 and landed in France on 16 July 1944. Returned from overseas service and arrived at the New York Port of Embarkation on 13 November 1945). Inactivated 15 November 1945 at Camp Kilmer, New

Jersey. Redesignated 494th Antiaircraft Artillery Automatic Weapons Battalion, allotted to the Organized Reserve Corps and assigned to First Army, 15 February 1949. Activated 4 March 1949 at Boston, Massachusetts. (Organized Reserve Corps redesignated 9 July 1952 as Army Reserve). Redesignated 1 January 1953 as the 494th Antiaircraft Artillery Battalion (Automatic Weapons). (Headquarters relocated to Needham, Massachusetts on 23 April 1958). Inactivated 1 May 1959 at Needham.

CAMPAIGN STREAMERS
World War II
Normandy
Northern France
Rhineland
England 1944

DECORATIONS
Belgian Fourragere 1940 (494th AAA Gun Bn cited; DAGO 43, 1950)

Cited in the Order of the Day of the Belgian Army for *DEFENSE OF ANTWERP* (494th AAA Gun Bn cited for period 25 Oct-28 Nov 1944; DAGO 43, 1950)

Cited in the Order of the Day of the Belgian Army for *DEFENSE OF ANTWERP HARBOR* (494th AAA Gun Bn cited for action on 16 Dec 1944; DAGO 43, 1950)

COAT OF ARMS
SHIELD: Per fess gules and or, four mullets of six points of the second each bearing a gunstone, three in chief, one and two, and one on a foot arched of the first.

CREST: That for the regiments and separate battalions of the Army Reserve: On a wreath of the colors (or and gules) the Lexington Minute Man proper. The statue of the Minute Man, Captain John Parker (H. H. Kitson, sculptor), stands on the common in Lexington, Massachusetts.

MOTTO: *Il tau epei tass* (Come Back A Victor Or Dead On Your Shield)

Scarlet is for Artillery. The gunstones on the mullets represent both artillery fire and the unit's World War II campaigns. The scarlet, yellow and black color scheme alludes to the Belgian national colors. Both the colors and the arched yellow band, representing a Roman bridge which is a typical historical landmark of the country, refer to Belgium for whose defense the unit was decorated.

DISTINCTIVE INSIGNIA
The insignia is the shield and motto of the coat of arms. The sample of the insignia depicted was approved for wear on 22 May 1956.

495th ANTIAIRCRAFT ARTILLERY MISSILE BATTALION

Constituted 15 June 1942 in the Army of the United States as the 495th Coast Artillery Battalion (Antiaircraft) (Gun) and activated 10 July 1942 in Iceland. Reorganized and redesignated 5 September 1943 as the 495th Antiaircraft Artillery Gun Battalion (Semimobile). (Moved to England on 6 November 1943 and landed in France on 23 June 1944). Inactivated 30 October 1945 at Bad Neustadt, Germany. Redesignated 22 September 1952 as the 495th Antiaircraft Artillery Battalion and allotted to the Regular Army. Activated 27 October 1952 at Fort Bliss, Texas. Reorganized and redesignated 10 August 1953 as the 495th Antiaircraft Artillery Missile Battalion. Inactivated 28 August 1958 at Fort Bliss.

CAMPAIGN STREAMERS
World War II
Normandy
Northern France
Rhineland
Central Europe
England 1944

DECORATIONS
Belgian Fourragere 1940 (495th AAA Gun Bn cited; DAGO 43, 1950)

Cited in the Order of the Day of the Belgian Army for *DEFENSE OF ANTWERP* (495th AAA Gun Bn cited for period 25 Oct-28 Nov 1944; DAGO 43, 1950)

Cited in the Order of the Day of the Belgian Army for *DEFENSE OF ANTWERP HARBOR* (495th AAA Gun Bn cited for action on 16 Dec 1944; DAGO 43, 1950)

COAT OF ARMS
SHIELD: Per fess arched abased or and gules, in chief on a pale between four endorses of the last a tower argent, door and windows sable, in base a fountain.

CREST: None

MOTTO: Forever First

The colors red and yellow are used for Artillery. The red pale and four endorses represent the five campaigns of the unit during World War II. The white tower, taken from the castle depicted on the coat of arms of Antwerp, symbolizes the defense of that city, an action for which the unit was cited and decorated. The fess is arched to indicate the "rim of the world", as it was there in Iceland that the battalion was initially activated, which is indicated by the fountain.

DISTINCTIVE INSIGNIA
The insignia is the shield and motto of the coat of arms. The sample of the insignia depicted was approved for wear on 9 June 1954.

495th ANTIAIRCRAFT ARTILLERY AUTOMATIC WEAPONS BATTALION

Constituted 19 December 1942 in the Army of the United States as the 391st Coast Artillery Battalion (Antiaircraft) (Automatic Weapons) and activated 10 January 1943 at Camp Davis, North Carolina. Redesignated 30 April 1943 as the 391st Antiaircraft Artillery Automatic Weapons Battalion (Semimobile). (Departed Boston Port of Embarkation 27 February 1944 for overseas service; arrived in England 8 March 1944 and landed in France on 14 July 1944. Returned from overseas service and arrived at the New York Port of Embarkation on 27 December 1945). Inactivated 27 December 1945 at Camp Kilmer, New Jersey. Allotted to the Organized Reserves 7 March 1947 and activated 24 March 1947 at Oklahoma City, Oklahoma. (Organized Reserves redesignated 25 March 1948 as Organized Reserve Corps). Redesignated 30 June 1949 as the 495th Antiaircraft Artillery Automatic Weapons Battalion and assigned to the 95th Infantry Division. (Headquarters relocated to Antlers, Oklahoma on 1 October 1950).

Redesignated 1 March 1952 as the 391st Antiaircraft Artillery Automatic Weapons Battalion.

CAMPAIGN STREAMERS
World War II
Normandy
Northern France
Rhineland

DECORATIONS
None

COAT OF ARMS
None

DISTINCTIVE INSIGNIA
None

496th ANTIAIRCRAFT ARTILLERY BATTALION

Constituted 19 December 1942 in the Army of the United States as the 496th Coast Artillery Battalion (Antiaircraft) (Gun) and activated 10 January 1943 at Camp Stewart, Georgia. Reorganized and redesignated 7 June 1943 as the 496th Antiaircraft Artillery Gun Battalion (Semimobile). (Departed Portland Sub Port of Embarkation 16 March 1944 for overseas service; arrived in New Guinea on 4 April 1944 and moved to the Philippine Islands on 3 May 1945. Returned from overseas service and arrived at the Los Angeles Port of Embarkation 12 January 1946). Inactivated 13 January 1946 at Camp Anza, Arlington, California. Redesignated 24 May 1949 as the 853d Antiaircraft Artillery Automatic Weapons Battalion. Redesignated 496th

Antiaircraft Artillery Gun Battalion and allotted to the Regular Army on 16 October 1952. Redesignated 26 August 1953 as the 496th Antiaircraft Artillery Battalion. Activated 15 September 1953 at Camp Stewart, Georgia; inactivated 20 December 1957 at Chicago, Illinois.

CAMPAIGN STREAMERS
World War II
New Guinea
Southern Philippines

DECORATIONS
Philippine Presidential Unit Citation, Streamer embroidered *17 OCTOBER 1944 TO 4 JULY 1945* (496th AAA Gun Bn cited; DAGO 47, 1950)

COAT OF ARMS
SHIELD: Per bend or and gules, a pile issuing from dexter chief between in chief a sun of eight rays and in base a stone war club head, all counterchanged.

CREST: None

MOTTO: *Defendores die Noctuque* (Defenders Night And Day)

The colors are red and yellow for Artillery. The division of the shield simulates rays and symbolizes the antiaircraft mission of the organization. The World War II service in the Pacific Theater is indicated by the sun from the flag and seal of the Philippine Islands and the war club head, of a type commonly used by the native warriors of New Guinea.

DISTINCTIVE INSIGNIA
The insignia is the shield and motto of the coat of arms. The sample of the insignia depicted was approved for wear on 18 August 1954.

497th ANTIAIRCRAFT ARTILLERY GUN BATTALION

Constituted 19 December 1942 in the Army of the United States as the 497th Coast Artillery Battalion (Antiaircraft) (Gun) and activated 20 January 1943 at Camp Stewart, Georgia. Reorganized and redesignated 7 June 1943 as the 497th Antiaircraft Artillery Gun Battalion (Semimobile). (Departed Seattle Port of Embarkation 2 November 1943 for overseas service and arrived at New Caledonia on 23 November 1943. After service on Guadalcanal and in New Guinea, moved to the Philippine Islands on 14 July 1945. Returned from overseas service and arrived at the San Francisco Port of Embarkation on 13 January 1946). Inactivated 15 January 1946 at Camp Stoneman, California.

CAMPAIGN STREAMERS
World War II
Pacific Theater without inscription

DECORATIONS
None

COAT OF ARMS
None

DISTINCTIVE INSIGNIA
None

498th COAST ARTILLERY BATTALION

Constituted 8 March 1942 in the Army of the United States as the 498th Coast Artillery Battalion (Antiaircraft) (Gun). (Detachment of Headquarters and Headquarters Battery and 1st Platoons of Batteries A and B activated 1 April 1942 at Aruba, Netherlands West Indies; inactivated 25 November 1943 at Aruba). Disbanded 25 November 1943.

CAMPAIGN STREAMERS
None

DECORATIONS
None

COAT OF ARMS
None

DISTINCTIVE INSIGNIA
None

498th ANTIAIRCRAFT ARTILLERY AUTOMATIC WEAPONS BATTALION

Constituted July 1923 in the Organized Reserves as 2d Battalion, 513th Artillery (Antiaircraft), Coast Artillery Corps and allotted to the Second Corps Area. Organized during October 1923 with Headquarters at Syracuse, New York. Redesignated 30 June 1924 as 2d Battalion, 513th Coast Artillery (Antiaircraft). Ordered into active military service, less personnel and equipment and organized 1 September 1942 at Fort Bliss, Texas. Reorganized and redesignated 20 January 1943 as the 200th Coast Artillery Battalion (Antiaircraft) (Automatic Weapons). Redesignated 19 March 1943 at Camp Pickett, Virginia as the 400th Coast Artillery Battalion (Antiaircraft) (Automatic Weapons). (Departed Hampton Roads Port of Embarkation 8 June 1943 for overseas service and arrived in North Africa on 22 June 1943. After service in Sicily, Italy, Corsica and France returned to Hampton Roads Port of Embarkation on 15 November 1945). Inactivated 15 November 1945 at Camp Patrick Henry, Virginia. Activated 21 February 1947 with Headquarters at Rochester, New York. (Organized Reserves redesignated 25 March 1948 as Organized Reserve Corps). Redesignated 8 July 1949 as the 498th Antiaircraft Artillery Automatic Weapons Battalion and assigned to the 98th Infantry Division.

Redesignated 4 April 1952 as the 400th Antiaircraft Artillery Automatic Weapons Battalion.

CAMPAIGN STREAMERS
World War II
Sicily (with arrowhead)
Naples-Foggia
Rome-Arno
Rhineland

DECORATIONS
None

COAT OF ARMS
None

DISTINCTIVE INSIGNIA
None

499th COAST ARTILLERY BATTALION

Constituted 8 March 1942 in the Army of the United States as the 499th Coast Artillery Battalion (Antiaircraft) (Gun). (1st Platoon of Battery A and 2d Platoon of Battery B activated 10 April 1942 at Curacao, Netherlands West Indies and inactivated 25 November 1943 at Curacao; detachment of Headquarters and Headquarters Battery activated 17 April 1942 at Curacao and inactivated 25 November 1943 at Curacao). Disbanded 25 November 1943.

CAMPAIGN STREAMERS
None

DECORATIONS
None

COAT OF ARMS
None

DISTINCTIVE INSIGNIA
None

500th ANTIAIRCRAFT ARTILLERY GUN BATTALION

Constituted 19 December 1942 in the Army of the United States as the 500th Coast Artillery Battalion (Antiaircraft) (Gun) and activated 20 January 1943 at Camp Stewart, Georgia. Redesignated 8 June 1943 as the 500th Antiaircraft Artillery Gun Battalion (Semimobile). Departed Boston Port of Embarkation for overseas service 1 August 1943 and arrived in Greenland 25 August 1943; Returned to the United States and arrived at the Boston Port of Embarkation 30 July 1944). Disbanded 20 September 1944 at Camp Davis, North Carolina.

CAMPAIGN STREAMERS
World War II
European Theater without inscription

DECORATIONS
None

COAT OF ARMS
None

DISTINCTIVE INSIGNIA
None

501st ANTIAIRCRAFT ARTILLERY BATTALION

Constituted 19 December 1942 in the Army of the United States as the 501st Coast Artillery Battalion (Antiaircraft) (Gun) and activated 20 February 1943 at Camp Edwards, Massachusetts. Redesignated 7 June 1943 as the 501st Antiaircraft Artillery Gun Battalion. (Departed San Francisco Port of Embarkation 16 December 1943 for overseas service; arrived in Hawaii on 21 December 1943 and landed on Saipan, Marianas Islands on 27 June 1944). Inactivated on Saipan, 25 February 1946. Allotted to the Regular Army and activated 15 January 1949 at Fort Bliss, Texas. Redesignated 20 July 1953 as the 501st Antiaircraft Artillery Battalion (Gun). Inactivated 20 December 1957 at Camp Hanford, Washington.

CAMPAIGN STREAMERS
World War II
Western Pacific

DECORATIONS
None

COAT OF ARMS
SHIELD: Gules two lightning flashes terminating in serpents crossed in saltire, in base a sea proper.

CREST: None

MOTTO: Our Strength, Your Protection

The colors scarlet and yellow are used for Artillery. The "lightning serpents" are used to represent the fire power of the battalion while the sea symbolizes war service in the Pacific Theater during World War II.

DISTINCTIVE INSIGNIA
The insignia is the shield and motto of the coat of arms. The sample of the insignia depicted was approved for wear on 17 May 1950.

502d ANTIAIRCRAFT ARTILLERY BATTALION

Constituted 19 December 1942 in the Army of the United States as the 502d Coast Artillery Battalion (Antiaircraft) (Gun) and activated 20 February 1943 at Camp Edwards, Massachusetts. Redesignated 7 June 1943 as the 502d Antiaircraft Artillery Gun Battalion (Semimobile). (Departed San Francisco Port of Embarkation 16 December 1943 for overseas service; arrived in Hawaii on 21 December 1943 and landed in the Philippine Islands on 20 October 1944. Moved to Okinawa on 1 April 1945. Returned to the United States and arrived at the Seattle Port of Embarkation on 13 January 1946). Inactivated 15 January 1946 at Fort Lawton, Washington. Allotted to the Regular Army on 15 October 1948. Activated 18 November 1948 at Fort Bliss, Texas. Redesignated 1 September 1953 as the 502d Antiaircraft Artillery Battalion. Inactivated 15 September 1958 at Eielson Air Force Base, Alaska.

CAMPAIGN STREAMERS
World War II
Leyte (with arrowhead)
Ryukyus

DECORATIONS
Philippine Presidential Unit Citation, Streamer embroidered *17 OCTOBER 1944 TO 4 JULY 1945* (502d AAA Gun Bn cited; DAGO 47, 1950)

COAT OF ARMS
SHIELD: Per saltire gules and or, in chief a falcon of the second, in fess a demi-sun in splendour of the first and a sun in splendour sable and in base a pheon of the second.

CREST: None

MOTTO: The Skies We Guard

Red and yellow are the colors used for Artillery. The falcon indicates mastery of the air. The black sun represents Alaskan service, the land of the midnight sun. The pheon symbolizes the assault landing on Leyte and also represents an early form of artillery or machine fired weapon. The demi-sun alludes to the fact that the Ryukyu Islands were a Japanese possession and denotes service in that area.

DISTINCTIVE INSIGNIA
The insignia is the shield and motto of the coat of arms. The sample of the insignia depicted was approved for wear on 21 May 1953.

503d AIRBORNE ANTIAIRCRAFT BATTALION

Constituted 19 December 1942 in the Army of the United States as the 503d Coast Artillery Battalion (Antiaircraft) (Gun) and activated 10 February 1943 at Camp Stewart, Georgia. Redesignated 7 June 1943 as the 503d Antiaircraft Artillery Gun Battalion (Semimobile). (Departed San Francisco Port of Embarkation 8 January 1944 for overseas service; arrived in Hawaii on 16 January 1944 and landed on Okinawa on 24 June 1945. Returned from overseas service and arrived at the Los Angeles Port of Embarkation on 20 January 1946). Inactivated 21 January 1946 at Camp Anza, Arlington, California. Redesignated as the 503d Airborne Antiaircraft Battalion and assigned to the 82d Airborne Division on 11 December 1947. Activated 15 December 1947 at Fort Bragg, North Carolina. Allotted to the Regular Army on 15 November 1948. Relieved from the 82d Airborne Division and inactivated 10 June 1949 at Camp Mackall, North Carolina.

CAMPAIGN STREAMERS
World War II
Ryukyus

DECORATIONS
None

COAT OF ARMS
None

DISTINCTIVE INSIGNIA
None

504th ANTIAIRCRAFT ARTILLERY MISSILE BATTALION

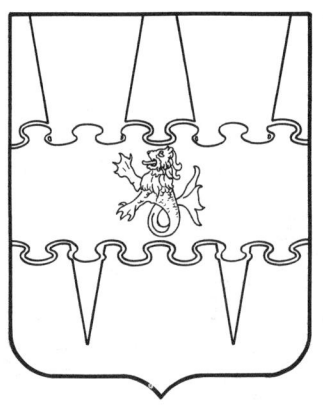 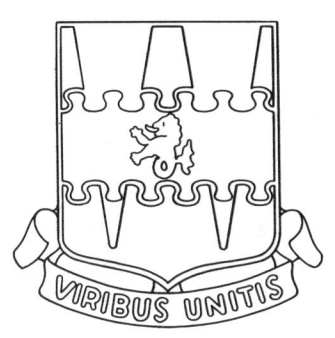

Constituted 8 February 1943 in the Army of the United States as the 504th Coast Artillery Battalion (Antiaircraft) (Gun) and activated 20 March 1943 at Camp Davis, North Carolina. Redesignated 7 June 1943 as the 504th Antiaircraft Artillery Gun Battalion (Semimobile). (Departed San Francisco Port of Embarkation 12 April 1944 for overseas service; arrived in Hawaii 19 April 1944, landed in the Philippine Islands 20 October 1944 and moved to Okinawa 1 April 1945). Inactivated 15 March 1946 on Okinawa. Allotted to the Regular Army 27 October 1948. Activated 20 November 1948 at Fort Bliss, Texas. Redesignated 24 July 1953 as the 504th Antiaircraft Artillery Battalion. Reorganized and redesignated 10 January 1955 as the 504th Antiaircraft Artillery Missile Battalion. Inactivated 1 September 1958 at Carleton, Michigan.

CAMPAIGN STREAMERS
World War II
Leyte (with arrowhead)
Ryukyus

DECORATIONS
Philippine Presidential Unit Citation, Streamer embroidered *17 OCTOBER 1944 TO 4 JULY 1945* (504th AAA Gun Bn cited; DAGO 47, 1950)

COAT OF ARMS
SHIELD: Gules, two piles issuing in chief or, overall a fess nebuly sable fimbriated of the second charged with a sea-lion of the like.

CREST: None

MOTTO: *Viribus Unitis* (With United Strength)

The colors red and yellow are those of Artillery. The two piles representing searchlight beams and the fess with a nebuly outline to symbolize clouds indicate the antiaircraft artillery functions of the organization. The sea-lion represents World War II service in the Philippines.

DISTINCTIVE INSIGNIA
The insignia is the shield and motto of the coat of arms. The sample of the insignia depicted was approved for wear on 11 May 1950.

505th ANTIAIRCRAFT ARTILLERY MISSILE BATTALION

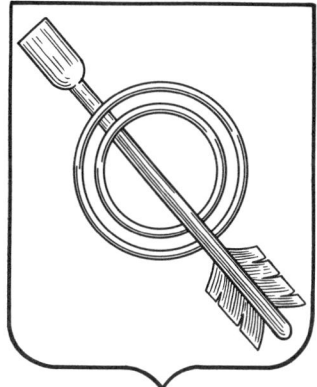 

Constituted 25 February 1943 in the Army of the United States as the 505th Coast Artillery Battalion (Antiaircraft) (Gun) and activated 10 April 1943 at Camp Stewart, Georgia. Redesignated 7 June 1943 as the 505th Antiaircraft Artillery Gun Battalion (Semimobile). (Departed Seattle Port of Embarkation 12 August 1944 for overseas service; arrived in Hawaii on 21 August 1944 and landed on Okinawa on 3 May 1945. Returned from overseas service and arrived at the San Francisco Port of Embarkation on 1 January 1946). Inactivated 3 January 1946 at Camp Stoneman, California. Allotted to the Regular Army on 14 May 1952. Activated 22 November 1952 at Fort Tilden, New York. Redesignated 3 August 1953 as the 505th Antiaircraft Artillery Battalion (Gun). Reorganized and redesignated 9 June 1954 as the 505th Antiaircraft Artillery Missile Battalion. Inactivated 1 September 1958 at Fort Tilden.

CAMPAIGN STREAMERS
World War II
Ryukyus

DECORATIONS
None

COAT OF ARMS

SHIELD: Gules, in bend a bird bolt enfiled with two concentric annulets (the map symbol for a military air base) or.

CREST: None

MOTTO: *Super Omnes* (Above All)

The colors scarlet and yellow are used for Artillery. The bird bolt, a type of arrow used for killing birds, symbolizes the antiaircraft mission of the organization. An air base in the Pacific was made possible by the capture of the Ryukyus; the map symbol represents the unit's service in that campaign.

DISTINCTIVE INSIGNIA

The insignia is the shield and motto of the coat of arms. The sample of the insignia depicted was approved for wear on 1 October 1953.

506th ANTIAIRCRAFT ARTILLERY MISSILE BATTALION

Constituted 25 February 1943 in the Army of the United States as the 506th Coast Artillery Battalion (Antiaircraft) (Gun) and activated 20 May 1943 at Camp Stewart, Georgia. Redesignated 7 June 1943 as the 506th Antiaircraft Artillery Gun Battalion. (Departed Seattle Port of Embarkation 17 June 1944 for overseas service; arrived in Hawaii on 25 June 1944 and landed on Iwo Jima, Volcano Islands on 25 February 1945). Inactivated 15 January 1946 on Iwo Jima. Allotted to the Regular Army on 19 November 1952. Activated 1 December 1952 at Logan Station, Philadelphia, Pennsylvania. Redesignated 24 July 1953 as the 506th Antiaircraft Artillery Battalion (Gun). Reorganized and redesignated 1 December 1954 as the 506th Antiaircraft Artillery Missile Battalion. Inactivated 1 September 1958 at Eureka, Pennsylvania.

CAMPAIGN STREAMERS
World War II
Air Offensive, Japan

DECORATIONS
Navy Unit Commendation, Streamer embroidered *IWO JIMA* (506th AAA Gun Bn cited for period 19-28 Feb 1945; DAGO 73, 1948)

COAT OF ARMS

SHIELD: Per fess abased or and barry wavy azure and argent, in chief the emblem of the city of Tokyo, gules.

CREST: None

MOTTO: *Volcani Vigor* (Strength Of Vulcan)

The emblem of the city of Tokyo – capital of Japan – represents the country as a whole and commemorates the service of the organization in that area during World War II. The field is red for Artillery. The blue and white wavy bars symbolize the Pacific Ocean around Iwo Jima where the organization was cited for extraordinary heroism.

DISTINCTIVE INSIGNIA
The insignia is the shield and motto of the coat of arms. The sample of the insignia depicted was approved for wear on 21 August 1953.

507th ANTIAIRCRAFT ARTILLERY BATTALION

Constituted 25 January 1943 in the Army of the United States as the 507th Coast Artillery Battalion (Antiaircraft) (Gun) and activated 20 May 1943 at Camp Stewart, Georgia. Redesignated 7 June 1943 as the 507th Antiaircraft Artillery Gun Battalion (Semimobile). (Departed San Francisco Port of Embarkation 12 July 1944 for overseas service; arrived in New Guinea on 31 July 1944 and moved to the Philippine Islands on 14 March 1945). Inactivated 5 April 1948 on Luzon, Philippine Islands. Redesignated 4 April 1949 as the 507th Antiaircraft Artillery Automatic Weapons Battalion. Activated 11 April 1949 at Otawa, Honshu, Japan. Allotted to the Regular Army 27 November 1951. Redesignated 25 November 1953 as the 507th Antiaircraft Artillery Battalion. Inactivated 22 June 1957 in Japan.

CAMPAIGN STREAMERS
World War II
New Guinea
Luzon

DECORATIONS
Philippine Presidential Unit Citation, Streamer embroidered *17 OCTOBER 1944 TO 4 JULY 1945* (507th AAA Gun Bn cited; DAGO 47, 1950)

COAT OF ARMS
SHIELD: Per chevron gules and or, in chief a Philippine sun and a Korean bell of the second; in base a falcon on a mailed fist of the first.

CREST: None

MOTTO: *Peto, Iacto, Deleo* (Seek–Strike–Destroy)

Red is the branch color for Artillery. The sun, taken from the Philippine flag, represents the service of the battalion in that area. Korea is noted for its bells, one of which is used to symbolize service in Korea. The falcon and the mailed fist signify the organization's striking power and the army's strength and guidance, respectively.

DISTINCTIVE INSIGNIA
The insignia is the shield and motto of the coat of arms. The sample of the insignia depicted was approved for wear on 5 June 1953.

508th ANTIAIRCRAFT ARTILLERY MISSILE BATTALION

Constituted 25 February 1943 in the Army of the United States as the 508th Coast Artillery Battalion (Antiaircraft) (Gun) and activated 20 May 1943 at Camp Stewart, Georgia. Redesignated 7 June 1943 as the 508th Antiaircraft Artillery Gun Battalion (Semimobile). (Departed San Francisco Port of Embarkation 14 June 1944 for overseas service; arrived in New Guinea on 12 July 1944 and landed in the Philippine Islands on 9 January 1945. Returned from overseas service and arrived at the San Francisco Port of Embarkation on 13 January 1946). Inactivated 15 January 1946 at Camp Stoneman, California. Redesignated 508th Antiaircraft Artillery Missile Battalion and allotted to the Regular Army on 28 January 1957. Activated 15 February 1957 at Lordstown, Ohio. Inactivated 1 September 1958 at Cleveland, Ohio.

CAMPAIGN STREAMERS
World War II
New Guinea
Luzon
Leyte

DECORATIONS
Philippine Presidential Unit Citation, Streamer embroidered *17 OCTOBER 1944 TO 4 JULY 1945* (508th AAA Gun Bn cited; DAGO 47, 1950)

COAT OF ARMS
SHIELD: Gules, a triple headed bird-bolt in bend or, a foot wavy azure, fimbriated of the second.

CREST: None

MOTTO: *Ancile Impervium* (Impervious Shield)

Scarlet and yellow are the colors used for Artillery. The three prongs of the bird-bolt allude to the battalion's three campaigns as an Antiaircraft Artillery Battalion. The wavy blue base represents the Pacific Ocean area in which these campaigns were fought.

DISTINCTIVE INSIGNIA

The insignia is the shield and motto of the coat of arms. Although the sample of the insignia depicted was approved for wear on 22 August 1958 it was never worn by this organization.

509th ANTIAIRCRAFT ARTILLERY MISSILE BATTALION

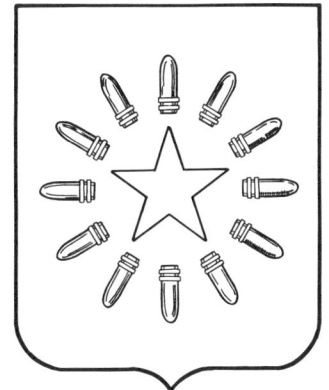 

Constituted 25 February 1943 in the Army of the United States as the 509th Antiaircraft Artillery Gun Battalion (Semimobile) and activated 10 June 1943 at Camp Edwards, Massachusetts. Inactivated 25 January 1945 at Camp Swift, Texas. (163d Antiaircraft Artillery Gun Battalion consolidated with the 509th Antiaircraft Artillery Gun Battalion on 2 February 1946). Allotted to the Regular Army and activated at Pittsburgh, Pennsylvania on 1 December 1952. Redesignated 24 July 1953 as the 509th Antiaircraft Artillery Battalion (Gun). Reorganized and redesignated 1 February 1955 as the 509th Antiaircraft Artillery Missile Battalion. Inactivated 1 September 1958 at Hickam, Pennsylvania.

CAMPAIGN STREAMERS
World War II
New Guinea (with arrowhead)
Luzon

DECORATIONS
Philippine Presidential Unit Citation, Streamer embroidered *17 OCTOBER 1944 TO 4 JULY 1945* (163d AAA Gun Bn cited; DAGO 47, 1950)

COAT OF ARMS
SHIELD: Gules, within a circle of twelve shells or, a mullet argent.

CREST: None

MOTTO: *Fidus Audax* (Faithful And Bold)

Scarlet and yellow are the colors used for Artillery. The functions of the organization are allegorically illustrated by the circle of shells denoting the organization as Artillery and being ready for action in any direction. The white star is symbolic of Texas, the place of activation.

DISTINCTIVE INSIGNIA
The insignia is the shield and motto of the coat of arms. The sample of the insignia depicted was approved for wear on 2 June 1954.

510th ANTIAIRCRAFT ARTILLERY GUN BATTALION

Constituted 25 February 1943 in the Army of the United States as the 510th Antiaircraft Artillery Gun Battalion (Semimobile) and activated 15 June 1943 at Camp Edwards, Massachusetts. (Departed San Francisco Port of Embarkation 27 June 1944 for overseas service; arrived in New Guinea on 20 July 1944 and landed in the Philippine Islands on 1 December 1944. Returned from overseas service and arrived at the Los Angeles Port of Embarkation on 17 January 1946). Inactivated 18 January 1946 at Camp Anza, Arlington, California. Allotted to the Regular Army, 19 July 1954.

CAMPAIGN STREAMERS
World War II
New Guinea
Leyte

DECORATIONS
Philippine Presidential Unit Citation, Streamer embroidered *17 OCTOBER 1944 TO 4 JULY 1945* (510th AAA Gun Bn cited; DAGO 47, 1950)

COAT OF ARMS
None

DISTINCTIVE INSIGNIA
None

511th ANTIAIRCRAFT ARTILLERY BATTALION

Constituted 25 February 1943 in the Army of the United States as the 511th Antiaircraft Artillery Gun Battalion (Semimobile) and activated 10 June 1943 at Camp Edwards, Massachusetts. Reorganized at Camp Pickett, Virginia and redesignated 1 May 1944 as the 808th Field Artillery Battalion (155mm Howitzer, Tractor Drawn). (Departed New York Port of Embarkation 24 September 1944 for overseas service; arrived in England on 30 September 1944 and landed in France on 3 October 1944. Returned from overseas service and arrived at the Hampton Roads Port of Embarkation on 23 October 1945). Inactivated 23 October 1945 at Camp Patrick Henry, Virginia. Allotted to the Organized Reserves and assigned to Seventh Army on 17 October 1946. Activated 28 October 1946 at Jacksonville, Florida. Released from Seventh Army and assigned to Third Army, 15 March 1947. (Organized Reserves redesignated 25 March 1948 as Organized Reserve Corps). Relocated to Gainesville, Florida on 1 January 1950. Inactivated 31 December 1950 at Gainesville. Redesignated 14 March 1952 as the 511th Antiaircraft Artillery Battalion.

CAMPAIGN STREAMERS
World War II
Rhineland
Central Europe

DECORATIONS
None

COAT OF ARMS
None

DISTINCTIVE INSIGNIA
None

511th ANTIAIRCRAFT ARTILLERY AUTOMATIC WEAPONS BATTALION

Constituted 13 August 1946 in the Regular Army as the 511th Antiaircraft Artillery Automatic Weapons Battalion (Philippine Scouts) and activated 28 December 1946 at Gufuki, Okinawa. Inactivated 1 May 1949 at Kubasaki, Okinawa. Disbanded 20 December 1951.

CAMPAIGN STREAMERS
None

DECORATIONS
None

COAT OF ARMS
None

DISTINCTIVE INSIGNIA
None

512th ANTIAIRCRAFT ARTILLERY GUN BATTALION

Constituted 25 February 1943 in the Army of the United States as the 512th Antiaircraft Artillery Gun Battalion (Semimobile) and activated 15 June 1943 at Camp Edwards, Massachusetts.

Redesignated 1 May 1944 as the 809th Field Artillery Battalion.

CAMPAIGN STREAMERS
None

DECORATIONS
None

COAT OF ARMS
None

DISTINCTIVE INSIGNIA
None

512th ANTIAIRCRAFT ARTILLERY GUN BATTALION

Constituted 13 August 1946 in the Regular Army as the 512th Antiaircraft Artillery Gun Battalion (Philippine Scouts) and activated 20 December 1946 at San Marcellino, Philippine Islands. Inactivated 30 April 1947 at Manila, Philippine Islands. Disbanded 20 December 1951.

CAMPAIGN STREAMERS
None

DECORATIONS
None

COAT OF ARMS
None

DISTINCTIVE INSIGNIA
None

513th ANTIAIRCRAFT ARTILLERY MISSILE BATTALION

Constituted 25 February 1943 in the Army of the United States as the 513th Antiaircraft Artillery Gun Battalion (Semimobile) and activated 10 June 1943 at Camp Edwards, Massachusetts. (Departed San Francisco Port of Embarkation 17 December 1944 for overseas service and arrived in the Philippine Islands on 2 January 1945). Inactivated 5 April 1946 in the Philippine Islands. Allotted to the Regular Army 19 November 1952. Activated 5 December 1952 at Fort Lawton, Washington. Redesignated 20 July 1953 as the 513th Antiaircraft Artillery Battalion (Gun). Reorganized and redesignated 20 December 1954 as the 513th Antiaircraft Artillery Missile Battalion. Inactivated 1 September 1958 at Poulsbo, Washington.

CAMPAIGN STREAMERS
World War II
Luzon
Leyte

DECORATIONS
Philippine Presidential Unit Citation, Streamer embroidered *17 OCTOBER 1944 TO 4 JULY 1945* (513th AAA Gun Bn cited; DAGO 47, 1950)

COAT OF ARMS
SHIELD: Gules, the Philippine sun or.

CREST: None

MOTTO: *Maximus Sub Soles* (Best Under The Sun)

The colors red and yellow are for Artillery. The Philippine sun represents combat service in that area.

DISTINCTIVE INSIGNIA
The insignia is the shield and motto of the coat of arms. The sample of the insignia depicted was approved for wear on 28 January 1954.

514th ANTIAIRCRAFT ARTILLERY MISSILE BATTALION

Constituted 25 February 1943 in the Army of the United States as the 514th Antiaircraft Artillery Gun Battalion (Semimobile) and activated 10 July 1943 at Camp Edwards, Massachusetts. (Departed Portland Sub Port of Embarkation 22 January 1945 for overseas service and arrived in Hawaii on 29 January 1945. After service on Eniwetok Island, Ulithi Island and Okinawa, returned from overseas service and arrived at the Los Angeles Port of Embarkation on 20 January 1946). Inactivated 21 January 1946 at Camp Anza, Arlington, California. Allotted to the Regular Army on 19 November 1952. Activated 26 December 1952 at Fort Banks, Massachusetts. Redesignated 3 August 1953 as the 514th Antiaircraft Artillery Battalion. Reorganized and redesignated 5 January 1955 as the 514th Antiaircraft Artillery Missile Battalion. Inactivated 1 September 1958 at Squantum, Massachusetts.

CAMPAIGN STREAMERS
World War II
Pacific Theater without inscription

DECORATIONS
None

COAT OF ARMS
SHIELD: Or, a palm tree issuing from a foot of the sea proper, in chief a mullet of eight points gules.

CREST: None

MOTTO: To Serve We Wait

The palm tree issuing from the sea symbolizes the Pacific Theater and represents the organization's service in that area during World War II. The eight-pointed star in Artillery red signifies a burst of flak, thus symbolizing the organization's function during its war service.

DISTINCTIVE INSIGNIA
The insignia is the shield and motto of the coat of arms. The sample of the insignia depicted was approved for wear on 6 January 1954.

516th ANTIAIRCRAFT ARTILLERY MISSILE BATTALION

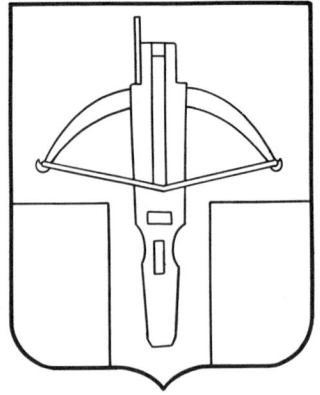 

Constituted 25 February 1943 in the Army of the United States as the 516th Antiaircraft Artillery Gun Battalion (Semimobile) and activated 1 October 1943 at Camp Haan, California. (Departed Portland Sub Port of Embarkation 22 January 1945 and arrived in Hawaii on 29 January 1945). Inactivated 30 November 1945 at Fort Weaver, Oahu, Territory of Hawaii. Allotted to the Regular Army and activated 5 January 1953 at Detroit, Michigan. Redesignated 24 July 1953 as the 516th Antiaircraft Artillery Battalion (Gun). Reorganized and redesignated 20 May 1954 as the 516th Antiaircraft Artillery Missile Battalion. Inactivated 1 September 1958 at Selfridge Air Force Base, Michigan.

CAMPAIGN STREAMERS
World War II
Pacific Theater without inscription

DECORATIONS
None

COAT OF ARMS
SHIELD: Per fess abased gules and or, a pale of the first; overall an arbalest of the second, garnished of the field.

CREST: None

MOTTO: *Protectae Vinemus* (We Come To Protect)

Red and yellow are used for Artillery organizations. The arbalest, a mechanical bow, alludes to the nature of the battalion.

DISTINCTIVE INSIGNIA
The insignia is the shield and motto of the coat of arms. The sample of the insignia depicted was approved for wear on 27 December 1954.

517th ANTIAIRCRAFT ARTILLERY GUN BATTALION

Constituted 25 February 1943 in the Army of the United States as the 517th Antiaircraft Artillery Gun Battalion (Semimobile) and activated 1 October 1943 at Camp Davis, North Carolina. Inactivated 27 December 1944 at Fort Jackson, South Carolina. Disbanded 20 December 1951.

CAMPAIGN STREAMERS
None

DECORATIONS
None

COAT OF ARMS
None

DISTINCTIVE INSIGNIA
None

518th ANTIAIRCRAFT ARTILLERY BATTALION

Constituted 25 February 1943 in the Army of the United States as the 518th Antiaircraft Artillery Gun Battalion (Semimobile) and activated 12 November 1943 in New Caledonia. Inactivated 15 February 1946 on Luzon, Philippine Islands. Allotted to the Regular Army 9 December 1948. Activated 15 January 1949 at Fort Bliss, Texas. Redesignated 20 July 1953 as the 518th Antiaircraft Artillery Battalion (Gun). Inactivated 20 December 1957 at Camp Hanford, Washington.

CAMPAIGN STREAMERS
World War II
Luzon

DECORATIONS
Philippine Presidential Unit Citation, Streamer embroidered *17 OCTOBER 1944 TO 4 JULY 1945* (518th AAA Gun Bn cited; DAGO 47, 1950)

COAT OF ARMS
SHIELD: Gules, on a pile or a sea-lion sejant-erect of the field.

CREST: None

MOTTO: *Tonans* (Thunderer)

The colors red and yellow are those of Artillery. The pile represents a searchlight beam and the traditional sea-lion from the coat of arms of Manila indicates the World War II service in the Philippine Islands.

DISTINCTIVE INSIGNIA
The insignia is the shield and motto of the coat of arms. The sample of the insignia depicted was approved for wear on 13 March 1950.

519th ANTIAIRCRAFT ARTILLERY BATTALION

Constituted 25 February 1943 in the Army of the United States as the 519th Antiaircraft Artillery Gun Battalion (Semimobile) and activated 1 June 1943 at the Teaneck Armory, West Englewood, New Jersey. (Departed New York Port of Embarkation 27 February 1944 for overseas service; arrived in England on 9 March 1944 and landed in France on 9 July 1944). Inactivated 6 May 1946 in France. Allotted to the Regular Army 9 December 1948. Activated 15 January 1949 at Fort Bliss, Texas. Redesignated 20 July 1953 as the 519th Antiaircraft Artillery Battalion (Gun). Inactivated 20 December 1957 at Camp Hanford, Washington.

CAMPAIGN STREAMERS
World War II
Normandy
Northern France
Rhineland

DECORATIONS
Belgian Fourragere 1940 (519th AAA Gun Bn cited; DAGO 43, 1950)

Cited in the Order of the Day of the Belgian Army for action at *ANTWERP* (519th AAA Gun Bn cited for period 25 Oct-28 Nov 1944; DAGO 43, 1950)

Cited in the Order of the Day of the Belgian Army for action at *ANTWERP HARBOR* (519th AAA Gun Bn cited for action on 16 Dec 1944; DAGO 43, 1950)

COAT OF ARMS
SHIELD: Gules, on a pile or a fleur-de-lis of the first and a bunch of blue grapes in pale proper.

CREST: None

MOTTO: To Hold The High Road

The colors red and yellow are those for Artillery. The pile represents a searchlight beam while the fleur-de-lis and grapes symbolize the World War II service in France and the Rhineland.

DISTINCTIVE INSIGNIA
The insignia is the shield and motto of the coat of arms. The sample of the insignia depicted was approved for wear on 12 April 1950.

520th COAST ARTILLERY BATTALION

Constituted 1 July 1924 in the Regular Army as the 1st Battalion, 3d Coast Artillery (Harbor Defense) and organized from former companies of the 3d Regiment of Artillery as follows:

Headquarters, 1st Battalion (subsequently Headquarters and Headquarters Battery, 1st Battalion) constituted new and activated 3 January 1941 in the Harbor Defenses of Los Angeles

25th Company, Coast Artillery Corps (constituted 11 January 1812 in the Regular Army as a company in the 3d Regiment of Artillery and organized at Sacket's Harbor, New York during July 1812 as Captain Roger Jones' Company, 3d Regiment of Artillery; redesignated as Captain A. C. W. Fanning's Company, 3d Regiment of Artillery in February 1814; redesignated 12 May 1814 as Captain A. C. W. Fanning's Company, Corps of Artillery; redesignated 17 May 1815 as Captain Roger Jones' Company, Corps of Artillery, Northern Division; redesignated 17 June 1816 as Company E, 3d Battalion, Corps of Artillery, Northern Division; redesignated 1 June 1821 as Company A, 3d Regiment of Artillery; redesignated 13 February 1901 as 25th Company, Coast Artillery, Artillery Corps; redesignated 2 February 1907 as 25th Company, Coast Artillery Corps; redesignated 2d Company, Fort Miley [California] in July 1916; redesignated 31 August 1917 as 19th Company, Coast Defenses of San Francisco; redesignated 25 October 1918 as Battery C, 18th Artillery [Coast Artillery Corps]; redesignated 2 December 1918 as 19th Company, Coast Defenses of San Francisco; and redesignated 1 June 1922 as 25th Company, Coast Artillery Corps), redesignated Battery A; inactivated 1 March 1930 at San Pedro, California and activated 1 July 1939 at Fort MacArthur, California

26th Company, Coast Artillery Corps (constituted 9 May 1794 in the Regular Army as a company in the Corps of Artillerists and Engineers and organized 7 August 1794 at Fort Johnston as Captain Michael Kalteisen's Company, Corps of Artillerists and Engineers; redesignated 3 March 1799 as Captain Michael Kalteisen's Company, 1st Regiment of Artillerists and Engineers; redesignated 1 June 1802 as Captain Michael Kalteisen's Company, Regiment of Artillerists; redesignated Captain George Peters' Company, Regiment of Artillerists in 1807; redesignated Captain Clarence Mulford's Company, Regiment of Artillerists in 1808; redesignated Lieutenant William Laval's Company, Regiment of Artillerists in 1811; redesignated Captain William Wilson's Company, 1st Regiment of Artillery in 1812; redesignated 12 May 1814 as Captain William Wilson's Company, Corps of Artillery; redesignated 17 May 1815 as Captain William Wilson's Company, Corps of Artillery, Southern Division; redesignated 21 August 1816 as Company B, 2d Battalion, Corps of Artillery. Southern Division; redesignated 1 June 1821 as Company B, 3d Regiment of Artillery; redesignated 13 February 1901 as 26th Company, Coast Artillery, Artillery Corps; redesignated 2 February 1907 as 26th Company, Coast Artillery Corps; redesignated 16 July 1916 as 1st Company, Fort Flager [Washington]; redesignated 31 August 1917 as 13th Company, Coast Defenses of Puget Sound; and redesignated 1 June 1922 as 26th Company, Coast Artillery Corps), redesignated Battery B; inactivated 1 March 1930 and activated 1 July 1940, both at Fort MacArthur

31st Company, Coast Artillery Corps (constituted 11 January 1812 in the Regular Army as a company in the 2d Regiment of Artillery and organized at Petersburg, Virginia later that year as Captain George W. Russell's Company, 2d Regiment of Artillery; redesignated 12 May 1814 as Captain John Peyton's Company, Corps of Artillery; redesignated 17 May 1815 as Captain John Peyton's Company, Corps of Artillery, Southern Division; redesignated Captain Hippolite H. Villard's Company, Corps of Artillery, Southern Division in 1815; redesignated Captain Ethan A. Allen's Company, Corps of Artillery, Southern Division early in 1816; redesignated 21 August 1816 as Company O, 2d Battalion, Corps of Artillery, Southern Division; redesignated 1 June 1821 as Company I, 3d Regiment of Artillery; redesignated 13 February 1901 as 31st Company, Coast Artillery, Artillery Corps; redesignated 2 February 1907 as 31st Company, Coast Artillery Corps; redesignated 20 July 1916 as 2d Company, Fort Caswell [North Carolina]; redesignated 24 July 1917 as Battery L, 8th Provisional Regiment, Coast Artillery Corps; redesignated 5 February 1918 as Battery L, 53d Artillery, Coast Artillery Corps; redesignated 15 July 1918 as Battery E, 53d Artillery, Coast Artillery Corps; and redesignated 1 June 1922 as 31st Company, Coast Artillery Corps), redesignated Battery C;

inactivated at San Diego, California and activated 2 December 1940 at Fort Rosecrans, California

27th Company, Coast Artillery Corps (constituted 9 May 1794 in the Regular Army as 4th Company, 2d Battalion, Corps of Artillerists and Engineers and organized later that year as Captain Donald G. Mitchell's Company, 2d Battalion, Corps of Artillerists and Engineers; redesignated as Captain Nehemiah Freeman's Company, Corps of Artillerists and Engineers in August 1798; redesignated 3 March 1799 as Captain Nehemiah Freeman's Company, 1st Regiment of Artillerists and Engineers; redesignated 16 March 1802 as Captain Richard S. Blackburn's Company, Regiment of Artillerists; redesignated 30 April 1803 as Captain John Saunders' Company, Regiment of Artillerists; redesignated 3 June 1809 as Captain William Wilson's Company, Regiment of Artillerists; redesignated 11 January 1812 as Captain William Wilson's Company, 1st Regiment of Artillery; redesignated 29 February 1812 as Captain Hannibal M. Allen's Company, 1st Regiment of Artillery; redesignated 16 August 1813 as Captain Hopley Yeaton's Company, 1st Regiment of Artillery; redesignated 12 May 1814 as Captain Hopley Yeaton's Company, Corps of Artillery; redesignated 17 May 1815 as Captain Hopley Yeaton's Company, Corps of Artillery, Southern Division; redesignated 21 August 1816 as Company K, 2d Battalion, Corps of Artillery, Southern Division; redesignated 1 June 1821 as Company D, 3d Regiment of Artillery; redesignated 13 February 1901 as 27th Company, Coast Artillery, Artillery Corps; redesignated 2 February 1907 as 27th Company, Coast Artillery Corps; redesignated as 7th Company, Fort Winfield Scott [California] in July 1916; redesignated 31 August 1917 as 7th Company, Coast Defenses of San Francisco; redesignated 22 December 1917 as 4th Antiaircraft Battery; demobilized 22 January 1919 at Fort Totten, New York; reconstituted and consolidated with active 3d Company, Coast Defenses of Los Angeles [organized 1 February 1918] and redesignated 27th Company, Coast Artillery Corps, 1 June 1922), redesignated Battery D; inactivated 1 February 1940 at Fort Rosecrans, activated 2 December 1940 at Fort MacArthur, inactivated 1 October 1942 at Fort MacArthur, and disbanded 18 October 1944.

Reorganized and redesignated 18 October 1944 as 520th Coast Artillery Battalion (Harbor Defense). Redesignated 1 December 1944 as the 3d Coast Artillery Battalion (Harbor Defense).

CAMPAIGN STREAMERS

War of 1812
Streamer without inscription

Indian Wars
Seminoles
Washington 1858

Mexican War
Monterey
Vera Cruz
Cerro Gordo

Civil War
Streamer without inscription

Chinese Relief Expedition
Streamer without inscription

Philippine Insurrection
Streamer without inscription

DECORATIONS
None

DECORATIONS
None

COAT OF ARMS
None

DISTINCTIVE INSIGNIA
None

521st COAST ARTILLERY BATTALION

Constituted 1 July 1924 in the Regular Army as 2d Battalion, 3d Coast Artillery (Harbor Defense) and organized from former companies of the 3d Regiment of Artillery as follows:

Headquarters (subsequently Headquarters and Headquarters Battery), 2d Battalion constituted new and organized 2 December 1940 in the Harbor Defenses of Los Angeles

28th Company, Coast Artillery Corps (constituted 27 April 1798 in the Regular Army as a company in the 2d Regiment of Artillerists and Engineers and organized as Captain John Lillie's Company, 2d Regiment of Artillerists and Engineers the following year; redesignated 1 April 1802 as Captain George Izard's Company, Regiment of Artillerists; redesignated as Captain Howell Cobb's Company, Regiment of Artillerists in June 1803; redesignated 1 February 1806 as Captain William Yate's Company, Regiment of Artillerists; redesignated as Captain Addison B. Armistead's Company, Regiment of Artillerists in 1807; redesignated 11 January 1812 as Captain Addison B. Armistead's Company, 2d Regiment of Artillery; redesignated 13 February 1813 as Lieutenant Adrian Niel's Company, Corps of Artillery, Southern Division; redesignated 21 August 1816 as Company I, 1st Battalion, Corps of Artillery, Southern Division; redesignated 1 June 1821 as Company E, 3d Regiment of Artillery; redesignated 13 February 1901 as 28th Company, Coast Artillery, Artillery Corps; redesignated 2 February 1907 as 28th Company, Coast Artillery Corps; redesignated 12 July 1916 as 1st Company, Fort Rosecrans [California]; redesignated 31 August 1917 as 1st Company, Coast Defenses of San Diego [2d Company, Coast Defenses of San Diego consolidated 13 October 1919 with 1st Company, Coast Defenses of San Diego]; and redesignated 1 June 1922 as 28th Company, Coast Artillery Corps), redesignated Battery E

34th Company, Coast Artillery Corps (constituted 3 March 1847 in the Regular Army as Company M, 3d Regiment of Artillery and organized 1 October 1847; redesignated 13 February 1901 as 34th Company, Coast Artillery, Artillery Corps; redesignated 2 February 1907 as 34th Company, Coast Artillery Corps; redesignated 1st Company, Fort Stevens [Oregon] in July 1916; redesignated 31 August 1917 as 1st Company, Coast Defenses of the Columbia; and redesignated 1 June 1922 as 34th Company, Coast Artillery Corps), redesignated Battery F and inactivated at Fort Stevens; activated 1 July 1939 at Fort Stevens, inactivated 1 February 1940 at Fort Stevens and activated 2 December 1940 at Fort MacArthur

35th Company, Coast Artillery Corps (constituted 2 March 1899 in the Regular Army as Company N, 3d Regiment of Artillery and organized at Angel Island, California during April 1899; redesignated 13 February 1901 as 35th Company, Coast Artillery, Coast Artillery Corps; redesignated 2 February 1907 as 35th Company, Coast Artillery Corps; redesignated 1 July 1916 as 1st Company, Fort Monroe [Virginia]; redesignated 31 August 1917 as 1st Company, Coast Defenses of Chesapeake Bay; and redesignated 1 June 1922 as 35th Company, Coast Artillery Corps), redesignated Battery G and inactivated at Fort Monroe; activated 1 June 1941 at Los Angeles, inactivated 29 August 1941 at Los Angeles and activated 14 February 1942 at Fort MacArthur

Reorganized and redesignated 18 October 1944 as 521st Coast Artillery Battalion (Harbor Defense). Disbanded 15 September 1945 at Fort MacArthur.

Reconstituted 28 June 1950 in the Regular Army as the 18th Antiaircraft Artillery Battalion.

CAMPAIGN STREAMERS
None

DECORATIONS
None

COAT OF ARMS
None

DISTINCTIVE INSIGNIA
None

522d COAST ARTILLERY BATTALION

Constituted 1 July 1924 in the Regular Army as 3d Battalion, 3d Coast Artillery (Harbor Defense) and organized 14 February 1942 at Fort MacArthur, California with Batteries H, I, and K which were constituted 1 September 1935 in the Regular Army. Reorganized and redesignated 18 October 1944 as the 522d Coast Artillery Battalion (Harbor Defense). Disbanded 15 September 1945 at Huntington Beach, California.

Reconstituted 28 June 1950 and consolidated with the 43d Antiaircraft Artillery Automatic Weapons Battalion.

CAMPAIGN STREAMERS
None

DECORATIONS
None

COAT OF ARMS
None

DISTINCTIVE INSIGNIA
None

523d ANTIAIRCRAFT ARTILLERY AUTOMATIC WEAPONS BATTALION

Constituted 30 June 1924 in the Organized Reserves as 2d Battalion, 625th Coast Artillery (Harbor Defense) and allotted to the Ninth Corps Area. Organized at San Diego, California during July 1924. Withdrawn from the Organized Reserves and allotted to the Regular Army on 1 September 1935. Redesignated 1 February 1940 as 2d Battalion, 19th Coast Artillery (Harbor Defense). Activated 3 January 1941 at Fort Rosecrans, California in the Harbor Defenses of San Diego. Reorganized and redesignated 18 October 1944 as the 523d Coast Artillery Battalion (Harbor Defense). Disbanded 15 September 1945 at Fort Rosecrans. Reconstituted 2 December 1946 in the Organized Reserves as the 523d Antiaircraft Artillery Automatic Weapons Battalion. (Organized Reserves redesignated 25 March 1948 as Organized Reserve Corps).

Consolidated 28 June 1950 with the 35th Antiaircraft Aircraft Gun Battalion.

CAMPAIGN STREAMERS
None

DECORATIONS
None

COAT OF ARMS
None

DISTINCTIVE INSIGNIA
None

HEADQUARTERS AND HEADQUARTERS DETACHMENT 524th COAST ARTILLERY BATTALION

Constituted 5 July 1946 as Headquarters and Headquarters Detachment, 524th Coast Artillery Battalion (Harbor Defense) and allotted to the Washington National Guard. Organized and Federally recognized 24 February 1948 at Bellingham.

Converted and redesignated 1 October 1949 as Medical Detachment, 240th Antiaircraft Artillery Gun Battalion.

CAMPAIGN STREAMERS
None

DECORATIONS
None

COAT OF ARMS
None

DISTINCTIVE INSIGNIA
None

HEADQUARTERS AND HEADQUARTERS DETACHMENT 525th COAST ARTILLERY BATTALION

Constituted 5 July 1946 as Headquarters and Headquarters Detachment, 525th Coast Artillery Battalion (Harbor Defense) and allotted to the National Guard of the State of Washington. Withdrawn from allotment to the Washington Army National Guard on 1 May 1949 and returned to Department of the Army control.

CAMPAIGN STREAMERS
None

DECORATIONS
None

COAT OF ARMS
None

DISTINCTIVE INSIGNIA
None

526th ANTIAIRCRAFT ARTILLERY MISSILE BATTALION

Constituted 2 May 1918 in the Regular Army as 1st Battalion, 71st Artillery (Coast Artillery Corps) and organized 12 May 1918 at Forts Strong and Andrews in the Coast Defenses of Boston. Demobilized 6 March 1919 at Camp Devens, Massachusetts. Reconstituted in the Regular Army as 1st Battalion, 71st Coast Artillery (Antiaircraft) (Semimobile) and activated at

Fort Story, Virginia, 1 July 1940. Reorganized at Washington, District of Columbia and redesignated 1 September 1943 as the 71st Antiaircraft Artillery Gun Battalion. (Batteries A, B, and C inactivated 26 December 1944 at Camp Gruber, Oklahoma). Reorganized with new batteries and redesignated 10 January 1945 as the 526th Antiaircraft Artillery Composite Battalion. Reorganized and redesignated 1 September 1945 as the 526th Antiaircraft Artillery Gun Battalion. Redesignated 3 August 1953 as the 526th Antiaircraft Artillery Battalion. Reorganized and redesignated 13 February 1954 as the 526th Antiaircraft Artillery Missile Battalion. Inactivated 1 September 1958 at Fort Hancock, New Jersey.

Consolidated 31 July 1959 with the 71st Artillery, a parent regiment under the Combat Arms Regimental System.

CAMPAIGN STREAMERS
World War I
Streamer without inscription

DECORATIONS
None

COAT OF ARMS
SHIELD: Or, on a canton gules a hurte fimbriated argent bearing three mullets, two and one of the like.

CREST: None

MOTTO: *Die et Nocte Vigilari* (Watchful Night And Day)

The shield, which bears the coat of arms of the former 504th Coast Artillery in the canton, indicates the descent of the 526th Antiaircraft Artillery Missile Battalion from that organization.

DISTINCTIVE INSIGNIA
The insignia is the shield and motto of the coat of arms. The sample of the insignia depicted was approved for wear on 1 May 1951.

527th ANTIAIRCRAFT ARTILLERY AUTOMATIC WEAPONS BATTALION

Constituted in the Louisiana National Guard as 2d Battalion 204th Coast Artillery (Antiaircraft) and organized from new and existing units as follows:

Headquarters, 2d Battalion 156th Infantry (organized and Federally recognized 7 July 1922 at New Iberia; relocated to New Orleans 30 August 1924 and relocated to Shreveport on 1 November 1931), redesignated 15 December 1939 as Headquarters, 2d Battalion

Service Company 156th Infantry (organized and Federally recognized 5 July 1922 at Monroe), redesignated 15 December 1939 as Headquarters Battery, 2d Battalion

Company H 156th Infantry (organized and Federally recognized 24 July 1925 at Minden), redesignated 21 December 1939 as Battery E

Company F 156th Infantry (organized 2 August 1909 at Ruston as Company F 1st Infantry, Louisiana National Guard; mustered into Federal service 25 June 1916 at Camp Stafford, Louisiana; mustered out at Camp Stafford 25 September 1916 and resumed State status; mustered into Federal service 10 April 1917 at Camp Nicholls, Louisiana and drafted into Federal service 5 August 1917; redesignated 27 September 1917 as Company F 156th Infantry and assigned to the 39th Division; demobilized 23 January 1919 at Camp Beauregard, Louisiana; reorganized and Federally recognized 25 January 1922 at Ruston as Company L 156th Infantry; and redesignated 1 May 1929 as Company F 156th Infantry), redesignated Battery F

Company G 156th Infantry (organized 24 August 1892 at Monroe as Company C 2d Battalion of Infantry, Louisiana National Guard and redesignated Company B 1st Infantry, Louisiana National Guard in 1897; mustered into Federal service 18 May 1898 at New Orleans as Company B 1st Louisiana Volunteer Infantry; mustered out 3 October 1898 at Jacksonville, Florida; reorganized 8 August 1899 at Monroe as Company D 1st Separate Battalion of Infantry, Louisiana National Guard; redesignated 6 December 1904 as Company D 1st Infantry, Louisiana National Guard; mustered into Federal service 25 June 1916 at Camp Stafford for Mexican border; mustered out 25 September 1916 at Camp Stafford and resumed State status; mustered into Federal service 10 April 1917 at Camp Nicholls and drafted into Federal service 5 August 1917; redesignated 27 September 1917 as Company D 156th Infantry and assigned to the 39th Division; demobilized 23 January 1919 at Camp Beauregard; reorganized and Federally recognized 9 December 1921 at Monroe as Company G, Infantry, Louisiana National Guard; and redesignated 4 August 1922 as Company G 156th Infantry), redesignated 26 December 1939 as Battery G

Headquarters Company 2d Battalion 156th Infantry (organized and Federally recognized 14 June 1921 at Natchidoches as 1st Separate Company of Infantry, Louisiana National Guard and redesignated 3 November 1921 as Company C 156th Infantry; redesignated 3 July 1922 as Headquarters Company 3d Battalion 156th Infantry and redesignated 1 May 1929 as Headquarters Company 2d Battalion 156th Infantry) redesignated 15 December 1939 as Battery H

Inducted into Federal service 6 January 1941 at home stations. Reorganized at San Diego, California and redesignated 10 September 1943 as 527th Antiaircraft Artillery Automatic Weapons Battalion (Semimobile). Inactivated 1 December 1944 at Camp Livingston, Louisiana.

Redesignated 27 May 1946 as 3d Battalion, 199th Infantry.

CAMPAIGN STREAMERS
World War I
Streamer without inscription

DECORATIONS
None

COAT OF ARMS
None

DISTINCTIVE INSIGNIA
None

527th ANTIAIRCRAFT ARTILLERY BATTALION

Constituted 27 May 1946 in the Louisiana National Guard as the 527th Antiaircraft Artillery Automatic Weapons Battalion. Redesignated 17 June 1946 as the 527th Antiaircraft Artillery Searchlight Battalion. Redesignated 1 December 1947 as the 527th Antiaircraft Artillery Gun Battalion and organized from new and existing units as follows:

Headquarters, 3d Squadron 108th Cavalry (organized and Federally recognized 15 March 1929 at New Orleans; consolidated 6 October 1940 with Headquarters, 105th Separate Battalion, Coast Artillery [Antiaircraft]; inducted into Federal service 6 January 1941 at New Orleans; redesignated 10 July 1942 as Headquarters, 105th Coast Artillery Battalion [Antiaircraft] [Automatic Weapons]; departed New York Port of Embarkation 5 August 1942 for overseas service; arrived in England 17 August 1942, moved to Scotland 24 September 1942 and landed in North Africa on 8 November 1942; arrived in Sicily on 11 July 1943 and moved to Italy on 15 September 1943; redesignated 1 July 1944 as Headquarters, 105th Antiaircraft Artillery Automatic Weapons Battalion [Self Propelled]; inactivated in Italy on 15 September 1945; withdrawn from consolidation with Headquarters, 105th Antiaircraft Artillery Automatic Weapons Battalion and redesignated 27 May 1946 as Headquarters and Headquarters Battery), reorganized and Federally recognized 23 May 1949 at New Orleans

Battery A 105th Antiaircraft Artillery Automatic Weapons Battalion (organized and Federally recognized 3 August 1924 at New Orleans as Service Troop 108th Cavalry; redesignated 15 March 1929 as Troop I 108th Cavalry; converted, reorganized and redesignated 6 October 1940 as Battery A 105th Separate Battalion, Coast Artillery [Antiaircraft]; inducted into Federal service 6 January 1941 at New Orleans; redesignated 10 July 1942 as Battery A 105th Coast Artillery Battalion; redesignated 1 July 1944 as Battery A 105th Antiaircraft Artillery Automatic Weapons Battalion; inactivated 15 September 1945 in Italy), reorganized and Federally recognized 23 May 1949 at New Orleans as Battery A

Battery B 105th Antiaircraft Artillery Automatic Weapons Battalion (organized and Federally recognized 6 October 1940 at New Orleans; inducted into Federal service 6 January 1941 at New Orleans; redesignated 10 July 1942 as Battery B 105th Coast Artillery Battalion; redesignated 1 July 1944 as Battery B 105th Antiaircraft Artillery Automatic Weapons

Battalion; inactivated 15 September 1945 in Italy), reorganized and Federally recognized 23 May 1949 at New Orleans as Battery B

Batteries C and D organized new and Federally recognized 23 May 1949 at New Orleans

Medical Department Detachment 105th Antiaircraft Artillery Automatic Weapons Battalion (organized and Federally recognized 24 June 1927 at New Orleans as Medical Department Detachment 108th Cavalry; redesignated in part as Medical Department Detachment 105th Separate Battalion, Coast Artillery [Antiaircraft] on 12 October 1940; inducted into Federal service 6 January 1941 at New Orleans; redesignated 10 July 1942 as Medical Department Detachment, 105th Coast Artillery Battalion; redesignated 1 July 1944 as Medical Department Detachment, 105th Antiaircraft Artillery Automatic Weapons Battalion; inactivated 15 September 1945 in Italy), reorganized and Federally recognized 23 May 1949 at New Orleans as Medical Department Detachment

Reorganized and redesignated 1 October 1949 as the 527th Antiaircraft Artillery Automatic Weapons Battalion. Reorganized and redesignated 1 October 1952 as the 527th Antiaircraft Artillery Gun Battalion. Redesignated 1 October 1953 as the 527th Antiaircraft Artillery Battalion (90mm Gun).

Consolidated 1 July 1959 with the 141st Artillery, a parent regiment under the Combat Arms Regimental System.

CAMPAIGN STREAMERS
World War I
Streamer without inscription

World War II
Algeria-French Morocco (with arrowhead)
Tunisia
Sicily (with arrowhead)
Naples-Foggia
Rome-Arno
North Apennines
Po Valley

DECORATIONS
French Croix de Guerre with Palm, World War II, Streamer embroidered *KASSERINE* (105th CA Bn cited for period 1 Jan-30 Apr 1943; DAGO 65, 1955)

COAT OF ARMS
SHIELD: Gules on a chevron cottised or a broken Lictor's axe of the field.

CREST: That for the regiments and separate battalions of the Louisiana Army National Guard: On a wreath of the colors (or and gules) a pelican in her piety affronte with three young in nest argent, armed and vulned proper.

MOTTO: Let There Be Fire

The colors red and yellow are for Artillery. The chevron with the broken Lictor's axe is symbolic of the defeat and collapse of Italy and its colonies. The chevron is suggestive of the arrowhead and the two cottises allude specifically to the two assault landings in the Mediterranean Theater during World War II.

DISTINCTIVE INSIGNIA
The insignia is the shield and motto of the coat of arms. The sample of the insignia depicted was approved for wear on 25 June 1954.

528th ARTILLERY BATTALION

Constituted 31 March 1924 in the Organized Reserves as the 528th Artillery Battalion, Coast Artillery Corps (Fixed Defenses), allotted to the First Corps area and assigned to the Harbor Defenses of Long Island Sound.

Redesignated 30 June 1924 as the 618th Coast Artillery Battalion (Harbor Defenses).

CAMPAIGN STREAMERS
None

DECORATIONS
None

COAT OF ARMS
None

DISTINCTIVE INSIGNIA
None

528th ANTIAIRCRAFT ARTILLERY GUN BATTALION

Constituted 1 October 1939 as 1st Battalion, 214th Coast Artillery (Antiaircraft) and allotted to the Georgia National Guard. Organized and Federally recognized 20 October 1939 with Headquarters, Headquarters Battery and Combat Train at Thomson and batteries at Augusta, Milledgeville, Monroe and Statesboro. Inducted into Federal service 25 November 1940 at home stations. (Departed San Francisco Port of Embarkation 24 September 1942 for overseas service; arrived in New Zealand 6 October 1942, moved to New Caledonia 27 November 1942 and landed on Guadalcanal on 30 January 1943). Reorganized on Guadalcanal and redesignated 11 November 1943 as 528th Antiaircraft Artillery Gun Battalion (Semimobile). (Returned to New Zealand 10 January 1944; moved to New Guinea 22 June 1944 and then to Morotai Island on 1 October 1944). Returned from overseas service and inactivated 28 December 1945 at Camp Stoneman, California.

Consolidated 19 July 1946 with the 101st Antiaircraft Artillery Automatic Weapons Battalion.

CAMPAIGN STREAMERS
World War II
Guadalcanal
New Guinea

DECORATIONS
None

COAT OF ARMS
None

DISTINCTIVE INSIGNIA
None

529th ANTIAIRCRAFT ARTILLERY AUTOMATIC WEAPONS BATTALION

Constituted in the Regular Army as 2d Battalion, 69th Artillery (Coast Artillery Corps) and organized 17 May 1918 at Fort Worden, Washington. Demobilized 5 March 1919 at Camp Eustis, Virginia. Reconstituted 22 January 1926 in the Regular Army as 2d Battalion, 69th Coast

Artillery (Antiaircraft). Activated 4 October 1939 at Fort Crockett, Texas; inactivated 1 February 1940 at Fort Crockett and activated 1 June 1940 at Fort Monroe, Virginia. Reorganized and redesignated 10 September 1943 as the 529th Antiaircraft Artillery Automatic Weapons Battalion. Inactivated 5 September 1945 at Fort Bliss, Texas. Activated 11 July 1946 at Fort Bliss; inactivated 4 January 1947 at Fort Bliss.

Redesignated 28 June 1950 as the 86th Antiaircraft Artillery Battalion.

CAMPAIGN STREAMERS
World War I
Streamer without inscription

DECORATIONS
None

COAT OF ARMS
None

DISTINCTIVE INSIGNIA
None

530th ANTIAIRCRAFT ARTILLERY AUTOMATIC WEAPONS BATTALION

Organized in the Washington National Guard as the 2d Battalion, 205th Coast Artillery (Antiaircraft) and Federally recognized 22 November 1939 with Headquarters at Olympia and batteries at Centralia, Kelso, Tacoma and Wenatchee. Inducted into Federal service 3 February 1941 at home stations. Reorganized at Santa Monica, California and redesignated 10 September 1943 as the 530th Antiaircraft Artillery Automatic Weapons Battalion. (Departed New York Port of Embarkation 16 December 1944 for overseas service and arrived in Scotland 21 December 1944; moved to England 23 December 1944 and landed in France on 8 March 1945. Returned from overseas service and arrived at the New York Port of Embarkation on 2 November 1945). Inactivated 3 November 1945 at Camp Shanks, New York.

Broken up 5 July 1946 and elements redesignated as follows: Headquarters Battery redesignated Battery C, 700th Antiaircraft Artillery Automatic Weapons Battalion; Battery C redesignated Battery D, 530th Antiaircraft Artillery Automatic Weapons Battalion; and Battery D redesignated Company G, 161st Infantry.

CAMPAIGN STREAMERS
World War II
Rhineland
Central Europe

DECORATIONS
None

COAT OF ARMS
None

DISTINCTIVE INSIGNIA
None

530th ANTIAIRCRAFT ARTILLERY BATTALION

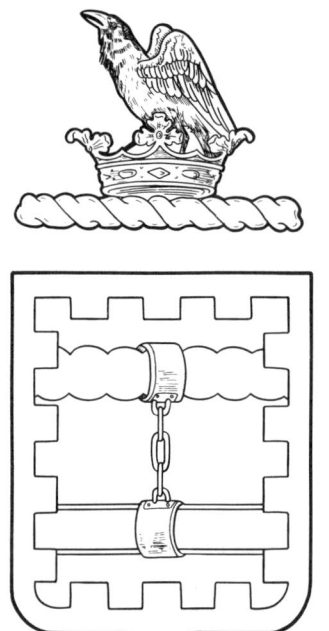

Constituted in the Washington National Guard as the 2d Battalion, 148th Field Artillery and organized from new and existing units at Tacoma as follows:

Headquarters organized new and Federally recognized 5 November 1930

Battery D organized new and Federally recognized 4 November 1930

Headquarters Battery, 146th Field Artillery (organized and Federally recognized 28 April 1921 at Tacoma as Headquarters Battery, Field Artillery, Washington National Guard; redesignated 1 May 1921 as Headquarters Battery, 146th Field Artillery), redesignated 1 February 1927 as Battery E

Battery F, 146th Field Artillery (organized and Federally recognized 30 September 1918 at Tacoma as Company F, 3d Infantry, Washington National Guard; redesignated 1 April 1921 as Battery F, Field Artillery, Washington National Guard; redesignated 1 May 1921 as Battery F, 146th Field Artillery), redesignated 1 February 1927 as Battery F

Reorganized and redesignated 3 September 1940 as 2d Battalion, 248th Coast Artillery (Harbor Defense). Inducted into Federal service 16 September 1940 at Tacoma. Inactivated 8 May 1944 at Camp Barkeley, Texas. Disbanded 14 June 1944. Reconstituted 25 August 1945 in the Washington National Guard. Redesignated 5 July 1946 as the 530th Antiaircraft Artillery Automatic Weapons Battalion. Reorganized and Federally recognized 14 April 1947 at Tacoma. Redesignated 1 October 1953 as the 530th Antiaircraft Artillery Battalion (Automatic Weapons) (Mobile). Reorganized and redesignated 1 January 1956 as the 530th Antiaircraft Artillery Battalion (75mm Gun).

Broken up 15 April 1959 and elements converted, reorganized and redesignated as follows: Headquarters and Headquarters Battery and Medical Detachment consolidated and redesignated 783d Transportation Company (Floating Craft Depot Maintenance); Batteries A and B consolidated, reorganized and redesignated Company D, 2d Battle Group, 161st Infantry and Battery C redesignated 506th Transportation Company (Harbor Craft).

CAMPAIGN STREAMERS
None

DECORATIONS
None

COAT OF ARMS
SHIELD: Gules, in chief a bar invected argent coupled by a fetterlock or to a bar in base vert fimbriated of the third, all within a bordure embattled of the last.

CREST: That for the regiments and separate battalions of the Washington State Army National Guard: On a wreath of the colors (or and gules) a raven with wings endorsed issuing out of a ducal coronet, all proper.

MOTTO: *Alta Peten* (Aiming At High Things)

The shield is that for the old 205th Coast Artillery within an embattled border.

DISTINCTIVE INSIGNIA
The insignia is the shield, crest and motto of the coat of arms. The sample of the insignia depicted was approved for wear on 11 September 1952.

531st ANTIAIRCRAFT ARTILLERY MISSILE BATTALION

Constituted 6 July 1942 in the Army of the United States as the 531st Coast Artillery Battalion (Antiaircraft) (Automatic Weapons) and activated 15 July 1942 at Fort Bliss, Texas. Redesignated 15 May 1943 as the 531st Antiaircraft Artillery Automatic Weapons Battalion (Mobile). (Departed Boston Port of Embarkation 11 February 1944 for overseas service; arrived in England 23 February 1944 and landed in France on 15 June 1944. Returned from overseas service and arrived at the New York Port of Embarkation on 1 January 1946). Inactivated 2 January 1946 at Camp Kilmer, New Jersey. Redesignated as the 531st Antiaircraft Artillery Battalion (Automatic Weapons) 30 June 1952 and allotted to the Regular Army. Activated 24 July 1952 at Fort Bliss, Texas. Reorganized and redesignated 15 June 1957 as the 531st Antiaircraft Artillery Missile Battalion. Inactivated 1 September 1958 at Ellsworth Air Force Base, South Dakota.

CAMPAIGN STREAMERS
World War II
Normandy
Northern France
Rhineland
Ardennes-Alsace
Central Europe

DECORATIONS

Meritorious Unit Commendation, Streamer embroidered *EUROPEAN THEATER 1944* (HHB 531st AAA AW Bn cited for period 16 Jun-15 Aug 1944; GO 100, Hq, 30th Inf Div dated 10 May 1945)

Meritorious Unit Commendation, Streamer embroidered *EUROPEAN THEATER 1944-1945* (HHB 531st AAA AW Bn cited for period 16 Aug 1944-15 Feb 1945; GO 129, Hq, 30th Inf Div dated 23 May 1945)

French Croix de Guerre with Palm, World War II, Streamer embroidered *FRANCE* (531st AAA AW Bn cited for period 15 Jun 1944-25 Apr 1945; DAGO 14, 1959)

Belgian Fourragere 1940 (531st AAA AW Bn cited; DAGO 43, 1950)

Cited in the Order of the Day of the Belgian Army for action in *DEFENSE OF BELGIUM* (531st AAA AW Bn cited for period 4-10 Sept 1944; DAGO 43, 1950)

Cited in the Order of the Day of the Belgian Army for action in the *ARDENNES* (531st AAA AW Bn cited for period 17-25 Jan 1945; DAGO 43, 1950)

COAT OF ARMS
SHIELD: Sable, a lion rampant between two fleurs-de-lis and in chief two battle axes in saltire, braced, all or.

CREST: None

MOTTO: *Dictimus igno* (We Speak With Fire)

The gold lion on a black shield recalls that the unit was cited by the Belgian Army and received the fourragere of that country for action in Belgium and in the Ardennes. The two fleurs-de-lis symbolize the organization's campaigns in Normandy and Northern France. The battle axe, a favorite Teutonic weapon and heraldic charge throughout the medieval period, is used to represent the Battalion's campaigns in the Rhineland and Central Europe.

DISTINCTIVE INSIGNIA
The insignia is the shield and motto of the coat of arms. The sample of the insignia depicted was approved for wear on 7 May 1953.

532d ANTIAIRCRAFT ARTILLERY AUTOMATIC WEAPONS BATTALION

Constituted 6 July 1942 in the Army of the United States as the 532d Separate Coast Artillery

Battalion (Antiaircraft) (Automatic Weapons) and activated 15 July 1942 at Fort Bliss, Texas. (Departed New York Port of Embarkation 27 February 1943 for overseas service and landed in North Africa 9 March 1943). Redesignated 12 December 1943 as the 532d Antiaircraft Artillery Automatic Weapons Battalion. (Moved to Italy 11 November 1943).

Reorganized at Montecatini, Italy on 19 December 1944 and redesignated 2d Battalion, 473d Infantry.

CAMPAIGN STREAMERS
World War II
Tunisia
Naples-Foggia
Rome-Arno
North Apennines

DECORATIONS
None

COAT OF ARMS
SHIELD: Per pale gules and or, a winged sea lion sejant, wings addorsed and elevated and charged with two annulets, in chief three spear heads, all counterchanged.

CREST: None

MOTTO: It Shall Flourish

The scarlet is for the Coast Artillery. The functions of the organization are illustrated by the heraldic sea lion which is a symbol of sea power and is emblematic of great courage, strong of body and a foe to fear. The spear heads betoken dexterity and nimbleness of wit. The annulets represent the ring hung from crossed beams at tournaments or jousts which had to be carried off on the tip of a participant's lance as he rode by at full tilt, thus further referring to the martial aspect of the Battalion. The numerical designation is indicated by the five inanimate symbols, the three spear heads and the two parts of the shield (532). The motto "It Shall Flourish" is expressive of the expected growth of the organization.

DISTINCTIVE INSIGNIA
The insignia is the shield and motto of the coat of arms. The insignia depicted was never made for nor worn by this organization.

532d ANTIAIRCRAFT ARTILLERY GUN BATTALION

Constituted 13 August 1946 in the Regulay Army as the 532d Antiaircraft Artillery Gun Battalion (Philippine Scouts). Activated 28 December 1946 on Okinawa; inactivated 1 May 1949 on Okinawa. Disbanded 20 December 1951.

CAMPAIGN STREAMERS
None

DECORATIONS
None

COAT OF ARMS
None

DISTINCTIVE INSIGNIA
None

533d ANTIAIRCRAFT ARTILLERY AUTOMATIC WEAPONS BATTALION

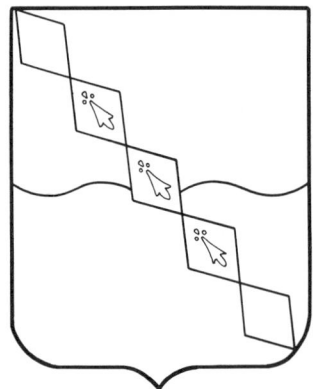

Constituted 6 July 1942 in the Army of the United States as the 533d Coast Artillery Battalion (Antiaircraft) (Automatic Weapons) and activated 15 July 1942 at Fort Bliss, Texas. (Departed New York Port of Embarkation 25 February 1943 for overseas service; arrived in North Africa 9 March 1943 and landed on Sardinia 17 November 1943). Redesignated 15 December 1943 as the 533d Antiaircraft Artillery Automatic Weapons Battalion (Mobile). (Moved to France on 8 November 1944. Returned from overseas service and arrived at the New York Port of Embarkation on 25 October 1945). Inactivated 26 October 1945 at Camp Kilmer, New Jersey.

CAMPAIGN STREAMERS
World War II
Rhineland
Ardennes-Alsace
Central Europe

DECORATIONS
None

COAT OF ARMS
SHIELD: Per fess wavy azure and gules five lozenges conjoined in bend or, the center three charged with an ermine spot sable.

CREST: None

MOTTO: We Take All Comers

The scarlet is the color of the Coast Artillery Corps; the blue representing the sky and the sea, the wavy division line denoting the sea and water. The lozenges, like all other square figures symbolize honesty and consistency and the ermine spots betoken dignity. The numerical designation is indicated by the five lozenges forming the band of protection, the center three and the three ermine spots (533). The motto is in the form of a challenge to all possible encroachment.

DISTINCTIVE INSIGNIA
The insignia is the shield and motto of the coat of arms. The insignia depicted was never made for nor worn by this organization.

534th ANTIAIRCRAFT ARTILLERY AUTOMATIC WEAPONS BATTALION

Constituted 6 July 1942 in the Army of the United States as the 534th Coast Artillery Battalion (Antiaircraft) (Automatic Weapons) and activated 15 July 1942 at Fort Bliss, Texas. (Departed New York Port of Embarkation 28 April 1943 for overseas service; arrived in North Africa on 11 May 1943 and landed at Salerno, Italy on 9 September 1943. Redesignated 12 December 1943 as the 534th Antiaircraft Artillery Automatic Weapons Battalion. (After service at Anzio and in France and Germany, returned from overseas service and arrived at the Hampton Roads Port of Embarkation on 19 October 1945). Inactivated 19 October 1945 at Camp Patrick Henry, Virginia.

Redesignated 9 December 1948 as 3d Antiaircraft Artillery Automatic Weapons Battalion.

CAMPAIGN STREAMERS
World War II
Naples-Foggia (with arrowhead)
Anzio (with arrowhead)
Rome-Arno
Southern France (with arrowhead)
Ardennes-Alsace
Central Europe

DECORATIONS
None

COAT OF ARMS
None

DISTINCTIVE INSIGNIA
None

535th ANTIAIRCRAFT ARTILLERY BATTALION

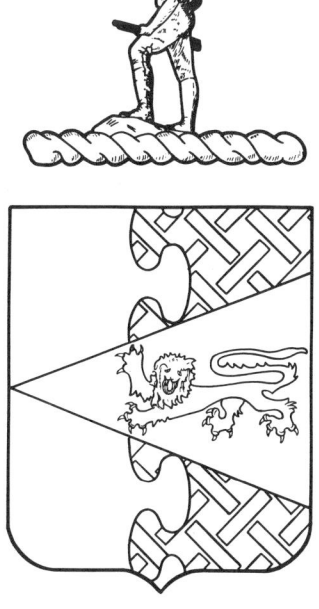

Constituted 6 July 1942 in the Army of the United States as the 535th Coast Artillery Battalion

(Antiaircraft) (Automatic Weapons) and activated 15 July 1942 at Camp Haan, California. Redesignated 15 May 1943 as the 535th Antiaircraft Artillery Automatic Weapons Battalion. (Departed New York Port of Embarkation for overseas service 11 February 1944; arrived in England on 23 February 1944 and landed in France on 6 June 1944). Inactivated 24 June 1946 in Germany. Allotted to the Organized Reserves 29 October 1946 and assigned to Second Army. Activated 14 November 1946 with Headquarters at Indianapolis, Indiana. (Organized Reserves redesignated Organized Reserve Corps on 25 March 1948). Redesignated 6 June 1950 as the 535th Antiaircraft Artillery Automatic Weapons Battalion (Mobile). Redesignated 3 October 1950 as the 535th Antiaircraft Artillery Automatic Weapons Battalion. Redesignated 1 April 1952 as the 535th Antiaircraft Artillery Automatic Weapons Battalion (Mobile). (Organized Reserve Corps redesignated Army Reserve on 9 July 1952). Redesignated 12 March 1954 as the 535th Antiaircraft Artillery Battalion (Automatic Weapons). Inactivated 1 May 1959 at Indianapolis.

CAMPAIGN STREAMERS
World War II
Normandy (with arrowhead)
Northern France
Rhineland
Ardennes-Alsace
Central Europe

DECORATIONS
Belgian Fourragere 1940 (535th AAA AW Bn cited; DAGO 43, 1950)

Cited in the Order of the Day of the Belgian Army for action in the *SIEGFRIED LINE* (535th AAA AW Bn cited for the period 18 Nov-16 Dec 1944; DAGO 43, 1950)

Cited in the Order of the Day of the Belgian Army for action on *ELSENBORN CREST* (535th AAA AW Bn cited for period 16 Dec 1944-20 Feb 1945; DAGO 43, 1950)

COAT OF ARMS
SHIELD: Per pale nebuly gules and fretty or and sable, on a pile issuant from sinister throughout of the second a lion passant guardant of the first.

CREST: That for the regiments and separate battalions of the Army Reserve: On a wreath of the colors (or and gules) the Lexington Minute Man proper. The statue of the Minute Man, Captain John Parker (H. H. Kitson, sculptor), stands on the common in Lexington, Massachusetts.

MOTTO: *Securitas per Vigiliam* (Security Through Vigilance)

The colors scarlet and yellow are for Artillery. The nebuly partition line, a heraldic representation of clouds, is pierced by a wedge to symbolize the antiaircraft mission of the battalion. The wedge shape also crosses the black interlaced bars of the fretty field which signifies the barrier of the Siegfried Line. The lion, taken from the coat of arms of Normandy refers to the area where the organization received its baptism of fire during World War II.

DISTINCTIVE INSIGNIA
The insignia is the shield and motto of the coat of arms. The sample of the insignia depicted was approved for wear on 28 January 1957.

536th ANTIAIRCRAFT ARTILLERY AUTOMATIC WEAPONS BATTALION

Constituted 6 July 1942 in the Army of the United States as the 536th Coast Artillery Battalion (Antiaircraft) (Automatic Weapons) and activated 15 July 1942 at Camp Stewart, Georgia. (Departed New York Port of Embarkation 27 April 1943 for overseas service and arrived in North Africa 11 May 1943. After service on Crozo Island and Malta, moved to Sicily 15 October 1943). Redesignated 13 November 1943 as 536th Antiaircraft Artillery Automatic Weapons Battalion. (Moved to Italy on 10 January 1944). Disbanded 16 November 1944 at Tirrenia, Italy, and personnel transferred to the 287th Quartermaster Battalion.

CAMPAIGN STREAMERS
World War II
Naples-Foggia
Anzio
Rome-Arno

DECORATIONS
None

COAT OF ARMS
SHIELD: Gules, a panther rampant or, armed and langued azure, grasping with its dexter paw a vulture displayed sable, fimbriated of the second.

CREST: None

MOTTO: With Pride And Honor

The scarlet is the color of the Coast Artillery. The functions of the organization are symbolized in that the panther heraldically signifies a brave man who will defend its position with its life; the vulture represents the treatment accorded to enemy encroachment. The motto, With Pride And Honor, is expressive of the manner in which the personnel performs its allotted duties.

DISTINCTIVE INSIGNIA
The insignia is the shield and motto of the coat of arms. The insignia depicted was never made for nor worn by this organization.

536th ANTIAIRCRAFT ARTILLERY GUN BATTALION

Constituted 13 August 1946 in the Regular Army as the 536th Antiaircraft Artillery Gun Battalion (Philippine Scouts). Activated 20 December 1946 at San Marcellino, Philippine Islands; inactivated 25 August 1947 at Manila, Philippine Islands. Disbanded 20 December 1951.

CAMPAIGN STREAMERS
None

DECORATIONS
None

COAT OF ARMS
None

DISTINCTIVE INSIGNIA
None

537th ANTIAIRCRAFT ARTILLERY BATTALION

Constituted 6 July 1942 in the Army of the United States as the 537th Coast Artillery Battalion (Antiaircraft) (Automatic Weapons) and activated 15 July 1942 at Camp Hulen, Texas. Redesignated 15 May 1943 as the 537th Antiaircraft Artillery Automatic Weapons Battalion (Mobile). (Departed New York Port of Embarkation 1 March 1944 for overseas service; arrived in England 7 March 1944 and landed in France on 17 June 1944). Inactivated 29 June 1946 in Germany. Allotted to the Organized Reserve Corps and assigned to the 90th Infantry Division on 21 February 1952. Activated 1 March 1952 with Headquarters at El Paso, Texas. (Organized Reserve Corps redesignated 9 July 1952 as Army Reserve). Redesignated 9 January 1953 as the 537th Antiaircraft Artillery Battalion (Automatic Weapons). (Headquarters relocated to Beaumont, Texas in 1957). Inactivated 1 April 1959 at Beaumont.

CAMPAIGN STREAMERS
World War II
Normandy
Northern France
Rhineland
Ardennes-Alsace
Central Europe

DECORATIONS
Meritorious Unit Commendation, Streamer embroidered *EUROPEAN THEATER 1944* (HHB 537th AAA AW Bn cited for period 17 Jun-31 Aug 1944; GO 519, Hq 90th Inf Div, dated 8 June 1945)

Meritorious Unit Commendation, Streamer embroidered *EUROPEAN THEATER 1944-1945* (HHB 537th AAA AW Bn cited for period 1 Sept 1944-28 Feb 1945; GO 519, Hq 90th Inf Div, dated 8 June 1945)

COAT OF ARMS
SHIELD: Or, on a bend nebuly azure between in chief a Texas longhorn steer's head erased and in base a pheon, point to base gules, a bow of the first.

CREST: That for the regiments and separate battalions of the Army Reserve: On a wreath of the colors (or and gules) the Lexington Minute Man proper. The statue of the Minute Man, Captain John Parker (H. H. Kitson, sculptor), stands on the common in Lexington, Massachusetts.

MOTTO: *Je Tiens Ferme* (I Hold Firm)

Scarlet is the color of the Coast Artillery Corps. The bend represents the scarf of a military commander and the nebuly outline of the bend, clouds, symbolizing the antiaircraft functions of the organization. The bow placed on the bend indicates the readiness in which the battalion holds itself at all times. The steer's head is for Texas, the State of activation and the pheon indicates nimbleness of wit and alertness of the personnel

DISTINCTIVE INSIGNIA
The insignia is the shield and motto of the coat of arms. The sample of the insignia depicted was approved for wear on 20 February 1957.

538th ANTIAIRCRAFT ARTILLERY AUTOMATIC WEAPONS BATTALION

Constituted 13 January 1941 in the Regular Army as 2d Battalion, 100th Coast Artillery (Antiaircraft) (Semimobile) (Colored) and activated 17 April 1941 at Camp Davis, North Carolina. Reorganized at Camp Stewart, Georgia and redesignated 20 April 1943 as the 538th Antiaircraft Artillery Automatic Weapons Battalion (Semimobile) (Colored). Disbanded 25 April 1944 at Camp Patrick Henry, Virginia.

CAMPAIGN STREAMERS
None

DECORATIONS
None

COAT OF ARMS
None

DISTINCTIVE INSIGNIA
None

539th ANTIAIRCRAFT ARTILLERY AUTOMATIC WEAPONS BATTALION

Constituted 13 January 1941 in the Regular Army as 2d Battalion, 79th Coast Artillery (Antiaircraft) (Mobile) and activated 1 June 1941 at Fort Bliss, Texas. Reorganized at Manchester, Connecticut and redesignated 1 September 1943 as the 539th Antiaircraft Artillery Automatic Weapons Battalion. Inactivated 10 August 1944 at Camp Rucker, Alabama. Disbanded 26 October 1944. Reconstituted 13 August 1946 in the Regular Army as the 539th Antiaircraft Artillery Automatic Weapons Battalion (Philippine Scouts) and activated 20 December 1946 at Manila, Philippine Islands. Inactivated 25 August 1947 at Manila. Disbanded 28 June 1950.

CAMPAIGN STREAMERS
None

DECORATIONS
None

COAT OF ARMS
None

DISTINCTIVE INSIGNIA
None

540th ANTIAIRCRAFT ARTILLERY AUTOMATIC WEAPONS BATTALION

Constituted 20 September 1942 in the Army of the United States as 2d Battalion, 701st Coast Artillery (Antiaircraft) and activated 1 October 1942 at Fort Totten, New York. Reorganized at Newport, Rhode Island and redesignated 1 September 1943 as 540th Antiaircraft Artillery Automatic Weapons Battalion (Semimobile). Inactivated 8 November 1944 at Camp Gordon, Georgia. Disbanded 20 December 1951.

CAMPAIGN STREAMERS
None

DECORATIONS
None

COAT OF ARMS
None

DISTINCTIVE INSIGNIA
None

541st ANTIAIRCRAFT ARTILLERY AUTOMATIC WEAPONS BATTALION

Constituted 19 January 1942 in the Army of the United States as 2d Battalion, 601st Coast Artillery (Antiaircraft) and activated 1 February 1942 at Fort Bliss, Texas. Reorganized at Philadelphia, Pennsylvania on 1 September 1943 and redesignated as 541st Antiaircraft Artillery Automatic Weapons Battalion (Semimobile). Inactivated 4 July 1944 at Camp Shelby, Mississippi. Disbanded 26 October 1944.

CAMPAIGN STREAMERS
None

DECORATIONS
None

COAT OF ARMS
None

DISTINCTIVE INSIGNIA
None

542d ANTIAIRCRAFT ARTILLERY BATTALION

Constituted 31 January 1942 in the Army of the United States as 2d Battalion, 602d Coast Artillery (Antiaircraft) and activated 1 March 1942 at Fort Bliss, Texas. Reorganized at New York, New York on 1 September 1943 and redesignated as 542d Antiaircraft Artillery Automatic Weapons Battalion (Mobile). (Departed New York Port of Embarkation 10 December 1944 for overseas service; arrived in England on 16 December 1944 and landed in France on 1 March 1945). Inactivated 11 December 1945 in Germany. Redesignated 542d Antiaircraft Artillery Battalion, allotted to the Regular Army and assigned to the 14th Armored Division on 25 February 1953.

CAMPAIGN STREAMERS
World War II
Rhineland
Central Europe

DECORATIONS
None

COAT OF ARMS
None

DISTINCTIVE INSIGNIA
None

543d ANTIAIRCRAFT ARTILLERY AUTOMATIC WEAPONS BATTALION

Constituted 31 January 1942 in the Army of the United States as 2d Battalion, 603d Coast Artillery (Antiaircraft) and activated 1 March 1942 at Camp Stewart, Georgia. Reorganized at Inglewood, California and redesignated 10 September 1943 as 543d Antiaircraft Artillery Automatic Weapons Battalion (Semimobile). Inactivated 5 September 1945 at Fort Bliss, Texas. Disbanded 20 December 1951.

CAMPAIGN STREAMERS
None

DECORATIONS
None

COAT OF ARMS
None

DISTINCTIVE INSIGNIA
None

544th ANTIAIRCRAFT ARTILLERY AUTOMATIC WEAPONS BATTALION

Constituted 31 January 1942 in the Army of the United States as 2d Battalion, 604th Coast Artillery (Antiaircraft) and activated 1 March 1942 at Fort Bliss, Texas. Reorganized at New York, New York on 1 September 1943 and redesignated as 544th Antiaircraft Artillery Automatic Weapons Battalion (Semimobile). Inactivated 11 August 1944 at Camp Chaffee, Arkansas. Disbanded 26 October 1944. Reconstituted 13 August 1946 in the Regular Army as the 544th Antiaircraft Artillery Automatic Weapons Battalion (Philippine Scouts). Activated 20 December 1946 at Manila, Philippine Islands; inactivated 30 April 1947 at Manila. Disbanded 20 December 1951.

CAMPAIGN STREAMERS
None

DECORATIONS
None

COAT OF ARMS
None

DISTINCTIVE INSIGNIA
None

545th ANTIAIRCRAFT ARTILLERY AUTOMATIC WEAPONS BATTALION

Constituted 31 January 1942 in the Army of the United States as 2d Battalion, 605th Coast Artillery (Antiaircraft) and activated 1 March 1942 at Camp Stewart, Georgia. Reorganized at Boston, Massachusetts on 1 September 1943 and redesignated as 545th Antiaircraft Artillery Automatic Weapons Battalion (Mobile). Inactivated 8 November 1944 at Camp Gordon, Georgia. Disbanded 20 December 1951.

CAMPAIGN STREAMERS
None

DECORATIONS
None

COAT OF ARMS
None

DISTINCTIVE INSIGNIA
None

546th ANTIAIRCRAFT ARTILLERY BATTALION

Constituted 19 December 1942 in the Army of the United States as the 546th Coast Artillery Battalion (Antiaircraft) (Automatic Weapons) and activated 10 January 1943 at Camp Haan, California. Redesignated 15 May 1943 as the 546th Antiaircraft Artillery Automatic Weapons Battalion (Mobile). (Departed New York Port of Embarkation 20 April 1944 for overseas service; arrived in England 2 May 1944 and landed in France on 14 July 1944. Returned from overseas service; arrived at the New York Port of Embarkation 20 March 1946). Inactivated 21 March 1946 at Camp Kilmer, New Jersey. Redesignated 546th Antiaircraft Artillery Battalion and allotted to the Regular Army 17 November 1953. Activated 20 November 1953 at Fort Bliss, Texas; inactivated 15 June 1957 at Carswell Air Force Base, Texas.

CAMPAIGN STREAMERS
World War II
Normandy
Northern France
Rhineland
Ardennes-Alsace
Central Europe

DECORATIONS
None

COAT OF ARMS
SHIELD: Gules and a quarter azure a lion rampant queue fourche or.

CREST: None

MOTTO: *Caelitus mihi Vires* (My Strength Is From Heaven)

The colors red and yellow are for Artillery. The lion symbolizes strength and courage. The lion reaching into the blue quarter represents the organization's function of defending the skies. The forked tail indicates the two times the unit has been active.

DISTINCTIVE INSIGNIA
The insignia is the shield and motto of the coat of arms. The sample of the insignia depicted was approved for wear on 3 May 1955.

547th ANTIAIRCRAFT ARTILLERY BATTALION

Constituted 19 December 1942 in the Army of the United States as the 547th Coast Artillery Battalion (Antiaircraft) (Automatic Weapons) and activated 10 January 1943 at Camp Haan, California. (Departed New York Port of Embarkation 24 August 1944 for overseas service; arrived in England 1 September 1944 and landed in France on 29 September 1944). Inactivated 29 June 1946 in Germany. Redesignated 547th Antiaircraft Artillery Battalion (Automatic Weapons), allotted to the Regular Army and assigned to the 9th Armored Division on 6 August 1953.

CAMPAIGN STREAMERS
World War II
Rhineland
Ardennes-Alsace
Central Europe

DECORATIONS
None

COAT OF ARMS
None

DISTINCTIVE INSIGNIA
None

548th ANTIAIRCRAFT ARTILLERY MISSILE BATTALION

Constituted 19 December 1942 in the Army of the United States as the 548th Coast Artillery Battalion (Antiaircraft) (Automatic Weapons) and activated 10 January 1943 at Camp Haan, California. Redesignated 27 May 1943 as the 548th Antiaircraft Artillery Automatic Weapons Battalion (Mobile). (Departed New York Port of Embarkation 20 September 1944 for overseas service; arrived in England 24 September 1944 and landed in France on 21 October 1944. Returned from overseas service and arrived at Boston Port of Embarkation 17 December 1945). Inactivated 18 December 1945 at Camp Myles Standish, Massachusetts. Redesignated 548th Antiaircraft Artillery Battalion and allotted to the Regular Army 17 November 1953. Activated 15 December 1953 at Fort Bliss, Texas. Reorganized and redesignated 1 March 1957 as the 548th Antiaircraft Artillery Missile Battalion. Inactivated 1 September 1958 at Loring Air Force Base, Maine.

CAMPAIGN STREAMERS
World War II
Rhineland
Central Europe

DECORATIONS
None

COAT OF ARMS
SHIELD: Or, two lightning bolts chevronwise gules, in base a hurt charged with a fleur-de-lis of the first.

CREST: None

MOTTO: Ever Vigilant

Red and yellow are the colors used for Artillery. The fleur-de-lis on the blue disk, used to represent water, is for service in Europe. The two lightning bolts refer to the campaigns of the Battalion during World War II and also allude to the unit's antiaircraft mission.

DISTINCTIVE INSIGNIA
The insignia is the shield and motto of the coat of arms. The sample of the insignia depicted was approved for wear on 22 April 1955.

549th ANTIAIRCRAFT ARTILLERY MISSILE BATTALION

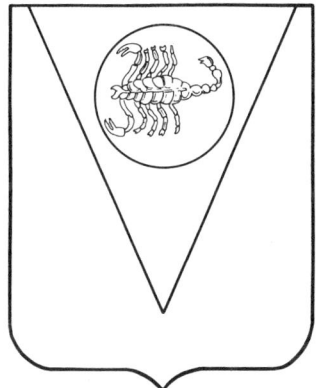
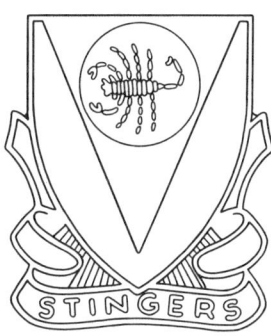

Constituted 19 December 1942 in the Army of the United States as the 549th Coast Artillery Battalion (Antiaircraft) (Automatic Weapons) and activated 20 January 1943 at Camp Edwards, Massachusetts. Redesignated 15 May 1943 as the 549th Antiaircraft Artillery Automatic Weapons Battalion (Mobile). (Departed New York Port of Embarkation 29 September 1944 for overseas service; arrived in England 9 October 1944 and landed in France on 1 December 1944. Returned from overseas service and arrived at the New York Port of Embarkation 7 March 1946). Inactivated 9 March 1946 at Camp Kilmer, New Jersey. Redesignated 549th Antiaircraft Artillery Gun Battalion and allotted to the Regular Army 16 June 1952. Activated 23 July 1952 at Camp Stewart, Georgia. Redesignated 8 June 1953 as the 549th Antiaircraft Artillery Battalion. Reorganized and redesignated 14 July 1958 as the 549th Antiaircraft Artillery Missile Battalion. Inactivated 1 September 1958 in Greenland.

CAMPAIGN STREAMERS
World War II
Rhineland
Ardennes-Alsace
Central Europe

DECORATIONS
None

COAT OF ARMS
SHIELD: Gules, in chief on a pale or a golp charged with a scorpion of the second.

CREST: None

MOTTO: Stingers

The colors red and yellow are for Artillery. The yellow triangle is used to symbolize a searchlight beam, thus indicating the origin of the Battalion as Coast Artillery (Antiaircraft). The purple grape symbolizes the Rhineland where the Battalion received its baptism of fire. The scorpion, which carries its stinger poised ready to strike upward, emphasizes the antiaircraft functions as well as preparedness and lethal striking power of the organization.

DISTINCTIVE INSIGNIA
The insignia is the shield and motto of the coat of arms. The sample of the insignia depicted was approved for wear on 27 March 1953.

550th ANTIAIRCRAFT ARTILLERY BATTALION

Constituted 19 December 1942 in the Army of the United States as the 550th Coast Artillery Battalion (Antiaircraft) (Automatic Weapons) and activated 10 January 1943 at Camp Edwards, Massachusetts. Redesignated 15 May 1943 as the 550th Antiaircraft Artillery Automatic Weapons Battalion (Mobile). (Departed Boston Port of Embarkation 21 October 1943 for overseas service; arrived in England 2 November 1943 and landed in France on 1 December 1944. Returned from overseas service and arrived at the Boston Port of Embarkation 1 November 1945). Inactivated 2 November 1945 at Camp Myles Standish, Massachusetts. Redesignated as the 550th Antiaircraft Artillery Gun Battalion and allotted to the Regular Army 16 June 1952. Activated 23 July 1952 at Camp Stewart, Georgia. Redesignated 8 May 1953 as the 550th Antiaircraft Artillery Battalion (Gun). Inactivated 20 December 1957 at Norfolk, Virginia.

CAMPAIGN STREAMERS
World War II
Normandy
Northern France
Rhineland
Ardennes-Alsace
Central Europe

DECORATIONS
French Croix de Guerre with Gold Star, World War II, Streamer embroidered *NORMANDY* (550th AAA AW Bn cited; DAGO 43, 1950)

COAT OF ARMS

SHIELD: Per chevron rayonne or and gules, a chevron rompu reversed and enhanced azure, that part over the second fimbriated of the first, in base a lion passant guardant of the like, langued of the field.

CREST: None

MOTTO: *Victoria cum Honore* (Victory With Honor)

Scarlet and yellow are colors used for the Artillery. The rayonne partition line symbolizes the fire power of the Battalion's guns. The blue chevron, broken and falling from above, alludes to the antiaircraft functions, while the lion from the coat of arms of the French province of Normandy refers to the area where the Battalion received its baptism of fire during World War II.

DISTINCTIVE INSIGNIA

The insignia is the shield and motto of the coat of arms. Sample of the insignia depicted with the motto *VICTORIA CUM HONOS* was approved for wear on the uniform on 22 May 1953. On 19 April 1954 the motto was changed to *VICTORIA CUM HONORE* and the revised insignia was unofficially worn until the Battalion was inactivated in 1957.

551st ANTIAIRCRAFT ARTILLERY MISSILE BATTALION

Constituted 19 December 1942 in the Army of the United States as the 551st Coast Artillery Battalion (Antiaircraft) (Automatic Weapons) and activated 20 January 1943 at Camp Edwards, Massachusetts. Redesignated 15 May 1943 as the 551st Antiaircraft Artillery Automatic Weapons Battalion (Mobile). (Departed Boston Port of Embarkation 22 June 1944 for overseas service; arrived in England 29 June 1944 and landed in France on 26 July 1944. Returned from overseas service and arrived at the New York Port of Embarkation 25 October 1945). Inactivated 26 October 1945 at Camp Shanks, New York. Redesignated as the 551st Antiaircraft Artillery Gun Battalion and allotted to the Regular Army 16 June 1952. Activated 23 July 1952 at Camp Stewart, Georgia. Redesignated 8 May 1953 as the 551st Antiaircraft Artillery Battalion (Gun). Reorganized and redesignated 17 August 1954 as the 551st Antiaircraft Artillery Missile Battalion. Inactivated 1 September 1958 at Los Angeles, California.

CAMPAIGN STREAMERS
World War II
Normandy
Northern France
Rhineland
Ardennes-Alsace
Central Europe

DECORATIONS
None

COAT OF ARMS
SHIELD: Gules, in fess an annulet or, over all five bird bolts, head to head of the like.

CREST: None

MOTTO: Guardian Of The Skies

The colors red and yellow are for Artillery. The bird bolts, arrows used for killing birds, symbolize antiaircraft and correspond in number to the campaigns of the organization in Europe during World War II. The metal ring represents a link of chain mail, thus symbolizing a strongly defended area. The charges combined indicate a "strike in the target ring".

DISTINCTIVE INSIGNIA
The insignia is the shield and motto of the coat of arms. The sample of the insignia depicted was approved for wear on 6 August 1953.

552d COAST ARTILLERY BATTALION

Constituted in the Organized Reserves as the 552d Coast Artillery Battalion (Antiaircraft) and organized during April 1926 at Los Angeles, California. Disbanded 5 September 1928 at Los Angeles.

CAMPAIGN STREAMERS
None

DECORATIONS
None

COAT OF ARMS
None

DISTINCTIVE INSIGNIA
None

552d ANTIAIRCRAFT ARTILLERY MISSILE BATTALION

Constituted 19 December 1942 in the Army of the United States as the 552d Coast Artillery

Battalion (Antiaircraft) (Automatic Weapons) and activated 20 February 1943 at Camp Hulen, Texas. Redesignated 15 May 1943 as the 552d Antiaircraft Artillery Automatic Weapons Battalion (Mobile). (Departed New York Port of Embarkation 6 February 1944 for overseas service; arrived in England 17 February 1944 and landed in France on 15 June 1944. Returned from overseas service and arrived at the New York Port of Embarkation 12 November 1945). Inactivated 14 November 1945 at Camp Kilmer, New Jersey. Redesignated 15 November 1948 as the 552d Antiaircraft Artillery Gun Battalion. Activated 22 November 1948 at Karlsruhe, Germany. Allotted to the Regular Army 15 November 1951. Redesignated 1 October 1953 as the 552d Antiaircraft Artillery Battalion. Reorganized and redesignated 8 October 1957 as the 552d Antiaircraft Artillery Missile Battalion. Inactivated 1 September 1958 at Camp Kilmer, New Jersey.

CAMPAIGN STREAMERS
World War II
Normandy
Northern France
Rhineland
Ardennes-Alsace
Central Europe

DECORATIONS
None

COAT OF ARMS
SHIELD: Per bend or and gules a fleur-de-lis and a bunch of grapes counterchanged.

CREST: None

MOTTO: Our Aim Is High

Red and yellow are the colors for Artillery. The fleur-de-lis of France and a bunch of grapes for the Rhineland and Central Europe are used to symbolize service in Europe during World War II.

DISTINCTIVE INSIGNIA
The insignia is the shield and motto of the coat of arms. The sample of the insignia depicted was approved for wear on 23 July 1951.

553d COAST ARTILLERY BATTALION

Constituted in the Organized Reserves as the 553d Coast Artillery Battalion (Antiaircraft), allotted to the First Corps area and organized during November 1924 with Headquarters at Boston, Massachusetts. Withdrawn from the First Corps area and allotted to the Second Corps area in January 1925. Disbanded 5 September 1928.

CAMPAIGN STREAMERS
None

DECORATIONS
None

COAT OF ARMS
None

DISTINCTIVE INSIGNIA
None

553d ANTIAIRCRAFT ARTILLERY BATTALION

Constituted 19 December 1942 in the Army of the United States as the 553d Coast Artillery Battalion (Antiaircraft) (Automatic Weapons) and activated 20 February 1943 at Camp Hulen, Texas. Redesignated 15 May 1943 as the 553d Antiaircraft Artillery Automatic Weapons Battalion (Mobile). (Departed New York Port of Embarkation 11 August 1944 for overseas service; arrived in England 22 August 1944 and landed in France on 21 September 1944. Returned from overseas service and arrived at the Boston Port of Embarkation on 29 October 1945). Inactivated 30 October 1945 at Camp Myles Standish, Massachusetts. Redesignated 9 February 1955 as the 553d Antiaircraft Artillery Battalion and allotted to the Regular Army. Activated 15 April 1955 at Camp Stewart, Georgia; inactivated 20 September 1956 at Camp Stewart.

CAMPAIGN STREAMERS
World War II
Rhineland
Ardennes-Alsace
Central Europe

DECORATIONS
None

COAT OF ARMS
None

DISTINCTIVE INSIGNIA
None

554th COAST ARTILLERY BATTALION

Constituted in the Organized Reserves as the 554th Coast Artillery Battalion (Antiaircraft). Disbanded 13 June 1924.

CAMPAIGN STREAMERS
None

DECORATIONS
None

COAT OF ARMS
None

DISTINCTIVE INSIGNIA
None

554th ANTIAIRCRAFT ARTILLERY MISSILE BATTALION

Constituted 19 December 1942 in the Army of the United States as the 554th Coast Artillery Battalion (Antiaircraft) (Automatic Weapons) and activated 20 February 1943 at Camp Hulen, Texas. Redesignated 15 May 1943 as the 554th Antiaircraft Artillery Automatic Weapons Battalion (Mobile). (Departed New York Port of Embarkation 1 March 1944 for overseas service; arrived in England 9 March 1944 and landed in France on 27 June 1944. Returned from overseas service and arrived at the Boston Port of Embarkation 24 October 1945). Inactivated 25 October 1945 at Camp Myles Standish, Massachusetts. Redesignated as the 554th Antiaircraft Artillery Battalion and allotted to the Regular Army, 16 June 1952. Activated 23 July 1952 at Camp Stewart, Georgia. Redesignated 8 May 1953 as the 554th Antiaircraft Artillery Battalion. Reorganized and redesignated 10 November 1954 as the 554th Antiaircraft Artillery Missile Battalion. Inactivated 1 September 1958 at Los Angeles, California.

CAMPAIGN STREAMERS
World War II
Normand
Northern France
Rhineland
Central Europe

DECORATIONS
None

COAT OF ARMS
SHIELD: Per saltire gules and or, four mullets of six points in cross counterchanged.

CREST: None

MOTTO: Beware Our Bursts

The shield is in the colors of the Artillery. The four stars represent flak bursts, one for each of the organization's campaigns in Europe during World War II.

DISTINCTIVE INSIGNIA
The insignia is the shield and motto of the coat of arms. The sample of the insignia depicted was approved for wear on 20 July 1953.

555th COAST ARTILLERY BATTALION

Constituted in the Organized Reserves as the 555th Coast Artillery Battalion (Antiaircraft); allotted to the Sixth Corps area and organized 7 January 1927 at Detroit, Michigan. Disbanded 5 September 1928. Reconstituted 11 April 1930 and consolidated with the 945th Coast Artillery.

CAMPAIGN STREAMERS
None

DECORATIONS
None

COAT OF ARMS
None

DISTINCTIVE INSIGNIA
None

555th ANTIAIRCRAFT ARTILLERY BATTALION

Constituted 19 December 1942 in the Army of the United States as the 555th Coast Artillery Battalion (Antiaircraft) (Automatic Weapons) and activated 20 February 1943 at Camp Hulen, Texas. Redesignated 15 May 1943 as the 555th Antiaircraft Artillery Automatic Weapons Battalion (Mobile). (Departed New York Port of Embarkation 28 August 1944 for overseas service; arrived in England 3 September 1944 and landed in France on 2 October 1944. Returned from overseas service and arrived at the New York Port of Embarkation on 8 December 1945). Inactivated 9 December 1945 at Camp Kilmer, New Jersey. Allotted to the Organized Reserve Corps and assigned to the 104th Infantry Division on 1 March 1952. Activated 1 March 1952 with Headquarters at Seattle, Washington. (Organized Reserve Corps redesignated 9 July 1952 as Army Reserve). Redesignated 15 November 1952 as the 555th Antiaircraft Artillery Battalion (Automatic Weapons). Relieved from the 104th Infantry Division and disbanded 11 June 1959 at Seattle.

CAMPAIGN STREAMERS
World War II
Rhineland
Central Europe

DECORATIONS
Presidential Unit Citation (Army), Streamer embroidered *ROER RIVER BRIDGEHEAD* (Btry A, 555th AAA AW Bn cited for period 23-25 Feb 1945; DAGO 64, 1948)

COAT OF ARMS
SHIELD: Gules, between two flanks, the dexter per pale wavy azure and or and the sinister reversed, a barrulet dancette of the last, in base a fleur-de-lis of the same.

CREST: That for the regiments and separate battalions of the Army Reserve: On a wreath of the colors (or and gules) the Lexington Minute Man proper. The statue of the Minute Man, Captain John Parker (H. H. Kitson, sculptor), stands on the common in Lexington, Massachusetts.

MOTTO: Alert, Able, Absolute

The colors red and yellow are for Artillery. The shield itself alludes to the State of Washington where the Battalion was activated and stationed after World War II. The two blue wavy sections, representing water, refer to Puget Sound and Lake Washington between which Seattle, the organization's headquarters was located. The jagged yellow line symbolizes Washington's mountainous terrain and also simulates three V's (the Roman numeral 5) and thus refers to the battalion's numerical designation. The fleur-de-lis indicates combat service in Europe during World War II.

DISTINCTIVE INSIGNIA
The insignia is the shield and motto of the coat of arms. The insignia depicted was never made for nor worn by this organization.

556th ANTIAIRCRAFT ARTILLERY AUTOMATIC WEAPONS BATTALION

Constituted 8 February 1943 in the Army of the United States as the 556th Coast Artillery Battalion (Antiaircraft) (Automatic Weapons) and activated 20 March 1943 at Camp Davis, North Carolina. Redesignated 15 May 1943 as the 556th Antiaircraft Artillery Automatic Weapons Battalion (Mobile). (Departed Boston Port of Embarkation 7 September 1944 for overseas service; arrived in England 14 September 1944 and landed in France on 18 September 1944). Inactivated 29 June 1946 in Belgium.

CAMPAIGN STREAMERS
World War II
Rhineland
Central Europe

DECORATIONS
None

COAT OF ARMS
None

DISTINCTIVE INSIGNIA
None

557th ANTIAIRCRAFT ARTILLERY BATTALION

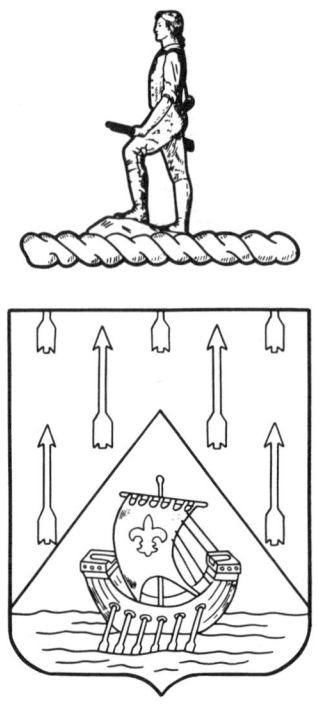 

Constituted 8 February 1943 in the Army of the United States as the 557th Coast Artillery Battalion (Antiaircraft) (Automatic Weapons) and activated 20 March 1943 at Camp Davis, North Carolina. Redesignated 15 May 1943 as the 557th Antiaircraft Artillery Automatic Weapons Battalion (Mobile). (Departed New York Port of Embarkation 23 July 1944 for overseas service; arrived in England 28 July 1944 and landed in France on 16 August 1944. Returned from overseas service and arrived at the Hampton Roads Port of Embarkation 13 December 1945). Inactivated 13 December 1945 at Camp Patrick Henry, Virginia. Allotted to the Organized Reserve Corps and assigned to the 84th Infantry Division, 13 February 1952. Activated 1 March 1952 with Headquarters at Madison, Wisconsin. Redesignated 15 December 1952 as the 557th Antiaircraft Artillery Battalion (Automatic Weapons). Relieved from the 84th Infantry Division and disbanded 18 May 1959 at Madison.

CAMPAIGN STREAMERS
World War II
Northern France
Rhineland
Ardennes-Alsace
Central Europe

DECORATIONS
Cited in the Order of the Day of the Belgian Army for action in *BELGIUM* (557th AAA AW Bn cited for period 3-13 Sept 1944; DAGO 43, 1950)

COAT OF ARMS
SHIELD: Per chevron or and gules, the first seme of arrows counterchanged, on the second upon a sea issuant from base a lymphad with oars and sail unfurled of the first charged with a fleur-de-lis azure.

CREST: That for the regiments and separate battalions of the Army Reserve: On a wreath of the colors (or and gules) the Lexington Minute Man proper. The statue of the Minute Man, Captain John Parker (H. H. Kitson, sculptor), stands on the common

in Lexington, Massachusetts.

MOTTO: Clear Skies

The colors red and yellow are used for Artillery. The upward thrust of the arrows and the triangular partition line symbolize the antiaircraft mission of the organization. The lymphad, taken from the coat of arms of Paris, and the fleur-de-lis commemorate the unit's service in Europe during World War II.

DISTINCTIVE INSIGNIA
The insignia is the shield and motto of the coat of arms. The sample of the insignia depicted was approved for wear on 31 January 1955.

558th ANTIAIRCRAFT ARTILLERY AUTOMATIC WEAPONS BATTALION

Constituted 8 February 1943 in the Army of the United States as the 558th Coast Artillery Battalion (Antiaircraft) (Automatic Weapons) and activated 20 March 1943 at Camp Davis, North Carolina. Redesignated 15 May 1943 as the 558th Antiaircraft Artillery Automatic Weapons Battalion (Mobile). (Departed New York Port of Embarkation 30 October 1944 for overseas service; arrived in England 12 November 1944 and landed in France on 4 February 1945. Returned from overseas service and arrived at the New York Port of Embarkation 13 November 1945). Inactivated 14 November 1945 at Camp Shanks, New York.

CAMPAIGN STREAMERS
World War II
Central Europe

DECORATIONS
None

COAT OF ARMS
None

DISTINCTIVE INSIGNIA
None

559th ANTIAIRCRAFT ARTILLERY BATTALION

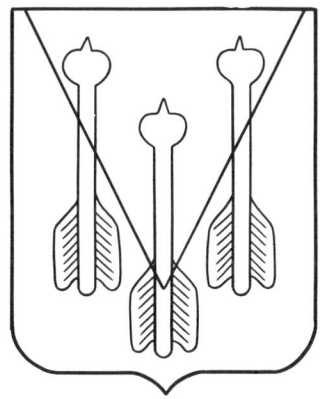 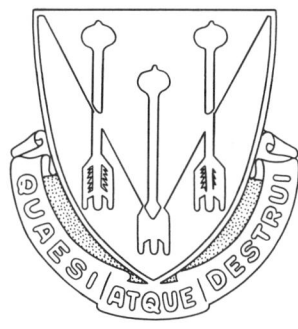

Constituted 8 February 1943 in the Army of the United States as the 559th Coast Artillery Battalion (Antiaircraft) (Automatic Weapons) and activated 20 March 1943 at Camp Davis,

North Carolina. Redesignated 15 May 1943 as the 559th Antiaircraft Artillery Automatic Weapons Battalion (Mobile). (Departed New York Port of Embarkation 24 July 1944 for overseas service; arrived in England 31 July 1944 and landed in France on 16 August 1944. Returned from overseas service and arrived at the New York Port of Embarkation 8 March 1946). Inactivated 9 March 1946 at Camp Kilmer, New Jersey. Redesignated 559th Antiaircraft Artillery Battalion and allotted to the Regular Army, 9 February 1955. Activated 15 May 1955 at Camp Stewart, Georgia; inactivated 20 September 1956 at Camp Stewart.

CAMPAIGN STREAMERS
World War II
Northern France
Rhineland
Central Europe

DECORATIONS
None

COAT OF ARMS
SHIELD: Gules, a pile or; overall three bosons palewise, points to chief, two and one counterchanged.

CREST: None

MOTTO: *Quaesi Atque Destrui* (Seek And Destroy)

The colors scarlet and yellow are used for Artillery. The unit's origin as Coast Artillery Antiaircraft is symbolized by the yellow triangle representing a searchlight beam. The three bosons—ancient weapons used to bring down birds—represent the three campaigns of the battalion in Europe during World War II.

DISTINCTIVE INSIGNIA
The insignia is the shield and motto of the coat of arms. The sample of the insignia depicted was approved for wear 10 July 1956.

560th ANTIAIRCRAFT ARTILLERY AUTOMATIC WEAPONS BATTALION

Constituted 25 February 1943 in the Army of the United States as the 560th Coast Artillery Battalion (Antiaircraft) (Automatic Weapons) and activated 10 April 1943 at Camp Stewart, Georgia. Redesignated 15 May 1943 as the 560th Antiaircraft Artillery Automatic Weapons Battalion (Mobile).

Converted and redesignated 7 December 1944 as the 72d Chemical Mortar Battalion.

CAMPAIGN STREAMERS
None

DECORATIONS
None

COAT OF ARMS
None

DISTINCTIVE INSIGNIA
None

561st ANTIAIRCRAFT ARTILLERY AUTOMATIC WEAPONS BATTALION

Constituted 25 February 1943 in the Army of the United States as the 561st Coast Artillery Battalion (Antiaircraft) (Automatic Weapons) and activated 10 April 1943 at Camp Stewart, Georgia. Redesignated 15 May 1943 as the 561st Antiaircraft Artillery Automatic Weapons Battalion (Mobile). Inactivated 8 November 1944 at Camp Gordon, Georgia. Disbanded 20 December 1951.

CAMPAIGN STREAMERS
None

DECORATIONS
None

COAT OF ARMS
None

DISTINCTIVE INSIGNIA
None

562d ANTIAIRCRAFT ARTILLERY AUTOMATIC WEAPONS BATTALION

Constituted 25 February 1943 in the Army of the United States as the 562d Coast Artillery Battalion (Antiaircraft) (Automatic Weapons) and activated 20 April 1943 at Camp Stewart, Georgia. Redesignated 15 May 1943 as the 562d Antiaircraft Artillery Automatic Weapons Battalion (Mobile). (Departed Boston Port of Embarkation 7 October 1944 for overseas service; arrived in England 15 October 1944 and landed in France on 18 October 1944. Returned from overseas service and arrived at the Boston Port of Embarkation on 29 October 1945). Inactivated 30 October 1945 at Camp Myles Standish, Massachusetts.

CAMPAIGN STREAMERS
World War II
Rhineland
Central Europe

DECORATIONS
None

COAT OF ARMS
None

DISTINCTIVE INSIGNIA
None

563d ANTIAIRCRAFT ARTILLERY BATTALION

Constituted 25 February 1943 in the Army of the United States as the 563d Coast Artillery Battalion (Antiaircraft) (Automatic Weapons) and activated 20 April 1943 at Camp Stewart, Georgia. Redesignated 15 May 1943 as the 563d Antiaircraft Artillery Automatic Weapons Battalion (Mobile). (Departed Boston Port of Embarkation 11 October 1944 for overseas service and landed in France on 18 October 1944. Returned from overseas service and arrived at the New York Port of Embarkation on 1 March 1946). Inactivated 2 March 1946 at Camp Kilmer, New Jersey. Redesignated 15 November 1955 as the 563d Antiaircraft Artillery Battalion and allotted to the Regular Army.

CAMPAIGN STREAMERS
World War II
Rhineland
Ardennes-Alsace
Central Europe

DECORATIONS
None

COAT OF ARMS
None

DISTINCTIVE INSIGNIA
None

564th ANTIAIRCRAFT ARTILLERY AUTOMATIC WEAPONS BATTALION

Constituted 25 February 1943 in the Army of the United States as the 564th Coast Artillery Battalion (Antiaircraft) (Automatic Weapons) and activated 20 April 1943 at Camp Stewart, Georgia. Redesignated 15 May 1943 as the 564th Antiaircraft Artillery Automatic Weapons Battalion (Mobile). (Departed New York Port of Embarkation 22 October 1944 for overseas service; arrived in England 2 November 1944 and landed in France on 29 December 1944. Returned from overseas service and arrived at the Boston Port of Embarkation on 13 November 1945). Inactivated 14 November 1945 at Camp Kilmer, New Jersey.

CAMPAIGN STREAMERS
World War II
European Theater without inscription

DECORATIONS
None

COAT OF ARMS
None

DISTINCTIVE INSIGNIA
None

565th ANTIAIRCRAFT ARTILLERY AUTOMATIC WEAPONS BATTALION

Constituted 25 February 1943 in the Army of the United States as the 565th Coast Artillery Battalion (Antiaircraft) (Automatic Weapons) and activated 10 April 1943 at Camp Stewart, Georgia. Redesignated 15 May 1943 as the 565th Antiaircraft Artillery Automatic Weapons Battalion (Mobile). (Departed New York Port of Embarkation 6 October 1944 for overseas service; arrived in England 18 October 1944 and landed in France on 15 December 1944). Inactivated 6 October 1945 in Germany.

CAMPAIGN STREAMERS
World War II
Rhineland
Ardennes-Alsace
Central Europe

DECORATIONS
None

COAT OF ARMS
None

DISTINCTIVE INSIGNIA
None

566th ANTIAIRCRAFT ARTILLERY AUTOMATIC WEAPONS BATTALION

Constituted 25 February 1943 in the Army of the United States as the 566th Coast Artillery Battalion (Antiaircraft) (Automatic Weapons) and activated 20 April 1943 at Camp Stewart, Georgia. Redesignated 15 May 1943 as the 566th Antiaircraft Artillery Automatic Weapons Battalion (Mobile). (Departed New York Port of Embarkation 30 October 1944 for overseas service; arrived in England 12 November 1944 and landed in France on 26 December 1944. Returned from overseas service and arrived at the New York Port of Embarkation on 11 December 1945). Inactivated 12 December 1945 at Camp Shanks, New York.

CAMPAIGN STREAMERS
World War II
Rhineland
Central Europe

DECORATIONS
None

COAT OF ARMS
None

DISTINCTIVE INSIGNIA
None

567th ANTIAIRCRAFT ARTILLERY AUTOMATIC WEAPONS BATTALION

Constituted 25 February 1943 in the Army of the United States as the 567th Coast Artillery Battalion (Antiaircraft) (Automatic Weapons) and activated 10 May 1943 at Camp Haan, California. Redesignated 15 May 1943 as the 567th Antiaircraft Artillery Automatic Weapons Battalion (Mobile). (Departed New York Port of Embarkation 14 October 1944 for overseas service; arrived in England 25 October 1944 and landed in France on 18 December 1944. Returned from overseas service and arrived at the New York Port of Embarkation 15 March 1946). Inactivated 16 March 1946 at Camp Kilmer, New Jersey.

CAMPAIGN STREAMERS
World War II
Northern France
Rhineland
Ardennes-Alsace
Central Europe

DECORATIONS
None

COAT OF ARMS
None

DISTINCTIVE INSIGNIA
None

568th ANTIAIRCRAFT ARTILLERY AUTOMATIC WEAPONS BATTALION

Constituted 25 February 1943 in the Army of the United States as the 568th Coast Artillery Battalion (Antiaircraft) (Automatic Weapons) and activated 10 May 1943 at Camp Haan, California. Redesignated 15 May 1943 as the 568th Antiaircraft Artillery Automatic Weapons Battalion (Mobile). (Departed New York Port of Embarkation 7 November 1944 for overseas service; arrived in England 18 November 1944 and landed in France on 19 November 1944. Returned from overseas service and arrived at the New York Port of Embarkation 22 November 1945). Inactivated 24 November 1945 at Camp Kilmer, New Jersey.

CAMPAIGN STREAMERS
World War II
Central Europe

DECORATIONS
None

COAT OF ARMS
None

DISTINCTIVE INSIGNIA
None

569th ANTIAIRCRAFT ARTILLERY AUTOMATIC WEAPONS BATTALION

Constituted 25 February 1943 in the Army of the United States as the 569th Coast Artillery Battalion (Antiaircraft) (Automatic Weapons) and activated 10 May 1943 at Camp Haan, California. Redesignated 15 May 1943 as the 569th Antiaircraft Artillery Automatic Weapons Battalion (Mobile). (Departed New York Port of Embarkation 7 November 1944 for overseas service; arrived in England 18 November 1944 and landed in France on 28 January 1945. Returned from overseas service and arrived at the New York Port of Embarkation on 16 February 1946). Inactivated 17 February 1946 at Camp Kilmer, New Jersey.

CAMPAIGN STREAMERS
World War II
Rhineland
Central Europe

DECORATIONS
None

COAT OF ARMS
None

DISTINCTIVE INSIGNIA
None

570th ANTIAIRCRAFT ARTILLERY AUTOMATIC WEAPONS BATTALION

Constituted 25 February 1943 in the Army of the United States as the 570th Antiaircraft Artillery Automatic Weapons Battalion (Self Propelled) and assigned to the Antiaircraft Command. Activated 10 June 1943 at Camp Edwards, Massachusetts; inactivated 30 June 1944 at Camp Edwards. Disbanded 26 October 1944 Reconstituted 13 August 1946 in the Regular Army as the 570th Antiaircraft Artillery Automatic Weapons Battalion (Philippine Scouts) and activated 20 December 1946 at San Fernando La Union, Philippine Islands. Inactivated 20 August 1947 at San Fernando La Union. Disbanded 20 December 1951.

CAMPAIGN STREAMERS
None

DECORATIONS
None

COAT OF ARMS
None

DISTINCTIVE INSIGNIA
None

571st ANTIAIRCRAFT ARTILLERY AUTOMATIC WEAPONS BATTALION

Constituted 25 February 1943 in the Army of the United States as the 571st Antiaircraft Artillery Automatic Weapons Battalion (Self Propelled) and activated 10 June 1943 at Camp Edwards, Massachusetts. (Departed Boston Port of Embarkation 10 November 1944 for overseas service; arrived in England 17 November 1944 and landed in France on 22 December 1944). Inactivated 10 September 1946 in Germany.

CAMPAIGN STREAMERS
World War II
Rhineland
Ardennes-Alsace
Central Europe

DECORATIONS
None

COAT OF ARMS
None

DISTINCTIVE INSIGNIA
None

572d ANTIAIRCRAFT ARTILLERY BATTALION

Constituted 25 February 1943 in the Army of the United States as the 572d Antiaircraft Artillery Automatic Weapons Battalion (Self Propelled) and activated 10 June 1943 at Camp Edwards, Massachusetts. (Departed New York Port of Embarkation 29 September 1944 for overseas service; arrived in England 10 October 1944 and landed in France on 26 November 1944. Returned from overseas service and arrived at the Hampton Roads Port of Embarkation on 24 November 1945). Inactivated 24 November 1945 at Camp Patrick Henry, Virginia. Redesignated 572d Antiaircraft Artillery Battalion, allotted to the Regular Army and assigned to the 12th Armored Division on 6 August 1953.

CAMPAIGN STREAMERS
World War II
Rhineland
Ardennes-Alsace
Central Europe

DECORATIONS
None

COAT OF ARMS
None

DISTINCTIVE INSIGNIA
None

573d ANTIAIRCRAFT ARTILLERY AUTOMATIC WEAPONS BATTALION

Constituted 25 February 1943 in the Army of the United States as the 573d Antiaircraft Artillery Automatic Weapons Battalion (Self Propelled) and activated 10 June 1943 at Camp Edwards, Massachusetts. (Departed New York Port of Embarkation 16 December 1944 for overseas service; arrived in England 21 December 1944 and landed in France on 5 March 1945. Returned from overseas service and arrived at the New York Port of Embarkation on 21 March 1946). Inactivated 22 March 1946 at Camp Kilmer, New Jersey.

CAMPAIGN STREAMERS
World War II
Rhineland
Central Europe

DECORATIONS
None

COAT OF ARMS
None

DISTINCTIVE INSIGNIA
None

574th ANTIAIRCRAFT ARTILLERY BATTALION

Constituted 25 February 1943 in the Army of the United States as the 574th Antiaircraft Artillery Automatic Weapons Battalion (Self Propelled) and activated 15 June 1943 at Camp Edwards, Massachusetts. (Departed New York Port of Embarkation 16 December 1944 for overseas service; arrived in England 21 December 1944 and landed in France on 10 March 1945). Inactivated 9 December 1945 in France. Redesignated 813th Antiaircraft Artillery Automatic Weapons Battalion, allotted to the Organized Reserve Corps and assigned to the 13th Armored Division, 17 May 1949. Activated 27 May 1949 with Headquarters at Los Angeles, California. (Headquarters relocated to San Diego, California on 7 July 1950). Relieved from the 13th Armored Division, redesignated 574th Antiaircraft Artillery Automatic Weapons Battalion and assigned to the 63d Infantry Division, 1 March 1952. Redesignated 15 November 1952 as the 574th Antiaircraft Artillery Battalion (Automatic Weapons). (Batteries C and D inactivated 8 February 1954 at San Diego). Relieved from the 63d Infantry Division and inactivated 1 May 1959 at San Diego.

CAMPAIGN STREAMERS
World War II
Rhineland
Ardennes-Alsace
Central Europe

DECORATIONS
None

COAT OF ARMS
SHIELD: Per fess gules and or, a bar counterchanged, three arrows palewise of the like, their heads terminating in fleurs-de-lis.

CREST: That for the regiments and separate battalions of the Army Reserve: On a wreath of the colors (or and gules) the Lexington Minute Man proper. The statue of the Minute Man, Captain John Parker (H. H. Kitson, sculptor), stands on the common in Lexington, Massachusetts.

MOTTO: *Cives Milites* (Citizen Soldiers)

Red and yellow are used for Artillery. The narrow yellow and red bars were suggested by the arms of Aragon and refer to the Spanish settlement of California, the battalion's home state. The three arrows terminating in fleurs-de-lis allude to the campaigns of the unit in Europe during World War II and also simulate its antiaircraft mission.

DISTINCTIVE INSIGNIA
The insignia is the shield and motto of the coat of arms. The insignia depicted was never made for nor worn by this organization.

575th ANTIAIRCRAFT ARTILLERY BATTALION

Constituted 25 February 1943 in the Army of the United States as the 575th Antiaircraft Artillery Automatic Weapons Battalion (Self Propelled) and activated 10 July 1943 at Fort Bliss, Texas. (Departed New York Port of Embarkation 30 October 1944 for overseas service; arrived in England 11 November 1944 and landed in France on 18 December 1944. Returned from overseas service and arrived at the Hampton Roads Port of Embarkation on 20 December 1945). Inactivated 20 December 1945 at Camp Patrick Henry, Virginia. Redesignated 575th Antiaircraft Artillery Battalion, allotted to the Regular Army and assigned to the 8th Armored Division on 6 August 1953.

CAMPAIGN STREAMERS
World War II
Rhineland
Ardennes-Alsace
Central Europe

DECORATIONS
None

COAT OF ARMS
None

DISTINCTIVE INSIGNIA
None

576th ANTIAIRCRAFT ARTILLERY AUTOMATIC WEAPONS BATTALION

Constituted 25 February 1943 in the Army of the United States as the 576th Antiaircraft Artillery Automatic Weapons Battalion (Self Propelled) and activated 15 July 1943 at Camp Davis, North Carolina. Assigned to the Replacement and School Command 14 December 1944. Inactivated 27 December 1944 at Camp Livingston, Louisiana. Disbanded 20 December 1951.

CAMPAIGN STREAMERS
None

DECORATIONS
None

COAT OF ARMS
None

DISTINCTIVE INSIGNIA
None

577th ANTIAIRCRAFT ARTILLERY AUTOMATIC WEAPONS BATTALION

Constituted 25 February 1943 in the Army of the United States as the 577th Antiaircraft Artillery Automatic Weapons Battalion (Mobile) and activated 10 July 1943 at Camp Edwards, Massachusetts. Assigned to the Replacement and School Command 23 November 1944. Inactivated 1 December 1944 at Camp Livingston, Louisiana. Disbanded 20 December 1951.

CAMPAIGN STREAMERS
None

DECORATIONS
None

COAT OF ARMS
None

DISTINCTIVE INSIGNIA
None

578th ANTIAIRCRAFT ARTILLERY AUTOMATIC WEAPONS BATTALION

Constituted 25 February 1943 in the Army of the United States as the 578th Antiaircraft Artillery Automatic Weapons Battalion (Self Propelled) and activated 10 July 1943 at Fort Sheridan, Illinois. Inactivated 1 December 1944 at Camp Livingston, Louisiana. Disbanded 20 December 1951.

CAMPAIGN STREAMERS
None

DECORATIONS
None

COAT OF ARMS
None

DISTINCTIVE INSIGNIA
None

579th ANTIAIRCRAFT ARTILLERY AUTOMATIC WEAPONS BATTALION

Constituted 25 February 1943 in the Army of the United States as the 579th Antiaircraft Artillery Automatic Weapons Battalion (Self Propelled) and activated 10 July 1943 at Camp Hulen, Texas. (Departed San Francisco Port of Embarkation 25 March 1945 for overseas service and arrived in the Philippine Islands on 30 April 1945). Inactivated 15 April 1946 at Yokohama, Japan.

CAMPAIGN STREAMERS
World War II
Luzon

DECORATIONS
Philippine Presidential Unit Citation, Streamer embroidered *17 OCTOBER 1944 TO 4 JULY 1945* (579th AAA AW Bn cited; DAGO 47, 1950)

COAT OF ARMS
None

DISTINCTIVE INSIGNIA
None

580th ANTIAIRCRAFT ARTILLERY AUTOMATIC WEAPONS BATTALION

Constituted 25 February 1943 in the Army of the United States as the 580th Antiaircraft Artillery Automatic Weapons Battalion (Mobile) and activated 1 October 1943 at Camp Stewart, Georgia. (Departed New York Port of Embarkation 16 December 1944 for overseas service; arrived in England 22 December 1944 and landed in France on 25 March 1945. Returned from overseas service and arrived at the New York Port of Embarkation on 30 November 1945). Inactivated 1 December 1945 at Camp Kilmer, New Jersey.

CAMPAIGN STREAMERS
World War II
Rhineland
Central Europe

DECORATIONS
None

COAT OF ARMS
None

DISTINCTIVE INSIGNIA
None

581st ANTIAIRCRAFT ARTILLERY AUTOMATIC WEAPONS BATTALION

Constituted 25 February 1943 in the Army of the United States as the 581st Antiaircraft Artillery Automatic Weapons Battalion (Mobile) and activated 1 October 1943 at Camp Stewart, Georgia (Departed New York Port of Embarkation 26 December 1944 for overseas service; arrived in England 7 January 1945 and landed in France on 9 March 1945. Returned from overseas service and arrived at the New York Port of Embarkation on 21 March 1946). Inactivated 23 March 1946 at Camp Kilmer, New Jersey.

CAMPAIGN STREAMERS
World War II
Rhineland
Central Europe

DECORATIONS
None

COAT OF ARMS
None

DISTINCTIVE INSIGNIA
None

582d ANTIAIRCRAFT ARTILLERY AUTOMATIC WEAPONS BATTALION

Constituted 25 February 1943 in the Army of the United States as the 582d Antiaircraft Artillery Automatic Weapons Battalion (Self Propelled) and activated 1 October 1943 at Fort Bliss, Texas. Inactivated 1 October 1945 at Fort Bliss. Disbanded 20 December 1951.

CAMPAIGN STREAMERS
None

DECORATIONS
None

COAT OF ARMS
None

DISTINCTIVE INSIGNIA
None

583d ANTIAIRCRAFT ARTILLERY AUTOMATIC WEAPONS BATTALION

Constituted 25 February 1943 in the Army of the United States as the 583d Antiaircraft Artillery Automatic Weapons Battalion (Self Propelled) and activated 1 October 1943 at Fort Bliss, Texas. Inactivated 9 May 1944 at Camp Chaffee, Arkansas. Disbanded 26 June 1944.

CAMPAIGN STREAMERS
None

DECORATIONS
None

COAT OF ARMS
None

DISTINCTIVE INSIGNIA
None

584th ANTIAIRCRAFT ARTILLERY AUTOMATIC WEAPONS BATTALION

Constituted 25 February 1943 in the Army of the United States as the 584th Antiaircraft Artillery Automatic Weapons Battalion (Mobile) and activated 1 October 1943 at Camp Davis, North Carolina. Inactivated 15 December 1944 at Camp Maxey, Texas. Disbanded 20 December 1951.

CAMPAIGN STREAMERS
None

DECORATIONS
None

COAT OF ARMS
None

DISTINCTIVE INSIGNIA
None

585th ANTIAIRCRAFT ARTILLERY AUTOMATIC WEAPONS BATTALION

Constituted 25 February 1943 in the Army of the United States as the 585th Antiaircraft Artillery Automatic Weapons Battalion (Self Propelled) and activated 1 October 1943 at Camp Hulen, Texas. Inactivated 6 May 1944 at Camp Chaffee, Arkansas. Disbanded 26 June 1944.

CAMPAIGN STREAMERS
None

DECORATIONS
None

COAT OF ARMS
None

DISTINCTIVE INSIGNIA
None

586th ANTIAIRCRAFT ARTILLERY AUTOMATIC WEAPONS BATTALION

Constituted 25 February 1943 in the Army of the United States as the 586th Antiaircraft Artillery Automatic Weapons Battalion (Semimobile) and activated 1 October 1943 at Camp Hulen, Texas. (Departed Seattle Port of Embarkation 5 March 1945 for overseas service; arrived in Hawaii 11 March 1945 and moved to Okinawa on 12 August 1945). Inactivated 10 March 1947 on Okinawa.

CAMPAIGN STREAMERS
World War II
Pacific Theater without inscription

DECORATIONS
None

COAT OF ARMS
None

DISTINCTIVE INSIGNIA
None

587th ANTIAIRCRAFT ARTILLERY AUTOMATIC WEAPONS BATTALION

Constituted 25 February 1943 in the Army of the United States as the 587th Antiaircraft Artillery Automatic Weapons Battalion (Mobile) and activated 1 October 1943 at Camp Hulen, Texas. Inactivated 29 October 1944 at Camp Maxey, Texas. Disbanded 20 December 1951.

CAMPAIGN STREAMERS
None

DECORATIONS
None

COAT OF ARMS
None

DISTINCTIVE INSIGNIA
None

588th ANTIAIRCRAFT ARTILLERY AUTOMATIC WEAPONS BATTALION

Constituted 25 February 1943 in the Army of the United States as the 588th Antiaircraft Artillery Automatic Weapons Battalion (Mobile) and activated 1 October 1943 at Camp Hulen, Texas. Inactivated 2 February 1945 at Fort Jackson, South Carolina. Disbanded 28 December 1951.

CAMPAIGN STREAMERS
None

DECORATIONS
None

COAT OF ARMS
None

DISTINCTIVE INSIGNIA
None

589th ANTIAIRCRAFT ARTILLERY AUTOMATIC WEAPONS BATTALION

Constituted 15 April 1942 in the Army of the United States as the 2d Battalion, 614th Coast Artillery (Antiaircraft) and activated 17 April 1942 at Fort Randolph, Canal Zone. (Moved to the United States and arrived at the New York Port of Embarkation on 3 October 1943). Reorganized at Camp Stewart, Georgia on 1 December 1943 and redesignated as the 589th Antiaircraft Artillery Automatic Weapons Battalion (Mobile). Inactivated 31 October 1944 at Camp Gordon, Georgia.

CAMPAIGN STREAMERS
World War II
American Theater without inscription

DECORATIONS
None

COAT OF ARMS
None

DISTINCTIVE INSIGNIA
None

590th ANTIAIRCRAFT ARTILLERY AUTOMATIC WEAPONS BATTALION

Constituted 4 December 1940 in the Regular Army as the 2d Battalion, 82d Coast Artillery (Antiaircraft) and allotted to the Panama Canal Department. Activated 7 December 1940 at Fort Randolph, Canal Zone. Reorganized at Camp Stewart, Georgia and redesignated 1 December 1943 as the 590th Antiaircraft Artillery Automatic Weapons Battalion (Self Propelled). Inactivated 10 May 1944 at Camp Pickett, Virginia. Disbanded 26 June 1944.

CAMPAIGN STREAMERS
World War II
American Theater without inscription

DECORATIONS
None

COAT OF ARMS
None

DISTINCTIVE INSIGNIA
None

591st ANTIAIRCRAFT ARTILLERY AUTOMATIC WEAPONS BATTALION

Constituted July 1923 in the Organized Reserves as the 2d Battalion, 517th Artillery (Antiaircraft), Coast Artillery Corps and allotted to the Ninth Corps area. Redesignated 1 July 1924 as the 2d Battalion, 517th Coast Artillery (Antiaircraft). Organized at San Francisco, California during August 1925. Withdrawn from the Organized Reserves 1 January 1938 and allotted to the Regular Army. Redesignated 1 August 1940 as the 2d Battalion, 78th Coast Artillery (Antiaircraft) (Semimobile). Activated 10 February 1941 at March Field Firing Center, California. (Departed San Francisco Port of Embarkation 15 April 1943 for overseas service and arrived on Attu Island in the Aleutians on 11 May 1943). Reorganized and redesignated 7 February 1944 as the 591st Antiaircraft Artillery Automatic Weapons Battalion. Inactivated 26 January 1945 at Camp Hood, Texas.

Redesignated 28 June 1950 as the 99th Antiaircraft Artillery Battalion.

CAMPAIGN STREAMERS
World War II
Aleutian Islands (with arrowhead)

DECORATIONS
Presidential Unit Citation (Army), Streamer embroidered *CHICAGO HARBOR-ATTU* (Btry F, 78th CA cited for period 18-26 May 1943; WDGO 10, 1944)

COAT OF ARMS
None

DISTINCTIVE INSIGNIA
None

592d ANTIAIRCRAFT ARTILLERY AUTOMATIC WEAPONS BATTALION

Constituted in the Missouri National Guard as 2d Battalion, 2d Artillery (Antiaircraft), Coast Artillery Corps, and organized from new and existing units as follows:

Headquarters and Headquarters Detachment organized new and Federally recognized 28 April 1921 at Springfield

Battery E organized new and Federally recognized 22 January 1921 at Anderson

Company B, 130th Machine Gun Battalion (organized at Springfield as *Springfield Light Guards* and redesignated 26 November 1883 as Company F 5th Infantry, Missouri Volunteer Militia; redesignated 15 October 1890 as Company F 2d Infantry, Missouri National Guard; mustered into Federal service 12 May 1898 at Jefferson Barracks as Company F 2d Missouri Volunteer Infantry; mustered out 3 March 1899 at Albany, Georgia and reorganized as Company M 2d Infantry, Missouri National Guard; disbanded at Springfield about 1905; reorganized 28 December 1908 at Springfield as Company K 2d Infantry, Missouri National Guard; mustered into Federal service 28 June 1916 at Nevada for service on the Mexican border; mustered out 13 January 1917 at Fort Riley, Kansas and resumed State status; drafted into Federal service 5 August 1917; redesignated 1 October 1917 as Company B 130th Machine Gun Battalion and assigned to the 35th Division; demobilized 7 May 1919 at Camp Funston), reorganized and Federally recognized 24 January 1921 at Springfield as Battery F

Company A 130th Machine Gun Battalion (organized 24 June 1909 at Webb City as Company I 2d Infantry, Missouri National Guard; mustered into Federal service 28 June 1916 at Webb City for service on the Mexican border; mustered out 13 January 1917 at Fort Riley, Kansas and resumed State status; drafted into Federal service 5 August 1917; redesignated 1 October 1917 as Company A 130th Machine Gun Battalion and assigned to the 35th Division; demobilized 7 May 1919 at Camp Funston), reorganized and Federally recognized 20 January 1921 at Webb City as Battery G

Redesignated 1 October 1921 as 2d Battalion, 203d Artillery (Antiaircraft), Coast Artillery Corps. Redesignated 19 April 1924 as 2d Battalion, 203d Coast Artillery (Antiaircraft). (Headquarters relocated to Lamar on 27 December 1927). Inducted into Federal service 16 September 1940 at home stations. (Departed Seattle Port of Embarkation 18 June 1942 for overseas service and arrived at Fort Randall, Alaska on 26 June 1942). Reorganized at Amchitka Island, Alaska and redesignated 12 February 1944 as 592d Antiaircraft Artillery Automatic Weapons Battalion (Mobile). (Returned from overseas service and arrived at the Seattle Port of Embarkation on 16 September 1944). Inactivated 10 November 1944 at Camp Maxey, Texas.

Redesignated 27 June 1946 as 196th Tank Battalion.

CAMPAIGN STREAMERS
World War I
Meuse-Argonne
Alsace 1918
Lorraine 1918

World War II
Aleutian Islands

DECORATIONS
None

COAT OF ARMS
None

DISTINCTIVE INSIGNIA
None

593d ANTIAIRCRAFT ARTILLERY AUTOMATIC WEAPONS BATTALION

Constituted in the Michigan National Guard as 2d Battalion, 210th Coast Artillery (Antiaircraft) and organized from new and existing units as follows:

Headquarters, 3d Squadron 106th Cavalry (organized and Federally recognized 15 July 1917 at Detroit as Headquarters, 1st Separate Squadron of Cavalry, Michigan National Guard; drafted into Federal service 5 August 1917 at Detroit; redesignated 23 September 1917 as Headquarters, 2d Battalion 119th Field Artillery and assigned to the 32d Division; demobilized 15 May 1919 at Camp Custer, Michigan; reorganized and Federally recognized 14 June 1921 at Detroit as Headquarters, 1st Separate Squadron of Cavalry; redesignated 1 July 1921 as Headquarters, 1st Squadron 106th Cavalry; redesignated 10 April 1929 as Headquarters, 3d Squadron 106th Cavalry), redesignated 20 September 1940 as Headquarters, 2d Battalion

Headquarters Battery 2d Battalion organized new and Federally recognized 10 October 1940 at Detroit

Troop I 106th Cavalry (organized and Federally recognized 14 June 1921 at Detroit as Headquarters Detachment, 1st Separate Squadron of Cavalry; redesignated 1 July 1921 as Headquarters Detachment 1st Squadron 106th Cavalry), redesignated 20 September 1940 as Battery E

Troop K 106th Cavalry (organized 30 January 1908 at Detroit as Troop B, Cavalry, Michigan National Guard; mustered into Federal service 19 June 1916 at Detroit for duty on Mexican border; mustered out 23 March 1917 at Detroit and resumed State status; drafted into Federal service 5 August 1917 at Detroit; redesignated 23 September 1917 as Battery D 119th Field Artillery and assigned to the 32d Division; demobilized 15 May 1919 at Camp Custer, Michigan; reorganized and Federally recognized 9 August 1920 at Detroit as Troop B, 1st Squadron of Cavalry, Michigan National Guard; redesignated 1 July 1921 as Troop B 106th Cavalry and redesignated 10 April 1929 as Troop K 106th Cavalry), redesignated 20 September 1940 as Battery F

Batteries G and H organized new and Federally recognized 20 September 1940 at Detroit

Inducted into Federal service 24 February 1941 at Detroit. (Departed Seattle Port of Embarkation 29 June 1942 for overseas service and arrived in Alaska on 5 July 1942). Reorganized on Adak Island and redesignated 14 February 1944 as 593d Antiaircraft Artillery Automatic Weapons Battalion. (Returned from overseas service and arrived at the Seattle Port of Embarkation on 16 September 1944). Inactivated 1 November 1944 at Camp Howze, Texas.

Redesignated 1 February 1949 as 146th Antiaircraft Artillery Automatic Weapons Battalion.

CAMPAIGN STREAMERS
World War I
Aisne-Marne
Oise-Aisne
Meuse-Argonne
Lorraine 1918
Alsace 1918
Champagne 1918

World War II
Aleutian Islands

DECORATIONS
French Croix de Guerre with Silver Star, World War I, Streamer embroidered *AISNE-MARNE* and *OISE-AISNE* (119th FA cited; WDGO 11, 1924)

COAT OF ARMS
None

DISTINCTIVE INSIGNIA
None

593d ANTIAIRCRAFT ARTILLERY AUTOMATIC WEAPONS BATTALION

Constituted 22 May 1946 as the 593d Antiaircraft Artillery Automatic Weapons Battalion and allotted to the Michigan National Guard. Organized and Federally recognized 1 November 1949 with Headquarters and Medical Detachment at Kingsford; Battery A at Manistee; Battery B at Iron River; Battery C at Baraga and Battery D at Ironwood.

Redesignated 1 October 1950 as the 300th Antiaircraft Artillery Gun Battalion.

CAMPAIGN STREAMERS
None

DECORATIONS
None

COAT OF ARMS
None

DISTINCTIVE INSIGNIA
None

594th ANTIAIRCRAFT ARTILLERY AUTOMATIC WEAPONS BATTALION

Constituted 28 March 1942 in the Army of the United States as the 2d Battalion, 503d Coast Artillery (Antiaircraft) (Semimobile) and activated 7 April 1942 at Fort Lewis, Washington. (Departed Seattle Port of Embarkation for overseas service 22 June 1942 and arrived in Alaska on 29 June 1942). Reorganized at Fort Glenn, Alaska and redesignated 8 February 1944 as the 594th Antiaircraft Artillery Automatic Weapons Battalion (Semimobile). (Returned to the United States and arrived at the Seattle Port of Embarkation on 6 August 1944). Inactivated 25 September 1944 at Camp Bowie, Texas.

CAMPAIGN STREAMERS
World War II
Aleutian Islands

DECORATIONS
None

COAT OF ARMS
None

DISTINCTIVE INSIGNIA
None

595th ANTIAIRCRAFT ARTILLERY AUTOMATIC WEAPONS BATTALION

Constituted 29 July 1921 in the Organized Reserves as the 2d Battalion, 509th Artillery (Antiaircraft), Coast Artillery Corps and allotted to the Ninth Corps area. Organized during November 1922 with Headquarters at Seattle, Washington. Redesignated 30 June 1924 as the 2d Battalion, 509th Coast Artillery (Antiaircraft). Withdrawn from the Organized Reserves and allotted to the Regular Army on 1 October 1933. Redesignated as the 2d Battalion, 75th Coast Artillery (Antiaircraft) and activated at Fort Lewis, Washington on 1 July 1940. (Departed Seattle Port of Embarkation 26 November 1940 and arrived at Fort Richardson, Alaska on 30 November 1940. Returned to the United States and arrived at the Seattle Port of Embarkation on 3 February 1944). Reorganized and redesignated 20 February 1944 as the 595th Antiaircraft Artillery Automatic Weapons Battalion. Inactivated 1 December 1944 at Camp Livingston, Louisiana.

Redesignated 28 June 1950 as the 90th Antiaircraft Artillery Battalion.

CAMPAIGN STREAMERS
World War II
Pacific Theater without inscription

DECORATIONS
None

COAT OF ARMS
None

DISTINCTIVE INSIGNIA
None

597th ANTIAIRCRAFT ARTILLERY AUTOMATIC WEAPONS BATTALION

Organized 27 September 1917 at Camp Pike, Arkansas as the 141st Machine Gun Battalion and assigned to the 39th Division. Redesignated 2 October 1918 as the 141st Antiaircraft Machine Gun Battalion. Demobilized 13 January 1919 at Camp Beauregard, Louisiana. Allotted to the Arkansas National Guard and reorganized as the 2d Battalion, 141st Artillery (Antiaircraft), Coast Artillery Corps with Headquarters Federally recognized 21 June 1921 at Little Rock and batteries at Nashville, Heber Springs, Blue Mountain, Ozark and Little Rock. Redesignated 1 December 1923 as the 2d Battalion, 206th Artillery (Antiaircraft), Coast Artillery Corps. Redesignated 22 April 1924 as the 2d Battalion, 206th Coast Artillery (Antiaircraft). Inducted into Federal service 6 January 1941 at home stations. (Departed Seattle Port of Embarkation 27 February 1942 for overseas service and arrived in Alaska on 8 March 1942. Returned from overseas service and arrived at the Seattle Port of Embarkation on 27 February 1944). Reorganized at Fort Bliss, Texas and redesignated 1 April 1944 as the 597th Antiaircraft Artillery Automatic Weapons Battalion (Mobile). (Departed New York Port of Embarkation 10 December 1944 for overseas service; arrived in England 16 December 1944 and landed in France on 2 March 1945. Returned from overseas service and arrived at the New York Port of Embarkation on 11 December 1945). Inactivated 12 December 1945 at Camp Kilmer, New Jersey.

Redesignated 27 May 1946 as the 445th Field Artillery Battalion.

CAMPAIGN STREAMERS
World War I
Streamer without inscription

World War II
Aleutian Islands
Rhineland
Central Europe

DECORATIONS
None

COAT OF ARMS
None

DISTINCTIVE INSIGNIA
None

598th ANTIAIRCRAFT ARTILLERY BATTALION

Constituted in the Minnesota National Guard as the 1st Battalion, 215th Coast Artillery (Antiaircraft) (Semimobile) and organized 1 July 1940 from elements of the 205th and 206th Infantry Regiments as follows:

Headquarters, 3d Battalion, 205th Infantry (organized and Federally recognized 30 April 1921 at St. Cloud as Headquarters, 3d Battalion, 5th Infantry, Minnesota National Guard and redesignated 1 December 1923 as Headquarters, 3d Battalion, 205th Infantry; relocated to Mankato on 26 November 1928 and to Luverne about 1930), redesignated Headquarters, 1st Battalion

Company L, 205th Infantry (organized 6 March 1908 at Redwood Falls as Company L, 2d Infantry, Minnesota National Guard; mustered into Federal service 26 June 1916 at Fort Snelling, Minnesota for service on the Mexican border; mustered out 24 January 1917 at Fort Snelling and resumed State status; called into Federal service 15 July 1917 at Redwood Falls and drafted into Federal service 5 August 1917; redesignated 1 October 1917 as Company L, 136th Infantry and assigned to the 34th Division; demobilized 18 February 1919 at Camp Grant, Illinois and consolidated with Company L, 5th Infantry, Minnesota National Guard [organized and Federally recognized 17 January 1919 at Redwood Falls]; redesignated 1 December 1923 as Company L, 205th Infantry), redesignated Headquarters Battery, 1st Battalion

Company E, 206th Infantry (organized prior to 1895 at Faribault as Company B, 2d Infantry, Minnesota National Guard; redesignated 4 May 1898 as Company B, 12th Minnesota Volunteer Infantry; mustered into Federal service 7 May 1898 at St. Paul; mustered out 5 November 1898 and returned to State control; reorganized at Faribault about 1900 as Company B, 2d Infantry, Minnesota National Guard; mustered into Federal service 26 June 1916 at Fort Snelling, Minnesota for service on the Mexican border; mustered out 24 January 1917 at Fort Snelling and resumed State status; called into Federal service 15 July 1917 at Faribault and drafted into Federal service 5 August 1917; redesignated 1 October 1917 as Company B, 136th Infantry and assigned to the 34th Division; demobilized 18 February 1919 at Camp Grant, Illinois and consolidated with Company H, 6th Infantry, Minnesota National Guard [organized and Federally recognized 30 January 1919 at Faribault]; redesignated 1 December 1923 as Company E, 206th Infantry), redesignated Battery A

Company D, 205th Infantry (organized 2 February 1908 at St. Peter as Company K, 2d Infantry, Minnesota National Guard; mustered into Federal service 26 June 1916 at Fort Snelling, Minnesota for service on the Mexican border; mustered out 24 January 1917 at Fort Snelling and resumed State status; called into Federal service 15 July 1917 at St. Peter and drafted into Federal service 5 August 1917; redesignated 1 October 1917 as Company K, 136th Infantry and assigned to the 34th Division; demobilized 18 February 1919 at Camp Grant, Illinois and consolidated with Company B, 5th Infantry, Minnesota National Guard [organized and Federally recognized 17 January 1919 at St. Peter]; redesignated 17 May 1921 as Headquarters Company, 1st Battalion, 5th Infantry; redesignated 1 November 1923 as

Company D, 5th Infantry; and redesignated 1 December 1923 as Company D, 205th Infantry), redesignated Battery B

Company A, 205th Infantry (organized at New Ulm prior to 1895 as Company A, 2d Infantry, Minnesota National Guard; redesignated 4 May 1898 as Company A, 12th Minnesota Volunteer Infantry; mustered into Federal service 7 May 1898 at St. Paul; mustered out 5 November 1898 and returned to State control; reorganized at New Ulm about 1900 as Company A, 2d Infantry, Minnesota National Guard; mustered into Federal service 26 June 1916 at Fort Snelling, Minnesota for service on the Mexican border; mustered out 24 January 1917 at Fort Snelling and resumed State status; called into Federal service 15 July 1917 at New Ulm and drafted into Federal service 5 August 1917; redesignated 1 October 1917 as Company A, 136th Infantry and assigned to the 34th Division; demobilized 18 February 1919 at Camp Grant, Illinois; reorganized and Federally recognized 17 May 1919 at New Ulm as Company A, 5th Infantry, Minnesota National Guard; redesignated 1 December 1923 as Company A, 205th Infantry), redesignated Battery C

Battery F, 125th Field Artillery (organized prior to 1903 at Olivia as Company H, 3d Infantry, Minnesota National Guard; mustered into Federal service 19 June 1916 at Fort Snelling, Minnesota for service on the Mexican border; mustered out 19 December 1916 at Fort Snelling and resumed State status; called into Federal service 24 July 1917 at Olivia and drafted into Federal service 5 August 1917; redesignated 1 October 1917 as Battery E, 125th Field Artillery and assigned to the 34th Division; demobilized 22 January 1919 at Camp Dodge, Iowa; reorganized and Federally recognized 24 July 1924 at Olivia as Battery F, 125th Field Artillery), redesignated Battery D

Inducted into Federal service 6 January 1941 at home stations. (Departed Seattle Port of Embarkation 29 August 1941 for overseas service and arrived at Fort Greely, Kodiak, Alaska on 3 September 1941. Returned from overseas service and arrived at the Seattle Port of Embarkation on 29 February 1944). Reorganized at Fort Bliss, Texas and redesignated 1 July 1944 as the 598th Antiaircraft Artillery Gun Battalion (Semimobile). Inactivated 29 October 1944 at Camp Maxey, Texas. Reorganized 21 June 1946 and organic elements redesignated, consolidated or disbanded as follows: Headquarters Battery redesignated Cannon Company, 135th Infantry; Battery A disbanded; Battery B redesignated Service Battery, 125th Field Artillery Battalion; Battery C redesignated Service Company, 135th Infantry; and Battery D consolidated with Headquarters and Headquarters Battery, 175th Field Artillery Battalion; concurrently, new organic batteries constituted and allotted to the Minnesota National Guard. Battalion reorganized at Duluth and Federally recognized 1 October 1946. Reorganized and redesignated 1 October 1949 as the 598th Antiaircraft Artillery Automatic Weapons Battalion (Mobile). Reorganized and redesignated 16 July 1951 as the 598th Antiaircraft Artillery Gun Battalion (90mm). Redesignated 1 October 1953 as the 598th Antiaircraft Artillery Battalion (90mm Gun).

Battalion broken up 22 February 1959 and elements converted and redesignated as follows: Headquarters and Headquarters Battery as Headquarters and Headquarters Detachment, 109th Transportation Battalion (Tactical Carrier); Battery A as the 114th Transportation Company (Tactical Carrier); Battery B as Battery B, 1st Howitzer Battalion, 125th Field Artillery; Battery C as the 224th Transportation Company (Tactical Carrier); and Battery D as the 535th Transportation Company (Tactical Carrier).

CAMPAIGN STREAMERS
World War II
Pacific Theater without inscription

DECORATIONS
None

COAT OF ARMS
None

DISTINCTIVE INSIGNIA
None

599th ANTIAIRCRAFT ARTILLERY AUTOMATIC WEAPONS BATTALION

Constituted in the Minnesota National Guard as the 2d Battalion, 215th Coast Artillery (Antiaircraft) (Semimobile) and organized 1 July 1940 from elements of the 205th Infantry as follows:

Headquarters, 2d Battalion, 205th Infantry (organized and Federally recognized 1 June 1921 at Luverne as Headquarters, 2d Battalion, 5th Infantry, Minnesota National Guard; redesignated 1 December 1923 as Headquarters, 2d Battalion, 205th Infantry and relocated to Mankato on 29 October 1930), redesignated Headquarters, 2d Battalion

Service Company, 205th Infantry (organized and Federally recognized 17 January 1919 at Mankato as Supply Company, 5th Infantry, Minnesota National Guard; redesignated 19 April 1921 as Service Company, 5th Infantry; redesignated 1 December 1923 as Service Company, 205th Infantry), redesignated Headquarters Battery, 2d Battalion

Company H, 205th Infantry (organized and Federally recognized 17 January 1919 at Luverne as Company H, 5th Infantry, Minnesota National Guard and redesignated 1 December 1923 as Company H, 205th Infantry), redesignated Battery E

Company F, 205th Infantry (organized 28 November 1905 at Worthington as Company F, 3d Infantry, Minnesota National Guard; redesignated 31 January 1908 as Company F, 2d Infantry; mustered into Federal service 26 June 1916 at Fort Snelling, Minnesota for service on the Mexican border; mustered out 24 January 1917 at Fort Snelling and resumed State status; called into Federal service 15 July 1917 at Worthington and drafted into Federal service 5 August 1917; redesignated 1 October 1917 as Company F, 136th Infantry and assigned to the 34th Division; demobilized 18 February 1919 at Camp Grant, Illinois and consolidated with Company F, 5th Infantry, Minnesota National Guard [organized and Federally recognized 17 January 1919 at Worthington]; redesignated 1 December 1923 as Company F, 205th Infantry), redesignated Battery F

Company G, 205th Infantry (organized and Federally recognized 19 May 1921 at Windom as Headquarters Company, 2d Battalion, 5th Infantry, Minnesota National Guard; redesignated 1 May 1923 as Company G, 5th Infantry; redesignated 1 December 1923 as Company G, 205th Infantry), redesignated Battery G

Company E, 205th Infantry (organized at Fairmont prior to 1895 as Company D, 2d Infantry, Minnesota National Guard; redesignated 4 May 1898 as Company D, 12th Minnesota Volunteer Infantry; mustered into Federal service 7 May 1898 at St. Paul; mustered out 5 November 1898 and returned to State control; reorganized at Fairmont about 1900 as Company E, 2d Infantry, Minnesota National Guard; mustered into Federal service 26 June 1916 at Fort Snelling, Minnesota for service on the Mexican border; mustered out 24 January 1917 at Fort Snelling and resumed State status; called into Federal service 15 July 1917 at Fairmont and drafted into Federal service 5 August 1917; redesignated 1 October 1917 as Company E, 136th Infantry and assigned to the 34th Division; demobilized 18 February 1919 at Camp Grant, Illinois and consolidated with Company G, 5th Infantry, Minnesota National Guard [organized and Federally recognized 17 January 1919 at Fairmont]; redesignated 1 May 1922 as Headquarters Company, 2d Battalion, 5th Infantry; redesignated 1 December 1923 as Headquarters Company, 2d Battalion, 205th Infantry and redesignated 1 October 1924 as Company E, 205th Infantry), redesignated Battery H

Inducted into Federal service 6 January 1941 at home stations. (Departed Seattle Port of Embarkation 29 August 1941 for overseas service and arrived at Fort Greely, Kodiak, Alaska on 3 September 1941. Returned from overseas service and arrived at the Seattle Port of Embarkation 29 February 1944). Reorganized at Fort Bliss, Texas and redesignated 1 July 1944 as the 599th Antiaircraft Artillery Automatic Weapons Battalion (Mobile). (Departed New York Port of Embarkation 10 December 1944 for overseas service; arrived in England 16 December 1944 and landed in France on 3 March 1945. Returned from overseas service and arrived at the Hampton Roads Port of Embarkation 7 December 1945). Inactivated 7 December 1945 at Camp Patrick Henry, Virginia.

Consolidated 28 June 1946 with the 135th Infantry.

CAMPAIGN STREAMERS
World War II
Pacific Theater without inscription
Rhineland
Central Europe

DECORATIONS
None

COAT OF ARMS
None

DISTINCTIVE INSIGNIA
None

601st ANTIAIRCRAFT ARTILLERY BATTALION

Constituted 19 January 1942 in the Army of the United States as 1st Battalion, 601st Coast Artillery (Antiaircraft) and activated 1 February 1942 at Fort Bliss, Texas. Reorganized at Philadelphia, Pennsylvania on 1 September 1943 and redesignated as 601st Antiaircraft Artillery Gun Battalion (Semimobile). (Departed New York Port of Embarkation 13 March 1944 for overseas service; arrived in England on 21 March 1944 and landed in France on 6 July 1944). Inactivated 31 December 1945 in Germany. Allotted to the Regular Army on 19 November 1952. Activated 1 January 1953 at Fort George G. Meade, Maryland. Redesignated 15 July 1953 as the 601st Antiaircraft Artillery Battalion. Inactivated 15 June 1957 at Andrews Air Force Base, Maryland.

CAMPAIGN STREAMERS
World War II
England 1944
Normandy
Northern France
Rhineland

DECORATIONS
Belgian Fourragere 1940 (601st AAA Gun Bn cited; DAGO 43, 1950)

Cited in the Order of the Day of the Belgian Army for action in defense of *ANTWERP* (601st AAA Gun Bn cited for period 25 Oct-28 Nov 1944; DAGO 43, 1950)

Cited in the Order of the Day of the Belgian Army for action in defense of *ANTWERP HARBOR* (601st AAA Gun Bn cited for action on 16 Dec 1944; DAGO 43, 1950)

COAT OF ARMS
SHIELD: Gules a condor volant in bend sinister or, the sinister wing severed, embrued proper, by a two handed sword of the second.

CREST: None

MOTTO: Clip Their Wings

Red is for Artillery. The condor is one of the largest and most powerful flying birds; this bird of prey, roosting and breeding at elevations of 10,000 to 16,000 feet, has been seen at elevations of over 23,000 feet. By preference it feeds on carrion and is exceedingly voracious and tenacious of life and can exist without food for over 40 days. The vanquished vulture of the skies is aptly symbolical of the antiaircraft functions of the organization, that of clearing the skies of such attacking birds of prey.

DISTINCTIVE INSIGNIA
The insignia is the shield and motto of the coat of arms. The insignia depicted was unofficially worn by this organization between 1953 and 1957.

602d ANTIAIRCRAFT ARTILLERY MISSILE BATTALION

Constituted 31 January 1942 in the Army of the United States as 1st Battalion, 602d Coast Artillery (Antiaircraft) and activated 1 March 1942 at Fort Bliss, Texas. Reorganized at New York, New York on 1 September 1943 and redesignated as 602d Antiaircraft Artillery Gun Battalion (Semimobile). (Departed New York Port of Embarkation 15 March 1944 for overseas service; arrived in England on 21 March 1944 and landed in France on 3 July 1944. Returned from overseas service and arrived at the New York Port of Embarkation on 25 January 1946). Inactivated 26 January 1946 at Camp Kilmer, New Jersey. Allotted to the Regular Army on 19 November 1952. Activated 1 January 1953 at Baltimore, Maryland. Redesignated 22 July 1953 as the 602d Antiaircraft Artillery Battalion. Reorganized and redesignated 22 September 1955 as the 602d Antiaircraft Artillery Missile Battalion. Inactivated 1 September 1958 at Laytonville, Maryland.

CAMPAIGN STREAMERS
World War II
Normandy
Northern France
Rhineland
Ardennes-Alsace

DECORATIONS
None

COAT OF ARMS
SHIELD: Sable, on a mullet gules fimbriated or, surmounted by two searchlight beams issuant from center base to dexter and sinister chief throughout a shell, point to chief, all of the third.

CREST: None

MOTTO: It Will Be Done

The star, in red for Artillery, alludes to Texas, the "Lone Star" State where the battalion was originally organized. The projectile and searchlight beams refer to the antiaircraft mission of the organization while the two searchlight beams form the letter "V" for victory.

DISTINCTIVE INSIGNIA
The insignia is the shield and motto of the coat of arms. The sample of the insignia depicted was originally approved on 29 March 1943 for wear by the 602d Coast Artillery.

603d ANTIAIRCRAFT ARTILLERY GUN BATTALION

Constituted 31 January 1942 in the Army of the United States as 1st Battalion, 603d Coast Artillery (Antiaircraft) and activated 1 March 1942 at Camp Stewart, Georgia. Reorganized at Burbank, California and redesignated 10 September 1943 as 603d Antiaircraft Artillery Gun Battalion (Semimobile). Inactivated 13 May 1944 at Camp Phillips, Kansas. Disbanded 26 June 1944.

CAMPAIGN STREAMERS
None

DECORATIONS
None

COAT OF ARMS
SHIELD: Gules a Greek mythological Gorgon-headed harpy pierced by a sword in bend, point to chief, all or.

CREST: None

MOTTO: Ready Willing And Able

The shield is in the colors of the Coast Artillery. The monstrous mythological creature, the harpy, sometimes represented as having a woman's head and bird's wings, tail, legs, and claws, and pierced with the trusty sword of the organization, is symbolic of the antiaircraft functions of the organization. The harpies were usually malign creatures who snatch up and carry off souls of the dead or execute divine vengeance by seizing and defiling the food of the victim; originally they seem to have been personification of devastating winds. These were the same creatures, according to the belief of the Greek and Romans, who were employed by the higher gods to carry out their ill bidding.

DISTINCTIVE INSIGNIA

The insignia is the shield and motto of the coat of arms. The sample of the insignia depicted was unofficially worn by this organization during 1943 and 1944.

604th ANTIAIRCRAFT ARTILLERY GUN BATTALION

Constituted 31 January 1942 in the Army of the United States as 1st Battalion, 604th Coast Artillery (Antiaircraft) and activated 1 March 1942 at Fort Bliss, Texas. Reorganized at New York, New York on 1 September 1943 and redesignated as 604th Antiaircraft Artillery Gun Battalion (Semimobile).

Redesignated 1 May 1944 as the 942d Field Artillery Battalion.

CAMPAIGN STREAMERS
None

DECORATIONS
None

COAT OF ARMS
SHIELD: Per bend azure and gules, on the first a silhouette of an aircraft with a broken wing bendsinisterwise argent, on the second an antiaircraft gun barrel in elevated position or.

CREST: None

MOTTO: *Facemus* (We Do)

The scarlet is the color of the Coast Artillery Corps. The functions of the organization are symbolized by the aircraft gun, the primary weapon of the battalion; the falling airplane represents the target of the antiaircraft falling from the blue, symbolizing the sky where the target is usually found.

DISTINCTIVE INSIGNIA
No distinctive insignia was approved for this organization.

605th COAST ARTILLERY BATTALION

Constituted July 1923 in the Organized Reserves as the 605th Artillery Battalion (Railway), Coast Artillery Corps (Fixed Defense) and allotted to the Ninth Corps area. Organized at Seattle Washington during November 1923 from existing companies as follows: 940th Company, Coast Artillery Corps redesignated Headquarters Battery; 930th Company, Coast Artillery Corps redesignated Battery A; and 931st Company, Coast Artillery Corps redesignated Battery B. Redesignated 30 June 1924 as the 605th Coast Artillery Battalion (Railway). Relocated to Los Angeles, California in 1930. Disbanded 22 August 1942 at Los Angeles.

CAMPAIGN STREAMERS
None

DECORATIONS
None

COAT OF ARMS
SHIELD: Per bend wavy gules and azure, in sinister chief a dragon rampant or.

CREST: That for the regiments and separate battalions of the Organized Reserves: On a wreath of the colors (or and gules) the Lexington Minute Man proper. The statue of the Minute Man, Captain John Parker (H. H. Kitson, sculptor), stands on the common in Lexington, Massachusetts.

MOTTO: *Vigilantia Immortalis* (Everlasting Vigilance)

The shield is partitioned per bend wavy, the red representing Artillery and the blue the Pacific Ocean. The dragon represents speed, alertness, mobility, courage, and power.

DISTINCTIVE INSIGNIA
The insignia is the shield and motto of the coat of arms. The sample of the insignia depicted was approved for wear on 22 March 1932.

605th ANTIAIRCRAFT ARTILLERY MISSILE BATTALION

Constituted 31 January 1942 in the Army of the United States as 1st Battalion, 605th Coast Artillery (Antiaircraft) and activated 1 March 1942 at Camp Stewart, Georgia. Reorganized at Boston, Massachusetts on 1 September 1943 and redesignated as 605th Antiaircraft Artillery Gun Battalion (Semimobile). (Departed New York Port of Embarkation 21 March 1944 for overseas service; arrived in England on 27 March 1944 and landed in France on 9 July 1944). Inactivated 29 June 1946 in France. Allotted to the Regular Army on 19 November 1952. Activated 16 February 1953 at Fort Dawes, Massachusetts. Redesignated 3 August 1953 as the 605th Antiaircraft Artillery Battalion. Reorganized and redesignated 19 April 1956 as the 605th Antiaircraft Artillery Missile Battalion. Inactivated 1 September 1958 at Nahant, Massachusetts.

CAMPAIGN STREAMERS
World War II
Normandy
Northern France
Rhineland

DECORATIONS
Belgian Fourragere 1940 (605th AAA Gun Bn cited; DAGO 43, 1950)

Cited in the Order of the Day of the Belgian Army for action in defense of *ANTWERP* (605th AAA Gun Bn cited for period 25 Oct-28 Nov 1944; DAGO 43, 1950)

Cited in the Order of the Day of the Belgian Army for action in defense of *ANTWERP HARBOR* (605th AAA Gun Bn cited for action on 16 Dec 1944; DAGO 43, 1950)

COAT OF ARMS
SHIELD: Gules, within a double tressure flory, counter flory a fretty or.

CREST: None

MOTTO: Visibility Unlimited

Medieval castles always used a moat as a first line of defense; such a moat is represented by the double tressure around the inside of the shield, the flowered border being the locks and safeguards employed to keep the moat in constant order. The fretty, symbolic of the net of additional protection encompassing the field of operations is also representative of the activities of keeping the enemy away from its objective.

DISTINCTIVE INSIGNIA
The insignia is the shield and motto of the coat of arms. The insignia depicted was unofficially worn by this organization between 1953 and 1958.

606th COAST ARTILLERY BATTALION

Constituted in the Regular Army as 1st Battalion, Howitzer Regiment, 30th Brigade, Coast Artillery Corps and organized 26 March 1918 in France from new and existing units as follows:

Headquarters, 1st Battalion organized new

Battery E, 52d Artillery, Coast Artillery Corps (constituted 2 March 1899 in the Regular Army as Battery O, 1st Regiment of Artillery and organized later that same year at Jackson Barracks, New Orleans, Louisiana; reorganized and redesignated 13 February 1901 as the 12th Company, Coast Artillery, Artillery Corps; redesignated 2 February 1907 as the 12th Company, Coast Artillery Corps; redesignated 3 July 1916 as the 2d Company, Fort H. G. Wright [New York]; redesignated 22 July 1917 as Battery E, 7th Provisional Regiment, Coast Artillery Corps; and redesignated 5 February 1918 as Battery E, 52d Artillery, Coast Artillery Corps), redesignated 1st Battery

Battery F, 52d Artillery, Coast Artillery Corps (constituted in the Regular Army as 2d Company, Fort Schuyler [New York] and organized 8 June 1917 at Fort Schuyler; redesignated 22 July 1917 as Battery F, 7th Provisional Regiment, Coast Artillery Corps; and redesignated 5 February 1918 as Battery F, 52d Artillery, Coast Artillery Corps), redesignated 2d Battery

Redesignated 7 August 1918 as 1st Battalion, 44th Artillery, Coast Artillery Corps. Inactivated 31 August 1921 at Camp Jackson, South Carolina. Redesignated 1 July 1924 as 1st Battalion, 44th Coast Artillery (155mm Gun). Activated 10 February 1941 at Camp Wallace, Texas with Negro enlisted personnel. Reorganized at Fort Ord, California and redesignated 5 June 1944 as the 606th Coast Artillery Battalion (155mm Gun) (Colored). Disbanded 3 August 1944 at Camp Livingston, Louisiana. Reconstituted in the Regular Army and consolidated with the 54th Armored Field Artillery Battalion on 28 June 1950.

CAMPAIGN STREAMERS
World War I
Champagne-Marne
St. Mihiel
Champagne 1918
Lorraine 1918

DECORATIONS
None

COAT OF ARMS
None

DISTINCTIVE INSIGNIA
None

606th ANTIAIRCRAFT ARTILLERY BATTALION

 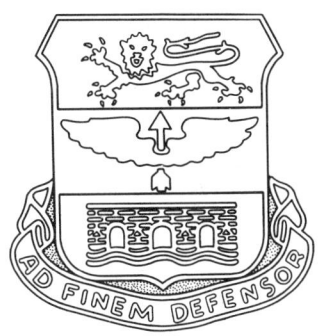

Constituted 25 February 1943 in the Army of the United States as the 120th Coast Artillery Battalion (Antiaircraft) (Gun) and activated 2 April 1943 at Camp Haan, California. Redesignated 28 June 1943 as the 120th Antiaircraft Artillery Gun Battalion (Mobile). (Departed New York Port of Embarkation 23 December 1943 for overseas service; arrived in England on 29 December 1943 and landed in France on 16 June 1944. Returned to the United States after the war and arrived at the Hampton Roads Port of Embarkation on 4 December 1945). Inactivated 4 December 1945 at Camp Patrick Henry, Virginia. Redesignated 5 December 1949 as the 606th Antiaircraft Artillery Gun Battalion. Allotted to the Regular Army on 5 December 1949. Activated 14 February 1953 at Lewiston, New York. Redesignated 3 August 1953 as the 606th Antiaircraft Artillery Battalion. Inactivated 20 December 1957 at Niagara Falls, New York.

CAMPAIGN STREAMERS
World War II
Normandy
Northern France
Rhineland
Ardennes-Alsace
Central Europe
England 1944

DECORATIONS
French Croix de Guerre with Gold Star, World War II, Streamer embroidered *NORMANDY* (120th AAA Gun Bn cited for period 1-31 July 1944; DAGO 43, 1950.

COAT OF ARMS
SHIELD: Gules, on a fess between a lion passant guardant and a triple-arched bridge over water or, a vol sable pierced by an arrow of the first.

CREST: None

MOTTO: *Ad Finem Defensor* (Defenders To The End)

The colors red and yellow are for Artillery. The antiaircraft mission of the battalion is depicted by the pierced wings. The lion, taken from the English quarter of the coat of arms of Great Britain, and the bridge, taken from the coat of arms of Pontorson, Normandy symbolize the first campaign of the organization in Europe during World War II and its distinguished valor in defense of the bridges of Normandy.

DISTINCTIVE INSIGNIA
The insignia is the shield and motto of the coat of arms. The sample of the insignia depicted was approved for wear on 25 March 1954.

607th COAST ARTILLERY BATTALION

Constituted in the Regular Army as 3d Battalion, Howitzer Regiment, 30th Brigade, Coast Artillery Corps and organized 26 March 1918 in France from new and existing units as follows:

Headquarters, 3d Battalion organized new

Battery I, 51st Artillery (constituted 10 July 1907 in the Regular Army as the 151st Company, Coast Artillery, Artillery Corps and organized 5 August 1907 at Fort Revere, Massachusetts; redesignated as 2d Company, Fort Andrews [Massachusetts] in July 1916; redesignated 21 July 1917 as Battery I, 6th Provisional Regiment, Coast Artillery Corps; and redesignated 5 February 1918 as Battery I, 51st Artillery, Coast Artillery Corps), redesignated 5th Battery

Battery K, 6th Artillery, Coast Artillery Corps (constituted 12 April 1808 in the Regular Army as a company in the Regiment of Light Artillery and organized early in 1814 as Lieutenant Francis Stribling's Company, Regiment of Light Artillery; redesignated 30 June 1814 as Captain Francis Stribling's Company, Regiment of Light Artillery; consolidated during May or June 1815 with Captain Adam Larrabee's Company, Regiment of Light Artillery [organized during 1814] and Captain Thomas Ketchum's Company, Regiment of Light Artillery [organized during 1814], reorganized and redesignated as Captain Nathan Towson's Company, Regiment of Light Artillery; and redesignated 22 May 1816 as Company D, Regiment of Light Artillery, redesignated 1 June 1821 as Company H, 1st Regiment of Artillery; redesignated 13 February 1901 as 7th Company, Coast Artillery, Artillery Corps; redesignated 2 February 1907 as 7th Company, Coast Artillery Corps; redesignated 30 June 1916 as 2d Company, Fort Banks [Massachusetts]; redesignated 21 July 1917 as Battery K, 6th Provisional Regiment, Coast Artillery Corps; redesignated 5 February 1918 as Battery K, 51st Artillery, Coast Artillery Corps), redesignated 6th Battery

Redesignated 7 August 1918 as 3d Battalion, 44th Artillery, Coast Artillery Corps. Inactivated 31 August 1921 at Camp Jackson, South Carolina. Redesignated 1 July 1924 as 3d Battalion, 44th Coast Artillery (155mm Gun). Activated 10 February 1941 at Camp Wallace, Texas with Negro enlisted personnel. Reorganized at Fort Ord, California and redesignated 5 June 1944 as the 607th Coast Artillery Battalion (155mm Gun) (Colored). Disbanded 31 July 1944 at Camp Rucker, Alabama. Reconstituted 28 June 1950 in the Regular Army and consolidated with the 44th Field Artillery Battalion.

CAMPAIGN STREAMERS

War of 1812
Canada

Indian Wars
Seminoles

Mexican War
Vera Cruz
Cerro Gordo
Contreras
Churubusco
Chapultepec
Vera Cruz 1847
Mexico 1847

Civil War
Sumter
Peninsula
Fredericksburg
Chancellorsville
Gettysburg
Wilderness
Spotsylvania
Cold Harbor

Petersburg
Virginia 1863

World War I
St. Mihiel
Alsace 1918
Lorraine 1918

DECORATIONS
None

COAT OF ARMS
None

DISTINCTIVE INSIGNIA
None

HEADQUARTERS AND HEADQUARTERS DETACHMENT 608th COAST ARTILLERY BATTALION

Constituted 26 June 1946 as Headquarters and Headquarters Detachment, 608th Coast Artillery Battalion (Harbor Defense) and allotted to the Massachusetts National Guard. Withdrawn from allotment to the Massachusetts Army National Guard on 1 May 1949 and returned to Department of the Army control.

CAMPAIGN STREAMERS
None

DECORATIONS
None

COAT OF ARMS
None

DISTINCTIVE INSIGNIA
None

609th COAST ARTILLERY BATTALION

Constituted 31 March 1924 in the Organized Reserves as the 609th Artillery Battalion (Railway), Coast Artillery Corps and allotted to the Third Corps area. Redesignated 30 June 1924 as the 609th Coast Artillery Battalion (Railway). Organized at Fort Monroe, Virginia during August 1925. Disbanded 5 September 1928 at Fort Monroe.

CAMPAIGN STREAMERS
None

DECORATIONS
None

COAT OF ARMS
None

DISTINCTIVE INSIGNIA
None

HEADQUARTERS AND HEADQUARTERS DETACHMENT 609th COAST ARTILLERY BATTALION

Constituted 26 June 1946 as Headquarters and Headquarters Detachment, 609th Coast Artillery Battalion (Harbor Defense) and allotted to the Massachusetts National Guard. Withdrawn from allotment to the Massachusetts Army National Guard on 1 May 1949 and returned to Department of the Army control.

CAMPAIGN STREAMERS
None

DECORATIONS
None

COAT OF ARMS
None

DISTINCTIVE INSIGNIA
None

HEADQUARTERS AND HEADQUARTERS DETACHMENT 610th COAST ARTILLERY BATTALION

Constituted 26 June 1946 as Headquarters and Headquarters Detachment, 610th Coast Artillery Battalion (Harbor Defense) and allotted to the Massachusetts National Guard. Withdrawn from allotment to the Massachusetts Army National Guard on 1 May 1949 and returned to Department of the Army control.

CAMPAIGN STREAMERS
None

DECORATIONS
None

COAT OF ARMS
None

DISTINCTIVE INSIGNIA
None

HEADQUARTERS AND HEADQUARTERS DETACHMENT 611th COAST ARTILLERY BATTALION

Constituted 27 September 1946 as Headquarters and Headquarters Detachment, 611th Coast Artillery Battalion (Harbor Defense) and allotted to the New York National Guard. Withdrawn from allotment to the New York Army National Guard on 1 May 1949 and returned to Department of the Army control.

CAMPAIGN STREAMERS
None

DECORATIONS
None

COAT OF ARMS
None

DISTINCTIVE INSIGNIA
None

HEADQUARTERS AND HEADQUARTERS DETACHMENT 612th COAST ARTILLERY BATTALION

Constituted 27 September 1946 as Headquarters and Headquarters Detachment, 612th Coast Artillery Battalion (Harbor Defense) and allotted to the New York National Guard. Withdrawn from allotment to the New York Army National Guard on 1 May 1949 and returned to Department of the Army control.

CAMPAIGN STREAMERS
None

DECORATIONS
None

COAT OF ARMS
None

DISTINCTIVE INSIGNIA
None

613th COAST ARTILLERY BATTALION

Constituted 31 March 1924 in the Organized Reserves as the 613th Artillery Battalion, Coast Artillery Corps (Fixed Defenses) and allotted to the First Corps area. Redesignated 30 June 1924 as the 613th Coast Artillery Battalion (Harbor Defense). Organized in the Harbor Defenses of Portland during November 1924 with Headquarters at Portland.

Redesignated 19 March 1926 as 613th Coast Artillery.

CAMPAIGN STREAMERS
None

DECORATIONS
None

COAT OF ARMS
None

DISTINCTIVE INSIGNIA
None

HEADQUARTERS AND HEADQUARTERS DETACHMENT 613th COAST ARTILLERY BATTALION

Constituted 2 July 1946 as Headquarters and Headquarters Detachment, 613th Coast Artillery Battalion (Harbor Defense) and allotted to the Virginia National Guard. Withdrawn from allotment to the Virginia National Guard 31 August 1948 and returned to Department of the Army control.

CAMPAIGN STREAMERS
None

DECORATIONS
None

COAT OF ARMS
None

DISTINCTIVE INSIGNIA
None

614th COAST ARTILLERY BATTALION

Constituted 31 March 1924 in the Organized Reserves as the 614th Artillery Battalion (Fixed Defenses), Coast Artillery Corps and allotted to the First Corps area. Redesignated 30 June 1924 as the 614th Coast Artillery Battalion (Harbor Defense). Organized in the Harbor Defenses of Portsmouth, New Hampshire during November 1924. Reorganized, expanded and redesignated 19 March 1926 as the 614th Coast Artillery (Harbor Defense). Reorganized and redesignated 9 May 1935 as the 614th Separate Coast Artillery Battalion (Harbor Defense). Withdrawn from the Organized Reserves and allotted to the Regular Army on 1 September 1935.

Reorganized, expanded and redesignated 1 February 1940 as the 22d Coast Artillery.

CAMPAIGN STREAMERS
None

DECORATIONS
None

COAT OF ARMS
None

DISTINCTIVE INSIGNIA
None

614th ANTIAIRCRAFT ARTILLERY BATTALION

Constituted 27 April 1942 in the Army of the United States as the 614th Tank Destroyer Battalion (Towed 3-inch Antitank Gun) (Colored) and activated 25 July 1942 at Camp Carson,

Colorado. (Departed New York Port of Embarkation for overseas service 27 August 1944 and landed in France on 7 September 1944. Returned from overseas service and arrived at the New York Port of Embarkation on 30 January 1946). Inactivated 31 January 1946 at Camp Kilmer, New Jersey. Redesignated 16 April 1947 as the 886th Field Artillery Battalion and allotted to the Organized Reserves. Activated 24 April 1947 with Headquarters at Columbus, Ohio. (Organized Reserves redesignated 25 March 1948 as Organized Reserve Corps). Reorganized and redesignated 10 September 1950 as the 886th Antiaircraft Artillery Gun Battalion. Redesignated 10 April 1952 as the 614th Antiaircraft Artillery Gun Battalion. (Organized Reserve Corps redesignated 9 July 1952 as Army Reserve). Redesignated 17 September 1953 as the 614th Antiaircraft Artillery Battalion. Relocated to Philadelphia, Pennsylvania on 21 September 1955. Inactivated 18 May 1959 at Philadelphia.

CAMPAIGN STREAMERS
World War II
Northern France
Rhineland
Ardennes-Alsace
Central Europe

DECORATIONS
None

COAT OF ARMS
SHIELD: Gules, a star of eight points or, on a chief of the last four fleurs-de-lis sable.

CREST: That for the regiments and separate battalions of the Army Reserve: On a wreath of the colors (or and gules) the Lexington Minute Man proper. The statue of the Minute Man, Captain John Parker (H. H. Kitson, sculptor), stands on the common in Lexington, Massachusetts.

MOTTO: *Osculun Mortis* (Kiss Of Death)

The shield is red for Artillery. The eight-pointed star represents an artillery shellburst. Black and golden orange were the colors of the Tank Destroyer forces of World War II; these colors, together with the four fleurs-de-lis refer to the service in Europe as a Tank Destroyer Battalion during World War II.

DISTINCTIVE INSIGNIA
The insignia is the shield and motto of the coat of arms. The sample of the insignia depicted was approved for wear on 10 July 1957.

615th ANTIAIRCRAFT ARTILLERY MISSILE BATTALION

Constituted 26 June 1954 as the 615th Antiaircraft Artillery Battalion (90mm Gun) and allotted to the Virginia Army National Guard. Organized and Federally recognized 13 September 1954 with Headquarters at South Norfolk and elements at Craddock, Smithfield, Camp Pendleton and South Norfolk. Reorganized and redesignated 15 February 1958 as the 615th Antiaircraft Artillery Missile Battalion (NIKE).

Consolidated 1 June 1959 with the 111th Artillery, a parent regiment under the Combat Army Regimental System.

CAMPAIGN STREAMERS
None

DECORATIONS
None

COAT OF ARMS

SHIELD: Gules, a mullet of eight points or.

CREST: That for the regiments and separate battalions of the Virginia Army National Guard: On a wreath of the colors (or and gules), "Virtus, the genius of the Commonwealth dressed as an Amazon, resting on a spear with one hand and holding a sword in the other, and treading on Tyranny, represented by a man prostrate, a crown falling from his head, a broken chain in his left hand and a scourge in his right" all proper.

MOTTO: *Percutite si Vultis* (Strike If You Will)

The shield is in the colors of Artillery. The mullet symbolizes an antiaircraft shellburst and represents the function of the unit.

DISTINCTIVE INSIGNIA

The insignia is the shield and motto of the coat of arms. Although the sample of the insignia depicted was approved for wear on 23 March 1960 it was never worn by this organization.

616th SEPARATE BATTALION COAST ARTILLERY

Constituted 1 July 1924 in the Organized Reserves as the 616th Coast Artillery Battalion (Harbor Defense) and allotted to the First Corps area. Organized at New Bedford, Massachusetts during December 1924. Expanded and redesignated 616th Coast Artillery (Harbor Defense) in 1926 by constitution of additional batteries which were subsequently organized in Taunton, Massachusetts, Providence and Woonsocket, Rhode Island by 11 January 1927. Withdrawn from the Organized Reserves, reorganized and redesignated as the 616th Separate Battalion, Coast Artillery (Harbor Defense), and allotted to the Regular Army on 1 September 1936.

Redesignated 1 February 1940 as the 23d Separate Battalion, Coast Artillery.

CAMPAIGN STREAMERS
None

DECORATIONS
None

COAT OF ARMS
None

DISTINCTIVE INSIGNIA
None

HEADQUARTERS AND HEADQUARTERS DETACHMENT 616th COAST ARTILLERY BATTALION

Constituted 2 July 1946 as Headquarters and Headquarters Detachment, 616th Coast Artillery Battalion (Harbor Defense) and allotted to the Virginia National Guard. Withdrawn from allotment to the Virginia National Guard 1 May 1949 and returned to Department of the Army control.

CAMPAIGN STREAMERS
None

DECORATIONS
None

COAT OF ARMS
None

DISTINCTIVE INSIGNIA
None

HEADQUARTERS AND HEADQUARTERS DETACHMENT 617th COAST ARTILLERY BATTALION

Constituted 2 July 1946 as Headquarters and Headquarters Detachment, 617th Coast Artillery Battalion (Harbor Defense) and allotted to the Virginia National Guard. Withdrawn from allotment to the Virginia National Guard 1 May 1949 and returned to Department of the Army control.

CAMPAIGN STREAMERS
None

DECORATIONS
None

COAT OF ARMS
None

DISTINCTIVE INSIGNIA
None

618th COAST ARTILLERY BATTALION

Constituted 31 March 1924 in the Organized Reserves as the 528th Artillery Battalion, Coast Artillery Corps (Fixed Defenses), allotted to the First Corps area and assigned to the Harbor Defenses of Long Island Sound. Redesignated 30 June 1924 as the 618th Coast Artillery Battalion (Harbor Defense). Organized from existing Coast Artillery Corps Companies (which had been constituted in July 1923) during July 1924 with Headquarters at New London, Connecticut. (Headquarters relocated to Bridgeport, Connecticut in September 1924; to Hartford, Connecticut in November 1925 and to Elizabeth, New Jersey in April 1937). Disbanded 18 October 1943.

CAMPAIGN STREAMERS
None

DECORATIONS
None

COAT OF ARMS
None

DISTINCTIVE INSIGNIA
None

620th COAST ARTILLERY BATTALION

Constituted 31 March 1924 in the Organized Reserves as the 620th Artillery, Coast Artillery Corps (Fixed Defenses) and allotted to the Second Corps area. Redesignated 30 June 1924 as the 620th Coast Artillery Battalion (Harbor Defense). Organized at Wilmington, Delaware during July 1924 from existing Coast Artillery Corps Companies (which had been constituted in July 1923).

Reorganized and redesignated 19 March 1926 as the 620th Coast Artillery (Harbor Defense).

CAMPAIGN STREAMERS
None

DECORATIONS
None

COAT OF ARMS
None

DISTINCTIVE INSIGNIA
None

623d COAST ARTILLERY BATTALION

Constituted 30 June 1924 in the Organized Reserves as the 623d Coast Artillery Battalion (Harbor Defense) and allotted to the Fourth Corps area. (Battery A organized at Jacksonville, Florida in June 1924; relocated to Atlanta, Georgia in October 1926 and to Columbia, South Carolina in April 1939). Disbanded 18 October 1943.

CAMPAIGN STREAMERS
None

DECORATIONS
None

COAT OF ARMS
None

DISTINCTIVE INSIGNIA
None

624th COAST ARTILLERY BATTALION

Constituted 31 March 1924 in the Organized Reserves as the 624th Artillery Battalion, Coast Artillery Corps (Fixed Defenses) and allotted to the Fourth Corps area. Redesignated 30 June 1924 as the 624th Coast Artillery Battalion (Harbor Defense). Organized during August 1924 from existing Coast Artillery Corps Companies (which had been constituted in July 1923). Withdrawn from the Fourth Corps area and allotted to the Eighth Corps area on 1 October 1933. Reorganized in Texas during April 1937 with Headquarters at San Antonio. Disbanded 18 October 1943.

CAMPAIGN STREAMERS
None

DECORATIONS
None

COAT OF ARMS
None

DISTINCTIVE INSIGNIA
None

629th COAST ARTILLERY BATTALION

Constituted 18 May 1922 in the Organized Reserves as the 907th Company, Coast Artillery Corps, allotted to the Ninth Corps area and assigned to the Coast Defenses of the Columbia. Redesignated 30 June 1924 as the 629th Coast Artillery Battery (Harbor Defense). Organized 25 July 1924 at Portland, Oregon. Reorganized, expanded and redesignated 19 March 1926 as the 629th Coast Artillery Battalion (Harbor Defense). Disbanded 18 October 1943.

CAMPAIGN STREAMERS
None

DECORATIONS
None

COAT OF ARMS
None

DISTINCTIVE INSIGNIA
None

630th ANTIAIRCRAFT ARTILLERY AUTOMATIC WEAPONS BATTALION

Constituted 5 May 1942 in the Army of the United States as 2d Battalion, 504th Coast Artillery (Antiaircraft) (Semimobile) and activated 1 July 1942 at Camp Hulen, Texas. Reorganized and redesignated 20 January 1943 as the 630th Coast Artillery Battalion (Antiaircraft) (Automatic Weapons). (Departed Boston Port of Embarkation 28 April 1943 for overseas service; arrived in North Africa on 12 May 1943 and landed in Italy on 9 September 1943). Redesignated 12 December 1943 as the 630th Antiaircraft Artillery Automatic Weapons Battalion. Inactivated 26 September 1945 near Florence, Italy.

Redesignated 18 June 1948 as the 43d Antiaircraft Artillery Automatic Weapons Battalion.

CAMPAIGN STREAMERS
World War II
Naples-Foggia (with arrowhead)
Rome-Arno
Po Valley
North Apennines

DECORATIONS
Meritorious Unit Commendation, Streamer embroidered *EUROPEAN THEATER* (630th AAA AW Bn cited for period 1 Feb-31 Mar 1945; GO 103, Hq Fifth Army, dtd 19 Aug 1945)

COAT OF ARMS
None

DISTINCTIVE INSIGNIA
None

633d ANTIAIRCRAFT ARTILLERY AUTOMATIC WEAPONS BATTALION

Constituted 25 February 1943 in the Army of the United States as the 633d Antiaircraft Artillery Automatic Weapons Battalion (Mobile) and organized 14 August 1943 at Honiton, England from personnel of the 1st Battalion, 244th Coast Artillery. Inactivated 6 October 1945 at Camp Shanks, New York. Disbanded 5 November 1948.

Reconstituted 1 March 1950 and consolidated with the 102d Antiaircraft Artillery Automatic Weapons Battalion.

CAMPAIGN STREAMERS
World War II
Normandy
Northern France
Rhineland
Ardennes-Alsace
Central Europe
England 1944

DECORATIONS
None

COAT OF ARMS
None

DISTINCTIVE INSIGNIA
None

633d ANTIAIRCRAFT ARTILLERY AUTOMATIC WEAPONS BATTALION

Constituted 1 April 1942 in the Army of the United States as 3d Battalion, 510th Coast Artillery (Antiaircraft) and activated 15 November 1942 at Fort Sheridan, Illinois. Reorganized at Fort Sheridan and redesignated 20 January 1943 as the 225th Coast Artillery Searchlight Battalion. Redesignated 3 March 1943 as the 225th Antiaircraft Artillery Searchlight Battalion. (Departed New York Port of Embarkation 23 December 1943 for the European Theater of Operations; arrived in England on 18 January 1944 and landed in France on 18 June 1944). Inactivated 31 December 1945 in Germany. Redesignated 5 November 1948 as the 633d Antiaircraft Artillery Automatic Weapons Battalion and allotted to the Organized Reserve Corps. Assigned to Second Army and activated 7 December 1948 at Philadelphia.

Redesignated 15 July 1949 as the 479th Antiaircraft Artillery Automatic Weapons Battalion.

CAMPAIGN STREAMERS
World War II
Normandy
Northern France
Rhineland
Central Europe

DECORATIONS
None

COAT OF ARMS
None

DISTINCTIVE INSIGNIA
None

633d ANTIAIRCRAFT ARTILLERY BATTALION

Constituted in the New York National Guard as 1st Battalion, 9th Coast Defense Command, Coast Artillery Corps and organized from new or existing units as follows:

Headquarters organized new and Federally recognized 19 July 1921 at New York City

13th Company, Coast Defenses of Sandy Hook (organized 10 October 1848 at New York City as a Company of Artillery in the 2d Regiment, 1st Brigade, New York State Militia; redesignated 29 September 1855 as Company B [*State Guard Company*], 55th Regiment, New York State Militia; redesignated 25 June 1859 as Company A 9th Regiment, New York State Militia; mustered into Federal service 8 June 1861 at Washington, District of Columbia; redesignated 7 December 1861 as Company A 83d New York Volunteer Infantry; mustered out 23 June 1864 at New York City and reorganized as Company A 9th Regiment, New York National Guard; mustered into Federal service 17 May 1898 at Peekskill as Company A 9th New York Volunteer Infantry; mustered out 15 November 1898 at New York City and resumed State status; redesignated 23 January 1908 as 13th Company, 9th Artillery District, Coast Artillery Corps; redesignated 10 August 1914 as 13th Company, 9th Coast Defense Command, Coast Artillery Corps; mustered into Federal service 19 July 1917 and drafted into Federal service on 5 August 1917; redesignated 11 January 1918 as 13th Company, Coast Defenses of Sandy Hook; and demobilized at Fort Hancock, New Jersey in December 1918), reorganized and Federally recognized 26 November 1920 as 13th Company, 9th Coast Defense Command

16th Company, Coast Defenses of Sandy Hook (organized prior to 1903 as Company D, 9th Regiment New York National Guard and redesignated 23 January 1908 as 16th Company, 9th Artillery District, Coast Artillery Corps; redesignated 10 August 1914 as 16th Company, 9th Coast Defense Command; mustered into Federal service 19 July 1917 at New York City and drafted into Federal service on 5 August 1917; redesignated 11 January 1918 as 16th Company, Coast Defenses of Sandy Hook; and demobilized at Fort Hancock in December 1918), reorganized and Federally recognized 30 June 1921 at New York City as 16th Company, 9th Coast Defense Command, Coast Artillery Corps

14th Company, Coast Defenses of Sandy Hook (organized 12 July 1852 at New York City as a Company in the 2d Regiment, 1st Brigade, New York State Militia; redesignated 12 June 1857 as Company G 55th Regiment, New York State Militia; redesignated 9 November 1857 as Company L 55th Regiment, New York State Militia; redesignated 3 May 1858 as Company K 55th Regiment, New York State Militia; redesignated 25 June 1859 as Company B 9th Regiment, New York State Militia; mustered into Federal service 8 June 1861 at Washington, District of Columbia; redesignated 7 December 1861 as Company B 83d New York Volunteer Infantry; mustered out 23 June 1864 at New York City and reorganized as Company B 9th Regiment, New York National Guard; mustered into Federal service 20 May 1898 at Peekskill as Company B 9th New York Volunteer Infantry; mustered out 15 November 1898 at New York City and resumed State status; redesignated 23 January 1908 as 14th Company, 9th Artillery District; Coast Artillery Corps; redesignated 10 August 1914 as 14th Company, 9th Coast Defense Command; mustered into Federal service 19 July 1917 at New York City and drafted into Federal service on 5 August 1917; redesignated 11 January 1918 as 14th Company, Coast Defenses of Sandy Hook; and demobilized at Fort Hancock in December 1918), reorganized and Federally recognized 28 June 1920 at New York City as 14th Company, 9th Coast Defense Command, Coast Artillery Corps

Redesignated 1 February 1924 as 1st Battalion 244th Artillery Coast Artillery Corps and reorganized to consist of Headquarters, Headquarters Detachment and Combat Train, 1st Battalion and Batteries A and B. Redesignated 14 May 1924 as 1st Battalion, 244th Coast Artillery (Tractor Drawn). Redesignated 15 March 1940 as 1st Battalion, 244th Coast Artillery (155mm Gun). Inducted into Federal service 16 September 1940 at New York City. Inactivated 14 August 1943 at Honiton, England and personnel reassigned to the 633d Antiaircraft Artillery Automatic Weapons Battalion. Disbanded 5 June 1944. Reconstituted 25 August 1945 in the New York National Guard. Broken up 27 September 1946; Headquarters and Headquarters Battery redesignated Headquarters and Headquarters Detachment, 259th Coast Artillery Battalion and Batteries A and B redesignated 952d and 953d Coast Artillery Batteries respectively. Headquarters and Headquarters Detachment, 952d and 953d Coast Artillery Batteries reorganized and Federally recognized 14 November 1947 at New York City. Headquarters and Headquarters Detachment, 259th Coast Artillery Battalion and 952d and 953d Coast Artillery Batteries consolidated, reorganized and redesignated 1 February 1950 as 102d Antiaircraft Artillery Automatic Weapons Battalion. Consolidated 1 March 1950 with the 633d Antiaircraft Artillery Automatic Weapons Battalion (activated 14 August 1943 at Honiton, England and inactivated 6 October 1945 at Camp Shanks, New York), reorganized and redesignated 633d Antiaircraft Artillery Automatic Weapons Battalion. Reorganized and redesignated 1 May 1950 as the 633d Antiaircraft Artillery Gun Battalion. Ordered into Federal service 15 May 1951 at New York City. Reorganized and redesignated 633d Antiaircraft Artillery Automatic Weapons Battalion about 1952. Released from active Federal service 14 April 1953 and resumed State status. Disbanded 1 October 1957 when Federal recognition was withdrawn.

CAMPAIGN STREAMERS

Civil War
Manassas
Antietam
Fredericksburg
Chancellorsville
Gettysburg
Wilderness
Spotsylvania
Cold Harbor
Virginia 1861
Virginia 1862
Virginia 1863
Virginia 1864

World War II
Normandy
Northern France
Rhineland
Ardennes-Alsace
Central Europe
England 1944

DECORATIONS
None

COAT OF ARMS

SHIELD: Gules, between in fess two fleurs-de-lis a sheathed Roman sword, point to base or, debruised by a cross patee argent charged with a hurt bearing the number "9" of the second within a bordure wavy of the second.

CREST: That for the regiments and separate battalions of the New York National Guard: On a wreath of the colors (or and gules) the full rigged ship *Half Moon*, all proper.

MOTTO: By Force If Necessary

The shield is that of the coat of arms of the 244th Coast Artillery, within a border to indicate descent from the 1st Battalion of that organization.

DISTINCTIVE INSIGNIA

The insignia is the shield and motto of the coat of arms. The sample of the insignia depicted was approved for wear on 30 January 1952.

634th ANTIAIRCRAFT ARTILLERY AUTOMATIC WEAPONS BATTALION

Constituted 25 February 1943 in the Army of the United States as the 634th Antiaircraft Artillery Automatic Weapons Battalion (Mobile) and organized 10 August 1943 at Honiton, England from personnel of the 2d Battalion, 61st Coast Artillery. (Arrived in France on 13 June 1944. Returned from overseas service and arrived at the New York Port of Embarkation on 4 October 1945). Inactivated 6 October 1945 at Camp Kilmer, New Jersey.

Consolidated 28 June 1950 with the 39th Antiaircraft Artillery Automatic Weapons Battalion.

CAMPAIGN STREAMERS
World War II
Normandy
Northern France
Rhineland
Ardennes-Alsace
Central Europe
England 1944

DECORATIONS
Presidential Unit Citation (Army), Streamer embroidered *ST. VITH* (634th AAA AW Bn cited for the period 16-21 Dec 1944; WDGO 108, 1945)

COAT OF ARMS
None

DISTINCTIVE INSIGNIA
None

635th ANTIAIRCRAFT ARTILLERY AUTOMATIC WEAPONS BATTALION

Constituted 25 February 1943 in the Army of the United States as the 635th Antiaircraft Artillery Automatic Weapons Battalion (Mobile) and organized 10 August 1943 at Honiton, England from personnel of the 3d Battalion, 61st Coast Artillery. (Moved to France on 9 July 1944. Returned to the United States after the war and arrived at the New York Port of Embarkation on 26 March 1946). Inactivated 27 March 1946 at Camp Kilmer, New Jersey.

Consolidated with the 52d Antiaircraft Artillery Battalion on 28 June 1950.

CAMPAIGN STREAMERS
World War II
Normandy
Northern France
Rhineland
Ardennes-Alsace
Central Europe
England 1944

DECORATIONS
None

COAT OF ARMS
None

DISTINCTIVE INSIGNIA
None

637th ANTIAIRCRAFT ARTILLERY AUTOMATIC WEAPONS BATTALION

Constituted 29 July 1921 in the Organized Reserves as the 2d Battalion, 508th Artillery (Antiaircraft), Coast Artillery Corps and allotted to the Eighth Corps area. Organized during March 1922 at El Paso, Texas. Redesignated 30 June 1924 as the 2d Battalion, 508th Coast Artillery (Antiaircraft). Withdrawn from the Eighth Corps area, allotted to the Third Corps area and reorganized 10 January 1927 at Pittsburgh, Pennsylvania. Ordered into active military service, less personnel and equipment, at Camp Stewart, Georgia on 1 September 1942. Reorganized at Camp Stewart and redesignated 20 January 1943 as the 637th Coast Artillery Battalion (Antiaircraft) (Automatic Weapons). (Departed New York Port of Embarkation 5 March 1943 for overseas service and landed in North Africa on 18 March 1943). Redesignated 19 November 1943 as the 637th Antiaircraft Artillery Automatic Weapons Battalion. Disbanded 22 July 1944 at Oran, Algeria.

CAMPAIGN STREAMERS
World War II
European Theater without inscription

DECORATIONS
None

COAT OF ARMS
None

DISTINCTIVE INSIGNIA
None

638th ANTIAIRCRAFT ARTILLERY AUTOMATIC WEAPONS BATTALION

Constituted 9 May 1942 in the Army of the United States as the 2d Battalion, 512th Coast Artillery (Antiaircraft) (Semimobile) and activated 15 June 1942 at Fort Bliss, Texas. Reorganized at Fort Bliss and redesignated 20 January 1943 as the 638th Coast Artillery Battalion (Antiaircraft) (Automatic Weapons). (Departed Hampton Roads Port of Embarkation 9 May 1943 for overseas service; arrived in North Africa 23 May 1943 and moved to Corsica on

10 January 1944). Redesignated 1 May 1944 as the 638th Antiaircraft Artillery Automatic Weapons Battalion (Mobile). (Relocated to Italy on 26 September 1944). Disbanded 1 October 1944 at Bagnoli, Italy.

CAMPAIGN STREAMERS
World War II
Naples-Foggia
Rome-Arno

DECORATIONS
None

COAT OF ARMS
None

DISTINCTIVE INSIGNIA
None

639th ANTIAIRCRAFT ARTILLERY AUTOMATIC WEAPONS BATTALION

Constituted in the Organized Reserves during July 1923 as the 2d Battalion, 514th Artillery, Coast Artillery Corps (Antiaircraft) and organized during October 1923 at Albany, New York. Redesignated 30 June 1924 as the 2d Battalion, 514th Coast Artillery (Antiaircraft). Withdrawn from the Organized Reserves and allotted to the Regular Army on 1 January 1938. Ordered into active military service, less personnel and equipment on 1 March 1942 at Camp Davis, North Carolina. Reorganized at Camp Davis and redesignated 26 May 1943 as 639th Coast Artillery Battalion (Antiaircraft) (Automatic Weapons). (Departed New York Port of Embarkation 29 September 1944 and landed in France on 10 October 1944. Returned from overseas service and arrived at the New York Port of Embarkation on 1 January 1946). Inactivated 2 January 1946 at Camp Kilmer, New Jersey. Activated 11 July 1946 at Fort Bliss, Texas; inactivated 4 January 1947 at Fort Bliss.

Redesignated 14 September 1948 as the 48th Antiaircraft Artillery Automatic Weapons Battalion.

CAMPAIGN STREAMERS
World War II
Rhineland
Ardennes-Alsace
Central Europe

DECORATIONS
Cited in the Order of the Day of the Belgian Army for action in the *ARDENNES* (Btry D 639th AAA AW Bn cited for period 17-25 Jan 1945; DAGO 43, 1950)

COAT OF ARMS
None

DISTINCTIVE INSIGNIA
None

641st ANTIAIRCRAFT ARTILLERY AUTOMATIC WEAPONS BATTALION

Constituted 31 January 1942 in the Army of the United States as the 2d Battalion, 501st Coast Artillery (Antiaircraft) (Semimobile) and activated 1 April 1942 at Camp Haan, California. Reorganized and redesignated 10 September 1943 as the 641st Antiaircraft Artillery Automatic Weapons Battalion (Semimobile). Disbanded 3 February 1945 at Shemya, Alaska.

CAMPAIGN STREAMERS
World War II
Aleutian Islands

DECORATIONS
None

COAT OF ARMS
None

DISTINCTIVE INSIGNIA
None

642d ANTIAIRCRAFT ARTILLERY AUTOMATIC WEAPONS BATTALION

Constituted 31 January 1942 in the Army of the United States as the 2d Battalion, 502d Coast Artillery (Antiaircraft) (Semimobile) and activated 1 May 1942 at Fort Sheridan, Illinois. Reorganized at Paterson, New Jersey and redesignated 1 September 1943 as the 642d Antiaircraft Artillery Automatic Weapons Battalion (Mobile). Inactivated 8 November 1944 at Camp Gordon, Georgia. Disbanded 9 November 1944.

CAMPAIGN STREAMERS
None

DECORATIONS
None

COAT OF ARMS
None

DISTINCTIVE INSIGNIA
None

643d ANTIAIRCRAFT ARTILLERY AUTOMATIC WEAPONS BATTALION

Constituted 29 July 1921 in the Organized Reserves as the 2d Battalion, 507th Artillery (Antiaircraft), Coast Artillery Corps and allotted to the Seventh Corps area. Organized during March 1922 with Headquarters at Fort Des Moines, Iowa. Redesignated 30 June 1924 as the 2d Battalion, 507th Coast Artillery (Antiaircraft). Withdrawn from the Organized Reserves and allotted to the Regular Army on 1 October 1933. Ordered into active military service, less personnel and equipment, and organized 1 August 1942 at Camp Haan, California. Reorganized and redesignated 10 September 1943 at North Long Beach, California as the 643d Antiaircraft Artillery Automatic Weapons Battalion (Mobile). Inactivated 25 February 1945 at Fort Bliss, Texas.

CAMPAIGN STREAMERS
None

DECORATIONS
None

COAT OF ARMS
None

DISTINCTIVE INSIGNIA
None

644th ANTIAIRCRAFT ARTILLERY AUTOMATIC WEAPONS BATTALION

Constituted 5 April 1946 in the Army of the United States as the 644th Antiaircraft Artillery Automatic Weapons Battalion. Activated 6 April 1946 at Eschenstruth, Germany; inactivated 20 January 1947 at Eschenstruth. Disbanded 10 October 1952.

CAMPAIGN STREAMERS
None

DECORATIONS
None

COAT OF ARMS
None

DISTINCTIVE INSIGNIA
None

646th ANTIAIRCRAFT ARTILLERY AUTOMATIC WEAPONS BATTALION

Constituted 2 November 1942 in the Army of the United States as the 485th Coast Artillery Battalion (Antiaircraft) (Automatic Weapons) and activated 10 February 1943 at Camp Hulen, Texas. Reorganized and redesignated 30 April 1943 as the 485th Antiaircraft Artillery Automatic Weapons Battalion (Semimobile). (Departed San Francisco Port of Embarkation 16 February 1944 for overseas service and arrived in Hawaii on 21 February 1944. Moved to the Philippine Islands on 20 October 1944 and participated in the initial landings on Okinawa on 1 April 1945). Inactivated 20 February 1946 on Okinawa. Redesignated 10 November 1949 as the 646th Antiaircraft Artillery Automatic Weapons Battalion.

Redesignated 16 October 1952 as the 485th Antiaircraft Artillery Automatic Weapons Battalion.

CAMPAIGN STREAMERS
World War II
Leyte (with arrowhead)
Ryukyus (with arrowhead)

DECORATIONS
Philippine Presidential Unit Citation, Streamer embroidered *17 OCTOBER 1944 TO 4 JULY 1945* (485th AAA AW Bn cited; DAGO 47, 1950)

COAT OF ARMS
None

DISTINCTIVE INSIGNIA
None

649th ANTIAIRCRAFT ARTILLERY BATTALION

Constituted 2 July 1946 as the 239th Field Artillery Battalion and allotted to the Texas National Guard. Organized and Federally recognized 3 June 1947 with Headquarters at Temple and elements at Belton, Cameron, Temple and Taylor. Reorganized and redesignated 1 March 1949 as the 649th Antiaircraft Artillery Automatic Weapons Battalion and assigned to the 49th Armored Division. Redesignated 1 October 1953 as the 649th Antiaircraft Artillery Battalion (Automatic Weapons) (Self Propelled).

Relieved from the 49th Armored Division and consolidated 16 March 1959 with the 112th Armor, a parent regiment under the Combat Arms Regimental System.

CAMPAIGN STREAMERS
None

DECORATIONS
None

COAT OF ARMS
None

DISTINCTIVE INSIGNIA
None

650th ANTIAIRCRAFT ARTILLERY BATTALION

Constituted 20 July 1940 as 2d Battalion, 261st Coast Artillery (Harbor Defense) and allotted to the New Jersey National Guard. Organized and Federally recognized 25 November 1940 at Jersey City. Redesignated 15 January 1941 as the 122d Separate Battalion Coast Artillery (Antiaircraft) (Gun). Inducted into Federal service 27 January 1941 at Jersey City. Redesignated 10 September 1943 as 122d Antiaircraft Artillery Gun Battalion (Semimobile). (Departed Seattle

Port of Embarkation 23 July 1944 for overseas service; arrived at Amchitka, Alaska 3 August 1944 and moved to Shemya, Alaska on 5 November 1944). Inactivated 3 February 1945 at Shemya. Redesignated 28 June 1946 as the 309th Antiaircraft Artillery Automatic Weapons Battalion. Reorganized and Federally recognized 15 April 1947 at Jersey City. Redesignated 650th Antiaircraft Artillery Automatic Weapons Battalion and assigned to the 50th Armored Division on 1 March 1949. Redesignated 1 October 1953 as the 650th Antiaircraft Artillery Battalion (Automatic Weapons) (Self Propelled).

Redesignated 1 May 1958 as the 165th Armored Field Artillery Battalion.

CAMPAIGN STREAMERS
World War II
Pacific Theater without inscription

DECORATIONS
None

COAT OF ARMS
SHIELD: Gules, in base an igloo proper, a bordure or.

CREST: That for the regiments and separate battalions of the New Jersey Army National Guard: On a wreath of the colors (or and gules) a lion's head erased or, collared four fusils gules.

MOTTO: *Haec Facta Scribemus* (On This Shield We Shall Write Our Deeds)

The shield is red for Artillery. The igloo symbolizes service in Alaska during World War II.

DISTINCTIVE INSIGNIA
The insignia is the shield and motto of the coat of arms. The sample of the insignia depicted was approved for wear on 10 February 1953.

651st AIRBORNE ANTIAIRCRAFT BATTALION

Constituted 15 July 1946 in the Organized Reserves as the 651st Airborne Antiaircraft Battalion and activated 6 August 1946 at Jacksonville, Florida. Assigned to the 108th Airborne Division on 20 September 1946. (Organized Reserves redesignated 25 March 1948 as the Organized Reserve Corps). Relieved from the 108th Airborne Division and disbanded 1 May 1952 at Jacksonville.

CAMPAIGN STREAMERS
None

DECORATIONS
None

COAT OF ARMS
None

DISTINCTIVE INSIGNIA
None

675th ANTIAIRCRAFT ARTILLERY AUTOMATIC WEAPONS BATTALION

Constituted 10 July 1946 as the 675th Antiaircraft Artillery Automatic Weapons Battalion and allotted to the Oregon National Guard. Withdrawn from allotment to the Oregon Army National Guard and returned to Department of the Army control about 1949.

CAMPAIGN STREAMERS
None

DECORATIONS
None

COAT OF ARMS
None

DISTINCTIVE INSIGNIA
None

677th ANTIAIRCRAFT ARTILLERY AUTOMATIC WEAPONS BATTALION

Constituted 9 July 1946 in the North Carolina National Guard as the 677th Antiaircraft Artillery Automatic Weapons Battalion and partially organized from new and existing units as follows:

Company A 630th Tank Destroyer Battalion (constituted 3 December 1941 in the Army of the United States and organized 15 December 1941 at Fort Jackson, South Carolina from personnel of the Antiaircraft and Antitank Platoons of the 1st and 2d Battalions of the 113th Field Artillery; allotted to the North Carolina National Guard on 21 February 1942; inactivated 31 March 1946 at Camp Kilmer, New Jersey), reorganized and Federally recognized 10 June 1947 at Red Springs as Headquarters and Headquarters Battery

Battery B 530th Field Artillery Battalion (organized 18 April 1914 at Raeford as Company G 2d Infantry, North Carolina National Guard; mustered into Federal service 16 June 1916 for Mexican border and drafted into Federal service 5 August 1917; redesignated 12 September 1917 as Company G 119th Infantry and assigned to the 30th Division; demobilized 17 April 1919 at Camp Jackson, South Carolina; reorganized at Raeford and Federally recognized 5 August 1921 as Machine Gun [Antiaircraft] Company, North Carolina National Guard; redesignated 8 November 1921 as Battery G [Machine Gun] 200th Artillery, Coast Artillery Corps [Antiaircraft]; redesignated 27 September 1924 as Battery G [Machine Gun] 200th Coast Artillery [Antiaircraft]; redesignated 1 December 1926 as Battery F 252d Coast Artillery [Harbor Defense]; redesignated 25 November 1929 as Battery F 252d Coast Artillery [Tractor Drawn]; inducted into Federal service 16 September 1940 at Raeford; reorganized and redesignated 20 May 1944 as Battery B 530th Field Artillery Battalion; inactivated 30 September 1945 at the Cecchignola Redeployment Training Center, Italy), reorganized and Federally recognized 10 March 1947 at Raeford as Battery A

Battery B organized new and Federally recognized 1 February 1959 at St. Pauls.

Redesignated 1 February 1949 as the 130th Antiaircraft Artillery Automatic Weapons Battalion.

CAMPAIGN STREAMERS
World War II
Normandy
Northern France
Rhineland
Ardennes-Alsace
Central Europe

DECORATIONS
None

COAT OF ARMS
None

DISTINCTIVE INSIGNIA
None

678th ANTIAIRCRAFT ARTILLERY BATTALION

Constituted 5 July 1946 in the South Carolina National Guard as the 678th Antiaircraft Artillery Automatic Weapons Battalion (Mobile) and organized from new and existing units as follows:

Headquarters, 2d Battalion 263d Coast Artillery (organized and Federally recognized 21 July 1923 at Beaufort as Headquarters, 1st Coast Defense Command, Coast Artillery Corps; redesignated 25 March 1924 as Headquarters, 1st Separate Battalion Coast Artillery, South Carolina National Guard; redesignated 31 July 1925 as Headquarters, 265th Coast Artillery Battalion [Harbor Defense]; redesignated 10 June 1930 as Headquarters, 1st Battalion 263d Coast Artillery; relocated to Dillon on 14 June 1930; relocated to Greenwood and redesignated Headquarters, 2d Battalion 263d Coast Artillery on 26 October 1939; inducted into Federal service 13 January 1941 at Greenwood; disbanded 1 October 1944 at Fort Moultrie, South Carolina and reconstituted 25 August 1945), reorganized and Federally recognized 15 April 1947 at Anderson as Headquarters and Headquarters Battery

Battery E 263d Coast Artillery (organized and Federally recognized 14 June 1930 at Anderson; inducted into Federal service 13 January 1941 at Anderson; redesignated 1 October 1944 as Battery C, Harbor Defense of Charleston; redesignated Battery E 263d Coast Artillery and inactivated 30 June 1945 at Fort Moultrie), consolidated with Headquarters and Headquarters Battery

Battery A organized new and Federally recognized 5 March 1947 at Seneca

Headquarters Company 2d Battalion 118th Infantry (organized and Federally recognized 25 October 1921 at Easley as Headquarters Company 2d Battalion, 1st Infantry, South Carolina National Guard; redesignated 19 December 1921 as Headquarters Company 2d Battalion, 118th Infantry; redesignated 1 May 1940 as Headquarters Detachment 2d Battalion, 118th Infantry; inducted into Federal serviced 16 September 1940 at Easley; redesignated 1 April 1942 as Headquarters Company 2d Battalion, 118th Infantry and inactivated 15 January 1946 at Camp Kilmer, New Jersey), reorganized and Federally recognized 12 March 1947 at Easley as Battery B

Searchlight Battery, 263d Coast Artillery (organized and Federally recognized 28 June 1934 at Greenville as Battery F 263d Coast Artillery; redesignated 15 April 1940 as Searchlight Battery, 263d Coast Artillery; inducted into Federal service 13 January 1941 at Greenville; disbanded 1 October 1944 at Fort Moultrie and reconstituted 25 August 1945), reorganized and Federally recognized 8 August 1945 at Greenville as Battery C

Battery D organized new and Federally recognized 29 April 1947 at Williamston

Medical Detachment organized new and Federally recognized 23 March 1949 at Williamston

Reorganized and redesignated 1 November 1952 as 678th Antiaircraft Artillery Gun Battalion (90mm). Redesignated 1 October 1953 as 678th Antiaircraft Artillery Battalion (90mm Gun).

Consolidated 1 April 1959 with 263d Artillery, a parent regiment under the Combat Arms Regimental System.

CAMPAIGN STREAMERS
None

DECORATIONS
None

COAT OF ARMS
None

DISTINCTIVE INSIGNIA
None

679th ANTIAIRCRAFT ARTILLERY AUTOMATIC WEAPONS BATTALION

Constituted 27 September 1946 as the 679th Antiaircraft Artillery Automatic Weapons Battalion (Semimobile) and allotted to the New York National Guard. Withdrawn from allotment to the New York Army National Guard and returned to Department of the Army control about 1950.

CAMPAIGN STREAMERS
None

DECORATIONS
None

COAT OF ARMS
None

DISTINCTIVE INSIGNIA
None

681st ANTIAIRCRAFT ARTILLERY AUTOMATIC WEAPONS BATTALION

Constituted 5 August 1946 in the California National Guard as the 681st Antiaircraft Artillery Automatic Weapons Battalion. Organized and Federally recognized 27 February 1947 with Headquarters at Belmont and batteries at Menlo Park, San Bruno, and San Mateo. (Headquarters relocated to San Mateo on 14 December 1947).

Redesignated 1 February 1949 as the 149th Antiaircraft Artillery Battalion.

CAMPAIGN STREAMERS
None

DECORATIONS
None

COAT OF ARMS
None

DISTINCTIVE INSIGNIA
None

682d ANTIAIRCRAFT ARTILLERY BATTALION

Constituted 5 August 1946 in the California National Guard as the 682d Antiaircraft Artillery Automatic Weapons Battalion and organized from new and existing units as follows:

Headquarters, 951st Antiaircraft Artillery Automatic Weapons Battalion (organized and Federally recognized 3 December 1924 at San Pedro as Headquarters, 2d Battalion, 251st Coast Artillery [Harbor Defense]; relocated to Long Beach and reorganized as Headquarters, 2d Battalion, 251st Coast Artillery [Antiaircraft]; inducted into Federal service 16 September 1940 at Long Beach; redesignated 1 March 1944 as Headquarters, 951st Antiaircraft Artillery Automatic Weapons Battalion and inactivated 29 December 1945 at Camp Stoneman, California), reorganized as Headquarters and Headquarters Battery and Federally recognized 2 June 1947 at Long Beach

Battery A, 951st Antiaircraft Artillery Automatic Weapons Battalion (organized as the 16th Company, 2d Coast Defense Command, Coast Artillery Corps and Federally recognized 24 September 1916 at San Pedro; drafted into Federal service 5 August 1917 at San Pedro; redesignated 4 September 1917 as the 5th Company, Coast Defenses of Los Angeles; redesignated 20 January 1918 as Battery D, 2d Antiaircraft Artillery Battalion; demobilized 19 January 1919 at Camp Dix, New Jersey; reorganized and Federally recognized 20 April 1922 at San Pedro as the 468th Company, Coast Artillery Corps, California National Guard; redesignated 6 October 1923 as Battery K, 250th Artillery, Coast Artillery Corps; redesignated 1 November 1924 as Battery E, 251st Coast Artillery; inducted into Federal service 16 September 1940 at San Pedro; redesignated 1 March 1944 as Battery A, 951st Antiaircraft Artillery Automatic Weapons Battalion and inactivated 29 December 1945 at Camp Stoneman), reorganized as Battery A and Federally recognized 11 December 1947 at San Pedro

Battery B organized new and Federally recognized 7 July 1947 at Compton

Battery C organized new and Federally recognized 20 October 1947 at Lynwood

Battery D organized new and Federally recognized 27 January 1948 at Norwalk

Medical Detachment organized new and Federally recognized 27 June 1947 at Long Beach

Reorganized and redesignated 1 January 1951 as the 682d Antiaircraft Artillery Gun Battalion. Redesignated 1 October 1953 as the 682d Antiaircraft Artillery Battalion.

Consolidated 1 May 1959 with the 251st Artillery, a parent regiment under the Combat Arms Regimental System.

CAMPAIGN STREAMERS
World War II
Central Pacific
Northern Solomons
Luzon (with arrowhead)

DECORATIONS
Philippine Presidential Unit Citation, Streamer embroidered *17 OCTOBER 1944 TO 4 JULY 1945* (951st AAA AW Bn cited; DAGO 47, 1950)

COAT OF ARMS
SHIELD: Or, on six pallets couped gules a fleur-de-lis encircled by a garland of laurel of the first.

CREST: That for the regiments and separate battalions of the California Army National Guard: On a wreath of the colors (or and gules) the setting sun behind a grizzly bear passant on a grassy field, all proper.

MOTTO: *Intrepide* (Undaunted)

Red and yellow are the colors for Artillery. The design is based on the coat of arms of the former 251st Coast Artillery and indicates the descent from elements of the 2d Battalion of that organization.

DISTINCTIVE INSIGNIA
The insignia is the shield and motto of the coat of arms. The sample of the insignia depicted was approved for wear on 12 December 1952.

683d ANTIAIRCRAFT ARTILLERY MISSILE BATTALION

Constituted 10 July 1946 as the 683d Antiaircraft Artillery Automatic Weapons Battalion and allotted to the Oregon National Guard. Withdrawn from allotment to the Oregon National Guard, redesignated 683d Antiaircraft Artillery Battalion (90mm Gun) and allotted to the Maryland Army National Guard on 1 November 1955. Organized and Federally recognized 21 November 1955 at Baltimore. Reorganized and redesignated 15 January 1958 as the 683d Antiaircraft Artillery Missile Battalion (NIKE).

Consolidated 1 March 1959 with the 70th Artillery, a parent regiment under the Combat Arms Regimental System.

CAMPAIGN STREAMERS
None

DECORATIONS
None

COAT OF ARMS

SHIELD: Per fess wavy gules and paly of six or and sable a bend counterchanged, in chief a five-bastioned fort of the second voided of the third.

CREST: That for the regiments and separate battalions of the Maryland Army National Guard: On a wreath of the colors (or and gules) a cross bottony per cross quarterly gules and argent.

MOTTO: O'er The Rampart We Watch

Scarlet and gold are used for Artillery. The five-pointed figure represents the "Star Fort", Fort McHenry, early defense of the city of Baltimore against hostile attack. The black and gold lower part of the shield is taken from the arms of Calvert, Lord Baltimore. The design refers to the battalion's place of activation and home station at Baltimore.

DISTINCTIVE INSIGNIA
The insignia is the shield and motto of the coat of arms. The sample of the insignia depicted was approved for wear on 27 June 1958.

684th ANTIAIRCRAFT ARTILLERY MISSILE BATTALION

Constituted 1 June 1956 as the 684th Antiaircraft Artillery Battalion (90mm Gun) and allotted to the Maryland Army National Guard. Organized and Federally recognized 1 October 1956 with Headquarters at Towson; Battery A at Catonsville; Batteries B and C at Baltimore and Battery D at Towson. (Headquarters relocated to Baltimore on 1 January 1957). Reorganized and redesignated 15 January 1958 as the 684th Antiaircraft Artillery Missile Battalion (NIKE). (Headquarters relocated to Towson on 15 February 1958).

Consolidated 1 March 1959 with the 70th Artillery, a parent regiment under the Combat Arms Regimental System.

CAMPAIGN STREAMERS
None

DECORATIONS
None

COAT OF ARMS
SHIELD: Paly of six or and sable, a bend counterchanged, on an inescutcheon gules a representation of *The Battle of Baltimore (1814) Monument* of the first.

CREST: That for the regiments and separate battalions of the Maryland Army National Guard: On a wreath of the colors (or and gules) a cross bottony per cross quarterly gules and argent.

MOTTO: The Shield Of Baltimore

Scarlet and yellow are used for Artillery. The black stripes and designs of the inner shield allude to the flag of the City of Baltimore and symbolizes the battalion's mission — to shield the city and state from air attack. The monument is also used upon the Seal of the city.

DISTINCTIVE INSIGNIA
The insignia is the shield and motto of the coat of arms. The sample of the insignia depicted was approved for wear on 10 July 1957.

685th ANTIAIRCRAFT ARTILLERY BATTALION

Constituted 8 July 1946 in the Massachusetts National Guard as the 685th Antiaircraft Artillery Automatic Weapons Battalion and organized from new and existing units as follows:

2d Platoon, Battery D, 747th Antiaircraft Artillery Automatic Weapons Battalion (organized and Federally recognized 8 December 1939 at Bourne as Battery H, 211th Coast Artillery and redesignated 6 May 1940 as 2d Platoon, Battery H, 211th Coast Artillery; inducted into active Federal service at Bourne on 16 September 1940; redesignated 16 September 1943 as 2d Platoon, Battery D, 747th Antiaircraft Artillery Automatic Weapons Battalion and inactivated 5 September 1945 at Fort Bliss, Texas), reorganized and Federally recognized 27 January 1948 at Bourne as Headquarters and Headquarters Battery

Battery A organized new at Middleboro and Federally recognized 28 June 1948

Battery B organized new at Plymouth and Federally recognized 9 February 1948

Battery C, 747th Antiaircraft Artillery Automatic Weapons Battalion (organized at Falmouth and Federally recognized 26 October 1939 as Battery G, 211th Coast Artillery; inducted into Federal service 16 September 1940 at Falmouth; redesignated 16 August 1943 as Battery C, 747th Antiaircraft Artillery Automatic Weapons Battalion, and inactivated 5 September 1945 at Fort Bliss), reorganized and Federally recognized at Falmouth as Battery C

2d Platoon, Battery C, 747th Antiaircraft Artillery Automatic Weapons Battalion (organized and Federally recognized 23 February 1940 at Barnstable as 2d Platoon, Battery G, 211th Coast Artillery; inducted into Federal service at Boston on 16 September 1940; redesignated 16 August 1943 as 2d Platoon, Battery C, 747th Antiaircraft Artillery Automatic Weapons Battalion and inactivated 5 September 1945 at Fort Bliss), reorganized and Federally recognized at Hyannis as Battery D

Medical Detachment, 747th Antiaircraft Artillery Automatic Weapons Battalion (organized 16 August 1943 at Vallejo, California and inactivated 5 September 1945 at Fort Bliss), reorganized and Federally recognized 9 February 1948 at Bourne as Medical Detachment

Reorganized and redesignated 1 January 1949 as the 685th Antiaircraft Artillery Gun Battalion. Ordered into active Federal service at Bourne on 1 May 1951. Released from active Federal service 31 January 1953 and reorganized in State service. Redesignated 1 October 1953 as the 685th Antiaircraft Artillery Battalion (90mm Gun).

Consolidated 1 May 1959 with the 211th Artillery, a parent regiment under the Combat Arms Regimental System.

CAMPAIGN STREAMERS
None

DECORATIONS
None

COAT OF ARMS
None

DISTINCTIVE INSIGNIA
None

686th ANTIAIRCRAFT ARTILLERY MISSILE BATTALION

Constituted 12 February 1959 as the 686th Antiaircraft Artillery Missile Battalion and allotted to the Maryland Army National Guard. Consolidated 1 March 1959 with the 70th Artillery, a parent regiment under the Combat Arms Regimental System.

CAMPAIGN STREAMERS
None

DECORATIONS
None

COAT OF ARMS
None

DISTINCTIVE INSIGNIA
None

687th ANTIAIRCRAFT ARTILLERY AUTOMATIC WEAPONS BATTALION

Constituted 27 September 1946 as the 687th Antiaircraft Artillery Automatic Weapons Battalion (Self Propelled) and allotted to the New York National Guard. Withdrawn from allotment to the New York Army National Guard and returned to Department of the Army control about 1949.

CAMPAIGN STREAMERS
None

DECORATIONS
None

COAT OF ARMS
None

DISTINCTIVE INSIGNIA
None

688th ANTIAIRCRAFT ARTILLERY BATTALION

Constituted 24 May 1946 in the Pennsylvania National Guard as the 688th Antiaircraft Artillery Automatic Weapons Battalion and organized from new and existing units as follows:

Headquarters and Headquarters Battery organized new and Federally recognized 12 December 1946 at Allentown

Battery A organized new and Federally recognized 7 November 1946 at Allentown

Battery B organized new and Federally recognized 18 December 1947 at Allentown

Company B, 805th Tank Destroyer Battalion (organized 29 July 1876 at Tamaqua as Company B, 8th Infantry, Pennsylvania National Guard; mustered into Federal service 12

May 1898 as Company B, 8th Infantry, Pennsylvania Volunteers and mustered out 7 March 1899 at Augusta, Georgia; reorganized 31 May 1899 at Tamaqua as Company B, 8th Infantry, Pennsylvania National Guard; mustered into Federal service 9 July 1916 for service on the Mexican border; mustered out 27 February 1917 and resumed State status; mustered into Federal service 15 July 1917 and drafted into Federal service 5 August 1917; redesignated 11 October 1917 as Company B, 112th Infantry and assigned to the 28th Division; demobilized 6 May 1919 at Camp Dix, New Jersey; redesignated 16 July 1919 as the 103d Ammunition Train; reorganized and Federally recognized 6 August 1921 at Tamaqua; reorganized in part as Troop B, 122d Quartermaster Squadron on 1 March 1940; consolidated with Troop C, 122d Quartermaster Squadron and redesignated 23 September 1940 as Company B, 105th Antitank Battalion; inducted into Federal service 3 February 1941 at Harrisburg; redesignated 15 December 1941 as Company B, 805th Tank Destroyer Battalion; and inactivated 2 November 1945 at Camp Hood, Texas), reorganized and Federally recognized 11 September 1946 at Tamaqua as Battery C

Battery D organized new and Federally recognized 30 March 1948 at Tamaqua

Medical Detachment organized new and Federally recognized 30 September 1946 at Allentown

Reorganized and redesignated 1 October 1951 as the 688th Antiaircraft Artillery Gun Battalion. Redesignated 1 October 1953 as the 688th Antiaircraft Artillery Battalion. Disbanded 18 October 1953 when Federal recognition was withdrawn.

CAMPAIGN STREAMERS
None

DECORATIONS
None

COAT OF ARMS
None

DISTINCTIVE INSIGNIA
None

689th ANTIAIRCRAFT ARTILLERY GUN BATTALION

Constituted in the Pennsylvania National Guard as the 1st Battalion, 176th Field Artillery (155mm Howitzer) and organized from new and existing units as follows:

Headquarters, 1st Battalion, 18th Infantry, Pennsylvania National Guard (organized and Federally recognized 31 July 1920 at Pittsburgh), redesignated 1 April 1921 as Headquarters, 1st Battalion

Company G, 18th Infantry, Pennsylvania National Guard (organized 14 December 1873 at Pittsburgh; mustered into Federal service 13 May 1898 at Mount Gretna as Company G, 18th Pennsylvania Volunteers; mustered out 22 October 1898 at Pittsburgh and resumed State status; mustered into Federal service 4 July 1916 at Mount Gretna for service on the Mexican border; mustered out 5 January 1917 and resumed State status; mustered into Federal service 14 April 1917 at Pittsburgh and drafted into Federal service 5 August 1917; consolidated 11 October 1917 with Company G, 111th Infantry; reconstituted 16 October 1919 in the Pennsylvania National Guard as Company G, 18th Infantry), reorganized and Federally recognized 5 April 1921 at Pittsburgh as Headquarters Battery and Combat Train 1st Battalion

Battery A organized new and Federally recognized 6 February 1922 at Pittsburgh

Company B, 18th Infantry, Pennsylvania National Guard (organized 1 February 1870 at Pittsburgh as 2d Company, *Duquesne Greys* and redesignated 30 November 1871 as Company B, 18th Infantry, Pennsylvania National Guard; mustered into Federal service 13 May 1898 at Mount Gretna as Company B, 18th Pennsylvania Volunteers; mustered out 22 October 1898 at Pittsburgh and resumed State status; mustered into Federal service 4 July 1916 at Mount Gretna for service on the Mexican border; mustered out 5 January 1917 and resumed State status; mustered into Federal service 14 April 1917 at Pittsburgh and drafted into Federal service on 5 August 1917; consolidated 11 October 1917 with Company B, 111th Infantry; reconstituted 16 October 1919 in the Pennsylvania National Guard as Company B, 18th Infantry; reorganized and Federally recognized 6 July 1920 at Pittsburgh), redesignated 1 April 1921 as Battery B

Inducted into Federal service 3 February 1941 at Pittsburgh. Reorganized and redesignated 12 March 1942 as the 176th Field Artillery Battalion (105mm Howitzer Truck Drawn). Inactivated 5 December 1945 at Camp Kilmer, New Jersey. Redesignated 24 May 1946 as the 689th Antiaircraft Artillery Automatic Weapons Battalion. Reorganized and Federally recognized 10 December 1946 with Headquarters at Pittsburgh and batteries at Pittsburgh and Coraopolis. Redesignated 1 June 1951 as the 689th Antiaircraft Artillery Gun Battalion (90mm). Disbanded 30 September 1953 at Pittsburgh when Federal recognition was withdrawn.

CAMPAIGN STREAMERS
World War I
Champagne-Marne
Aisne-Marne
Oise-Aisne
Meuse-Argonne
Champagne 1918
Lorraine 1918

World War II
Northern France
Rhineland
Ardennes-Alsace
Central Europe

DECORATIONS
None

COAT OF ARMS
SHIELD: Sable, a fess checky argent and azure between three high explosive shells each debruised by a leopard's face or.

CREST: That for the regiments and separate battalions of the Pennsylvania Army National Guard: On a wreath of the colors (or and sable) a lion rampant guardant proper, holding in dexter paw a naked scimitar argent, hilted or and in sinister an escutcheon argent, on a fess sable three plates.

MOTTO: Puebla To The Marne

This battalion was organized at Pittsburgh and Battery B was originally organized as 2d Company, *Duquesne Greys*. The shield is that of William Pitt and later the City of Pittsburgh with the three gold discs replaced by three high explosive shells, each charged with a leopard's face from the arms of Duquesne.

DISTINCTIVE BADGE
The badge is the shield, crest and motto of the coat of arms on a red projectile. The sample of the badge depicted was originally approved 15 October 1924 for wear by the 176th Field Artillery.

690th ANTIAIRCRAFT ARTILLERY BATTALION

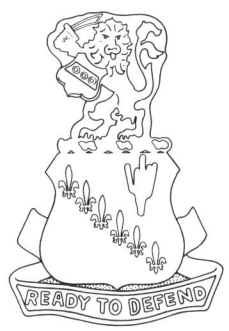

Constituted 24 May 1946 in the Pennsylvania National Guard as the 690th Antiaircraft Artillery Automatic Weapons Battalion, Self Propelled and organized from new and existing units as follows:

Company F 119th Cavalry Reconnaissance Squadron, Mechanized (organized 31 December 1914 at Harrisburg as Provisional Supply Company 8th Infantry, Pennsylvania National Guard; mustered into Federal service 9 July 1916 at Mount Gretna for Mexican border; redesignated 7 September 1916 as Supply Company 8th Infantry, Pennsylvania National Guard; mustered out 27 February 1917 and resumed State status; mustered into Federal service 15 July 1917 at Harrisburg and drafted into Federal service on 5 August 1917; consolidated 11 October 1917 with Supply Company 112th Infantry; reconstituted 16 October 1919 in the Pennsylvania National Guard as Supply Company, 8th Infantry; reorganized and Federally recognized 14 July 1920 at Harrisburg; redesignated 1 June 1921 as Service Troop 104th Cavalry; redesignated 1 April 1929 as Troop K 104th Cavalry; redesignated 23 September 1940 as Troop F 104th Cavalry; inducted into Federal service 17 February 1941 at Harrisburg; redesignated 1 January 1944 as Company F 119th Cavalry Reconnaissance Squadron, Mechanized and inactivated 15 August 1944 at Camp Gruber, Oklahoma), reorganized and Federally recognized 18 February 1947 at Harrisburg as Headquarters and Headquarters Battery

Battery A 107th Field Artillery Battalion (organized and Federally recognized 24 August 1920 at Harrisburg as Battery A 1st Field Artillery, Pennsylvania National Guard; redesignated 1 April 1921 as Battery A 107th Field Artillery; inducted into Federal service 17 February 1941 at Harrisburg; redesignated 17 February 1942 as Battery A 107th Field Artillery Battalion and inactivated 27 October 1945 at Camp Shelby, Mississippi), reorganized and Federally recognized 6 November 1946 at Harrisburg as Battery A

Headquarters Battery 73d Antiaircraft Artillery Gun Battalion (organized and Federally recognized 1 June 1922 at Lebanon as Headquarters Detachment 2d Battalion 213th Artillery, Coast Artillery Corps; redesignated 1 August 1924 as Headquarters Detachment 2d Battalion 213th Coast Artillery; redesignated 1 April 1939 as Headquarters Detachment and Combat

Train 1st Battalion 213th Coast Artillery; redesignated 15 December 1939 as Headquarters Battery and Combat Train 1st Battalion 213th Coast Artillery; inducted into Federal service 15 September 1940 at Lebanon; redesignated 23 March 1944 as Headquarters Battery 73d Antiaircraft Artillery Gun Battalion and inactivated 25 January 1945 in France), reorganized and Federally recognized 7 November 1946 at Lebanon as Battery B

Detachment 1, Battery A 73d Antiaircraft Artillery Gun Battalion (organized 10 September 1842 at Pottsville as *Independent Blues of Pottsville*; assigned to 1st Battalion, Schuylkill County Volunteers on 18 April 1844; redesignated *Washington Artillerists* and attached to Schuylkill County Volunteers in 1845; mustered into Federal service as Company B 1st Regiment, Pennsylvania Volunteer Infantry; mustered out 27 July 1848 and reverted to State control; reorganized 22 February 1850 as *Washington Artillerists* and attached to Schuylkill County Volunteers; mustered into Federal service 18 April 1861 at Harrisburg as *Washington Artillerists*, Pennsylvania Volunteers and redesignated Company H 25th Pennsylvania Volunteer Infantry the following month; mustered out of Federal service 29 July 1861 at Harrisburg and resumed State status; mustered into Federal service 1 October 1861 at Harrisburg as Company G 48th Pennsylvania Volunteer Infantry; mustered out 17 July 1865 and returned to State control; reorganized 7 September 1870 at Pottsville as *Gowen Guards*; redesignated 30 June 1874 as Company F 7th Infantry, Pennsylvania National Guard; redesignated 4 November 1879 as the *Washington Artillerists*; redesignated 30 November 1881 as an unassigned infantry company and attached to the 3d Brigade, Pennsylvania National Guard; redesignated 18 June 1883 as Company F 4th Infantry, Pennsylvania National Guard; mustered into Federal service 9 May 1898 at Mount Gretna as Company F 4th Pennsylvania Volunteers; mustered out of Federal service 16 November 1898 and resumed State status; mustered into Federal service 8 July 1916 at Mount Gretna for Mexican border; redesignated 10 August 1916 as Company C, Engineer Battalion, Pennsylvania National Guard; mustered out 28 February 1917 and resumed State status; redesignated 13 July 1917 as Company C 1st Engineers, Pennsylvania National Guard; mustered into Federal service 15 July 1917 at Pottsville and drafted into Federal service on 5 August 1917; redesignated 11 October 1917 as Company C 103d Engineers and assigned to the 28th Division; demobilized 16 May 1919 at Camp Dix, New Jersey; reorganized and Federally recognized 6 June 1922 at Pottsville as Service Battery 213th Artillery, Coast Artillery Corps; redesignated 1 August 1924 as Service Battery 213th Coast Artillery; redesignated 15 December 1939 as Detachment 1, Battery A 213th Coast Artillery; inducted into Federal service 15 September 1940 at Pottsville; redesignated 23 March 1944 as Detachment 1, Battery A 73d Antiaircraft Artillery Gun Battalion and inactivated 25 January 1945 in France), reorganized and Federally recognized 10 December 1946 at Pottsville as Battery C

Battery B 899th Antiaircraft Artillery Automatic Weapons Battalion (organized at Pottsville during 1831 as *National Light Infantry* of Pottsville; assigned to the 30th Regiment, Pennsylvania Militia on 5 May 1832 and later reassigned to 1st Regiment, Schuylkill County Volunteers; mustered into Federal service 18 April 1861 at Harrisburg as *National Light Infantry*, Pennsylvania Volunteers and redesignated Company D 25th Pennsylvania Volunteer Infantry in May 1861; mustered out 1 August 1861 and resumed State status; mustered into Federal service 23 September 1861 at Harrisburg as Company A 96th Pennsylvania Volunteer Infantry; mustered out 21 October 1864 and returned to State control; reorganized 3 October 1870 at Pottsville as *Pottsville Light Infantry*; redesignated 30 June 1874 as Company G 7th Infantry, Pennsylvania National Guard; redesignated 8 July 1881 as Company H 8th Infantry, Pennsylvania National Guard; mustered into Federal service 12 May 1898 at Mount Gretna as Company H 8th Pennsylvania Volunteers; mustered out 7 March 1899 at Augusta, Georgia and resumed State status; mustered into Federal service 9 July 1916 at Mount Gretna for Mexican border; mustered out 1 March 1917 and resumed State status; mustered into Federal service 15 July 1917 at Pottsville and drafted into Federal service on 5 August 1917; consolidated 11 October 1917 with Company H 112th Infantry; reorganized and Federally recognized 6 June 1922 at Pottsville as Headquarters Battery 213th Artillery, Coast Artillery Corps; redesignated 1 August 1924 as Headquarters Battery 213th Coast Artillery; redesignated 1 April 1939 as Battery F 213th Coast Artillery; inducted into Federal service 15 September 1940 at Pottsville; redesignated 14 March 1944 as Battery B 899th Antiaircraft Artillery Automatic Weapons Battalion and inactivated 13 February 1945 in France), reorganized and Federally recognized 22 October 1946 at Pottsville as Battery D

Medical Detachment organized new and Federally recognized 6 November 1946 at

Harrisburg

Redesignated 1 October 1953 as the 690th Antiaircraft Artillery Battalion (Automatic Weapons) (Self Propelled). Disbanded 18 October 1953 at home stations when Federal recognition was withdrawn.

CAMPAIGN STREAMERS

Civil War
Antietam
Fredericksburg
Wilderness
Spotsylvania
Cold Harbor
Petersburg
Appomattox
Virginia 1862

World War I
Champagne-Marne
Aisne-Marne
Oise-Aisne
Meuse-Argonne
Champagne 1918
Lorraine 1918

World War II
Naples-Foggia
Rome-Arno
Rhineland

DECORATIONS
None

COAT OF ARMS
SHIELD: Argent, six fleurs-de-lis palewise in bend azure, in chief a giant cactus vert.

CREST: That for the regiments and separate battalions of the Pennsylvania Army National Guard: On a wreath of the colors (argent and azure) a lion rampant guardant proper, holding in dexter paw a naked scimitar argent, hilted or and in sinister an escutcheon argent, on a fess sable three plates.

MOTTO: Ready To Defend

The shield is silver or white, the old color of the Infantry. The giant cactus represents Mexican border service while the six fleurs-de-lis represent service in France during World War I.

DISTINCTIVE INSIGNIA
The insignia is the shield crest and motto of the coat of arms. The insignia depicted was never made for nor worn by this organization.

691st ANTIAIRCRAFT ARTILLERY AUTOMATIC WEAPONS BATTALION

Constituted 2 July 1946 in the Virginia National Guard as the 691st Antiaircraft Artillery Automatic Weapons Battalion and organized from new and existing units as follows:

Headquarters Battery, 111th Field Artillery Battalion (organized 26 June 1856 at Portsmouth as *Old Dominion Guard* and assigned to 7th Regiment, Virginia Volunteers; reassigned to 3d Regiment, Virginia Volunteers later that year; mustered into active State service 20 April 1861 at Portsmouth; redesignated 1 July 1861 as Company K, 9th Virginia Infantry, Confederate States Army; surrendered 9 April 1865 at Appomattox Court House; reorganized 5 December 1877 at Portsmouth as *Old Dominion Guard*; redesignated 29 August 1882 as Company E, 4th Regiment of Infantry, Virginia Volunteers; redesignated 19 April 1894 as Company A, 3d Battalion of Infantry, Virginia Volunteers; mustered into Federal service 21 May 1898 at Richmond as Company L, 4th Virginia Volunteer Infantry; mustered out 27 April 1899 at Savannah, Georgia and returned to State control; reorganized 4 September 1900 at Portsmouth as *Old Dominion Guard*, Virginia Volunteers; redesignated 1 October 1900 as Company L, 71st Infantry, Virginia Volunteers; redesignated 1 September

1908 as Company L, 4th Infantry, Virginia Volunteers; mustered into Federal service 6 April 1917 at Portsmouth and drafted into Federal service on 5 August 1917; consolidated with Company K 4th Infantry, Virginia Volunteers [originally organized at Portsmouth in 1792 as *Portsmouth Rifles*], reorganized and redesignated 4 October 1917 as Machine Company, 116th Infantry and assigned to the 29th Division; demobilized 30 May 1919 at Camp Lee, Virginia; reorganized and Federally recognized 27 February 1924 at Portsmouth as Headquarters Detachment and Combat Train, 1st Battalion 111th Field Artillery; reorganized and redesignated 16 October 1924 as Headquarters Battery and Combat Train, 1st Battalion 111th Field Artillery; reorganized and redesignated 1 July 1940 as Headquarters Battery, 1st Battalion 111th Field Artillery; inducted into Federal service 3 February 1941 at Portsmouth; redesignated 12 March 1942 as Headquarters Battery, 111th Field Artillery Battalion; inactivated 6 January 1946 at Camp Kilmer, New Jersey), reorganized and Federally recognized 13 December 1946 at Portsmouth as Headquarters and Headquarters Battery

Battery A organized new and Federally recognized 23 June 1947 at Suffolk

Battery B organized new and Federally recognized 25 February 1947 at Franklin

Battery C 111th Field Artillery Battalion (organized 15 February 1809 at Portsmouth as *Portsmouth Light Artillery* and assigned to 4th Regiment of Artillery, Virginia Militia; mustered into Federal service for defense of Craney Island, Virginia on 22 June 1813, then mustered out; mustered into active State service 20 April 1861 at Portsmouth as Captain Cary F. Grimes' Company, Virginia Light Artillery [also known as *Grimes' Battery*]; Captain Grimes killed in action 17 September 1862 at Antietam and unit redesignated 18 September 1862 as Captain John H. Thompson's Company, Virginia Light Artillery; disbanded 4 October 1862 at Winchester when artillery of Army of Northern Virginia reorganized; reorganized at Portsmouth 18 July 1891 as Battery C [*Grimes' Battery*] 1st Battalion of Artillery, Virginia Volunteers; redesignated 1 September 1908 as Battery C, 1st Battalion of Field Artillery, Virginia Volunteers; mustered into Federal service 18 June 1916 for Mexican border duty; mustered out at Richmond 22 March 1917 and resumed State status; mustered into Federal service 2 July 1917 at Portsmouth; redesignated 4 August 1917 as Battery C, 1st Regiment of Virginia Field Artillery; drafted into Federal service 5 August 1917; redesignated 15 September 1917 as Battery C, 111th Field Artillery and assigned to the 29th Division; demobilized 2 June 1919 at Camp Lee, Virginia; reorganized and Federally recognized 4 May 1921 at Portsmouth as Battery C, Field Artillery, Virginia National Guard; redesignated 30 May 1921 as Battery C 1st Battalion Field Artillery, Virginia National Guard; redesignated 21 November 1921 as Battery C 111th Field Artillery; inducted into Federal service 3 February 1941 at Portsmouth; redesignated 12 March 1942 as Battery C 111th Field Artillery Battalion; and inactivated 6 January 1946 at Camp Kilmer, New Jersey), reorganized and Federally recognized 10 February 1947 at Portsmouth as Battery C

Headquarters Company, 3d Battalion 176th Infantry (organized 27 June 1921 at Parksley as 7th Company, 2d Provisional Regiment, Virginia National Guard; redesignated 12 October 1921 as Company K 1st Infantry, Virginia National Guard; redesignated 9 March 1922 as Company K 183d Infantry; reorganized and redesignated 19 January 1924 as Headquarters Company, 3d Battalion 183d Infantry and relocated to Onancock; redesignated 22 February 1929 as Headquarters Company, 3d Battalion 1st Infantry, Virginia National Guard; redesignated 1 January 1941 as Headquarters Company 3d Battalion 176th Infantry; inducted into Federal service 3 February 1941 at Onancock; and inactivated 10 July 1944 at Fort Benning, Georgia), reorganized and Federally recognized 1 July 1947 at Onancock as Battery D

Medical Detachment organized new and Federally recognized 4 November 1947 at Portsmouth

Redesignated 1 February 1949 as the 129th Antiaircraft Artillery Automatic Weapons Battalion.

CAMPAIGN STREAMERS
War of 1812
Streamer without inscription

Civil War (Confederate service)
Peninsula
Second Manassas
Sharpsburg
Virginia 1861

World War I
Streamer without inscription

World War II
Normandy (with arrowhead)
Northern France
Rhineland
Central Europe

DECORATIONS
French Croix de Guerre with Palm, World War II, Streamer embroidered BEACHES OF NORMANDY (29th Inf Div cited for action on 6 June 1944; DAGO 43, 1950)

COAT OF ARMS
None

DISTINCTIVE INSIGNIA
None

692d ANTIAIRCRAFT ARTILLERY AUTOMATIC WEAPONS BATTALION

Constituted 5 August 1946 in the Florida National Guard as the 692d Antiaircraft Artillery Battalion and organized from new and existing units as follows:

Headquarters, 1st Battalion 265th Coast Artillery (Harbor Defense) (organized and Federally recognized 7 December 1929 at Jacksonville; inducted into Federal service 6 January 1941 at Jacksonville; disbanded 31 July 1944 in Alaska; and reconstituted 5 July 1946 in the Florida National Guard) reorganized and Federally recognized 3 December 1946 at Jacksonville as Headquarters and Headquarters Battery

Battery A organized new and Federally recognized 23 February 1948 at Palatka

Service Company, 124th Infantry (organized and Federally recognized 18 July 1917 at St. Augustine as Supply Company, 1st Infantry, Florida National Guard; drafted into Federal service 5 August 1917; redesignated 1 October 1917 as Supply Company, 56th Depot Brigade and assigned to the 31st Division; disbanded 1 November 1917 at Camp Wheeler, Georgia; reorganized and Federally recognized 1 March 1921 at St. Augustine as Service Company, 1st Infantry, Florida National Guard; redesignated 7 December 1921 as Service Company, 154th Infantry; redesignated 28 May 1924 as Service Company, 124th Infantry; inducted into Federal service 25 November 1940 at St. Augustine; inactivated 2 March 1944 at Fort Jackson, South Carolina; activated 5 April 1944 in Australia; inactivated 16 December 1945 at Camp Stoneman, California) reorganized and Federally recognized 6 June 1949 at St. Augustine as Battery B

Battery A, 265th Coast Artillery (organized and Federally recognized 25 May 1921 at Jacksonville as 1st Company, Coast Artillery Corps, Florida National Guard; redesignated 29 May 1922 as 437th Coast Artillery Company; assigned to 1st Separate Battalion, Coast Artillery, Florida National Guard on 9 February 1924; redesignated 4 April 1924 as Battery A, 1st Separate Battalion, Coast Artillery, Florida National Guard; redesignated 22 July 1925 as Battery A 265th Coast Artillery Battalion; redesignated 20 November 1929 as Battery A, 265th Coast Artillery; inducted into Federal service 6 January 1941 at Jacksonville; disbanded 31 July 1944 in Alaska; reconstituted 5 July 1946 in the Florida National Guard), reorganized and

Federally recognized 20 September 1948 at Jacksonville as Battery C

Battery D, 265th Coast Artillery (organized and Federally recognized 1 July 1929 at Daytona Beach as Battery D, 265th Coast Artillery Battalion and redesignated 20 November 1929 as Battery D, 265th Coast Artillery; redesignated 1 January 1930 as Battery C, 265th Coast Artillery; redesignated 15 April 1940 as Battery D, 265th Coast Artillery; inducted into Federal service 6 January 1941 at Daytona Beach; disbanded 31 July 1944 in Alaska; and reconstituted 5 July 1946 in the Florida National Guard), reorganized and Federally recognized 20 September 1948 at Daytona Beach as Battery D

Medical Detachment organized new and Federally recognized 12 June 1947 at Jacksonville

Redesignated 1 February 1949 as the 148th Antiaircraft Artillery Automatic Weapons Battalion.

CAMPAIGN STREAMERS
World War II
Pacific Theater without inscription

DECORATIONS
None

COAT OF ARMS
None

DISTINCTIVE INSIGNIA
None

693d ANTIAIRCRAFT ARTILLERY AUTOMATIC WEAPONS BATTALION

Constituted 1 October 1920 as 2d Battalion, 6th Infantry and allotted to the Illinois National Guard. Converted and redesignated 19 March 1921 as 2d Battalion, 1st Artillery (Antiaircraft), Coast Artillery Corps. Redesignated 13 December 1921 as 2d Battalion, 202d Artillery (Antiaircraft), Coast Artillery Corps. Organized and Federally recognized 15 May 1922 at Chicago. Redesignated 7 December 1923 as 2d Battalion, 202d Artillery (Antiaircraft), Coast Artillery Corps. Redesignated 26 August 1924 as 2d Battalion, 202d Coast Artillery (Antiaircraft). Inducted into Federal service 16 September 1940 at Chicago. Reorganized at Bremerton, Washington and redesignated 10 September 1943 as 396th Antiaircraft Artillery Automatic Weapons Battalion. Inactivated 9 January 1945 at Camp Livingston, Louisiana. Redesignated 5 July 1946 as 693d Antiaircraft Artillery Automatic Weapons Battalion. Reorganized and Federally recognized 13 December 1946 at Chicago.

Redesignated 1 February 1949 as the 133d Antiaircraft Artillery Automatic Weapons Battalion.

CAMPAIGN STREAMERS
None

DECORATIONS
None

COAT OF ARMS
None

DISTINCTIVE INSIGNIA
None

694th ANTIAIRCRAFT ARTILLERY AUTOMATIC WEAPONS BATTALION

Constituted 31 May 1946 as the 694th Antiaircraft Artillery Automatic Weapons Battalion (Self Propelled) and allotted to the Michigan National Guard. Withdrawn from allotment to the Michigan Army National Guard and returned to Department of the Army control about 1949.

CAMPAIGN STREAMERS
None

DECORATIONS
None

COAT OF ARMS
None

DISTINCTIVE INSIGNIA
None

695th ANTIAIRCRAFT ARTILLERY AUTOMATIC WEAPONS BATTALION

Constituted 31 May 1946 as the 695th Antiaircraft Artillery Automatic Weapons Battalion (Self Propelled) and allotted to the Michigan National Guard. Withdrawn from allotment to the Michigan Army National Guard and returned to Department of the Army control about 1949.

CAMPAIGN STREAMERS
None

DECORATIONS
None

COAT OF ARMS
None

DISTINCTIVE INSIGNIA
None

696th ANTIAIRCRAFT ARTILLERY AUTOMATIC WEAPONS BATTALION

Constituted 2 July 1946 in the Texas National Guard as the 696th Antiaircraft Artillery Automatic Weapons Battalion and organized from new and existing units as follows:

Headquarters Company, 2d Battalion, 141st Infantry (organized 18 July 1905 at El Paso as Company K, 4th Infantry, Texas National Guard; mustered into Federal Service 18 May 1916 for Mexican border duty; mustered out 24 May 1917 at Fort Sam Houston, Texas and resumed State status; mustered into Federal service 11 April 1917 at Fort Sam Houston and drafted into Federal service 5 August 1917; redesignated 15 October 1917 as Company G, 144th Infantry and assigned to the 36th Division; demobilized 21 June 1919 at Camp Bowie, Texas; reorganized and Federally recognized 11 May 1922 at El Paso as Headquarters Company, 2d Battalion, 141st Infantry; redesignated 1 May 1940 as Headquarters Detachment, 2d Battalion, 141st Infantry; inducted into Federal service 25 November 1940 at El Paso; redesignated 1 April 1942 as Headquarters Company, 2d Battalion, 141st Infantry; inactivated 22 December 1945 at Camp Patrick Henry, Virginia), reorganized and Federally recognized 2 December 1946 at El Paso as Headquarters and Headquarters Battery

Company E, 141st Infantry (organized and Federally recognized 21 November 1923 at El Paso; inducted into Federal service 25 November 1940 and inactivated 22 December 1945 at Camp Patrick Henry), reorganized and Federally recognized 20 May 1947 at El Paso as Battery A

Company H, 141st Infantry (organized and Federally recognized 11 May 1922 at El Paso; inducted into Federal service 25 November 1940 at El Paso and inactivated 22 December 1945 at Camp Patrick Henry), reorganized and Federally recognized 2 December 1946 at El Paso as Battery B

Batteries C and D organized new and Federally recognized 2 December 1946 at El Paso

Redesignated 1 May 1949 as the 136th Antiaircraft Artillery Automatic Weapons Battalion.

CAMPAIGN STREAMERS
World War I
Meuse-Argonne

World War II
Naples-Foggia (with arrowhead)
Anzio
Rome-Arno
Southern France (with arrowhead)
Rhineland
Ardennes-Alsace
Central Europe

DECORATIONS
Presidential Unit Citation (Army), Streamer embroidered COLMAR POCKET (2d Bn 141st Inf cited for period 7-19 Dec 1944; WDGO 56, 1946)

French Croix de Guerre with Palm, World War II, Streamer embroidered VOSGES (141st Inf cited for period 24 Nov-2 Dec 1944; DAGO 43, 1950)

COAT OF ARMS
None

DISTINCTIVE INSIGNIA
None

697th ANTIAIRCRAFT ARTILLERY BATTALION

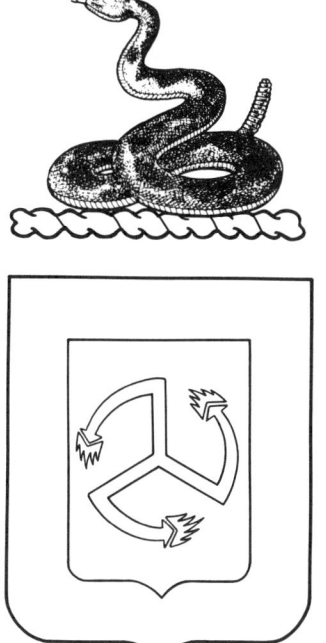

Organized in the New Mexico National Guard as Headquarters, 3d Squadron, 111th Cavalry and Federally recognized 14 July 1929 at Carlsbad. Relocated to Clovis on 1 May 1936. Converted, reorganized and redesignated 26 April 1940 as Headquarters, 2d Battalion, 207th Coast Artillery (Antiaircraft). Redesignated 1 July 1940 as Headquarters, 2d Battalion, 200th Coast Artillery (Antiaircraft). Inducted into Federal service 6 January 1941 at Clovis. Surrendered to Japanese *14th Army*, 9 April 1942 on Luzon. Formally inactivated 2 April 1946 at Fort Mills, Philippine Islands. Redesignated 31 May 1946 as Headquarters, 697th Antiaircraft Artillery Automatic Weapons Battalion. Reorganized and Federally recognized 2 November 1947 at Carlsbad; remainder of battalion organized from new and existing units as follows:

Battery F, 200th Coast Artillery (organized 15 September 1909 at Carlsbad as Company B, 1st Infantry, New Mexico National Guard; mustered into Federal service 16 July 1916 at Carlsbad for service on the Mexican border; mustered out 5 April 1917 at Columbus and resumed State status; mustered into Federal service 11 June 1917 and drafted into Federal service 5 August 1917; redesignated 20 October 1917 as Company B, 143d Machine Gun Battalion and assigned to the 40th Division; relieved from the 40th Division and demobilized 30 April 1919 at Camp Grant, Illinois; reorganized and Federally recognized 28 July 1920 at Carlsbad as Troop B, 1st Cavalry, New Mexico National Guard; redesignated 2 May 1922 as Troop B, 111th Cavalry; redesignated 15 March 1929 as Troop I, 111th Cavalry; converted, reorganized and redesignated 26 April 1940 as Battery F, 207th Coast Artillery [Antiaircraft]; redesignated 1 July 1940 as Battery F, 200th Coast Artillery [Antiaircraft]; inducted into Federal service 6 January 1941 at Carlsbad; surrendered to Japanese *14th Army* on Luzon; formally inactivated 2 April 1946 at Fort Mills, Philippine Islands), reorganized and Federally recognized 27 June 1947 at Carlsbad as Headquarters Battery

Battery A organized new and Federally recognized 25 September 1947 at Roswell

Battery B organized new and Federally recognized 13 October 1947 at Carlsbad

Battery C organized new and Federally recognized 2 November 1947 at Artesia

Battery D organized new and Federally recognized 28 June 1947 at Hobbs

Medical Detachment organized new and Federally recognized 12 February 1949 at Roswell

Headquarters relocated to Artesia on 1 October 1952. Redesignated 1 October 1953 as the 697th Antiaircraft Artillery Battalion (Automatic Weapons) (Mobile).

Consolidated 1 September 1959 with the 200th Artillery, a parent regiment under the Combat Arms Regimental System.

CAMPAIGN STREAMERS
World War II
Philippine Islands

DECORATIONS
Presidential Unit Citation (Army), Streamer embroidered *CLARK FIELD* (200th Coast Arty cited for period 8-22 Dec 1941; WDGO 14, 1942)

Presidential Unit Citation (Army), Streamer embroidered *BATAAN* (200th Coast Arty cited for period 7 Jan-8 Mar 1942; WDGO 14, 1942)

Presidential Unit Citation (Army), Streamer embroidered *DEFENSE OF THE PHILIPPINES* (Mil & Naval Forces of the US engaged in the defense of the Philippines cited for the period 7 Dec 1941-10 May 1942; WDGO 22, 1942 as amended by WDGO 46, 1948)

Philippine Presidential Unit Citation, Streamer embroidered *7 DECEMBER 1941 TO 10 MAY 1942* (200th Coast Arty cited; DAGO 43, 1950)

COAT OF ARMS
SHIELD: Or, an Avanyu sable; a bordure gules.

CREST: That for the regiments and separate battalions of the New Mexico Army National Guard: On a wreath of the colors (or and sable) a coiled rattlesnake proper.

MOTTO: *Defensores Patriae* (Guardians Of The Country)

The colors red and yellow are used for Artillery. The Avanyu is a figure representing happiness and prosperity and was widely used by the ancient Pueblo Indians in New Mexico. The shield is that of the old 111th Cavalry within a gold border to represent descent from that regiment.

DISTINCTIVE INSIGNIA
The insignia is the shield and motto of the coat of arms. The sample of the insignia depicted was approved for wear on 13 August 1953.

698th ANTIAIRCRAFT ARTILLERY MISSILE BATTALION

Constituted 27 May 1942 in the Illinois National Guard as the 3d Battalion, 202d Coast Artillery (Antiaircraft) and activated 15 June 1942 at Bremerton, Washington. Reorganized and redesignated 10 September 1943 as the 242d Antiaircraft Artillery Searchlight Battalion. Inactivated 23 June 1944 at Camp Van Dorn, Mississippi. Disbanded 26 June 1944. Reconstituted 27 May 1946 in the Illinois National Guard. Redesignated 5 July 1946 as the 698th Antiaircraft Artillery Gun Battalion. Reorganized and Federally recognized 14 February 1947 at Chicago. Ordered into active Federal service 1 May 1951 at Chicago. Released from active Federal service 1 February 1953 and resumed State status. Redesignated 1 October 1953 as the 698th Antiaircraft Artillery Battalion (90mm Gun). (133d Antiaircraft Artillery Battalion consolidated with 698th Antiaircraft Artillery Battalion on 28 February 1954). Reorganized and redesignated 27 February 1958 as the 698th Antiaircraft Artillery Missile Battalion (NIKE).

Reorganized and redesignated 1 March 1959 as the 202d Combat Arms Regiment, a parent regiment under the Combat Arms Regimental System.

CAMPAIGN STREAMERS
World War II
Normandy
Northern France
Rhineland
Ardennes-Alsace
Central Europe
Pacific Theater without inscription

DECORATIONS
French Croix de Guerre with Palm, World War II, Streamer embroidered *MOSELLE* (106th Cav Recon Sqn cited for period 20 Aug 1944-10 Feb 1945; DAGO 43, 1950)

French Croix de Guerre with Palm, World War II, Streamer embroidered *CAEN-FALAISE* (106th Cav Recon Sqn cited for period 5-20 Aug 1944; DAGO 43, 1950)

Fourragere in the colors of the French Croix de Guerre, World War II (106th Cav Recon Sqn cited; DAGO 43, 1950)

COAT OF ARMS
SHIELD: Azure, three piles in point or, overall a winged projectile palewise wings displayed gules, that portion on the field fimbriated of the second; all within a double bordure of the third and of the second.

CREST: That for the regiments and separate battalions of the Illinois Army National Guard: On a wreath of the colors (or and azure) upon a grassy field the blockhouse of old Fort Dearborn proper.

MOTTO: Citizen Soldiers

The shield is that of the old 202d Coast Artillery within a red and yellow border to indicate the descent from the 3d Battalion of that regiment. The three piles on the blue field are representative of Coast Artillery and its area of operations. The winged projectile is red for Artillery and the wings indicate the antiaircraft nature of the unit.

DISTINCTIVE INSIGNIA
The insignia is the shield and motto of the coat of arms. The sample of the insignia depicted was approved for wear on 17 June 1954.

700th ANTIAIRCRAFT ARTILLERY BATTALION

Constituted 5 July 1946 in the Washington National Guard as the 700th Antiaircraft Artillery Automatic Weapons Battalion and organized from new and existing units as follows:

Headquarters, 1st Battalion, 248th Coast Artillery (Harbor Defense) (organized at Seattle during 1909 as Headquarters, Coast Artillery Reserve, Washington National Guard and redesignated Headquarters, Coast Artillery Corps, Washington National Guard in 1915; redesignated 5 May 1916 as Headquarters, First Coast Defense Command, Washington National Guard; drafted into Federal service 5 August 1917 and subsequently demobilized in the Coast Defenses of Puget Sound, Washington; reconstituted 26 January 1921 in the Washington National Guard as Headquarters, 1st Coast Defense Command; reorganized and Federally recognized 13 November 1923 at Aberdeen as Headquarters, 1st Battalion, Coast Artillery Corps, Washington National Guard; redesignated 1 March 1924 as Headquarters, 1st Battalion, 248th Artillery, Coast Artillery Corps; redesignated 1 May 1924 as Headquarters, 1st Battalion, 248th Coast Artillery [Harbor Defense]; relocated to Olympia on 24 September 1928; redesignated 1 October 1933 as Headquarters, 248th Coast Artillery Battalion [Harbor Defense]; redesignated 1 September 1935 as Headquarters, 1st Battalion, 248th Coast Artillery; relocated to Aberdeen on 20 November 1939; inducted into Federal service 16 September 1940 at Aberdeen; inactivated 8 May 1944 at Camp Barkeley, Texas; disbanded 14 June 1944 and reconstituted 25 August 1945 in the Washington National Guard), reorganized and Federally recognized 19 March 1947 at Aberdeen as Headquarters and Headquarters Battery

Headquarters Battery, 248th Coast Artillery (organized and Federally recognized 28 November 1939 at Aberdeen as Headquarters Detachment, 1st Battalion, 248th Coast Artillery and redesignated 1 January 1940 as Headquarters Battery, 248th Coast Artillery; inducted into Federal service 16 September 1940; inactivated 8 May 1944 at Camp Barkeley; disbanded 14 June 1944 and reconstituted 25 August 1945 in the Washington National Guard), reorganized and Federally recognized 29 September 1947 at Aberdeen as Battery A

Battery B organized new and Federally recognized 12 November 1947 at Shelton

Headquarters Battery, 205th Antiaircraft Artillery Group (organized and Federally recognized 8 November 1939 at Olympia as Headquarters Battery, 205th Coast Artillery [Antiaircraft]; inducted into Federal service 3 February 1941 at Olympia; redesignated 10 September 1943 as Headquarters Battery, 205th Antiaircraft Artillery Group and inactivated 24 August 1944 at Camp Bowie, Texas), reorganized and Federally recognized 9 July 1947 at Olympia as Battery C

Battery D organized new and Federally recognized 29 July 1947 at Port Orchard

Medical Detachment organized new and Federally recognized 17 May 1947 at Aberdeen

Battalion assigned to the 41st Infantry Division on 1 February 1949. Redesignated 1 October 1953 as the 700th Antiaircraft Artillery Battalion (Automatic Weapons) (Self Propelled).

Relieved from the 41st Infantry Division and consolidated 15 April 1959 with the 248th Artillery, a parent regiment under the Combat Arms Regimental System.

CAMPAIGN STREAMERS
None

DECORATIONS
None

COAT OF ARMS
SHIELD: Gules, on a chief embattled or a fleur-de-lis of the first.

CREST: That for the regiments and separate battalions of the Washington Army National Guard: On a wreath of the colors (or and gules) a raven with wings endorsed issuing out of a ducal coronet, all proper.

MOTTO: *Facillime Princeps* (Most Easily The First, Or Foremost)

The shield is red for Artillery. During World War II the organization occupied forts in the Harbor Defenses of Puget Sound. The chief is embattled to represent this service.

DISTINCTIVE INSIGNIA
The insignia is the shield, crest and motto of the coat of arms. The sample of the insignia depicted was originally approved 12 May 1924 for wear by the 248th Coast Artillery.

701st ANTIAIRCRAFT ARTILLERY BATTALION

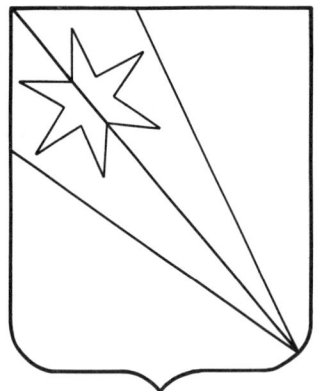 

Constituted 20 September 1942 in the Army of the United States as the 1st Battalion, 701st Coast Artillery (Antiaircraft) and activated 1 October 1942 at Fort Totten, New York. Reorganized and redesignated 1 September 1943 as the 701st Antiaircraft Artillery Gun Battalion (Semimobile). Inactivated 9 November 1944 at Camp Maxey, Texas. Allotted to the Regular Army on 19 November 1952. Activated 1 February 1953 at Pittsburgh, Pennsylvania. Redesignated 24 July 1953 as the 701st Antiaircraft Artillery Battalion (Gun). Inactivated 20 December 1957 at Pittsburgh.

CAMPAIGN STREAMERS
None

DECORATIONS
None

COAT OF ARMS
SHIELD: Per bend or and gules, on a pile issuing from dexter chief a mullet of six points, all counterchanged.

CREST: None

MOTTO: Steel Shield

The shield is in the colors of Artillery. The pile and mullet are functional symbolism — the pile representing the artillery cone of fire and the mullet, a burst of flak.

DISTINCTIVE INSIGNIA
The insignia is the shield and motto of the coat of arms. The sample of the insignia depicted was approved for wear on 8 October 1954.

702d ANTIAIRCRAFT ARTILLERY GUN BATTALION

Constituted 20 June 1946 as the 702d Antiaircraft Artillery Gun Battalion and allotted to the Maryland National Guard. Withdrawn from allotment to the Maryland National Guard and returned to Department of the Army control on 2 September 1947.

CAMPAIGN STREAMERS
None

DECORATIONS
None

COAT OF ARMS
None

DISTINCTIVE INSIGNIA
None

703d ANTIAIRCRAFT ARTILLERY BATTALION

Constituted 17 September 1923 in the Maine National Guard as 1st Battalion, 240th Artillery (Fixed Defense) and organized from new and existing units as follows:

Headquarters, 1st Battalion organized new and Federally recognized 9 January 1924 at Bath

301st Company, 1st Coast Defense Command, Coast Artillery Corps (organized at Portland during 1803 as *Portland Light Infantry*; in Federal service for a short period during 1812 but not in combat; assigned to the Maine Volunteer Militia in 1848; redesignated 21 June 1854 as Company A 1st Regiment, Maine Volunteer Militia; mustered into Federal service 3 May 1861 at Portland; mustered out at Portland 5 August 1861 and resumed State status; consolidated 28 September 1861 with Company C 10th Maine Volunteer Infantry; [Company C 10th Maine Volunteer Infantry mustered out 8 May 1863 at Portland]; reorganized at Portland during 1868 as *Portland Light Infantry*; redesignated 5 April 1873 as Company A 1st Infantry, Maine Volunteer Militia; mustered into Federal service at Augusta during May 1898 as Company A 1st Maine Volunteer Infantry; mustered out in October 1898 and resumed State status; redesignated 1 January 1910 as 1st Company, Coast Artillery Corps, Maine National Guard; called into Federal service 25 July 1917 and drafted into Federal service on 5 August 1917; redesignated 11 August 1917 as 7th Company, Fort Williams [Maine]; redesignated 31 August 1917 as 17th Company, Coast Defenses of Portland; demobilized at Fort Williams during January 1919 and consolidated with 1st Company, Coast Artillery Corps, Maine National Guard which had been reorganized and Federally recognized 11 May 1918 at Portland; and redesignated 10 January 1922 as 301st Company, 1st Coast Defense Command, Coast Artillery Corps), redesignated Battery A

306th Company, 1st Coast Defense Command, Coast Artillery Corps (organized prior to 1903 at Sanford as Company F 1st Infantry, Maine National Guard; redesignated 1 January 1910 as 6th Company, Coast Artillery Corps, Maine National Guard; called into Federal service 25 July 1917 and drafted into Federal service 5 August 1917; redesignated 11 August 1917 as 3d Company, Fort Levett [Maine]; redesignated 31 August 1917 as 23d Company, Coast Defenses of Portland; demobilized at Fort Levett during December 1918; reorganized and Federally recognized 3 November 1920 at Sanford as 6th Company, Coast Artillery Corps, Maine National Guard; and redesignated 9 January 1922 as 306th Company, 1st Coast Defense Command, Coast Artillery Corps), redesignated Battery B

307th Company, 1st Coast Defense Command Coast Artillery Corps, Maine National Guard (organized prior to 1895 at Brunswick as Company K 1st Infantry, Maine National Guard; mustered into Federal service at Augusta as Company K 1st Maine Volunteer Infantry during May 1898; mustered out during October 1898 and resumed State status; redesignated 1 January 1910 as 10th Company, Coast Artillery Corps, Maine National Guard; disbanded 20 November 1911 at Brunswick but reorganized at Brunswick on 23 April 1912; called into Federal service 25 July 1917 and drafted into Federal service on 5 August 1917; redesignated 11 August 1917 as 4th Company, Fort Preble [Maine]; redesignated 31 August 1917 as 21st Company, Coast Defenses of Portland; demobilized at Fort Preble during December 1918; reorganized and Federally recognized 28 March 1922 at Brunswick as 307th Company, 1st Coast Defense Command, Coast Artillery Corps), redesignated Battery C

311th Company, 1st Coast Defense Command, Coast Artillery Corps (organized at Portland in 1807 as *Portland Mechanic Blues*; in Federal service for short period during 1812 but not in combat; assigned to the Maine Volunteer Militia in 1818; redesignated 21 June 1854 as Company B 1st Regiment, Maine Volunteer Militia; mustered into Federal service 3 May 1861 at Portland; mustered out at Portland 5 August 1861 and resumed State status; redesignated 28 September 1861 as Company B 10th Maine Volunteer Infantry; mustered into Federal service 3 August 1851 at Cape Elizabeth; mustered out 8 May 1863 at Portland and resumed State status; mustered into Federal service 17 December 1863 at Augusta as Company B 29th Maine Volunteer Infantry; mustered out 21 June 1866 at Hilton Head, South Carolina; reorganized about 1870 at Portland as *Portland Mechanic Blues*; redesignated 5 April 1873 as Company B 1st Infantry, Maine Volunteer Militia; mustered into Federal service at Augusta during May 1898 as Company B 1st Maine Volunteer Infantry; mustered out during October 1898 and resumed State status; redesignated 1 January 1910 as 2d Company, Coast Artillery Corps, Maine National Guard; called into Federal service 25 July 1917 and drafted into Federal service 5 August 1917; redesignated 11 August 1917 as 2d Company, Fort Levett [Maine]; redesignated 31 August 1917 as 22d Company, Coast Defenses of Portland; redesignated 1 January 1918 as Battery D 54th Artillery, Coast Artillery Corps; demobilized 13 March 1919 at Camp Devens, Massachusetts; reorganized and Federally recognized 15 May 1922 at Portland as 308th Company, 1st Coast Defense Command, Coast Artillery Corps; and redesignated 20 June 1922 as 311th Company, 1st Coast Defense Command, Coast Artillery Corps), redesignated Battery D

Redesignated 16 April 1924 as 1st Battalion, 240th Coast Artillery (Harbor Defense). (Headquarters relocated to Portland on 11 September 1924). Inducted into Federal service 16 September 1940 at Portland. Consolidated with regimental Headquarters and Headquarters Battery, reorganized and redesignated 7 October 1944 as 185th Coast Artillery Battalion (Harbor Defense). Inactivated 1 April 1945 at Peaks Island, Maine. Redesignated 21 May 1946 as 703d Antiaircraft Artillery Gun Battalion. Reorganized and Federally recognized 6 February 1947 with Headquarters at South Portland and batteries at Bath, Brunswick, Rockland and South Portland. Ordered into active Federal service 14 August 1950 at South Portland. Released from active Federal service 13 April 1952 and resumed State status. Redesignated 1 October 1953 as 703d Antiaircraft Artillery Battalion.

Battalion broken up 15 May 1959 and elements converted, reorganized and redesignated or consolidated as follows: Headquarters and Headquarters Battery redesignated Troop F 103d Armored Cavalry; Battery A redesignated Troop D 103d Armored Cavalry; Battery B redesignated Howitzer Battery, 3d Battalion 103d Armored Cavalry; Battery C redesignated Tank Company, 3d Squadron 103d Armored Cavalry; and Battery D consolidated with Battery B 1st Automatic Weapons Battalion, 240th Artillery

CAMPAIGN STREAMERS
War of 1812
Streamer without inscription

Civil War
Valley
Manassas
Antietam
Shenandoah
Louisiana 1864

DECORATIONS
None

COAT OF ARMS
SHIELD: Argent, on a bend azure ten mullets of the field between a portcullis gules and a phoenix of the like rising out of flames proper.

CREST: That for the regiments and separate battalions of the Maine Army National Guard; On a wreath of the colors (argent and gules) a pine tree proper.

MOTTO: *Semper Primus et Fidelis* (Always First And Faithful)

Red is the color for Artillery and the portcullis symbolizes the former harbor defense mission. The phoenix is taken from the crest of the City of Portland, seaport and chief gateway of Maine and indicates the location of the Headquarters of the Battalion. It was also the crest of the Harbor Defenses of Portland of which the organization was a part during World War I. Additionally it symbolizes the successive rejuvenations of the organization following the major wars in which the battalion has participated. The blue symbolizes service as Infantry during the Civil War while the stars represent the various campaigns and battles in which the organization participated during that war.

DISTINCTIVE INSIGNIA
The insignia is the shield and motto of the coat of arms. The sample of the insignia depicted was originally approved on 18 May 1929 for wear by the 240th Coast Artillery.

704th ANTIAIRCRAFT ARTILLERY MISSILE BATTALION

Constituted in the Massachusetts National Guard as 1st Battalion, 1st Coast Defense Command, Coast Artillery Corps and Federally recognized 14 March 1921 with Headquarters at Medford and Batteries at Boston and New Bedford. Redesignated 1 October 1923 as 1st Battalion, 241st Artillery, Coast Artillery Corps. Redesignated 30 April 1924 as 1st Battalion, 241st Coast Artillery (Harbor Defense). (Headquarters relocated to Boston about 1925; to Fall River on 7 June 1939 and back to Boston on 28 June 1940). Inducted into Federal service at home stations on 16 September 1940. Reorganized and redesignated 7 October 1944 as 241st Coast Artillery Battalion (Harbor Defense). Inactivated 1 April 1945 at Fort Warren, Massachusetts. Redesignated 8 July 1946 as 704th Antiaircraft Artillery Gun Battalion and reorganized from existing units as follows:

Headquarters and Headquarters Detachment, 241st Coast Artillery Battalion reorganized and Federally recognized 3 February 1948 at Boston as Headquarters and Headquarters Battery

Battery D, 241st Coast Artillery Battalion (organized 6 August 1798 at Boston as the *City Guards*, Massachusetts Militia and redesignated 25 April 1842 as Company A 2d Battalion of Artillery, Massachusetts Volunteer Militia; redesignated 4 June 1844 as Company D, 5th Regiment of Artillery; redesignated 26 February 1855 as Company D, 2d Regiment of Infantry; redesignated 24 January 1861 as Company D, 1st Regiment of Infantry; mustered into Federal service at Boston on 25 May 1861 as Company D, 1st Regiment, Massachusetts Volunteers and mustered out 25 May 1864 at Boston; reorganized at Boston 18 May 1866 as Company D, 10th Regiment of Infantry; redesignated 7 September 1866 as Company D, 1st Regiment of Infantry; redesignated 14 July 1876 as Company D, 1st Battalion of Infantry; redesignated 3 December 1878 as Company D, 1st Regiment of Infantry; redesignated 1 June 1897 as Battery D, 1st Regiment of Heavy Artillery; mustered into Federal service at Fort Warren 9 May 1898 as Battery D, 1st Massachusetts Volunteer Heavy Artillery; mustered out 14 November 1898 and resumed State status; redesignated 1 November 1905 as 1st Company, Coast Artillery, Artillery Corps; redesignated 15 November 1907 as 1st Company, Coast Artillery Corps, Massachusetts National Guard; called into Federal service 25 July 1917, mustered into Federal service at Boston 3 August 1917, and drafted into Federal service 5 August 1917; redesignated 31 August 1917 as 16th Company, Coast Defenses of Boston; demobilized 4 December 1919 at Fort Revere; reorganized at Boston and Federally recognized 18 October 1920 as 1st Company, 1st Coast Defense Command, Coast Artillery

Corps; redesignated 1 January 1922 as 321st Company, 1st Coast Defense Command, Coast Artillery Corps; redesignated 1 October 1923 as Battery D, 241st Artillery, Coast Artillery Corps; redesignated 30 April 1924 as Battery D, 241st Coast Artillery; and inducted into Federal service at Boston 16 September 1940); redesignated 7 October 1944 as Battery D, 241st Coast Artillery Battalion and inactivated 1 April 1945 at Boston), reorganized and Federally recognized 6 April 1948 at Boston as Battery A

Battery B, 241st Coast Artillery Battalion (organized 21 August 1852 at Boston as Company B [*Maverick Rifles*], 3d Battalion of Light Infantry, Massachusetts Volunteer Militia and redesignated 26 February 1855 as Company B, 2d Regiment of Infantry; redesignated 24 January 1861 as Company B, 1st Regiment of Infantry; mustered into Federal service at Boston 23 May 1861 as Company B, 1st Regiment, Massachusetts Volunteers, and mustered out 25 May 1864 at Boston; reorganized at Boston 27 July 1865 as 73d Unattached Company, Massachusetts Volunteer Militia; redesignated 10 August 1865 as Company I, 7th Regiment of Infantry; redesignated 3 August 1870 as Company D, 1st Battalion of Infantry; disbanded at Boston 11 May 1872; reorganized 10 June 1872 at Boston as Company D, 1st Battalion of Infantry, Massachusetts Volunteer Militia; redesignated 3 March 1874 as Company D, 4th Battalion of Infantry; redesignated 3 December 1878 as Company L, 1st Regiment of Infantry; redesignated 1 June 1897 as Battery L, 1st Regiment of Heavy Artillery; mustered into Federal service at Fort Warren, Massachusetts on 9 May 1898 as Battery L, 1st Massachusetts Volunteer Heavy Artillery; mustered out 14 November 1898 at Boston and resumed State status; redesignated 1 November 1905 as 11th Company, Coast Artillery, Artillery Corps, Massachusetts Volunteer Militia; redesignated 15 November 1907 as 11th Company, Coast Artillery Corps, Massachusetts National Guard; assigned to 1st Coast Defense Command, Coast Artillery Corps on 11 January 1917; called into Federal service 25 July 1917, mustered in 3 August 1917, and drafted in 5 August 1917; redesignated 31 August 1917 as 26th Company, Coast Defenses of Boston; redesignated 18 December 1917 as Battery B, 55th Artillery, Coast Artillery Corps; demobilized at Camp Winfield Scott, California during February 1919; reorganized at Boston and Federally recognized 13 September 1920 as 11th Company, 1st Coast Defense Command, Coast Artillery Corps; redesignated 1 January 1922 as 319th Company, 1st Coast Defense Command, Coast Artillery Corps; redesignated 1 October 1923 as Battery L, 241st Artillery, Coast Artillery Corps; redesignated 30 April 1924 as Battery L, 241st Coast Artillery; redesignated 1 June 1940 as Battery B, 241st Coast Artillery; and inducted into Federal service at Boston on 16 September 1940; redesignated 7 October 1944 as Battery B, 241st Coast Artillery Battalion and inactivated 1 April 1945 at Fort Warren), reorganized and Federally recognized 13 April 1948 at Boston as Battery B

Battery C, 241st Coast Artillery Battalion (organized 2 August 1798 at Boston as the *Boston Light Infantry*, and assigned to the 2d Regiment of Light Infantry, Massachusetts Militia; mustered into Federal service at Boston 1 July 1814, mustered out 30 July 1814 at Boston and resumed State status; reassigned to the 1st Regiment of Light Infantry, Massachusetts Militia on 1 July 1834; redesignated 25 April 1842 as Company A, 1st Regiment of Light Infantry, Massachusetts Volunteer Militia; redesignated 26 February 1855 as Company A, 1st Regiment of Infantry; redesignated 1 March 1859 as Company A, 2d Battalion of Infantry; redesignated 3 August 1862 as Company A, 43d Regiment of Infantry; mustered into Federal service at Camp Meigs, Massachusetts 20 October 1862 as Company A, 43d Regiment, Massachusetts Volunteers, mustered out at Boston 30 July 1863; reorganized at Boston 10 September 1864 as Company A, 43d Regiment of Infantry; redesignated 22 September 1864 as 24th Unattached Company; redesignated 10 August 1866 as Company A, 7th Regiment of Infantry; redesignated 20 July 1870 as Company A, 1st Battalion of Infantry; redesignated 25 March 1874 as Company A, 4th Battalion of Infantry; redesignated 3 December 1878 as Company K, 1st Regiment of Infantry; redesignated 1 June 1897 as Battery K, 1st Regiment of Heavy Artillery; mustered into Federal service at Fort Warren, Massachusetts as Battery K, 1st Massachusetts Volunteer Heavy Artillery, mustered out at Boston 14 November 1898 and resumed State status; redesignated 1 November 1905 as 2d Company, Coast Artillery, Artillery Corps; redesignated 15 November 1907 as 2d Company, Coast Artillery Corps, Massachusetts National Guard; assigned to the 1st Coast Defense Command, Coast Artillery Corps on 11 January 1917; called into Federal service 25 July 1917, mustered into Federal service at Boston 3 August 1917, and drafted into Federal service 5 August 1917; redesignated 31 August 1917 as 17th Company, Coast Defenses of Boston; demobilized 4 December 1918 at Fort Revere, Massachusetts; reorganized at Boston and Federally recognized 27 December 1920 as 2d Company, 1st Coast Defense Command, Coast Artillery Corps;

redesignated 1 January 1922 as 322d Company, 1st Coast Defense Command, Coast Artillery Corps; redesignated 1 October 1923 as Battery K, 241st Artillery, Coast Artillery Corps; redesignated 30 April 1924 as Battery K, 241st Coast Artillery; redesignated 1 June 1940 as Battery C, 241st Coast Artillery; and inducted into Federal service on 16 September 1940 at Boston; redesignated 7 October 1944 as Battery C, 241st Coast Artillery Battalion, and inactivated 1 April 1945 in the Harbor Defenses of Boston), reorganized and Federally recognized 28 June 1948 at Boston as Battery C

Company K, 101st Infantry (organized 26 January 1903 at Hingham as Company K, 5th Regiment of Infantry, Massachusetts Volunteer Militia; mustered into Federal service at Framingham for service on the Mexican border; mustered out 10 November 1916 at Boston and resumed State status; called into Federal service 25 July 1917 and drafted into Federal service on 5 August 1917; redesignated 12 February 1918 as Company K, 3d Pioneer Infantry; demobilized 4 August 1919 at Camp Devens, Massachusetts; reorganized and Federally recognized 23 August 1920 at Hingham as 9th Company, 1st Coast Defense Command, Coast Artillery Corps; redesignated 1 January 1922 as 329th Company, 1st Coast Defense Command, Coast Artillery Corps; redesignated 7 June 1923 as Company K, 101st Infantry; inducted into Federal service at Hingham on 16 January 1941; inactivated 29 December 1945 at Camp Patrick Henry, Virginia), reorganized and Federally recognized 15 March 1948 at Hingham as Battery D

Medical Detachment, 241st Coast Artillery Battalion (organized and Federally recognized 7 June 1922 at Boston as Medical Department Detachment, 1st Coast Defense Command, Coast Artillery Corps; redesignated 1 October 1923 as Medical Department Detachment, 241st Artillery, Coast Artillery Corps; redesignated 30 April 1924 as Medical Department Detachment, 241st Coast Artillery; inducted into active Federal service at Boston on 16 September 1940; redesignated 7 October 1944 as Medical Detachment, 241st Coast Artillery Battalion and inactivated 1 April 1945 at Fort Warren), reorganized and Federally recognized at Boston as Medical Detachment

Battalion ordered into active Federal service at Boston on 16 March 1951. Released from active Federal service 15 March 1953 and resumed State status. Redesignated 1 October 1953 as 704th Antiaircraft Artillery Battalion. Reorganized and redesignated 1 February 1958 as the 704th Antiaircraft Artillery Missile Battalion.

Consolidated 1 May 1959 with the 241st Artillery, a parent regiment under the Combat Arms Regimental System.

CAMPAIGN STREAMERS

Civil War
Bull Run
Peninsula
Manassas
Fredericksburg
Chancellorsville
Gettysburg
Wilderness
Spotsylvania
Maryland 1861
Virginia 1863

World War I
Meuse-Argonne

DECORATIONS
None

COAT OF ARMS

SHIELD: Per bend azure and gules, in chief a lozenge argent and in base a falcon close or upon a mount proper; on a canton gules fimbriated or a dexter arm embowed, grasping a broad sword of the last.

CREST: That for the regiments and separate battalions of the Massachusetts Army National Guard: On a wreath of the colors (argent and azure) a dexter arm embowed, clothed blue and ruffed white proper, grasping a broad sword argent, the pommel and hilt or.

MOTTO: *Vigilantia* (Vigilance)

The shield is blue and red and commemorates the service of elements of the battalion as both Infantry and Artillery. In the canton is the device of the old *Roxbury Artillery*. The white diamond was the device of the badge of the III Corps of the Army of the Potomac during the Civil War and the falcon on the green hill represents Montfaucon in France where elements of the battalion served during World War I.

DISTINCTIVE INSIGNIA

The insignia is the shield and motto of the coat of arms. The sample of the insignia depicted was originally approved on 31 January 1928 for wear by the 241st Coast Artillery.

705th ANTIAIRCRAFT ARTILLERY BATTALION

Constituted in the Rhode Island Militia as 2d Battalion, 1st Light Infantry and organized at Providence during January 1872 from new and existing companies. Redesignated 1st Battalion of Infantry, Rhode Island Militia in May 1875. Redesignated 1 June 1887 as 1st Battalion, 1st Regiment of Infantry, Brigade Rhode Island Militia. Mustered into Federal service at Quonset Point during May 1898 as 1st Battalion, 1st Rhode Island Volunteer Infantry. Mustered out 30 March 1899 at Columbia, South Carolina and resumed State status. Redesignated 15 April 1907 as 1st Battalion, 1st Regiment of Infantry, Rhode Island National Guard. Converted and reorganized 4 November 1908 as separate companies of the 1st Coast Artillery District, Rhode Island National Guard. (These companies continued independent existence in 1st Coast Defense Command, Coast Artillery Corps; Coast Artillery Corps, Rhode Island National Guard and in the Coast Defenses of Narragansett Bay until demobilized at Fort Getty, Rhode Island in December 1918). Reorganized as 2d Battalion, 1st Coast Defense Command, Coast Artillery Corps and Federally recognized 12 May 1921 with Headquarters at Providence and batteries at Woonsocket, Westerly and Providence. Redesignated 1 October 1923 as 2d Battalion 243d Artillery, Coast Artillery Corps. Redesignated 11 July 1924 as 2d Battalion, 243d Coast Artillery (Harbor Defense). Inducted into Federal service 16 September 1940 at home stations. Inactivated 10 April 1944 at Camp Forrest, Tennessee. Disbanded 7 October 1944. Reconstituted 25 August 1945 and allotted to the Rhode Island National Guard. Redesignated 2 July 1946 as the 705th Antiaircraft Artillery Gun Battalion (Semimobile). Reorganized and Federally recognized 4 December 1946 with Headquarters at Providence and batteries at

Natick, East Greenwich, Pawtucket and Westerly. Ordered into active Federal service 14 August 1950 at home stations. Released from active Federal service 13 July 1952 and resumed State status. Redesignated 1 October 1953 as the 705th Antiaircraft Artillery Battalion (90mm Gun).

Consolidated 1 April 1959 with the 243d Artillery, a parent regiment under the Combat Arms Regimental System.

CAMPAIGN STREAMERS
Civil War
Bull Run

DECORATIONS
None

COAT OF ARMS
SHIELD: Gules, overall and on a saltire azure, fimbriated argent, a maple leaf of the last, in dexter on a chief embattled of the like a palm tree vert; a bordure of the first.

CREST: That for the regiments and separate battalions of the Rhode Island Army National Guard: On a wreath of the colors (argent and gules) an anchor paleways or.

MOTTO: *Rideau de fer* (Curtain Of Iron)

The shield (less one charge) of the coat of arms of the old 243d Coast Artillery placed within a red border represents the descent of the organization from the 2d Battalion of that regiment. Red is for Artillery and the blue saltire is for Civil War service. The embattled chief refers to service in the Coast Defenses of Narragansett Bay during World War I.

DISTINCTIVE INSIGNIA
The insignia is the shield and motto of the coat of arms. The sample of the insignia depicted was approved for wear on 23 June 1954.

706th ANTIAIRCRAFT ARTILLERY GUN BATTALION

Constituted 27 September 1946 as the 706th Antiaircraft Artillery Gun Battalion (Mobile) and allotted to the New York National Guard. Withdrawn from allotment to the New York National Guard and returned to Department of the Army control on 1 April 1951.

CAMPAIGN STREAMERS
None

DECORATIONS
None

COAT OF ARMS
None

DISTINCTIVE INSIGNIA
None

707th ANTIAIRCRAFT ARTILLERY MISSILE BATTALION

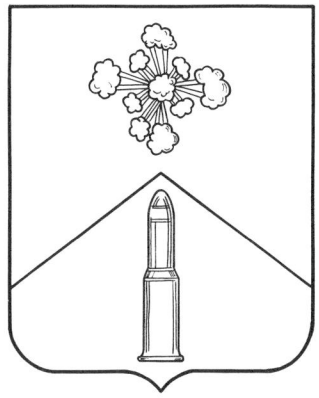
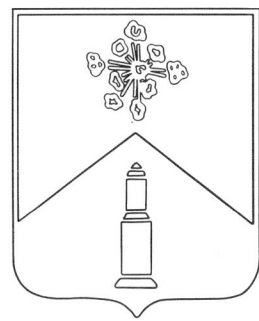

Constituted 24 May 1946 as the 707th Antiaircraft Artillery Gun Battalion (90mm) and allotted to the Pennsylvania National Guard. Organized and Federally recognized 2 December 1946 at Philadelphia. Ordered into active Federal service 14 August 1950 at Philadelphia. Released from active Federal service 13 June 1952 and resumed State status. Redesignated 1 October 1953 as the 707th Antiaircraft Artillery Battalion (90mm Gun). Reorganized and redesignated 15 February 1958 as the 707th Antiaircraft Artillery Missile Battalion (NIKE).

Consolidated 1 June 1959 with the 166th Artillery, a parent regiment under the Combat Arms Regimental System.

CAMPAIGN STREAMERS
None

DECORATIONS
None

COAT OF ARMS
SHIELD: Per chevron gules and or, in chief a shell burst of the second and in base a fixed round of ammunition of the first.

CREST: That for the regiments and separate battalions of the Pennsylvania Army National Guard: On a wreath of the colors (or and gules) a lion rampant guardant proper, holding in dexter paw a naked scimitar argent, hilted or and in sinister an escutcheon argent, on a fess sable three plates.

MOTTO: None

The colors red and yellow are used for Artillery. The 90mm Artillery shell pointing skyward and the shell burst represent antiaircraft artillery.

DISTINCTIVE INSIGNIA

The insignia is the shield and motto of the coat of arms. The sample of the insignia depicted was approved for wear on 26 September 1952.

708th ANTIAIRCRAFT ARTILLERY MISSILE BATTALION

Constituted 24 May 1946 in the Pennsylvania National Guard as the 708th Antiaircraft Artillery Gun Battalion (Semimobile) and organized from new and existing units as follows:

Headquarters, 967th Field Artillery Battalion (organized and Federally recognized 9 November 1921 at Pittsburgh as Headquarters, 2d Battalion 176th Field Artillery; inducted into Federal service 3 February 1941 at Pittsburgh; redesignated 12 March 1942 as Headquarters, 2d Battalion 228th Field Artillery; redesignated 1 March 1943 as Headquarters, 967th Field Artillery Battalion and inactivated 2 December 1945 at Camp Patrick Henry, Virginia), reorganized and Federally recognized 12 January 1948 at Pittsburgh as Headquarters and Headquarters Battery

Battery A 967th Field Artillery Battalion (organized 5 September 1831 at Pittsburgh as *Duquesne Greys*; mustered into Federal service 16 December 1846 as Company K 1st Pennsylvania Volunteers and served in Mexico; mustered out 25 July 1848 and returned to State control; reorganized 20 August 1849 at Pittsburgh as *Duquesne Greys*; mustered into Federal service 25 April 1861 at Pittsburgh as Company D 12th Pennsylvania Volunteer Infantry; mustered out 5 August 1861 and returned to State control; reorganized 26 August 1869 at Pittsburgh as *Duquesne Greys*; redesignated 1 February 1870 as 1st Company, *Duquesne Greys*; redesignated 30 November 1871 as Company A 18th Infantry, Pennsylvania National Guard; mustered into Federal service 13 May 1898 at Mount Gretna as Company A 18th Pennsylvania Volunteers; mustered out 22 October 1898 at Pittsburgh and resumed State status; mustered into Federal service 4 July 1916 at Mount Gretna for Mexican border; mustered out 5 January 1917 and resumed State status; mustered into Federal service 14 April 1917 at Pittsburgh and drafted into Federal service on 5 August 1917; consolidated 11 October 1917 with Company A 111th Infantry; former Company A 18th Infantry reconstituted 16 October 1919 in the Pennsylvania National Guard; reorganized and Federally recognized

30 July 1920 at Pittsburgh; redesignated 1 April 1921 as Company D 176th Field Artillery; inducted into Federal service 3 February 1941 at Pittsburgh; redesignated 12 March 1942 as Battery D 228th Field Artillery; redesignated 1 March 1943 as Battery A 976th Field Artillery Battalion and inactivated 2 December 1945 at Camp Patrick Henry, Virginia), reorganized and Federally recognized 29 March 1948 at Pittsburgh as Battery A

Battery B organized new and Federally recognized 15 March 1949 at Pittsburgh

Battery C organized new and Federally recognized 28 June 1949 at Pittsburgh

Battery C 724th Antiaircraft Artillery Gun Battalion (organized 26 July 1898 at Pittsburgh as Company I 17th Infantry, Pennsylvania National Guard and redesignated 1 July 1899 as Company I 18th Infantry, Pennsylvania National Guard; mustered into Federal service 4 July 1916 at Mount Gretna for Mexican border; mustered out 5 January 1917 and resumed State status; mustered into Federal service 14 April 1917 at Pittsburgh and drafted into Federal service 5 August 1917; consolidated 11 October 1917 with Company I 111th Infantry; former Company I 18th Infantry reconstituted 16 October 1919 in the Pennsylvania National Guard; reorganized and Federally recognized 29 July 1920 at Pittsburgh; redesignated 1 April 1921 as Battery F 176th Field Artillery; inducted into Federal service 3 February 1941 at Pittsburgh; redesignated 12 March 1942 as Battery F 228th Field Artillery; redesignated 1 March 1943 as Battery C 967th Field Artillery Battalion; inactivated 2 December 1945 at Camp Patrick Henry, Virginia; redesignated 24 May 1946 as Battery C 724th Antiaircraft Artillery Searchlight Battalion; reorganized and Federally recognized 25 June 1948 at Pittsburgh as Battery C 724th Antiaircraft Artillery Gun Battalion), redesignated 3 November 1949 as Battery D

Medical Detachment organized new and Federally recognized 27 January 1948 at Pittsburgh

Battalion ordered into active Federal service 1 May 1951 at Pittsburgh. Released from active Federal service 28 February 1953 and resumed State status. Reorganized and redesignated 1 February 1958 as the 708th Antiaircraft Artillery Missile Battalion (NIKE). (Headquarters relocated to Blawnox on 14 March 1958).

Consolidated 1 June 1959 with the 176th Artillery, a parent regiment under the Combat Arms Regimental System.

CAMPAIGN STREAMERS
World War I
Champagne-Marne
Aisne-Marne
Oise-Aisne
Meuse-Argonne
Champagne 1918
Lorraine 1918

World War II
Normandy
Northern France
Rhineland
Central Europe

DECORATIONS
None

COAT OF ARMS
SHIELD: Sable, a fess checky argent and azure between three high explosive shells each debruised by a leopard's face or, within a bordure of the last.

CREST: That for the regiments and separate battalions of the Pennsylvania Army National

Guard: On a wreath of the colors (argent and sable) a lion rampant guardant proper holding in dexter paw a naked scimitar argent, hilted or and in sinister an escutcheon argent, on a fess sable three plates.

MOTTO: We Will Be Vigilant

The design is that of the coat of arms for the old 176th Field Artillery and the gold border shows descent from elements of that regiment.

DISTINCTIVE INSIGNIA
The insignia is the shield and motto of the coat of arms. The sample of the insignia depicted was approved for wear on 26 October 1954.

709th ANTIAIRCRAFT ARTILLERY MISSILE BATTALION

Constituted 24 May 1946 as the 709th Antiaircraft Artillery Gun Battalion (120mm) and allotted to the Pennsylvania National Guard. Organized and federally recognized 30 October 1947 at Philadelphia. Ordered into active Federal service 14 August 1950 at Philadelphia. Released from active Federal service 13 August 1952 and resumed State status. Redesignated 14 August 1952 as the 709th Antiaircraft Artillery Gun Battalion (90mm). Redesignated 1 October 1953 as the 709th Antiaircraft Artillery Battalion (90mm Gun). Reorganized and redesignated 15 February 1958 as the 709th Antiaircraft Artillery Missile Battalion (NIKE). (Headquarters relocated to Media 5 April 1958).

Consolidated 1 June 1959 with the 166th Artillery, a parent regiment under the Combat Arms Regimental System.

CAMPAIGN STREAMERS
None

DECORATIONS
None

COAT OF ARMS

SHIELD: Gules a flight of arrows issuant from sinister base bendwise or.

CREST: That for the regiments and separate battalions of the Pennsylvania Army National Guard: On a wreath of the colors (or and gules) a lion rampant guardant proper, holding in dexter paw a naked scimitar argent, hilted or and in sinister an escutcheon argent, on a fess sable three plates.

MOTTO: *Patria, Valor, Gloria* (Country, Valor, Glory)

Red and yellow are the colors for Artillery. The flight of arrows symbolizes in heraldic terms the fire power of the organization's principal arm as well as the military aspirations of the organization.

DISTINCTIVE INSIGNIA

The insignia is the shield and motto of the coat of arms. The insignia depicted was unofficially worn between 1952 and 1959.

710th ANTIAIRCRAFT ARTILLERY MISSILE BATTALION

Constituted 2 July 1946 as the 710th Antiaircraft Artillery Gun Battalion (Semimobile) and allotted to the Virginia National Guard. Organized and Federally recognized 15 October 1946 with Headquarters at Newport News and elements at Williamsburg, Hampton, and Newport News. Ordered into active Federal service 14 August 1950 at home stations. Released from active Federal service 13 April 1952 and resumed State status. Redesignated 1 October 1953 as the 710th Antiaircraft Artillery Battalion (90mm Gun). Reorganized and redesignated 15 February 1958 as the 710th Antiaircraft Artillery Missile Battalion (NIKE).

Consolidated 1 June 1959 with the 111th Artillery, a parent regiment under the Combat Arms Regimental System.

CAMPAIGN STREAMERS
None

DECORATIONS
None

COAT OF ARMS
None

DISTINCTIVE INSIGNIA
None

711th ANTIAIRCRAFT ARTILLERY BATTALION

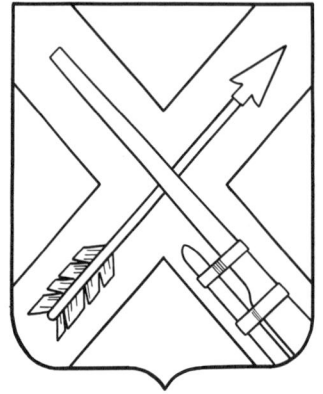

Constituted 24 July 1946 in the Alabama National Guard as the 711th Antiaircraft Artillery Gun Battalion and organized from new and existing units as follows:

Company A, Coast Artillery Battalion, Alabama National Guard (organized at Mobile in 1836 as the *Mobile Artillery Company* [also known as *Alabama Artillery* and *Alabama State Artillery*]; mustered into Federal service about May 1836 at Mobile as a company in Colonel Smith's *Regiment of Alabama Mounted Volunteers*; mustered out 27 July 1836 at Mobile and resumed State status; mustered into Federal service 23 May 1846 at Mobile as a company in Colonel J. M. Withers' 1st Alabama Volunteers; mustered out 16 June 1846 at Mobile and resumed State status; reorganized, consolidated with existing volunteer artillery companies in the Mobile area, redesignated *Alabama State Artillery Battalion* and mustered into Confederate States service in August 1863; surrendered 4 May 1865 with the Army of the Department of Alabama and Mississippi; reorganized as the State Artillery Company in July 1872; redesignated Battery A, Field Artillery, Alabama State Troops in 1887; redesignated about 1894 as Battery A, 1st Artillery Battalion, Alabama State Troops; reorganized and redesignated 14 January 1908 as Company A, Coast Artillery Battalion, Alabama National Guard; mustered out of State service 28 February 1910; and reconstituted 24 July 1946), reorganized as Headquarters and Headquarters Battery and Federally recognized 9 January 1947 at Mobile

Battery A organized new and Federally recognized 28 March 1947 at Mobile

Battery B organized new and Federally recognized 19 February 1947 at Bay Minette

Battery C, 104th Antiaircraft Artillery Automatic Weapons Battalion (organized and Federally recognized 1 October 1939 at Luverne as Service Company [less Band Section] 106th Medical Regiment and redesignated 1 December 1939 as Headquarters and Service Company [less Band Section], 106th Medical Regiment; converted and redesignated 14 November 1940 as Battery C, 104th Separate Battalion, Coast Artillery [Antiaircraft Artillery]; inducted into Federal service 10 February 1941 at Luverne; redesignated 15 June 1944 as Battery C, 104th Antiaircraft Artillery Automatic Weapons Battalion; and inactivated 31 January 1946 at Saijo, Japan), reorganized and Federally recognized 17 February 1947 at

Luverne as Battery C

Battery D organized new and Federally recognized 18 February 1947 at Atmore

Medical Department Detachment, Special Troops, 31st Division (organized and Federally recognized 30 June 1936 at Mobile; inducted into Federal service 25 November 1940 at Mobile; disbanded 10 February 1942 at Camp Bowie, Texas; and reconstituted 25 August 1945 in the Alabama National Guard), reorganized and Federally recognized 21 February 1947 at Mobile as Medical Detachment

Battalion ordered into active Federal service 4 September 1950 at home stations. Released from active Federal service 3 September 1952 and resumed State status. Redesignated 1 October 1953 as the 711th Antiaircraft Artillery Battalion (90mm Gun).

Converted and redesignated 2 May 1959 as the 711th Signal Battalion.

CAMPAIGN STREAMERS
Indian Wars
Creeks

Civil War (Confederate service)
Alabama 1865

DECORATIONS
None

COAT OF ARMS
SHIELD: Gules, on a saltire or the barrel of an antiaircraft artillery gun issuing from sinister base sable and an arrow gules.

CREST: That for the regiments and separate battalions of the Alabama Army National Guard: On a wreath of the colors (or and gules), a slip of cotton plant with full bursting boll proper.

MOTTO: Smash To The Stars

The colors red and yellow are used for Artillery. The saltire, taken from the State flag of Alabama, alludes to the Confederate flag and symbolizes Civil War service. The arrow refers to service in the Indian Wars against the Creeks. The antiaircraft artillery gun represents the function of the organization as an Artillery unit.

DISTINCTIVE INSIGNIA
The insignia is the shield and motto of the coat of arms. The sample of the insignia depicted was approved for wear on 10 June 1955.

712th ANTIAIRCRAFT ARTILLERY BATTALION

Constituted 5 July 1946 in the Florida National Guard as the 712th Antiaircraft Artillery Gun Battalion (Semimobile) and organized from new and existing units as follows:

Battery F, 265th Coast Artillery (organized and Federally recognized 2 October 1939 at Miami; inducted into Federal service 6 January 1941 at Miami; disbanded 31 July 1944 in Alaska and reconstituted 5 July 1946), reorganized and Federally recognized 17 December 1946 at Miami as Headquarters and Headquarters Battery

Battery E, 265th Coast Artillery (organized at Key West during June 1888 as *Island City Guards*; redesignated Company A, 5th Battalion, Florida State Troops in 1893 and redesignated Company I, 2d Infantry, Florida State Troops in 1902; mustered into Federal service 21 June 1916 for Mexican border duty; mustered out 17 March 1917 and resumed State status; drafted into Federal service 5 August 1917 at Key West; redesignated 6 October 1917 as Company I, 124th Infantry and assigned to the 31st Division; demobilized 14 January 1919 at Camp Gordon, Georgia; reorganized and Federally recognized 29 June 1923 at Key West as the 438th Company, Coast Artillery Corps; assigned to the 1st Separate Battalion of Coast Artillery, Florida National Guard on 31 October 1923; redesignated 9 February 1924 as Battery B, 1st Separate Battalion of Coast Artillery, Florida National Guard; redesignated 22 July 1925 as Battery B, 265th Coast Artillery Battalion; redesignated 20 November 1929 as Battery B, 265th Coast Artillery Battalion; redesignated 1 January 1930 as Battery E, 265th Coast Artillery; inducted into Federal service 6 January 1941 at Key West; disbanded 31 January 1944 in Alaska and reconstituted 5 July 1946), reorganized and Federally recognized 14 July 1947 at Key West as Battery A

Clearing Company, 105th Medical Battalion (constituted 18 September 1917 in the National Guard as Headquarters Company, 116th Field Artillery and assigned to the 31st Division; organized at Camp Wheeler, Georgia during October 1917; demobilized 16 January 1919 at Camp Gordon, Georgia; reconstituted 14 December 1921 in the Florida National Guard as Headquarters Battery, 116th Field Artillery; reorganized and Federally recognized 24 October 1923 at Fort Meyers; redesignated 13 January 1937 as Company F, 106th Medical Regiment; redesignated 1 January 1940 as Company E, 106th Medical Regiment; inducted into Federal service 25 November 1940 at Fort Meyers; redesignated 1 March 1942 as Clearing Company, 106th Medical Battalion and inactivated 18 December 1945 at Camp Stoneman, California), reorganized and Federally recognized 9 January 1950 at Fort Meyers as Battery B

Headquarters Battery, 31st Division Artillery (organized and Federally recognized 25 January 1927 at Avon Park as Headquarters Battery, 56th Field Artillery Brigade; inducted into Federal service 25 November 1940 at Avon Park; redesignated 27 February 1942 as Headquarters Battery, 31st Division Artillery and inactivated 21 December 1945 at Camp Stoneman, California), reorganized and Federally recognized 5 July 1945 at Avon Park as Battery C

Service Battery, 116th Field Artillery Battalion (constituted 18 September 1917 in the National Guard as Battery F, 116th Field Artillery and assigned to the 31st Division; organized at Camp Wheeler, Georgia during October 1917; demobilized 16 January 1919 at Camp Gordon, Georgia; reconstituted 14 December 1921 and allotted to the Florida National Guard; reorganized and Federally recognized 19 September 1923 at Arcadia; redesignated 1 April 1937 as Service Battery, 116th Field Artillery; inducted into Federal service 25 November 1940 at Arcadia; redesignated 27 February 1942 as Service Battery, 116th Field Artillery Battalion and inactivated 20 December 1945 at Camp Stoneman, California), reorganized and Federally recognized 15 April 1947 at Arcadia as Battery D

Ordered into active Federal service 1 May 1951 at home stations. Released from active Federal service 30 April 1953 and resumed State status. (Headquarters relocated to Sarasota on 22 June 1953). Redesignated 1 October 1953 as the 712th Antiaircraft Artillery Battalion (90mm Gun).

Consolidated 15 April 1959 with the 265th Artillery, a parent regiment under the Combat Arms Regimental System.

CAMPAIGN STREAMERS
World War I
Streamer without inscription

World War II
New Guinea (with arrowhead)
Southern Philippines

DECORATIONS
Philippine Presidential Unit Citation, Streamer embroidered *17 OCTOBER 1944 TO 4 JULY 1945* (31st Inf Div cited; DAGO 47, 1950)

COAT OF ARMS
SHIELD: Gules a five-bastioned fort within a palm wreath or.

CREST: That for the regiments and separate battalions of the Florida Army National Guard: On a wreath of the colors (or and gules) an alligator statant proper.

MOTTO: Avow Ardent Avenge

Red and yellow are used for Artillery. The five-bastioned fort represents the old Spanish forts of Florida and is indicative of the battalion's location. The wreath of palm, a symbol of victory, is for service in the Pacific area, the palm being common both in Florida and on the islands of the Pacific.

DISTINCTIVE INSIGNIA
The insignia is the shield and motto of the coat of arms. The sample of the insignia depicted was approved for wear on 26 April 1954.

713th ANTIAIRCRAFT ARTILLERY BATTALION

Constituted 5 July 1946 in the South Carolina National Guard as the 713th Antiaircraft Artillery Gun Battalion (Semimobile) and organized from new and existing units as follows:

Headquarters, 1st Battalion, 263d Coast Artillery (organized and Federally recognized 15 June 1930 at Florence as Headquarters, 2d Battalion, 263d Coast Artillery; redesignated 26 October 1939 as Headquarters, 1st Battalion, 263d Coast Artillery; inducted into Federal service 13 January 1941 at Florence; disbanded 25 August 1945 at Fort Moultrie, South Carolina and reconstituted 25 August 1945), reorganized as Headquarters and Headquarters Battery and Federally recognized 4 April 1947 at Lancaster

Battery A, 107th Antiaircraft Artillery Automatic Weapons Battalion (organized and Federally recognized 27 June 1922 at Lancaster as the 429th Company, 1st Coast Defense Command, Coast Artillery Corps; redesignated 25 March 1924 as Battery C, 1st Separate Battalion, Coast Artillery, South Carolina National Guard; redesignated 31 July 1925 as Battery C, 263d Coast Artillery Battalion; redesignated 10 June 1930 as Battery C, 263d Coast Artillery; redesignated 23 October 1939 as Battery H, 263d Coast Artillery; redesignated 15 April 1940 as Battery I, 263d Coast Artillery; redesignated 10 December 1940 as Battery A, 107th Separate Battalion, Coast Artillery; inducted into Federal service 10 February 1941 at Lancaster; redesignated 13 November 1943 as Battery A, 107th Antiaircraft Artillery Automatic Weapons Battalion and inactivated 5 December 1944 at Pouzzila, Italy), consolidated with Headquarters and Headquarters Battery

Battery A organized new and Federally recognized 21 October 1947 at York

Battery B organized new and Federally recognized 10 February 1947 at Camden

Battery C, 263d Coast Artillery (organized and Federally recognized 5 October 1939 at Cheraw as Battery H, 263d Coast Artillery; redesignated 23 October 1939 as Battery C, 263d Coast Artillery; inducted into Federal service 13 January 1941 at Cheraw; redesignated 1 October 1944 as Battery A, Harbor Defense of Charleston; redesignated 30 June 1945 as Battery C, 263d Coast Artillery and inactivated at Fort Moultrie), reorganized and Federally recognized 18 March 1947 at Cheraw as Battery C

Headquarters Battery, 1st Battalion, 263d Coast Artillery (organized and Federally recognized 15 April 1940 at Florence and inducted into Federal service 13 January 1941 at Florence; disbanded 1 October 1944 at Fort Moultrie and reconstituted 25 August 1945), reorganized and Federally recognized 21 March 1947 at Florence as Battery D

Medical Detachment organized new and Federally recognized 1 March 1949 at Florence

Ordered into active Federal service 14 August 1950 at home stations. Released from active Federal service 13 June 1952 and resumed State status. Redesignated 1 October 1953 as the 713th Antiaircraft Artillery Battalion (90mm Gun).

Consolidated 1 April 1959 with the 263d Artillery, a parent regiment under the Combat Arms Regimental System.

CAMPAIGN STREAMERS
None

DECORATIONS
None

COAT OF ARMS
None

DISTINCTIVE INSIGNIA
None

714th ANTIAIRCRAFT ARTILLERY GUN BATTALION

Constituted 31 May 1946 as the 714th Antiaircraft Artillery Gun Battalion (Mobile) and allotted to the Michigan National Guard. Withdrawn from allotment to the Michigan Army National Guard and returned to Department of the Army control about 1949.

CAMPAIGN STREAMERS
None

DECORATIONS
None

COAT OF ARMS
None

DISTINCTIVE INSIGNIA
None

715th ANTIAIRCRAFT ARTILLERY GUN BATTALION

Constituted in the Army of the United States as the 192d Coast Artillery Battalion (Harbor Defense) and organized 7 October 1944 at Fort Tilden, New York from former batteries of the 245th Coast Artillery. Inactivated 1 April 1945 at Fort Tilden. Redesignated 27 September 1946 as the 715th Antiaircraft Artillery Gun Battalion and allotted to the New York National Guard. Reorganized and Federally recognized 19 January 1948 at Brooklyn. Ordered into active Federal service 14 August 1950 at Brooklyn. Released from active Federal service 13 June 1952 and resumed State status. Redesignated 1 October 1953 as the 715th Antiaircraft Artillery Battalion (90mm Gun).

Redesignated 1 April 1955 as the 715th Field Artillery Battalion.

CAMPAIGN STREAMERS
Civil War
Gettysburg

DECORATIONS
None

COAT OF ARMS
SHIELD: Per chevron azure and gules a chevron gray, fimbriated or between in chief the Corps badge of the VII Army Corps of the Civil War (a crescent holding a star within its horns, both reversed) and a Roman sword, point down, both of the last and in base a fleur-de-lis argent, all within a bordure of the fourth.

CREST: That for the regiments and separate battalions of the New York Army National Guard: On a wreath of the colors (or and gules) the full rigged ship *Half Moon*, all proper.

MOTTO: *Victoria Signum Nostrum* (Victory Is Our Motto)

The shield is that of the 245th Coast Artillery within a gold border to indicate the descent of the battalion from that regiment.

DISTINCTIVE INSIGNIA
The insignia is the shield and motto of the coat of arms. The sample of the insignia depicted was approved for wear on 4 March 1952.

716th ANTIAIRCRAFT ARTILLERY BATTALION

Constituted 19 April 1921 in the New Mexico National Guard as Headquarters, 2d Squadron, 1st Cavalry. Redesignated 2 May 1922 as Headquarters, 2d Squadron, 111th Cavalry. Organized and Federally recognized 3 August 1923 at Santa Fe. Relocated to Deming 9 August 1928; to Roswell 12 April 1933 and back to Deming on 4 August 1938. Converted, reorganized and

redesignated 26 April 1940 as Headquarters, 1st Battalion, 207th Coast Artillery [Antiaircraft]. Redesignated 1 July 1940 as Headquarters, 1st Battalion, 200th Coast Artillery [Antiaircraft]. Inducted into Federal service 6 January 1941 at Deming. Surrendered to Japanese *14th Army* 9 April 1942 on Luzon. Formally inactivated 2 April 1946 at Fort Mills, Philippine Islands. Redesignated 31 May 1946 as Headquarters, 716th Antiaircraft Artillery Gun Battalion. Reorganized and Federally recognized 27 September 1947 at Las Cruces; remainder of battalion organized from new and existing units as follows:

Headquarters Battery, 200th Coast Artillery (organized 9 February 1914 at Deming as Company I, 1st Infantry, New Mexico National Guard; mustered into Federal service 16 July 1916 for Mexican border; mustered out 5 April 1917 at Columbus and resumed State status; mustered into Federal service 11 June 1917 at Deming and drafted into Federal service 5 August 1917; consolidated 20 October 1917 with Company B 144th Machine Gun Battalion [Company B 144th Machine Gun Battalion demobilized 30 April 1919 at Camp Grant, Illinois]; reorganized and Federally recognized 18 June 1921 at Deming as Troop C 1st Cavalry, New Mexico National Guard; redesignated 2 May 1922 as Troop C 111th Cavalry; redesignated 15 March 1929 as Troop E 111th Cavalry; converted, reorganized and redesignated 26 April 1940 as Headquarters Battery, 207th Coast Artillery [Antiaircraft]; redesignated 1 July 1940 as Headquarters Battery, 200th Coast Artillery [Antiaircraft]; inducted into Federal service 6 January 1941 at Deming; surrendered 9 April 1942 to Japanese *14th Army* on Luzon; formally inactivated 2 April 1946 at Fort Mills), reorganized and Federally recognized 27 September 1947 at Deming as Headquarters Battery

Headquarters Company, 120th Engineer Combat Battalion (organized at Las Cruces prior to 1903 as Company A 1st Infantry, New Mexico National Guard; mustered into Federal service 16 July 1916 for Mexican border; mustered out 5 April 1917 at Columbus and resumed State status; mustered into Federal service 11 June 1917 at Las Cruces and drafted into Federal service 5 August 1917; redesignated 21 October 1917 as Company A 143d Machine Gun Battalion and assigned to the 40th Division; relieved from the 40th Division and demobilized 30 April 1919 at Camp Grant, Illinois; reorganized and Federally recognized 20 June 1921 at Las Cruces as Headquarters and Service Company, 1st Engineers, New Mexico National Guard; redesignated 2 May 1922 as Headquarters and Service Company, 137th Engineers; redesignated 23 February 1923 as Headquarters and Service Company, 120th Engineers; inducted into Federal service 16 September 1940 at Las Cruces; reorganized and redesignated 11 February 1942 as Headquarters Company, 120th EngineerNattalion; redesignated 1 August 1942 as Headquarters Company, 120th Engineer Combat Battalion; inactivated 26 November 1945 at Camp Bowie, Texas), recognized and Federally recognized 26 September 1947 at Las Cruces as Battery A

Battery G, 200th Coast Artillery (organized prior to 1903 at Silver City as Company D, 1st Infantry, New Mexico National Guard and redesignated Company H, 1st Infantry about 1915; mustered into Federal service 16 July 1916 for Mexican border; mustered out 5 April 1917 at Columbus and resumed State status; mustered into Federal service 11 June 1917 at Silver City and drafted into Federal service 5 August 1917; consolidated 20 October 1917 with Company C 143d Machine Gun Battalion [Company C 143d Machine Gun Battalion redesignated 7 March 1918 as Company D 144th Machine Gun Battalion and demobilized 30 April 1919 at Camp Grant, Illinois]; reorganized and Federally recognized 11 May 1923 at Silver City as Troop F 111th Cavalry; converted, reorganized and redesignated 26 April 1940 as Battery G, 207th Coast Artillery [Antiaircraft]; redesignated 1 July 1940 as Battery G, 200th Coast Artillery [Antiaircraft]; inducted into Federal service 6 January 1941 at Silver City; surrendered 9 April 1942 to Japanese *14th Army* on Luzon; formally inactivated 2 April 1946 at Fort Mills), reorganized and Federally recognized 24 June 1947 at Silver City as Battery B

Battery C organized new and Federally recognized 4 November 1947 at Lordsburg

Battery D organized new and Federally recognized 9 November 1947 at Truth or Consequences

Ordered into active Federal service 14 August 1950 at home stations. Released from active Federal service 13 August 1952 and resumed State status. Redesignated 1 October 1953 as the 716th Antiaircraft Artillery Battalion (90mm Gun).

Consolidated 1 September 1959 with the 200th Artillery, a parent regiment under the Combat Arms Regimental System.

CAMPAIGN STREAMERS
World War I
Streamer without inscription

World War II
Philippine Islands

DECORATIONS
Presidential Unit Citation (Army), Streamer embroidered *CLARK FIELD* (200th Coast Arty cited for period 8-22 Dec 1941; WDGO 14, 1942)

Presidential Unit Citation (Army), Streamer embroidered *BATAAN* (200th Coast Arty cited for period 7 Jan-8 Mar 1942; WDGO 14, 1942)

Presidential Unit Citation (Army), Streamer embroidered *DEFENSE OF THE PHILIPPINES* (Mil & Naval Forces of the US engaged in the defense of the Philippines cited for the period 7 Dec 1941-10 May 1942; WDGO 22, 1942 as amended by WDGO 46, 1948)

Philippine President Unit Citation, Streamer embroidered *7 DECEMBER 1941 TO 10 MAY 1942* (200th Coast Arty cited; DAGO 43, 1940)

COAT OF ARMS
SHIELD: Sable, an Avanyu or.

CREST: That for the regiments and separate battalions of the New Mexico Army National Guard: On a wreath of the colors (or and sable) a coiled rattlesnake proper.

MOTTO: Anything, Anywhere, Anytime

The Avanyu, a figure representing happiness and prosperity, was used by the old 111th Cavalry but the colors have been reversed to indicate the descent from that regiment.

DISTINCTIVE INSIGNIA
The insignia is the shield and motto of the coat of arms. The sample of the insignia depicted was approved for wear on 13 July 1954.

717th ANTIAIRCRAFT ARTILLERY BATTALION

Organized in the New Mexico National Guard as Headquarters, 120th Engineers and Federally recognized 8 June 1924 at Las Cruces. Inducted into Federal service 16 September 1940 at Las Cruces. Redesignated 11 February 1942 as Headquarters, 120th Engineer Battalion. Redesignated 1 August 1942 as Headquarters, 120th Engineer Combat Battalion. Inactivated 26 November 1945 at Camp Bowie, Texas. Redesignated 31 May 1946 as Headquarters, 717th Antiaircraft Artillery Gun Battalion. Reorganized and Federally recognized 23 June 1947 at Albuquerque; remainder of battalion organized from new and existing units as follows:

Company A 120th Engineer Combat Battalion (organized and Federally recognized 2 March 1928 at Albuquerque as Company D 120th Engineers; inducted into Federal service 16 September 1940 at Albuquerque; redesignated 11 February 1942 as Company A 120th Engineer Battalion; redesignated 1 August 1942 as Company A 120th Engineer Combat Battalion; and inactivated 26 November 1945 at Camp Bowie), reorganized and Federally recognized 30 September 1947 at Albuquerque as Headquarters Battery

Battery A organized new and Federally recognized 6 November 1947 at Farmington

Battery A 200th Coast Artillery (organized at Albuquerque in 1916 as Headquarters Company, 1st Infantry, New Mexico National Guard; mustered into Federal service 16 July 1916 for Mexican border; mustered out 5 April 1917 at Columbus and resumed State status; mustered into Federal service 11 June 1917 at Albuquerque and drafted into Federal service 5 August 1917; broken up 20 October 1917 and personnel assigned to 115th Train Headquarters, Train and Military Police, 40th Division; [115th Train Headquarters, Train and Military Police demobilized 2 May 1919 at Camp Kearney, California]; reorganized and Federally recognized 26 July 1920 at Albuquerque as Troop A 1st Cavalry, New Mexico National Guard; redesignated 28 May 1921 as Headquarters Troop, 1st Cavalry; redesignated 2 May 1922 as Headquarters Troop, 111th Cavalry; converted, reorganized and redesignated 26 April 1940 as Battery A, 207th Coast Artillery [Antiaircraft]; redesignated 1 July 1940 as Battery A, 200th Coast Artillery [Antiaircraft]; inducted into Federal service 6 January 1941 at Albuquerque; surrendered 9 April 1942 to Japanese *14th Army* on Luzon; formally inactivated 2 April 1946 at Fort Mills), reorganized and Federally recognized 1 October 1947 at Albuquerque as Battery B

Company B 120th Engineer Combat Battalion (organized and Federally recognized 24 January 1924 at Socorro as Company E 120th Engineers; inducted into Federal service 16 September 1940 at Socorro; redesignated 11 February 1942 as Company B 120th Engineer Battalion; redesignated 1 August 1942 as Company B 120th Engineer Combat Battalion; and inactivated 26 November 1945 at Camp Bowie, Texas), reorganized and Federally recognized 28 September 1947 at Socorro as Battery C

Battery D 200th Coast Artillery (organized and Federally recognized 29 June 1940 at Gallup; inducted into Federal service 6 January 1941 at Gallup; surrendered 9 April 1942 to Japanese *14th Army* on Luzon; formally inactivated 2 April 1946 at Fort Mills), reorganized and Federally recognized 24 January 1947 at Gallup as Battery D

Medical Department Detachment, 200th Coast Artillery (organized and Federally recognized 25 July 1929 at Albuquerque as Medical Department Detachment, 111th Cavalry; redesignated 26 April 1940 as Medical Department Detachment, 207th Coast Artillery [Antiaircraft]; redesignated 1 July 1940 as Medical Department Detachment, 200th Coast Artillery [Antiaircraft]; inducted into Federal service 6 January 1941 at Albuquerque; surrendered 9 April 1942 to Japanese *14th Army* on Luzon; formally inactivated 2 April 1946 at Fort Mills), reorganized and Federally recognized 23 December 1948 at Albuquerque as Medical Detachment

Ordered into active Federal service 1 May 1951 at home stations. Released from active Federal service 28 February 1953 and resumed State status. Redesignated 1 October 1953 as 717th Antiaircraft Artillery Battalion (90mm Gun).

Consolidated 1 September 1959 with the 200th Artillery, a parent regiment under the Combat Arms Regimental System.

CAMPAIGN STREAMERS
World War II
Philippine Islands
Sicily (with arrowhead)
Naples-Foggia (with arrowhead)
Rome-Arno
Anzio
Southern France (with arrowhead)
Northern France
Rhineland
Ardennes-Alsace
Central Europe

DECORATIONS
Presidential Unit Citation (Army), Streamer embroidered *CLARK FIELD* (200th Coast Arty cited for period 8-22 Dec 1941; WDGO 14, 1942)

Presidential Unit Citation (Army), Streamer embroidered *BATAAN* (200th Coast Arty cited for period 7 Jan-8 Mar 1942; WDGO 14, 1942)

Presidential Unit Citation (Army), Streamer embroidered *DEFENSE OF THE PHILIPPINES* (Mil & Naval Forces of the US engaged in the defense of the Philippines cited for the period 7 Dec 1941-10 May 1942; WDGO 22, 1942 as amended by WDGO 46, 1948)

Presidential Unit Citation (Army), Streamer embroidered *BLIES RIVER* (Co B 120th Engr Cbt Bn cited for period 13-15 Mar 1945; WDGO 84, 1945)

Meritorious Unit Commendation, Streamer embroidered *EUROPEAN THEATER* (Hq, 120th Engr Cbt Bn cited for period 15 Aug 1944-31 Jan 1945; GO 196, Hq 45th Inf Div dated 31 May 1945)

Philippine Presidential Unit Citation, Streamer embroidered *7 DECEMBER 1941 TO 10 MAY 1942* (200th Coast Arty cited; DAGO 43, 1950)

French Croix de Guerre with Palm, World War II, Streamer embroidered *ACQUAFONDATA* (120th Engr Cbt Bn cited for period 1-31 Jan 1944; DAGO 43, 1950)

COAT OF ARMS
SHIELD: Or, an Avanyu sable. (The Avanyu is a Pueblo Indian device not unlike the device of the Isle of Man conventionalized, which is blazoned three legs embowed conjoined at the thighs, the three arms of the Avanyu each ending in a triangular head bearing five points).

CREST: That for the regiments and separate battalions of the New Mexico Army National Guard: On a wreath of the colors (or and sable) a coiled rattlesnake proper.

MOTTO: *Pro Civitate et Patria* (For State And Country)

The Avanyu device used by the Pueblo Indians is another form of the triskelion, a lucky talisman and symbolic of energy, motion and victory. It is also emblematic of "the whirling sun" and "lighting in air" which allude to the fire power and antiaircraft mission of the unit.

DISTINCTIVE INSIGNIA
The insignia is the shield, crest and motto of the coat of arms. The sample of the insignia depicted was originally approved on 12 July 1926 for wear by the 111th Cavalry.

718th ANTIAIRCRAFT ARTILLERY BATTALION

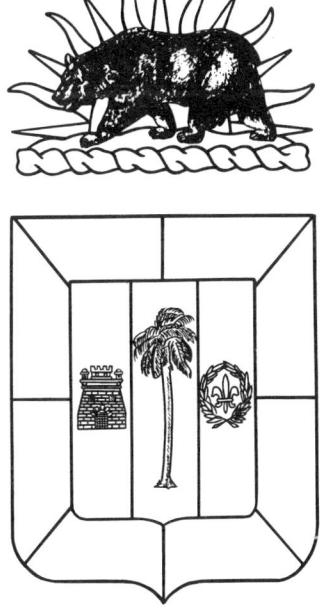

Constituted in the California National Guard as 2d Battalion, 250th Coast Artillery (Harbor Defense) and organized from existing units as follows:

Headquarters, 2d Battalion organized new and Federally recognized 7 February 1925 at San Francisco

2d Separate Battery, Coast Artillery Corps, California National Guard (organized 27 February 1911 at San Francisco as 10th Company, Coast Artillery Corps, California National Guard; mustered into Federal service 12 April 1917 at San Francisco and drafted into Federal service on 5 August 1917; redesignated 31 August 1917 as 30th Company, Coast Defenses of

San Francisco; redesignated 21 May 1918 as Supply Company, 67th Artillery, Coast Artillery Corps; demobilized 23 April 1919 at the Presidio of San Francisco; reorganized at San Francisco as 2d Separate Battery, Coast Artillery Corps, California National Guard and Federally recognized 28 August 1924), redesignated 1 November 1924 as Headquarters Detachment and Combat Train, 2d Battalion

Battery C, 250th Artillery, Coast Artillery Corps (organized about 1900 as Company C, 1st Battalion of Heavy Artillery, California National Guard and redesignated 11 May 1907 as Company L, 5th Infantry, California National Guard; redesignated 21 April 1909 as 3d Company, Coast Artillery Corps, California National Guard; mustered into Federal service 12 April 1917 at San Francisco and drafted into Federal service on 5 August 1917; redesignated 31 August 1917 as 23d Company, Coast Defenses of San Francisco; redesignated 27 April 1918 as Battery C, 1st Army Artillery Park; demobilized 26 May 1919 at Presidio of San Francisco; reorganized and Federally recognized 28 June 1919 at San Francisco as Separate Company D, Infantry, California National Guard; redesignated 1 February 1921 as 3d Company, 1st Coast Defense Command, Coast Artillery Corps; redesignated 9 January 1922 as 459th Company, 1st Coast Defense Command, Coast Artillery Corps; redesignated 6 October 1923 as Battery C, 250th Artillery, Coast Artillery Corps), redesignated 1 November 1924 as Battery C

Battery D, 250th Artillery, Coast Artillery Corps (organized prior to 1900 as Company D, 1st Infantry, California National Guard and redesignated 11 May 1907 as Company M, 5th Infantry, California National Guard; redesignated 21 April 1909 as 4th Company, Coast Artillery Corps, California National Guard; mustered into Federal service 12 April 1917 at San Francisco and drafted into Federal service on 5 August 1917; redesignated 31 August 1917 as 24th Company, Coast Defenses of San Francisco; redesignated 27 April 1918 as Battery C, 1st Army Artillery Park; demobilized 26 May 1919 at Presidio of San Francisco; reorganized and Federally recognized 28 June 1919 at San Francisco as Separate Company D, Infantry, California National Guard; redesignated 1 February 1921 as 4th Company, 1st Coast Defense Command, Coast Artillery Corps; redesignated 9 January 1922 as 462d Company, 1st Coast Defense Command, Coast Artillery Corps; redesignated 6 October 1923 as Battery D, 250th Artillery, Coast Artillery Corps), redesignated 1 November 1924 as Battery D

Redesignated 15 March 1940 as 2d Battalion, 250th Coast Artillery (155mm Gun). Inducted into Federal service 16 September 1940 at San Francisco. Reorganized at Camp Gruber, Oklahoma and redesignated 18 May 1944 as the 536th Field Artillery Battalion (8 Inch Howitzer, Truck Drawn). (Departed Hampton Roads Port of Embarkation 18 February 1945 for overseas service and arrived in Italy on 1 March 1945). Inactivated 25 November 1945 in Italy. Redesignated 5 August 1946 as the 718th Antiaircraft Artillery Gun Battalion. Reorganized and Federally recognized 31 January 1949 at San Francisco. Ordered into active Federal service at San Francisco on 15 May 1951. Released from active Federal service 14 May 1953 and resumed State status. Redesignated 1 October 1953 as the 718th Antiaircraft Artillery Battalion. (Headquarters relocated to Alameda on 1 July 1954). Battalion disbanded when Federal recognition was withdrawn on 30 November 1954.

CAMPAIGN STREAMERS
World War I
St. Mihiel
Meuse-Argonne

World War II
North Apennines
Po Valley

DECORATIONS
None

COAT OF ARMS
SHIELD: Gules a pale argent charged with a palm tree proper, in dexter fess a tower triple towered and in sinister a fleur-de-lis encircled by a garland of laurel, all or within a bordure gyronny of the last and of the first.

CREST: That for the regiments and separate battalions of the California Army National Guard: On a wreath of the colors (argent and gules) the setting sun behind a grizzly bear passant on a grassy field, all proper.

MOTTO: *Rien a pas beau* (Nothing Is In Vain)

The shield is red for Artillery. The castle is for service during the War with Spain; the palm tree is for the Philippine Insurrection and the wreathed fleur-de-lis commemorates service in France during World War I. The shield is that of the 250th Coast Artillery within a red and yellow border to represent the descent from the 2d Battalion of that organization.

DISTINCTIVE INSIGNIA
The insignia is the shield and motto of the coat of arms. The sample of the insignia depicted was approved for wear on 13 June 1952.

718th ANTIAIRCRAFT ARTILLERY BATTALION

Organized in the California Army National Guard as the 718th Antiaircraft Artillery Battalion (90mm Gun) and Federally recognized 12 April 1955 with Headquarters and Headquarters Battery and Batteries A and C at Los Angeles and Batteries B and D at Long Beach. (Headquarters relocated to Long Beach on 10 September 1956). Battalion disbanded when Federal recognition was withdrawn on 12 June 1957.

CAMPAIGN STREAMERS
None

DECORATIONS
None

COAT OF ARMS
None

DISTINCTIVE INSIGNIA
None

719th ANTIAIRCRAFT ARTILLERY BATTALION

Constituted 5 August 1946 as the 719th Antiaircraft Artillery Gun Battalion and allotted to the California National Guard. Organized and Federally recognized 22 September 1947 at Alameda. Redesignated 1 October 1953 as the 719th Antiaircraft Artillery Battalion (90mm Gun). Disbanded 28 February 1958 at Alameda when Federal recognition was withdrawn.

CAMPAIGN STREAMERS
None

DECORATIONS
None

COAT OF ARMS
SHIELD: Per fess gules and azure a fess dancette to chief or, on the second a fess couped, enhanced of the third.

CREST: That for the regiments and separate battalions of the California Army National Guard: On a wreath of the colors (or and gules) the setting sun behind a grizzly bear passant on a grassy field, all proper.

MOTTO: *Ultima Ratio Regum* (The Last Reasoning Of Kings)

The colors scarlet and yellow are used for Artillery. The blue represents San Francisco Bay and the yellow rectangle is for Alameda Island, the home area of the battalion. The jagged yellow area alludes to the Diablo Mountains.

DISTINCTIVE INSIGNIA
The insignia is the shield and motto of the coat of arms. The sample of the insignia depicted was approved for wear on 29 January 1957.

720th ANTIAIRCRAFT ARTILLERY MISSILE BATTALION

Constituted 5 August 1946 in the California National Guard as the 720th Antiaircraft Artillery Gun Battalion and organized from new and existing units as follows:

Battery C, 951st Antiaircraft Artillery Automatic Weapons Battalion (organized and Federally recognized 14 April 1936 at Long Beach as Service Battery [less Band Section], 251st Coast Artillery; redesignated 4 January 1938 as Battery G, 251st Coast Artillery; inducted into Federal service 16 September 1940 at Long Beach; redesignated 1 March 1944 as Battery C, 951st Antiaircraft Artillery Automatic Weapons Battalion and inactivated 29 December 1945 at Camp Stoneman, California) reorganized as Headquarters and Headquarters Battery and Federally recognized 10 April 1947 at Long Beach

Battery D, 951st Antiaircraft Artillery Automatic Weapons Battalion (organized and Federally recognized 24 January 1938 at Long Beach as Battery H, 251st Coast Artillery; inducted into Federal service 16 September 1940 at Long Beach; redesignated 1 March 1944 as Battery D, 951st Antiaircraft Artillery Automatic Weapons Battalion and inactivated 29 December 1945 at Camp Stoneman) reorganized as Battery A and Federally recognized 13 November 1947 at Long Beach

Battery B organized new and Federally recognized 13 November 1947 at Long Beach

Battery C organized new and Federally recognized 19 May 1948 at Gardena

Battery D organized new and Federally recognized 17 January 1949 at Long Beach

Medical Detachment organized new and Federally recognized 10 April 1947 at Long Beach

Redesignated 1 October 1953 as the 720th Antiaircraft Artillery Battalion. Reorganized and redesignated 1 June 1957 as the 720th Antiaircraft Artillery Missile Battalion (NIKE).

Consolidated 1 May 1959 with the 251st Artillery, a parent regiment under the Combat Arms Regimental System.

CAMPAIGN STREAMERS
World War II
Central Pacific
Northern Solomons
Luzon (with arrowhead)

DECORATIONS
Philippine Presidential Unit Citation, Streamer embroidered *17 OCTOBER 1944 TO 4 JULY 1945* (951st AAA AW Bn cited; DAGO 47, 1950)

COAT OF ARMS
SHIELD: Gules, on six pallets couped or a fleur-de-lis encircled by a garland of laurel of the first.

CREST: That for the regiments and separate battalions of the California Army National Guard: On a wreath of the colors (or and gules) the setting sun behind a grizzly bear passant on a grassy field, all proper.

MOTTO: *Deo Patriae Amicis* (For My God, My Country, And My Friends)

Red and yellow are the colors for Artillery. The design is based on the coat of arms of the former 251st Coast Artillery and indicates the descent from elements of the 2d Battalion of that organization.

DISTINCTIVE INSIGNIA
The insignia is the shield and motto of the coat of arms. The sample of the insignia depicted was approved for wear on 9 October 1953.

722d ANTIAIRCRAFT ARTILLERY BATTALION

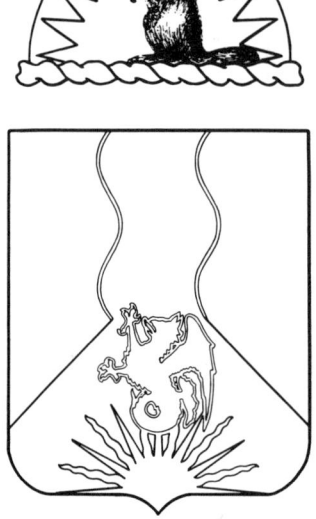

Constituted in the Oregon National Guard as Coast Artillery Corps (Fixed Defenses), Oregon National Guard and organized from new and existing units as follows:

Headquarters (organized 20 May 1887 at Portland as Headquarters, 2d Regiment, Oregon

Infantry; mustered into Federal service at Portland as Headquarters, 2d Oregon Volunteer Infantry in May 1898; mustered out 7 August 1899 at San Francisco, California; reorganized 3 May 1900 at Eugene as Headquarters, 4th Regiment, Oregon Infantry; converted and redesignated 17 July 1907 as Headquarters, 4th Infantry, Oregon National Guard; converted and redesignated 12 December 1911 as Headquarters, Coast Artillery Corps, Oregon National Guard; drafted into Federal service 5 August 1917 at Fort Stevens, Oregon; demobilized 20 November 1918 in the Coast Defenses of the Columbia) reorganized and Federally recognized 22 March 1921 at Salem

1st Company, Coast Artillery Corps, Oregon National Guard, organized new and Federally recognized 30 June 1919 at Ashland

2d Company, Coast Artillery Corps, Oregon National Guard, organized new and Federally recognized 30 June 1919 at Marshfield

3d Company, Coast Artillery Corps, Oregon National Guard, organized new and Federally recognized 24 March 1920 at Newport

5th Company, Coast Defenses of the Columbia (organized at Albany prior to 1895 as Company G, 2d Infantry, Oregon National Guard; mustered into Federal service in May 1898 as Company G, 2d Oregon Volunteer Infantry; mustered out 7 August 1899 at San Francisco, California and reorganized at Albany in 1900 as Company G, 2d Infantry; redesignated 17 July 1907 as Company G, 4th Infantry, Oregon National Guard; converted and redesignated 13 December 1911 as 5th Company, Coast Artillery Corps, Oregon National Guard; drafted into Federal service 5 August 1917 at Fort Stevens, Oregon; redesignated 15 January 1918 as 5th Company, Coast Defenses of the Columbia; demobilized 14 December 1918 at Fort Canby, Washington), reorganized and Federally recognized 22 March 1921 at Albany as 4th Company, Coast Artillery Corps, Oregon National Guard

Medical Detachment organized new and Federally recognized 13 April 1921 at Albany

(Reorganized 31 March 1922 and 1st through 4th Companies redesignated 483d through 486th Companies, Coast Artillery Corps, Oregon National Guard). Reorganized and redesignated 12 December 1923 as 1st Battalion, 249th Artillery, Coast Artillery Corps. Redesignated 18 April 1924 as 1st Battalion, 249th Coast Artillery (Harbor Defense). Inducted into Federal service 16 September 1940 at home stations. Reorganized and redesignated 18 October 1944 as the 249th Coast Artillery Battalion (Harbor Defense). Inactivated 15 September 1945 at Fort Stevens, Oregon. Redesignated 10 July 1946 as the 722d Antiaircraft Artillery Gun Battalion. Reorganized and Federally recognized 31 January 1950 with Headquarters at Portland and batteries at Portland, Redmond, Gresham and Salem. Reorganized and redesignated 16 July 1951 as the 722d Antiaircraft Artillery Automatic Weapons Battalion. Redesignated 1 October 1953 as the 722d Antiaircraft Artillery Battalion (Automatic Weapons) (Self Propelled).

Reorganized and redesignated 1 April 1959 as the 249th Artillery, a parent regiment under the Combat Arms Regimental System.

CAMPAIGN STREAMERS
War with Spain
Manila

Philippine Insurrection
Manila
Malolos
San Isidro

DECORATIONS
None

COAT OF ARMS
SHIELD: Per chevron gules and azure, from partition line to chief a pale wavy of the second

fimbriated or, issuant from base a setting sun of the last, at nombril point a sea griffin of the first, fringed of the fourth.

CREST: That for the regiments and separate battalions of the Oregon Army National Guard: On a wreath of the colors (or and gules) a demi disc gules charged with the setting sun with twelve light rays or (the shoulder sleeve insignia of the 41st Division), behind a beaver sejant proper.

MOTTO: *Cede Nullis* (Surrender To None)

The shield is red for Artillery. The blue portion represents the mouth of the Columbia River, the station of the 249th Coast Artillery. The setting sun is taken from the Oregon State Seal while the sea griffin is the mythical guardian of treasure on land and sea.

DISTINCTIVE INSIGNIA
The insignia is the shield and motto of the coat of arms. The sample of the insignia depicted was originally approved on 8 May 1928 for wear by the 249th Coast Artillery.

724th ANTIAIRCRAFT ARTILLERY MISSILE BATTALION

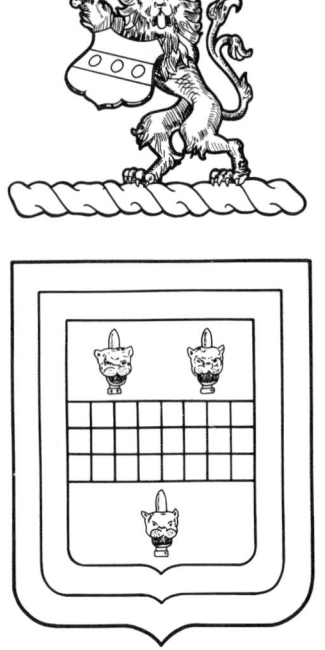
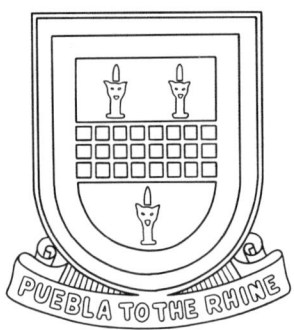

Organized and Federally recognized 16 November 1921 at Pittsburgh as Headquarters Battery and Combat Train, 2d Battalion, 176th Field Artillery. Reorganized and redesignated 1 July 1940 as Headquarters Battery, 2d Battalion, 176th Field Artillery. Inducted into Federal service 3 February 1941 at Pittsburgh. Redesignated 12 March 1942 as Headquarters Battery, 2d Battalion, 228th Field Artillery. Redesignated 1 March 1943 as Headquarters Battery, 967th Field Artillery Battalion. Inactivated 2 December 1945 at Camp Patrick Henry, Virginia. Redesignated 24 May 1946 as Headquarters and Headquarters Battery, 724th Antiaircraft Artillery Searchlight Battalion. Reorganized and Federally recognized 16 December 1947 at Pittsburgh. Redesignated Headquarters and Headquarters Battery, 724th Antiaircraft Artillery Gun Battalion (Mobile) in 1947. Reorganized and redesignated 1 October 1949 as Headquarters and Headquarters Battery, 724th Antiaircraft Artillery Automatic Weapons Battalion (Mobile). Remainder of Battalion organized from new and existing units as follows:

Battery A, 688th Field Artillery Battalion (organized and Federally recognized 26 September 1949 at Everett), redesignated 1 June 1950 as Battery A

Battery B organized new and Federally recognized 8 August 1950 at Pittsburgh

Battery C, 967th Artillery Battalion (organized 26 July 1898 at Pittsburgh as Company I, 17th Infantry, Pennsylvania National Guard and redesignated 1 July 1899 as Company I, 18th Infantry, Pennsylvania National Guard; mustered into Federal service 4 July 1916 at Mount Gretna for service on the Mexican border; mustered out 5 January 1917 and resumed State status; mustered into Federal service 14 April 1917 at Pittsburgh and drafted into Federal service 5 August 1917; consolidated 11 October 1917 with Company I, 111th Infantry; former Company I, 18th Infantry reconstituted 16 October 1919 in the Pennsylvania National Guard; reorganized and Federally recognized 29 July 1920 at Pittsburgh; redesignated 1 April 1921 as Battery F, 176th Field Artillery; inducted into Federal service 3 February 1941 at Pittsburgh; redesignated 12 March 1942 as Battery F, 228th Field Artillery; redesignated 1 March 1943 as Battery C, 967th Field Artillery Battalion and inactivated 2 December 1945 at Camp Patrick Henry, Virginia), reorganized and Federally recognized 25 June 1948 at Pittsburgh as Battery C

Service Battery, 176th Field Artillery Battalion (organized and Federally recognized 1 July 1940 at Pittsburgh as an element of Headquarters Battery, 176th Field Artillery; redesignated 1 January 1941 as Service Battery, 176th Field Artillery; inducted into Federal service 3 February 1941 at Pittsburgh; redesignated 12 March 1942 as Service Battery, 176th Field Artillery Battalion and inactivated 5 December 1945 at Camp Kilmer, New Jersey), reorganized and Federally recognized 9 June 1949 at Pittsburgh as Battery D

Medical Detachment organized new and Federally recognized 10 November 1947 at Pittsburgh

Battalion reorganized and redesignated 1 October 1951 as the 724th Antiaircraft Artillery Gun Battalion (90mm). Redesignated 1 October 1953 as the 724th Antiaircraft Artillery Battalion (90mm Gun). Reorganized and redesignated 1 February 1958 as the 724th Antiaircraft Artillery Missile Battalion (NIKE). (Headquarters relocated to Moon Run on 14 March 1958).

Consolidated 1 June 1959 with the 176th Artillery, a parent regiment under the Combat Arms Regimental System.

CAMPAIGN STREAMERS
World War II
Normandy
Northern France
Rhineland
Central Europe

DECORATIONS
None

COAT OF ARMS
SHIELD: Sable, a fess checky argent and azure between three high explosive shells each debruised by a leopard's face or, all within a bordure per bordure gules and of the fourth.

CREST: That for the regiments and separate battalions of the Pennsylvania Army National Guard: On a wreath of the colors (argent and sable) a lion rampant guardant proper holding in dexter paw a naked scimitar argent, hilted or and in sinister an escutcheon argent, on a fess sable three plates.

MOTTO: We Will Be Vigilant

The design is that of the coat of arms for the old 176th Field Artillery and the gold and red border shows descent from elements of that regiment.

DISTINCTIVE INSIGNIA
The insignia is the shield and motto of the coat of arms. The insignia depicted was unofficially worn by this battalion between 1954 and 1959.

725th ANTIAIRCRAFT ARTILLERY BATTALION

Constituted 9 July 1946 as the 725th Antiaircraft Artillery Searchlight Battalion and allotted to the North Carolina National Guard. Redesignated 725th Antiaircraft Artillery Automatic Weapons Battalion in 1949. Organized and Federally recognized 10 January 1950 with Headquarters at Whiteville and batteries at Shallotte, Fair Bluff, Bladenboro and Benson. Redesignated 1 October 1953 as 725th Antiaircraft Artillery Battalion (Automatic Weapons) (Self Propelled).

Redesignated 28 October 1954 as the 130th Antiaircraft Artillery Battalion (Automatic Weapons) (Self Propelled).

CAMPAIGN STREAMERS
None

DECORATIONS
None

COAT OF ARMS
SHIELD: Per fess nebuly arched azure and gules, three projectiles in bend or.

CREST: That for the regiments and separate battalions of the North Carolina Army National Guard: On a wreath of the colors (or and gules) a hornet's nest hanging from a bough beset with thirteen hornets, all proper.

MOTTO: *Dux Vitae Ratio* (The Guide Of Life Is Common Sense)

Red is for Artillery. The division of the shield is arched and nebuly to represent the sky and

810

clouds. The three projectiles, spaced at close intervals, symbolize the rapid fire of automatic weapons.

DISTINCTIVE INSIGNIA
The insignia is the shield and motto of the coat of arms. The sample of the insignia depicted was approved for wear on 11 August 1954.

726th ANTIAIRCRAFT ARTILLERY BATTALION

Constituted 31 May 1946 in the New Mexico National Guard as the 726th Antiaircraft Artillery Searchlight Battalion and organized from new and existing units as follows:

Headquarters organized new and Federally recognized 23 June 1947 at Albuquerque

Battery C 200th Coast Artillery (organized at Santa Fe in 1916 as Supply Company, 1st Infantry, New Mexico National Guard; mustered into Federal service 16 July 1916 for Mexican border; mustered out 5 April 1917 at Columbus and resumed State status; mustered into Federal service 11 June 1917 at Santa Fe and drafted into Federal service 5 August 1917; redesignated 20 October 1917 as Company B 115th Train, Headquarters and Military Police and assigned to the 40th Division; demobilized 25 April 1919 at Camp Kearny, California; reorganized and Federally recognized 11 April 1921 at Santa Fe as Troop D 1st Cavalry, New Mexico National Guard; redesignated 2 May 1922 as Troop D 111th Cavalry; redesignated 10 June 1922 as Troop E 111th Cavalry; redesignated 15 March 1929 as Troop B 111th Cavalry; converted, reorganized and redesignated 26 April 1940 as Battery C, 207th Coast Artillery [Antiaircraft]; redesignated 1 July 1940 as Battery C, 200th Coast Artillery [Antiaircraft]; inducted into Federal service 6 January 1941 at Santa Fe; surrendered 9 April 1942 to Japanese *14th Army* on Luzon; formally inactivated 2 April 1946 at Fort Mills), reorganized and Federally recognized 29 September 1947 at Santa Fe as Headquarters Battery

Battery H 200th Coast Artillery (organized and Federally recognized 12 May 1929 at Taos as Troop K 111th Cavalry; redesignated 26 April 1940 as Battery H, 207th Coast Artillery [Antiaircraft]; redesignated 1 July 1940 as Battery H, 200th Coast Artillery [Antiaircraft]; inducted into Federal service 6 January 1941 at Taos; surrendered 9 April 1942 to Japanese

14th Army on Luzon; formally inactivated 2 April 1946 at Fort Mills), reorganized and Federally recognized 29 September 1947 at Taos as Battery A

Company C 120th Engineer Combat Battalion (organized and Federally recognized 13 November 1923 at Las Vegas as Company F 120th Engineers; inducted into Federal service 16 September 1940 at Las Vegas; redesignated 11 February 1942 as Company C 120th Engineer Battalion; redesignated 1 August 1942 as Company C 120th Engineer Combat Battalion; inactivated 26 November 1945 at Camp Bowie, Texas), reorganized and Federally recognized 26 June 1947 at Las Vegas as Battery B

Headquarters Company 804th Tank Destroyer Battalion (organized and Federally recognized 10 October 1940 at Santa Fe as Headquarters Company,. 104th Antitank Battalion; inducted into Federal service 6 January 1941 at Santa Fe; redesignated 15 December 1941 as Headquarters Company, 804th Tank Destroyer Battalion; and inactivated 10 December 1945 at Camp Hood, Texas), reorganized and Federally recognized 7 November 1947 at Santa Fe as Battery C

Battery D organized new and Federally recognized 21 October 1948 at Espanola

Reorganized and redesignated 1 December 1947 as 726th Antiaircraft Artillery Gun Battalion. Ordered into active Federal service 14 August 1950 at home stations. Released from active Federal service 13 May 1952 and resumed State status. Redesignated 1 October 1953 as 726th Antiaircraft Artillery Battalion (90mm Gun).

Consolidated 1 September 1959 with the 200th Artillery, a parent regiment under the Combat Arms Regimental System.

CAMPAIGN STREAMERS
World War II
Philippine Islands

DECORATIONS
Presidential Unit Citation (Army), Streamer embroidered *CLARK FIELD* (200th Coast Arty cited for period 8-22 Dec 1941; WDGO 14, 1942)

Presidential Unit Citation (Army), Streamer embroidered *BATAAN* (200th Coast Arty cited for period 7 Jan-8 Mar 1942; WDGO 14, 1942)

Presidential Unit Citation (Army), Streamer embroidered *DEFENSE OF THE PHILIPPINES* (Mil & Naval Forces of the US engaged in the defense of the Philippines cited for the period 7 Dec 1941-10 May 1942; WDGO 22, 1942 as amended by WDGO 46, 1948)

Philippine Presidential Unit Citation, Streamer embroidered *7 DECEMBER 1941 TO 10 MAY 1942* (200th Coast Arty cited; DAGO 43, 1950)

COAT OF ARMS
SHIELD: Or, an Avanyu sable; a bordure gyronny of the first and gules.

CREST: That for the regiments and separate battalions of the New Mexico Army National Guard: On a wreath of the colors (or and sable) a coiled rattlesnake proper.

MOTTO: *Miras Arriba* (Keep Your Goal High)

The shield is that of the coat of arms of the old 111th Cavalry within a red and yellow border to represent the descent from that regiment. The Avanyu is a figure representing happiness and prosperity and was used by the ancient Pueblo Indians in New Mexico.

DISTINCTIVE INSIGNIA
The insignia is the shield and motto of the coat of arms. The sample of the insignia depicted was approved for wear on 28 September 1953.

727th ANTIAIRCRAFT ARTILLERY MACHINE GUN BATTALION

Constituted 10 July 1943 in the Army of the United States as the 727th Machine Gun Battalion (less Battery A) and assigned to the 10th Light Division. Activated, less Battery A, 15 July 1943 at Camp Haan, California; concurrently, Antiaircraft Battery, Mountain Training Center reorganized and redesignated Battery A.

Redesignated 6 November 1944 as the 10th Mountain Infantry Antitank Battalion

CAMPAIGN STREAMERS
None

DECORATIONS
None

COAT OF ARMS
None

DISTINCTIVE INSIGNIA
None

728th ANTIAIRCRAFT ARTILLERY MISSILE BATTALION

Constituted 5 August 1946 in the California National Guard as the 728th Antiaircraft Artillery Searchlight Battalion and organized from new and existing units as follows:

Headquarters, 535th Field Artillery Battalion (organized and Federally recognized 15 October 1921 at San Francisco as Headquarters, 1st Battalion, 1st Coast Defense Command, Coast Artillery Corps and redesignated 6 October 1923 as Headquarters, 1st Battalion 250th Artillery, Coast Artillery Corps [Fixed Defense]; redesignated 1 November 1924 as Headquarters, 1st Battalion 250th Coast Artillery [Harbor Defense]; redesignated 15 March

1940 as Headquarters, 1st Battalion 250th Coast Artillery [155mm Gun]; inducted into Federal service 16 September 1940 at San Francisco; redesignated 18 May 1944 as Headquarters, 535th Field Artillery Battalion [8 Inch Howitzer, Truck Drawn]; and inactivated 29 November 1945 at Camp Shanks, New York), reorganized and Federally recognized 3 March 1947 at San Francisco as Headquarters and Headquarters Battery

Battery A, 535th Field Artillery Battalion (organized about 1900 as Company B, 1st Battalion of Heavy Artillery, California National Guard and redesignated 11 May 1907 as Company H, 5th Infantry, California National Guard; redesignated 21 April 1909 as 1st Company, Coast Artillery Corps, California National Guard; mustered into Federal service 12 April 1917 at San Francisco and drafted into Federal service on 5 August 1917; redesignated 31 August 1917 as 21st Company, Coast Defenses of San Francisco; redesignated 2 March 1918 as Battery A, 1st Army Artillery Park; demobilized 26 May 1919 at Presidio of San Francisco; reorganized and Federally recognized 15 July 1920 at San Francisco as 1st Company, 1st Coast Defense Command, Coast Artillery Corps; redesignated 9 January 1922 as 459th Company, 1st Coast Defense Command, Coast Artillery Corps; redesignated 6 October 1923 as Battery A, 250th Artillery, Coast Artillery Corps; redesignated 1 November 1924 as Battery A, 250th Coast Artillery; inducted into Federal service 16 September 1940 at San Francisco; redesignated 18 May 1944 as Battery A, 535th Field Artillery Battalion and inactivated 29 November 1945 at Camp Shanks, New York), reorganized and Federally recognized 21 March 1949 at San Francisco as Battery A

Battery B organized new and Federally recognized 17 April 1950 at San Francisco

Battery B, 535th Field Artillery Battalion (organized about 1900 as Company A, 1st Battalion of Heavy Artillery, California National Guard and redesignated 11 May 1907 as Company K, 5th Infantry, California National Guard; redesignated 21 April 1909 as 2d Company, Coast Artillery Corps, California National Guard; mustered into Federal service 12 April 1917 at San Francisco and drafted into Federal service on 5 August 1917; redesignated 31 August 1917 as 22d Company, Coast Defenses of San Francisco; redesignated 2 March 1918 as Battery B, 1st Army Artillery Park; demobilized 26 May 1919 at Presidio of San Francisco; reorganized and Federally recognized 17 February 1921 at San Francisco as 2d Company, 1st Coast Defense Command, Coast Artillery Corps; redesignated 9 January 1922 as 460th Company, 1st Coast Defense Command, Coast Artillery Corps; redesignated 6 October 1923 as Battery B, 250th Artillery, Coast Artillery Corps; redesignated 1 November 1924 as Battery B, 250th Coast Artillery; inducted into Federal service 16 September 1940 at San Francisco; redesignated 18 May 1944 as Battery B, 535th Field Artillery Battalion and inactivated 29 November 1945 at Camp Shanks, New York), reorganized and Federally recognized 8 July 1948 at San Francisco as Battery C

Battery D organized new and Federally recognized 17 April 1950 at San Francisco

Medical Detachment organized new and Federally recognized 5 May 1947 at San Francisco

Redesignated 1 December 1947 as the 728th Antiaircraft Artillery Gun Battalion. Ordered into active Federal service 15 May 1951. Relieved from active Federal service 14 May 1953 and resumed State status. Redesignated 1 October 1953 as the 728th Antiaircraft Artillery Battalion. (Headquarters relocated to Alameda on 15 November 1954). Reorganized and redesignated 1 March 1958 as the 728th Antiaircraft Artillery Missile Battalion. (Headquarters relocated to Berkeley on 1 June 1958).

Consolidated 1 May 1959 with the 250th Artillery, a parent regiment under the Combat Arms Regimental System.

CAMPAIGN STREAMERS
World War I
St. Mihiel
Meuse-Argonne

World War II
Central Europe
Pacific Theater without inscription

DECORATIONS
None

COAT OF ARMS

SHIELD: Gules a pale argent charged with a palm tree proper, in dexter fess a tower triple towered and in sinister a fleur-de-lis encircled by a garland of laurel, all or.

CREST: That for the regiments and separate battalions of the California National Guard: On a wreath of the colors (argent and gules) the setting sun behind a grizzly bear passant on a grassy field, all proper.

MOTTO: *Oram Occidentalem Defendimus* (We Defend The Western Coast)

The shield is red for Artillery. The castle is for service during the War with Spain; the palm tree is for the Philippine Insurrection and the wreathed fleur-de-lis commemorates service in France during World War I.

DISTINCTIVE INSIGNIA

The insignia is the shield and motto of the coat of arms. The sample of the insignia depicted was originally approved on 5 August 1925 for wear by the 250th Coast Artillery.

729th ANTIAIRCRAFT ARTILLERY MACHINE GUN BATTALION

Constituted 21 July 1943 in the Army of the United States as the 729th Antiaircraft Artillery Machine Gun Battalion and assigned to the 89th Light Division. Activated 24 July 1943 at Camp Haan, California. Relieved from the 89th Light Division and disbanded 15 June 1944 at Camp Butner, North Carolina.

CAMPAIGN STREAMERS
None

DECORATIONS
None

COAT OF ARMS
None

DISTINCTIVE INSIGNIA
None

730th ANTIAIRCRAFT ARTILLERY BATTALION

Organized as the 8th Company, Coast Artillery Corps, California National Guard and Federally recognized 11 May 1921 at San Diego. Redesignated 9 January 1922 as the 466th Company, 1st Coast Defense Command, Coast Artillery Corps. Redesignated 6 October 1923 as Battery H, 250th Artillery, Coast Artillery Corps. Redesignated 1 November 1924 as Battery C, 251st Coast Artillery. Redesignated 1 January 1930 as Battery A, 251st Coast Artillery. Inducted into Federal service 16 September 1940 at San Diego. (Departed Los Angeles Port of Embarkation 17 November 1940 for overseas service and arrived at Fort Shafter, Hawaii on 23 November 1940; subsequently served in the Fiji Islands, on Bougainville and in the Philippine Islands). Reorganized and redesignated 1 March 1944 as Battery A, 746th Antiaircraft Artillery Gun Battalion. (Returned from overseas service and arrived at the San Francisco Port of Embarkation on 13 January 1946). Inactivated 15 January 1946 at Camp Stoneman, California. Redesignated 5 August 1946 as Headquarters and Headquarters Battery, 730th Antiaircraft Artillery Searchlight Battalion; concurrently, remainder of battalion constituted new and allotted to the California National Guard. Reorganized and Federally recognized 25 October 1947 with Headquarters at San Diego and batteries at Compton, El Cajon and National City. Redesignated 1 December 1947 as the 730th Antiaircraft Artillery Gun Battalion (Mobile). (Headquarters relocated to National City on 30 September 1949). Redesignated 1 October 1953 as the 730th Antiaircraft Artillery Battalion (90mm Gun).

Consolidated 1 May 1959 with the 251st Artillery, a parent regiment under the Combat Arms Regimental System.

CAMPAIGN STREAMERS
World War I
Meuse-Argonne

World War II
Central Pacific
Northern Solomons
Leyte
Southern Philippines

DECORATIONS
Philippine Presidential Unit Citation, Streamer embroidered *17 OCTOBER 1944 TO 4 JULY*

1945 (746th AAA AW Bn cited; DAGO 47, 1950)

COAT OF ARMS

SHIELD: Gules, a ship of Cabrillo's time or, on a canton of the last a fleur-de-lis encircled by a garland of laurel azure.

CREST: That for the regiments and separate battalions of the California Army National Guard: On a wreath of the colors (or and gules) the setting sun behind a grizzly bear passant on a grassy field, all proper.

MOTTO: *Al Tirar* (Let's Shoot)

The shield is red for Artillery. The ship and the canton were taken from the coat of arms of the old 251st Coast Artillery and commemorate the descent from that organization. The ship is representative of that of Don Juan Rodriguez Cabrillo, a Portuguese explorer who discovered San Diego Harbor.

DISTINCTIVE INSIGNIA

The insignia is the shield and motto of the coat of arms. The sample of the insignia depicted was approved for wear on 8 December 1953.

731st ANTIAIRCRAFT ARTILLERY MACHINE GUN BATTALION

Constituted 10 July 1943 in the Army of the United States as the 731st Antiaircraft Artillery Machine Gun Battalion and assigned to the 71st Light Division. Activated 15 July 1943 at Camp Haan, California. Relieved from the 71st Light Division and disbanded 26 May 1944 at Fort Benning, Georgia.

CAMPAIGN STREAMERS
None

DECORATIONS
None

COAT OF ARMS
None

DISTINCTIVE INSIGNIA
None

732d ANTIAIRCRAFT ARTILLERY BATTALION

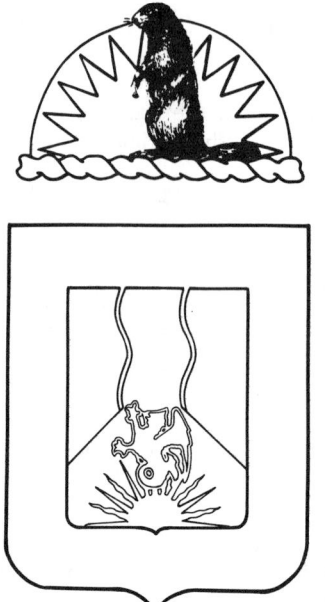

Constituted in the Oregon National Guard as the 171st Coast Artillery Battalion (Harbor Defense) and organized 18 October 1944 from former batteries of the 249th Coast Artillery as follows:

Headquarters, 2d Battalion, 249th Coast Artillery (organized and Federally recognized 17 April 1926 at Albany and relocated to Junction City on 2 February 1931, to Klamath Falls on 8 May 1931, to Medford on 1 April 1932, to Ashland on 11 June 1937 and to Salem on 15 April 1940; inducted into Federal service 16 September 1940), redesignated Headquarters

Headquarters Battery, 2d Battalion, 249th Coast Artillery (organized and Federally recognized 15 April 1940 at Salem; and inducted into Federal service 16 September 1940 at Salem), redesignated Headquarters Detachment

Company C, 249th Coast Artillery (organized and Federally recognized 22 April 1940 at Klamath Falls and inducted into Federal service 16 September 1940 at Klamath Falls), redesignated Battery A

Company D, 249th Coast Artillery (organized at Albany prior to 1895 as Company G, 2d Infantry, Oregon National Guard; mustered into Federal service in May 1898 as Company G, 2d Oregon Volunteer Infantry; mustered out 7 August 1899 at San Francisco, California and reorganized at Albany in 1900 as Company G, 2d Infantry; redesignated 17 July 1907 as Company G, 4th Infantry, Oregon National Guard; converted and redesignated 13 December 1911 as 5th Company, Coast Artillery Corps, Oregon National Guard; drafted into Federal service 5 August 1917 at Fort Stevens, Oregon; redesignated 15 January 1918 as 5th Company, Coast Defenses of the Columbia; demobilized 14 December 1918 at Fort Canby, Washington; reorganized and Federally recognized 31 March 1922 at Albany as the 483d Company, Coast Artillery Corps, Oregon National Guard; redesignated 12 December 1923 as Battery A, 249th Artillery, Coast Artillery Corps; redesignated 18 April 1924 as Battery A, 249th Coast Artillery; redesignated 14 April 1940 as Battery D, 249th Coast Artillery; and inducted into Federal service 16 September 1940 at Albany), redesignated Battery B

Battalion inactivated 15 September 1945 at Fort Canby. Redesignated 10 July 1946 as the 965th Field Artillery Battalion. Reorganized and Federally recognized 13 November 1947 with Headquarters at Klamath Falls. Redesignated 1 February 1949 as the 732d Antiaircraft Artillery Gun Battalion (90mm). (Headquarters relocated to Ashland on 12 May 1949). Reorganized and redesignated 16 July 1951 as the 732d Antiaircraft Artillery Automatic Weapons Battalion. Redesignated 1 October 1953 as the 732d Antiaircraft Artillery Battalion (Automatic Weapons) (Self Propelled).

Consolidated 1 April 1959 with the 249th Artillery, a parent regiment under the Combat Arms Regimental System.

CAMPAIGN STREAMERS
None

DECORATIONS
None

COAT OF ARMS
SHIELD: Per chevron gules and azure, from partition line to chief a pale wavy of the second fimbriated or, issuant from base a setting sun of the last, at nombril point a sea griffin of the first fringed of the fourth, all within a bordure also of the fourth.

CREST: That for the regiments and separate battalions of the Oregon Army National Guard: On a wreath of the colors (or and gules) a demi disc gules charged with the setting sun with twelve light rays or (the shoulder sleeve insignia of the 41st Division) behind a beaver sejant proper.

MOTTO: *Attempto* (I Dare)

The coat of arms is that of the old 249th Coast Artillery within a border to indicate the descent from that regiment.

DISTINCTIVE INSIGNIA
The insignia is the shield and motto of the coat of arms. The sample of the insignia depicted was approved for wear on 16 May 1952.

734th ANTIAIRCRAFT ARTILLERY BATTALION

Constituted 25 February 1943 in the Army of the United States as the 734th Antiaircraft Artillery Gun Battalion (Semimobile) and activated 20 July 1943 at Camp Edwards, Massachusetts. (Departed San Francisco Port of Embarkation 11 November 1944 for overseas service; arrived in New Guinea 1 December 1944 and moved to the Philippine Islands on 31 March 1945). Inactivated 25 February 1946 at Pampanga, Philippine Islands. Allotted to the Regular Army 19 November 1952. Activated 20 March 1953 at Chicago, Illinois. Redesignated 24 July 1953 as the 734th Antiaircraft Artillery Battalion (Gun). Inactivated 15 June 1957 at Chicago.

CAMPAIGN STREAMERS
World War II
Luzon

DECORATIONS
Philippine Presidential Unit Citation, Streamer embroidered *17 OCTOBER 1944 TO 4 JULY 1945* (734th AAA AW Gun Bn cited; DAGO 47, 1950)

COAT OF ARMS
SHIELD: Per chevron reversed or and gules, on the first a sea lion holding in dexter paw a sword and on the second two 120mm guns issuant from base saltirewise, all counterchanged.

CREST: None

MOTTO: *Pax per Tormenta* (Peace Through Artillery)

The colors scarlet and yellow are used for Artillery. The guns symbolize the heavy protective fire power of the battalion's antiaircraft artillery. The sea lion, from the coat of arms of Manila, represents service in the Philippine Islands during World War II.

DISTINCTIVE INSIGNIA
The insignia is the shield and motto of the coat of arms. The sample of the insignia depicted was approved for wear on 10 February 1954.

736th ANTIAIRCRAFT ARTILLERY BATTALION

Constituted 4 May 1921 in the Delaware National Guard as 1st Battalion, 198th Artillery (Antiaircraft), Coast Artillery Corps, and organized from new or former elements of the 1st Delaware Infantry as follows:

Headquarters, 1st Battalion organized new and Federally recognized 15 July 1921 at Wilmington

Company L, 59th Pioneer Infantry (organized and Federally recognized 22 June 1917 at Wilmington as Company L, 1st Delaware Infantry and mustered into Federal service 25 July 1917 at Wilmington; redesignated 17 January 1918 as Company L, 59th Pioneer Infantry and demobilized 8 July 1919 at Camp Dix, New Jersey), reorganized and Federally recognized 15 July 1921 at Wilmington as Headquarters Detachment and Combat Train, 1st Battalion

3d Company (Antiaircraft Artillery), Delaware Coast Artillery Corps (organized prior to 1903 as Company D, 1st Delaware Infantry; mustered into Federal service 8 July 1916 for duty on the Mexican border and mustered out 15 February 1917; mustered into Federal service at Wilmington 25 July 1917; redesignated 17 January 1918 as Company F, 59th Pioneer Infantry;ldemobilized 7 August 1919 at Camp Dix, New Jersey; reorganized and Federally recognized 17 February 1921 as 3d Company [Antiaircraft Artillery], Delaware Coast Artillery Corps), redesignated Battery A

2d Company (Antiaircraft Artillery), Delaware Coast Artillery Corps (organized prior to 1903 at Wilmington as Company F, 1st Delaware Infantry; mustered into Federal service 8 July 1916 for duty on the Mexican border, mustered out 15 February 1917 and reverted to State control; mustered into Federal service at Wilmington 25 July 1917; redesignated 17 January 1918 as Company G, 59th Pioneer Infantry; demobilized 8 July 1919 at Camp Dix, New Jersey; reorganized and Federally recognized 26 January 1921 at Wilmington as 2d Company [Antiaircraft Artillery], Delaware Coast Artillery Corps), redesignated Battery B

5th Company (Antiaircraft Artillery), Delaware Coast Artillery Corps (organized prior to 1903 as Company C, 1st Delaware Infantry; mustered into Federal service 8 July 1916 for duty on the Mexican border and mustered out 15 February 1917; mustered into Federal service 25 July 1917 at Wilmington; redesignated 17 January 1918 as Company C, 59th Pioneer Infantry; demobilized 7 August 1919 at Camp Upton, New York; reorganized and Federally recognized 11 April 1921 at Wilmington as 5th Company [Antiaircraft Artillery], Delaware Coast Artillery Corps), redesignated Battery C

1st Company (Antiaircraft Artillery), Delaware Coast Artillery Corps (organized prior to 1903 as Company A, 1st Delaware Infantry; mustered into Federal service 8 July 1916 for duty on the Mexican border and mustered out 15 February 1917; mustered into Federal service 25 July 1917 at Wilmington; redesignated 17 January 1918 as Company H, 59th Pioneer Infantry; demobilized 8 July 1919 at Camp Dix, New Jersey; reorganized and Federally recognized 26 January 1921 at Wilmington as 1st Company [Antiaircraft Artillery], Delaware Coast Artillery Corps), redesignated Battery D

Redesignated 16 August 1924 as 1st Battalion, 198th Coast Artillery (Antiaircraft). Inducted into Federal service 16 September 1940 at Wilmington. (Departed Charleston Port of Embarkation 27 January 1942 for overseas service and arrived on Bora Bora 17 February 1942. Following service at Efate, New Hebrides and on Guadalcanal moved to the Treasury Islands on 6 November 1943). Redesignated 1 March 1944 as the 736th Antiaircraft Artillery Gun Battalion. (Relocated to New Guinea on 9 February 1945 and moved to the Philippine Islands on 15 July 1945. Returned from overseas service and arrived at the San Francisco Port of Embarkation on 31 December 1945). Inactivated 2 January 1946 at Camp Stoneman, California. Reorganized and Federally recognized 16 October 1946 with Headquarters at Wilmington and elements at Newark, New Castle and Wilmington. Ordered into active Federal service 14 August 1950 at home stations. Released from active Federal service 28 August 1952 and resumed State status. Redesignated 1 October 1953 as 736th Antiaircraft Artillery Battalion (90mm Gun). (Headquarters relocated to New castle 20 January 1958).

Reorganized and consolidated 1 April 1959 with the 198th Artillery, a parent regiment under the Combat Arms Regimental System.

CAMPAIGN STREAMERS
World War I
Meuse-Argonne

World War II
Northern Solomons (with arrowhead)

DECORATIONS
None

COAT OF ARMS
SHIELD: Argent, a fleur-de-lis gules; on a chief azure eleven mullets, five and six or.

CREST: That for the regiments and separate battalions of the Delaware Army National Guard: On a wreath of the colors (argent and gules) a griffin's head erased gules, eared and beaked or, langued gules, collared sable, fimbriated argent and thereon three plates.

MOTTO: First Regiment Of First State

The shield is white, the old Infantry color, and red, the color for Artillery. The eleven mullets represent the eleven battles and campaigns in which the organization served during the Civil War while the red fleur-de-lis is for service in France during World War I.

DISTINCTIVE INSIGNIA
The insignia is the shield and motto of the coat of arms. The sample of the insignia depicted was originally approved on 12 July 1934 for wear by the 198th Coast Artillery.

737th ANTIAIRCRAFT ARTILLERY MISSILE BATTALION

Constituted 21 May 1942 in the Army of the United States as 1st Battalion, 608th Coast Artillery (Antiaircraft) and activated 15 November 1942 at Fort Bliss, Texas. Reorganized 20 January 1943 at Fort Bliss and redesignated 737th Coast Artillery Battalion (Antiaircraft) (Gun) (Semimobile) (Separate). (Departed San Francisco Port of Embarkation 16 August 1943 for overseas service and arrived on New Caledonia on 4 September 1943). Redesignated 1 November 1943 as 737th Antiaircraft Artillery Gun Battalion (Semimobile). (After service on Guadalcanal, Tulagi and Emirau Island and in the Philippines, returned to San Francisco Port of Embarkation on 20 January 1946). Inactivated 22 January 1946 at Camp Stoneman, California. Allotted to the Regular Army on 19 November 1952. Activated 15 March 1953 at New York, New York. Redesignated 3 August 1953 as the 737th Antiaircraft Artillery Battalion (Gun). Reorganized and redesignated 2 March 1956 as the 737th Antiaircraft Artillery Missile Battalion. Inactivated 1 September 1958 at Camp Shanks, New York.

CAMPAIGN STREAMERS
World War II
Bismarck Archipelago
Luzon

DECORATIONS
Philippine Presidential Unit Citation, Streamer embroidered *17 OCTOBER 1944 TO 4 JULY 1945* (737th AAA Gun Bn cited; DAGO 47, 1950)

COAT OF ARMS
SHIELD: Per chevron gules and or, in base a mullet of seven points azure charged with a Philippine sun of the second

CREST: None

MOTTO: *Patriae Vigil* (Sentinel Of Country)

Red and yellow are used for Artillery organizations. The seven pointed star, suggested by the Australian flag is for combat service in the Bismarck Archipelago, an Australian mandate. The sun, taken from the Philippine flag represents combat service on Luzon during World War II.

DISTINCTIVE INSIGNIA
The insignia is the shield and motto of the coat of arms. The sample of the insignia depicted was approved for wear on 13 October 1954.

738th ANTIAIRCRAFT ARTILLERY MISSILE BATTALION

Constituted 21 May 1942 in the Army of the United States as 1st Battalion, 609th Coast Artillery (Antiaircraft) and activated 10 December 1942 at Camp Edwards, Massachusetts. Reorganized at Camp Edwards and 1st Battalion redesignated 20 January 1943 as 738th Coast Artillery Battalion (Antiaircraft) (Gun) (Separate). Redesignated 7 June 1943 as 738th Antiaircraft Artillery Gun Battalion (Semimobile). (Departed San Francisco Port of Embarkation 6 January 1944 for overseas service; arrived in Hawaii on 15 January 1944 and moved to Saipan on 1 September 1944). Inactivated 25 February 1946 on Saipan. Allotted to the Regular Army on 19 November 1952. Activated 1 March 1953 at Philadelphia, Pennsylvania. Redesignated 20 July 1953 as 738th Antiaircraft Artillery Battalion (Gun). Reorganized and redesignated 9 July 1954 as the 738th Antiaircraft Artillery Missile Battalion. Inactivated 1 September 1958 at Lumberton, New Jersey.

CAMPAIGN STREAMERS
World War II
Western Pacific

DECORATIONS
None

COAT OF ARMS

SHIELD: Or, three dragons' heads erased, conjoined in one neck, the faces looking to the chief, dexter, and sinister sides gules, incensed proper, the uppermost head affixed by a wreath of laurel of the third.

CREST: None

MOTTO: Try To Pass

The scarlet is the color for Artillery. The functions of the battalion are allegorically represented by the fabulous dragons' heads, alert in all directions, breathing fire and thus indicating their readiness to oppose all encroachments. The laurel has been added for design and represents the wreaths anciently bestowed upon victors. The motto, "Try To Pass", expresses a challenge to all.

DISTINCTIVE INSIGNIA

The insignia is the shield and motto of the coat of arms. The sample of the insignia depicted was approved for wear on 13 October 1953.

739th ANTIAIRCRAFT ARTILLERY MISSILE BATTALION

 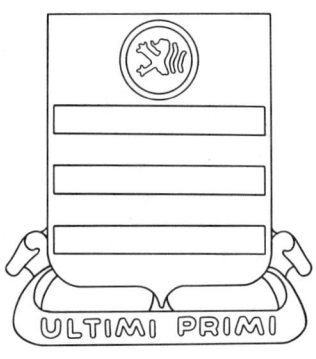

Constituted 21 May 1942 in the Army of the United States as 1st Battalion, 610th Coast Artillery (Antiaircraft) and activated 10 December 1942 at Camp Davis, North Carolina. Reorganized at Camp Davis and redesignated 20 January 1943 as 739th Coast Artillery Battalion (Antiaircraft) (Gun) (Separate). Redesignated 7 June 1943 as the 739th Antiaircraft Artillery Gun Battalion (Semimobile). (Departed San Francisco Port of Embarkation 18 September 1943 for overseas service and arrived in the Fiji Islands 2 October 1943. Moved to New Guinea on 1 December 1944 and relocated to the Philippine Islands on 12 March 1945). Inactivated 11 February 1946 on Mindanao, Philippine Islands. Allotted to the Regular Army on 19 November 1952. Activated 1 April 1953 in Korea; inactivated 20 December 1954 in Korea. Redesignated 16 November 1955 as the 739th Antiaircraft Artillery Missile Battalion. Activated 2 January 1956 at Fort Banks, Massachusetts; inactivated 1 September 1958 at Bristol, Rhode Island.

CAMPAIGN STREAMERS

World War II
Luzon
Southern Philippines

Korean War
Third Korean Winter
Korea, Summer 1953

DECORATIONS

Philippine Presidential Unit Citation, Streamer embroidered *17 OCTOBER 1944 TO 4 JULY 1945* (739th AAA Gun Bn cited; DAGO 47, 1950)

Republic of Korea Presidential Unit Citation, Streamer embroidered *KOREA* (739th AAA Gun Bn cited for period 1 Apr 1953-1 May 1954; DAGO 51, 1957)

COAT OF ARMS

SHIELD: Barry of six gules and or, in chief of the last a lion rampant naissant double queued of the first within an annulet azure.

CREST: None

MOTTO: *Ultimi Primi* (The Last Shall Be First)

In the scarlet of the Coast Artillery Corps the protective duties of the organization are indicated by the demi lion, the king of beasts, heraldically being the lively image of a good soldier who must be valiant of courage, strong of body and a foe to fear. The annulet represents the ring hung from a crossbeam at medieval tournaments or jousts which had to be carried off on the tip of the participant's lance as he rode by at full tilt. The chief division of the shield signifies honor and authority and anciently was granted for successful performance in war.

DISTINCTIVE INSIGNIA

The insignia is the shield and motto of the coat of arms. The sample of the insignia depicted was approved for wear on 6 January 1954.

740th ANTIAIRCRAFT ARTILLERY MISSILE BATTALION

 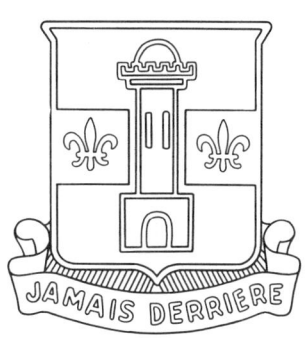

Constituted 21 May 1942 in the Army of the United States as 1st Battalion, 611th Coast Artillery (Antiaircraft) and activated 10 December 1942 at Fort Bliss, Texas. Reorganized 20 January 1943 at Fort Bliss and redesignated as 740th Coast Artillery Battalion (Antiaircraft) (Gun) (Separate). Redesignated 7 June 1943 as the 740th Antiaircraft Artillery Gun Battalion (Semimobile). (Departed New York Port of Embarkation 11 February 1944 for overseas service; arrived in England on 23 February 1944 and landed in France on 16 July 1944). Inactivated 9 July 1946 in France. Allotted to the Regular Army on 19 November 1952. Activated 14 April 1953 at the Presidio of San Francisco, California. Redesignated 20 July 1953 as the 740th Antiaircraft Artillery Battalion (Gun). Reorganized and redesignated 9 July 1954 as the 740th Antiaircraft Artillery Missile Battalion. Inactivated 1 September 1958 at San Francisco, California.

CAMPAIGN STREAMERS

World War II
England 1944
Normandy
Northern France

DECORATIONS
Belgian Fourragere 1940 (740th AAA Gun Bn cited; DAGO 43, 1950)

Cited in the Order of the Day of the Belgian Army for action in defense of ANTWERP (740th AAA Gun Bn cited for period 25 Oct-28 Nov 1944; DAGO 43, 1950)

Cited in the Order of the Day of the Belgian Army for action in defense of ANTWERP HARBOR (740th AAA Gun Bn cited for action on 16 Dec 1944; DAGO 43, 1950)

COAT OF ARMS
SHIELD: Gules, on a fess or two fleurs-de-lis sable, in pale overall a tower argent, fimbriated of the first, door and windows of the third.

CREST: None

MOTTO: *Jamais Derriere* (Never Behind)

The colors red and yellow are used for Artillery. The yellow fess and black fleurs-de-lis represents the World War II campaigns of the organization. The white tower, taken from the castle which appears on the arms of Antwerp, symbolizes the defense of that city for which the battalion was cited and decorated.

DISTINCTIVE INSIGNIA
The insignia is the shield and motto of the coat of arms. The sample of the insignia depicted was approved for wear on 12 July 1954.

741st ANTIAIRCRAFT ARTILLERY MISSILE BATTALION

Constituted 21 May 1942 in the Army of the United States as 1st Battalion, 612th Coast Artillery (Antiaircraft) (Colored) and activated 1 September 1942 at Camp Stewart, Georgia. Reorganized at Camp Stewart on 20 January 1943 and redesignated as 741st Coast Artillery Battalion (Antiaircraft) (Gun) (Separate) (Colored). Redesignated 8 June 1943 as 741st Antiaircraft Artillery Gun Battalion (Semimobile) (Colored). (Departed San Francisco Port of Embarkation 7 September 1943 for overseas service; arrived in Australia 1 October 1943 and moved to New Guinea on 14 October 1943). Inactivated 30 January 1945 at Milne Bay, New Guinea. Redesignated 741st Antiaircraft Artillery Missile Battalion and allotted to the Regular Army on 12 December 1956. Activated 1 January 1957 at Fort Hancock, New Jersey. Inactivated 1 September 1958 at Fairfield, Connecticut.

CAMPAIGN STREAMERS
World War II
New Guinea

DECORATIONS
None

COAT OF ARMS
SHIELD: Per chevron reversed gules and sable a pile or charged with a stylized flying fox-bat of the second, garnished of the third.

CREST: None

MOTTO: *Animis Opibusque Parati* (Ready In Soul And Resource)

The colors yellow and scarlet are for Artillery. The flying fox, a large marauding bat indigenous to New Guinea, is used with the inverted triangle to symbolize marauding aircraft caught by a searchlight beam. It thus represents both the wartime function and the New Guinea campaign of the unit.

DISTINCTIVE INSIGNIA
The insignia is the shield and motto of the coat of arms. The sample of the insignia depicted was approved for wear on 31 March 1958.

742d ANTIAIRCRAFT ARTILLERY GUN BATTALION

Constituted 21 May 1942 in the Army of the United States as 1st Battalion, 613th Coast Artillery (Antiaircraft) (Colored) and activated 10 December 1942 at Camp Stewart, Georgia. Reorganized at Camp Stewart on 20 January 1943 and redesignated 742d Coast Artillery Battalion (Antiaircraft) (Gun) (Separate) (Colored). Redesignated 7 June 1943 as the 742d Antiaircraft Artillery Gun Battalion (Semimobile) (Colored). (Departed San Francisco Port of Embarkation 29 September 1943 for overseas service; arrived on Espiritu Santo 16 October 1943 and moved to New Britain on 20 May 1944. After service in New Guinea moved to the Philippines on 11 August 1945). Inactivated 11 February 1946 at Subic Bay, Luzon, Philippine Islands.

CAMPAIGN STREAMERS
World War II
Bismarck Archipelago

DECORATIONS
None

COAT OF ARMS
None

DISTINCTIVE INSIGNIA
None

743d ANTIAIRCRAFT ARTILLERY GUN BATTALION

Constituted 13 January 1941 in the Regular Army as 1st Battalion, 94th Coast Artillery (Antiaircraft) (Semimobile) and activated 17 April 1941 at Camp Davis, North Carolina. (Departed New York Port of Embarkation 18 February 1942 for overseas service and arrived in Australia on 28 March 1942; Battery D sent to New Guinea upon arrival but subsequently rejoined Battalion in Australia). Reorganized in Australia and redesignated 15 May 1943 as the 743d Coast Artillery Battalion (Antiaircraft). (Following service on Kiriwina Island and Goodenough Island, landed at Tanahmerah Bay, New Guinea on 2 January 1944). Redesignated 15 June 1944 as the 743d Antiaircraft Artillery Gun Battalion. (Moved to the Philippine Islands on 14 July 1945). Inactivated 30 May 1947 at San Fernando, Luzon, Philippine Islands.

Redesignated 13 October 1948 as the 36th Antiaircraft Artillery Gun Battalion.

CAMPAIGN STREAMERS
World War II
East Indies
New Guinea (with arrowhead)

DECORATIONS
Presidential Unit Citation (Army), Streamer embroidered *PAPUA* (Btry D 94th CA cited for period 23 Jul 1942-23 Jan 1943; WDGO 21, 1943)

COAT OF ARMS
None

DISTINCTIVE INSIGNIA
None

744th ANTIAIRCRAFT ARTILLERY BATTALION

Constituted in the New Hampshire National Guard as 1st Battalion, 197th Artillery (Antiaircraft), Coast Artillery Corps and organized from new and existing units as follows:

Headquarters, 1st Battalion organized new and Federally recognized 9 June 1922 at Laconia

Headquarters Detachment and Combat Train, 1st Battalion organized new and Federally recognized 9 June 1922 at Charlestown

Company E, First Army Headquarters Regiment (organized 14 April 1891 at Concord as Company E 3d Infantry, New Hampshire National Guard; mustered into Federal service during May 1898 as Company E 1st New Hampshire Volunteer Infantry; mustered out 1 November 1898 and resumed State status; redesignated 20 January 1900 as Company E 2d

Infantry, New Hampshire National Guard; redesignated 27 April 1909 as Company E 1st Infantry, New Hampshire National Guard; mustered into Federal service 10 July 1916 for Mexican border; mustered out 20 February 1917 and resumed State status; called into Federal service 25 July 1917 at Concord and drafted into Federal service on 5 August 1917; redesignated 11 February 1918 as Company E, First Army Headquarters Regiment and demobilized at Camp Devens, Massachusetts during June 1919), reorganized and Federally recognized 22 December 1921 at Concord as Battery A

8th Company, Coast Defense of Portsmouth (organized 22 July 1817 at Dover as 1st Company of Light Infantry and assigned to the 25th Regiment, New Hampshire State Militia; chartered 27 June 1835 as *Strafford Guards*; mustered into Federal service at Concord during May 1861 as Company A 1st New Hampshire Volunteer Infantry; mustered out 9 August 1861 and resumed State status; redesignated Company A 1st Infantry, New Hampshire National Guard in 1878; mustered into Federal service during May 1898 as Company F 1st New Hampshire Volunteer Infantry; mustered out 1 November 1898 and resumed State status; redesignated 1 January 1900 as Company A 2d Infantry, New Hampshire National Guard; redesignated 27 April 1909 as 4th Company, Coast Artillery Corps, New Hampshire National Guard; called into Federal service 25 July 1917 at Dover and drafted into Federal service on 5 August 1917; redesignated 6 August 1917 as 7th Company, Fort Constitution [New Hampshire]; redesignated 29 August 1917 as 8th Company, Coast Defense of Portsmouth and demobilized at Fort Constitution during December 1918), reorganized and Federally recognized 17 March 1922 as Battery B

6th Company, Coast Defense of Portsmouth (organized 15 April 1861 at Laconia as *Laconia Volunteers* and mustered into Federal service 21 May 1861 at Portsmouth as Company F 2d New Hampshire Volunteer Infantry; redesignated 21 June 1864 as Company F, 2d New Hampshire Volunteer Veteran Infantry; mustered out 19 December 1865 and returned to State control; reorganized 17 September 1866 at Laconia as Company G 2d Infantry, New Hampshire Volunteer State Militia; redesignated 16 October 1886 as Company K 3d Infantry, New Hampshire National Guard; mustered into Federal service during May 1898 as Company K 1st New Hampshire Volunteer Infantry; mustered out 1 November 1898 and resumed State status; redesignated 20 January 1900 as Company K 2d Infantry, New Hampshire National Guard; redesignated 27 April 1909 as 2d Company, Coast Artillery Corps, New Hampshire National Guard; called into Federal service 25 July 1917 and drafted into Federal service on 5 August 1917; redesignated 6 August 1917 as 5th Company, Fort Constitution; redesignated 29 August 1917 as 6th Company, Coast Defense of Portsmouth and demobilized at Fort Constitution in December 1918), reorganized and Federally recognized 30 March 1922 at Laconia as Battery C

1st Company, Coast Artillery Corps, New Hampshire National Guard (organized 20 May 1861 at Portsmouth as *Goodwin Guards* and mustered into Federal service 21 May 1861 at Portsmouth as Company A 2d New Hampshire Volunteer Infantry; redesignated 21 June 1864 as Company A 2d New Hampshire Volunteer Veteran Infantry; mustered out 19 December 1865 and returned to State control; reorganized 21 February 1866 at Portsmouth as Company A 3d Infantry, New Hampshire Volunteer State Militia; mustered into Federal service during May 1898 as Company A 1st New Hampshire Volunteer Infantry; mustered out 1 November 1898 and resumed State status; redesignated 1 January 1900 as Company B 2d Infantry, New Hampshire National Guard; redesignated 27 April 1909 as 1st Company, Coast Artillery Corps, New Hampshire National Guard; called into Federal service 25 July 1917 and drafted into Federal service on 5 August 1917; redesignated 6 August 1917 as 4th Company, Fort Constitution; redesignated 29 August 1917 as 9th Company, Coast Defense of Portsmouth; demobilized at Fort Constitution during December 1918 and reconstituted 2 September 1920 as 1st Company, Coast Artillery Corps, New Hampshire National Guard), reorganized and Federally recognized 16 February 1922 at Portsmouth as Battery D

Redesignated 23 April 1924 as 1st Battalion, 197th Coast Artillery (Antiaircraft). Inducted into Federal service 16 September 1940 at home stations. (Departed San Francisco Port of Embarkation 18 February 1942 for overseas service and arrived in Australia on 22 March 1942). Redesignated 15 May 1943 as 744th Coast Artillery Battalion (Antiaircraft) (Gun). Redesignated 15 June 1944 as 744th Antiaircraft Artillery Gun Battalion (Mobile). (After service in New Guinea and on Morotai Island, returned from overseas service and arrived at the San Francisco Port of Embarkation on 26 December 1945). Inactivated 29 December 1945 at Camp Stoneman,

California. Reorganized and Federally recognized 4 April 1947 with Headquarters at Laconia and batteries at Concord, Franklin, Laconia and Rochester. Redesignated 1 October 1953 as the 744th Antiaircraft Artillery Battalion (90mm Gun).

Consolidated 1 February 1959 with the 197th Artillery, a parent regiment under the Combat Arms Regimental System.

CAMPAIGN STREAMERS
Civil War
Bull Run
Peninsula
Manassas
Fredericksburg
Gettysburg
Cold Harbor
Petersburg
Appomattox
Virginia 1864

World War II
East Indies
New Guinea (with arrowhead)

DECORATIONS
None

COAT OF ARMS
SHIELD: Azure, in base a lion passant guardant or, and in fess a lozenge and a fleur-de-lis argent; on a chief gules, fimbriated of the second a winged projectile, wings inverted of the last.

CREST: That for the regiments and separate battalions of the New Hampshire Army National Guard: On a wreath of the colors (or and azure) two pine branches saltirewise proper crossed behind a bundle of five arrows palewise argent, bound together by a ribbon gules, the ends entwining the branches.

MOTTO: *A bas l'Avion* (Down With The Plane)

The shield is blue and refers to early service as infantry. The chief is red for Artillery while the white lozenge represents Civil War service.

DISTINCTIVE INSIGNIA
The insignia is the shield and motto of the coat of arms. The sample of the insignia depicted was originally approved 11 October 1927 for wear by the 197th Coast Artillery.

745th ANTIAIRCRAFT ARTILLERY BATTALION

Constituted 16 May 1940 in the Connecticut National Guard as 1st Battalion 208th Coast Artillery (Antiaircraft) and organized from new and existing units as follows:

Headquarters, 1st Battalion organized new and Federally recognized 13 November 1940 at Wethersfield

Headquarters Battery and Combat Train, 1st Battalion organized new and Federally recognized 26 September 1940 at West Hartford

Troop B 21st Reconnaissance Squadron (organized and Federally recognized 1 February 1926 at Hartford as 118th Veterinary Company, 118th Medical Regiment; redesignated 1 January 1937 as Veterinary Company, 118th Medical Regiment; and redesignated 1 May 1939 as Troop B, 21st Reconnaissance Squadron), redesignated Battery A

Troop B 110th Cavalry (chartered 19 May 1788 at Hartford as *Governor's Independent Troop of Horse Guards* and redesignated 1st Company of Governor's Horse Guards in May 1854; redesignated 6 March 1911 as Troop B, Cavalry, Connecticut National Guard; redesignated 17 June 1915 as Troop B 5th Militia Cavalry, Connecticut National Guard; mustered into Federal service 20 June 1916 for duty on the Mexican border; mustered out 28 October 1916 and resumed State status; redesignated 3 May 1917 as Troop B 1st Separate Squadron of Cavalry, Connecticut National Guard; redesignated 19 May 1917 as Troop B 3d Separate Squadron of Cavalry, Connecticut National Guard; mustered into Federal service 25 July 1917 at Hartford; redesignated 22 August 1917 as Company B 101st Machine Gun Battalion and assigned to the 26th Division; demobilized 29 April 1919 at Camp Devens, Massachusetts; reorganized and Federally recognized 25 March 1920 as Troop B, Connecticut Cavalry; redesignated 12 December 1923 as Troop B 1st Separate Squadron of Cavalry, Connecticut National Guard; redesignated 3 May 1929 as Troop B 122d Cavalry; relocated to West Hartford on 6 February 1931 and redesignated 10 June 1937 as Troop B 110th Cavalry), redesignated Battery B

Troop A 110th Cavalry (organized and Federally recognized 2 May 1917 at Hartford as Troop C 1st Separate Squadron of Cavalry, Connecticut National Guard; redesignated 19 May 1917 as Troop L 3d Squadron of Cavalry, Connecticut National Guard; mustered into Federal service 25 July 1917 at Hartford and drafted into Federal service 5 August 1917; redesignated 22 August 1917 as Company C 101st Machine Gun Battalion and assigned to the 26th Division; demobilized 29 April 1919 at Camp Devens, Massachusetts; reorganized and Federally recognized 9 March 1923 as Troop C 1st Separate Squadron of Cavalry, Connecticut National Guard; redesignated 3 May 1929 as Troop A 122d Cavalry; relocated to West Hartford on 6 February 1931 and redesignated 10 June 1937 as Troop A 110th Cavalry), redesignated Battery C

Machine Gun Troop, 110th Cavalry (chartered at New Haven as Second Company of the Governor's Horse Guards in October 1808; dissolved at New Haven in 1847 but reorganized at New Haven on 8 May 1861; redesignated 5 July 1901 as Troop A, Cavalry, Connecticut National Guard; redesignated 17 June 1915 as Troop A 5th Militia Cavalry, Connecticut National Guard; mustered into Federal service at New Haven 20 June 1916 for Mexican border duty; mustered out 4 November 1916 and resumed State status; redesignated 3 May 1917 as Troop A 1st Separate Squadron of Cavalry, Connecticut National Guard; redesignated 19 May 1917 as Troop A 3d Separate Squadron of Cavalry, Connecticut National Guard; mustered into Federal service 25 July 1917 at New Haven and drafted into Federal service 5 August 1917; redesignated 22 August 1917 as Company A 101st Machine Gun Battalion and assigned to the 26th Division; redesignated 18 January 1918 as Company D 102d Machine Gun Battalion; demobilized 29 April 1919 at Camp Devens, Massachusetts; reorganized and Federally recognized 19 April 1920 at New Haven as Troop A, Connecticut Cavalry; redesignated 12 December 1923 as Troop A 1st Separate Squadron of Cavalry, Connecticut National Guard; redesignated 3 May 1929 as Headquarters Troop 122d Cavalry; redesignated 14 December 1936 as Machine Gun Troop 122d Cavalry; and redesignated 10 June 1937 as Machine Gun Troop 110th Cavalry), redesignated Battery D

Inducted into Federal service at home stations. Reorganized and redesignated 15 June 1943 as 745th Separate Coast Artillery Battalion (Antiaircraft) (Gun). Redesignated 15 June 1944 as 745th Antiaircraft Artillery Gun Battalion. Inactivated 7 January 1946 at Camp Stoneman, California. Reorganized and Federally recognized 16 September 1947 with Headquarters at Norwich and batteries at Norwich, West Hartford, New London and New Haven. Ordered into active Federal service 14 August 1950 at home stations. Released from active Federal service 13 April 1952 and resumed State status. Redesignated 1 October 1953 as the 745th Antiaircraft Artillery Battalion (90mm Gun).

Battalion broken up 1 May 1959 and elements converted and/or redesignated as follows: Headquarters and Headquarters Battery at Norwich redesignated Company B 162d Transportation Battalion; Battery A at Norwich redesignated Battery C 2d Gun Battalion 192d Artillery; Battery B at New Haven redesignated Battery D 3d Gun Battalion 242d Artillery; Battery C at Groton redesignated Company A 162d Transportation Battalion; and Battery D at West Hartford redesignated Headquarters and Headquarters Battery 1st Missile Battalion

192d Artillery.

CAMPAIGN STREAMERS
World War I
Champagne-Marne
Aisne-Marne
St. Mihiel
Meuse-Argonne
Ile de France 1918
Lorraine 1918

World War II
Papua
East Indies
New Guinea (with arrowhead)
Luzon

DECORATIONS
Presidential Unit Citation (Army), Streamer embroidered *PAPUA* (208th CA cited for period 23 Jul 1942-23 Jan 1943; WDGO 21, 1943)

Philippine Presidential Unit Citation, Streamer embroidered *17 OCTOBER 1944 TO 4 JULY 1945* (745th AAA Gun Bn cited; DAGO 47, 1950)

COAT OF ARMS
None

DISTINCTIVE INSIGNIA
None

746th ANTIAIRCRAFT ARTILLERY GUN BATTALION

Constituted 1 November 1924 in the California National Guard as 1st Battalion, 251st Coast Artillery (Harbor Defense) and organized from new and existing units as follows:

Headquarters organized new and Federally recognized 7 November 1924 at San Diego

Battery E 250th Artillery, Coast Artillery Corps (organized 12 October 1881 at San Diego as *San Diego City Guard* and redesignated 22 July 1885 as Company B, 7th Separate Battalion, Infantry, California National Guard; redesignated 5 May 1888 as Company B 7th Infantry, California National Guard; redesignated 8 February 1890 as Company B 9th Infantry; redesignated 7 December 1895 as Company B, 7th Infantry; mustered into Federal service 9 May 1898 at the Presidio of San Francisco as Company B 7th California Volunteer Infantry; mustered out 2 December 1898 at Los Angeles and resumed State status; redesignated 29 June 1909 as 5th Company, 1st Coast Defense Command, Coast Artillery Corps; called into Federal service 12 April 1917 and drafted into Federal service on 5 August 1917; redesignated 31 August 1917 as 5th Company, Coast Defenses of San Diego; redesignated 15 January 1918 as Company B 2d Antiaircraft Battalion; demobilized 15 January 1919 at Camp Dix, New Jersey; reorganized and Federally recognized 15 March 1921 at San Diego as 5th Company, Coast Artillery Corps, California National Guard; redesignated 9 January 1922 as 463d Company, 1st Coast Defense Command, Coast Artillery Corps; and redesignated 6 October 1923 as Battery E 250th Artillery, Coast Artillery Corps), redesignated Battery A

Battery F 250th Artillery, Coast Artillery Corps (organized 16 May 1911 at San Diego as 8th Company, 1st Coast Defense Command, Coast Artillery; mustered into Federal service 12 April 1917 at San Diego and drafted into Federal service 5 August 1917; redesignated 31 August 1917 as 6th Company, Coast Defenses of San Diego; redesignated 1 January 1918 as Battery B, 65th Artillery, Coast Artillery Corps; demobilized 28 February 1919 at Camp Lewis, Washington; reorganized and Federally recognized 15 March 1921 as 6th Company, Coast Artillery Corps, California National Guard; redesignated 9 January 1922 as 464th Company,

1st Coast Defense Command, Coast Artillery Corps; and redesignated 9 January 1922 as Battery F 250th Artillery, Coast Artillery Corps), redesignated as Battery B

Battery H 250th Artillery, Coast Artillery Corps (organized and Federally recognized 11 May 1921 at San Diego as 8th Company, Coast Artillery Corps, California National Guard; redesignated 9 January 1922 as 466th Company, 1st Coast Defense Command, Coast Artillery Corps and redesignated 6 October 1923 as Battery H 250th Artillery, Coast Artillery Corps) redesignated Battery C (subsequently redesignated Battery A on 1 January 1930 when former Battery A was redesignated Headquarters Detachment and Combat Train, 1st Battalion; new Battery C organized and Federally recognized 13 April 1936 at San Diego)

Battery D organized new and Federally recognized 4 October 1937 at San Diego

Reorganized and redesignated 1 January 1930 as 1st Battalion, 251st Coast Artillery (Antiaircraft). Inducted into Federal service 16 September 1940 at San Diego. (Departed Los Angeles Port of Embarkation 17 November 1940 for overseas service and arrived at Fort Shafter, Hawaii on 23 November 1940; subsequently served in the Fiji Islands, on Bougainville and in the Philippine Islands). Reorganized and redesignated 1 March 1944 as the 746th Antiaircraft Artillery Gun Battalion. (Returned from overseas service and arrived at the San Francisco Port of Embarkation on 13 January 1946). Inactivated 15 January 1946 at Camp Stoneman, California.

Broken up 5 August 1946 and elements redesignated or consolidated as follows: Headquarters as Headquarters and Headquarters Battery, 251st Antiaircraft Artillery Group; Headquarters Battery consolidated with Headquarters and Headquarters Battery, 251st Antiaircraft Artillery Group; Battery A as Headquarters and Headquarters Battery, 730th Antiaircraft Artillery Searchlight Battalion; Battery B as Headquarters and Headquarters Battery, 746th Antiaircraft Artillery Gun Battalion; Battery C consolidated with Headquarters and Headquarters Battery, 730th Antiaircraft Artillery Searchlight Battalion; and Battery D consolidated with Headquarters and Headquarters Battery, 746th Antiaircraft Artillery Gun Battalion.

CAMPAIGN STREAMERS
World War I
Meuse-Argonne

World War II
Central Pacific
Northern Solomons
Leyte
Southern Philippines

DECORATIONS
Philippine Presidential Unit Citation, Streamer embroidered *17 OCTOBER 1944 TO 4 JULY 1945* (746th AAA Gun Bn cited; DAGO 47, 1950)

COAT OF ARMS
None

DISTINCTIVE INSIGNIA
None

746th ANTIAIRCRAFT ARTILLERY BATTALION

Constituted in the California National Guard as 8th Company, 1st Coast Defense Command, Coast Artillery Corps and organized 16 May 1911 at San Diego. Mustered into Federal service 12 April 1917 at San Diego and drafted into Federal service on 5 August 1917. Redesignated 31 August 1917 as 6th Company, Coast Defenses of San Diego. Redesignated 1 January 1918 as Battery B 65th Artillery, Coast Artillery Corps. Demobilized 28 February 1919 at Camp Lewis, Washington. Reorganized as 6th Company, Coast Artillery Corps, California National Guard and Federally recognized 15 March 1921 at San Diego. Redesignated 9 January 1922 as 464th Company, 1st Coast Defense Command, Coast Artillery Corps. Redesignated 6 October 1923 as Battery F 250th Artillery, Coast Artillery Corps. Redesignated 1 November 1924 as Battery B 251st Coast Artillery. Inducted into Federal service 16 September 1940 at San Diego. (Departed Los Angeles Port of Embarkation 17 November 1940 for overseas service and arrived at Fort Shafter, Hawaii on 23 November 1940; subsequently served in the Fiji Islands, on Bougainville and in the Philippine Islands). Redesignated 1 March 1944 as Battery B 746th Antiaircraft Artillery Gun Battalion. (Returned from overseas service and arrived at the San Francisco Port of Embarkation on 13 January 1946). Inactivated 15 January 1946 at Camp Stoneman, California. Redesignated 5 August 1946 as Headquarters and Headquarters Battery, 746th Antiaircraft Artillery Gun Battalion; concurrently, remainder of battalion constituted new and allotted to the California National Guard. Reorganized and Federally recognized 24 February 1947 at San Diego. Ordered into active Federal service 14 August 1950 at San Diego. Released from active Federal service 13 June 1952 and resumed State status. Redesignated 1 October 1953 as 746th Antiaircraft Artillery Battalion.

Consolidated 1 May 1959 with the 251st Artillery, a parent regiment under the Combat Arms Regimental System.

CAMPAIGN STREAMERS

World War I
St. Mihiel
Meuse-Argonne
Lorraine 1918

World War II
Central Pacific
Northern Solomons
Leyte
Southern Philippines

DECORATIONS
Philippine Presidential Unit Citation, Streamer embroidered *7 OCTOBER 1944 TO 4 JULY 1945* (746th AAA Gun Bn cited; DAGO 47, 1950)

COAT OF ARMS
SHIELD: Or, six pallets couped gules, a ship of Cabrillo's time argent; on a canton azure a fleur-de-lis encircled by a garland of laurel of the first.

CREST: That for the regiments and separate battalions of the California Army National Guard: On a wreath of the colors (or and gules) the setting sun behind a grizzly bear passant on a grassy field, all proper.

MOTTO: We Aim To Hit

The shield is red for Artillery. The six couped pallets produce a diminished bordure effect on the shield and represent the six batteries comprising the 251st Coast Artillery at the time of its organization in 1924 as a Harbor Defense unit. The ship is representative of the ship of Don Juan Rodriguez Cabrillo, a Portuguese explorer who discovered San Diego Harbor. The charges on the canton, a fleur-de-lis within a garland of laurel, are from the coat of arms of the 250th Coast Artillery and represent the source of many elements of the parent regiment when it was first organized.

DISTINCTIVE INSIGNIA
The insignia is the shield and motto of the coat of arms. The sample of the insignia depicted was originally approved on 16 June 1928 for wear by the 251st Coast Artillery.

747th ANTIAIRCRAFT ARTILLERY AUTOMATIC WEAPONS BATTALION

Organized at Boston in 1874 as First Corps Cadets, Massachusetts Volunteer Militia to consist of four companies, one of which was originally organized 16 October 1741 at Boston as the Independent Corps of Cadets in the Massachusetts Militia. Reorganized and redesignated 22 May 1917 as 1st Battalion, 101st Engineers and assigned to the 26th Division. Demobilized 29 April 1919 at Camp Devens, Massachusetts. Reorganized as 1st Separate Battalion of Infantry, Massachusetts National Guard and Federally recognized 19 July 1921 at Boston. Redesignated 14 March 1922 as the 211th Machine Gun Battalion (Antiaircraft), Coast Artillery Corps. Redesignated 31 March 1923 as 2d Battalion, 211th Artillery (Antiaircraft), Coast Artillery Corps. Redesignated 30 April 1924 as 2d Battalion (Machine Gun), 211th Coast Artillery (Antiaircraft). (Headquarters relocated to Plymouth on 6 May 1940). Inducted into Federal service 16 September 1940 at Boston. Reorganized and redesignated 16 August 1943 as the 747th Antiaircraft Artillery Automatic Weapons Battalion. Inactivated 5 September 1945 at Fort Bliss, Texas.

Consolidated with the 772d Antiaircraft Artillery Gun Battalion and redesignated 8 July 1946 as the 211th Cavalry Reconnaissance Squadron, Mechanized.

CAMPAIGN STREAMERS
World War I
Champagne-Marne
Aisne-Marne
St. Mihiel
Meuse-Argonne
Ile de France 1918
Lorraine 1918

DECORATIONS
None

COAT OF ARMS
None

DISTINCTIVE INSIGNIA
None

747th ANTIAIRCRAFT ARTILLERY BATTALION

Constituted 1 June 1940 in the Massachusetts National Guard as the 4th Battalion, 241st Coast Artillery (Harbor Defense) and organized at Fall River from new and existing units. Inducted into Federal service at Fall River on 16 September 1940. Redesignated 13 September 1943 as 3d Battalion, 8th Coast Artillery. Inactivated 18 April 1944 at Camp Shelby, Mississippi and disbanded 31 May 1944. Reconstituted 25 August 1945 in the Massachusetts National Guard. Redesignated 8 July 1946 as the 747th Antiaircraft Artillery Automatic Weapons Battalion (Semimobile). Reorganized at Fall River and Federally recognized 26 January 1948. Reorganized and redesignated 1 July 1951 as the 747th Antiaircraft Artillery Gun Battalion (90mm). Redesignated 1 October 1953 as the 747th Antiaircraft Artillery Battalion (90mm Gun).

Consolidated 1 May 1959 with the 211th Artillery, a parent regiment under the Combat Arms Regimental System.

CAMPAIGN STREAMERS
None

DECORATIONS
None

COAT OF ARMS
None

DISTINCTIVE INSIGNIA
None

748th ANTIAIRCRAFT ARTILLERY GUN BATTALION

Constituted 10 January 1942 in the Army of the United States as the 25th Separate Coast Artillery Battalion (Harbor Defense) and activated 22 January 1942 in the Harbor Defenses of Sandy Hook, New Jersey. (Departed New York Port of Embarkation 29 April 1942 for overseas service and arrived in Iceland on 10 May 1942). Reorganized and redesignated 28 October 1943 as the 748th Antiaircraft Artillery Gun Battalion. (Returned from overseas service and arrived at the New York Port of Embarkation on 14 June 1945). Disbanded 22 June 1945 at Camp Kilmer,

New Jersey.

CAMPAIGN STREAMERS
World War II
European Theater without inscription

DECORATIONS
None

COAT OF ARMS
SHIELD: Gules, a fess or, in chief a wolf passant proper, in base two barrulets wavy argent.

CREST: None

MOTTO: *Cave Adsum* (Beware, I Am Here)

The shield is red for Artillery while the yellow horizontal band, representing the overseas service of the organization, is the heraldic symbol of military pre-eminence or girdle of honor anciently signifying that the bearer must always be in readiness to undergo the business of public weal. The wolf in the upper portion of the shield represents the enemy staved off by the golden girdle of the organization, the foreign service being indicated by the white wavy bands in base representing the ocean between the station in Iceland and the United States.

DISTINCTIVE INSIGNIA
The insignia is the shield and motto of the coat of arms. The insignia depicted was never made for nor worn by this organization.

749th ANTIAIRCRAFT ARTILLERY BATTALION

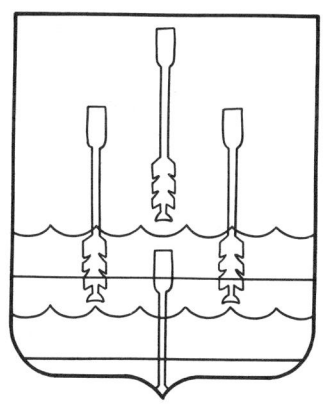
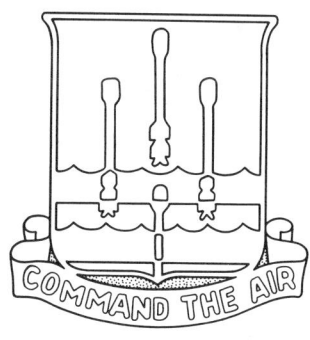

Constituted 10 January 1942 in the Army of the United States as the 26th Separate Coast Artillery Battalion (Harbor Defense) and activated 28 January 1942 at Fort McKinley in the Harbor Defenses of Portland, Maine. (Departed Boston Port of Embarkation 21 August 1942 for overseas service and arrived in Iceland on 31 August 1942). Reorganized and redesignated 28 October 1943 as the 749th Antiaircraft Artillery Gun Battalion. (Moved to England on 1 July 1944 and landed in France on 25 August 1944). Inactivated 25 November 1945 in Germany. Allotted to the Regular Army on 19 November 1952. Activated 1 April 1953 at New York, New York. Redesignated 3 August 1953 as the 749th Antiaircraft Artillery Battalion (Gun). Inactivated 20 December 1957 at New York.

CAMPAIGN STREAMERS
World War II
Northern France
Rhineland
Central Europe
Ground Combat-Europe

DECORATIONS
None

COAT OF ARMS
SHIELD: Gules, a bar gemel in base engrailed to chief or, overall issuant from base a flight of four bird bolts counterchanged.

CREST: None

MOTTO: Command The Air

Red and yellow are for Artillery. The indented bars symbolize the ocean and the historic Harbor Defense service of the unit. The bird bolts indicate both the antiaircraft mission of the battalion and its four campaigns in Europe during World War II.

DISTINCTIVE INSIGNIA
The insignia is the shield and motto of the coat of arms. The sample of the insignia depicted was approved for wear on 12 July 1954.

750th ANTIAIRCRAFT ARTILLERY GUN BATTALION

Constituted 15 January 1918 in the Regular Army as 2d Battalion, 64th Regiment, Coast Artillery Corps and organized 17 May 1918 at Pensacola, Florida. Demobilized 2 April 1919 at Camp Eustis, Virginia. Reconstituted 2 May 1921 in the Regular Army as 2d Battalion, Hawaiian Antiaircraft Regiment and activated 3 June 1921 at Fort Ruger, Hawaii. Redesignated 2 June 1922 as 2d Battalion, 64th Artillery (Antiaircraft). Redesignated 20 February 1924 as 2d Battalion, 64th Coast Artillery (Antiaircraft) (Semimobile). Reorganized and redesignated 12 December 1943 as the 750th Antiaircraft Artillery Gun Battalion (Semimobile). Inactivated 10 December 1946 at Fort Shafter, Hawaii.

Redesignated 28 June 1950 as the 83d Antiaircraft Artillery Battalion.

CAMPAIGN STREAMERS
World War I
Streamer without inscription

World War II
Central Pacific

DECORATIONS
None

COAT OF ARMS
None

DISTINCTIVE INSIGNIA
None

751st ANTIAIRCRAFT ARTILLERY MISSILE BATTALION

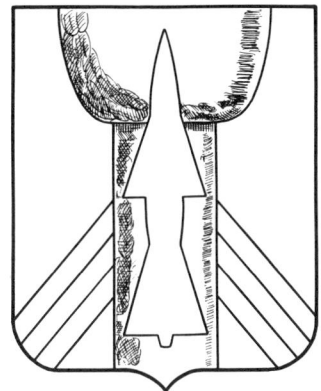 

Constituted 4 November 1943 in the Army of the United States as Headquarters and Headquarters Battery, 751st Antiaircraft Artillery Gun Battalion and activated 12 December 1943 at Fort Kamehameha, Hawaii; concurrently, remainder of battalion organized from existing units as follows:

Battery F, 93d Coast Artillery (constituted 13 January 1941 in the Regular Army and activated 25 January 1941 at Camp Davis, North Carolina), redesignated Battery A

Battery H, 93d Coast Artillery (constituted 13 January 1941 in the Regular Army and activated 25 January 1941 at Camp Davis, North Carolina), redesignated Battery B

Battery C, 64th Coast Artillery (constituted 15 January 1918 in the Regular Army as Battery C, 64th Artillery, Coast Artillery Corps and activated 17 May 1918 at Pensacola, Florida; demobilized 2 April 1919 at Camp Eustis, Virginia; reconstituted 2 May 1921 in the Regular Army as Battery C, Hawaiian Antiaircraft Regiment and activated 3 June 1921 at Fort Ruger, Hawaii; redesignated 2 June 1922 as Battery C, 64th Artillery [Antiaircraft], Coast Artillery Corps and redesignated 20 February 1924 as Battery C, 64th Coast Artillery [Antiaircraft]), redesignated Battery C

Battery F, 64th Coast Artillery (constituted 15 January 1918 in the Regular Army as Battery F, 64th Artillery, Coast Artillery Corps and activated 17 May 1918 at Pensacola, Florida; demobilized 2 April 1919 at Camp Eustis, Virginia; reconstituted 2 May 1921 in the Regular Army as Battery F, Hawaiian Antiaircraft Regiment and activated 3 June 1921 at Fort Ruger, Hawaii; redesignated 2 June 1922 as Battery F, 64th Artillery [Antiaircraft], Coast Artillery Corps and redesignated 20 February 1924 as Battery F, 64th Coast Artillery [Antiaircraft]), redesignated Battery D

Battalion, less Batteries C and D inactivated 25 February 1946 at Fort Shafter, Hawaii; concurrently, Batteries C and D inactivated on Saipan. Redesignated 22 March 1956 as the 751st Antiaircraft Artillery Missile Battalion and allotted to the Regular Army. Activated 1 May 1956 at Fort Banks, Massachusetts; inactivated 1 September 1958 at Coventry, Rhode Island.

CAMPAIGN STREAMERS
World War I
Streamer without inscription

World War II
Central Pacific
Western Pacific

DECORATIONS
None

COAT OF ARMS

SHIELD: Gules, two chevronels or, overall on a chamorro stone column of the like a guided missile sable.

CREST: None

MOTTO: Rise To Fight

Scarlet and yellow are the colors used for Artillery. The chamorro stone column found in the islands of the Western Pacific commemorates the service of the organization in that area during World War II while the guided missile refers to the function of the battalion. The chevronels from the coat of arms of Governor Winthrop allude to Fort Banks, Massachusetts where the battalion was activated following World War II.

DISTINCTIVE INSIGNIA

The insignia is the shield and motto of the coat of arms. The sample of the insignia depicted was approved for wear on 14 December 1956.

752d ANTIAIRCRAFT ARTILLERY BATTALION

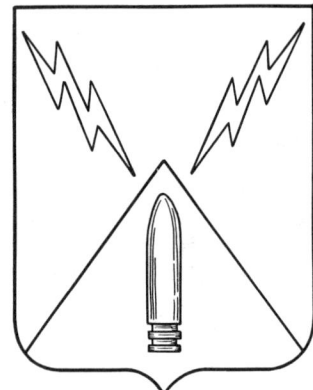 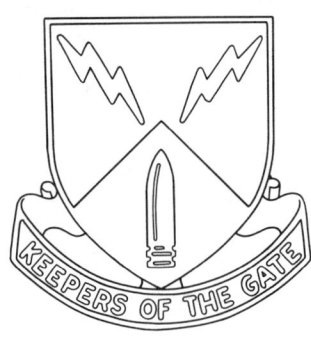

Constituted 13 January 1941 in the Regular Army as 2d Battalion, 95th Coast Artillery (Antiaircraft) (Semimobile) and activated 17 April 1941 at Camp Davis, North Carolina. (Departed San Francisco Port of Embarkation 26 December 1941 for overseas service and arrived in Hawaii on 7 January 1942). Reorganized in Hawaii and redesignated 12 December 1943 as the 752d Antiaircraft Artillery Gun Battalion. (Moved to Saipan 6 February 1945 and to Iwo Jima on 11 April 1945). Inactivated 5 June 1948 on Saipan. Activated 14 April 1953 at San Francisco, California. Redesignated 20 July 1953 as the 752d Antiaircraft Artillery Battalion. Inactivated 15 June 1957 at Fort Scott, California.

CAMPAIGN STREAMERS
World War II
Air Offensive, Japan
Western Pacific

DECORATIONS
None

COAT OF ARMS

SHIELD: Per chevron gules and or, two flashes in chevron inverted of the second, in base a projectile palewise sable.

CREST: None

MOTTO: Keepers Of The Gate

Red is for Artillery. The projectile symbolizes the battalion's function. The two flashes represent the campaigns of the organization in the Pacific Theater during World War II.

DISTINCTIVE INSIGNIA
The insignia is the shield and motto of the coat of arms. The sample of the insignia depicted was approved for wear on 25 November 1953.

753d ANTIAIRCRAFT ARTILLERY BATTALION

Constituted 13 January 1941 in the Regular Army as 2d Battalion, 96th Coast Artillery (Antiaircraft) (Semimobile) and activated 15 April 1941 at Camp Davis, North Carolina. (Departed San Francisco Port of Embarkation 27 February 1942 for overseas service and arrived in Hawaii on 10 March 1942). Reorganized in Hawaii and redesignated 12 December 1943 as the 753d Antiaircraft Artillery Gun Battalion. (Moved to Kwajalein Atoll in the Marshall Islands on 4 February 1944 and returned to Hawaii on 28 July 1945). (161st Antiaircraft Artillery Gun Battalion consolidated with the 753d Antiaircraft Artillery Gun Battalion on 28 February 1946). Redesignated 28 January 1955 as the 753d Antiaircraft Artillery Battalion. Inactivated 22 June 1957 at Tomioka, Honshu, Japan.

CAMPAIGN STREAMERS
World War II
Eastern Mandates
New Guinea
Luzon (with arrowhead)

DECORATIONS
Philippine Presidential Unit Citation, Streamer embroidered *17 OCTOBER 1944 TO 4 JULY 1945* (161st AAA Gun Bn cited; DAGO 47, 1950)

COAT OF ARMS
SHIELD: Gules, within a saltire parted and fretty argent a shell or, a bordure of the last.

CREST: On a wreath of the colors (or and gules) a griffin passant gules.

MOTTO: *Petimus et Vastimus* (We Seek And Destroy)

The coat of arms is that of the 96th Coast Artillery within a gold border to indicate the descent of the battalion from that regiment. The shield is red for Artillery. The crisscrossing searchlight beams and the shell refer to the operations of the battalion. The crest, a griffin possessing the dual nature of eagle and lion, symbolizes mastery of sky and land, paralleling the objectivity of the organization.

DISTINCTIVE INSIGNIA
The insignia is the shield and motto of the coat of arms. The sample of the insignia depicted was approved for wear on 3 September 1952.

754th ANTIAIRCRAFT ARTILLERY GUN BATTALION

Constituted 15 July 1941 in the Regular Army as 2d Battalion, 97th Coast Artillery (Antiaircraft) (Semimobile) and activated 9 October 1941 in Hawaii. Reorganized at Hickam Field, Hawaii and redesignated 12 December 1943 as the 754th Antiaircraft Artillery Gun Battalion. Inactivated 23 January 1946 at Hickam Field.

CAMPAIGN STREAMERS
World War II
Central Pacific

DECORATIONS
None

COAT OF ARMS
None

DISTINCTIVE INSIGNIA
None

755th ANTIAIRCRAFT ARTILLERY GUN BATTALION

Constituted 13 January 1941 in the Regular Army as 2d Battalion, 98th Coast Artillery (Antiaircraft) (Semimobile) and activated 11 July 1941 at Schofield Barracks, Hawaii. Reorganized in Hawaii and redesignated 12 December 1943 as the 755th Antiaircraft Artillery Gun Battalion (Semimobile). Inactivated 18 February 1946 at Camp Malokole, Hawaii.

CAMPAIGN STREAMERS
World War II
Central Pacific

DECORATIONS
None

COAT OF ARMS
None

DISTINCTIVE INSIGNIA
None

761st ANTIAIRCRAFT ARTILLERY GUN BATTALION

Constituted 25 February 1943 in the Army of the United States as the 761st Antiaircraft Artillery Gun Battalion (Semimobile). Activated 15 September 1943 at Fort Sherman, Canal Zone; disbanded 1 February 1946 at Fort Sherman.

CAMPAIGN STREAMERS
World War II
American Theater without inscription

DECORATIONS
None

COAT OF ARMS
None

DISTINCTIVE INSIGNIA
None

762d ANTIAIRCRAFT ARTILLERY GUN BATTALION

Constituted 25 February 1943 in the Army of the United States as the 762d Antiaircraft Artillery Gun Battalion (Semimobile) and activated 15 September 1943 at Fort Randolph, Canal Zone. (Returned from overseas service and arrived at the New Orleans Port of Embarkation on 9 September 1944). Disbanded 5 September 1945 at Fort Bliss, Texas.

CAMPAIGN STREAMERS
World War II
American Theater without inscription

DECORATIONS
None

COAT OF ARMS
None

DISTINCTIVE INSIGNIA
None

763d ANTIAIRCRAFT ARTILLERY GUN BATTALION

Constituted 25 February 1943 in the Army of the United States as the 763d Antiaircraft Artillery Gun Battalion (Semimobile). Activated 15 September 1943 at Fort Sherman, Canal Zone; disbanded 1 February 1946 at Fort Sherman.

CAMPAIGN STREAMERS
World War II
American Theater without inscription

DECORATIONS
None

COAT OF ARMS
None

DISTINCTIVE INSIGNIA
None

764th ANTIAIRCRAFT ARTILLERY BATTALION

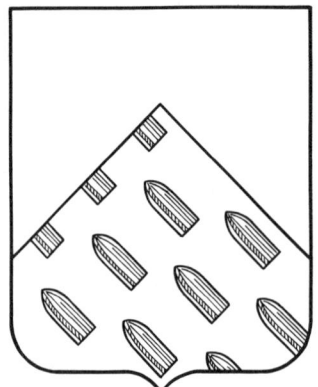 

Constituted 25 February 1943 in the Army of the United States as the 764th Antiaircraft Artillery Gun Battalion (Semimobile) and activated 15 September 1943 at Fort Randolph, Canal Zone. Allotted to the Regular Army 9 November 1951. Redesignated 1 July 1953 as the 764th Antiaircraft Artillery Battalion (Gun). Inactivated 1 September 1958 at Fort Clayton, Canal Zone.

CAMPAIGN STREAMERS
World War II
American Theater without inscription

DECORATIONS
None

COAT OF ARMS
SHIELD: Per chevron gules and or, in base seme of projectiles bendwise of the first.

CREST: None

MOTTO: *Honos Habet Onus* (Honor Brings Responsibility)

Red and yellow are used for Artillery. The field strewn with projectiles is symbolic of the battalion's function in the defense of America, as well as indicating the character of the organization – antiaircraft.

DISTINCTIVE INSIGNIA
The insignia is the shield and motto of the coat of arms. The sample of the insignia depicted was approved for wear on 5 March 1953.

765th ANTIAIRCRAFT ARTILLERY GUN BATTALION

Constituted 25 February 1943 in the Army of the United States as the 765th Antiaircraft Artillery Gun Battalion (Semimobile). Activated 15 September 1943 at Fort Clayton, Canal Zone; disbanded 1 February 1946 at Fort Clayton.

CAMPAIGN STREAMERS
World War II
American Theater without inscription

DECORATIONS
None

COAT OF ARMS
None

DISTINCTIVE INSIGNIA
None

766th ANTIAIRCRAFT ARTILLERY GUN BATTALION

Constituted 25 February 1943 in the Army of the United States as the 766th Coast Artillery Battalion (Gun) (Semimobile) and activated 15 September 1943 at Fort Clayton, Canal Zone. Reorganized and redesignated 1 February 1946 as the 766th Antiaircraft Artillery Gun Battalion. Inactivated 15 April 1946 at Fort Clayton.

CAMPAIGN STREAMERS
World War II
American Theater without inscription

DECORATIONS
None

COAT OF ARMS
None

DISTINCTIVE INSIGNIA
None

767th ANTIAIRCRAFT ARTILLERY AUTOMATIC WEAPONS BATTALION

Constituted 25 February 1943 in the Army of the United States as the 767th Antiaircraft Artillery Automatic Weapons Battalion (Semimobile). Activated 15 September 1943 at Fort Kobbe, Canal Zone; disbanded 1 February 1946 at Fort Kobbe.

CAMPAIGN STREAMERS
World War II
American Theater without inscription

DECORATIONS
None

COAT OF ARMS
None

DISTINCTIVE INSIGNIA
None

768th ANTIAIRCRAFT ARTILLERY BATTALION

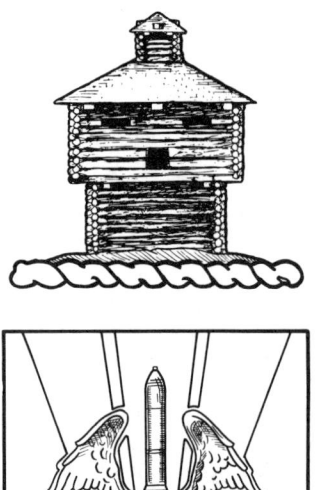

Constituted 1 October 1920 as 1st Battalion, 6th Infantry and allotted to the Illinois National Guard. Converted and redesignated 19 March 1921 as 1st Battalion, 1st Artillery (Antiaircraft), Coast Artillery Corps. Redesignated 7 December 1923 as 1st Battalion, 202d Artillery (Antiaircraft), Coast Artillery Corps. Organized at Chicago and Federally recognized 26 August 1924 as 1st Battalion, 202d Coast Artillery (Antiaircraft). Inducted into Federal service 16 September 1940 at Chicago. Reorganized at Bremerton, Washington and redesignated 10 September 1943 as the 768th Antiaircraft Artillery Gun Battalion. (Departed Seattle Port of Embarkation 22 July 1944 for overseas service; arrived at Adak Island, Alaska 2 August 1944 and moved to Camp Earle, Alaska on 19 November 1944). Inactivated 3 February 1945 at Camp Earle. Reorganized and Federally recognized 13 December 1948 at Chicago. Ordered into active Federal service 15 May 1951 at Chicago. Released from active Federal service 11 April 1953 and resumed State status. Redesignated 1 October 1953 as the 768th Antiaircraft Artillery Battalion (Gun). (121st Tank Battalion consolidated 16 March 1954 with the 768th Antiaircraft Artillery Battalion).

Consolidated 27 February 1958 with the 698th Antiaircraft Artillery Missile Battalion.

CAMPAIGN STREAMERS
World War II
Normandy
Northern France
Rhineland
Ardennes-Alsace
Central Europe
Pacific Theater without inscription

DECORATIONS
French Croix de Guerre with Palm, World War II, Streamer embroidered *MOSELLE* (106th Cav Recon Sqn cited for period 20 Aug 1944-10 Feb 1945; DAGO 43, 1950)

French Croix de Guerre with Palm, World War II, Streamer embroidered *CAEN-FALAISE*

(106th Cav Recon Sqn cited for period 5-20 Aug 1944; DAGO 43, 1950)

Fourragere in the colors of the French Croix de Guerre, World War II (106th Cav Recon Sqn cited; DAGO 43, 1950)

COAT OF ARMS
SHIELD: Azure, three piles in point or, overall a winged projectile palewise wings displayed gules, that portion on the field fimbriated of the second.

CREST: That for the regiments and separate battalions of the Illinois Army National Guard: On a wreath of the colors (or and azure) upon a grassy field the blockhouse of old Fort Dearborn proper.

MOTTO: *Arte et Armis* (By Skill And Arms)

The three piles on the blue field are representative of Coast Artillery and its area of operations. The winged projectile is red for Artillery and the wings indicate the antiaircraft nature of the unit.

DISTINCTIVE INSIGNIA
The insignia is the shield, crest and motto of the coat of arms. The sample of the insignia depicted was originally approved on 20 April 1926 for wear by the 202d Coast Artillery.

769th ANTIAIRCRAFT ARTILLERY GUN BATTALION

Constituted in the Louisiana National Guard as 1st Battalion, 204th Coast Artillery (Antiaircraft) and organized from new and existing units as follows:

Headquarters, 1st Battalion organized new and Federally recognized 15 December 1939 at Shreveport

Detachment of Staff Section-Service Company, 156th Infantry (organized and Federally recognized 18 December 1936 at Shreveport), redesignated 19 December 1939 as Headquarters Battery and Combat Train, 1st Battalion

Company E, 156th Infantry (organized and Federally recognized 19 November 1928 at Shreveport as Company C, 156th Infantry and redesignated 1 May 1929 as Company E, 156th Infantry), redesignated 15 December 1939 as Battery A

Detachment 1, Company E, 156th Infantry (organized and Federally recognized 19 November 1928 at Shreveport as Detachment 1, Company C, 156th Infantry and redesignated 1 May 1929 as Detachment 1, Company E, 156th Infantry), redesignated 15 December 1939 as Battery B

Batteries C and D organized new and Federally recognized 15 December 1939 at Shreveport

Battalion inducted into Federal service 6 January 1941 at home stations. Reorganized at San Diego, California and redesignated 10 September 1943 as the 769th Antiaircraft Artillery Gun Battalion (Semimobile).

Reorganized at Fort Sill, Oklahoma and designated 4 January 1945 as the 2d Rocket Battalion (Motorized) (4.5" Rocket).

CAMPAIGN STREAMERS
None

DECORATIONS
None

COAT OF ARMS
None

DISTINCTIVE INSIGNIA
None

769th ANTIAIRCRAFT ARTILLERY BATTALION

Organized early in 1861 at Baton Rouge as the *Baton Rouge Fencibles*, Louisiana Militia Force and mustered into State service 30 May 1861 as Captain Andrew Herron's Company (*Baton Rouge Fencibles*), 7th Louisiana Volunteer Infantry. Mustered into Confederate States Army as Company B, 7th Louisiana Infantry (Pelican Regiment). Surrendered 9 April 1865 at Appomattox Court House, Virginia with the Army of Northern Virginia, Confederate States Army. Reorganized at Baton Rouge in 1877 as the *Baton Rouge Zouaves*. Reorganized 30 March 1878 as part of the Louisiana Special Militia Force. Disbanded early in 1880 but reorganized 26 May 1883 as the *Baton Rouge Light Guards*. Redesignated 12 June 1883 as the *Governor's Rifles* (also known as *Governor's Guards*). Mustered into State service 12 July 1883 as Company A, St. John Battalion, Special Militia Force. Disbanded 13 March 1884 at Baton Rouge. Reorganized 20 April 1886 at Baton Rouge as the *State Fencibles* (also known as the *Baton Rouge Fencibles*) and designated as Company A, 1st Battalion of Infantry, 2d Brigade, Special Militia Force. (Company A disbanded 31 August 1891 when 1st Battalion of Infantry was dissolved. 1st Battalion was reorganized to consist of five companies and Company A was reorganized during December 1891). Disbanded 31 January 1899. Reorganized as Company M, 1st Infantry, Louisiana National Guard and mustered into State service on 13 October 1904. Disbanded 29 January 1908 but reorganized 7 October 1908 as Company E, 1st Infantry, Louisiana National Guard. Mustered into Federal service 28 July 1916 at Camp Stafford, Louisiana for service on the Mexican border. Mustered out 25 September 1916 at Camp Stafford and resumed State status. Mustered into Federal service 10 April 1917 at Camp Nicholls, Louisiana and drafted into Federal service 5 August 1917. Redesignated 27 September 1917 as Company H, 156th Infantry and assigned to the 39th Division. Demobilized 23 January 1919 at Camp Beauregard, Louisiana. Reorganized and Federally recognized 6 July 1922 at Baton Rouge as Headquarters Company, 156th Infantry. Reorganized and redesignated 6 December 1923 as Howitzer Company, 156th Infantry. Reorganized and redesignated 1

December 1926 as Company A, 156th Infantry. Inducted into Federal service 25 November 1940 at Baton Rouge. Inactivated 22 March 1946 at Camp Kilmer, New Jersey. Reorganized and Federally recognized 3 June 1947 at Baton Rouge. Converted, reorganized and redesignated 1 June 1948 as Headquarters and Headquarters Battery, 769th Antiaircraft Artillery Gun Battalion; subsequently, remainder of battalion organized in Eastern Louisiana as follows: Battery A organized new and Federally recognized 30 June 1948 at Baton Rouge; Battery B organized new and Federally recognized 30 June 1948 at Baton Rouge; Battery C organized new and Federally recognized 27 September 1948 at Plaquemine; Battery D organized new and Federally recognized 18 June 1948 at Donaldsonville. Reorganized and redesignated 1 October 1949 as the 769th Antiaircraft Artillery Automatic Weapons Battalion. Redesignated 1 October 1953 as the 769th Antiaircraft Artillery Automatic Weapons Battalion (Automatic Weapons).

Redesignated 1 July 1959 as the 769th Signal Battalion.

CAMPAIGN STREAMERS
Civil War (Confederate service)
Peninsula
Second Manassas
Sharpsburg
Fredericksburg
Chancellorsville
Gettysburg
Wilderness
Spotsylvania
Cold Harbor
Petersburg
Shenandoah
Appomattox
Virginia 1861

World War I
Streamer without inscription

World War II
Northern France

DECORATIONS
None

COAT OF ARMS
SHIELD: Per fess gules and or, in chief a mullet of six points of the second and in base a pale azure.

CREST: That for the regiments and separate battalions of the Louisiana Army National Guard: On a wreath of the colors (or and gules) a pelican in her piety affronte with three young in nest argent, armed and vulned proper.

MOTTO: *Dieu avec nous* (God With Us)

The colors red and yellow are used for Artillery. Blue represents the Infantry origin and the campaigns of the organization. The six pointed star, symbolizing an air burst of an artillery shell refers to the mission of the battalion.

DISTINCTIVE INSIGNIA
The insignia is the shield and motto of the coat of arms. The sample of the insignia depicted was approved for wear on 3 December 1954.

770th ANTIAIRCRAFT ARTILLERY MISSILE BATTALION

Organized in the Washington National Guard as 1st Battalion, 205th Coast Artillery (Antiaircraft) and Federally recognized 30 November 1939 at Seattle. Inducted into Federal service 3 February 1941 at Seattle. Reorganized at Santa Monica, California and redesignated 10 September 1943 as the 770th Antiaircraft Artillery Gun Battalion (Semimobile). Inactivated 10 February 1944 at Santa Monica. Reorganized and Federally recognized 12 May 1947 at Seattle. Ordered into active Federal service 14 August 1950 at Seattle. Released from active Federal service 13 July 1952 and resumed State status. Redesignated 1 October 1953 as 770th Antiaircraft Artillery Battalion (120mm Gun). Reorganized and redesignated 2 January 1958 as the 770th Antiaircraft Artillery Missile Battalion.

Consolidated 15 April 1959 with the 205th Artillery, a parent regiment under the Combat Arms Regimental System.

CAMPAIGN STREAMERS
None

DECORATIONS
None

COAT OF ARMS
SHIELD: Gules, in chief a bar invected argent coupled by a fetterlock or to a bar in base vert, fimbriated of the second.

CREST: That for the regiments and separate battalions of the Washington Army National Guard: On a wreath of the colors (argent and gules) a raven with wings endorsed issuing out of a ducal coronet, all proper.

MOTTO: *Res Verae* (Data Correct)

The shield is red for Artillery. The silver bar represents clouds while the green bar is representative of the earth. The fetterlock coupling the two symbolizes the idea of the link between the earth and things above.

DISTINCTIVE INSIGNIA
The insignia is the shield and motto of the coat of arms. The sample of the insignia depicted was approved for wear on 13 December 1951.

771st ANTIAIRCRAFT ARTILLERY GUN BATTALION

Organized during May and June 1806 at New York, New York as four companies of artillery and assigned to the Battalion of Artillery, First Brigade, Major Andrew Sitcher, commanding, on 26 July 1806. Reorganized and redesignated 5 April 1807 as a battalion of the 3d Regiment of Artillery, New York State Militia. Reorganized 25 August 1808 as 2d (Infantry) Battalion, 3d Regiment of Artillery. Redesignated 13 June 1812 as 2d Battalion, 11th Regiment of Artillery. Mustered into Federal service 15 September 1812 at New York City; mustered out 15 December 1812 and resumed State status. Mustered into Federal service 2 September 1814 at New York City; mustered out 2 December 1814 and resumed State status. Redesignated 27 January 1825 as a battalion of the 2d Regiment of Artillery. Withdrawn from the 2d Regiment of Artillery on 1 October 1825 and designated Battalion of National Guards. Reorganized and redesignated 6 May 1826 as a battalion of the 27th Regiment of Artillery. Redesignated 27 July 1847 as 1st Battalion, 7th Regiment of Infantry (National Guard), New York State Militia. Mustered into Federal service 26 April 1861 at Washington, District of Columbia; mustered out 3 June 1861 at New York City and resumed State status. Mustered into Federal service 19 June 1862 at Fort Federal Hill, Maryland for Federal service beginning 25 May 1862; mustered out 5 September 1862 at New York City and resumed State status. Mustered into Federal service 17 June 1863 at New York City; mustered out 21 July 1863 at New York City and resumed State status. Mustered into Federal service 26 June 1916 at New York City for Mexican border duty; mustered out 2 December 1916 at New York City and resumed State status. Called into Federal service 15 July 1917 and drafted into Federal service 5 August 1917. Redesignated 1 October 1917 as 1st Battalion, 107th Infantry and assigned to the 27th Division. Demobilized 2 April 1919 at Camp Upton, New York. Reorganized and Federally recognized 27 October 1921 at New York City. Converted and redesignated 9 September 1940 as 1st Battalion 207th Coast Artillery (Antiaircraft). Inducted into Federal service 10 February 1941 at New York City. Reorganized and redesignated 21 April 1943 as 771st Antiaircraft Artillery Gun Battalion. Inactivated 15 January 1946 on Guam, Marianas Islands.

Consolidated 27 September 1946 with the 107th Infantry.

CAMPAIGN STREAMERS
War of 1812
Streamer without inscription

Civil War
Streamer without inscription

World War I
Ypres-Lys
Somme Offensive
Flanders 1918

World War II
Western Pacific

DECORATIONS
Portuguese *Ordem da Torre e Espada* (Order of Tower and Sword), Streamer embroidered *FRANCE* (107th Inf cited; WDGO 11, 1924)

COAT OF ARMS
SHIELD: Per chevron gules and gray, a chevron embattled to chief rompu enhanced argent between in chief, the cipher of the regiment of 1824 (the script monogram "NG") and a lion rampant, both or and in base the cap device of 1815 as worn in 1915 (a flaming bomb charged with the number 7 sable) of the like, within a bordure of the fourth.

CREST: None

MOTTO: *Pro Gloria et Libera* (For Glory And Liberty)

The shield is that of the coat of arms of the 107th Infantry, New York National Guard within a gold border, representing the descent from the 1st battalion of that regiment.

DISTINCTIVE INSIGNIA
Although no distinctive insignia was approved for this organization, an insignia consisting of the shield and motto of the coat of arms is known to exist.

771st ANTIAIRCRAFT ARTILLERY GUN BATTALION

Constituted 27 September 1946 in the New York National Guard as the 176th Military Police Battalion and organized at Brooklyn from new and existing units as follows:

Headquarters, 3d Battalion 245th Coast Artillery (organized and Federally recognized 25 March 1920 at Brooklyn as Headquarters, 3d Battalion, 13th Coast Defense Command, Coast Artillery Corps and redesignated 1 January 1924 as Headquarters, 3d Battalion 245th Artillery, Coast Artillery Corps; redesignated 14 May 1924 as Headquarters, 3d Battalion 245th Coast Artillery; inducted into Federal service 16 September 1944 at Brooklyn and disbanded 7 October 1944 at Fort Hancock, New Jersey; reconstituted 25 August 1945 in the New York National Guard), reorganized and Federally recognized 31 March 1948 at Brooklyn as Headquarters and Headquarters Detachment

Company A organized new and Federally recognized 31 March 1948 at Brooklyn

Headquarters Battery, 4th Battalion 245th Coast Artillery (organized and Federally recognized 5 June 1940 at Brooklyn and inducted into Federal service 16 September 1940 at Brooklyn; disbanded 7 October 1940 at Fort Hancock and reconstituted 25 August 1945 in the New York National Guard), reorganized and Federally recognized 22 June 1948 at Brooklyn as Company B

Battery E, 192d Coast Artillery Battalion (organized at Brooklyn prior to 1903 as Company K, 13th Heavy Artillery, National Guard, State of New York and redesignated 1 September 1906 as Company K, 13th Coast Artillery Corps; redesignated 23 January 1908 as 10th Company, 13th Artillery District, Coast Artillery Corps; redesignated 10 August 1914 as 10th Company, 13th Coast Defense Command; mustered into Federal service 23 July 1917 at Brooklyn and drafted into Federal service 5 August 1917; redesignated 22 January 1918 as 25th Company, Coast Defenses of Southern New York and demobilized at Fort Tilden, New

York in December 1918; reorganized at Brooklyn and Federally recognized 17 June 1920 as 10th Company, 13th Coast Defense Command, Coast Artillery Corps; redesignated 28 January 1922 as 366th Company, 13th Coast Defense Command, Coast Artillery Corps; redesignated 1 January 1924 as Battery K, 245th Artillery, Coast Artillery Corps; redesignated 14 May 1924 as Battery K, 245th Coast Artillery; inducted into Federal service 16 September 1940 at Brooklyn; redesignated 7 October 1944 as Battery E, 192d Coast Artillery Battalion; and inactivated 1 April 1945 at Fort Tilden), reorganized and Federally recognized 24 February 1949 at Brooklyn as Company C

Medical Detachment organized new and Federally recognized 22 June 1948 at Brooklyn

Consolidated with the 180th Tank Battalion (constituted 3 December 1941 in the Army of the United States as the 771st Tank Destroyer Battalion; activated 15 December 1941 at Fort Ethan Allen, Vermont with personnel from the 186th and 187th Field Artillery Regiments of the New York National Guard; inactivated 1 December 1945 at the New York Port of Embarkation; redesignated 180th Tank Battalion and allotted to the New York National Guard on 27 September 1946), reorganized and redesignated 1 February 1950 as the 771st Antiaircraft Artillery Automatic Weapons Battalion. Reorganized and redesignated 1 September 1950 as the 771st Antiaircraft Artillery Gun Battalion (90mm). Disbanded 30 November 1952 at Brooklyn when Federal recognition was withdrawn.

CAMPAIGN STREAMERS
World War II
Rhineland
Central Europe

DECORATIONS
None

COAT OF ARMS
None

DISTINCTIVE INSIGNIA
None

771st ANTIAIRCRAFT ARTILLERY BATTALION

Organized in the New York National Guard as Company H, 101st Armored Cavalry and Federally recognized 19 July 1951 at Rochester. Converted and redesignated 23 May 1956 as Headquarters and Headquarters Battery, 771st Antiaircraft Artillery Battalion (Automatic Weapons) (Mobile); concurrently, remainder of battalion organized by activation of newly constituted units at Richfield Springs, Dansville, Catskill and Norwich. Battalion broken up and elements disbanded or consolidated and redesignated as follows: Headquarters and Headquarters Battery and Battery A consolidated, reorganized and redesignated 29 November 1958 as Company D, 27th Reconnaissance Battalion and Batteries B, C and D disbanded when Federal recognition was withdrawn on 1 October 1958.

CAMPAIGN STREAMERS
None

DECORATIONS
None

COAT OF ARMS
None

DISTINCTIVE INSIGNIA
None

772d ANTIAIRCRAFT ARTILLERY GUN BATTALION

Constituted 31 March 1923 in the Massachusetts National Guard as 1st Battalion, 211th Artillery (Antiaircraft), Coast Artillery Corps. Redesignated 30 April 1924 as 1st Battalion (Gun), 211th Coast Artillery (Antiaircraft) and organized from new and existing units as follows:

Headquarters, 1st Battalion organized new and Federally recognized 19 May 1939 at Belmont

Headquarters Detachment, 2d Battalion, 211th Coast Artillery (organized and Federally recognized 14 March 1922 at Boston as Headquarters Company, 1st Separate Battalion Infantry, Massachusetts National Guard; redesignated 14 March 1922 as Headquarters Detachment, 211th Machine Gun Battalion [Antiaircraft], Coast Artillery Corps; redesignated 31 May 1923 as Headquarters Detachment, 2d Battalion 211th Artillery [Antiaircraft], Coast Artillery Corps; and redesignated 30 April 1924 as Headquarters Detachment, 2d Battalion 211th Coast Artillery [Antiaircraft]), redesignated 21 June 1929 as Headquarters Detachment and Combat Train, 1st Battalion

Battery G, 211th Artillery (organized at Boston in 1874 as Company A, First Corps Cadets, Massachusetts Volunteer Militia; redesignated 22 May 1917 as Company A, 1st Regiment Engineers, Massachusetts National Guard; called into Federal service at Boston 25 July 1917; drafted into Federal service 5 August 1917; redesignated 18 August 1917 as Company A, 101st Engineers and assigned to the 26th Division; demobilized 29 April 1919 at Camp Devens, Massachusetts; reorganized and Federally recognized 14 March 1922 at Boston as Battery G, 211th Machine Gun Battalion [Antiaircraft], Coast Artillery Corps; and redesignated 31 May 1923 as Battery G, 211th Artillery [Antiaircraft], Coast Artillery Corps), redesignated 30 April 1924 as Battery B and further redesignated Battery A on 1 January 1927

Battery E, 211th Coast Artillery (chartered 16 October 1741 in the Massachusetts Militia as the Independent Company of Cadets and organized 19 October 1741 at Boston, Lieutenant Colonel Benjamin Pollard, commanding; [formally returned its colors to the British commander at Boston on 15 August 1774]; reorganized 1776-1777 in the Massachusetts Militia following the British evacuation of Boston and served in active State service as an element of the Boston Regiment, Suffolk County Brigade; redesignated 23 July 1780 as a company in the 16th Massachusetts Regiment, Continental Line; mustered out of Continental Army 20 June 1784; reorganized 19 October 1786 at Boston as Independent Company of Cadets, Massachusetts Militia; mustered into Federal service 26 May 1862 as the Boston Cadet Company and stationed at Fort Warren where it guarded Confederate prisoners of war; mustered out of Federal service 2 July 1862 and resumed State status; redesignated Company B, First Corps Cadets, Massachusetts Volunteer Militia in 1874; reorganized and redesignated 22 May 1917 as Company B, 1st Regiment Engineers, Massachusetts National Guard; called into Federal service at Boston, 25 July 1917; drafted into Federal service 5 August 1917; redesignated Company B, 101st Engineers and assigned to the 26th Division 18 August 1917; demobilized at Camp Devens, Massachusetts, 29 April 1919; reorganized and Federally recognized 11 May 1921 at Boston as Company A, 1st Separate Battalion, Infantry, Massachusetts National Guard; redesignated 14 March 1922 as Battery E, 211th Machine Gun Battalion [Antiaircraft], Coast Artillery Corps; redesignated 31 May 1923 as Battery E, 211th Artillery [Antiaircraft], Coast Artillery Corps; and redesignated 30 April 1924 as Battery E, 211th Coast Artillery [Antiaircraft]), redesignated 1 January 1927 as Battery B

Battery C organized new and Federally recognized 8 March 1939 at Boston

Battery D organized new and Federally recognized 11 May 1939 at Boston

Inducted into Federal service 16 September 1940 at Boston. Reorganized and redesignated 16 August 1943 as 772d Antiaircraft Artillery Gun Battalion. Inactivated 30 May 1944 at Camp Howze, Texas. Disbanded 26 June 1944. Reconstituted 25 August 1945 in the Massachusetts National Guard.

Consolidated 8 July 1946 with the 211th Cavalry Reconnaissance Squadron, Mechanized.

CAMPAIGN STREAMERS
World War I
Champagne-Marne
Aisne-Marne
St. Mihiel
Meuse-Argonne
Ile de France 1918
Lorraine 1918

DECORATIONS
None

COAT OF ARMS
None

DISTINCTIVE INSIGNIA
None

772d ANTIAIRCRAFT ARTILLERY MISSILE BATTALION

Constituted in the Massachusetts National Guard as 2d Battalion, 1st Coast Defense Command, Coast Artillery Corps and Federally recognized 22 November 1920 with Headquarters at Roslindale and companies at Boston, New Bedford, Chelsea, and Fall River. Redesignated 25 September 1923 as 2d Battalion, 241st Artillery, Coast Artillery Corps. Redesignated 30 April 1924 as 2d Battalion, 241st Coast Artillery (Harbor Defense). (Headquarters relocated to Boston about 1925 and to Chelsea on 28 June 1940). Inducted into Federal service 16 September 1940 at home stations. Reorganized and redesignated 7 October 1944 as the 187th Coast Artillery Battalion (Harbor Defense). Battalion, less Batteries C and E, inactivated 1 April 1945 at Fort Ruckman, Massachusetts; concurrently, Batteries C and E redesignated Batteries C and B respectively, Harbor Defenses of Boston. (Batteries C and B, Harbor Defenses of Boston inactivated 30 June 1946 at Forts Warren and Dawes, Massachusetts and reverted to former designations as elements of the 187th Coast Artillery Battalion). Redesignated 8 July 1946 as the 772d Antiaircraft Artillery Gun Battalion.

Reorganized and Federally recognized 29 January 1948 with Headquarters at Chelsea and batteries at Chelsea, Fort Banks and Winthrop. Reorganized and redesignated 1 October 1949 as 772d Antiaircraft Artillery Automatic Weapons Battalion (Mobile). Reorganized and redesignated 1 July 1951 as 772d Antiaircraft Artillery Gun Battalion (90mm). (Headquarters relocated to Boston on 13 May 1952). Redesignated 1 October 1953 as 772d Antiaircraft Artillery Battalion (90mm Gun). (Headquarters relocated to Chelsea on 4 November 1957). Reorganized and redesignated 1 February 1958 as 772d Antiaircraft Artillery Missile Battalion.

Consolidated 1 May 1959 with the 241st Artillery, a parent regiment under the Combat Arms Regimental System.

CAMPAIGN STREAMERS
Civil War
Bull Run
Peninsula
Manassas
Fredericksburg
Gettysburg
Wilderness
Spotsylvania
Maryland 1861
Virginia 1863

DECORATIONS
None

COAT OF ARMS
SHIELD: Per bend azure and gules, in chief a lozenge argent and in base a falcon close upon a mount or, on a canton of the second, fimbriated of the last a dexter arm embowed, grasping a broad sword gold; all within a bordure of the last.

CREST: That for the regiments and separate battalions of the Massachusetts Army National Guard: On a wreath of the colors (argent and azure) a dexter arm embowed, clothed blue and ruffed white proper, grasping a broad sword argent, the pommel and hilt or.

MOTTO: *Posset* (It Is Able)

The shield is the coat of arms approved for the old 241st Coast Artillery within a gold border to indicate descent from that regiment.

DISTINCTIVE INSIGNIA
The insignia is the shield and motto of the coat of arms. The sample of the insignia depicted was never made for nor worn by this organization.

773d ANTIAIRCRAFT ARTILLERY MISSILE BATTALION

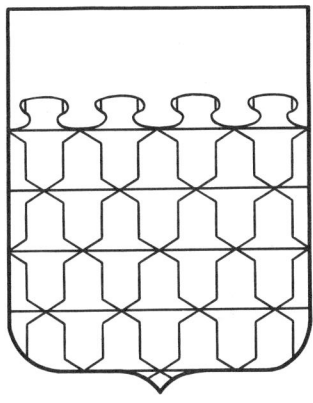

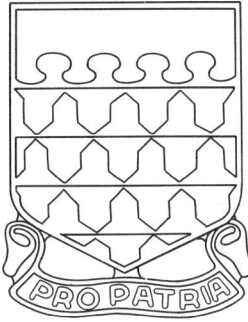

Organized in the National Guard, State of New York as companies of the 1st Battalion, 12th Regiment and activated at New York City as follows: Companies A and B on 16 November 1859; Company D on 16 July 1884 and Company C on 3 June 1885. (Companies A and B mustered into Federal service 2 May 1861 at Washington, District of Columbia and mustered out on 5 August 1861; mustered into Federal service 31 May 1862, surrendered to Confederate forces at Harpers Ferry, West Virginia, paroled 16 September 1862 and mustered out 12 October 1862; mustered into Federal service 16 June 1863 at New York City and mustered out 20 July 1863). 1st Battalion, 12th Regiment mustered into Federal service 13 May 1898 at Peekskill as elements of the 12th New York Volunteer Infantry. Mustered out 20 April 1899 at New York City and resumed State status. Mustered into Federal service 28 June 1916 at New York City for service on the Mexican border; mustered out 10 March 1917 and resumed State status. Mustered into Federal service 22 July 1917 and drafted into Federal service on 5 August 1917. Redesignated 4 January 1918 as 1st Battalion, 52d Pioneer Infantry. Demobilized 23 January 1919 at Camp Dix, New Jersey. Reorganized at New York City and Federally recognized 9 December 1921 as 1st Battalion, 212th Artillery (Antiaircraft), Coast Artillery Corps. Redesignated 14 May 1924 as 1st Battalion, 212th Coast Artillery (Antiaircraft). Inducted into Federal service 10 February 1941 at New York City. Reorganized at Seattle, Washington and redesignated 10 September 1943 as the 773d Antiaircraft Artillery Gun Battalion (Semimobile). Inactivated 13 May 1944 at Camp Phillips, Kansas. Disbanded 26 June 1944. Reconstituted 25 August 1945 in the New York National Guard. Reorganized and Federally recognized 6 October 1947 at New York City. Ordered into active Federal service 1 May 1951 at New York City. Released from active Federal service 30 April 1953 and resumed State status. Redesignated 1 October 1953 as the 773d Antiaircraft Artillery Battalion (90mm Gun). Reorganized and redesignated 15 February 1958 as the 773d Antiaircraft Artillery Missile Battalion (NIKE). (Headquarters and Headquarters Battery relocated to the Bronx on 20 July 1958; other batteries subsequently relocated to Kensico and Spring Valley).

Reorganized and redesignated 16 March 1959 as the 212th Artillery, a parent regiment under the Combat Arms Regimental System.

CAMPAIGN STREAMERS
Civil War
Virginia 1861
West Virginia 1861
West Virginia 1862
Maryland 1862

World War II
Meuse-Argonne

DECORATIONS
None

COAT OF ARMS
SHIELD: Vair, a chief nebuly gules.

CREST: That for the regiments and separate battalions of the New York National Guard: On a wreath of the colors (argent and azure) the full rigged ship *Half Moon*, all proper.

MOTTO: *Pro Patria* (For Country)

The shield of vair represents the location of the battalion in southern New York where fur constituted a major part of the early trade of this region. Vair originated from the fur of a kind of squirrel (the vair) which was blue-gray on the back and white underneath. The red chief is for Artillery and the nebuly partition line is the heraldic symbol for clouds, the field of antiaircraft fire.

DISTINCTIVE INSIGNIA
The insignia is the shield and motto of the coat of arms. The sample of the insignia depicted was originally approved on 14 February 1928 for wear by the 212th Coast Artillery.

774th ANTIAIRCRAFT ARTILLERY GUN BATTALION

Constituted in the Minnesota National Guard as 1st Battalion of Infantry and organized during 1880 at St. Paul and Minneapolis to consist of *Minneapolis Light Infantry, Minneapolis Zouave Guards, St. Paul Guards* and *Allen Light Guards*, all organized during 1879. Redesignated 1st Battalion, 1st Infantry, Minnesota National Guard in 1883. Redesignated 4 May 1898 as 1st Battalion, 13th Minnesota Volunteer Infantry. Mustered into Federal service 7 May 1898 at Camp Ramsey, Minnesota and mustered out 3 October 1899 at San Francisco, California. Reorganized about 1900 at Minneapolis and St. Paul as 1st Battalion, 1st Infantry, Minnesota National Guard. Mustered into Federal service 30 June 1916 at Fort Snelling, Minnesota for service on the Mexican border. Mustered out 14 March 1917 at Fort Snelling and resumed State status. Called into Federal service 25 March 1917; mustered into Federal service 7 April 1917 at Fort Snelling and drafted into Federal service 5 August 1917. Redesignated 1st Battalion, 135th Infantry and assigned to the 34th Division. Demobilized 18 February 1919 at Camp Grant, Illinois and consolidated with 1st Battalion, 6th Infantry, Minnesota National Guard (organized and Federally recognized 30 January 1919 at St. Paul). Redesignated 1 December 1923 as 1st Battalion, 206th Infantry. Converted, reorganized and redesignated 1 July 1940 as 1st Battalion, 216th Coast Artillery (Antiaircraft) (Semimobile). Inducted into Federal service 6 January 1941 at St. Paul. Reorganized at San Francisco, California and redesignated 10 September 1943 as the 774th Antiaircraft Artillery Gun Battalion. Inactivated 8 June 1944 at Camp Howze, Texas. Disbanded 26 June 1944. Reconstituted 25 August 1945 in the Minnesota National Guard.

Redesignated 21 June 1946 as the 256th Antiaircraft Artillery Automatic Weapons Battalion.

CAMPAIGN STREAMERS
World War I
Streamer without inscription

DECORATIONS
None

COAT OF ARMS
None

DISTINCTIVE INSIGNIA
None

775th ANTIAIRCRAFT ARTILLERY GUN BATTALION

Constituted in the Minnesota National Guard as 1st Battalion, 217th Coast Artillery (Antiaircraft) (Semimobile) and organized 1 July 1940 from existing and new units as follows:

Headquarters, 3d Battalion, 206th Infantry (organized and Federally recognized 29 April 1921 at St. Paul as Headquarters, 3d Battalion, 6th Infantry, Minnesota National Guard; redesignated 1 December 1923 as Headquarters, 3d Battalion, 206th Infantry; relocated to Long Prairie on 10 June 1925; relocated to Sauk Centre on 3 December 1938), relocated to St. Paul on 1 July 1940 and redesignated Headquarters, 1st Battalion

Headquarters Detachment, 3d Battalion, 205th Infantry (organized and Federally recognized 31 May 1921 at Benson as Company I, 5th Infantry, Minnesota National Guard; redesignated 1 December 1923 as Company I, 205th Infantry; redesignated 1 February 1925 as Headquarters Company, 3d Battalion, 205th Infantry; and redesignated 1 May 1940 as Headquarters Detachment, 3d Battalion, 205th Infantry), redesignated Headquarters Battery, 1st Battalion

Company K, 205th Infantry (organized and Federally recognized 17 January 1919 at Morris as Company K, 5th Infantry, Minnesota National Guard and redesignated 1 December 1923 as Company K, 205th Infantry), redesignated Battery B

Company G, 206th Infantry (organized and Federally recognized 14 January 1921 at Alexandria as Company L, 6th Infantry, Minnesota National Guard; redesignated 1 December 1923 as Company L, 206th Infantry; and redesignated 1 March 1927 as Company G, 206th Infantry), redesignated Battery C

Company I, 206th Infantry (organized and Federally recognized 10 February 1920 at Long Prairie as Company I, 6th Infantry, Minnesota National Guard and redesignated 1 December 1923 as Company I, 206th Infantry), redesignated Battery D

Inducted into Federal service 10 February 1941 at home stations. Reorganized at Oakland, California and redesignated 10 September 1943 as the 775th Antiaircraft Artillery Gun Battalion (Semimobile). Inactivated 6 May 1944 at Camp Phillips, Kansas. Consolidated 21 June 1946 with the 136th Infantry.

CAMPAIGN STREAMERS
None

DECORATIONS
None

COAT OF ARMS
None

DISTINCTIVE INSIGNIA
None

776th ANTIAIRCRAFT ARTILLERY AUTOMATIC WEAPONS BATTALION

Constituted 8 February 1943 in the Army of the United States as the 776th Coast Artillery Battalion (Antiaircraft) (Automatic Weapons) and activated 20 March 1943 at Camp Davis, North Carolina. Reorganized and redesignated 30 April 1943 as the 776th Antiaircraft Artillery Automatic Weapons Battalion (Semimobile). (Departed Boston Port of Embarkation 28 February 1944 for overseas service; arrived in England on 8 March 1944 and landed in France on 24 July 1944. Returned from overseas service and arrived at the Boston Port of Embarkation on 25 November 1945). Inactivated 26 November 1945 at Camp Myles Standish, Massachusetts.

Redesignated 13 October 1948 as the 22d Antiaircraft Artillery Automatic Weapons Battalion.

CAMPAIGN STREAMERS
World War II
Normandy
Northern France
Rhineland
Central Europe
England 1944

DECORATIONS
None

COAT OF ARMS
None

DISTINCTIVE INSIGNIA
None

777th ANTIAIRCRAFT ARTILLERY AUTOMATIC WEAPONS BATTALION

Constituted 8 February 1943 in the Army of the United States as the 777th Coast Artillery Battalion (Antiaircraft) (Automatic Weapons) and activated 20 March 1943 at Fort Sheridan, Illinois. Redesignated 1 May 1943 as the 777th Antiaircraft Artillery Automatic Weapons Battalion. (Departed New York Port of Embarkation 18 April 1944 for overseas service; arrived in England on 26 April 1944 and landed in France on 20 July 1944). Inactivated 30 June 1946 in Germany.

Redesignated 13 October 1948 as the 23d Antiaircraft Artillery Automatic Weapons Battalion.

CAMPAIGN STREAMERS
World War II
Normandy
Northern France
Rhineland
Ardennes-Alsace
Central Europe
England 1944

DECORATIONS
French Croix de Guerre with Gold Star, World War II, Streamer embroidered *AVRANCHES* (777th AAA AW Bn cited for period 1-3 Aug 1944; DAGO 43, 1950)

COAT OF ARMS
None

DISTINCTIVE INSIGNIA
None

778th ANTIAIRCRAFT ARTILLERY AUTOMATIC WEAPONS BATTALION

Constituted 8 February 1943 in the Army of the United States as the 778th Coast Artillery Battalion (Antiaircraft) (Automatic Weapons) and activated 10 March 1943 at Camp Haan, California. Redesignated 1 May 1943 as the 778th Antiaircraft Artillery Automatic Weapons Battalion. (Departed New York Port of Embarkation for overseas service 14 October 1944; arrived in England 25 October 1944 and landed in France on 19 December 1944. Returned from overseas service and arrived at the New York Port of Embarkation on 30 April 1946). Inactivated 1 May 1946 at Camp Kilmer, New Jersey.

Redesignated 13 October 1948 as the 25th Antiaircraft Artillery Automatic Weapons Battalion.

CAMPAIGN STREAMERS
World War II
Northern France
Rhineland
Ardennes-Alsace
Central Europe

DECORATIONS
Presidential Unit Citation (Army), Streamer embroidered *LUXEMBOURG* (Btry C 778th AAA AW Bn cited for period 7-12 Feb 1945; WDGO 19, 1947 as amended by DAGO 74, 1948)

COAT OF ARMS
None

DISTINCTIVE INSIGNIA
None

779th ANTIAIRCRAFT ARTILLERY AUTOMATIC WEAPONS BATTALION

Constituted 8 February 1943 in the Army of the United States as the 779th Coast Artillery Battalion (Antiaircraft) (Automatic Weapons) and activated 10 March 1943 at Camp Haan, California. Reorganized and redesignated 30 April 1943 as the 779th Antiaircraft Artillery Automatic Weapons Battalion (Semimobile). (Departed Seattle Port of Embarkation 10 August 1944 for overseas service; arrived in Hawaii on 17 August 1944 and landed on Okinawa on 13 April 1945). Inactivated 31 March 1946 at Seoul, Korea.

CAMPAIGN STREAMERS
World War II
Ryukyus

DECORATIONS
None

COAT OF ARMS
None

DISTINCTIVE INSIGNIA
None

780th ANTIAIRCRAFT ARTILLERY AUTOMATIC WEAPONS BATTALION

Constituted 8 February 1943 in the Army of the United States as the 780th Coast Artillery Battalion (Antiaircraft) (Automatic Weapons) and activated 10 March 1943 at Camp Haan, California. Reorganized and redesignated 30 April 1943 as the 780th Antiaircraft Artillery Automatic Weapons Battalion (Semimobile). Inactivated 31 July 1944 at Camp Van Dorn, Mississippi. Disbanded 26 October 1944.

CAMPAIGN STREAMERS
None

DECORATIONS
None

COAT OF ARMS
None

DISTINCTIVE INSIGNIA
None

781st ANTIAIRCRAFT ARTILLERY AUTOMATIC WEAPONS BATTALION

Constituted 8 February 1943 in the Army of the United States as the 781st Coast Artillery Battalion (Antiaircraft) (Automatic Weapons) and activated 20 March 1943 at Camp Haan, California. Reorganized and redesignated 30 April 1943 as the 781st Antiaircraft Artillery Automatic Weapons Battalion (Semimobile). Inactivated 5 August 1944 at Camp Maxey, Texas. Disbanded 26 October 1944.

CAMPAIGN STREAMERS
None

DECORATIONS
None

COAT OF ARMS
None

DISTINCTIVE INSIGNIA
None

782d ANTIAIRCRAFT ARTILLERY AUTOMATIC WEAPONS BATTALION

Constituted 8 February 1943 in the Army of the United States as the 782d Coast Artillery Battalion (Antiaircraft) (Automatic Weapons) and activated 20 March 1943 at Camp Haan, California. Reorganized and redesignated 30 April 1943 as the 782d Antiaircraft Artillery Automatic Weapons Battalion (Semimobile). Inactivated 12 June 1944 at Camp Haan. Disbanded 26 June 1944.

CAMPAIGN STREAMERS
None

DECORATIONS
None

COAT OF ARMS
None

DISTINCTIVE INSIGNIA
None

783d ANTIAIRCRAFT ARTILLERY AUTOMATIC WEAPONS BATTALION

Constituted 8 February 1943 in the Army of the United States as the 783d Coast Artillery Battalion (Antiaircraft) (Automatic Weapons) and activated 20 March 1943 at Camp Haan, California. Reorganized and redesignated 30 April 1943 as the 783d Antiaircraft Artillery Automatic Weapons Battalion (Semimobile). Inactivated 25 July 1944 at Camp Haan. Disbanded 26 October 1944.

CAMPAIGN STREAMERS
None

DECORATIONS
None

COAT OF ARMS
None

DISTINCTIVE INSIGNIA
None

784th ANTIAIRCRAFT ARTILLERY AUTOMATIC WEAPONS BATTALION

Constituted 25 February 1943 in the Army of the United States as the 784th Coast Artillery Battalion (Antiaircraft) (Automatic Weapons) and activated 10 April 1943 at Fort Bliss, Texas. Redesignated 30 April 1943 as the 784th Antiaircraft Artillery Automatic Weapons Battalion. (Departed Boston Port of Embarkation 7 April 1944 for overseas service; arrived in England 10 April 1944 and landed in France 14 July 1944). Inactivated 31 December 1945 in Germany.

Redesignated 13 October 1948 as the 26th Antiaircraft Artillery Automatic Weapons Battalion.

CAMPAIGN STREAMERS
World War II
Normandy
Northern France
Rhineland
Central Europe

DECORATIONS
Belgian Fourragere 1940 (784th AAA AW Bn cited; DAGO 43, 1950)

Cited in the Order of the Day of the Belgian Army for action in the defense of *LIEGE* (784th AAA AW Bn cited for period 27 Nov-14 Dec 1944; DAGO 43, 1950)

Cited in the Order of the Day of the Belgian Army for defense of the *MEUSE RIVER* area (784th AAA AW Bn cited for period 16 Dec 1944-25 Jan 1945; DAGO 43, 1950)

COAT OF ARMS
None

DISTINCTIVE INSIGNIA
None

785th ANTIAIRCRAFT ARTILLERY BATTALION

Constituted 25 February 1943 in the Army of the United States as the 785th Coast Artillery Battalion (Antiaircraft) (Automatic Weapons) and activated 10 April 1943 at Fort Bliss, Texas. Reorganized and redesignated 30 April 1943 as the 785th Antiaircraft Artillery Automatic Weapons Battalion (Semimobile). (Departed San Francisco Port of Embarkation 7 April 1944 for overseas service and arrived on New Guinea 13 May 1944. After service on Morotai Island, moved to the Philippine Islands on 12 January 1946). Inactivated 10 April 1946 on Luzon, Philippine Islands. Allotted to the Organized Reserve Corps on 22 February 1952. Assigned to the 96th Infantry Division and activated 1 March 1952 with Headquarters at Billings, Montana.

(Organized Reserve Corps redesignated 9 July 1952 as Army Reserve). Redesignated 15 November 1952 as the 785th Antiaircraft Artillery Battalion (Automatic Weapons) (Self Propelled). Inactivated 1 June 1959 at Billings.

CAMPAIGN STREAMERS
World War II
New Guinea

DECORATIONS
None

COAT OF ARMS
SHIELD: Gules, on a rocket bendwise a bird of paradise or.

CREST: That for the regiments and separate battalions of the Army Reserve: On a wreath of the colors (or and gules) the Lexington Minute Man proper. The statue of the Minute Man, Captain John Parker (H. H. Kitson, sculptor), stands on the common in Lexington, Massachusetts.

MOTTO: *Furor Caelorum* (Fury Of The Skies)

The shield is red and yellow for Artillery. The bird of paradise, an especial celebrity among the numerous and beautiful birds of New Guinea where the battalion served during World War II, commemorates service in that area. The rocket is a symbol of Antiaircraft Artillery fire.

DISTINCTIVE INSIGNIA
The insignia is the shield and motto of the coat of arms. The insignia depicted was never made for nor worn by this organization.

786th ANTIAIRCRAFT ARTILLERY AUTOMATIC WEAPONS BATTALION

Constituted 25 February 1943 in the Army of the United States as the 786th Coast Artillery Battalion (Antiaircraft) (Automatic Weapons) and activated 20 April 1943 at Fort Bliss, Texas. Reorganized and redesignated 30 April 1943 as the 786th Antiaircraft Artillery Automatic Weapons Battalion (Semimobile). Inactivated 27 July 1944 at Camp Swift, Texas. Disbanded 26 October 1944.

CAMPAIGN STREAMERS
None

DECORATIONS
None

COAT OF ARMS
None

DISTINCTIVE INSIGNIA
None

787th ANTIAIRCRAFT ARTILLERY AUTOMATIC WEAPONS BATTALION

Constituted 25 February 1943 in the Army of the United States as the 787th Coast Artillery Battalion (Antiaircraft) (Automatic Weapons) and activated 20 April 1943 at Camp Hulen, Texas. Redesignated 30 April 1943 as the 787th Antiaircraft Artillery Automatic Weapons

Battalion. (Departed New York Port of Embarkation 11 August 1944 for overseas service; arrived in England 22 August 1944 and landed in France on 22 September 1944). Inactivated 27 June 1946 in Germany.

Redesignated 13 October 1948 as the 29th Antiaircraft Artillery Automatic Weapons Battalion.

CAMPAIGN STREAMERS
World War II
Rhineland
Ardennes-Alsace

DECORATIONS
Belgian Fourragere 1940 (787th AAA AW Bn cited; DAGO 43, 1950)

Cited in the Order of the Day of the Belgian Army for action in the defense of *ANTWERP* (787th AAA AW Bn cited for period 25 Oct-28 Nov 1944; DAGO 43, 1950)

Cited in the Order of the Day of the Belgian Army for action in the defense of *ANTWERP HARBOR* (787th AAA AW Bn cited for action on 16 Dec 1944; DAGO 43, 1950)

COAT OF ARMS
None

DISTINCTIVE INSIGNIA
None

788th ANTIAIRCRAFT ARTILLERY AUTOMATIC WEAPONS BATTALION

Constituted 25 February 1943 in the Army of the United States as the 788th Coast Artillery Battalion (Antiaircraft) (Automatic Weapons) and activated 20 April 1943 at Camp Hulen, Texas. Redesignated 30 April 1943 as the 788th Antiaircraft Artillery Automatic Weapons Battalion. (Departed New York Port of Embarkation 11 August 1944 for overseas service; arrived in England 22 August 1944 and landed in France on 23 September 1944). Inactivated 29 June 1946 in France.

Redesignated 13 October 1948 as the 39th Antiaircraft Artillery Automatic Weapons Battalion, Mobile.

CAMPAIGN STREAMERS
World War II
Northern France
Rhineland
Ardennes-Alsace
Central Europe

DECORATIONS
None

COAT OF ARMS
None

DISTINCTIVE INSIGNIA
None

789th ANTIAIRCRAFT ARTILLERY BATTALION

Constituted 25 February 1943 in the Army of the United States as the 789th Coast Artillery Battalion (Antiaircraft) (Automatic Weapons) and activated 20 April 1943 at Camp Stewart, Georgia. Reorganized and redesignated 30 April 1943 as the 789th Antiaircraft Artillery Automatic Weapons Battalion (Semimobile). (Departed New York Port of Embarkation 13 May 1944 for overseas service; arrived in England 25 May 1944 and landed in France on 19 September 1944). Inactivated 18 December 1945 in Germany. Redesignated 9 February 1955 as the 789th Antiaircraft Artillery Battalion and allotted to the Regular Army. Activated 15 June 1955 at Camp Stewart, Georgia; inactivated 20 September 1956 at Camp Stewart.

CAMPAIGN STREAMERS
World War II
Northern France
Rhineland
Ardennes-Alsace
Central Europe

DECORATIONS
Belgian Fourragere 1940 (789th AAA AW Bn cited; DAGO 43, 1950)

Cited in the Order of the Day of the Belgian Army for action in the defense of ANTWERP (789th AAA AW Bn cited for period 25 Oct-28 Nov 1944; DAGO 43, 1950)

Cited in the Order of the Day of the Belgian Army for the defense of ANTWERP HARBOR (789th AAA AW Bn cited for action on 16 Dec 1944; DAGO 43, 1950)

COAT OF ARMS
SHIELD: Gules, in base on a gunstone fimbriated and emitting to chief four lightning bolts or a lion rampant of the last.

CREST: None

MOTTO: Set With Nerve

The colors scarlet and yellow are used for Artillery. The gunstone and lightning flashes pointing upward simulate the antiaircraft mission of the battalion, the four flashes also alluding to the battalion's four campaigns during World War II. The rampant lion from the coat of arms of Belgium commemorates the Belgian Fourragere awarded the battalion for action in the defense of Antwerp.

DISTINCTIVE INSIGNIA
The insignia is the shield and motto of the coat of arms. The insignia depicted was never made for nor worn by this organization.

790th ANTIAIRCRAFT ARTILLERY AUTOMATIC WEAPONS BATTALION

Constituted 25 February 1943 in the Army of the United States as the 790th Coast Artillery Battalion (Antiaircraft) (Automatic Weapons) (Colored) and activated 20 April 1943 at Camp Stewart, Georgia. Reorganized and redesignated 30 April 1943 as the 790th Antiaircraft Artillery Automatic Weapons Battalion (Semimobile) (Colored). Disbanded 24 April 1944 at Camp Patrick Henry, Virginia.

CAMPAIGN STREAMERS
None

DECORATIONS
None

COAT OF ARMS
None

DISTINCTIVE INSIGNIA
None

791st ANTIAIRCRAFT ARTILLERY AUTOMATIC WEAPONS BATTALION

Constituted 25 February 1943 in the Army of the United States as the 791st Coast Artillery Battalion (Antiaircraft) (Automatic Weapons) and activated 20 April 1943 at Camp Stewart, Georgia. Reorganized and redesignated 30 April 1943 as the 791st Antiaircraft Artillery Automatic Weapons Battalion (Semimobile). (Departed Boston Port of Embarkation 3 July 1944 for overseas service; arrived in England 12 July 1944 and landed in France 18 August 1944. Returned from overseas service and arrived at the New York Port of Embarkation on 2 September 1945). Inactivated 8 April 1946 at Camp Kilmer, New Jersey.

CAMPAIGN STREAMERS
World War II
Northern France

DECORATIONS
None

COAT OF ARMS
None

DISTINCTIVE INSIGNIA
None

792d ANTIAIRCRAFT ARTILLERY AUTOMATIC WEAPONS BATTALION

Constituted 25 February 1943 in the Army of the United States as the 792d Coast Artillery Battalion (Antiaircraft) (Automatic Weapons) and activated 20 April 1943 at Camp Stewart, Georgia. Redesignated 30 April 1943 as the 792d Antiaircraft Artillery Automatic Weapons Battalion. (Departed Boston Port of Embarkation 27 February 1944 for overseas service; arrived in England 11 March 1944 and landed in France on 16 October 1944. Returned from overseas service and arrived at the New York Port of Embarkation on 27 November 1945). Inactivated 28 November 1945 at Camp Kilmer, New Jersey.

Redesignated 25 June 1948 as the 46th Antiaircraft Artillery Automatic Weapons Battalion.

CAMPAIGN STREAMERS
World War II
Normandy
Northern France
Rhineland
Central France
England 1944

DECORATIONS
None

COAT OF ARMS
None

DISTINCTIVE INSIGNIA
None

793d ANTIAIRCRAFT ARTILLERY AUTOMATIC WEAPONS BATTALION

Constituted 25 February 1943 in the Army of the United States as the 793d Coast Artillery Battalion (Antiaircraft) (Automatic Weapons) and activated 20 April 1943 at Camp Stewart, Georgia. Redesignated 30 April 1943 as the 793d Antiaircraft Artillery Automatic Weapons Battalion. (Departed Seattle Port of Embarkation 15 November 1944 for overseas service and arrived in Hawaii on 23 November 1944). Inactivated 31 December 1945 at Schofield Barracks, Hawaii.

CAMPAIGN STREAMERS
World War II
Pacific Theater without inscription

DECORATIONS
None

COAT OF ARMS
None

DISTINCTIVE INSIGNIA
None

794th ANTIAIRCRAFT ARTILLERY AUTOMATIC WEAPONS BATTALION

Constituted 25 February 1943 in the Army of the United States as the 794th Coast Artillery Battalion (Antiaircraft) (Automatic Weapons) and activated 20 April 1943 at Camp Stewart, Georgia. Redesignated 30 April 1943 as the 794th Antiaircraft Artillery Automatic Weapons Battalion. (Departed New York Port of Embarkation 5 October 1944 for overseas service; arrived in England 13 October 1944 and landed in France on 16 October 1944. Returned from overseas service and arrived at the New York Port of Embarkation on 16 January 1946). Inactivated 20 January 1946 at Camp Kilmer, New Jersey.

CAMPAIGN STREAMERS
World War II
Central Europe

DECORATIONS
None

COAT OF ARMS
None

DISTINCTIVE INSIGNIA
None

795th ANTIAIRCRAFT ARTILLERY AUTOMATIC WEAPONS BATTALION

Constituted 25 February 1943 in the Army of the United States as the 795th Coast Artillery Battalion (Antiaircraft) (Automatic Weapons) and activated 20 April 1943 at Camp Stewart, Georgia. Redesignated 30 April 1943 as the 795th Antiaircraft Artillery Automatic Weapons Battalion. (Departed Boston Port of Embarkation 7 April 1944 for overseas service; arrived in England 16 April 1944 and landed in France on 18 July 1944). Inactivated 31 December 1945 in Germany.

Redesignated 25 June 1948 as the 42d Antiaircraft Artillery Automatic Weapons Battalion.

CAMPAIGN STREAMERS
World War II
Normandy
Northern France
Rhineland
Central Europe

DECORATIONS
None

COAT OF ARMS
None

DISTINCTIVE INSIGNIA
None

796th ANTIAIRCRAFT ARTILLERY AUTOMATIC WEAPONS BATTALION

Constituted 25 February 1943 in the Army of the United States as the 796th Coast Artillery Battalion (Antiaircraft) (Automatic Weapons) and activated 20 April 1943 at Camp Stewart, Georgia. Redesignated 30 April 1943 as the 796th Antiaircraft Artillery Automatic Weapons Battalion (Self Propelled). (Departed New York Port of Embarkation 11 August 1944 for overseas service; arrived in England 22 August 1944 and landed in France on 23 September 1944. Returned from overseas service and arrived in the New York Port of Embarkation on 16 April 1946). Inactivated 17 April 1946 at Camp Kilmer, New Jersey.

Redesignated 25 June 1948 as the 57th Antiaircraft Artillery Automatic Weapons Battalion.

CAMPAIGN STREAMERS
World War II
Rhineland
Ardennes-Alsace
Central Europe

DECORATIONS

President Unit Citation (Army), Streamer embroidered *BASTOGNE* (Btry B, 796th AAA AW Bn cited for period 18-27 Dec 1944; WDGO 17, 1945)

COAT OF ARMS
None

DISTINCTIVE INSIGNIA
None

797th ANTIAIRCRAFT ARTILLERY AUTOMATIC WEAPONS BATTALION

Constituted 25 February 1943 in the Army of the United States as the 797th Coast Artillery Battalion (Antiaircraft) (Automatic Weapons) and activated 16 April 1943 at Camp Haan, California. Redesignated 30 April 1943 as the 797th Antiaircraft Artillery Automatic Weapons Battalion (Mobile). Inactivated 1 November 1944 at Camp Howze, Texas. Disbanded 10 October 1952.

CAMPAIGN STREAMERS
None

DECORATIONS
None

COAT OF ARMS
None

DISTINCTIVE INSIGNIA
None

798th ANTIAIRCRAFT ARTILLERY AUTOMATIC WEAPONS BATTALION

Constituted 25 February 1943 in the Army of the United States as the 798th Coast Artillery Battalion (Antiaircraft) (Automatic Weapons). Redesignated 30 April 1943 as the 798th Antiaircraft Artillery Automatic Weapons Battalion (Mobile) and activated at Camp Haan, California. (Departed Boston Port of Embarkation 10 November 1944 for overseas service; arrived in England 17 November 1944 and landed in France on 6 February 1945. Returned from overseas service and arrived at the New York Port of Embarkation on 23 October 1945). Inactivated 24 October 1945 at Camp Shanks, New York.

Redesignated 18 June 1948 as the 58th Antiaircraft Artillery Automatic Weapons Battalion.

CAMPAIGN STREAMERS
World War II
Rhineland
Central Europe

DECORATIONS
None

COAT OF ARMS
None

DISTINCTIVE INSIGNIA
None

799th ANTIAIRCRAFT ARTILLERY AUTOMATIC WEAPONS BATTALION

Constituted 25 February 1943 in the Army of the United States as the 799th Coast Artillery Battalion (Antiaircraft) (Automatic Weapons) and activated 16 April 1943 at Camp Haan, California. Redesignated 30 April 1943 as the 799th Antiaircraft Artillery Automatic Weapons Battalion (Semimobile). Inactivated 19 July 1944 at Camp Gruber, Oklahoma. Disbanded 26 October 1944.

CAMPAIGN STREAMERS
None

DECORATIONS
None

COAT OF ARMS
None

DISTINCTIVE INSIGNIA
None

800th ANTIAIRCRAFT ARTILLERY AUTOMATIC WEAPONS BATTALION

Constituted 25 February 1943 in the Army of the United States as the 800th Coast Artillery Battalion (Antiaircraft) (Automatic Weapons) and activated 16 April 1943 at Camp Haan, California. Reorganized and redesignated 30 April 1943 as the 800th Antiaircraft Artillery Automatic Weapons Battalion (Semimobile). Inactivated 12 June 1944 at Camp Haan. Disbanded 26 June 1944.

CAMPAIGN STREAMERS
None

DECORATIONS
None

COAT OF ARMS
None

DISTINCTIVE INSIGNIA
None

804th ANTIAIRCRAFT ARTILLERY BATTALION

Constituted 30 August 1940 in the New Mexico National Guard as the 104th Antitank Battalion and organized from new and existing units as follows:

Headquarters organized new and Federally recognized 5 November 1940 at Roswell

Headquarters Company organized new and Federally recognized 10 October 1940 at Santa Fe

Battery A 158th Field Artillery (organized at Roswell during February 1910 as Light Battery A, New Mexico National Guard and redesignated Battery A, Field Artillery in 1911; mustered into Federal service 15 May 1916 at Roswell for Mexican border; mustered out 23 March 1917 and resumed State status; called into Federal service 21 April 1917 at Roswell and drafted into Federal service on 5 August 1917; redesignated 1 October 1917 as Battery A 146th Field Artillery and assigned to the 41st Division; relieved from the 41st Division and demobilized 26 June 1919 at Fort D. A. Russell, Wyoming; reorganized and Federally recognized 27 June 1921 at Roswell as Battery A 1st Field Artillery, New Mexico National Guard; redesignated 5 January 1922 as Battery C 158th Field Artillery; redesignated 10 February 1922 as Battery A 158th Field Artillery); redesignated 9 September 1940 as Company A

Company B organized new and Federally recognized 4 October 1940 at Raton

Company C organized new and Federally recognized 9 October 1940 at Tucumcari

Medical Detachment organized new and Federally recognized 4 October 1940 at Raton

Inducted into Federal service 6 January 1941 at home stations. Redesignated 15 December 1941 as the 804th Tank Destroyer Battalion (Self Propelled). (Departed New York Port of Embarkation 5 August 1942 for overseas service and arrived in England 17 August 1942; moved to North Africa 31 March 1943 and landed in Italy on 8 February 1944. Returned from overseas service and arrived at the Hampton Roads Port of Embarkation on 31 July 1945). Inactivated 10 December 1945 at Camp Hood, Texas. Redesignated 31 May 1946 as 804th Antiaircraft Artillery Automatic Weapons Battalion. Reorganized and Federally recognized 3 October 1947 with Headquarters at Tucumcari and batteries at Portales, Raton, Clovis and Clayton. Redesignated

1 October 1953 as 804th Antiaircraft Artillery Battalion (Automatic Weapons) (Mobile). Reorganized and redesignated 1 May 1956 as 804th Antiaircraft Artillery Battalion (75mm Gun).

Consolidated 1 September 1959 with the 200th Artillery, a parent regiment under the Combat Arms Regimental System.

CAMPAIGN STREAMERS
World War II
Rome-Arno
North Apennines
Po Valley

DECORATIONS
French Croix de Guerre with Palm, World War II, Streamer embroidered *CENTRAL ITALY* (804th TD Bn cited for period 1 Dec 1943-31 Jul 1944; DAGO 43, 1950)

COAT OF ARMS
SHIELD: Azure, five fleurs-de-lis in saltire argent.

CREST: That for the regiments and separate battalions of the New Mexico Army National Guard: On a wreath of the colors (argent and azure) a coiled rattlesnake proper.

MOTTO: *Adelante* (Forward)

The five fleurs-de-lis represent the five major engagements of an element of the organization during World War I.

DISTINCTIVE BADGE
On an inverted blue projectile five silver fleurs-de-lis below a arrow silver chief. The motto, *ADELANTE*, is silver on a blue scroll. The sample of the badge depicted was approved for wear on 15 January 1953.

811th ANTIAIRCRAFT ARTILLERY AUTOMATIC WEAPONS BATTALION

Constituted 13 May 1944 in the Army of the United States as the 811th Antiaircraft Artillery Automatic Weapons Battalion (Semimobile) and assigned to the Central Pacific Area. Activated 26 May 1944 at Camp Malokole, Hawaii; inactivated 29 November 1945 at Fort Shafter, Hawaii.

CAMPAIGN STREAMERS
World War II
Pacific Theater without inscription

DECORATIONS
None

COAT OF ARMS
None

DISTINCTIVE INSIGNIA
None

813th ANTIAIRCRAFT ARTILLERY AUTOMATIC WEAPONS BATTALION

Constituted 25 February 1943 in the Army of the United States as the 574th Coast Artillery Battalion (Antiaircraft) (Automatic Weapons) and redesignated 30 April 1943 as the 574th Antiaircraft Artillery Automatic Weapons Battalion (Self Propelled). Activated 15 June 1943 at Camp Edwards, Massachusetts. (Departed New York Port of Embarkation 16 December 1944 for overseas service; arrived in England 21 December 1944 and landed in France on 10 March 1945). Inactivated 9 December 1945 in France. Redesignated 813th Antiaircraft Artillery Automatic Weapons Battalion, allotted to the Organized Reserve Corps and assigned to the 13th Armored Division on 17 May 1949. Activated 27 May 1949 with Headquarters at Los Angeles, California. (Headquarters relocated to San Diego, California on 7 July 1950).

Redesignated 1 March 1952 as the 574th Antiaircraft Artillery Automatic Weapons Battalion.

CAMPAIGN STREAMERS
World War II
Rhineland
Ardennes-Alsace
Central Europe

DECORATIONS
None

COAT OF ARMS
None

DISTINCTIVE INSIGNIA
None

815th ANTIAIRCRAFT ARTILLERY AUTOMATIC WEAPONS BATTALION

Constituted 25 February 1943 in the Army of the United States as the 815th Coast Artillery Battalion (Antiaircraft) (Automatic Weapons) and activated 16 April 1943 at Camp Haan, California. Redesignated 30 April 1943 as the 815th Antiaircraft Artillery Automatic Weapons Battalion (Mobile). (Departed New York Port of Embarkation 4 December 1944 for overseas service; arrived in England 12 December 1944 and landed in France on 6 March 1945. Returned from overseas service and arrived at the New York Port of Embarkation on 1 March 1946). Inactivated 2 March 1946 at Camp Kilmer, New Jersey.

CAMPAIGN STREAMERS
World War II
Rhineland
Central Europe

DECORATIONS
None

COAT OF ARMS
None

DISTINCTIVE INSIGNIA
None

816th ANTIAIRCRAFT ARTILLERY AUTOMATIC WEAPONS BATTALION

Constituted 25 February 1943 in the Army of the United States as the 816th Coast Artillery Battalion (Antiaircraft) (Automatic Weapons). Redesignated 816th Antiaircraft Artillery Automatic Weapons Battalion (Semimobile) and activated 30 April 1943 at Camp Haan, California. Inactivated 28 July 1944 at Camp Swift, Texas. Disbanded 26 October 1944.

CAMPAIGN STREAMERS
None

DECORATIONS
None

COAT OF ARMS
None

DISTINCTIVE INSIGNIA
None

817th ANTIAIRCRAFT ARTILLERY AUTOMATIC WEAPONS BATTALION

Constituted 25 February 1943 in the Army of the United States as the 817th Coast Artillery Battalion (Antiaircraft) (Automatic Weapons) and activated 2 April 1943 at Camp Haan, California. Reorganized and redesignated 30 April 1943 as the 817th Antiaircraft Artillery Automatic Weapons Battalion (Semimobile). Inactivated 4 November 1944 at Camp Maxey, Texas. Disbanded 10 October 1952.

CAMPAIGN STREAMERS
None

DECORATIONS
None

COAT OF ARMS
None

DISTINCTIVE INSIGNIA
None

818th ANTIAIRCRAFT ARTILLERY AUTOMATIC WEAPONS BATTALION

Constituted 25 February 1943 in the Army of the United States as the 818th Coast Artillery Battalion (Antiaircraft) (Automatic Weapons). Redesignated 818th Antiaircraft Artillery Automatic Weapons Battalion (Semimobile) and activated 30 April 1943 at Camp Haan, California. Inactivated 25 July 1944 at Camp Swift, Texas. Disbanded 26 October 1944.

CAMPAIGN STREAMERS
None

DECORATIONS
None

COAT OF ARMS
None

DISTINCTIVE INSIGNIA
None

819th ANTIAIRCRAFT ARTILLERY AUTOMATIC WEAPONS BATTALION

Constituted 25 February 1943 in the Army of the United States as the 819th Coast Artillery Battalion (Antiaircraft) (Automatic Weapons) (Colored) and activated 20 April 1943 at Camp Stewart, Georgia. Reorganized and redesignated 30 April 1943 as the 819th Antiaircraft Artillery Automatic Weapons Battalion (Semimobile) (Colored). Disbanded 1 May 1944 at Indiantown Gap Military Reservation, Annville, Pennsylvania.

CAMPAIGN STREAMERS
None

DECORATIONS
None

COAT OF ARMS
None

DISTINCTIVE INSIGNIA
None

820th ANTIAIRCRAFT ARTILLERY AUTOMATIC WEAPONS BATTALION

Constituted 25 February 1943 in the Army of the United States as the 820th Coast Artillery Battalion (Antiaircraft) (Automatic Weapons). Redesignated 30 April 1943 as the 820th Antiaircraft Artillery Automatic Weapons Battalion (Semimobile). Activated 20 May 1943 at Fort Bliss, Texas. Inactivated 29 July 1944 at Camp Swift, Texas. Disbanded 26 October 1944.

CAMPAIGN STREAMERS
None

DECORATIONS
None

COAT OF ARMS
None

DISTINCTIVE INSIGNIA
None

821st ANTIAIRCRAFT ARTILLERY AUTOMATIC WEAPONS BATTALION

Constituted 25 February 1943 in the Army of the United States as the 821st Coast Artillery Battalion (Antiaircraft) (Automatic Weapons). Redesignated 30 April 1943 as the 821st Antiaircraft Artillery Automatic Weapons Battalion (Semimobile). Activated 20 May 1943 at

Fort Bliss, Texas. Inactivated 4 November 1944 at Camp Howze, Texas. Disbanded 10 October 1952.

CAMPAIGN STREAMERS
None

DECORATIONS
None

COAT OF ARMS
None

DISTINCTIVE INSIGNIA
None

822d ANTIAIRCRAFT ARTILLERY AUTOMATIC WEAPONS BATTALION

Constituted 25 February 1943 in the Army of the United States as the 822d Coast Artillery Battalion (Antiaircraft) (Automatic Weapons). Redesignated 30 April 1943 as the 822d Antiaircraft Artillery Automatic Weapons Battalion (Semimobile). Activated 10 May 1943 at Camp Haan, California. Inactivated 5 August 1944 at Camp Maxey, Texas. Disbanded 26 October 1944.

CAMPAIGN STREAMERS
None

DECORATIONS
None

COAT OF ARMS
None

DISTINCTIVE INSIGNIA
None

823d ANTIAIRCRAFT ARTILLERY AUTOMATIC WEAPONS BATTALION

Constituted 25 February 1943 in the Army of the United States as the 823d Coast Artillery Battalion (Antiaircraft) (Automatic Weapons). Redesignated 30 April 1943 as the 823d Antiaircraft Artillery Automatic Weapons Battalion (Semimobile). Activated 10 May 1943 at Camp Haan, California. Inactivated 5 August 1944 at Camp Maxey, Texas. Disbanded 26 October 1944.

CAMPAIGN STREAMERS
None

DECORATIONS
None

COAT OF ARMS
None

DISTINCTIVE INSIGNIA
None

824th ANTIAIRCRAFT ARTILLERY AUTOMATIC WEAPONS BATTALION

Constituted 25 February 1943 in the Army of the United States as the 824th Coast Artillery Battalion (Antiaircraft) (Automatic Weapons). Redesignated 30 April 1943 as the 824th Antiaircraft Artillery Automatic Weapons Battalion (Semimobile). Activated 24 May 1943 at Camp Haan, California. Inactivated 14 November 1944 at Camp Howze, Texas. Disbanded 10 October 1952.

CAMPAIGN STREAMERS
None

DECORATIONS
None

COAT OF ARMS
None

DISTINCTIVE INSIGNIA
None

832d ANTIAIRCRAFT ARTILLERY AUTOMATIC WEAPONS BATTALION

Constituted 25 February 1943 in the Army of the United States as the 832d Coast Artillery Battalion (Antiaircraft) (Automatic Weapons). Redesignated 30 April 1943 as the 832d Antiaircraft Artillery Automatic Weapons Battalion (Semimobile). Activated 24 May 1943 at Camp Haan, California. Inactivated 15 August 1944 at Camp Maxey, Texas. Disbanded 26 October 1944.

CAMPAIGN STREAMERS
None

DECORATIONS
None

COAT OF ARMS
None

DISTINCTIVE INSIGNIA
None

833d ANTIAIRCRAFT ARTILLERY AUTOMATIC WEAPONS BATTALION

Constituted 25 February 1943 in the Army of the United States as the 833d Coast Artillery Battalion (Antiaircraft) (Automatic Weapons). Redesignated 30 April 1943 as the 833d Antiaircraft Artillery Automatic Weapons Battalion (Semimobile). Activated 24 May 1943 at Camp Haan, California. Inactivated 8 November 1944 at Camp Howze, Texas. Disbanded 10 October 1952.

CAMPAIGN STREAMERS
None

DECORATIONS
None

COAT OF ARMS
None

DISTINCTIVE INSIGNIA
None

834th ANTIAIRCRAFT ARTILLERY AUTOMATIC WEAPONS BATTALION

Constituted 25 February 1943 in the Army of the United States as the 834th Coast Artillery Battalion (Antiaircraft) (Automatic Weapons). Redesignated 30 April 1943 as the 834th Antiaircraft Artillery Automatic Weapons Battalion (Self Propelled). Activated 24 May 1943 at Camp Haan, California. (Departed Portland Sub Port of Embarkation 22 January 1945 for overseas service; arrived in Hawaii 30 January 1945 and landed on Okinawa on 26 April 1945). Inactivated 30 June 1946 at Inchon, Korea.

CAMPAIGN STREAMERS
World War II
Ryukyus

DECORATIONS
None

COAT OF ARMS
None

DISTINCTIVE INSIGNIA
None

835th ANTIAIRCRAFT ARTILLERY AUTOMATIC WEAPONS BATTALION

Constituted 25 February 1943 in the Army of the United States as the 835th Coast Artillery Battalion (Antiaircraft) (Automatic Weapons). Redesignated 30 April 1943 as the 835th Antiaircraft Artillery Automatic Weapons Battalion (Semimobile). Activated 24 May 1943 at Camp Haan, California. Inactivated 8 November 1944 at Camp Howze, Texas. Disbanded 10 October 1952.

CAMPAIGN STREAMERS
None

DECORATIONS
None

COAT OF ARMS
None

DISTINCTIVE INSIGNIA
None

836th ANTIAIRCRAFT ARTILLERY AUTOMATIC WEAPONS BATTALION

Constituted 25 February 1943 in the Army of the United states as the 836th Coast Artillery Battalion (Antiaircraft) (Automatic Weapons). Redesignated 30 April 1943 as the 836th Antiaircraft Artillery Automatic Weapons Battalion (Semimobile). Activated 20 May 1943 at Camp Edwards, Massachusetts. Inactivated 12 December 1944 at Camp Livingston, Louisiana. Disbanded 10 October 1952.

CAMPAIGN STREAMERS
None

DECORATIONS
None

COAT OF ARMS
None

DISTINCTIVE INSIGNIA
None

837th ANTIAIRCRAFT ARTILLERY AUTOMATIC WEAPONS BATTALION

Constituted 25 February 1943 in the Army of the United States as the 837th Coast Artillery Battalion (Antiaircraft) (Automatic Weapons). Redesignated 30 April 1943 as the 837th Antiaircraft Artillery Automatic Weapons Battalion (Semimobile). Activated 20 May 1943 at Fort Sheridan, Illinois. Inactivated 1 December 1944 at Camp Livingston, Louisiana. Disbanded 10 October 1952.

CAMPAIGN STREAMERS
None

DECORATIONS
None

COAT OF ARMS
None

DISTINCTIVE INSIGNIA
None

838th ANTIAIRCRAFT ARTILLERY AUTOMATIC WEAPONS BATTALION

Constituted 25 February 1943 in the Army of the United States as the 838th Coast Artillery Battalion (Antiaircraft) (Automatic Weapons). Redesignated 30 April 1943 as the 838th Antiaircraft Artillery Automatic Weapons Battalion (Semimobile). Activated 20 May 1943 at Camp Hulen, Texas. (Departed New York Port of Embarkation 1 December 1944 for overseas service; arrived in England 12 December 1944 and landed in France on 8 February 1945. Returned from overseas service and arrived at the New York Port of Embarkation on 3 April 1946). Inactivated 4 April 1946 at Camp Kilmer, New Jersey.

CAMPAIGN STREAMERS
World War II
Rhineland
Central Europe

DECORATIONS
None

COAT OF ARMS
None

DISTINCTIVE INSIGNIA
None

839th ANTIAIRCRAFT ARTILLERY AUTOMATIC WEAPONS BATTALION

Constituted 25 February 1943 in the Army of the United States as the 839th Coast Artillery Battalion (Antiaircraft) (Automatic Weapons). Redesignated 30 April 1943 as the 839th Antiaircraft Artillery Automatic Weapons Battalion (Semimobile). Activated 20 May 1943 at Fort Bliss, Texas. (Departed Boston Port of Embarkation 2 December 1944 for overseas service; arrived in England 12 December 1944 and landed in France on 4 March 1945). Inactivated 6 October 1945 in France.

CAMPAIGN STREAMERS
World War II
Rhineland
Central Europe

DECORATIONS
None

COAT OF ARMS
None

DISTINCTIVE INSIGNIA
None

840th ANTIAIRCRAFT ARTILLERY AUTOMATIC WEAPONS BATTALION

Constituted 25 February 1943 in the Army of the United States as the 840th Coast Artillery Battalion (Antiaircraft) (Automatic Weapons). Redesignated 30 April 1943 as the 840th Antiaircraft Artillery Automatic Weapons Battalion (Semimobile). Activated 20 May 1943 at Camp Stewart, Georgia. (Departed Seattle Port of Embarkation 15 November 1944 for overseas service and arrived in Hawaii on 23 November 1944). Inactivated 8 April 1946 at West Aiea, Oahu, Hawaii.

CAMPAIGN STREAMERS
World War II
Pacific Theater without inscription

DECORATIONS
None

COAT OF ARMS
None

DISTINCTIVE INSIGNIA
None

841st ANTIAIRCRAFT ARTILLERY AUTOMATIC WEAPONS BATTALION

Constituted 25 February 1943 in the Army of the United States as the 841st Coast Artillery Battalion (Antiaircraft) (Automatic Weapons). Redesignated 30 April 1943 as the 841st Antiaircraft Artillery Automatic Weapons Battalion (Semimobile). Activated 20 May 1943 at Camp Stewart, Georgia. Inactivated 11 November 1944 at Camp Howze, Texas. Disbanded 10 October 1952.

CAMPAIGN STREAMERS
None

DECORATIONS
None

COAT OF ARMS
None

DISTINCTIVE INSIGNIA
None

842d ANTIAIRCRAFT ARTILLERY AUTOMATIC WEAPONS BATTALION

Constituted 25 February 1943 in the Army of the United States as the 842d Coast Artillery Battalion (Antiaircraft) (Automatic Weapons). Redesignated 30 April 1943 as the 842d Antiaircraft Artillery Automatic Weapons Battalion (Semimobile). Activated 20 May 1943 at Camp Stewart, Georgia. (Departed Seattle Port of Embarkation 15 November 1944 for overseas service and arrived in Hawaii on 23 November 1944). Inactivated 25 January 1946 on Oahu, Hawaii.

CAMPAIGN STREAMERS
World War II
Pacific Theater without inscription

DECORATIONS
None

COAT OF ARMS
None

DISTINCTIVE INSIGNIA
None

843d ANTIAIRCRAFT ARTILLERY AUTOMATIC WEAPONS BATTALION

Constituted 25 February 1943 in the Army of the United States as the 843d Coast Artillery Battalion (Antiaircraft) (Automatic Weapons). Redesignated 30 April 1943 as the 843d Antiaircraft Artillery Automatic Weapons Battalion (Air Transportable). Activated 20 May 1943 at Camp Stewart, Georgia. (Departed Los Angeles Port of Embarkation 29 June 1944 for overseas service and arrived in India on 7 August 1944. After service in Burma and China returned from overseas service and arrived at the New York Port of Embarkation on 5 November 1945). Inactivated 7 November 1945 at Camp Kilmer, New Jersey.

CAMPAIGN STREAMERS
World War II
China Defensive
India-Burma

DECORATIONS
None

COAT OF ARMS
None

DISTINCTIVE INSIGNIA
None

844th ANTIAIRCRAFT ARTILLERY AUTOMATIC WEAPONS BATTALION

Constituted 25 February 1943 in the Army of the United States as the 844th Coast Artillery Battalion (Antiaircraft) (Automatic Weapons). Redesignated 30 April 1943 as the 844th Antiaircraft Artillery Automatic Weapons Battalion (Semimobile). Activated 20 May 1943 at Camp Stewart, Georgia. Reorganized and redesignated 15 December 1943 as the 844th Antiaircraft Artillery Automatic Weapons Battalion (Air Transportable). Disbanded 5 August 1944 at Camp Stewart.

CAMPAIGN STREAMERS
None

DECORATIONS
None

COAT OF ARMS
None

DISTINCTIVE INSIGNIA
None

844th ANTIAIRCRAFT ARTILLERY AUTOMATIC WEAPONS BATTALION

Constituted 24 January 1942 in the Army of the United States as Headquarters and Headquarters Battery, 2d Battalion, 50th Coast Artillery (155mm Gun) (Mobile) and activated 1 February 1942 at Camp Pendleton, Virginia. Reorganized in the Admiralty Islands and redesignated 5 April 1944 as Headquarters and Headquarters Detachment, 43d Coast Artillery Battalion (155mm Gun). (Relocated to Pitylu Island on 16 April 1944. Returned from overseas service and arrived at the Los Angeles Port of Embarkation on 30 December 1945). Inactivated 31 December 1945 at Camp Anza, Arlington, California. Redesignated Headquarters and

Headquarters Detachment, 844th Coast Artillery Battalion (Harbor Defense), allotted to the Organized Reserves and assigned to Sixth Army on 6 May 1947. Activated 2 June 1947 at San Francisco, California. (Organized Reserves redesignated 25 March 1948 as the Organized Reserve Corps). Reorganized and redesignated 28 April 1948 as Headquarters and Headquarters Battery, 844th Antiaircraft Artillery Automatic Weapons Battalion; concurrently, 860th Coast Artillery Gun Battery redesignated Battery A; 865th Coast Artillery ATB Battery redesignated Battery B; 329th Coast Artillery ATB Battery redesignated Battery C; 810th Coast Artillery ATB Battery redesignated Battery D; and Medical Detachment, 844th Coast Artillery Battalion redesignated Medical Detachment, 844th Antiaircraft Artillery Automatic Weapons Battalion. Inactivated 31 August 1950 at San Francisco.

CAMPAIGN STREAMERS
World War II
Bismarck Archipelago
New Guinea

DECORATIONS
None

COAT OF ARMS
None

DISTINCTIVE INSIGNIA
None

845th ANTIAIRCRAFT ARTILLERY AUTOMATIC WEAPONS BATTALION

Constituted 25 February 1943 in the Army of the United States as the 845th Coast Artillery Battalion (Antiaircraft) (Automatic Weapons). Redesignated 30 April 1943 as the 845th Antiaircraft Artillery Automatic Weapons Battalion (Air Transportable). Activated 20 May 1943 at Camp Stewart, Georgia. Inactivated 10 May 1944 at Camp Pickett, Virginia. Disbanded 26 June 1944.

CAMPAIGN STREAMERS
None

DECORATIONS
None

COAT OF ARMS
None

DISTINCTIVE INSIGNIA
None

HEADQUARTERS AND HEADQUARTERS DETACHMENT 845th COAST ARTILLERY BATTALION

Constituted 24 January 1942 in the Army of the United States as Headquarters and Headquarters Battery, 1st Battalion, 50th Coast Artillery (155mm Gun) (Mobile) and activated 1 February 1942 at Camp Pendleton, Virginia. Reorganized and redesignated 2 February 1944 as Headquarters and Headquarters Detachment, 42d Coast Artillery Battalion (155mm Gun). (Departed Seattle Port of Embarkation 16 February 1944 for overseas service and arrived on Attu Island on 5 March 1944. Returned from overseas service and arrived at the Seattle Port of Embarkation on 26 November 1945). Inactivated 29 November 1945 at Fort Lawton, Washington. Redesignated Headquarters and Headquarters Detachment, 845th Coast Artillery Battalion (Harbor Defense), allotted to the Organized Reserves and assigned to Sixth

Army, 6 May 1947. Activated 2 June 1947 at Los Angeles, California. (Organized Reserves redesignated 25 March 1948 as Organized Reserve Corps). Inactivated 6 June 1948 at Los Angeles.

CAMPAIGN STREAMERS
World War II
Pacific Theater without inscription

DECORATIONS
None

COAT OF ARMS
None

DISTINCTIVE INSIGNIA
None

846th ANTIAIRCRAFT ARTILLERY AUTOMATIC WEAPONS BATTALION

Constituted 25 February 1943 in the Army of the United States as the 846th Coast Artillery Battalion (Antiaircraft) (Automatic Weapons) (Colored). Redesignated 30 April 1943 as the 846th Antiaircraft Artillery Automatic Weapons Battalion (Semimobile) (Colored). Activated 20 May 1943 at Camp Stewart, Georgia. Disbanded 24 April 1944 at Camp Patrick Henry, Virginia.

CAMPAIGN STREAMERS
None

DECORATIONS
None

COAT OF ARMS
None

DISTINCTIVE INSIGNIA
None

HEADQUARTERS AND HEADQUARTERS DETACHMENT 846th COAST ARTILLERY BATTALION

Constituted 28 April 1942 in the Army of the United States as Headquarters and Headquarters Battery, 3d Battalion, 47th Coast Artillery (155mm Gun) (Truck Drawn) and activated 15 April 1943 at Camp Pendleton, Virginia. Reorganized and redesignated 15 March 1944 as Headquarters and Headquarters Detachment, 38th Coast Artillery Battalion (155mm Gun). (Moved to Hawaii during summer of 1944. After service in the Philippine Islands and on New Caledonia moved to Okinawa on 24 June 1945). Inactivated 1 October 1945 at Kin, Okinawa. Redesignated Headquarters and Headquarters Detachment, 846th Coast Artillery Battalion (Harbor Defense), allotted to the Organized Reserves and assigned to Sixth Army on 6 May 1947. Activated 2 June 1947 at San Diego, California. (Organized Reserves redesignated 25 March 1948 as Organized Reserve Corps). Inactivated 1 March 1949 at San Diego.

CAMPAIGN STREAMERS
World War II
Leyte
Ryukyus

DECORATIONS
Philippine Presidential Unit Citation, Streamer embroidered *17 OCTOBER 1944 TO 4 JULY 1945* (38th CA Bn cited; DAGO 47, 1950)

COAT OF ARMS
None

DISTINCTIVE INSIGNIA
None

847th ANTIAIRCRAFT ARTILLERY GUN BATTALION

Constituted 25 July 1944 in the Army of the United States as the 53d Coast Artillery Battalion (Harbor Defense) and activated 13 August 1944 at Fort Shafter, Territory of Hawaii. Inactivated 10 April 1945 at Fort Shafter. Headquarters and Headquarters Detachment redesignated Headquarters and Headquarters Detachment, 847th Coast Artillery Battalion (Harbor Defense) and organic batteries redesignated separate batteries of Coast Artillery on 6 May 1947; concurrently, these elements allotted to the Organized Reserves, assigned to Sixth Army and Headquarters and Headquarters Detachment activated at Oakland, California. (Organized Reserves redesignated 25 March 1948 as Organized Reserve Corps). Headquarters and Headquarters Detachment, 847th Coast Artillery Battalion (Harbor Defense) redesignated Headquarters and Headquarters Battery, 847th Antiaircraft Artillery Gun Battalion on 25 February 1949; concurrently, former batteries redesignated organic elements of the 847th Antiaircraft Artillery Gun Battalion and Battalion activated at Oakland. Battalion inactivated 18 August 1950 at Oakland.

CAMPAIGN STREAMERS
World War II
Pacific Theater without inscription

DECORATIONS
None

COAT OF ARMS
None

DISTINCTIVE INSIGNIA
None

851st ANTIAIRCRAFT ARTILLERY AUTOMATIC WEAPONS BATTALION

Constituted 3 November 1942 in the Army of the United States as the 476th Coast Artillery Battalion (Antiaircraft) (Automatic Weapons) and activated 15 November 1942 at Fort Sheridan, Illinois. Reorganized and redesignated 30 April 1943 as the 476th Antiaircraft Artillery Automatic Weapons Battalion (Semimobile). (Departed San Francisco Port of Embarkation 27 October 1943 for overseas service and arrived in Australia on 13 November 1943. After service in New Guinea and on Biak Island, moved to the Philippine Islands on 9 February 1945). Inactivated 15 December 1945 at Zamboanga, Mindanao, Philippine Islands. Redesignated 24 May 1949 as the 851st Antiaircraft Artillery Automatic Weapons Battalion.

Redesignated 16 October 1952 as the 476th Antiaircraft Artillery Automatic Weapons Battalion.

CAMPAIGN STREAMERS
World War II
New Guinea (with arrowhead)
Luzon
Southern Philippines

DECORATIONS
Presidential Unit Citation (Army), Streamer embroidered *BIAK ISLAND* (476th AAA AW Bn cited for period 27 May-3 Jun 1944; WDGO 45, 1945)

Philippine Presidential Unit Citation, Streamer embroidered *17 OCTOBER 1944 TO 4 JULY 1945* (476th AAA AW Bn cited; DAGO 47, 1950)

COAT OF ARMS
None

DISTINCTIVE INSIGNIA
None

852d ANTIAIRCRAFT ARTILLERY MISSILE BATTALION

Constituted 2 November 1942 in the Army of the United States as the 487th Coast Artillery Battalion (Antiaircraft) (Automatic Weapons) and activated 10 December 1942 at Camp Haan, California. Reorganized and redesignated 30 April 1943 as the 487th Antiaircraft Artillery Automatic Weapons Battalion (Semimobile). (Departed Portland Sub Port of Embarkation 31 March 1944 for overseas service and arrived on New Guinea on 12 May 1944. After service on Noemfoor Island, moved to the Philippine Islands on 17 April 1945). Inactivated 15 February 1946 in the Philippine Islands. Redesignated 24 May 1949 as the 852d Antiaircraft Artillery Automatic Weapons Battalion. Redesignated 852d Antiaircraft Artillery Missile Battalion and allotted to the Regular Army on 7 February 1956. Activated 2 March 1956 at Milwaukee, Wisconsin; inactivated 1 September 1958 at Milwaukee.

CAMPAIGN STREAMERS
World War II
New Guinea (with arrowhead)
Luzon
Southern Philippines

DECORATIONS
Philippine Presidential Unit Citation, Streamer embroidered *17 OCTOBER 1944 TO 4 JULY 1945* (487th AAA AW Bn cited; DAGO 47, 1950)

COAT OF ARMS
SHIELD: Per fess wavy gules and or, issuant to chief two demi Philippine lions and in base a six pointed star charged with a pheon, all counterchanged.

CREST: None

MOTTO: Forever Alert

The colors scarlet and yellow are for Artillery. The six pointed star represents an air burst by a missile. The pheon, an artillery prototype is for the assault landing on New Guinea during World War II. The two sea lions from the Philippine coat of arms represent the two campaigns of the unit in that area.

DISTINCTIVE INSIGNIA
The insignia is the shield and motto of the coat of arms. The sample of the insignia depicted was approved for wear on 17 December 1957.

853d ANTIAIRCRAFT ARTILLERY AUTOMATIC WEAPONS BATTALION

Constituted 19 December 1942 in the Army of the United States as the 496th Coast Artillery Battalion (Antiaircraft) (Gun) and activated 10 January 1943 at Camp Stewart, Georgia. Reorganized and redesignated 7 June 1943 as the 496th Antiaircraft Artillery Gun Battalion (Semimobile). (Departed Portland Sub Port of Embarkation 16 March 1944 for overseas service; arrived in New Guinea on 4 April 1944 and moved to the Philippine Islands on 3 May 1945. Returned from overseas service and arrived at the Los Angeles Port of Embarkation 12 January 1946). Inactivated 13 January 1946 at Camp Anza, Arlington, California. Redesignated 24 May 1949 as the 853d Antiaircraft Artillery Automatic Weapons Battalion.

Redesignated 16 October 1952 as the 496th Antiaircraft Artillery Gun Battalion.

CAMPAIGN STREAMERS
World War II
New Guinea
Southern Philippines

DECORATIONS
Philippine Presidential Unit Citation, Streamer embroidered *17 OCTOBER 1944 TO 4 JULY 1945* (496th AAA AW Bn cited; DAGO 47, 1950)

COAT OF ARMS
None

DISTINCTIVE INSIGNIA
None

854th ANTIAIRCRAFT ARTILLERY AUTOMATIC WEAPONS BATTALION

Constituted 3 November 1942 in the Army of the United States as the 478th Coast Artillery Battalion (Antiaircraft) (Automatic Weapons) and activated 20 November 1942 at Camp Davis, North Carolina. Reorganized and redesignated 30 April 1943 as the 478th Antiaircraft Artillery Automatic Weapons Battalion (Semimobile). (Departed San Francisco Port of Embarkation 27 September 1943 for overseas service and arrived in Australia on 15 October 1943. After service in New Guinea, moved to the Philippine Islands on 22 February 1945. Returned from overseas service and arrived at the San Francisco Port of Embarkation on 2 January 1946). Inactivated 4 January 1946 at Camp Stoneman, California. Redesignated 24 May 1949 as the 854th Antiaircraft Artillery Automatic Weapons Battalion.

Redesignated 16 October 1952 as the 478th Antiaircraft Artillery Automatic Weapons Battalion.

CAMPAIGN STREAMERS
World War II
New Guinea
Leyte
Southern Philippines (with arrowhead)

DECORATIONS
Philippine Presidential Unit Citation, Streamer embroidered *17 OCTOBER 1944 TO 4 JULY 1945* (478th AAA AW Bn cited; DAGO 47, 1950)

COAT OF ARMS
None

DISTINCTIVE INSIGNIA
None

860th ANTIAIRCRAFT ARTILLERY AUTOMATIC WEAPONS BATTALION

Constituted 25 February 1943 in the Army of the United States as the 860th Coast Artillery Battalion (Antiaircraft) (Automatic Weapons). Redesignated 30 April 1943 as the 860th Antiaircraft Artillery Automatic Weapons Battalion (Self Propelled). Assigned to the Caribbean Defense Command on 18 August 1943. Activated 5 September 1943 at Fort Brooke, Puerto Rico. Inactivated 1 June 1944 at Camp Tortuguero, Puerto Rico. Disbanded 1 November 1944. Reconstituted 10 March 1949 in the Organized Reserve Corps. Assigned to Sixth Army on 28 March 1949. Activated 18 April 1949 at Los Angeles, California; inactivated 15 September 1950 at Los Angeles.

CAMPAIGN STREAMERS
World War II
American Theater without inscription

DECORATIONS
None

COAT OF ARMS
None

DISTINCTIVE INSIGNIA
None

861st ANTIAIRCRAFT ARTILLERY AUTOMATIC WEAPONS BATTALION

Constituted 25 February 1943 in the Army of the United States as the 861st Coast Artillery Battalion (Antiaircraft) (Automatic Weapons). Redesignated 30 April 1943 as the 861st Antiaircraft Artillery Automatic Weapons Battalion (Semimobile). Activated 5 November 1943 at Fort Kamehameha, Hawaii. (Arrived in the Philippine Islands on 8 December 1944 and landed in Okinawa on 1 April 1945). Inactivated 30 January 1946 on Okinawa. Allotted to the Organized Reserve Corps on 10 May 1949. Activated 1 April 1949 at Lansing, Michigan. Assigned to Fifth Army on 21 May 1949. Inactivated 4 December 1950 at Lansing.

CAMPAIGN STREAMERS
World War II
Leyte
Ryukyus

DECORATIONS
Philippine Presidential Unit Citation, Streamer embroidered *17 OCTOBER 1944 TO 4 JULY 1945* (861st AAA AW Bn cited; DAGO 47, 1950)

COAT OF ARMS
None

DISTINCTIVE INSIGNIA
None

862d ANTIAIRCRAFT ARTILLERY AUTOMATIC WEAPONS BATTALION

Constituted 25 February 1943 in the Army of the United States as the 862d Coast Artillery Battalion (Antiaircraft) (Automatic Weapons). Redesignated 30 April 1943 as the 862d Antiaircraft Artillery Automatic Weapons Battalion (Semimobile). Activated 10 May 1943 at Fort Ord, California. (Departed San Francisco Port of Embarkation 11 July 1943 for overseas service and arrived on Adak Island on 25 July 1943. After service on Kiska Island and at Fort Greely, Kodiak, returned from overseas service and arrived at the Seattle Port of Embarkation on 8 May 1944). Inactivated 7 August 1944 at Camp Van Dorn, Mississippi. Disbanded 26 October 1944.

CAMPAIGN STREAMERS
World War II
Aleutian Islands

DECORATIONS
None

COAT OF ARMS
None

DISTINCTIVE INSIGNIA
None

863d ANTIAIRCRAFT ARTILLERY AUTOMATIC WEAPONS BATTALION

Constituted 25 February 1943 in the Army of the United States as the 863d Coast Artillery Battalion (Antiaircraft) (Automatic Weapons). Redesignated 30 April 1943 as the 863d Antiaircraft Artillery Automatic Weapons Battalion (Semimobile). Activated 1 June 1943 at Fort Totten, New York. (Departed New York Port of Embarkation 21 March 1944 for overseas service; arrived in England 29 March 1944 and landed in France on 12 July 1944. Returned from overseas service and arrived at the Boston Port of Embarkation on 25 November 1945). Inactivated 26 November 1945 at Camp Myles Standish, Massachusetts. Allotted to the Organized Reserve Corps on 8 March 1949. Assigned to Fifth Army and activated 5 April 1949 at Chicago, Illinois. Inactivated 15 November 1950 at Chicago.

CAMPAIGN STREAMERS
World War II
Normandy
Northern France
Rhineland
Ardennes-Alsace
Central Europe

DECORATIONS
Presidential Unit Citation (Army), Streamer embroidered *ARDENNES* (863d AAA AW Bn cited for period 16-23 Dec 1944; WDGO 84, 1945)

Belgian Fourragere 1940 (Btry A 863d AAA AW Bn cited; DAGO 47, 1950)

Cited in the Order of the Day of the Belgian Army for action in the defense of *LIEGE* (Btry A 863d AAA AW Bn cited for period 27 Nov-14 Dec 1944; DAGO 43, 1950)

Cited in the Order of the Day of the Belgian Army for defense of the *MEUSE RIVER* (Btry A 863d AAA AW Bn cited for period 16 Dec 1944-25 Jan 1945; DAGO 43, 1950)

COAT OF ARMS
None

DISTINCTIVE INSIGNIA
None

864th ANTIAIRCRAFT ARTILLERY AUTOMATIC WEAPONS BATTALION

Constituted in the Regular Army as 3d Battalion, 64th Coast Artillery and organized at Fort Shafter, Hawaii: Headquarters and Headquarters Detachment and Combat Train, 3d Battalion and Battery I on 31 October 1925; and Batteries K and L on 1 July 1928. Reorganized and redesignated 12 December 1943 as the 864th Antiaircraft Artillery Automatic Weapons Battalion (Semimobile). Inactivated 5 June 1948 on Saipan.

Redesignated 28 June 1950 as the 94th Antiaircraft Artillery Battalion.

CAMPAIGN STREAMERS
World War II
Central Pacific
Western Pacific

DECORATIONS
None

COAT OF ARMS
None

DISTINCTIVE INSIGNIA
None

865th ANTIAIRCRAFT ARTILLERY MISSILE BATTALION

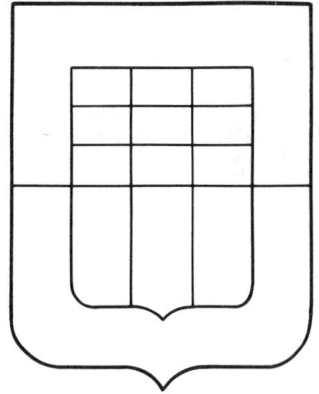 

Constituted 27 May 1942 in the Regular Army as 3d Battalion, 93d Coast Artillery (Antiaircraft) (Semimobile) and activated 15 June 1942 in Hawaii. Reorganized and redesignated 12 December 1943 as the 865th Antiaircraft Artillery Automatic Weapons Battalion (Semimobile). Redesignated 20 April 1953 as the 865th Antiaircraft Artillery Battalion (Automatic Weapons). Inactivated 20 December 1954 at Inchon, Korea. Redesignated 26 May 1955 as the 865th Antiaircraft Artillery Missile Battalion. Activated 1 June 1955 at Los Angeles, California; inactivated 1 September 1958 at Fort MacArthur, California.

CAMPAIGN STREAMERS
World War II
Central Pacific
Western Pacific

Korean War
UN Summer-Fall Offensive
Second Korean Winter
Korea Summer-Fall 1952
Third Korean Winter
Korea Summer 1953

DECORATIONS
None

COAT OF ARMS
SHIELD: Per fess sable and or, in chief a bar of the second, overall a pale counterchanged; all within a bordure per fess of the second and gules.

CREST: None

MOTTO: *Impenetrabile nos Sumus* (We Are Impenetrable)

Scarlet and yellow are the colors for Artillery. Black suggests the metal from which the battalion's weapons are made. The divisions of the shield – the upper half divided into nine parts and the lower into three – represent the numerical designation of the parent organization.

DISTINCTIVE INSIGNIA
The insignia is the shield and motto of the coat of arms. The sample of the insignia depicted was approved for wear on 15 September 1953.

866th ANTIAIRCRAFT ARTILLERY AUTOMATIC WEAPONS BATTALION

Constituted 27 May 1942 in the Regular Army as 3d Battalion, 95th Coast Artillery (Antiaircraft) (Semimobile) and activated 15 June 1942 in Hawaii. Reorganized in Hawaii and redesignated 12 December 1943 as the 866th Antiaircraft Artillery Automatic Weapons Battalion (Semimobile). (Moved to the Philippine Islands 20 October 1944 and landed on Okinawa on 26 April 1945). Inactivated 30 September 1946 on Luzon, Philippine Islands.

Redesignated 13 October 1948 as the 4th Antiaircraft Artillery Automatic Weapons Battalion.

CAMPAIGN STREAMERS
World War II
Leyte
Ryukyus

DECORATIONS
Philippine Presidential Unit Citation, Streamer embroidered *17 OCTOBER 1944 TO 4 JULY 1945* (866th AAA AW Bn cited; DAGO 47, 1950)

COAT OF ARMS
None

DISTINCTIVE INSIGNIA
None

867th ANTIAIRCRAFT ARTILLERY BATTALION

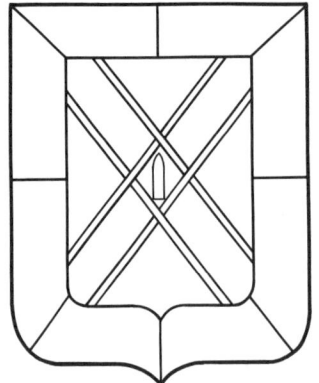 

Constituted 27 May 1942 in the Regular Army as 3d Battalion, 96th Coast Artillery (Antiaircraft) (Semimobile) and activated 15 June 1942 at Schofield Barracks, Hawaii. Reorganized in Hawaii and redesignated 12 December 1943 as the 753d Antiaircraft Artillery Gun Battalion (Semimobile). (Moved to Kwajalein Atoll in the Marshall Islands on 6 February 1944 and returned to Hawaii on 27 September 1944). Redesignated 14 February 1949 as the 867th Antiaircraft Artillery Automatic Weapons Battalion, Mobile. Redesignated 1 October 1950 as the 867th Antiaircraft Artillery Battalion. Inactivated 1 November 1957 at Fort Richardson, Alaska.

CAMPAIGN STREAMERS
World War II
Eastern Mandates
Western Pacific

DECORATIONS
None

COAT OF ARMS
SHIELD: Gules, within a saltire parted and fretty argent a shell or; a bordure gyronny or and gules.

CREST: None

MOTTO: *Caeli Causa Liberi* (For The Freedom Of The Skies)

The coat of arms is that of the 96th Coast Artillery within a red and yellow border to indicate the descent of the battalion from that regiment. The shield is red for Artillery. The crisscrossing searchlight beams and the shell refer to the operations of the battalion.

DISTINCTIVE INSIGNIA
The insignia is the shield and motto of the coat of arms. The sample of the insignia depicted was approved for wear on 12 November 1954.

868th ANTIAIRCRAFT ARTILLERY AUTOMATIC WEAPONS BATTALION

Constituted 27 May 1942 in the Regular Army as 3d Battalion, 97th Coast Artillery (Antiaircraft) (Semimobile) and activated 15 June 1942 in Hawaii. Reorganized at Hickam Field, Hawaii and redesignated 12 December 1943 as the 868th Antiaircraft Artillery Automatic Weapons Battalion. (Relocated to Guam on 10 September 1944). Inactivated 15 January 1946 on Guam.

CAMPAIGN STREAMERS
World War II
Western Pacific

DECORATIONS
None

COAT OF ARMS
None

DISTINCTIVE INSIGNIA
None

869th ANTIAIRCRAFT ARTILLERY AUTOMATIC WEAPONS BATTALION

Constituted 27 May 1942 in the Regular Army as 3d Battalion, 98th Coast Artillery (Antiaircraft) (Semimobile) and activated 18 June 1942 at Hickam Field, Hawaii. Reorganized in Hawaii and redesignated 12 December 1943 as the 869th Antiaircraft Artillery Automatic Weapons Battalion (Semimobile). Inactivated 29 October 1945 at Fort Shafter, Hawaii.

CAMPAIGN STREAMERS
World War II
Pacific Theater without inscription

DECORATIONS
None

COAT OF ARMS
None

DISTINCTIVE INSIGNIA
None

870th ANTIAIRCRAFT ARTILLERY BATTALION

Constituted 2 June 1913 in the New York National Guard as 2d Battalion, 15th Infantry (Colored). Organized and Federally recognized 29 June 1916 at New York City. Mustered into Federal service 25 July 1917 at Camp Whitman, New York and drafted into Federal service on 5 August 1917. Redesignated 1 March 1918 as 2d Battalion, 369th Infantry and assigned to the 93d Division. Relieved from the 93d Division and demobilized 28 February 1919 at Camp Upton, New York. Consolidated with the 2d Battalion, 15th Infantry, New York Guard (organized 31 July 1918 at New York City) and redesignated 11 October 1921 as 2d Battalion, 369th Infantry (Colored). Reorganized and Federally recognized 3 November 1924 at New York City. Converted, reorganized and redesignated 30 August 1940 as 2d Battalion, 369th Coast Artillery (Antiaircraft) (Colored). Inducted into Federal service 13 January 1941 at New York City. (Departed San Francisco Port of Embarkation 16 June 1942 for overseas service and arrived in Hawaii on 21 June 1942). Reorganized at Barber's Point, Hawaii and redesignated 12 December 1943 as the 870th Antiaircraft Artillery Automatic Weapons Battalion (Semimobile) (Colored). (Moved to Okinawa on 10 May 1945. Returned from overseas service and arrived at the Seattle Port of Embarkation on 13 January 1946). Inactivated 15 January 1946 at the Fort Lawton Staging Area, Seattle, Washington. Reorganized and Federally recognized 30 October 1947 at New York City. Reorganized and redesignated 1 September 1951 as the 870th Antiaircraft Artillery Gun Battalion (90mm). Redesignated 1 October 1953 as the 870th Antiaircraft Artillery Battalion (90mm Gun).

Redesignated 1 April 1955 as the 970th Field Artillery Battalion.

CAMPAIGN STREAMERS
World War I
Champagne-Marne
Meuse-Argonne
Champagne 1918
Alsace 1918

World War II
Ryukyus

DECORATIONS
French Croix de Guerre with Silver Star, World War I, Streamer embroidered *MEUSE-ARGONNE* (369th Inf cited; WDGO 11, 1924)

COAT OF ARMS
SHIELD: Per chevron azure and gules, a chevron wavy argent between in chief five poplar trees or and in base a rattlesnake ready to strike of the third, all within a bordure of the fourth.

CREST: That for the regiments and separate battalions of the New York Army National Guard: On a wreath of the colors (argent and azure) the full-rigged ship *Half Moon*, all proper.

MOTTO: *Noli me Calcare* (Don't Tread On Me)

The use of the shield of the coat of arms of the old 369th Infantry within a yellow border commemorates the descent from that regiment. The red, white and blue of the shield represents the Tricolor of France and commemorates the fact that the entire combat service of the organization during World War I was with the French Army. The wavy chevron commemorates the first front line sector held by the organization at the junction of the Aisne and Tourbe Rivers in the general outline of a wavy chevron. The five poplar trees represent the Argonne Forest and the five days of combat during the Meuse-Argonne offensive. The rattlesnake perpetuates the distinctive insignia adopted in April 1918 and worn by the organization throughout the remainder of its service in France.

DISTINCTIVE INSIGNIA
The insignia is the shield and motto of the coat of arms. The sample of the insignia depicted was approved for wear on 18 March 1955.

871st ANTIAIRCRAFT ARTILLERY AUTOMATIC WEAPONS BATTALION

Constituted 13 January 1941 in the Regular Army as 2d Battalion, 99th Coast Artillery (Antiaircraft) (Semimobile) (Colored) and activated 15 April 1941 at Camp Davis, North Carolina. (Departed New York Port of Embarkation 26 April 1942 for overseas service and arrived at Fort Read, Trinidad on 10 May 1942. Returned from overseas service and arrived at the New York Port of Embarkation 4 December 1943). Reorganized at Camp Stewart, Georgia and redesignated 29 February 1944 as the 871st Antiaircraft Artillery Automatic Weapons Battalion (Colored). (Departed San Francisco Port of Embarkation 20 January 1945 for overseas service and arrived in New Guinea on 4 February 1945). Disbanded 18 March 1945 at Hollandia, New Guinea.

CAMPAIGN STREAMERS
World War II
American Theater without inscription
Pacific Theater without inscription

DECORATIONS
None

COAT OF ARMS
None

DISTINCTIVE INSIGNIA
None

886th ANTIAIRCRAFT ARTILLERY GUN BATTALION

Constituted 27 April 1942 in the Army of the United States as the 614th Tank Destroyer Battalion (Towed 3 Inch Antitank Gun) (Colored) and activated 25 July 1942 at Camp Carson, Colorado. (Departed New York Port of Embarkation 27 August 1944 for overseas service and landed in France on 7 September 1944. Returned from overseas service and arrived at the New York Port of Embarkation on 30 January 1946). Inactivated 31 January 1946 at Camp Kilmer, New Jersey. Redesignated 16 April 1947 as the 886th Field Artillery Battalion and allotted to the Organized Reserves. Activated 24 April 1947 with Headquarters at Columbus, Ohio. (Organized Reserves redesignated 25 March 1948 as Organized Reserve Corps). Reorganized and redesignated 10 September 1950 as the 886th Antiaircraft Artillery Gun Battalion.

Redesignated 10 April 1952 as the 614th Antiaircraft Artillery Gun Battalion.

CAMPAIGN STREAMERS
World War II
Northern France
Rhineland
Ardennes-Alsace
Central Europe

DECORATIONS
None

COAT OF ARMS
None

DISTINCTIVE INSIGNIA
None

891st ANTIAIRCRAFT ARTILLERY AUTOMATIC WEAPONS BATTALION

Constituted 25 February 1943 in the Army of the United States as the 891st Coast Artillery Battalion (Antiaircraft) (Automatic Weapons). Redesignated 30 April 1943 as the 891st Antiaircraft Artillery Automatic Weapons Battalion (Semimobile). Assigned to the Caribbean Defense command on 18 August 1943. Activated 15 September 1943 at Fort Kobbe, Canal Zone. (Returned from overseas service and arrived at the New Orleans Port of Embarkation on 9 September 1944). Inactivated 5 September 1945 at Fort Bliss, Texas.

CAMPAIGN STREAMERS
World War II
American Theater without inscription

DECORATIONS
None

COAT OF ARMS
None

DISTINCTIVE INSIGNIA
None

892d ANTIAIRCRAFT ARTILLERY AUTOMATIC WEAPONS BATTALION

Constituted 25 February 1943 in the Army of the United States as the 892d Coast Artillery Battalion (Antiaircraft) (Automatic Weapons). Redesignated 30 April 1943 as the 892d Antiaircraft Artillery Automatic Weapons Battalion (Semimobile). Assigned to the Caribbean Defense command on 18 August 1943. Activated 5 September 1943 at Fort Brooke, Puerto Rico. Disbanded 1 June 1944 at Camp O'Reilly, Puerto Rico.

CAMPAIGN STREAMERS
World War II
American Theater without inscription

DECORATIONS
None

COAT OF ARMS
None

DISTINCTIVE INSIGNIA
None

893d ANTIAIRCRAFT ARTILLERY AUTOMATIC WEAPONS BATTALION

Constituted in the Regular Army as 2d Battalion, 62d Artillery (Antiaircraft), Coast Artillery Corps and organized 14 September 1922 from new and existing units as follows:

Headquarters and Headquarters Detachment, 2d Battalion constituted new and activated at Fort Totten, New York

30th Company, Coast Artillery Corps (constituted 12 April 1808 in the Regular Army as a company in the Regiment of Light Artillery and organized later that year as Captain George Peters' Company, Regiment of Light Artillery; redesignated as Captain Josiah G. Talfair's Company, Regiment of Light Artillery in 1809; redesignated as Captain William Campbell's Company, Regiment of Light Artillery in 1811; redesignated as Captain James Gibson's Company, Regiment of Light Artillery in 1812; redesignated as Captain Arthur W. Thornton's Company, Regiment of Light Artillery in 1813; and redesignated 22 May 1816 as Company F, Regiment of Light Artillery; redesignated 1 June 1821 as Company H, 3d Regiment of Artillery; reorganized and redesignated 13 February 1901 as 30th Company, Coast Artillery, Artillery Corps; redesignated 2 February 1907 as the 30th Company, Coast Artillery Corps; redesignated 1st Company, Fort Worden [Washington] in 1916; redesignated 31 August 1917 as 1st Company, Coast Defenses of Puget Sound; redesignated 1 June 1922 as the 30th Company, Coast Artillery Corps), redesignated Battery E

32d Company, Coast Artillery Corps (constituted 5 July 1838 in the Regular Army as Company K, 3d Regiment of Artillery and organized the following month at Fort Monroe, Virginia; redesignated 13 February 1901 as the 32d Company, Coast Artillery, Artillery Corps; redesignated 2 February 1907 as the 32d Company, Coast Artillery Corps; redesignated 20 July 1916 as the 3d Company, Fort Baker [California]; redesignated 31 August 1917 as the 12th Company, Coast Defenses of San Francisco; redesignated 25 October 1918 as Battery A, 18th Artillery, Coast Artillery Corps; redesignated 2 December 1918 as 12th Company, Coast Defenses of San Francisco; inactivated 16 September 1921 at Fort Winfield Scott, California; and redesignated 1 June 1922 as the 32d Company, Coast Artillery Corps), redesignated Battery F

Battery B, 62d Artillery Battalion (constituted 7 November 1907 in the Regular Army as the 165th Company (Torpedo), Coast Artillery Corps and activated 20 November 1907 at Fort Monroe, Virginia; redesignated 30 June 1916 as 4th Company, Fort Totten [New York]; redesignated 31 August 1917 as 1st Company, Coast Defenses of Eastern New York;

demobilized 30 September 1919; reconstituted in the Regular Army, consolidated with Battery B, 2d Antiaircraft Artillery Battalion [organized at Fort Totten in September 1921] and redesignated Battery B, 62d Artillery Battalion [Antiaircraft], Coast Artillery Corps, 1 June 1922; and inactivated 14 September 1922 at Fort Totten), redesignated Battery G

Company C, 62d Artillery Battalion (constituted 7 November 1907 in the Regular Army as the 167th Company, Coast Artillery Corps and activated 20 November 1907 at Fort Monroe, Virginia; redesignated 30 June 1916 as 5th Company, Fort Totten; redesignated 31 August 1917 as 5th Company, Coast Defenses of Eastern New York; redesignated 2d Company, Coast Defenses of Eastern New York in October 1919; disbanded 1 June 1921 at Fort Totten; reconstituted 1 June 1922 in the Regular Army, consolidated with Battery C, 2d Antiaircraft Battalion and redesignated Battery C, 62d Artillery Battalion [Antiaircraft], Coast Artillery Corps), redesignated Battery H and concurrently inactivated at Fort Totten

Batteries G and H activated 1 July 1939 at Fort Totten. (Battalion departed New York Port of Embarkation 31 August 1942 for overseas service; arrived in England 6 September 1942 and landed in North Africa on 11 November 1942). Reorganized and redesignated 24 March 1944 as the 893d Antiaircraft Artillery Automatic Weapons Battalion. (After service in Sicily and Italy, landed in Southern France on 16 August 1944). Inactivated 14 December 1945 in Germany.

Redesignated 13 October 1948 as the 50th Antiaircraft Artillery Automatic Weapons Battalion.

CAMPAIGN STREAMERS
Mexican War
Cerro Gordo
Contreras
Churubusco
Molino del Rey
Chapultepec

Indian Wars
Seminoles

War with Spain
Manila

Philippine Insurrection
Manila
Malolos
Luzon 1899

World War II
Algeria-French Morocco
Rome-Arno
Southern France
Rhineland
Central Europe

DECORATIONS
None

COAT OF ARMS
None

DISTINCTIVE INSIGNIA
None

894th ANTIAIRCRAFT ARTILLERY AUTOMATIC WEAPONS BATTALION

Constituted 2 May 1918 in the Regular Army as 2d Battalion, 67th Artillery, Coast Artillery Corps and organized 21 May 1918 at Fort Winfield Scott, California. Demobilized 23 April 1919 at the Presidio of San Francisco, California. Reconstituted 22 January 1926 in the Regular Army as 2d Battalion, 67th Coast Artillery (Antiaircraft) and activated 10 February 1941 at Fort Bragg, North Carolina. (Departed New York Port of Embarkation 13 January 1943 for overseas service and arrived in North Africa on 28 January 1943). Reorganized and redesignated 23 May 1944 as the 894th Antiaircraft Artillery Automatic Weapons Battalion. (After service in Italy, landed in Southern France on 1 September 1944). Inactivated 14 December 1945 in Germany.

Redesignated 13 October 1948 as the 5th Antiaircraft Artillery Automatic Weapons Battalion.

CAMPAIGN STREAMERS
World War I
Streamer without inscription

World War II
Tunisia
Naples-Foggia
Rome-Arno
Southern France
Rhineland
Ardennes-Alsace
Central Europe

DECORATIONS
None

COAT OF ARMS
None

DISTINCTIVE INSIGNIA
None

895th ANTIAIRCRAFT ARTILLERY AUTOMATIC WEAPONS BATTALION

Constituted 1 June 1918 in the Regular Army as 2d Battalion, 68th Artillery, Coast Artillery Corps and organized at Fort Terry, New York. Demobilized 1 March 1919 at Fort Wadsworth, New York. Reconstituted 22 January 1926 in the Regular Army as 2d Battalion, 68th Coast Artillery (Antiaircraft). Activated 4 November 1939 at Fort Williams, Maine. (Departed New York Port of Embarkation 2 November 1942 for overseas service and arrived in North Africa on 11 November 1942. Following service in Sicily moved to Italy on 31 October 1943). Reorganized at Santa Maria, Italy and redesignated 4 June 1944 as the 895th Antiaircraft Artillery Automatic Weapons Battalion. (After service in France returned from overseas service and arrived at the New York Port of Embarkation on 5 January 1946). Inactivated 6 January 1946 at Camp Kilmer, New Jersey.

Redesignated 13 October 1948 as the 8th Antiaircraft Artillery Automatic Weapons Battalion.

CAMPAIGN STREAMERS
World War I
Streamer without inscription

World War II
Sicily
Naples-Foggia
Anzio (with arrowhead)
Rome-Arno
Southern France (with arrowhead)
Rhineland
Ardennes-Alsace
Central Europe

DECORATIONS
None

COAT OF ARMS
None

DISTINCTIVE INSIGNIA
None

896th ANTIAIRCRAFT ARTILLERY AUTOMATIC WEAPONS BATTALION

Constituted 29 July 1921 in the Organized Reserves as 2d Battalion, 503d Artillery (Antiaircraft), Coast Artillery Corps and allotted to the Third Corps area. Organized during March 1922 with Headquarters at Tyrone, Pennsylvania. Redesignated 30 June 1924 as 2d Battalion, 503d Coast Artillery (Antiaircraft). Withdrawn from the Organized Reserves and allotted to the Regular Army on 1 October 1933. Redesignated 1 July 1940 as 2d Battalion, 74th Coast Artillery (Antiaircraft) and activated 3 January 1941 at Fort Monroe, Virginia. (Departed New York Port of Embarkation 28 April 1943 for overseas service and landed in North Africa on 11 May 1943. Moved to Sardinia and stationed at Cagliari where it was redesignated as the 896th Antiaircraft Artillery Automatic Weapons Battalion on 1 May 1944. Moved to Corsica on 1 September 1944 and landed in Southern France on 13 October 1944). Inactivated 9 July 1946 in France.

Redesignated 15 September 1948 as the 15th Antiaircraft Artillery Automatic Weapons Battalion.

CAMPAIGN STREAMERS
World War II
Rome-Arno
Rhineland

DECORATIONS
None

COAT OF ARMS
None

DISTINCTIVE INSIGNIA
None

897th ANTIAIRCRAFT ARTILLERY AUTOMATIC WEAPONS BATTALION

Constituted 31 January 1942 in the Army of the United States as 2d Battalion, 90th Coast Artillery (Antiaircraft) (Semimobile) (Colored) and activated 1 May 1942 at Camp Stewart, Georgia. (Departed New York Port of Embarkation 2 April 1943 for overseas service and arrived in North Africa on 12 April 1943). Reorganized at Oran, Algeria and redesignated 25 May 1944 as the 897th Antiaircraft Artillery Automatic Weapons Battalion. (Landed in Southern France on 9 September 1944). Disbanded 15 September 1944 at St. Tropez, France.

CAMPAIGN STREAMERS
World War II
Southern France

DECORATIONS
None

COAT OF ARMS
None

DISTINCTIVE INSIGNIA
None

898th ANTIAIRCRAFT ARTILLERY AUTOMATIC WEAPONS BATTALION

Constituted 23 July 1940 in the New York National Guard as 2d Battalion, 209th Coast Artillery (Antiaircraft). Organized in northwestern New York State and Federally recognized 16 October 1940 with Headquarters at Rochester. Inducted into Federal service 10 February 1941 at home stations. (Departed New York Port of Embarkation 11 May 1942 for overseas service; arrived in Northern Ireland on 18 May 1942 and moved to England on 12 December 1942. Landed in North Africa on 3 January 1943 and moved to Italy on 28 October 1943). Reorganized at Montesarcchio, Italy and redesignated 18 March 1944 as the 898th Antiaircraft Artillery Automatic Weapons Battalion (Mobile). (Following service on Corsica and in France, returned from overseas service and arrived at the Boston Port of Embarkation on 2 November 1945). Inactivated 3 November 1945 at Camp Myles Standish, Massachusetts.

Redesignated 16 March 1953 as the 336th Antiaircraft Artillery Gun Battalion.

CAMPAIGN STREAMERS
World War II
Tunisia
Naples-Foggia
Rome-Arno
Rhineland
Ardennes-Alsace
Central Europe

DECORATIONS
None

COAT OF ARMS
None

DISTINCTIVE INSIGNIA
None

898th ANTIAIRCRAFT ARTILLERY AUTOMATIC WEAPONS BATTALION

Constituted in the New York National Guard as 3d Battalion, 3d Infantry and organized from existing units at Rochester with Headquarters Federally recognized 8 October 1920. Redesignated 1 May 1921 as 3d Battalion, 108th Infantry and further redesignated 1 May 1929 as 2d Battalion, 108th Infantry. Inducted into Federal service 15 October 1940 at Rochester. Inactivated 7 April 1946 at Camp Stoneman, California. Redesignated 27 September 1946 as the 898th Antiaircraft Artillery Automatic Weapons Battalion. Reorganized and Federally recognized 17 September 1947 at Rochester.

Redesignated 1 February 1949 as the 127th Antiaircraft Artillery Automatic Weapons Battalion.

CAMPAIGN STREAMERS
World War I
Ypres-Lys
Somme Offensive
Flanders 1918

World War II
Bismarck Archipelago
Leyte
Luzon
Southern Philippines (with arrowhead)

DECORATIONS
Philippine Presidential Unit Citation, Streamer embroidered *17 OCTOBER 1944 TO 4 JULY 1945* (108th Inf cited; DAGO 47, 1950)

COAT OF ARMS
None

DISTINCTIVE INSIGNIA
None

899th ANTIAIRCRAFT ARTILLERY BATTALION

Constituted in the Pennsylvania National Guard as 2d Separate Battalion of Infantry and organized from new and existing units as follows:

Headquarters organized new and Federally recognized 1 November 1919 at Lancaster; Major William C. Rehm, commanding

Company A, 109th Machine Gun Battalion (organized 7 September 1916 in Federal service at El Paso, Texas as Machine Gun Company, 4th Infantry, Pennsylvania National Guard; mustered out at Lancaster 15 January 1917 and assumed State status; mustered into Federal service 15 July 1917 and drafted into Federal service 5 August 1917; redesignated 11 October 1917 as Company A, 109th Machine Gun Battalion and assigned to the 28th Division; and demobilized 4 May 1919 at Camp Dix, New Jersey), reorganized and Federally recognized 7 August 1920 at Lancaster as Company A

Company D, 151st Machine Gun Battalion (organized 17 June 1898 at Lancaster as Company B, 11th Infantry, Pennsylvania National Guard; redesignated 8 August 1899 as Company K, 4th Infantry, Pennsylvania National Guard; mustered into Federal service 15 July 1917 and drafted into Federal service 5 August 1917; redesignated 15 August 1917 as Company K, 149th Machine Gun Battalion and assigned to the 42d Division; redesignated 1 September 1917 as Company B, 149th Machine Gun Battalion; redesignated 24 March 1918 as Company D, 151st Machine Gun Battalion; and demobilized 10 May 1919 at Camp

Gordon, Georgia), reorganized and Federally recognized 29 July 1920 at Lancaster as Company B

Company D, 150th Machine Gun Battalion (organized 15 June 1898 at Reading as Company A [*Reading Rifles*], 11th Infantry, Pennsylvania National Guard; redesignated 8 August 1899 as Company I, 4th Infantry, Pennsylvania National Guard; mustered into Federal service 15 July 1917 and drafted into Federal service 5 August 1917; redesignated 15 August 1917 as Company I, 149th Machine Gun Battalion and assigned to the 42d Division; redesignated 1 September 1917 as Company A, 149th Machine Gun Battalion; redesignated 24 March 1918 as Company D, 150th Machine Gun Battalion; and demobilized 5 May 1919 at Camp Grant, Illinois), reorganized and Federally recognized 15 July 1921 at Reading as Company C

Company D, 109th Machine Gun Battalion (organized 11 August 1893 at Lebanon as the *Lebanon Rifles* and redesignated 6 July 1896 as Company H, 4th Infantry, Pennsylvania National Guard; mustered into Federal service 9 May 1898; mustered out 16 November 1898 and resumed State status; mustered into Federal service 8 July 1916 for Mexican border duty; mustered out 15 January 1917 and resumed State status; mustered into Federal service 15 July 1917 and drafted into Federal service 5 August 1917; redesignated 11 October 1917 as Company D, 107th Machine Gun Battalion and assigned to the 28th Division; redesignated 20 February 1918 as Company D, 109th Machine Gun Battalion; and demobilized 4 May 1919 at Camp Dix, New Jersey), reorganized and Federally recognized 23 July 1920 at Lebanon as Company D

Converted and redesignated 1 May 1922 as 2d Battalion, 213th Artillery (Antiaircraft), Coast Artillery Corps. Redesignated 1 August 1924 as 2d Battalion, 213th Coast Artillery (Antiaircraft). (Headquarters relocated to Reading on 15 October 1929. Inducted into Federal service 15 September 1940 at home stations. Reorganized at Castel Volturno, Italy and redesignated 14 March 1944 as the 899th Antiaircraft Artillery Automatic Weapons Battalion. Inactivated 13 February 1945 at St. Martin Vesubie, France. Reorganized and Federally recognized 8 October 1946 with Headquarters at Lancaster and batteries at Lancaster, Columbia and Lebanon. Assigned to the 28th Infantry Division on 1 February 1949. Ordered into active Federal service 5 September 1950 at home stations. Redesignated 1 April 1953 as the 899th Antiaircraft Artillery Battalion (Automatic Weapons) (Self Propelled). (899th Antiaircraft Artillery Battalion [NGUS] organized and Federally recognized 20 August 1953 with Headquarters at Lancaster). Released from active Federal service and resumed State status on 15 June 1954; concurrently, Federal recognition withdrawn from 899th Antiaircraft Artillery Battalion (NGUS). (Headquarters relocated to Hershey on 1 January 1958).

Relieved from the 28th Infantry Division, reorganized and consolidated 1 June 1959 with the 213th Artillery, a parent regiment under the Combat Arms Regimental System.

CAMPAIGN STREAMERS
World War I
Champagne-Marne
Aisne-Marne
Oise-Aisne
St. Mihiel
Meuse-Argonne
Champagne 1918
Lorraine 1918

World War II
Algeria-French Morocco (with arrowhead)
Naples-Foggia (with arrowhead)
Rome-Arno
Rhineland

DECORATIONS
None

COAT OF ARMS
SHIELD: Gules, seven fleurs-de-lis in pairle or.

CREST: That for the regiments and separate battalions of the Pennsylvania Army National Guard: On a wreath of the colors (or and gules) a lion rampant guardant proper holding in dexter paw a naked scimitar argent, hilted or and in sinister an escutcheon argent, on a fess sable three plates.

MOTTO: *Procede Usque ad Mortem* (Proceed Until Death)

The shield is red for Artillery while the seven fleurs-de-lis represent seven campaigns in France during World War I.

DISTINCTIVE INSIGNIA
The insignia is the shield and motto of the coat of arms. The sample of the insignia depicted was approved for wear on 4 September 1951.

900th ANTIAIRCRAFT ARTILLERY AUTOMATIC WEAPONS BATTALION

Constituted 13 April 1942 in the Army of the United States as 2d Battalion, 505th Coast Artillery (Antiaircraft) and activated 1 June 1942 at Camp Edwards, Massachusetts. (Departed New York Port of Embarkation 8 December 1942 for overseas service and arrived in England on 13 December 1942. After service in North Africa, landed at Salerno, Italy on 9 September 1943). Reorganized at Santa Maria, Italy and redesignated 14 March 1944 as the 900th Antiaircraft Artillery Automatic Weapons Battalion (Mobile). Disbanded 14 January 1945 at Montecatini, Italy and personnel reassigned to 3d Battalion, 473d Infantry.

CAMPAIGN STREAMERS
World War II
Naples-Foggia
Rome-Arno
North Apennines

DECORATIONS
None

COAT OF ARMS
None

DISTINCTIVE INSIGNIA
None

901st ANTIAIRCRAFT ARTILLERY AUTOMATIC WEAPONS BATTALION

Constituted in the Army of the United States as the 901st Antiaircraft Artillery Automatic Weapons Battalion (Semimobile) and activated 15 September 1943 at Fort Davis, Canal Zone. Disbanded 1 February 1946 at Fort Davis.

CAMPAIGN STREAMERS
World War II
American Theater without inscription

DECORATIONS
None

COAT OF ARMS
None

DISTINCTIVE INSIGNIA
None

902d ANTIAIRCRAFT ARTILLERY AUTOMATIC WEAPONS BATTALION

Constituted in the Army of the United States as the 902d Antiaircraft Artillery Automatic Weapons Battalion (Semimobile) and activated 15 September 1943 at Fort Gulick, Canal Zone. Disbanded 15 April 1946 at Fort Gulick.

CAMPAIGN STREAMERS
World War II
American Theater without inscription

DECORATIONS
None

COAT OF ARMS
None

DISTINCTIVE INSIGNIA
None

903d ANTIAIRCRAFT ARTILLERY BATTALION

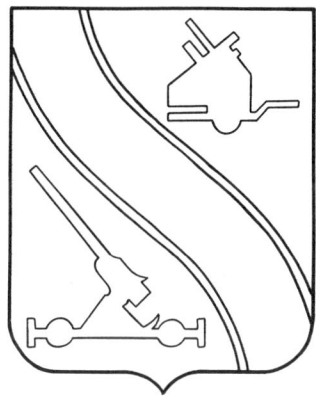 

Constituted in the Army of the United States as the 903d Antiaircraft Artillery Automatic Weapons Battalion (Semimobile) and activated 15 September 1943 at Fort Clayton, Canal Zone. Redesignated 22 September 1950 as the 903d Antiaircraft Artillery Automatic Weapons Battalion, Mobile. Allotted to the Regular Army on 19 October 1951. Redesignated 3 November 1952 as the 903d Antiaircraft Artillery Battalion (Automatic Weapons). Inactivated 15 December 1957 at Fort Clayton.

CAMPAIGN STREAMERS
World War II
American Theater without inscription

DECORATIONS
None

COAT OF ARMS
SHIELD: Gules, a bend reverse arched and arched azure fimbriated or between in chief the silhouette of an M55 quadruple .50 caliber machine gun mount and in base the silhouette of a 40mm automatic antiaircraft weapon, both of the last.

CREST: None

MOTTO: Ever On Watch

Red and yellow are the colors for Artillery. The bend in the form of a reversed curve symbolizes the Panama Canal, and the two pieces of artillery are representative of the weapons used by the battalion.

DISTINCTIVE INSIGNIA
The insignia is the shield and motto of the coat of arms. The sample of the insignia depicted was approved for wear on 30 July 1953.

906th ANTIAIRCRAFT ARTILLERY AUTOMATIC WEAPONS BATTALION

Constituted in the Army of the United States as the 906th Antiaircraft Artillery Automatic Weapons Battalion (Semimobile) and activated 15 September 1943 at Fort Clayton, Canal Zone. Disbanded 1 February 1946 at Fort Clayton.

CAMPAIGN STREAMERS
World War II
American Theater without inscription

DECORATIONS
None

COAT OF ARMS
None

DISTINCTIVE INSIGNIA
None

910th ANTIAIRCRAFT ARTILLERY AUTOMATIC WEAPONS BATTALION

Constituted in the Regular Army as 3d Battalion, 66th Regiment, Coast Artillery Corps, and organized 1 March 1918 with Headquarters at Fort Adams, Rhode Island. Demobilized 20 March 1919 at Camp Upton, New York. Reconstituted 27 May 1942 in the Regular Army as 3d Battalion, 66th Coast Artillery (Antiaircraft). Redesignated 2d Battalion, 66th Coast Artillery (Antiaircraft) (Automatic Weapons) and activated 25 August 1942 at Camp Buchanan, Fort Miles, Puerto Rico. Reorganized and redesignated 6 November 1943 as the 910th Antiaircraft Artillery Automatic Weapons Battalion. (Returned from overseas service and arrived at the New York Port of Embarkation on 4 December 1943. Departed New York Port of Embarkation on 1 December 1944; arrived in England 12 December 1944 and landed in France on 14 February 1945. Returned from overseas service and arrived at the New York Port of Embarkation on 9 February 1946). Inactivated 10 February 1946 at Camp Kilmer, New Jersey.

Redesignated 13 October 1948 as the 11th Antiaircraft Artillery Automatic Weapons Battalion.

CAMPAIGN STREAMERS
World War I
Streamer without inscription

World War II
American Theater without inscription
Rhineland
Central Europe

DECORATIONS
None

COAT OF ARMS
None

DISTINCTIVE INSIGNIA
None

913th ANTIAIRCRAFT ARTILLERY AUTOMATIC WEAPONS BATTALION

Constituted 16 October 1943 in the Army of the United States as the 913th Antiaircraft Artillery Automatic Weapons Battalion (Semimobile) and activated 6 November 1943 at San Juan, Puerto Rico. Disbanded 1 June 1944 at Camp O'Reilly, Puerto Rico.

CAMPAIGN STREAMERS
World War II
American Theater without inscription

DECORATIONS
None

COAT OF ARMS
None

DISTINCTIVE INSIGNIA
None

925th ANTIAIRCRAFT ARTILLERY AUTOMATIC WEAPONS BATTALION

Constituted 5 September 1928 in the Organized Reserves as 2d Battalion, 562d Coast Artillery (Antiaircraft) and allotted to the Third Corps area. Redesignated 30 November 1928 as 2d Battalion, 917th Coast Artillery (Antiaircraft) and organized in Virginia during 1929. Withdrawn from the Organized Reserves 1 October 1933 and allotted to the Regular Army. Redesignated 2d Battalion, 70th Coast Artillery (Antiaircraft) and activated at Fort Monroe, Virginia on 4 November 1939. (Departed New York Port of Embarkation 23 January 1942 for overseas service and arrived in Australia on 27 February 1942. After service in New Caledonia, moved to Guadalcanal on 10 November 1943). Reorganized and redesignated 10 November 1943 as the 925th Antiaircraft Artillery Automatic Weapons Battalion (Semimobile). (Moved to New Georgia on 22 November 1943 and after service on Green Island and Bougainville, landed in the Philippine Islands on 11 March 1945). Inactivated 31 August 1946 on Luzon, Philippine Islands.

Redesignated 13 October 1948 as the 21st Antiaircraft Artillery Automatic Weapons Battalion.

CAMPAIGN STREAMERS
World War II
Northern Solomons
Bismarck Archipelago
Leyte

DECORATIONS
Philippine Presidential Unit Citation, Streamer embroidered *17 OCTOBER 1944 TO 4 JULY 1945* (925th AAA AW Bn cited; DAGO 47, 1950)

COAT OF ARMS
None

DISTINCTIVE INSIGNIA
None

932d ANTIAIRCRAFT ARTILLERY AUTOMATIC WEAPONS BATTALION

Constituted in the Army of the United States as the 932d Antiaircraft Artillery Automatic Weapons Battalion (Semimobile) and activated 15 September 1943 in the Galapagos Islands. (Returned from overseas service and arrived at the New Orleans Port of Embarkation on 13 June 1944). Inactivated 18 August 1944 at Camp Butner, North Carolina.

CAMPAIGN STREAMERS
World War II
American Theater without inscription

DECORATIONS
None

COAT OF ARMS
None

DISTINCTIVE INSIGNIA
None

933d ANTIAIRCRAFT ARTILLERY MISSILE BATTALION

 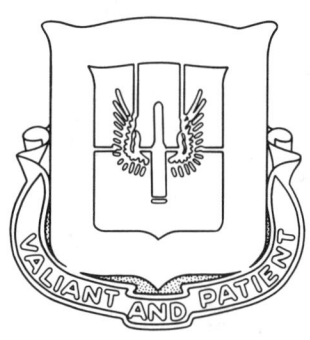

Constituted 29 July 1921 in the Organized Reserves as 2d Battalion, 502d Artillery (Antiaircraft), Coast Artillery Corps and allotted to the Second Corps area. Organized during November 1921 at New York, New York. Redesignated 30 June 1924 as 2d Battalion, 502d Coast Artillery (Antiaircraft). Withdrawn from the Organized Reserves 1 October 1933 and allotted to the Regular Army. Redesignated 1 August 1940 as 2d Battalion, 76th Coast Artillery (Antiaircraft) (Colored). Activated 10 February 1941 at Fort Bragg, North Carolina. (Departed San Francisco Port of Embarkation 10 August 1942 for overseas service and arrived on Espiritu Santo, New Hebrides on 2 September 1942). Reorganized and redesignated 1 November 1943 as the 933d Antiaircraft Artillery Automatic Weapons Battalion. (After service in the Russell and Admiralty Islands returned to the United States and arrived at the Los Angeles Port of Embarkation on 30 December 1945). Inactivated 31 December 1945 at Camp Anza, Arlington, California. Activated 30 June 1946 at Yokohama, Japan. Redesignated 1 June 1949 as the 933d Antiaircraft Artillery Automatic Weapons Battalion, Mobile. Redesignated 1 April 1954 as the 933d Antiaircraft Artillery Battalion (Automatic Weapons). Inactivated 13 May 1955 at Inchon, Korea. Redesignated 23 November 1955 as the 933d Antiaircraft Artillery Missile Battalion. Activated 15 December 1955 at Fort MacArthur, California. Inactivated 1 September 1958 at Pasadena, California.

CAMPAIGN STREAMERS
World War II
Northern Solomons

Korea
UN Defensive
UN Offensive
CCF Intervention
First UN Counteroffensive
CCF Spring Offensive
UN Summer-Fall Offensive
Second Korean Winter
Korea, Summer-Fall 1952
Third Korean Winter
Korea, Summer 1953

DECORATIONS
Republic of Korea Presidential Unit Citation, Streamer embroidered *KOREA* (933d AAA AW Bn cited for period 16 Sep 1950-1 May 1954; DAGO 51, 1957)

COAT OF ARMS
SHIELD: Per fess, to chief per pale of three azure, argent and tenne, to base gules, overall a winged round of fixed antiaircraft ammunition, the wings displayed or; a bordure of the last.

CREST: None

MOTTO: Valiant And Patient

The shield is red for Artillery. The place of activation, New York City, is represented by the city colors of blue, white and orange. The winged projectile refers to the antiaircraft functions of the organization while the gold border represents the descent from the old 76th Coast Artillery of which this battalion was a part.

DISTINCTIVE INSIGNIA
The insignia is the shield and motto of the coat of arms. The sample of the insignia depicted was approved for wear on 21 May 1953.

938th ANTIAIRCRAFT ARTILLERY AUTOMATIC WEAPONS BATTALION

Constituted 29 July 1921 in the Organized Reserves as 2d Battalion, 505th Artillery (Antiaircraft), Coast Artillery Corps and allotted to the Fifth Corps area. Organized during December 1921 in Ohio. Redesignated 30 June 1924 as 2d Battalion, 505th Coast Artillery (Antiaircraft). Withdrawn from the Organized Reserves 1 October 1933 and allotted to the Regular Army. Redesignated 1 August 1940 as 2d Battalion, 77th Coast Artillery (Antiaircraft) (Semimobile) (Colored). Activated 10 February 1941 at Fort Bragg, North Carolina. (Departed New York Port of Embarkation 9 April 1942 for overseas service; arrived on Tongatabu Island, South Tonga Islands 9 May 1942 and moved to New Hebrides on 18 April 1943). Reorganized and redesignated 1 November 1943 as the 938th Antiaircraft Artillery Automatic Weapons Battalion (Colored). (Moved to New Georgia on 12 December 1943 and to New Guinea on 6 February 1945). Disbanded 15 February 1945 at Finschhafen, New Guinea.

Reconstituted 13 October 1948 as the 38th Antiaircraft Artillery Automatic Weapons Battalion.

CAMPAIGN STREAMERS
World War II
Northern Solomons

DECORATIONS
None

COAT OF ARMS
None

DISTINCTIVE INSIGNIA
None

HEADQUARTERS AND HEADQUARTERS DETACHMENT 941st COAST ARTILLERY BATTALION

Constituted 10 August 1942 in the Army of the United States as Battery K, 197th Coast Artillery. Activated 15 August 1942 in Federal service at Townsville, Queensland, Australia. Redesignated 15 May 1943 as Battery B, 237th Antiaircraft Artillery Searchlight Battalion. Inactivated 29 December 1945 at Camp Anza, Arlington, California. Redesignated 23 May 1946 as Headquarters and Headquarters Detachment, 941st Coast Artillery Battalion (Harbor Defense) and allotted to the New Hampshire National Guard. Withdrawn from allotment to the New Hampshire National Guard 1 May 1949 and returned to Department of the Army control.

CAMPAIGN STREAMERS
World War II
East Indies
New Guinea
Leyte
Luzon
Southern Philippines (with arrowhead)

DECORATIONS
Philippine Presidential Unit Citation, Streamer embroidered *17 OCTOBER 1944 TO 4 JULY 1945* (237th AAA SL Bn cited; DAGO 47, 1950)

COAT OF ARMS
None

DISTINCTIVE INSIGNIA
None

945th ANTIAIRCRAFT ARTILLERY AUTOMATIC WEAPONS BATTALION

Constituted 4 May 1921 in the Delaware National Guard as 2d Battalion, 198th Artillery (Antiaircraft), Coast Artillery Corps, and organized from new and existing units as follows:

Headquarters, 2d Battalion organized new and Federally recognized 16 June 1921 at Dover

Company I, 59th Pioneer Infantry (organized and Federally recognized 22 June 1917 at Dover as Company I, 1st Delaware Infantry; mustered into Federal service 25 July 1917 at Dover and drafted into Federal service on 5 August 1917; redesignated 17 January 1918 as Company I, 59th Pioneer Infantry and demobilized 8 July 1919 at Camp Dix, New Jersey), reorganized and Federally recognized 16 June 1921 at Dover as Headquarters Detachment, 2d Battalion

Company K, 59th Pioneer Infantry (organized at Newark prior to 1903 as Company B, 1st Delaware Infantry; mustered into Federal service 8 July 1916 for service on the Mexican border; mustered out 15 February 1917 and resumed State status; mustered into Federal service 25 July 1917 and drafted into Federal service on 5 August 1917; redesignated 17 January 1918 as Company K, 59th Pioneer Infantry; demobilized 8 July 1919 at Camp Dix, New Jersey), reorganized and Federally recognized 4 May 1921 at Newark as Battery E

7th Company (Antiaircraft Artillery), Delaware Coast Artillery Corps (organized prior to 1903 at Milford as Company B, 1st Delaware Infantry; mustered into Federal service 8 July 1916 for service on the Mexican border; mustered out 15 February 1917 and resumed State status; mustered into Federal service 25 July 1917 at Milford and drafted into Federal service on 5 August 1917; redesignated 17 January 1918 as Company B, 59th Pioneer Infantry; demobilized 7 August 1919 at Camp Upton, New York; reorganized at Milford as 7th Company [Antiaircraft Artillery], Delaware Coast Artillery Corps and Federally recognized 2 May 1921), redesignated 4 May 1921 as Battery F

4th Company (Antiaircraft Artillery), Delaware Coast Artillery Corps (organized 28 February 1906 at Dover as Company G, 1st Delaware Infantry; mustered into Federal service 8 July 1916 for service on the Mexican border; mustered out 15 February 1917 and resumed State status; mustered into Federal service 25 July 1917 at Dover and drafted into Federal service on 5 August 1917; redesignated 17 January 1918 as Company A, 59th Pioneer Infantry; demobilized 8 July 1919 at Camp Dix, New Jersey; reorganized at Dover as 4th Company [Antiaircraft Artillery], Delaware Coast Artillery Corps and Federally recognized 19 February 1921), redesignated 4 May 1921 as Battery G

Battery H (Antiaircraft), Delaware Coast Artillery Corps (organized prior to 1903 at New Castle as Company H, 1st Delaware Infantry; mustered into Federal service 8 July 1916 for service on the Mexican border; mustered out 15 February 1917 and resumed State status; mustered into Federal service at New Castle 25 July 1917 and drafted into Federal service on 5 August 1917; redesignated 17 January 1918 as Company E, 59th Pioneer Infantry; demobilized 8 July 1919 at Camp Dix, New Jersey; reorganized at New Castle as Battery H [Antiaircraft], Delaware Coast Artillery Corps and Federally recognized 12 April 1921), redesignated 4 May 1921 as Battery H

Redesignated 16 August 1924 as 2d Battalion, 198th Coast Artillery (Antiaircraft). Inducted into Federal service 16 September 1940 at home stations. (Departed Charleston Port of Embarkation 27 January 1942 for overseas service and arrived on Bora Bora 17 February 1942). Redesignated 1 March 1944 as the 945th Antiaircraft Artillery Automatic Weapons Battalion. (After service on Efate, New Hebrides, Guadalcanal, in the Treasury Islands and New Guinea, moved to the Philippine Islands on 15 July 1945). Inactivated 15 February 1946 on Hokkaido, Japan. Reorganized and Federally recognized 17 October 1946 with Headquarters at Dover and batteries at Laurel, Georgetown, Milford and Seaford.

Redesignated 24 October 1949 as the 193d Antiaircraft Artillery Gun Battalion.

CAMPAIGN STREAMERS
World War I
Meuse-Argonne

World War II
Northern Solomons (with arrowhead)

DECORATIONS
None

COAT OF ARMS
None

DISTINCTIVE INSIGNIA
None

945th ANTIAIRCRAFT ARTILLERY BATTALION

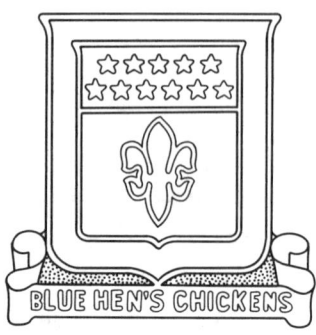

Organized during 1831 as a Light Infantry Battalion and attached to the 8th Regiment of Delaware Militia, with companies as follows: *Georgetown Minute Men*, organized 19 July 1831, Captain Edward L. Wells, commanding; Captain Coulter's Volunteer Company of Light Infantry, organized 14 September 1831; Captain Thomas McIlwain's Volunteer Company of Light Infantry, organized 15 November 1831; and Captain Gilley G. Short's Volunteer Company of Light Infantry, organized 17 November 1831. Battalion broken up 30 June 1846 and elements attached to 13th Regiment of Delaware Militia. Reorganized as elements of 1st Delaware Volunteer Infantry during April 1861. Mustered into Federal service at Wilmington 16 May 1861; mustered out 16 August 1861 at Wilmington and resumed State status. Mustered into Federal service 10 October 1861 at Washington, District of Columbia; mustered out 12 July 1865 near Munson's Hill, Virginia and reverted to State control. (1st Delaware Volunteer Infantry reorganized as 1st Delaware Zouave Regiment, Delaware State Volunteers by organization of Company A in 1869; redesignated as the 1st Regiment of Infantry, Organized Militia of Delaware in 1880 and 1st Regiment of Infantry, Delaware National Guard on 17 April 1885. Mustered into Federal service at Middletown as 1st Delaware Volunteer Infantry; mustered out 19 December 1898 and resumed State status). Reorganized 22 June 1917 as 1st Battalion, 1st Delaware Infantry with companies at Laurel, Georgetown, Milford and Dover. Called into Federal service 25 July 1917 and drafted into Federal service on 5 August 1917. Redesignated 17 January 1918 as 1st Battalion, 59th Pioneer Infantry. Demobilized 8 July 1919 at Camp Dix, New Jersey. Reconstituted 16 November 1920 as Separate Battalion, Delaware Coast Artillery Corps and subsequently organized from new and existing units as follows:

Headquarters organized new and Federally recognized 9 July 1936 at Dover

Headquarters Detachment organized new and Federally recognized 9 July 1936 at Laurel

Battery A organized new and Federally recognized 24 March 1924 at Laurel

Battery B, 261st Coast Artillery Battalion (originally organized at Georgetown in 1799 as 1st Company of Light Infantry, 8th Regiment of Delaware Militia, Captain Benton Harris, commanding; under the command of Captain John Kollock mustered into Federal service 2 March 1813 at Lewes, mustered out 4 May 1813 and resumed State status; mustered into Federal service 6 May 1813 at Lewes, mustered out 31 July 1813 and resumed State status;

mustered into Federal service 6 August 1814 at Lewes, mustered out 11 January 1815 and resumed State status; reorganized 6 March 1827 as 1st Company of Light Infantry, 1st Battalion, 8th Regiment of Delaware Infantry; reorganized 19 July 1831 as *Georgetown Minute Men*, Captain Edward L. Wells, commanding; redesignated 30 June 1846 as *Kirkwood Rifle Corps*, Captain Caleb R. Layton, commanding; redesignated Company G, 1st Delaware Volunteer Infantry in April 1861 and mustered into Federal service 16 May 1861 at Wilmington, mustered out 16 August 1861 at Wilmington and resumed State status; mustered into Federal service 10 October 1861 at Wilmington, mustered out 12 July 1865 near Munson's Hill, Virginia; reorganized at Georgetown during October 1881 as Company G, 1st Regiment, Delaware Volunteers; redesignated 17 April 1885 as Company G, 1st Regiment, Delaware National Guard; disbanded at Georgetown in 1894; reorganized and Federally recognized 22 June 1917 at Milford as Company K, 1st Delaware Infantry; mustered into Federal service at Milford 25 July 1917 and drafted into Federal service on 5 August 1917; redesignated Company D, 59th Pioneer Infantry; demobilized 8 July 1919 at Camp Dix, New Jersey; reconstituted 16 November 1920 as Battery B, Separate Battalion, Delaware Coast Artillery Corps; redesignated 14 March 1924 as Battery B, 1st Separate Battalion, Delaware Coast Artillery [Harbor Defense] and redesignated 10 July 1925 as Battery B, 261st Coast Artillery Battalion [Harbor Defense]), reorganized and Federally recognized 8 July 1936 at Georgetown as Battery B

Battery C organized new and Federally recognized 8 May 1940 at Laurel

Battalion redesignated 10 July 1925 as the 261st Coast Artillery Battalion (Harbor Defense). Redesignated 15 April 1940 as 1st Battalion, 261st Coast Artillery (Harbor Defense). Redesignated 261st Coast Artillery Battalion (Harbor Defense) and inducted into Federal service 27 January 1941. Battalion broken up and elements redesignated, inactivated or disbanded as follows: Headquarters and Headquarters Battery inactivated 20 April 1944 at Fort Jackson, South Carolina and disbanded 1 October 1944; Batteries A, B and C redesignated 1 October 1944 as Batteries E, F and G, respectively, 21st Coast Artillery Battalion (Harbor Defense). Reorganized as the 945th Antiaircraft Artillery Automatic Weapons Battalion and Federally recognized 24 October 1949 with Headquarters at Georgetown and batteries at Laurel, Dagsboro, Milford and Seaford. Redesignated 1 October 1953 as the 945th Antiaircraft Artillery Battalion (Automatic Weapons).

Redesignated 20 November 1956 as the 280th Antiaircraft Artillery Battalion.

CAMPAIGN STREAMERS
War of 1812
Delaware 1813
Delaware 1814
Delaware 1815

Civil War
Peninsula
Antietam
Fredericksburg
Chancellorsville
Gettysburg
Wilderness
Spotsylvania
Cold Harbor
Petersburg
Appomattox
Virginia 1863

World War I
Meuse-Argonne

DECORATIONS
None

COAT OF ARMS
SHIELD: Argent, a fleur-de-lis gules; on a chief azure eleven mullets, five and six or; overall a bordure of the second.

CREST: That for the regiments and separate battalions of the Delaware Army National Guard: On a wreath of the colors (argent and gules) a griffin's head erased azure, eared and beaked or, langued gules, collared sable, fimbriated argent and thereon three plates.

MOTTO: Blue Hen's Chickens

The shield of the coat of arms is that of the old 198th Coast Artillery while the red border indicates a close association with that organization.

DISTINCTIVE INSIGNIA
The insignia is the shield and motto of the coat of arms. The sample of the insignia depicted was approved for wear on 16 June 1955.

945th ANTIAIRCRAFT ARTILLERY BATTALION

Organized in the Delaware Army National Guard as the 945th Antiaircraft Artillery Battalion (75mm Gun) and Federally recognized 20 November 1956 with Headquarters at Laurel and batteries at Laurel and Seaford.

Consolidated 1 April 1959 with the 198th Artillery, a parent regiment under the Combat Arms Regimental System.

CAMPAIGN STREAMERS
None

DECORATIONS
None

COAT OF ARMS
SHIELD: Per bend or and gules, in chief a gamecock azure and in base a fountain.

CREST: That for the regiments and separate battalions of the Delaware Army National Guard: On a wreath of the colors (or and gules) a griffin's head erased azure, eared and beaked or, langued gules, collared sable, fimbriated argent and thereon three plates.

MOTTO: Liberty And Independence

The colors red and yellow are used for Artillery. The Blue Hen gamecock is the State bird of Delaware and refers to the legend of the Blue Hen's Chickens carried by the troops of Delaware in the Revolution. The fountain is taken from the coat of arms of the former 261st Coast Artillery Battalion to show partial descent and longevity through that battalion.

DISTINCTIVE INSIGNIA
The insignia is the shield and motto of the coat of arms. The insignia depicted was never made for nor worn by this organization.

947th ANTIAIRCRAFT ARTILLERY GUN BATTALION

Constituted 13 May 1944 in the Army of the United States as the 947th Antiaircraft Artillery Gun Battalion (Semimobile) and activated 26 May 1944 at Aiea, Hawaii. (Moved to Iwo Jima on 14 March 1945). Inactivated 15 January 1946 on Iwo Jima.

CAMPAIGN STREAMERS
World War II
Air Offensive Japan

DECORATIONS
None

COAT OF ARMS
None

DISTINCTIVE INSIGNIA
None

948th ANTIAIRCRAFT ARTILLERY GUN BATTALION

Constituted 13 May 1944 in the Army of the United States as the 948th Antiaircraft Artillery Gun Battalion (Semimobile) and activated 26 May 1944 at Schofield Barracks, Hawaii. (Moved to Ie Shima on 4 June 1945. Returned from overseas service and arrived at the Los Angeles Port of Embarkation on 20 January 1946). Inactivated 21 January 1946 at Camp Anza, Arlington, California.

CAMPAIGN STREAMERS
World War II
Ryukyus

DECORATIONS
None

COAT OF ARMS
None

DISTINCTIVE INSIGNIA
None

950th ANTIAIRCRAFT ARTILLERY BATTALION

Constituted in the Georgia National Guard as the 3d Battalion, 200th Infantry and Federally recognized 8 May 1924 with Headquarters at Elberton and companies at Cedartown, Calhoun and Elberton. Redesignated 9 June 1924 as 3d Battalion, 122d Infantry. Converted and reorganized 29 October 1939 as 2d Battalion, 214th Coast Artillery. Inducted into Federal service 25 November 1940 at home stations. (Departed San Francisco Port of Embarkation 24 September 1942 for overseas service; arrived in New Zealand 6 October 1942, moved to New Caledonia 27 November 1942 and landed on Guadalcanal on 30 January 1943). Reorganized on Guadalcanal and redesignated 11 November 1943 as the 950th Antiaircraft Artillery Automatic Weapons Battalion (Semimobile). (Returned to New Zealand 11 January 1944; moved to New Guinea on 23 June 1944 and landed in the Philippine Islands on 9 January 1945. Returned from overseas service and arrived at the San Francisco Port of Embarkation on 27 December 1945). Inactivated 28 December 1945 at Camp Stoneman, California. Reorganized and Federally recognized 20 June 1947 with Headquarters at Elberton and batteries at Monroe, Thomson and Elberton. Redesignated 1 October 1953 as the 950th Antiaircraft Artillery Battalion.

Consolidated 1 July 1959 with the 214th Artillery, a parent regiment under the Combat Arms Regimental System.

CAMPAIGN STREAMERS
World War II
Guadalcanal
New Guinea
Leyte
Luzon (with arrowhead)

DECORATIONS
Presidential Unit Citation (Army), Streamer embroidered *CORREGIDOR* (Btry A 950th AAA AW Bn cited for period 16-28 Feb 1945; WDGO 53, 1945)

Philippine Presidential Unit Citation, Streamer embroidered *17 OCTOBER 1944 TO 4 JULY 1945* (950th AAA AW Bn cited; DAGO 47, 1950)

COAT OF ARMS

SHIELD: Gules a chevronel debased azure fimbriated or, below three shell bursts one and two of the third.

CREST: That for the regiments and separate battalions of the Georgia Army National Guard: On a wreath of the colors (or and gules) a boar's head erased gules, in the mouth an oak branch vert, fructed or.

MOTTO: We Hear And Strike

The shield is scarlet, the color for Artillery. The chevron, indicative of strength and support, is blue and refers to the origin of the organization. The three shell bursts commemorate its mission as antiaircraft artillery.

DISTINCTIVE INSIGNIA

The insignia is the shield and motto of the coat of arms. The sample of the insignia depicted was originally approved 14 October 1940 for wear by the 214th Coast Artillery.

951st ANTIAIRCRAFT ARTILLERY AUTOMATIC WEAPONS BATTALION

Constituted 1 August 1924 in the California National Guard as 2d Battalion, 251st Coast Artillery (Harbor Defense). Organized and Federally recognized 3 December 1924 with Headquarters at San Pedro. Redesignated 1 January 1930 as 2d Battalion, 251st Coast Artillery (Antiaircraft) with batteries at Long Beach and San Pedro; concurrently, Headquarters relocated to Long Beach. Inducted into Federal service 16 September 1940 at home stations. (Departed Los Angeles Port of Embarkation 17 November 1940 for overseas service and arrived at Fort Shafter, Hawaii on 23 November 1940; subsequently served in the Fiji Islands, on Bougainville and in the Philippine Islands). Reorganized and redesignated 1 March 1944 as the 951st Antiaircraft Artillery Automatic Weapons Battalion. (Returned from overseas service and arrived at the San Francisco Port of Embarkation on 26 December 1945). Inactivated 29 December 1945 at Camp Stoneman, California.

Battalion broken up and its elements redesignated as follows: Headquarters and Headquarters Battery as Headquarters and Headquarters Battery, 682d Antiaircraft Artillery Automatic Weapons Battalion; Battery A as Battery A, 682d Antiaircraft Artillery Automatic Weapons Battalion; Battery B as Headquarters and Headquarters Battery, 234th Antiaircraft Artillery Group; Battery C as Headquarters and Headquarters Battery, 720th Antiaircraft Artillery Gun Battalion and Battery D as Battery A, 720th Antiaircraft Artillery Gun Battalion.

CAMPAIGN STREAMERS
World War II
Central Pacific
Northern Solomons
Luzon (with arrowhead)

DECORATIONS

Philippine Presidential Unit Citation, Streamer embroidered *17 OCTOBER 1944 TO 4 JULY 1945* (951st AAA AW Bn cited; DAGO 47, 1950)

COAT OF ARMS
None

DISTINCTIVE INSIGNIA
None

951st ANTIAIRCRAFT ARTILLERY BATTALION

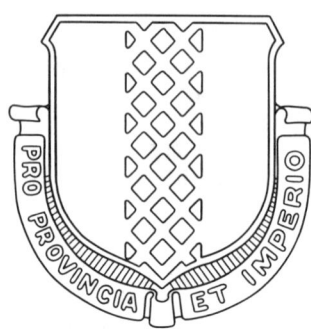

Constituted 5 August 1946 in the California National Guard as the 951st Antiaircraft Artillery Automatic Weapons Battalion and Federally recognized 20 March 1947 with Headquarters and Headquarters Battery and Batteries A and B at Richmond and Batteries C and D at Vallejo. Reorganized and redesignated 1 January 1951 as the 951st Antiaircraft Artillery Gun Battalion. Redesignated 1 October 1953 as the 951st Antiaircraft Artillery Battalion.

Consolidated 1 May 1959 with the 250th Artillery, a parent regiment under the Combat Arms Regimental System.

CAMPAIGN STREAMERS
None

DECORATIONS
None

COAT OF ARMS
SHIELD: Gules, a pale or fretty of the first.

CREST: That for the regiments and separate battalions of the California Army National Guard: On a wreath of the colors (argent and gules) the setting sun behind a grizzly bear passant on a grassy field, all proper.

MOTTO: *Pro Provincia et Imperio* (For State And Country)

Red and yellow are used for Artillery organizations. The red fretty lines on the yellow allude to the sky criss-crossed by antiaircraft fire, thus simulating a net through which no enemy aircraft can penetrate. The yellow pale also represents the Golden State.

DISTINCTIVE INSIGNIA
The insignia is the shield and motto of the coat of arms. The sample of the insignia depicted was approved for wear on 3 December 1952.

967th ANTIAIRCRAFT ARTILLERY MISSILE BATTALION

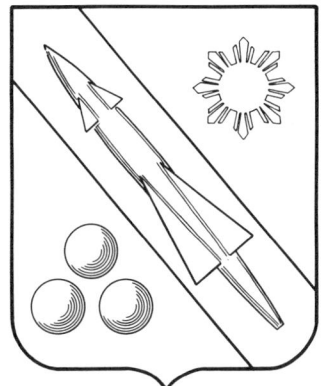 

Constituted 25 February 1943 in the Army of the United States as the 967th Coast Artillery Battalion (Antiaircraft) (Gun). Redesignated 30 April 1943 as the 967th Antiaircraft Artillery Gun Battalion (Semimobile). Activated 1 November 1943 on Guadalcanal. (Moved to Green Island on 15 February 1944. After service at Bougainville and in the Philippine Islands, returned from overseas service and arrived at the San Francisco Port of Embarkation on 26 December 1945). Inactivated 28 December 1945 at Camp Stoneman, California. Redesignated 967th Antiaircraft Artillery Missile Battalion and allotted to the Regular Army on 2 February 1956. Activated 1 March 1956 at Fort Hancock, New Jersey. Inactivated 1 September 1958 at West Haven, Connecticut.

CAMPAIGN STREAMERS
World War II
Northern Solomons (with arrowhead)
Bismarck Archipelago
Leyte

DECORATIONS
Philippine Presidential Unit Citation, Streamer embroidered *17 OCTOBER 1944 TO 4 JULY 1945* (967th AAA Gun Bn cited; DAGO 47, 1950)

COAT OF ARMS
SHIELD: Or, on a bend gules between in sinister chief a Philippine sun and in dexter base three pomeis, one and two, a guided missile of the first.

CREST: None

MOTTO: In Defense Of Freedom

Scarlet and yellow are the colors used for Artillery. The missile represents the organization's special mission as an Antiaircraft Artillery Missile Battalion. The green discs, symbolic of jungle island areas indicate the three campaigns in the Pacific during World War II. The sun device from the Philippine flag refers to the Philippine Presidential Unit Citation awarded to the unit for its service in the Philippine Islands.

DISTINCTIVE INSIGNIA
The insignia is the shield and motto of the coat of arms. The sample of the insignia depicted was approved for wear on 7 February 1957.

972d ANTIAIRCRAFT ARTILLERY BATTALION

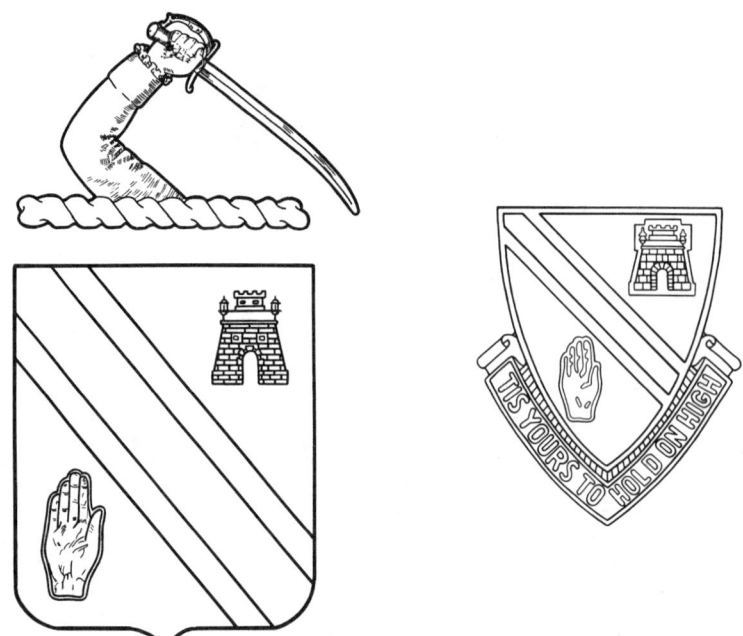

Constituted 2 September 1863 as a Company of Infantry in the Independent Division, Massachusetts Volunteer Militia and organized 10 September 1863 at Boston as the Unattached Company of Infantry, Captain Lewis Gaul, commanding. Redesignated 20 August 1864 as the 14th Unattached Company, Massachusetts Volunteer Militia. Redesignated 20 August 1866 as Company A, 2d Battalion of Infantry, 1st Brigade, Massachusetts Volunteer Militia. Disbanded 6 July 1876 at Boston. Reorganized 1 June 1877 at Boston as an Unattached Company of Infantry and assigned to the 1st Brigade, Massachusetts Volunteer Militia on 25 June 1877. Redesignated 3 December 1878 as Company L, 6th Regiment of Infantry, Massachusetts Volunteer Infantry. Mustered into Federal service 13 May 1898 at Boston as Company L, 6th Regiment, Massachusetts Volunteer Infantry; mustered out 21 January 1899 and resumed State status. Mustered into Federal service at Boston 6 April 1917 and drafted into Federal service on 5 August 1917. Redesignated 1st Separate Company, Infantry, 30 November 1917. Redesignated 1 January 1918 as Company L, 372d Infantry (Colored) and assigned to the 93d Division. Demobilized 6 March 1919 at Camp Sherman, Ohio. Reorganized 20 June 1919 at Boston as Company L, 6th Infantry (Provisional), Massachusetts National Guard. Disbanded 12 July 1920 at Boston. Reconstituted 30 November 1920 as 2d Separate Battalion of Infantry, Massachusetts National Guard and expanded to consist of Headquarters and Headquarters Company, and Companies A, B, C, and D. Reorganized and Federally recognized 15 March 1922 at Boston. Redesignated 1 January 1925 as 3d Battalion, 372d Infantry (Colored). Inducted into Federal service 10 March 1941 at Boston. Inactivated 31 January 1946 at Schofield Barracks, Hawaii. Redesignated 8 July 1946 as the 272d Field Artillery Battalion (155mm Howitzer-Towed). Reorganized and Federally recognized 5 November 1947 at Boston. Ordered into active Federal service at Boston 18 September 1950. Released from active Federal service 17 January 1955 and resumed State status. Reorganized and redesignated 1 January 1956 as the 972d Antiaircraft Artillery Battalion (75mm Gun).

Consolidated 1 May 1959 with the 241st Artillery, a parent regiment under the Combat Arms Regimental System.

CAMPAIGN STREAMERS
War with Spain
Puerto Rico

World War I
Meuse-Argonne
Lorraine 1918
Alsace 1918

World War II
Pacific Theater without inscription

DECORATIONS
French Croix de Guerre with Palm, World War I, Streamer embroidered *MEUSE-ARGONNE* (372d Inf cited; WDGO 11, 1924)

COAT OF ARMS
SHIELD: Azure, on a bend between a castle or and a dexter hand gules, fimbriated of the second, a bendlet of the third.

CREST: That for the regiments and separate battalions of the Massachusetts National Guard: On a wreath of the colors (or and azure) a dexter arm embowed, clothed blue and ruffled white proper, the hand grasping a broad sword argent, the pommel and hilt or.

MOTTO: Tis Yours To Hold On High

The shield is blue for Infantry and the castle, from the Puerto Rican occupation medal, denotes service in Puerto Rico during the War with Spain. The red hand and gold bend charged with the red bendlet commemorate service in France during World War I. The red hand was the insignia of the French 157th Division to which the 372d Infantry was attached during the Meuse-Argonne offensive. The bend charged with the bendlet indicates the service in the defensive sectors in Alsace and Lorraine. The arms of Alsace bear a gold bend and the arms of Lorraine a red bend.

DISTINCTIVE INSIGNIA
The insignia is the shield and motto of the coat of arms. The sample of the insignia depicted was originally approved on 16 August 1929 for wear by the 3d Battalion, 372d Infantry.

977th ANTIAIRCRAFT ARTILLERY AUTOMATIC WEAPONS BATTALION

Constituted 8 June 1943 in the Army of the United States as the 977th Antiaircraft Artillery Automatic Weapons Battalion (Semimobile) and activated 22 June 1943 in Iceland. (Returned from overseas service and arrived at the New York Port of Embarkation on 14 June 1945). Disbanded 22 June 1945 at Camp Kilmer, New Jersey.

CAMPAIGN STREAMERS
World War II
European Theater without inscription

DECORATIONS
None

COAT OF ARMS
None

DISTINCTIVE INSIGNIA
None

979th ANTIAIRCRAFT ARTILLERY MISSILE BATTALION

Organized in the Michigan Army National Guard as the 979th Field Artillery Battalion (NGUS) and Federally recognized 23 February 1953 at Detroit. Redesignated 1 February 1955 as the 979th Antiaircraft Artillery Battalion (90mm Gun). (979th Field Artillery Battalion [organized and Federally recognized 10 April 1939 at Detroit as 2d Battalion, 182d Field Artillery; inducted into Federal service 7 April 1941 at Detroit; redesignated 1 March 1943 as the 949th Field Artillery Battalion; inactivated 1 December 1945 at Camp Kilmer, New Jersey; reorganized and Federally recognized 30 January 1950 at Detroit as 979th Field Artillery Battalion; ordered into active Federal service 23 January 1951 and released from active Federal service on 3 April 1955] consolidated with the 979th Antiaircraft Artillery Battalion on 4 April 1955). Reorganized and redesignated 1 March 1958 as the 979th Antiaircraft Artillery Missile Battalion (NIKE).

Consolidated 15 March 1959 with the 177th Artillery, a parent regiment under the Combat Arms Regimental System.

CAMPAIGN STREAMERS
World War II
Northern France
Rhineland
Ardennes-Alsace
Central Europe

DECORATIONS
None

COAT OF ARMS
SHIELD: Gules, seme of quatrefoils voided or, a fess sable fimbriated of the second, all within a bordure of the like.

CREST: That for the regiments and separate battalions of the Michigan Army National Guard: On a wreath of the colors (or and gules) a griffin segreant or.

MOTTO: Mobile Might

The use of the coat of arms of the 182d Field Artillery within a border refers to the descent of the organization from that regiment. The background of the shield, seme of quatrefoils in gold on the red field is taken from the coat of arms of Count Pontchartrain who was the Minister of Marine in France at the time Detroit was founded. The black fess across the center of the shield is taken from the coat of arms of Cadillac, the founder of the city of Detroit, who was sent here by Count Pontchartrain. The field of red, substituted for the field of blue of Pontchartrain's arms, symbolizes the arm of service, Artillery, to which the 182d Field Artillery belonged.

DISTINCTIVE INSIGNIA
The insignia is the shield and motto of the coat of arms. The sample of the insignia depicted was originally approved on 3 September 1952 for wear by the 979th Field Artillery Battalion.

993d ANTIAIRCRAFT ARTILLERY SEARCHLIGHT BATTALION

Constituted 4 June 1946 in the Army of the United States as the 993d Antiaircraft Artillery Searchlight Battalion. Activated 28 June 1946 in Hawaii; inactivated 25 October 1946 in Hawaii.

Redesignated 23 November 1951 as the 56th Antiaircraft Artillery Gun Battalion.

CAMPAIGN STREAMERS
None

DECORATIONS
None

COAT OF ARMS
None

DISTINCTIVE INSIGNIA
None

APPENDIX 1

Coats of Arms and Distinctive Insignia

COATS OF ARMS AND DISTINCTIVE INSIGNIA

In his quest for recognition in combat and to distinguish his personal achievements, man has used distinctive marks since primitive times. The Phoenician builders left their marks upon the foundation stones of the Temple of Jerusalem and the walls of Baalbec. In Assyria and Babylonia the names and signs of early kings were stamped upon sun-dried bricks. Defensive weapons provided a way for decorative figures and marks to be placed on shields and trapping. Greek vases and Roman monumental sculptures furnish examples. The famous Bayeux Tapestry, a contemporary depiction of the Norman Conquest, displays distinctive emblems upon banners and some of the shields of the Normans and the English. Through all of these times no definite system appears to have been followed, for it is evident that such devices were of individual choice and quite temporary in nature.

The First Crusade brought together an allied army made up of elements from many of the nations of Europe. The leaders displayed a miscellany of pole standards bearing symbols and banners embroidered or painted with their devices, but the shield of the individual Crusader was plain. Bohemund's loosely organized and poorly disciplined crusaders met the Turkish Saracens at Doryleum on 1 July 1097. The better organized Muslims repeatedly hit the crusaders in swiftly shifting maneuvers with much confusion resulting among the Christians. The distinctly painted shields of the Saracen leaders, held aloft, were obvious and effective unit controls in the ensuing melee. The fortunate arrival of Crusader reinforcements saved the day, but the lessons of this battle made lasting impressions on the Christian leaders. Before the attack on Antioch in October the Crusader Army was reorganized, including the adoption of the initial elements of organized European armory. Military leaders recognized the value of the painted shield for instant identification of the fully armored knight in combat. At the battle of Hastings, William the Conqueror was forced to bare his head to convince his men that he still lived.

True heraldry began in the second quarter of the 12th century when it appeared almost simultaneously in several countries of western Europe. It is reasonably assumed that the rapid spread of the new idea was due in part to the association between warriors of different lands during the First Crusade and their use of symbols in Palestine. The earliest known instance of an heraldic shield occurred 25 years after the First Crusade (1147-49). It must be assumed that there was a more valid reason for the development of heraldry in Europe, the most obvious being the popularity of tournaments in the first half of the 12th century when knights from various countries gathered for feats of arms. These tournaments were occasions for display and pageantry and it would be natural for individual participants to adopt some device for identification purposes. The closed helm rendered the fully-armored knight unrecognizable, the easiest manner by which he could be recognized was through the use of some device painted on his shield.

In the 12th century heralds were responsible for the conduct of tournaments. During these tournaments they proclaimed the name of each entry and acted as masters of ceremonies and counselors. Immediate recognition of all armorial bearings became a skill of the profession.

Throughout their early histories there was a close association between heralds and minstrels. Many heralds wandered from court to court and collected and spread stories of feats of arms and of the individuals who performed them. The opinions of the heralds were potent factors in court circles. Heralds began marshaling state ceremonies, then carried messages of state and military, and even became ambassadors. By the early 14th century Rolls of Arms began to appear and the heralds' duties grew from mere recognition of arms to the surveying of arms. Kings and great nobles retained heralds in their permanent service and the heralds' duties progressed into professional responsibility for the control of armorial bearings.

Inevitably, disputes of arms arose among knights, particularly at gatherings such as tournaments and military events over which the Earl Marshal of England and his senior, the Constable, had jurisdictions. The Court of Chivalry of the Constable and Marshal heard and decided these disputes. Heralds were granted standing in the court and the Earl Marshal became their recognized superior of state.

In 1484 the English heralds of the Royal Household, and their pursuivants, were incorporated by charter of Richard III and granted a house in London. Visitations through the provinces were made by the heralds to correct, record, and control armorial bearings. In time heralds began devising and granting arms. Thus developed the College of Arms which exists to this day as the controlling authority for armorial bearings in England. Similar central authorities exist in many other countries of the world.

The Language of Heraldry

Heraldry is picture-writing in which every symbol has a meaning. Every element of a coat of arms including the shape of the shield itself has significance attached to it.

A complete coat of arms consists of a shield, a crest and a motto. The shield, which is the most important part of the arms, consists of a field upon which are placed the charges or figures that form the coat of arms. The *dexter* side of the shield is on the viewer's left; the *sinister* on the viewer's right. The upper portion of the shield is referred to as the *chief* and the lower part the *base*. The heraldic tinctures comprise two metals and eight colors as follows:

Metals

Or - gold   *Argent* - silver

Colors

Gules - red   *Purpure* - purple
Azure - blue   *Tenne* - orange
Sable - black   *Buff* - buff
Vert - green   *Sanguine* - maroon

Shields of more than one tincture are divided by partition or dividing lines into various forms. When the line is perpendicular it is called *per pale*; horizontal, *per fess*; diagonal lines from dexter chief to sinister base, *per bend*; diagonal dexter and diagonal sinister crossing at the center of the shield, *per saltire*; divided by two lines, one rising from the dexter and one rising from the sinister base and meeting in the center of the shield, *per chevron*.

The crest (from the Latin *cresta*, the tuft or comb which grows upon the heads of many birds) was originally placed upon the top of the helmet of chieftains so that their followers could readily distinguish them in battle. A crest is always placed upon a wreath of six skeins or twists composed of the principal metal and principal color of the shield alternately, in the order named. This wreath (torse) represents the piece of cloth which the knight twisted around the top of his helmet and by means of which the actual crest was attached. The crest for each organization of the Army National Guard is that approved for all Army National Guard regiments and separate battalions of that state, while the crest for all organizations of the Army Reserve is the Lexington Minute Man.

Mottoes are perhaps more ancient than coats of arms. Many of the older ones were originally war-cries and selected with deep sincerity in the expression of their thought. Some mottoes are of an idealistic or exalted nature. While many mottoes are expressed in Latin, the use of English is the accepted practice today. A handful of mottoes are in the more unusual languages such as French, German, Greek, Italian, Hawaiian and American Indian. One organization which served in Siberia during World War I has its motto in Russian.

Heraldry in the United States Army

Through usage over the centuries International Law provides that a belligerent is authorized to carry arms openly only when he is subject to the command of a responsible superior and equipped with a distinctive uniform, including insignia, which may be recognized at a distance. During the Revolutionary War the American forces used distinctive uniforms and markings (facings) to identify their personnel and units.

The American Congress, after having obtained the views of the New England Governors and of General Washington, resolved on 4 November 1775 that the clothing for the Army be paid for by stoppages of the men's pay, "that it by dyed brown and the distinction of regiments made in the facings". The facings for the infantry were white lapels, cuff linings, and standing capes.

The Quartermaster General was the heraldic authority for the United States Army from 1780 until 1961 and during these more than 180 years was the source of supply, the designer, and the point of reference, although the mission was not assigned to him by formal directive until 1924. Between 1919 and 1924 staff supervision of the heraldic program was the responsibility of the Supply Division, General Staff, and each coat of arms, distinctive insignia and shoulder sleeve insignia required the personal approval of the Chief of Staff. This was changed when The Adjutant General issued a letter (file: AG 424.5 Coats of Arms [11-22-24] [Misc] D, dated 18 December 1924) to The Quartermaster General advising, "The Quartermaster General is charged with supervision over the design of individual regimental coats of arms, regimental insignia and trimmings and shoulder sleeve insignia and will make suitable recommendation to The Adjutant General in each case, including a statement as to whether or not, in his opinion, the design submitted meets the requirements of regulations and the established policies of the War Department. The Quartermaster General will be furnished with such records, now in the files of the Equipment Branch, General Staff, as may be necessary to enable him to carry out these instructions".

The same directive assigned certain responsibilities to The Adjutant General when it advised that, "The Adjutant General is authorized to approve or disapprove the design of and to take appropriate action upon correspondence relating to individual regimental coats of arms, regimental insignia and trimmings and shoulder sleeve insignia, in accordance with regulations and established War Department policies. All cases not covered by existing regulations or policies and all recommendations for changes in same thought necessary or desirable will be forwarded to the Supply Division, General Staff, for appropriate action". On 8 October 1942 the authority of The Adjutant General to approve the designs of coats and distinctive insignia was delegated to The Quartermaster General (file: 2d endorsement, AG 421.7 Insignia [9-15-42] OP-I, Office of The Adjutant General, 8 October 1942).

In 1949 the Munitions Board, acting for the Army, Navy, and Air Force directed that "the Department of the Army be responsible for meeting the requirements of all three departments for the research, design and development for heraldic items subject to the approval of the Secretary of the Department concerned". Thereafter, the Secretary of the Army directed that "The Quartermaster General will assume the above-stated responsibility for the Department of the Army".

In 1957 Public Law 85-263 provided that the Secretary of the Army may design flags, insignia, badges, medals, seals, decorations, guidons, streamers, finial pieces for flagstaffs, buttons, buckles, awards, trophies, marks, emblems, rosettes, scrolls, braids, ribbons, knots, tabs, cords, and similar items for another military department upon the request of and approval by that department. The Army also was authorized to advise other departments and agencies on matters of heraldry. In 1959 Army Regulations 700-14 and Air Force Regulation 900-11 gave the Quartermaster General of the Army the responsibility to furnish heraldic facilities and services in implementation of Public Law 85-263.

In September 1960 The Institute of Heraldry, U.S. Army, was established and located at Cameron Station in Alexandria, Virginia, to which The Quartermaster General delegated the authority for all major operational activities of the heraldic program.

The Institute of Heraldry:
    a. Provides heraldic service to the Department of Defense and other government agencies upon request to include research, design and development; and acts as advisor to non-government agencies, organizations and individuals when appropriate.
    b. Designs, develops, and recommends heraldic items (as coats of arms, seals, insignia, flags, decorations, medals, markings, etc.) and acts upon matters pertaining to their wear, display, and use; and furnishes advice concerning the development of prototypes of heraldic items.
    c. Prepares heraldic drawings, paintings, and models for use in displays, illustration of publications, and manufacturing processes.
    d. In matters pertaining to the manufacture of heraldic items, recommends specifications and purchase descriptions, acts in matters of authorization of manufacturing firms, and monitors quality control of their production for sale through the Army-Air Force Exchange Service and commercial outlets to military units and personnel.
    e. Performs historical research regarding uniforms, flags, decorations, and other heraldic material, including cataloging, recording and preparing studies of customs and backgrounds pertaining thereto; charts unit histories to determine design and redesign of coats of arms and distinctive insignia.
    f. Maintains a library of heraldry.

Coats of Arms and Distinctive Insignia

Each regiment and separate battalion (fixed type) of the United States Army is authorized a coat of arms for display on the organizational flag and a distinctive insignia (erroneously referred to as the "unit crest") for wear on the uniform. The coat of arms is a heraldic representation of the organization's history, tradition, ideals, and accomplishments. Each is distinctive to the organization for which approved and serves as an inspiration and an incentive for unity of purpose. The elements of the coat of arms are embroidered on the organization color — the central element of which is the American eagle. The shield of the coat of arms is on the eagle's breast; a scroll bearing the motto is held in its beak with the crest placed above its head.

The distinctive insignia of the regiment or separate battalion is generally based on all or some portion of the coat of arms. Most consist of the shield and motto, some consist only of the shield of the coat of arms, and a few consist of the crest only or the crest and motto.

The Coat of Arms

Widespread use of coats of arms by the regiments and separate battalions of the United States Army is a relatively modern practice. A few regiments are known to have adopted unofficial coats of arms during the nineteenth century but not until 1902 did the War Department first encourage the regiments of the Army to design coats of arms for use on stationery and wear as regimental insignia on distinctive organizational mess jackets. Although this practice was no longer sanctioned after 1911, organizations continued to adopt for unofficial use such devices up to and throughout World War I. On 18 August 1919 the first major step was taken by the War Department to officially recognize a coat of arms for each regiment of the United States Army when it authorized the placing in the corners of the regiment's color an appropriate device to represent the wars, or other incidents connected with the organization's history. Additionally, a device distinctive of the organization was authorized to be placed on the eagle on the color and regimental commanders were invited to submit suggested devices for approval by the War Department. Some suggestions for devices to designate wars included a cactus for the Mexican War, a palm tree for the Philippine Insurrection, a conventional castle for the War with Spain and a laurel wreath for World War I.

The order was universally misunderstood by the Army and the War Department attempted to clarify the matter in November of that year when it published Circular No. 527 which stated:

"1. It is the desire of the War Department to cultivate in every possible way a healthy esprit de corps in every organization. Heretofore there has been comparatively little attention paid to the history of organizations by the members as a whole, and there has been nothing to bring any previous feat of arms to the attention of any officer or man except by those who deliberately made it their business to read and investigate. In order that the deeds of the regiment can be made familiar to all they must be continually set before them and this can be done in many ways; but as one means toward this end the design of organization colors has been recently changed to give each a color essentially its own, differing in design from every other color by perpetuating thereon historical events of the organization. The wars in which the regiment engaged will be shown by symbols in the corners. These will be standard for the Army. Suggestions as to their design are desired. The names of battles will be embroidered on the color itself where they can be easily read, instead of on silver bands which required a close inspection, and finally a device peculiar to that organization will be placed over the coat of arms of the United States.

2. As a flag is a symbol of the country, so should any device placed thereon represent events by symbolism; or to put it another way a flag is a heraldic emblem and everything placed on it must be heraldic in character. This points to either a regular coat of arms or a badge as the form to be taken by these distinctive organization devices. Regiments which already have satisfactory coats of arms should submit them for approval; others should design either a coat of arms or a badge. Whatever is used must conform to the rules of heraldry.

3. Another advantage in this is the fact that these same devices will be suitable in other ways to bring the regimental history home to every member, for example, on stationery, on pins, watch charms, etc., for civilian clothes, on tablets for headquarters, mess rooms, etc., possibly on the white mess jacket, all of which should promote esprit de corps.

4. In designing a coat of arms or badge, the following points should govern:

    a. If possible, some symbol should be used to commemorate the birth or initial service of the organization; if organized from some one state or section of the country an identification of the unit therewith should have good results. The organization of a regiment, like the birth of an individual, is an important event in its history.

    b. The first war in which the regiment took part should be commemorated. This also can be likened to the individual whose "baptism of fire" is always his most important engagement, his bearing on that occasion having an ineradicable effect on his future service.

Points on the shield and Lines of Partition

A complete coat of arms consists of the shield, crest and motto. The shield is the most important part of the arms and on it are placed the charges and various lines of partition and ordinaries. The shield illustrated at the right locates the different parts and points as follows:

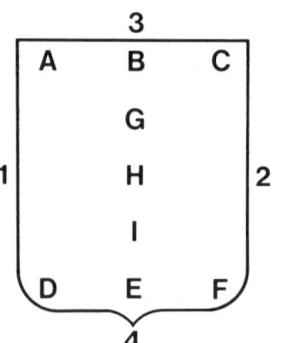

1. Dexter side
2. Sinister side
3. Chief
4. Base

A. Dexter chief
B. Middle chief
C. Sinister chief
D. Dexter base

E. Middle base
F. Sinister base
G. Honor point
H. Fess point
I. Nombril point

Lines of Partition (Shown divided Per Fess)

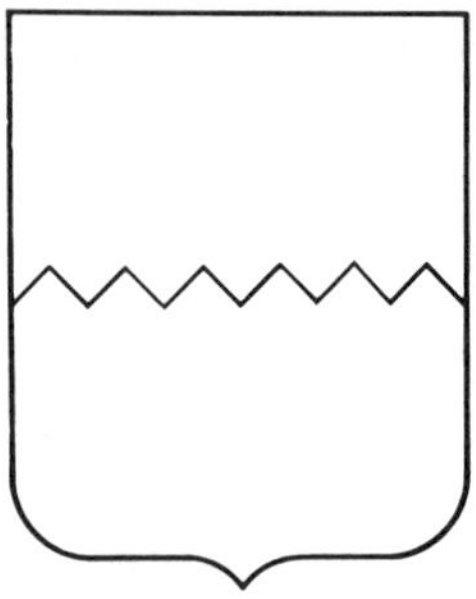

Indented 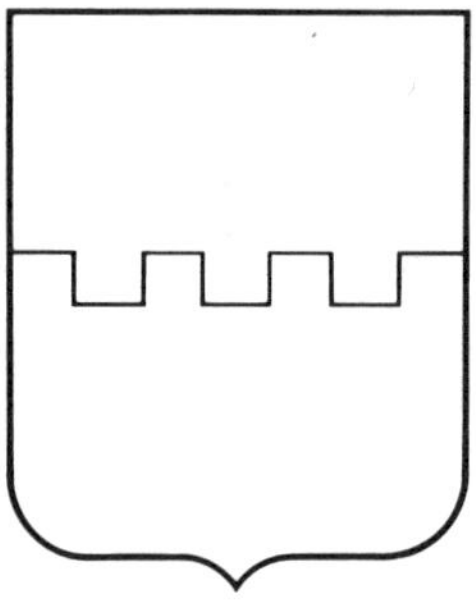 *Embattled*  *Dancetty* 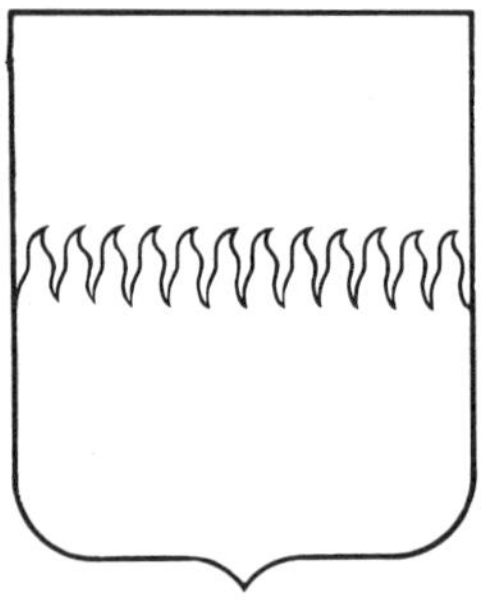 *Rayonne*

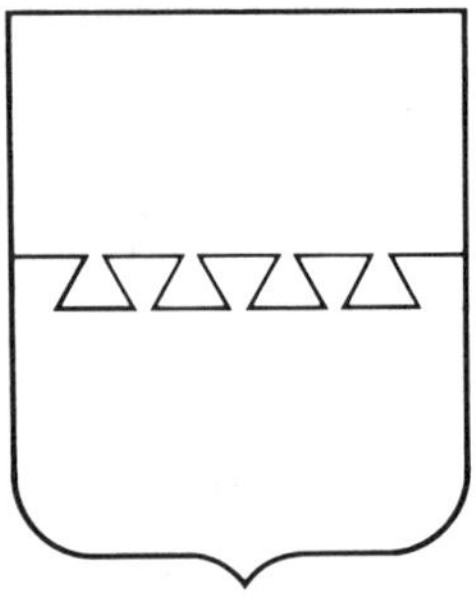

Dovetailed 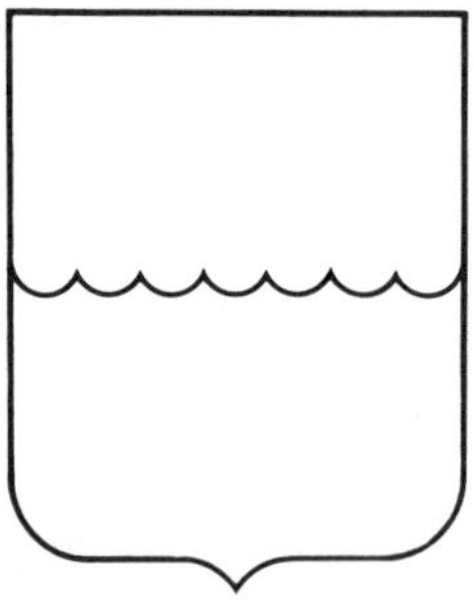 *Engrailed* 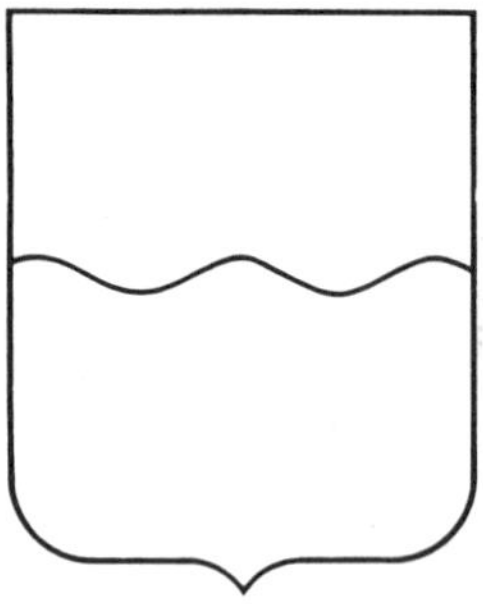 *Wavy* 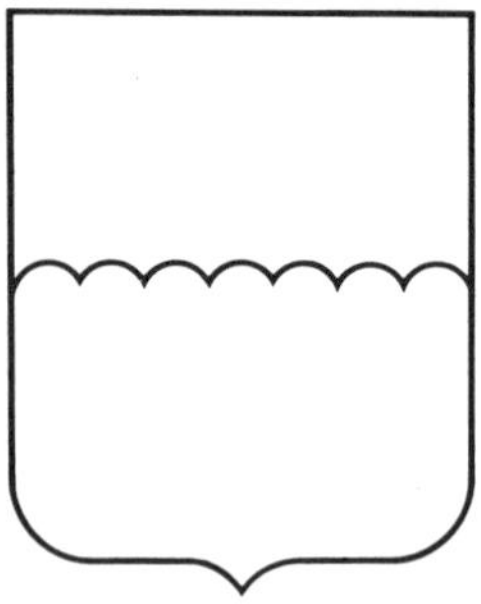 *Invected*

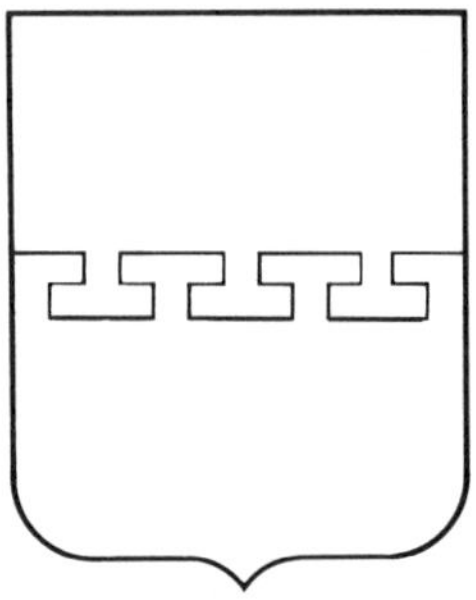

Potenty 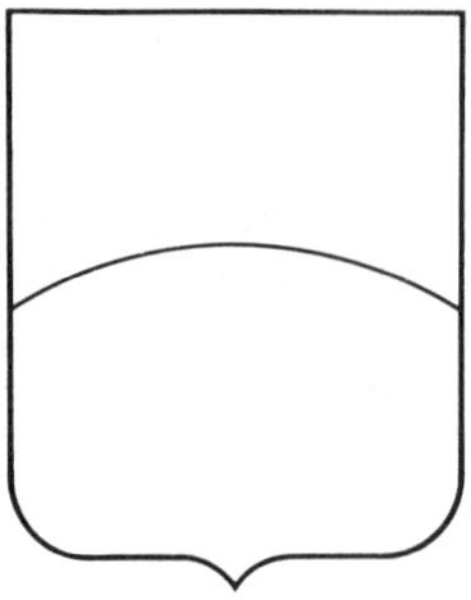 *Arched* 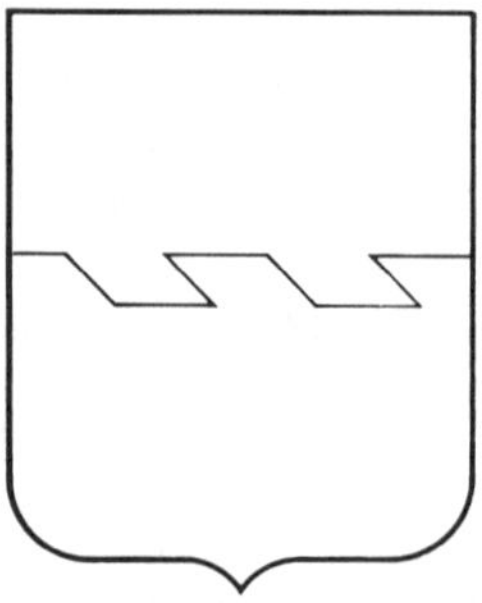 *Raguly*  *Nebuly*

Four Methods of Partition (Dividing the Shield)

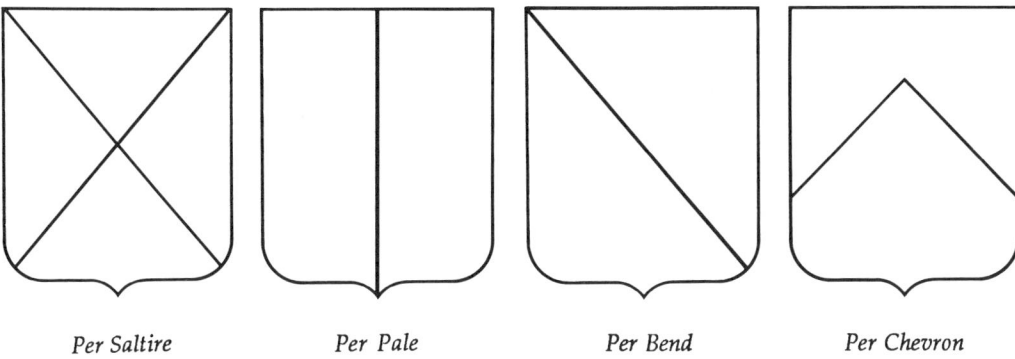

Per Saltire   *Per Pale*   *Per Bend*   *Per Chevron*

Twelve Ordinaries (Shown using various Lines of Partition Styles)

Fess Embattled    *Bar Dancetty*    *Bend Raguly*    *Bendlet Wavy*

Pile Indented    *Pallets* 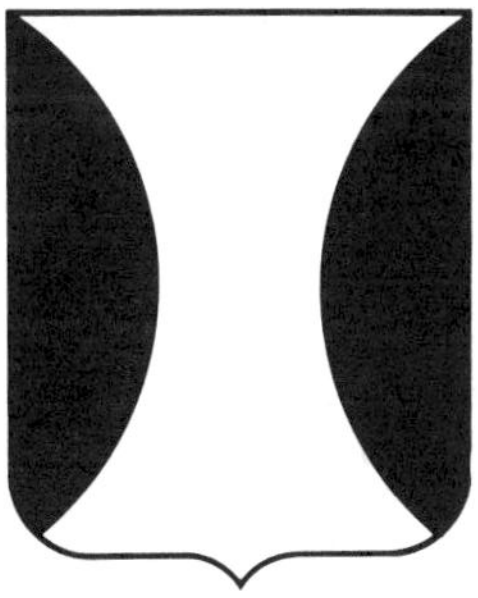   *Flaunches*    *Chief Rayonne*

Chevron Invected 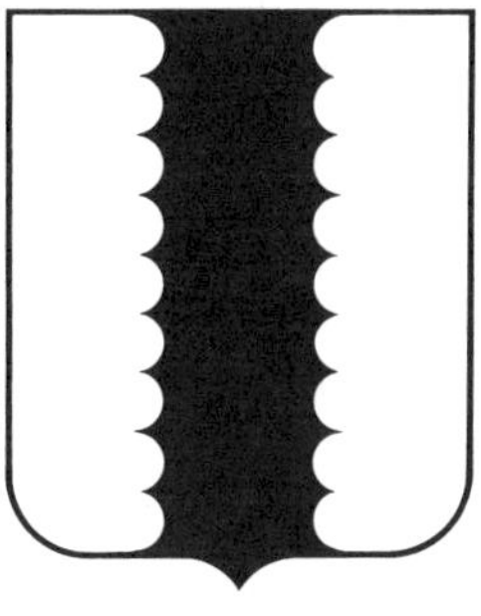   *Pale Engrailed*    *Cross*    *Saltire*

c. A particularly brilliant feat of arms should be the subject of the main part of the device or coat of arms and the more ancient that feat the better; in other words, the oldest services should be chosen to symbolize rather than the most recent, other things being equal. The tendency will be to enlarge on recent events because of personal participation therein. This should be carefully avoided.

d. For new organizations plenty of room should be left on the coat of arms for symbols to be placed in the future. They should not be overloaded and in all cases the arms should be as simple as possible."

This, then, was the beginning of the program which has provided coats of arms for the regiments and separate battalions of the Army and, except for a short period during and after World War II, has been in continuous effect for more than half a century. The use of devices in the corners of the regimental colors to represent the wars of the organization was never implemented, the suggested devices were instead incorporated into the organizational coats of arms.

Throughout the twenties and thirties, War Department policy dictated that the organizational color would not be issued until the coat of arms had been approved. The major mobilization at the beginning of World War II forced the War Department to issue flags to organizations which had no approved coat of arms. The overwhelming requirement for new coats of arms and the lack of history for the newly activated organizations caused the War Department to suspend the approval of new coats of arms after 1943. The only approvals between then and 1951 were for organizations that had served overseas during World War I.

Distinctive Insignia

Pride in organization and the desire to be recognized have been important to members of the United States Army since its very beginning. The general practice of distinguishing between the various regiments of the Army began during the Revolutionary War when each regiment identified itself by the colors of its facings (uniform collars, lapels, and cuffs). One regiment carried the matter of personal identification one step further. At the defense of Charleston (South Carolina) in 1776 the 1st South Carolina Regiment arrived wearing small silver metal crescents, inscribed *ultima ratio* on their hats. This is the earliest known use of a distinctive badge by any organization of the United States Army.

The use of regimental facings gave way to the practice of wearing the insignia of the branch of service and the regimental number early in the nineteenth century, a practice still in use today. While this was adequate for organizational identification, it did not provide the individual touch which so many regiments apparently desired. During the Mexican War the Regiment of Mounted Riflemen (now the 3d Armored Cavalry Regiment) wore a small gold trumpet on their cuffs, and at the beginning of the Civil War, one regiment (the 13th Pennsylvania Reserves, officially known to the rest of the Union Army as the *Bucktails*) reported to its rendezvous point at Harrisburg wearing strips of fur on their forage caps. Another regiment, the 5th Maryland (now the 175th Infantry) wore small silver bottony crosses on their uniforms.

The Civil War added a new dimension to the field of unit identification. Heretofore it had been restricted to the small unit level; now such identification was extended to include the Corps and its organic divisions. While such badges may be considered the forerunner to the shoulder sleeve insignia of World War I, the fact that they were made of metal and worn as a distinctive insignia is reason enough to document the reasons for their adoption.

The origin of the Corps badge is credited to General Philip Kearny, who early in the Civil War mistakenly reprimanded several officers whom he thought were under his command. When advised of his error, he apologized and said he would do something about it. He then directed his officers to wear a red patch on their caps. The practice became very popular not only with his officers but with the men who also used it unofficially for identification with their command. By the end of the war, almost every Corps in the Union Army had adopted a distinctive badge which followed a similar pattern; red for its first division, white for the second and blue for the third.

Shortly after the beginning of the War with Spain, reports reached the War Department from organizations then being formed that devices to facilitate identification of major formations were desired. Although Corps badges were not suggested, the adoption of a flag with a suitable device for each brigade or higher unit was recommended, as well as an ornament for the campaign hat to identify the regiment and company of the wearer. On 9 June 1898 the Secretary of War authorized designating flags and Corps badges for the Army Corps in existence but, at the insistence of Civil War Veterans, said that the designs would not duplicate any devices used during the Civil War. The War Department issued General Order 99 on 15 July 1898 which prescribed the patterns, but the scope was greater than those used during the Civil War. For instance, the Seventh Army Corps of Jacksonville, Florida, defined the magnitude when it issued its General Order 19 on 26 July 1898 which read:

"In order that there may be a badge to distinguish the different Divisions, Brigades and other organizations to which the Commissioned Officers and enlisted men belong, a seven-pointed star is hereby authorized to be worn on the front of the hat by all members of the Seventh Army Corps. For Infantry this star to be: Red for the First Division, White for the Second Division, and Blue for the Third Division; the number of the Brigade to be placed in the centre and made of white metal. For Cavalry: A yellow star with number of Regiment in the centre, number to be made of white metal. The Corps Commander and Staff to wear a star with red centre, white circle and blue points. The Division Commanders and Staff, a plain star of their Division color. The Brigade Commanders and Staff a star of the same color as their Division but with the number of the Brigade in centre in white metal. For Line Officers, the same as Brigade. For Engineer Officers and enlisted men, the color of star to be scarlet, edged with white. For Ordnance, magenta. For Medical and Hospital Corps, green. For Signal Corps, orange. The star herein mentioned shall be one and one-quarter inches in diameter. A sample of this star can, upon application, be seen at the office of the Chief Quartermaster of the Corps."

On 17 July 1902 the Staff Corps and Departments, the Corps of Artillery and the Regiments of Cavalry and Infantry of the Army were authorized to wear mess jackets. To personalize these jackets, the Secretary of War authorized the adoption of some distinctive ornamentation such as a coat of arms or device on 31 December 1902 for wear on the cuffs or lapels. Many regiments adopted such devices, but when the mess jacket was standardized in 1911 the authority for wear of regimental insignia was withdrawn. The regimental insignia remained popular and continued to be used until the end of World War I.

The first organization of the Army to wear an insignia in an overseas theater allegedly was the Tank Corps of the American Expeditionary Forces. In June 1918, while attached to the British Tank Center in France, each man of the Corps wore on his left shoulder strap a ribbon one and one-half inches wide, consisting of three equal stripes of yellow, red and blue. This ultimately evolved into a triangular sleeve insignia worn during the Meuse-Argonne offensive in September 1918, long before shoulder sleeve insignia were officially permitted to be worn in the AEF.

Although the trend was toward the use of shoulder sleeve insignia customized for regimental identification, some organizations, generally Aero Squadrons in England and France wore a small metal replica of their squadron insignia. The 94th Aero Squadron is known to have has its insignia made overseas and the famous "hat-in-the-ring" insignia was proudly worn by its top ace, Captain Eddie Rickenbacker.

Views on the adoption and wear of distinctive insignia surfaced periodically during 1919 and 1920. On 25 November 1919 in Circular 527 the War Department pointed out the possible use of regimental coats of arms as distinctive insignia, and in a Memorandum prepared in 1920 by Colonel Robert E. Wyllie, Chief of the Equipment Branch, Operations Division, General Staff, G-4, he indicated that coats of arms must be capable of being reproduced as collar insignia.

Regimental coats of arms and badges were reinstated on 29 April 1920 when War Department Circular No. 161 authorized their wear on the collar of the white uniform and on the lapels of the mess jacket. This Circular also permitted enlisted men for the first time to wear items on the uniform which were not furnished by the Quartermaster Corps, provided such articles had been approved by the Quartermaster General. While it did not provide for the wear of distinctive insignia by enlisted men, at least it removed the restriction against their wear.

In a conversation with members of the General Staff on 15 July 1921, the Secretary of War stated that he agreed in principle with the theory that regiments of the Army should be permitted to wear some distinctive badge or trimming on the uniform to identify them with their past achievements and traditions. He cited the case of the 3d Cavalry which, during the war with Mexico, wore green trimmings as the Regiment of Mounted Riflemen and trimmed its mess jackets in green, which some years before the War Department had ordered removed. Another organization cited was the 1st Cavalry, which had a regimental custom of wearing a small gilt dragoon button referring to its organization in 1833 as the First Dragoons. The Secretary concluded by stating that the War Department should consider the use of devices that would symbolize the history of the organizations and promote esprit de corps in the Army comparable to that of some of the more famous British regiments, such as the

Black Watch, the Gordon Highlanders, and the Coldstream Guards.

The conversation ultimately led to the publication of War Department Circular No. 244 in September 1921. It formally announced to the Army that regiments of the Regular Army and National Guard were entitled to wear distinctive insignia or trimmings on their uniforms as a means of promoting esprit de corps. The first approval took place on 18 March 1922 when the 51st Artillery was issued a formal letter of authorization by the War Department.

Originally the regimental insignia worn on the mess jacket and the service uniform were not of the same finish. The insignia for the mess jacket was brightly polished and enameled, while that worn on the service uniform, like the uniform buttons and branch of service insignia, was bronze without enamel. In a study made by the War Department early in 1923 it was found that 18 organizations wore only the highly polished and enameled insignia, two organizations only the bronze insignia, and eight organizations, both types. Two other organizations wore no metal insignia; the 3d Infantry wore a buff and black strap, and the 14th Cavalry a yellow and blue ribbon. In this study it was pointed out that the bronze insignia was mistaken at a short distance for the usual uniform insignia and added no color to the uniform. Further, the bronze insignia were not as attractive as the enameled insignia for promoting esprit de corps and pride in the organization. The study concluded by recommending no additional approvals of bronze insignia. War Department Circular No. 24, published on 27 March 1923, stated, "the wearing of regimental insignia of the metal badge type in bronze metal will not be authorized for any additional organizations and those organizations heretofore authorized to wear the devices in bronze will effect a gradual change to the bright metal and enamel type as the supply of insignia of bronze metal on hand becomes exhausted".

The intent of the War Department was to limit the authorization of distinctive insignia to the regiments of the Army, but almost immediately after the new regulation went into effect an insignia was approved for the U.S. Military Academy Detachment of Troops as an exception to policy. In his letter of transmittal, The Adjutant General pointed out that although the small separate detachments at the Military Academy were not authorized distinctive insignia, the device was authorized in view of the nature of the duty at the Military Academy, and that the detachments as a whole were considered to be equivalent to a regiment. It was the first approval for an organization which, in fact, was neither color-bearing nor a regiment, and that approval set in motion certain forces which have plagued the Army ever since. While an exception to policy may occur once without ill effects, the second time it becomes policy. In time new categories of organizations were authorized distinctive insignia, until by the beginning of World War II every organization in the Army was authorized to adopt one if it so desired.

Independent battalions or their equivalent were authorized distinctive insignia on 31 December 1926 and on 28 March 1928, company-size organizations were included for the first time when Army Regulations were revised to substitute *organizations* for *regiments and independent battalions*. The first approval under the new regulations occurred on 4 January 1928, almost two months prior to the date of the change, and the approval was for a badge instead of a distinctive insignia. Although many company-size organizations of the Regular Army failed to adopt distinctive badges, the change was well received in other circles, as evidenced by the many approvals made for Special Troop companies of the National Guard divisions during 1928 and 1929.

On 28 August 1941 the last remaining barriers were removed and regulations were revised to permit installations and War Department overhead units to adopt distinctive badges. Needless to say, the War Department was overwhelmed with requests from units wishing to adopt distinctive insignia or badges. Manufacturers could not keep abreast of the demand for insignia and sometimes took as long as six months to deliver the items. The new policy caused some misgivings at the War Department and commanders were subsequently directed to disapprove all requests for insignia unless:

- The circumstances were so unusual that the individuals of the organization affected could not properly perform their military duties without the insignia in question.
- The insignia would be useful to the organization even if it was not received for more than six months from the date of approval.
- The insignia could be worn by the organization if ordered overseas.

The action served to reduce the number of requests for new insignia arriving at the War Department but the use of brass, a critical war material, in the manufacture of distinctive insignia was another matter of major concern. A study made by the War Department indicated that it required approximately 55-1/2 tons of brass annually to meet the

- Fredericksburg 9 Nov-15 Dec 1862
- Murfreesborough 26 Dec 1862-4 Jan 1863
- Chancellorsville 27 Apr-6 May 1863
- Gettysburg 29 Jun-3 Jul 1863
- Vicksburg 29 Mar-4 Jul 1863
- Chickamauga 16 Aug-22 Sept 1863
- Chattanooga 23-27 Nov 1863
- Wilderness 4-7 May 1864
- Atlanta 7 May-2 Sept 1864
- Spotsylvania 8-21 May 1864
- Cold Harbor 22 May-3 Jun 1864
- Petersburg 4 Jun 1864-2 Apr 1865
- Shenandoah 7 Aug-28 Nov 1864
- Franklin 17-30 Nov 1864
- Nashville 1-16 Dec 1864
- Appomattox 3-9 Apr 1865

INDIAN WARS

- Miami Jan 1790-Aug 1795
- Tippecanoe 21 Sept-18 Nov 1811
- Creeks 27 Jul 1813-9 Aug 1814
  Feb 1836-Jul 1837
- Seminoles 20 Nov 1817-31 Oct 1818
  28 Dec 1835-14 Aug 1842
  15 Dec 1855-May 1858
- Black Hawk 26 Apr-30 Sept 1832
- Comanches 1867-1875
- Modocs 1872-1873
- Apaches 1873 and 1885-1886
- Little Big Horn 1876-1877
- Nez Perces 1877
- Bannocks 1878
- Cheyennes 1878-1879
- Utes Sept 1879-Nov 1880
- Pine Ridge Nov 1890-Jan 1891

WAR WITH SPAIN

- Santiago 22 Jun-11 Jul 1898
- Puerto Rico 25 Jul-13 Aug 1898
- Manila 31 Jul-13 Aug 1898

CHINA RELIEF EXPEDITION

- Tientsin 13 Jul 1900
- Yang-tsun 6 Aug 1900
- Peking 14-15 Aug 1900

PHILIPPINE INSURRECTION

- Manila 4 Feb-17 Mar 1899
- Iloilo 8-12 Feb 1899
- Malolos 24 Mar-16 Aug 1899
- Laguna de Bay 8-17 Apr 1899
- San Isidro 21 Apr-30 May 1899
  15 Oct-19 Nov 1899
- Zapote River 13 Jun 1899

---

* For Confederate service, campaign honors to indicate Bull Run, Manassas, and Antietam, use inscription: First Manassas, Second Manassas, and Sharpsburg, respectively.

- Cavite 7-13 Oct 1899
  4 Jan-9 Feb 1900
- Tarlac 5-20 Nov 1899
- San Fabian 6-19 Nov 1899
- Mindanao 4 Jul 1902-31 Dec 1904
  22 Oct 1905
- Jolo 1-24 May 1905; 6-8 Mar 1906
  11-15 Jun 1913

MEXICAN EXPEDITION

- Mexico 1916-1917 14 Mar 1916
  -17 Feb 1917

WORLD WAR I

- Cambrai 20 Nov-4 Dec 1917
- Somme Defensive 21 Mar-6 Apr 1918
- Lys 9-27 Apr 1918
- Aisne 27 May-5 Jun 1918
- Montdidier-Noyon 9-13 Jun 1918
- Champagne-Marne 15-18 Jul 1918
- Aisne-Marne 18 Jul-6 Aug 1918
- Somme Offensive 8 Aug-11 Nov 1918
- Oise-Aisne 18 Aug-11 Nov 1918
- Ypres-Lys 19 Aug-11 Nov 1918
- St. Mihiel 12-16 Sept 1918
- Meuse-Argonne 26 Sept-11 Nov 1918
- Vittorio Veneto 24 Oct-4 Nov 1918

WORLD WAR II – AMERICAN THEATER

- Antisubmarine 7 Dec 1941-2 Sept 1945
- Ground Combat 7 Dec 1941-2 Sept 1945
- Air Combat 7 Dec 1941-2 Sept 1945

WORLD WAR II – ASIATIC-PACIFIC THEATER

- Philippine Islands 7 Dec 1941
  -10 May 1942
- Burma 1942 7 Dec 1941- 26 May 1942
- Central Pacific 7 Dec 1941-6 Dec 1943
- East Indies 1 Jan-22 Jul 1942
- India-Burma 2 Apr 1942-28 Jan 1945
- Air Offensive, Japan 17 Apr 1942
  -2 Sept 1945
- Aleutian Islands 3 Jun 1942-24 Aug 1943
- China Defensive 4 Jul 1942-4 May 1945
- Papua 23 Jul 1942-23 Jan 1943
- Guadalcanal 7 Aug 1942-21 Feb 1943
- New Guinea 24 Jan 1943-31 Dec 1944
- Northern Solomons 22 Feb 1943
  -21 Nov 1944
- Eastern Mandates (Air) 7 Dec 1943
  -16 Apr 1944
  (Ground) 31 Jan-14 Jun 1944
- Bismarck Archipelago 15 Dec 1943
  -27 Nov 1944
- Western Pacific (Air) 17 Apr 1944
  -2 Sept 1945
  (Ground) 15 June 1944-2 Sept 1945

Although a single citation did not carry with it the right to display a streamer, it did count as an award and if the organization was cited a second time for distinguished service, it normally was awarded the Belgian Fourragere.

The only foreign decorations that authorized members of a decorated unit to wear an emblem symbolic of the award on their uniforms were the French and Belgian Fourrageres, the Netherlands Orange Lanyard, the Philippine Presidential Unit Citation, the Republic of Korea Presidential Unit Citation and the Republic of Vietnam Gallantry Cross and Civil Actions Honor Medal. Of these, only the French Fourragere was authorized for temporary wear. In other words, members of a unit awarded the French Fourragere could wear the Fourragere on their uniforms as long as they were members of the decorated unit. Upon leaving the unit they could no longer wear the Fourragere unless they were assigned to the unit during the period for which it was decorated. No temporary wear of emblems representing other foreign awards was authorized; they could only be worn by individuals who were with the unit during the period for which it was cited.

Behind the campaign streamers is immortalized the history of the Army. Here in strips of rayon is epitomized the courage, endurance, loyalty, patience, determination, and dedication of an Army now more than 200 years old and whose service to the nation cannot be measured in dollars. In the service of the Republic, these regiments have been annihilated by sword and disease, yet the only recognition for this heroism may be but a name on a strip of rayon. Five months of the most difficult, agonizing and tragic period of the Army is symbolized in the words "Philippine Islands" on the Asiatic-Pacific campaign streamer for the 59th, 60th, 200th and 515th Coast Artillery (Antiaircraft) Regiments.

Colonel William Travis, commanding the American forces at the Alamo, in February 1836, wrote in a message to "the People of Texas and All Americans in the World"

"...I am besieged by a thousand or more of the Mexicans under Santa Anna ...I have answered the demand (to surrender) with a cannon shot, and our flag waves proudly from the walls. I shall never surrender nor retreat ..."

Symbols of unit achievement or bravery help to maintain and stimulate the spirit of "never surrender nor retreat". U.S. Army units at the Meuse-Argonne, Myitkyina, Remagen Bridge, Bastogne and Inchon, and elsewhere throughout the world have shown the enemy that this spirit lives on in the modern American fighting man.

The battles, campaigns and wars in which the United States Army has participated as represented in its campaign streamers are as follows:

REVOLUTIONARY WAR

- Lexington — 19 Apr 1775
- Ticonderoga — 10 May 1775
- Boston — 17 Jun 1775-17 Mar 1776
- Quebec — 28 Aug 1775-Jul 1776
- Charleston — 28-29 Jun 1776
- Long Island — 26-29 Aug 1776
- Trenton — 26 Dec 1776
- Princeton — 3 Jan 1777
- Saratoga — 2 Jul-17 Oct 1777
- Brandywine — 11 Sept 1777
- Germantown — 4 Oct 1777
- Monmouth — 28 Jun 1778
- Savannah — 29 Dec 1778, 16 Sept-10 Oct 1779
- Charleston — 29 Mar-12 May 1780
- Cowpens — 17 Jan 1781
- Guilford Court House — 15 Mar 1781
- Yorktown — 28 Sept-19 Oct 1781

WAR OF 1812

- Canada — 18 Jun 1812-17 Feb 1815
- Chippewa — 5 Jul 1814
- Lundy's Lane — 25 Jul 1814
- Bladensburg — 17-29 Aug 1814
- McHenry — 13 Sept 1814
- New Orleans — 23 Sept 1814-8 Jan 1815

MEXICAN WAR

- Palo Alto — 8 May 1846
- Resaca de la Palma — 9 May 1846
- Monterrey — 21 Sept 1846
- Buena Vista — 22-23 Feb 1847
- Vera Cruz — 9-29 Mar 1847
- Contreras — 18-20 Aug 1847
- Churubusco — 20 Aug 1847
- Molino del Rey — 8 Sept 1847
- Chapultepec — 13 Sept 1847

CIVIL WAR

- Sumter — 12-13 Apr 1861
- Bull Run* — 16-22 Jul 1861
- Henry and Donelson — 6-16 Feb 1862
- Mississippi River — 6 Feb 1862-9 Jul 1863
- Peninsula — 17 Mar-3 Aug 1862
- Shiloh — 6-7 Apr 1862
- Valley — 15 May-17 Jun 1862
- Manassas* — 7 Aug-2 Sept 1862
- Antietam* — 3-17 Sept 1862

Campaign And Decoration Streamers

The Antiaircraft Artillery Battalion which normally consisted of a Headquarters and Headquarters Battery or Detachment and three or four lettered companies was classified as a color bearing unit. It carried two flags; a battalion and a National color. The term "color" when used alone implies the National color, or Stars and Stripes, while the term "colors" implies the National color and the organizational or battalion color collectively. The field of the organizational color was red for Artillery upon which was displayed a spread American eagle in shades of brown. On its breast was the coat of arms of the battalion and in its beak a ribbon inscribed with the organizational motto. Below the eagle was another ribbon bearing the designation of the battalion. The organizational color not only identified the unit but also represented the spirit and tradition of the organization. It also served as the carrier for the various decoration and campaign streamers awarded the battalion for achievement and war service.

Another flag long associated with antiaircraft artillery was the guidon. This was a red swallow-tailed flag carried by each battery as a unit marker and displayed in yellow the branch of service insignia between the battery letter above and the battalion number below.

While the first antiaircraft battalions were serving in France during World War I, the practice was to inscribe campaign participation on flagstaff silver bands. But silver bands were in short supply during 1918 and the AEF was authorized local procurement and use of ribbon or streamers as a substitute. In four foot lengths these ribbons were inscribed with the names of special battles and major operations of recipient organizations. These ribbons were in effect the forerunner of the modern day campaign streamers.

On 3 June 1920 hand embroidered silk streamers were adopted to replace all previous methods of displaying honors and decorations. The original War Department directive prescribed a silk streamer for each war in which the organization had served in a theater of operations, in the colors of the campaign ribbon for the different wars. Each streamer (at that time 2-3/4 inches wide and 3 feet long for standards and the same width but 4 feet long for colors) was inscribed with the name of the battle or campaign in which the organization had participated. Inscriptions for streamers were announced in orders published by the War Department. Shortly thereafter a streamer was adopted to show "Mention in Orders" for meritorious service in action. This was a blue silk streamer with the name of the action embroidered in white. This streamer was never utilized and in 1942 became the streamer for the Distinguished Unit Citation (now the Presidential Unit Citation [Army]).

Specific criteria for battle honors (now called campaign participation credit) has been refined and was contained in Army Regulations for many years. These honors were included in the Army Registers of 1866 through 1877, usually at the head of the list of officers of each regiment. These listings were eventually dropped from the Army Register owing to the difficulty in gathering full and reliable data. After 1877 such credits were confirmed, when possible, by The Adjutant General. In recent years this activity has been the responsibility of The Chief of Military History, U.S. Army and since 1920 a definite and fixed policy has been applied. The criteria have been changed a number of times over the years and are currently set forth in Army Regulations 870-5.

Just as the experienced soldier is known by the decorations and service ribbons he wears on his uniform, so is the well-tried military unit known by the decorations and campaign streamers it carries on its colors. Many of the honors which the fighting man can earn have a counterpart that can be given the unit for a like degree of service or achievement. For example, a campaign streamer with inscription is comparable to a theater service ribbon with battle star while many unit decorations are comparable to individual decorations. The Presidential Unit Citation (PUC) is awarded for the same degree of heroism required for the award of a Distinguished Service Cross to an individual; the Meritorious Unit Commendation (MUC), Navy Unit Commendation (NUC) (when awarded for merit), and Air Force Outstanding Unit Award (AFOUA) are awarded for the same degree of achievement warranting the award of the Legion of Merit; the Valorous Unit Award (VUA) and the Navy Unit Commendation (for bravery) are awarded for the same degree of bravery as that required for the award of a Silver Star.

Grateful foreign governments have awarded decorations to numerous Army units for outstanding action in combat. Probably the best known of these is the French Croix de Guerre which was earned by Army units in both World Wars. All foreign decorations carry with them the right to display a symbol on the decorated unit's color. Numerous AAA battalions were cited in the Order of the Day of the Belgian Army for their outstanding efforts in battle.

APPENDIX 2

Campaign And Decoration Streamers

requirements for existing insignia. Consequently, on 2 January 1943, the War Department announced that no further distinctive insignia would be approved or manufactured for the duration of the war. The duration lasted until 2 August 1947 when the ban was lifted and the organizations having approved insignia were authorized to have them manufactured. The prohibition on insignia for units not having one authorized was not lifted until 1951.

Prior to the ban being lifted the matter of organizational priorities was carefully studied and it was decided that company-size organizations would no longer be allowed to adopt distinctive badges because there were too many company-size organizations and too few personnel in the heraldic program to process them. The new policy, approved 14 February 1951, stated that distinctive insignia would be limited to color-bearing units and service schools, but those organizations having an insignia by virtue of a previous authority would be allowed to retain them.

Prior to World War II the Army consisted generally of regiments and fixed type battalions, all classified as color-bearing and entitled to a distinctive insignia. The demands of war forced the reorganization of all regiments, except infantry, into groups and battalions. Many of these battalions were further reorganized as flexible or non-color-bearing organizations. Especially affected were the support organizations such as Quartermaster, Ordnance, Transportation, Medical, Signal and, in some instances, Engineer battalions. The post-World War II policy dictated that these organizations were not entitled to coats of arms and distinctive insignia, a policy not understood and resented when such personnel saw sister color-bearing battalions wearing their distinctive insignia. Although the denial of coats of arms continued, the problem was partially resolved by authorization for wear of inherited insignia, if one existed.

Although non-color-bearing organizations at all echelons persisted in efforts to obtain distinctive insignia through the fifties and early sixties, their requests were consistently denied. When the Vietnam War was at its zenith in the mid-sixties, a new spirit seemed to prevail. On 25 March 1965 a distinctive badge was authorized for wear by the non-color-bearing units of the 1st Armored Division and authorization for a distinctive badge was quickly extended to other divisions. This was followed on 22 November 1965 by the authorization of a distinctive badge for the non-color-bearing units of each separate brigade and finally, on 5 January 1966, each flexible battalion was authorized its own distinctive badge.

In 1967 a new look was taken of the categories of organizations authorized distinctive insignia which resulted in further expansion to include such organizations as Major Commands, Armies, Corps, Logistical Commands, Groups and Hospitals. The separate company still failed to win approval, perhaps because there were still "too many of them and too few of us".

- Leyte 17 Oct 1944-1 Jul 1945
- Luzon 15 Dec 1944-4 Jul 1945
- Central Burma 29 Jan-15 Jul 1945
- Southern Philippines 27 Feb-4 Jul 1945
- Ryukyus 26 Mar-2 Jul 1945
- China Offensive 5 May-2 Sept 1945

WORLD WAR II – EUROPEAN-AFRICAN-MIDDLE EASTERN THEATER

- Egypt-Libya 11 Jun 1942-12 Feb 1943
- Air Offensive Europe 4 Jul 1942-5 Jun 1944
- Algeria-French Morocco 8-11 Nov 1942
- Tunisia (Air) 12 Nov 1942-13 May 1943
  (Ground) 17 Nov 1942-13 May 1943
- Sicily (Air) 14 May-17 Aug 1943
  (Ground) 9 Jul-17 Aug 1943
- Naples-Foggia (Air) 18 Aug 1943 -21 Jan 1944
  (Ground) 9 Sept 1943-21 Jan 1944
- Anzio 22 Jan-24 May 1944
- Rome-Arno 22 Jan-9 Sept 1944
- Normandy 6 Jun-24 Jul 1944
- Northern France 25 Jul-14 Sept 1944
- Southern France 15 Aug-14 Sept 1944
- North Apennines 10 Sept 1944-4 Apr 1945
- Rhineland 15 Sept 1944-21 Mar 1945
- Ardennes-Alsace 16 Dec 1944-25 Jan 1945
- Central Europe 22 Mar-11 May 1945
- Po Valley 5 Apr-8 May 1945

KOREAN WAR

- UN Defensive 27 Jun-15 Sept 1950
- UN Offensive 16 Sept-2 Nov 1950
- CCF Intervention 3 Nov 1950-24 Jan 1951
- First UN Counteroffensive 25 Jan -21 Apr 1951
- CCF Spring Offensive 22 Apr-8 Jul 1951
- UN Summer-Fall Offensive 9 Jul -27 Nov 1951
- Second Korean Winter 28 Nov 1951 -30 Apr 1952
- Korea, Summer-Fall 1952 1 May -30 Nov 1952
- Third Korean Winter 1 Dec 1952 -30 Apr 1953
- Korea, Summer 1953 1 May -27 Jul 1953

VIETNAM MILITARY OPERATIONS

- Vietnam Advisory Campaign 15 Mar 1962 -7 Mar 1965
- Vietnam Defense Campaign 8 Mar 1965 -24 Dec 1965
- Vietnam Counteroffensive 25 Dec 1965 -30 Jun 1966
- Vietnam Counteroffensive Phase II 1 Jul 1966-31 May 1967
- Vietnam Counteroffensive Phase III 1 Jun 1967-29 Jan 1968
- Tet Counteroffensive 30 Jan 1968 -1 Apr 1968
- Vietnam Counteroffensive Phase IV 2 Apr 1968-30 Jun 1968
- Vietnam Counteroffensive Phase V 1 Jul 1968-1 Nov 1968
- Vietnam Counteroffensive Phase VI 2 Nov 1968-22 Feb 1969
- Tet 1969 Counteroffensive 23 Feb 1969 -8 Jun 1969
- Vietnam Summer-Fall 1969 9 Jun 1969-31 Oct 1969
- Vietnam Winter-Spring 1970 1 Nov 1969-30 Apr 1970
- Sanctuary Counteroffensive 1 May 1970 -30 June 1970
- Vietnam Counteroffensive Phase VII 1 Jul 1970-30 Jun 1971
- Consolidation I 1 Jul 1971-30 Nov 1971
- Consolidation II 1 Dec 1971-29 Mar 1972
- Cease Fire 30 Mar 1972-28 Jan 1973

ARMED FORCES EXPEDITIONS

- Grenada 23 Oct-21 Nov 1983
- Panama 20 Dec 1989-31 Jan 1990

SOUTHWEST ASIA

- Defense of Saudi Arabia 1990-1991
  2 Aug 1990-16 Jan 1991

- Liberation of Kuwait 1991
  (17 Jan 1991-TBA)

APPENDIX 3

Glossary of Lineage Terms

GLOSSARY OF LINEAGE TERMS

ACTIVATE. To bring into being or establish a unit that has been constituted. This term is not used when referring to Army National Guard Units (see ORGANIZE).

ALLOT. To assign a unit to one of the components of the United States Army. The present components are the Regular Army, the Army National Guard, and the Army Reserve (formerly the Organized Reserves and the Organized Reserve Corps). During World War I, units were allotted to the National Army and during World War II to the Army of the United States. Army National Guard units were generally allotted to a particular state or group of states. Except for Army National Guard units, units may be withdrawn from one component and allotted to another. Such changes in allotment do not change the history, lineage, and honors of the units.

ARMY COMPOSITION OR COMPONENTS. Currently the Regular Army, Army National Guard of the United States, Army National Guard while in the service of the United States, and the Army Reserve.

Until 1898 the land forces of the United States consisted of the Regular Army and such temporary forces as were organized by call of the President or by special statutes for specific purposes.

In 1898 the organized and active land forces of the United States consisted of the Regular Army and the militia of the several States when called into the service of the United States. In time of war the two branches were designated the Regular Army and the Volunteer Army.

In 1914 the land forces consisted of the Regular Army, the organized militia while in the service of the United States, and such volunteer forces as Congress authorized.

1916: the Regular Army, the Volunteer Army, the Officers' Reserve Corps, the National Guard while in the service of the United States, and such other land forces as authorized by law.

1920: the Regular Army, the National Guard while in the service of the United States, and the Organized Reserves including the Officers' Reserve Corps and the Enlisted Reserve Corps.

1933: the Regular Army, the National Guard of the United States, the National Guard while in the service of the United States, the Officers' Reserve Corps, the Organized Reserves, and the Enlisted Reserve Corps.

1941: the Regular Army, the National Guard of the United States, the National Guard while in the service of the United States, the Officers' Reserve Corps, Organized Reserves, the Enlisted Reserve Corps, and persons inducted into the land forces of the United States under the Selective Training and Service Act of 1940.

ARMY NATIONAL GUARD. Units allotted to the several states. Before about 1954 the title did not include the word *Army*, which was added to distinguish the organizations from Air National Guard counterparts.

ARMY RESERVE. A component of the Army from 1952 to present (originally designated Organized Reserves under the National Defense Act of 1916 as amended in 1920, redesignated Organized Reserve Corps in 1948).

ARMY OF THE UNITED STATES. In all early acts, AUS had reference only to the Regular Army. In 1920 the term was extended to include the Regular Army, the National Guard while in the service of the United States, and the Organized Reserves. Beginning in 1941, AUS took on an additional meaning when many new units not included in the Mobilization Plans were constituted and activated in the AUS rather than in the Regular Army, National Guard, or Organized Reserves (which were provided for in the various Troop Programs). The Army Reorganization Act of 1950 declared the term AUS synonymous with the term Army, again giving it the same meaning it had in the 1920-1941 period. Consequently, a unit designated in the AUS in the 1941-1950 period and active after 1950 was normally placed in an Army component by DA directive.

ASSIGN. To make a unit part of a larger organization and place it under that organization's command and control until relieved from assignment. As a general rule, only divisional and separate brigade assignments exist in unit lineages.

CONSOLIDATE. To merge or combine two or more units into one new unit. The new unit may retain the designation of one of the original units or may have a new designation, but it inherits the history, lineage, and honors of all the units affected by the merger. In the Army

National Guard, personnel of the units are generally combined in the new unit. In the Regular Army and Army Reserve, units are usually consolidated when they are inactive or when only one of the units is active; therefore, personnel and equipment are seldom involved.

CONSTITUTE. To place the designation of a new unit on the official rolls of the Army. Such action is authorized only by the Secretary of the Army after provisions have been made for the inclusion of the unit in a DA Troop Program.

CONVERT. To transfer a unit from one branch of the Army to another; for example, from Infantry to Engineers. Such a move always requires a redesignation with the unit adopting the name of its new branch; however, there is no break in the historical continuity of the unit. If the unit is active, it must also be reorganized under a new table of organization and equipment (TOE).

DEMOBILIZE. To remove the designation of a unit from the official rolls of the Army. If the unit is active, it must also be inactivated. This term is used in unit lineages only when referring to the period immediately after World War I.

DESIGNATION. The official title of a unit, consisting usually of a number and a name.

DISBAND. To remove the designation of a unit from the official rolls of the Army. If the unit is active, it must also be inactivated. In the Army National Guard, this term generally is used when referring to the period before World War I.

ELEMENT. A unit that is assigned to or is part of a larger organization. (See also ORGANIC ELEMENT).

FEDERAL RECOGNITION. Acceptance of an Army National Guard unit by the Federal government after the unit has been inspected by a Federal representative and found to be properly housed, equipped, and organized according to Army requirements. Federal recognition may be withdrawn when the unit no longer meets these requirements or when the need no longer exists.

FEDERAL SERVICE. Active duty of an Army National Guard unit while under the control of the United States government, rather than under the control of its home state. Units enter Federal service by order of the President of the United States, as authorized by Congress. The phrase, "called into Federal service", was used for most wars through World War I. Units called into Federal service could not be sent into a foreign country without specific Congressional authorization; this was circumvented in some instances when units were "mustered into Federal service". The World War I draft had the effect of discharging National Guard personnel from the Guard and making them subject to the laws and regulations of the Army of the United States as selective service personnel. The phrase, "inducted into Federal service", was used during World War II. Since World War II the phrase "ordered into active Federal service", has been used. A unit remains in Federal service until released by the Federal government at which time it reverts to the control of its home state.

INACTIVATE. To place a unit not currently needed in an inoperative status without assigned personnel or equipment. When referring to the Army National Guard, this term was used only during and immediately after World War II for units in Federal service. Such units were retained on the rolls of the Army and most were reorganized in their home states.

NATIONAL ARMY. Composed of organizations from the additional military force authorized by the President by Act of 18 May 1917 and normally manned by drafted personnel.

NATIONAL GUARD. See ARMY NATIONAL GUARD.

NATIONAL GUARD OF THE UNITED STATES (NGUS). As used in this volume, a NGUS unit was a temporary organization within a state which took the place of a unit in Federal service during the Korean War. It had the same designation and was usually organized in the same general areas as the replaced unit.

ORGANIC ELEMENT. A unit that is an integral part of a larger organization; for example, a lettered company of a battalion.

ORGANIZE. To assign personnel and equipment to a unit and make it operative; i.e., capable of performing its mission. For Army National Guard units this term is used instead of activate.

RECONSTITUTE. To restore to the official rolls of the Army a unit that has been disbanded or demobilized. This can be done only by authority of the Secretary of the Army and the unit must again be allotted to an Army component. The reconstituted unit may have a new designation but it retains its former history, lineage, and honors.

REDESIGNATE. To change a unit's official name or number, or both. Redesignation is a change of title only; the unit's history, lineage, and honors remain the same.

REORGANIZE. To change the structure of a unit in accordance with a new table of organization and equipment (TOE), or to change from one type of unit to another within the same branch of the Army; for example, from Infantry to Airborne Infantry. (For reorganizations involving a new branch, see CONVERT.) When referring to the Army National Guard, the term also means to organize an inactive unit again.

TABLE OF ORGANIZATION AND EQUIPMENT (TOE). A table that prescribed the normal mission, organizational structure, personnel, and equipment authorized a military unit.

INDEX TO AAA AND COAST ARTY BATTALIONS

Page

1st AA Bn (1921-1922)	51
1st AAA Msl Bn (1950-1959)	52
2d AA Bn (1921-1922)	54
2d AAA Bn (1950-1961)	55
3d AA Bn (1921-1922)	58
3d Abn AA Bn (1943-1945)	59
3d Coast Arty Bn (1944-1945)	60
3d AAA Bn (1948-1961)	63
4th Coast Arty Bn (1944-1950)	64
4th AAA Bn (1948-1958)	66
5th AAA Bn (1948-1961)	68
6th AAA AW Bn (1950-1963)	69
7th AAA AW Bn (1943-1946)	71
7th AAA AW Bn (1946-1950)	72
7th AAA Bn (1950-1965)	73
8th AAA Bn (1948-1959)	74
9th Abn AA Bn (1943-1945)	75
9th AAA Msl Bn (1950-1958)	76
10th AAA Msl Bn (1950-1958)	78
11th AAA Msl Bn (1950-1958)	79
12th Abn AA Bn (1943-1944)	80
12th AAA Bn (1950-1961)	81
13th Abn AA Bn (1943-1944)	83
13th AAA Bn (1944-1958)	83
14th Abn AA Bn (1943-1944)	84
14th AAA Bn (1950-1957)	85
15th Abn AA Bn (1943-1944)	86
15th AAA Bn (1948-1957)	86
16th Abn AA Bn (1944-1945)	88
17th Abn AA Bn (1944-1945)	90
17th Abn AA Bn (1948-1949)	90
18th Abn AA Bn (1944-1945)	91
18th AAA Msl Bn (1950-1961)	91
19th AAA Bn (1950-1957)	93
20th Coast Arty Bn (1944-1950)	94
20th AAA Bn (1950-1958)	94
21st Coast Arty Bn (1944-1950)	96
21st AAA Bn (1948-1959)	97
22d AAA Bn (1948-1958)	98
23d Coast Arty Bn (1940-1943)	99
23d AAA Bn (1948-1958)	100
24th Coast Arty Bn (1942-1945)	101
24th AAA Msl Bn (1950-1960)	102
25th Coast Arty Bn (1942-1943)	103
25th AAA Msl Bn (1948-1963)	104
26th Coast Arty Bn (1942-1943)	105
26th AAA Bn (1948-1965)	106
27th Coast Arty Bn (1942-1950)	107
27th AAA Bn (1950-1958)	108
28th AAA Msl Bn (1950-1958)	109
29th Coast Arty Bn (1942-1944)	110
29th AAA Bn (1948-1957)	111
30th AAA Bn (1948-1957)	112
31st Coast Arty Bn (1943-1945)	113
31st AAA AW Bn (1950-1953)	113
32d Coast Arty Bn (1943-1944)	114
32d AAA Bn (1948-1957)	115
33d Coast Arty Bn (1944-1950)	115
33d AAA Bn (1950-1957)	116
34th Coast Arty Bn (1943-1944)	117

	Page
34th AAA Msl Bn (1948-1958)	118
35th Coast Arty Bn (1943-1946)	119
35th AAA Bn (1948-1957)	119
36th Coast Arty Bn (1943-1946)	120
36th AAA Msl Bn (1948-1958)	121
37th Coast Arty Bn (1944-1946)	122
37th AAA Bn (1948-1957)	122
38th Coast Arty Bn (1944-1947)	123
38th AAA Msl Bn (1948-1958)	124
39th AAA Bn (1948-1961)	125
40th AAA Bn (1948-1959)	126
41st Arty Bn (1922-1924)	127
41st AAA Bn (1948-1959)	128
42d Coast Arty Bn (1944-1947)	129
42d AAA Bn (1948-1961)	130
43d Coast Arty Bn (1943-1947)	131
43d AAA Bn (1948-1961)	132
44th Coast Arty Bn (1942)	133
44th Coast Arty Bn (1944-1950)	133
44th AAA Msl Bn (1950-1958)	134
45th Coast Arty Bn (1944-1950)	135
45th AAA Msl Bn (1950-1963)	136
46th Coast Arty Bn (1944)	137
46th AAA Bn (1948-1958)	138
47th AAA Bn (1948-1957)	139
48th Coast Arty Bn (1944-1950)	140
48th AAA Bn (1948-1958)	140
49th Coast Arty Bn (1944-1950)	141
49th AAA Msl Bn (1950-1958)	142
50th AAA Bn (1948-1961)	143
51st Coast Arty Bn (1944-1950)	146
51st AAA Bn (1950-1956)	147
52d Coast Arty Bn (1944-1950)	148
52d AAA Bn (1950-1961)	149
53d Coast Arty Bn (1944-1947)	150
53d AAA Bn (1950-1963)	150
54th Coast Arty Bn (1944-1950)	151
54th AAA Msl Bn (1950-1959)	152
55th Coast Arty Bn (1944-1946)	154
56th Coast Arty Bn (1944-1950)	154
56th AAA Msl Bn (1951-1958)	155
57th Coast Arty Bn (1945-1947)	155
57th AAA Bn (1948-1958)	156
58th Coast Arty Bn (1945-1948)	157
58th AAA AW Bn (1948-1956)	157
59th AAA Bn (1947-1959)	158
60th AAA Bn (1946-1959)	160
61st Arty Bn (1922-1924)	162
61st Coast Arty Bn (1946-1950)	163
61st AAA AW Bn (1950-1961)	164
62d AAA Bn (1944-1961)	166
63d AAA Msl Bn (1943-1958)	169
64th AAA Bn (1943-1957)	170
65th AAA Bn (1943-1959)	171
66th AAA Msl Bn (1943-1958)	172
67th AAA Msl Bn (1944-1961)	173
68th AAA Bn (1944-1959)	175
69th AAA Bn (1943-1957)	176
70th AAA Bn (1943-1959)	177
71st AAA Gun Bn (1943-1945)	178
71st AAA Msl Bn (1949-1959)	179
72d AAA Gun Bn (1944-1950)	180
73d AAA Gun Bn (1944-1950)	181

Unit	Page
73d AAA Bn (1950-1958)	182
74th AAA Msl Bn (1944-1958)	183
75th AAA Msl Bn (1944-1958)	184
76th AAA Bn (1943-1957)	185
77th AAA Bn (1943-1957)	186
78th AAA Msl Bn (1944-1959)	187
79th AAA Msl Bn (1943-1958)	189
80th AA Bn (1942-1958)	190
81st Abn AAA Bn (1942-1957)	191
82d AAA Bn (1948-1957)	193
83d AAA Msl Bn (1950-1958)	194
84th Abn AA Bn (1946-1952)	195
85th AAA Msl Bn (1943-1958)	196
86th AAA Gun Bn (1944-1946)	197
86th AAA Msl Bn (1950-1958)	198
87th AAA Gun Bn (1944-1945)	199
88th AAA Bn (1948-1957)	199
89th AAA Bn (1943-1957)	200
90th AAA Gun Bn (1944)	201
90th AAA Bn (1950-1957)	202
91st AAA Bn (1950-1958)	203
92d AAA Bn (1949-1957)	204
93d AAA Bn (1943-1957)	205
94th AAA Gun Bn (1944-1955)	206
94th AAA AW Bn (1950-1958)	206
95th AAA Msl Bn (1943-1958)	207
96th AAA Bn (1943-1958)	208
97th AAA Bn (1943-1957)	209
98th AAA Bn (1943-1957)	210
99th AAA Gun Bn (1944)	211
99th AAA Bn (1950-1959)	211
100th AAA Gun Bn (1944)	212
101st AAA Bn (1940-1959)	213
102d AAA AW Bn (1940-1947)	216
102d AAA AW Bn (1950)	217
102d AAA Bn (1950-1958)	219
102d AAA Bn (1958-1959)	220
103d AAA AW Bn (1940-1946)	221
104th AAA AW Bn (1940-1946)	223
104th AAA Bn (1946-1954)	224
104th AAA Bn (1953-1959)	226
105th AAA AW Bn (1940-1946)	227
105th AAA Bn (1946-1959)	228
106th AAA AW Bn (1940-1946)	230
106th AAA AW Bn (1950-1952)	232
106th AAA Bn (1952-1955)	234
106th AAA Bn (1955-1957)	235
106th AAA Bn (1957-1958)	237
106th AAA Msl Bn (1958-1959)	237
107th AAA Bn (1943-1959)	238
108th AAA Bn (1942-1959)	240
109th AAA Gun Bn (1942-1946)	241
109th AAA Msl Bn (1954-1959)	242
110th AAA Gun Bn (1942-1946)	243
110th AAA Bn (1954-1957)	243
111th AAA Gun Bn (1942-1952)	244
112th AAA Gun Bn (1942-1953)	244
113th AAA Gun Bn (1942-1949)	244
113th AAA Bn (1949-1959)	245
114th AAA Bn (1942-1959)	247
115th AAA Bn (1943-1959)	248
116th AAA Gun Bn (1943-1948)	249
116th AAA Msl Bn (1955-1959)	250

	Page
117th AAA Gun Bn (1943-1952)	251
118th AAA Bn (1943-1953)	251
119th AAA Gun Bn (1943-1948)	252
120th AAA Gun Bn (1943-1949)	252
120th AAA Bn (1949-1959)	253
121st AAA Gun Bn (1941-1945)	255
122d AAA Gun Bn (1941-1946)	255
122d AAA Bn (1946-1955)	256
123d AAA Bn (1941-1959)	257
124th AAA Bn (1943-1959)	258
125th AAA Gun Bn (1943-1946)	259
125th AAA Msl Bn (1951-1959)	260
126th AAA Bn (1943-1950)	260
126th AAA Bn (1949-1959)	261
127th AAA Gun Bn (1943-1946)	262
127th AAA AW Bn (1949-1952)	263
127th AAA Bn (1952-1959)	264
128th AAA Bn (1943-1959)	266
129th AAA Gun Bn (1943-1945)	267
129th AAA Bn (1949-1959)	268
130th Coast Arty Bn (1942-1944)	270
130th AAA Bn (1949-1954)	271
130th AAA Bn (1954-1959)	272
131st AAA Gun Bn (1943-1948)	273
132d AAA Gun Bn (1943-1948)	274
132d AAA Bn (1949-1959)	274
133d AAA Gun Bn (1943-1948)	275
133d AAA Bn (1949-1954)	276
133d AAA Bn (1954-1959)	277
134th AAA Bn (1943-1959)	278
135th AAA Gun Bn (1943-1949)	279
135th AAA Bn (1949-1959)	280
136th AAA Gun Bn (1943-1950)	281
136th AAA Bn (1949-1959)	282
137th AAA Gun Bn (1943-1945)	284
137th AAA Bn (1949-1959)	284
138th AAA Gun Bn (1943-1944)	285
138th AAA Bn (1949-1959)	286
139th AAA Gun Bn (1943-1945)	287
140th AAA Gun Bn (1943-1945)	287
140th AAA Bn (1949-1954)	288
141st AAA Bn (1943-1953)	289
142d AAA Gun Bn (1943-1950)	289
142d AAA Bn (1949-1959)	290
143d AAA Gun Bn (1943-1952)	291
144th AAA Gun Bn (1943-1944)	292
144th AAA Bn (1949-1954)	292
145th AAA Gun Bn (1943-1944)	293
145th AAA Bn (1949-1959)	294
146th AAA Gun Bn (1943-1944)	295
146th AAA Bn (1949-1959)	296
147th AAA Gun Bn (1943-1952)	297
148th AAA Gun Bn (1943-1944)	298
148th AAA Bn (1949-1959)	298
149th AAA Gun Bn (1943-1944)	300
149th AAA Bn (1949-1959)	300
150th AAA Bn (1946-1959)	301
151st Abn AA Bn (1942-1944)	303
151st AAA Bn (1955-1959)	303
152d Abn AA Bn (1942-1948)	305
153d Abn AA Bn (1942-1946)	305
154th Abn AA Bn (1943-1952)	306
155th Abn AA Bn (1942-1948)	306

	Page
156th AAA Bn (1949-1959)	307
157th AAA AW Bn (1946-1949)	308
158th AAA Gun Bn (1950-1951)	309
158th AAA Msl Bn (1955-1959)	309
159th Abn AA Bn (1946-1952)	310
161st AAA Gun Bn (1943-1946)	311
161st AAA Bn (1955-1959)	311
162d AAA Gun Bn (1943-1959)	311
163d AAA Gun Bn (1943-1946)	312
164th AAA Gun Bn (1943-1952)	312
165th AAA Gun Bn (1943-1946)	313
166th AAA Gun Bn (1943-1952)	313
167th AAA Bn (1943-1956)	314
168th AAA Msl Bn (1943-1958)	315
169th Coast Arty Bn (1944-1950)	316
169th AAA Bn (1949-1959)	317
170th Coast Arty Bn (1944-1950)	318
170th AAA Bn (1954-1959)	319
171st Coast Arty Bn (1944-1946)	320
171st Coast Arty Bn (1946-1949)	321
172d Coast Arty Bn (1944-1950)	321
173d Coast Arty Bn (1944-1950)	322
174th Coast Arty Bn (1944-1950)	323
175th Coast Arty Bn (1944-1952)	324
176th AAA Msl Bn (1944-1958)	326
177th AAA Bn (1944-1959)	327
178th Coast Arty Bn (1944-1946)	328
179th AAA Msl Bn (1944-1959)	329
180th AAA Bn (1944-1959)	330
181st Coast Arty Bn (1944-1950)	331
182d AAA Gun Bn (1946-1952)	332
182d AAA Bn (1952-1959)	332
183d AAA AW Bn (1946-1949)	333
184th AAA Gun Bn (1943-1950)	334
185th Coast Arty Bn (1944-1946)	334
186th Coast Arty Bn (1944-1946)	336
187th Coast Arty Bn (1944-1946)	336
187th Coast Arty Bn (1946-1949)	337
188th Coast Arty Bn (1944-1946)	337
188th Coast Arty Bn (1946-1949)	338
188th AAA Bn (1955-1959)	339
189th Coast Arty Bn (1944-1945)	341
189th Coast Arty Bn (1946-1949)	342
190th Coast Arty Bn (1944-1945)	343
192d Coast Arty Bn (1944-1945)	344
192d Coast Arty Bn (1946-1949)	344
193d AAA Bn (1949-1959)	345
194th AAA Gun Bn (1946-1949)	347
195th AAA Bn (1943-1958)	347
196th AAA AW Bn (1943-1952)	348
197th AAA AW Bn (1943-1950)	349
197th AAA Bn (1955-1959)	350
198th AAA AW Bn (1943-1947)	351
199th AAA Bn (1943-1955)	352
200th Coast Arty Bn (1943)	353
201st AAA Bn (1943-1958)	354
202d AAA AW Bn (1943-1949)	355
202d AAA Bn (1952-1959)	356
203d AAA AW Bn (1943-1950)	357
203d AAA Bn (1949-1959)	358
204th AAA Bn (1943-1959)	360
205th AAA AW Bn (1943-1952)	361
206th AAA AW Bn (1943-1952)	362

	Page
207th AAA AW Bn (1943-1947)	362
208th AAA AW Bn (1943-1944)	363
209th AAA AW Bn (1943-1948)	363
210th AAA Bn (1943-1959)	364
211th AAA Msl Bn (1943-1959)	366
212th AAA AW Bn (1943-1949)	368
213th AAA AW Bn (1943-1950)	369
213th AAA Bn (1950-1959)	370
214th AAA Gun Bn (1943-1950)	372
215th AAA Gun Bn (1943-1944)	373
216th AAA Bn (1943-1959)	374
217th AAA Gun Bn (1943-1948)	375
217th AAA Bn (1954-1959)	376
218th AAA Gun Bn (1943-1952)	377
219th AAA Gun Bn (1943-1944)	377
220th AAA Bn (1943-1957)	378
221st Coast Arty Bn (1944-1945)	379
222d AAA SL Bn (1943-1950)	379
223d AAA SL Bn (1943-1952)	379
224th AAA SL Bn (1943-1946)	380
225th AAA Bn (1943-1952)	380
226th AAA SL Bn (1942-1945)	381
227th AAA SL Bn (1942-1947)	381
227th AAA Msl Bn (1954-1959)	382
228th AAA SL Bn (1942-1943)	383
229th AAA SL Bn (1942-1946)	383
230th AAA SL Bn (1942-1946)	384
231st AAA SL Bn (1942-1946)	384
232d AAA SL Bn (1942-1952)	385
233d AAA SL Bn (1942-1946)	385
234th AAA Gun Bn (1942-1946)	386
235th AAA Gun Bn (1942-1952)	386
236th AAA SL Bn (1942-1945)	386
237th AAA SL Bn (1943-1946)	387
237th Coast Arty Bn (1946-1950)	388
238th AAA Bn (1943-1959)	389
239th AAA SL Bn (1942-1944)	390
240th AAA Msl Bn (1943-1959)	391
241st AAA SL Bn (1943-1959)	391
241st Coast Arty Bn (1944-1946)	392
241st Coast Arty Bn (1946-1949)	396
242d AAA SL Bn (1943-1946)	396
242d Coast Arty Bn (1944-1946)	397
243d AAA SL Bn (1943-1947)	399
243d AAA Msl Bn (1946-1959)	400
244th AAA SL Bn (1943-1946)	402
244th AAA Gun Bn (1950)	402
245th AAA SL Bn (1943-1959)	403
245th AAA Msl Bn (1944-1959)	404
246th AAA SL Bn (1943-1944)	405
247th AAA SL Bn (1943-1946)	406
248th Coast Arty Bn (1933-1935)	408
248th AAA SL Bn (1943-1958)	410
248th AAA Msl Bn (1954-1959)	410
249th AAA SL Bn (1943-1944)	411
249th Coast Arty Bn (1944-1946)	412
249th Coast Arty Bn (1946-1949)	414
250th AAA Bn (1943-1959)	414
251st AAA SL Bn (1943-1944)	415
252d AAA SL Bn (1943-1945)	416
253d AAA SL Bn (1943-1951)	416
254th AAA SL Bn (1943-1944)	416
255th AAA AW Bn (1943-1950)	417

	Page
256th AAA AW Bn (1943-1946)	417
256th AAA Bn (1946-1959)	419
257th AAA AW Bn (1943-1946)	420
257th AAA Bn (1946-1959)	421
258th AAA Bn (1953-1959)	422
259th Coast Arty Bn (1943-1946)	423
259th Coast Arty Bn (1946-1950)	424
259th AAA Msl Bn (1950-1959)	426
260th AAA Bn (1943-1954)	428
261st Coast Arty Bn (1925-1944)	430
262d Coast Arty Bn (1942-1944)	432
263d Coast Arty Bn (1925-1930)	433
263d Coast Arty Bn (1946-1949)	433
264th Coast Arty Bn (1942-1944)	433
265th Coast Arty Bn (1925-1929)	434
265th AAA Bn (1946-1959)	435
266th Coast Arty Bn (1942-1944)	436
267th Coast Arty Bn (1942-1954)	437
268th Coast Arty Bn (1942-1945)	437
270th Coast Arty Bn (1946-1949)	438
271st AAA Msl Bn (1946-1959)	439
272d AAA AW Bn (1946-1949)	440
275th AAA SL Bn (1943-1944)	441
276th AAA Bn (1942-1954)	441
277th Coast Arty Bn (1944-1954)	442
278th AAA AW Bn (1944-1953)	442
278th AAA Bn (1953-1959)	443
279th AAA Bn (1944-1959)	444
280th AAA Bn (1956-1959)	446
281st Coast Arty Bn (1943-1945)	448
282d Coast Arty Bn (1943-1954)	448
283d Coast Arty Bn (1943-1945)	449
283d AAA Bn (1946-1959)	449
284th AAA AW Bn (1945-1952)	451
285th Coast Arty Bn (1943-1950)	451
286th Coast Arty Bn (1943-1944)	452
286th AAA Bn (1952-1959)	453
287th Coast Arty Bn (1943-1944)	454
288th Coast Arty Bn (1943-1950)	455
289th Coast Arty Bn (1944)	456
289th Coast Arty Bn (1946-1950)	456
290th Coast Arty Bn (1944)	457
291st Coast Arty Bn (1944)	458
292d Coast Arty Bn (1944)	459
293d AAA SL Bn (1943-1944)	459
294th AAA SL Bn (1943-1950)	460
295th AAA SL Bn (1943-1950)	460
296th AAA SL Bn (1943-1948)	461
297th AAA SL Bn (1943-1952)	461
297th AAA Msl Bn (1956-1959)	461
298th AAA SL Bn (1943-1950)	463
298th AAA Bn (1956-1959)	463
299th AAA SL Bn (1944-1946)	464
300th AAA SL Bn (1944-1955)	465
300th AAA Bn (1950-1959)	465
301st Coast Arty BB Bn (1941-1944)	466
302d AA Balloon Bn (1941-1944)	467
303d Coast Arty BB Bn (1941-1943)	468
304th Coast Arty BB Bn (1941-1943)	469
305th Coast Arty BB Bn (1941-1944)	469
306th Coast Arty BB Bn (1942-1943)	470
307th Coast Arty BB Bn (1942-1943)	471
308th Coast Arty BB Bn (1942-1943)	472

Unit	Page
308th AAA Bn (1946-1955)	473
309th Coast Arty BB Bn (1942-1943)	474
309th AAA AW Bn (1946-1949)	475
310th Coast Arty BB Bn (1942-1943)	475
310th AAA AW Bn (1946-1952)	476
311th Coast Arty BB Bn (1942-1943)	476
311th AAA AW Bn (1946-1954)	477
312th Coast Arty BB Bn (1942-1943)	478
313th AA Balloon Bn (1942-1944)	478
313th AAA Bn (1949-1959)	479
314th AAA Bn (1946-1959)	480
315th Coast Arty BB Bn (1942-1943)	482
316th AA Balloon Bn (1942-1944)	483
317th AA Balloon Bn (1942-1944)	483
317th AAA Bn (1949-1959)	484
318th AA Balloon Bn (1942-1944)	485
318th AAA Gun Bn (1948-1952)	486
319th AA Balloon Bn (1942-1944)	486
319th AAA Bn (1949-1957)	487
320th AA Balloon Bn (1942-1945)	488
321st AA Balloon Bn (1942-1944)	489
321st AAA AW Bn (1946-1950)	489
322d AAA AW Bn (1946-1952)	490
323d AAA AW Bn (1946-1952)	490
324th AAA Gun Bn (1943-1949)	491
325th AAA Bn (1943-1959)	491
326th AAA SL Bn (1943-1952)	492
326th AAA Bn (1955-1959)	492
327th AAA SL Bn (1943-1952)	493
327th AAA Bn (1955-1959)	494
328th AAA SL Bn (1942-1944)	494
329th AAA SL Bn (1943-1952)	494
330th AAA SL Bn (1943-1952)	495
330th AAA Bn (1954-1959)	495
331st AAA SL Bn (1944-1961)	497
332d AAA SL Bn (1943-1944)	498
333d AAA SL Bn (1944)	498
334th AAA SL Bn (1944)	498
335th AAA SL Bn (1944)	499
336th AAA SL Bn (1943-1946)	499
336th AAA Gun Bn (1946-1953)	500
336th AAA Gun Bn (1953-1957)	501
337th AAA Bn (1944-1959)	503
338th AAA SL Bn (1944)	504
339th AAA SL Bn (1944-1946)	504
340th AAA Msl Bn (1943-1959)	505
341st AAA SL Bn (1943-1944)	506
341st AAA Bn (1955-1959)	507
342d AAA SL Bn (1943-1946)	508
343d AAA SL Bn (1943-1946)	508
343d AAA Gun Bn (1949-1952)	508
344th AAA SL Bn (1943-1946)	509
345th AAA SL Bn (1943-1946)	509
346th AAA SL Bn (1943-1946)	510
347th AAA SL Bn (1944)	510
348th AAA SL Bn (1943-1944)	511
350th AAA SL Bn (1942-1946)	511
351st AAA Msl Bn (1942-1958)	512
352d AAA SL Bn (1942-1952)	512
353d AAA SL Bn (1942-1946)	513
354th AAA SL Bn (1942-1944)	514
355th AAA SL Bn (1942-1944)	515
356th AAA SL Bn (1943-1945)	515

	Page
357th AAA SL Bn (1942-1945)	516
358th AAA SL Bn (1942-1952)	516
359th AAA SL Bn (1942-1952)	517
360th AAA SL Bn (1943-1944)	517
361st AAA SL Bn (1942-1944)	518
362d AAA SL Bn (1943-1945)	518
363d AAA SL Bn (1943-1952)	518
364th AAA Bn (1949-1959)	519
365th AAA SL Bn (1943-1944)	519
365th AAA Bn (1949-1959)	520
366th AAA SL Bn (1943-1944)	520
367th AAA SL Bn (1943-1944)	521
367th AAA Bn (1956-1959)	521
368th AAA SL Bn (1943-1944)	521
369th AAA Bn (1943-1955)	522
370th AAA SL Bn (1943-1944)	523
371st AAA SL Bn (1943-1944)	524
372d AAA SL Bn (1943-1944)	524
372d AAA Bn (1948-1950)	524
373d AAA SL Bn (1944-1946)	525
374th AAA SL Bn (1943-1945)	525
374th AAA Bn (1949-1959)	526
375th AAA AW Bn (1947-1950)	526
376th AAA Bn (1942-1959)	527
377th AAA Bn (1942-1959)	529
378th AAA Bn (1942-1950)	530
379th AAA AW Bn (1942-1950)	531
380th AAA Msl Bn (1943-1959)	532
381st AAA AW Bn (1942-1943)	533
382d AAA AW Bn (1942-1950)	533
383d AAA Bn (1942-1959)	534
384th AAA AW Bn (1943-1950)	535
385th AAA Bn (1943-1959)	536
386th AAA AW Bn (1942-1950)	537
387th AAA Bn (1942-1954)	538
388th AAA Bn (1943-1959)	539
389th AAA AW Bn (1942-1952)	539
390th AAA AW Bn (1942-1950)	540
391st AAA Bn (1942-1959)	541
392d AAA AW Bn (1943-1950)	542
393d AAA AW Bn (1942-1944)	542
393d AAA Gun Bn (1947-1952)	543
394th AAA AW Bn (1942-1945)	543
394th AAA Gun Bn (1947-1950)	544
395th AAA AW Bn (1942-1945)	544
396th AAA AW Bn (1943-1946)	545
396th AAA AW Bn (1946-1949)	545
397th AAA Bn (1942-1959)	546
398th AAA Bn (1942-1959)	547
399th AA Balloon Bn (1942-1943)	548
399th AAA AW Bn (1946-1952)	549
400th AAA Bn (1943-1959)	550
401st AAA Msl Bn (1942-1958)	551
402d AAA Gun Bn (1942-1944)	552
402d AAA AW Bn (1949-1952)	553
403d AAA Gun Bn (1942-1945)	554
403d AAA AW Bn (1949-1952)	554
404th Coast Arty Bn (1946-1949)	555
405th AAA Bn (1942-1959)	556
406th AAA Gun Bn (1942-1944)	557
407th AAA Gun Bn (1942-1950)	558
409th AAA Gun Bn (1942-1945)	558
410th AAA Gun Bn (1942-1944)	559

	Page
411th AAA Bn (1942-1959)	560
412th AAA AW Bn (1946-1949)	561
413th AAA Gun Bn (1942-1950)	562
414th AAA Bn (1942-1959)	563
415th AAA AW Bn (1942-1944)	564
416th AAA Bn (1946-1953)	564
417th AAA SL Bn (1942-1944)	565
418th AAA Bn (1946-1959)	565
419th Coast Arty Bn (1942-1944)	565
420th Coast Arty Bn (1942-1944)	566
420th AAA Bn (1946-1959)	566
421st AAA Bn (1941-1944)	567
421st AAA Bn (1948-1959)	567
422d AAA Bn (1942-1944)	568
422d AAA Bn (1952-1959)	569
423d AAA Bn (1941-1945)	570
424th AAA AW Bn (1942-1944)	571
425th AAA Bn (1946-1958)	572
427th AAA Bn (1942-1944)	573
427th AAA AW Bn (1949-1950)	573
428th Coast Arty Bn (1942-1943)	574
428th Coast Arty Bn (1948)	574
429th AAA Bn (1942-1944)	574
429th AAA AW Bn (1947-1950)	575
430th AAA Bn (1942-1959)	576
431st AAA AW Bn (1942-1950)	577
432d AAA Bn (1942-1954)	578
433d AAA Msl Bn (1942-1958)	579
434th AAA AW Bn (1942-1951)	580
435th AAA AW Bn (1942-1944)	581
436th AAA Msl Bn (1942-1958)	581
437th AAA AW Bn (1942-1944)	582
438th AAA Bn (1942-1959)	583
439th AAA Gun Bn (1942-1950)	584
440th AAA Bn (1942-1955)	585
441st AAA Msl Bn (1942-1958)	585
442d AAA AW Bn (1942-1944)	586
443d AAA Bn (1942-1958)	587
444th Abn AA Bn (1942-1949)	588
445th AAA Bn (1942-1959)	589
446th AAA Bn (1942-1959)	590
447th AAA Bn (1942-1959)	591
448th AAA Bn (1942-1959)	593
449th AAA Gun Bn (1942-1950)	594
450th AAA Bn (1942-1957)	595
451st AAA Bn (1942-1957)	596
452d AAA AW Bn (1942-1948)	597
452d AAA AW Bn (1949)	598
453d AAA Bn (1942-1959)	599
454th AAA Bn (1942-1959)	600
455th AAA AW Bn (1942-1950)	601
456th AAA Bn (1942-1955)	602
457th AAA Bn (1942-1959)	602
458th AAA AW Bn (1942-1944)	603
458th AAA Bn (1948-1959)	604
459th AAA Bn (1942-1955)	605
460th AAA Bn (1942-1959)	606
461st AAA Bn (1942-1959)	607
462d AAA AW Bn (1942-1948)	608
462d AAA Gun Bn (1949-1950)	609
463d AAA Bn (1942-1959)	609
464th AAA Bn (1942-1959)	611
465th AAA Msl Bn (1942-1958)	612

	Page
466th AAA Bn (1942-1959)	613
467th AAA AW Bn (1942-1949)	614
468th AAA AW Bn (1942-1950)	615
469th AAA Bn (1942-1959)	615
470th AAA Bn (1942-1959)	617
471st AAA Bn (1942-1959)	618
472d AAA AW Bn (1942-1952)	620
473d AAA AW Bn (1942-1949)	621
474th AAA Bn (1942-1956)	622
475th AAA AW Bn (1942-1946)	623
476th AAA AW Bn (1942-1952)	623
476th AAA AW Bn (1949-1952)	624
477th AAA AW Bn (1942-1948)	624
477th AAA AW Bn (1949-1952)	625
478th AAA Bn (1942-1958)	626
478th AAA AW Bn (1949-1952)	627
479th AAA AW Bn (1942-1944)	627
479th AAA AW Bn (1949-1952)	628
480th AAA AW Bn (1942-1945)	628
481st AAA Bn (1942-1959)	629
482d AAA Bn (1942-1959)	630
483d AAA Msl Bn (1942-1958)	631
484th AAA AW Bn (1942-1948)	632
485th AAA Msl Bn (1942-1958)	632
485th AAA AW Bn (1949-1952)	633
486th AAA Bn (1942-1959)	634
487th AAA AW Bn (1942-1949)	635
487th AAA Bn (1949-1954)	636
488th AAA AW Bn (1942-1944)	636
489th AAA Bn (1942-1959)	637
490th AAA AW Bn (1942-1952)	638
491st AAA Bn (1942-1959)	639
492d AAA AW Bn (1942-1944)	640
492d Abn AA Bn (1946-1952)	640
493d AAA AW Bn (1942-1944)	641
494th AAA Bn (1942-1959)	641
495th AAA Msl Bn (1942-1958)	643
495th AAA AW Bn (1949-1952)	644
496th AAA Bn (1942-1957)	644
497th AAA Gun Bn (1942-1946)	645
498th Coast Arty Bn (1942-1943)	646
498th AAA AW Bn (1949-1952)	646
499th Coast Arty Bn (1942-1943)	647
500th AAA Gun Bn (1942-1944)	647
501st AAA Bn (1942-1957)	648
502d AAA Bn (1942-1958)	649
503d Abn AA Bn (1942-1949)	650
504th AAA Msl Bn (1943-1958)	650
505th AAA Msl Bn (1943-1958)	651
506th AAA Msl Bn (1943-1958)	652
507th AAA Bn (1943-1957)	653
508th AAA Msl Bn (1943-1958)	654
509th AAA Msl Bn (1943-1958)	655
510th AAA Gun Bn (1943-1954)	656
511th AAA Bn (1943-1952)	656
511th AAA AW Bn (1946-1951)	657
512th AAA Gun Bn (1943-1944)	657
512th AAA Gun Bn (1946-1951)	657
513th AAA Msl Bn (1943-1958)	658
514th AAA Msl Bn (1943-1958)	659
516th AAA Msl Bn (1943-1958)	660
517th AAA Gun Bn (1943-1951)	660
518th AAA Bn (1943-1957)	661

	Page
519th AAA Bn (1943-1957)	662
520th Coast Arty Bn (1944)	663
521st Coast Arty Bn (1944-1950)	665
522d Coast Arty Bn (1944-1950)	666
523d AAA AW Bn (1944-1950)	666
524th Coast Arty Bn (1946-1949)	666
525th Coast Arty Bn (1946-1949)	667
526th AAA Msl Bn (1945-1959)	667
527th AAA AW Bn (1943-1946)	668
527th AAA Bn (1946-1959)	670
528th Arty Bn (1924)	672
528th AAA Gun Bn (1943-1946)	672
529th AAA AW Bn (1943-1950)	672
530th AAA AW Bn (1943-1946)	673
530th AAA Bn (1946-1959)	674
531st AAA Msl Bn (1942-1958)	675
532d AAA AW Bn (1942-1944)	676
532d AAA Gun Bn (1946-1951)	677
533d AAA AW Bn (1942-1945)	678
534th AAA AW Bn (1942-1948)	679
535th AAA Bn (1942-1959)	679
536th AAA AW Bn (1942-1944)	681
536th AAA Gun Bn (1946-1951)	682
537th AAA Bn (1942-1959)	682
538th AAA AW Bn (1943-1944)	683
539th AAA AW Bn (1943-1950)	684
540th AAA AW Bn (1943-1951)	684
541st AAA AW Bn (1943-1944)	684
542d AAA Bn (1943-1953)	685
543d AAA AW Bn (1943-1951)	685
544th AAA AW Bn (1943-1951)	686
545th AAA AW Bn (1943-1951)	686
546th AAA Bn (1942-1957)	687
547th AAA Bn (1942-1953)	688
548th AAA Msl Bn (1942-1958)	688
549th AAA Msl Bn (1942-1958)	689
550th AAA Bn (1942-1957)	690
551st AAA Msl Bn (1942-1958)	691
552d Coast Arty Bn (1926-1928)	692
552d AAA Msl Bn (1942-1958)	692
553d Coast Arty Bn (1924-1928)	693
553d AAA Bn (1942-1956)	694
554th Coast Arty Bn (1924)	694
554th AAA Msl Bn (1942-1958)	695
555th Coast Arty Bn (1927-1930)	696
555th AAA Bn (1942-1959)	696
556th AAA AW Bn (1943-1946)	697
557th AAA Bn (1943-1959)	698
558th AAA AW Bn (1943-1945)	699
559th AAA Bn (1943-1956)	699
560th AAA AW Bn (1943-1944)	700
561st AAA AW Bn (1943-1951)	701
562d AAA AW Bn (1943-1945)	701
563d AAA Bn (1943-1955)	701
564th AAA AW Bn (1943-1945)	702
565th AAA AW Bn (1943-1945)	702
566th AAA AW Bn (1943-1945)	703
567th AAA AW Bn (1943-1946)	703
568th AAA AW Bn (1943-1945)	704
569th AAA AW Bn (1943-1946)	704
570th AAA AW Bn (1943-1951)	705
571st AAA AW Bn (1943-1946)	705
572d AAA Bn (1943-1953)	706

Entry	Page
573d AAA AW Bn (1943-1946)	706
574th AAA Bn (1943-1959)	707
575th AAA Bn (1943-1953)	708
576th AAA AW Bn (1943-1951)	708
577th AAA AW Bn (1943-1951)	709
578th AAA AW Bn (1943-1951)	709
579th AAA AW Bn (1943-1946)	709
580th AAA AW Bn (1943-1945)	710
581st AAA AW Bn (1943-1946)	710
582d AAA AW Bn (1943-1951)	711
583d AAA AW Bn (1943-1944)	711
584th AAA AW Bn (1943-1951)	711
585th AAA AW Bn (1943-1944)	712
586th AAA AW Bn (1943-1947)	712
587th AAA AW Bn (1943-1951)	712
588th AAA AW Bn (1943-1951)	713
589th AAA AW Bn (1943-1944)	713
590th AAA AW Bn (1943-1944)	714
591st AAA AW Bn (1943-1945)	714
592d AAA AW Bn (1944-1946)	715
593d AAA AW Bn (1944-1949)	716
593d AAA AW Bn (1946-1950)	717
594th AAA AW Bn (1944)	717
595th AAA AW Bn (1944-1950)	718
597th AAA AW Bn (1944-1946)	718
598th AAA Bn (1944-1959)	719
599th AAA AW Bn (1944-1946)	721
601st AAA Bn (1943-1957)	722
602d AAA Msl Bn (1943-1958)	723
603d AAA Gun Bn (1943-1944)	724
604th AAA Gun Bn (1943-1944)	725
605th Coast Arty Bn (1923-1942)	726
605th AAA Msl Bn (1943-1958)	727
606th Coast Arty Bn (1944-1950)	728
606th AAA Bn (1949-1957)	729
607th Coast Arty Bn (1944-1950)	730
608th Coast Arty Bn (1946-1949)	731
609th Coast Arty Bn (1924-1928)	731
609th Coast Arty Bn (1946-1949)	731
610th Coast Arty Bn (1946-1949)	732
611th Coast Arty Bn (1946-1949)	732
612th Coast Arty Bn (1946-1949)	733
613th Coast Arty Bn (1924-1926)	733
613th Coast Arty Bn (1946-1948)	733
614th Coast Arty Bn (1924-1940)	734
614th AAA Bn (1952-1959)	734
615th AAA Msl Bn (1954-1959)	736
616th Coast Arty Bn (1924-1940)	737
616th Coast Arty Bn (1946-1949)	737
617th Coast Arty Bn (1946-1949)	738
618th Coast Arty Bn (1924-1943)	738
620th Coast Arty Bn (1924-1926)	739
623d Coast Arty Bn (1924-1943)	739
624th Coast Arty Bn (1924-1943)	739
629th Coast Arty Bn (1926-1943)	740
630th AAA AW Bn (1943-1948)	740
633d AAA AW Bn (1943-1950)	741
633d AAA AW Bn (1948-1949)	741
633d AAA Bn (1950-1957)	742
634th AAA AW Bn (1943-1950)	744
635th AAA AW Bn (1943-1950)	744
637th AAA AW Bn (1943-1944)	745
638th AAA AW Bn (1943-1944)	745

	Page
639th AAA AW Bn (1943-1948)	746
641st AAA AW Bn (1943-1945)	747
642d AAA AW Bn (1943-1944)	747
643d AAA AW Bn (1943-1945)	747
644th AAA AW Bn (1946-1952)	748
646th AAA AW Bn (1949-1952)	748
649th AAA Bn (1946-1959)	749
650th AAA Bn (1949-1958)	749
651st Abn AA Bn (1946-1952)	750
675th AAA AW Bn (1946-1949)	751
677th AAA AW Bn (1946-1949)	751
678th AAA Bn (1946-1959)	752
679th AAA AW Bn (1946-1950)	753
681st AAA AW Bn (1946-1949)	753
682d AAA Bn (1946-1959)	754
683d AAA Msl Bn (1946-1959)	756
684th AAA Msl Bn (1956-1959)	757
685th AAA Bn (1946-1959)	758
686th AAA Msl Bn (1959)	759
687th AAA AW Bn (1946-1949)	759
688th AAA Bn (1946-1953)	759
689th AAA Gun Bn (1946-1953)	761
690th AAA Bn (1946-1953)	763
691st AAA AW Bn (1946-1949)	765
692d AAA AW Bn (1946-1949)	767
693d AAA AW Bn (1946-1949)	768
694th AAA AW Bn (1946-1949)	769
695th AAA AW Bn (1946-1949)	769
696th AAA AW Bn (1946-1949)	769
697th AAA Bn (1946-1959)	771
698th AAA Msl Bn (1946-1959)	773
700th AAA Bn (1946-1959)	774
701st AAA Bn (1943-1957)	776
702d AAA Gun Bn (1946-1947)	776
703d AAA Bn (1946-1959)	777
704th AAA Msl Bn (1946-1959)	780
705th AAA Bn (1946-1959)	783
706th AAA Gun Bn (1946-1951)	784
707th AAA Msl Bn (1946-1959)	785
708th AAA Msl Bn (1946-1959)	786
709th AAA Msl Bn (1946-1959)	788
710th AAA Msl Bn (1946-1959)	789
711th AAA Bn (1946-1959)	790
712th AAA Bn (1946-1959)	792
713th AAA Bn (1946-1959)	794
714th AAA Gun Bn (1946-1949)	795
715th AAA Gun Bn (1946-1955)	795
716th AAA Bn (1946-1959)	796
717th AAA Bn (1946-1959)	799
718th AAA Bn (1946-1954)	801
718th AAA Bn (1955-1957)	803
719th AAA Bn (1946-1958)	804
720th AAA Msl Bn (1946-1959)	805
722d AAA Bn (1946-1959)	806
724th AAA Msl Bn (1946-1959)	808
725th AAA Bn (1946-1954)	810
726th AAA Bn (1946-1959)	811
727th AAA MG Bn (1943-1944)	813
728th AAA Msl Bn (1946-1959)	813
729th AAA MG Bn (1943-1944)	815
730th AAA Bn (1946-1959)	816
731st AAA MG Bn (1943-1944)	817
732d AAA Bn (1949-1959)	818

	Page
734th AAA Bn (1943-1957)	819
736th AAA Bn (1944-1959)	820
737th AAA Msl Bn (1943-1958)	822
738th AAA Msl Bn (1943-1958)	823
739th AAA Msl Bn (1943-1958)	824
740th AAA Msl Bn (1943-1958)	825
741st AAA Msl Bn (1943-1958)	826
742d AAA Gun Bn (1943-1946)	827
743d AAA Gun Bn (1943-1948)	827
744th AAA Bn (1943-1959)	828
745th AAA Bn (1943-1959)	830
746th AAA Gun Bn (1944-1946)	832
746th AAA Bn (1946-1959)	834
747th AAA AW Bn (1943-1946)	835
747th AAA Bn (1946-1959)	836
748th AAA Gun Bn (1943-1945)	836
749th AAA Bn (1943-1957)	837
750th AAA Gun Bn (1943-1950)	838
751st AAA Msl Bn (1943-1958)	839
752d AAA Bn (1943-1957)	840
753d AAA Bn (1943-1957)	841
754th AAA Gun Bn (1943-1946)	842
755th AAA Gun Bn (1943-1946)	842
761st AAA Gun Bn (1943-1946)	843
762d AAA Gun Bn (1943-1945)	843
763d AAA Gun Bn (1943-1946)	843
764th AAA Bn (1943-1958)	844
765th AAA Gun Bn (1943-1946)	844
766th AAA Gun Bn (1943-1946)	845
767th AAA AW Bn (1943-1946)	845
768th AAA Bn (1943-1958)	846
769th AAA Gun Bn (1943-1945)	847
769th AAA Bn (1948-1959)	848
770th AAA Msl Bn (1943-1959)	850
771st AAA Gun Bn (1943-1946)	851
771st AAA Gun Bn (1950-1952)	852
771st AAA Bn (1956-1958)	853
772d AAA Gun Bn (1943-1946)	854
772d AAA Msl Bn (1946-1959)	855
773d AAA Msl Bn (1943-1959)	857
774th AAA Gun Bn (1943-1946)	858
775th AAA Gun Bn (1943-1946)	859
776th AAA AW Bn (1943-1948)	860
777th AAA AW Bn (1943-1948)	860
778th AAA AW Bn (1943-1948)	861
779th AAA AW Bn (1943-1946)	861
780th AAA AW Bn (1943-1944)	862
781st AAA AW Bn (1943-1944)	862
782d AAA AW Bn (1943-1944)	863
783d AAA AW Bn (1943-1944)	863
784th AAA AW Bn (1943-1948)	863
785th AAA Bn (1943-1959)	864
786th AAA AW Bn (1943-1944)	865
787th AAA AW Bn (1943-1948)	865
788th AAA AW Bn (1943-1948)	866
789th AAA Bn (1943-1956)	867
790th AAA AW Bn (1943-1944)	868
791st AAA AW Bn (1943-1946)	868
792d AAA AW Bn (1943-1945)	868
793d AAA AW Bn (1943-1945)	869
794th AAA AW Bn (1943-1946)	869
795th AAA AW Bn (1943-1948)	870
796th AAA AW Bn (1943-1948)	870

Unit	Page
797th AAA AW Bn (1943-1952)	871
798th AAA AW Bn (1943-1948)	871
799th AAA AW Bn (1943-1944)	872
800th AAA AW Bn (1943-1944)	872
804th AAA Bn (1946-1959)	873
811th AAA AW Bn (1944-1945)	874
813th AAA AW Bn (1949-1952)	875
815th AAA AW Bn (1943-1946)	875
816th AAA AW Bn (1943-1944)	876
817th AAA AW Bn (1943-1952)	876
818th AAA AW Bn (1943-1944)	876
819th AAA AW Bn (1943-1944)	877
820th AAA AW Bn (1943-1944)	877
821st AAA AW Bn (1943-1952)	877
822d AAA AW Bn (1943-1944)	878
823d AAA AW Bn (1943-1944)	878
824th AAA AW Bn (1943-1952)	879
832d AAA AW Bn (1943-1944)	879
833d AAA AW Bn (1943-1952)	879
834th AAA AW Bn (1943-1946)	880
835th AAA AW Bn (1943-1952)	880
836th AAA AW Bn (1943-1952)	881
837th AAA AW Bn (1943-1952)	881
838th AAA AW Bn (1943-1946)	881
839th AAA AW Bn (1943-1945)	882
840th AAA AW Bn (1943-1946)	882
841st AAA AW Bn (1943-1952)	883
842d AAA AW Bn (1943-1946)	883
843d AAA AW Bn (1943-1945)	884
844th AAA AW Bn (1943-1944)	884
844th AAA AW Bn (1947-1950)	884
845th AAA AW Bn (1943-1944)	885
845th Coast Arty Bn (1947-1948)	885
846th AAA AW Bn (1943-1944)	886
846th Coast Arty Bn (1946-1949)	886
847th AAA Gun Bn (1949-1950)	887
851st AAA AW Bn (1949-1952)	887
852d AAA Msl Bn (1949-1958)	888
853d AAA AW Bn (1949-1952)	889
854th AAA AW Bn (1949-1952)	889
860th AAA AW Bn (1943-1950)	890
861st AAA AW Bn (1943-1950)	890
862d AAA AW Bn (1943-1944)	891
863d AAA AW Bn (1943-1950)	891
864th AAA AW Bn (1943-1950)	892
865th AAA Msl Bn (1943-1958)	892
866th AAA AW Bn (1943-1948)	893
867th AAA Bn (1943-1957)	894
868th AAA AW Bn (1943-1946)	894
869th AAA AW Bn (1943-1945)	895
870th AAA Bn (1943-1955)	896
871st AAA AW Bn (1944-1945)	897
886th AAA Gun Bn (1950-1952)	898
891st AAA AW Bn (1943-1945)	898
892d AAA AW Bn (1943-1944)	899
893d AAA AW Bn (1944-1948)	899
894th AAA AW Bn (1944-1948)	900
895th AAA AW Bn (1944-1948)	901
896th AAA AW Bn (1944-1948)	902
897th AAA AW Bn (1944)	902
898th AAA AW Bn (1944-1953)	903
898th AAA AW Bn (1946-1949)	903
899th AAA Bn (1944-1959)	904

	Page
900th AAA AW Bn (1944-1945)	906
901st AAA AW Bn (1943-1946)	906
902d AAA AW Bn (1943-1946)	907
903d AAA Bn (1943-1957)	907
906th AAA AW Bn (1943-1946)	908
910th AAA AW Bn (1943-1948)	908
913th AAA AW Bn (1943-1944)	909
925th AAA AW Bn (1943-1948)	909
932d AAA AW Bn (1943-1944)	910
933d AAA Msl Bn (1949-1958)	910
938th AAA AW Bn (1943-1948)	911
941st Coast Arty Bn (1946-1949)	912
945th AAA AW Bn (1944-1949)	912
945th AAA Bn (1949-1956)	914
945th AAA Bn (1956-1959)	916
947th AAA Gun Bn (1944-1946)	917
948th AAA Gun Bn (1944-1946)	917
950th AAA Bn (1943-1959)	918
951st AAA AW Bn (1944-1946)	919
951st AAA Bn (1946-1959)	920
967th AAA Msl Bn (1943-1958)	921
972d AAA Bn (1956-1959)	922
977th AAA AW Bn (1943-1945)	923
979th AAA Msl Bn (1955-1959)	924
993d AAA SL Bn (1946-1951)	925